# WHITAKER'S

## — AND —

# WHO'S WHO

## OUR GOVERNMENT

# 2016

B L O O M S B U R Y

LONDON · OXFORD · NEW YORK · NEW DELHI · SYDNEY

Bloomsbury Publishing
An imprint of Bloomsbury Publishing Plc

50 Bedford Square
London
WC1B 3DP
UK

1385 Broadway
New York
NY 10018
USA

www.bloomsbury.com

WHITAKER'S, the W Trident logo, the 'WHO'S WHO PUBLISHED ANNUALLY SINCE 1849'
belt logo and the Diana logo are trademarks of Bloomsbury Publishing Plc

British Library Cataloguing-in-Publication Data
A catalogue record for this book is available from the British Library.

ISBN:   PB:   978-1-4729-2780-4

2 4 6 8 10 9 7 5 3 1

Whitaker's content typeset in the UK by RefineCatch Limited, Bungay, Suffolk NR35 1EF
Printed and bound in Great Britain by CPI Group (UK) Ltd, Croydon CR0 4YY

To find out more about our authors and books visit www.bloomsbury.com. Here you will find
extracts, author interviews, details of forthcoming events and the option to sign up for our
newsletters.

# CONTENTS

PREFACE

## WHITAKER'S

## WHO'S WHO

# PREFACE

*Whitaker's and Who's Who: Our Government 2016* combines the parliamentary and governmental information contained in the most recent edition of *Whitaker's*, including full UK General Election 2015 results, with *Who's Who* biographies for all 650 sitting MPs, including those new to the 2015 parliament, and for all ministers of state. Using *Our Government 2016* it is possible to find out who your MP is, their majority in the 2015 General Election, whether they hold a position in the Cabinet or a Government Department and, using the *Who's Who* biographies, all about their education, career and recreations and interests. This is in context with the *Whitaker's* material which details how parliament works, the structure of government and how much government ministers and MPs are paid. It is a unique combination of information: essential reference for anyone interested in politics and the people in power.

The first edition of *Whitaker's* appeared in December 1868, following Joseph Whitaker's decision to publish his collection of facts, figures and commentary on the year in the form of an almanack. From the very start, *Whitaker's* included 'A large amount of Information Respecting the Government' and this has continued to the present day. *Whitaker's 2016* is the ultimate single-volume reference source gathered from the most up-to-date authoritative sources available. The fully updated 148th edition includes a comprehensive overview of the entire infrastructure of the UK, in-depth profiles of every country of the world, astronomical and tidal data for 2016, guides to UK law, education and taxation, colour infographics and reviews of the year in everything from archaeology to opera.

*Who's Who* is the recognised source book of information on people of influence and interest in all fields. The latest edition, *Who's Who 2016*, contains more than 33,000 biographies, approximately one thousand of these making their first appearance in *Who's Who*. They are of all kinds of people from all parts of the world and from all walks of life: arts, business and finance, church, civil service, education, entertainment, sport, government, law, local government, media, medicine, professional institutions, science and trade unions. Each entry is in a standard form, full name and present post being followed by date of birth and family details, education, career in date order, publications, recreations and address. The entries are carefully updated both from information supplied by biographees on their annual proofs and from many independent sources of reference.

The *Whitaker's* and *Who's Who* editorial teams hope you enjoy this, the first ever collaboration between these two renowned reference works.

# WHITAKER'S

**PARLIAMENT**
The House of Lords
The House of Commons
Parliamentary Information
Political Parties
Members of Parliament
General Election 2015 Results
Manifesto Commitments

**THE GOVERNMENT**
The Cabinet
Government Departments
    Executive Agencies
    Non-ministerial Government Departments

**THE YEAR 2014–15**
Parliament: The Year in Review

# PARLIAMENT

The UK constitution is not contained in any single document but has evolved over time, formed by statute, common law and convention. A constitutional monarchy, the UK is governed by ministers of the crown in the name of the sovereign, who is head both of the state and of the government.

The organs of government are the legislature (parliament), the executive and the judiciary. The executive comprises HM government (the cabinet and other ministers), government departments and local authorities. The judiciary pronounces on the law, both written and unwritten, interprets statutes and is responsible for the enforcement of the law; the judiciary is independent of both the legislature and the executive.

## THE MONARCHY

The sovereign personifies the state and is, in law, an integral part of the legislature, head of the executive, head of the judiciary, commander-in-chief of all armed forces of the crown and supreme governor of the Church of England. In the Channel Islands and the Isle of Man, which are crown dependencies, the sovereign is represented by a lieutenant-governor. In the member states of the Commonwealth of which the sovereign is head of state, her representative is a governor-general; in UK overseas territories the sovereign is usually represented by a governor, who is responsible to the British government.

Although in practice the powers of the monarchy are now very limited, and restricted mainly to the advisory and ceremonial, there are important acts of government which require the participation of the sovereign. These include summoning, proroguing and dissolving parliament, giving royal assent to bills passed by parliament, appointing important office-holders, eg government ministers, judges, bishops and governors, conferring peerages, knighthoods and other honours, and granting pardon to a person wrongly convicted of a crime. The sovereign appoints the prime minister; by convention this office is held by the leader of the political party which enjoys, or can secure, a majority of votes in the House of Commons. In international affairs the sovereign, as head of state, has the power to declare war and make peace, to recognise foreign states and governments, to conclude treaties and to annex or cede territory. However, as the sovereign entrusts executive power to ministers of the crown and acts on the advice of her ministers, which she cannot ignore, royal prerogative powers are in practice exercised by ministers, who are responsible to parliament.

Ministerial responsibility does not diminish the sovereign's importance to the smooth working of government. She holds meetings of the Privy Council (see below), gives audiences to her ministers and other officials at home and overseas, receives accounts of cabinet decisions, reads dispatches and signs state papers; she must be informed and consulted on every aspect of national life; and she must show complete impartiality.

### COUNSELLORS OF STATE

If the sovereign travels abroad for more than a few days or suffers from a temporary illness, it is necessary to appoint members of the royal family, known as counsellors of state, under letters patent to carry out the chief functions of the monarch, including the holding of Privy Councils and giving royal assent to acts passed by parliament. The normal procedure is to appoint three or four members of the royal family among those members remaining in the UK, provided they are over 21. There are currently five counsellors of state.

In the event of the sovereign on accession being under the age of 18 years, or by infirmity of mind or body, rendered incapable of performing the royal functions, provision is made for a regency.

## THE PRIVY COUNCIL

The sovereign in council, or Privy Council, was the chief source of executive power until the system of cabinet government developed. Its main function today is to advise the sovereign on the approval of various statutory functions and acts of the royal prerogative. These powers are exercised through orders in council and royal proclamations, approved by the Queen at meetings of the Privy Council. The council is also able to exercise a number of statutory duties without approval from the sovereign, including powers of supervision over the registering bodies for the medical and allied professions. These duties are exercised through orders of council.

Although appointment as a privy counsellor is for life, only those who are currently government ministers are involved in the day-to-day business of the council. A full council is summoned only on the death of the sovereign or when the sovereign announces his or her intention to marry.

There are a number of advisory Privy Council committees whose meetings the sovereign does not attend. Some are prerogative committees, such as those dealing with legislative matters submitted by the legislatures of the Channel Islands and the Isle of Man or with applications for charters of incorporation; and some are provided for by statute, eg those for the universities of Oxford and Cambridge and some Scottish universities.

Administrative work is carried out by the Privy Council Office under the direction of the Lord President of the Council, a cabinet minister.

## JUDICIAL COMMITTEE OF THE PRIVY COUNCIL

Supreme Court Building, Parliament Square,
London SW1P 3BD
T 020-7960 1500 W www.jcpc.uk

The Judicial Committee of the Privy Council is the court of final appeal from courts of the UK dependencies, courts of independent Commonwealth countries which have retained the right of appeal and courts of the Channel Islands and the Isle of Man. It also hears very occasional appeals from a number of ancient and ecclesiastical courts.

The committee is composed of privy counsellors who hold, or have held, high judicial office. Only three or five judges hear each case, and these are usually justices of the supreme court.
*Chief Executive,* Jenny Rowe, CB

## PARLIAMENT

Parliament is the supreme law-making authority and can legislate for the UK as a whole or for any parts of it separately (the Channel Islands and the Isle of Man are crown dependencies and not part of the UK). The main functions of parliament are to pass laws, to enable the government to raise taxes and to scrutinise government policy and administration, particularly proposals for expenditure. International treaties and agreements are customarily presented to parliament before ratification.

Parliament can trace its roots to two characteristics of Anglo-Saxon rule: the *witan* (a meeting of the king, nobles and advisors) and the *moot* (county meetings where local matters were discussed). However, it was the parliament that Simon de Montfort called in 1265 that is accepted as the forerunner to modern parliament, as it included non-noble representatives from counties, cities and towns alongside the nobility. The nucleus of early parliaments at the beginning of the 14th century were the officers of the king's household and the king's judges, joined by such ecclesiastical

and lay magnates as the king might summon to form a prototype 'House of Lords', and occasionally by the knights of the shires, burgesses and proctors of the lower clergy. By the end of Edward III's reign a 'House of Commons' was beginning to appear; the first known Speaker was elected in 1377.

Parliamentary procedure is based on custom and precedent, partly formulated in the standing orders of both houses of parliament. Each house has the right to control its own internal proceedings and to commit for contempt. The system of debate in the two houses is similar; when a motion has been moved, the Speaker proposes the question as the subject of a debate. Members speak from wherever they have been sitting. Questions are decided by a vote on a simple majority. Draft legislation is introduced, in either house, as a bill. Bills can be introduced by a government minister or a private member, but in practice the majority of bills which become law are introduced by the government. To become law, a bill must be passed by each house (for parliamentary stages, *see* Parliamentary Information) and then sent to the sovereign for the royal assent, after which it becomes an act of parliament.

Proceedings of both houses are public, except on extremely rare occasions. The minutes (called *Votes and Proceedings in the Commons,* and *Minutes of Proceedings in the Lords)* and the speeches *(The Official Report of Parliamentary Debates,* Hansard) are published daily. Proceedings are also recorded for transmission on radio and television and stored in the Parliamentary Recording Unit before transfer to the National Sound Archive. Television cameras have been allowed into the House of Lords since 1985 and into the House of Commons since 1989; committee meetings may also be televised.

The Fixed Term Parliament Act 2011 fixed the duration of a parliament at five years in normal circumstances, the term being reckoned from the date given on the writs for the new parliament. The term of a parliament has been prolonged by legislation in such rare circumstances as the two World Wars (31 January 1911 to 25 November 1918; 26 November 1935 to 15 June 1945). The life of a parliament is divided into sessions, usually of one year in length, beginning and ending most often in May.

### DEVOLUTION

The Scottish parliament and the National Assembly for Wales have legislative power over all devolved matters, ie matters not reserved to Westminster or otherwise outside its powers. The Northern Ireland Assembly has legislative authority in the fields previously administered by the Northern Ireland departments. The assembly was suspended in October 2002 and dissolved in April 2003, before being reinstated on 8 May 2007.

# THE HOUSE OF LORDS

London SW1A 0PW
T 020-7219 3107
E hlinfo@parliament.uk W www.parliament.uk

The House of Lords is the second chamber, or 'Upper House', of the UK's bicameral parliament. Until the beginning of the 20th century, the House of Lords had considerable power, being able to veto any bill submitted to it by the House of Commons. Since the introduction of the Parliament Acts 1911 and 1949, however, it has no powers over money bills and its power of veto over public legislation has been reduced over time to the power to delay bills for up to one session of parliament (usually one year). Today the main functions of the House of Lords are to contribute to the legislative process, to act as a check on the government, and to provide a forum of expertise. Its judicial role as final court of appeal ended in 2009 with the establishment of a new UK Supreme Court.

The House of Lords has a number of select committees. Some relate to the internal affairs of the house – such as its management and administration – while others carry out important investigative work on matters of public interest. The main committees are: the Communications Committee; the Constitution Committee; the Economic Affairs Committee; the European Union Committee; and the Science and Technology Committee. House of Lords' investigative committees look at broad issues and do not mirror government departments as the select committees in the House of Commons do.

The Constitutional Reform Act 2005 significantly altered the judicial function of the House of Lords and the role of the Lord Chancellor as a judge and its presiding officer. The Lord Chancellor is no longer the presiding officer of the House of Lords nor head of the judiciary in England and Wales, but remains a cabinet minister (the Lord Chancellor and Secretary of State for Justice), and is currently a member of the House of Commons. The function of the presiding officer of the House of Lords was devolved to the newly created post of the Speaker of the House of Lords, commonly known as Lord Speaker. The first Lord Speaker elected by the House was the Rt. Hon. Baroness Hayman on 4 July 2006.

Membership of the House of Lords comprises mainly of life peers created under the Life Peerages Act 1958, along with 92 hereditary peers and a small number of Lords of Appeal in Ordinary, ie law lords, who were created under the Appellate Jurisdiction Act 1876*. The Archbishops of Canterbury and York, the Bishops of London, Durham and Winchester, and the 21 senior diocesan bishops of the Church of England are also members. The House of Lords Act 1999 provides for 92 hereditary peers to remain in the House of Lords until further reform of the House has been carried out. Of these, 75 (42 Conservative, 28 crossbench, three Liberal Democrat and two Labour) are elected by hereditary peers in their political party or crossbench grouping. In addition, 15 office holders were elected by the whole house. Two hereditary peers with royal duties, the Earl Marshal and the Lord Great Chamberlain, have also remained members. Since November 2002, by-elections have been held to fill vacancies left by deaths of hereditary peers. Under the House of Lords Reform Act 2014 elected hereditary peers may also retire or resign permanently from the house. By-elections must be held within three months following the permanent retirement or death of an elected hereditary peer and take place under the Alternative Vote System.

Peers are disqualified from sitting in the house if they are:

• aliens, ie any peer who is not a British citizen, a Commonwealth citizen (under the British Nationality Act 1981) or a citizen of the Republic of Ireland
• under the age of 21
• undischarged bankrupts or, in Scotland, those whose estate is sequestered
• holders of a disqualifying judicial office
• members of the European parliament
• convicted of treason

Bishops cease to be members of the house when they retire.

Members who do not wish to attend sittings of the House of Lords may apply for leave of absence for the duration of a parliament. Since the passage of the House of Lords Reform Act 2014, members of the House may also retire permanently by giving notice in writing to the Clerk of the Parliaments.

Members of the House of Lords, who are not paid a salary, may claim a daily allowance of £300 (or may elect to claim a reduced daily allowance of £150) per sitting day – but only if they attend a sitting of the House and/or committee proceedings.
* Although the office of Lord of Appeal in Ordinary no longer exists, law lords created under the Appellate Jurisdiction Act 1876 remain members of the House. Those in office at the time of the establishment of the Supreme Court became justices of the UK Supreme Court and are not permitted to sit or vote in the House of Lords until they retire.

## COMPOSITION *as at 1 September 2015*

| | |
|---|---|
| Archbishops and bishops | 25 |
| Life peers under the Appellate Jurisdiction Act 1876 and the Life Peerages Act 1958 | 664 |
| Peers under the House of Lords Act 1999 | 86 |
| *Total* | 775 |

## 12 Parliament

STATE OF THE PARTIES *as at 1 September 2015†*

| Conservative | 225 |
| Labour | 211 |
| Liberal Democrat | 101 |
| Crossbench | 176 |
| Archbishops and bishops | 25 |
| Non-affiliated | 20 |
| Other parties | 17 |
| *Total* | 775 |

† Excluding 34 peers on leave of absence and eight disqualified as senior members of the judiciary

HOUSE OF LORDS PAY FOR SENIOR STAFF 2015–16
Senior staff are placed in the following pay bands according to their level of responsibility and taking account of other factors such as experience and marketability.

| Judicial group 4 | £176,226 |
| Senior band 3 | £104,000–£139,829 |
| Senior band 2 | £85,000–£124,845 |
| Senior band 1A | £69,000–£105,560 |
| Senior band 1 | £63,500–£93,380 |
| Band A1 | £60,824–£74,998 |
| Band A2 | £49,329–£61,741 |

OFFICERS AND OFFICIALS
The house is presided over by the Lord Speaker, whose powers differ from those of the Speaker of the House of Commons. The Lord Speaker has no power to rule on matters of order because the House of Lords is self-regulating. The maintenance of the rules of debate is the responsibility of all the members who are present.

A panel of deputy speakers is appointed by Royal Commission. The first deputy speaker is the Chair of Committees, a salaried officer of the house appointed at the beginning of each session. He or she chairs a number of 'domestic' committees relating to the internal affairs of the house . The first deputy speaker is assisted by a panel of deputy chairs, headed by the salaried Principal Deputy Chair of Committees, who is also chair of the European Union Committee of the house.

The Clerk of the Parliaments is the accounting officer and the chief permanent official responsible for the administration of the house. The Gentleman Usher of the Black Rod is responsible for security and other services and also has royal duties as secretary to the Lord Great Chamberlain.
*Lord Speaker* (£101,664), Rt. Hon. Baroness D'Souza, CMG
*Chair of Committees* (£84,524), Rt. Hon. Lord Laming, CBE
*Principal Deputy Chair of Committees* (£79,076), Lord Boswell of Aynho

*Clerk of the Parliaments* (Judicial Group 4), David Beamish
*Clerk Assistant* (Senior Band 3), Edward Ollard
*Reading Clerk and Clerk of the Overseas Office* (Senior Band 3), Simon Burton
*Gentleman Usher of the Black Rod and Serjeant-at-Arms* (Senior Band 2), Lt.-Gen. David Leakey, CMG, CBE
*Yeoman Usher of the Black Rod and Deputy Serjeant-at-Arms* (Band A1), Neil Baverstock
*Commissioner for Lords' Standards,* Paul Kernagham, CBE, QPM
*Counsel to the Chair of Committees* (Senior Band 2), Peter Milledge; P. Hardy
*Registrar of Lords' Interests* (Senior Band 1A), Brendan Keith
*Clerk of Committees* (Senior Band 2), Dr F. P. Tudor
*Legal Adviser to the Human Rights Committee* (Senior Band 2), Murray Hunt
*Director of Information Services and Librarian* (Senior Band 2), Dr Elizabeth Hallam Smith
*Director of Facilities* (Senior Band 2), Carl Woodall
*Finance Director* (Senior Band 1A), Andrew Makower
*Director of Parliamentary Digital Service* (Senior Band 1A), Rob Greig
*Director of Human Resources* (Senior Band 1A), Tom Mohan
*Clerk of Legislation* (Senior Band 1A), Jake Vaughan
*Principal Clerk of Select Committees* (Senior Band 1A), Christopher Johnson, DPHIL
*Director of Parliamentary Archives* (Senior Band 1), Adrian Brown

LORD GREAT CHAMBERLAIN'S OFFICE
*Lord Great Chamberlain,* Marquess of Cholmondeley, KCVO
*Secretary to the Lord Great Chamberlain,* Lt.-Gen. David Leakey, CMG, CBE

SELECT COMMITTEES
The main House of Lords select committees, as at July 2015, are as follows:
*Administration and Works* – *Chair,* Rt. Hon. Lord Laming, CBE; *Clerk,* Chris Atkinson
*Communications* – *Chair,* Lord Best, OBE; *Clerk,* Anna Murphy
*Constitution* – *Chair,* Lord Lang of Monkton, PC; *Clerk,* Antony Willott
*Delegated Powers and Regulatory Reform* – *Chair,* Baroness Fookes, DBE; *Clerk,* Christine Salmon Percival
*Economic Affairs* – *Chair,* Lord Hollick; *Clerk,* Ayeesha Waller
*Equality Act 2010 and Disability* – *Chair,* Baroness Deech, DBE; *Clerk,* Michael Collon
*European Union* – *Chair,* Lord Boswell of Aynho; *Principal Clerk,* Christopher Johnson, DPHIL; *Clerk,* Stuart Stoner
*European Union* – *Sub-committees:*

*Energy and Environment – Chair,* Baroness Scott of Needham Market; *Clerk,* Patrick Milner

*External Affairs – Chair,* Lord Tugendhat; *Clerk,* Eva George

*Financial Affairs – Chair,* Baroness Falkner of Margravine; *Clerk,* John Turner

*Home Affairs – Chair,* Baroness Prashar; *Clerk,* Theodore Pembroke

*Internal Market – Chair,* Lord Whitty; *Clerk,* Alicia Cunningham

*Justice – Chair,* Baroness Kennedy of the Shaws; *Clerk,* Megan Conway

*House – Chair,* Baroness D'Souza, CMG, PC; *Clerk,* Rob Whiteway

*Hybrid Instruments – Chair,* Rt. Hon. Lord Laming, CBE; *Clerk,* vacant

*Information – Chair,* Baroness Donaghy, CBE; *Clerk,*

*Liaison – Chair,* Rt. Hon. Lord Laming, CBE; *Clerk,* Philippa Tudor

*National Policy for the Built Environment – Chair,* Baroness O'Cathain, OBE; *Clerk,* Matthew Smith

*Privileges and Conduct – Chair,* Rt. Hon. Lord Laming, CBE; *Clerk,* Chloe Mawson

*Procedure – Chair,* Rt. Hon. Lord Laming, CBE; *Clerk,* Chloe Mawson

*Refreshment – Chair,* Rt. Hon. Lord Laming, CBE; *Clerk,* Chris Atkinson

*Science and Technology – Chair,* Earl of Selborne, GBE; *Clerk,* Chris Clarke

*Secondary Legislation Scrutiny – Chair,* Lord Trefgarne, PC; *Clerk,* vacant

*Selection Committee – Chair,* Rt. Hon. Lord Laming, CBE; *Clerk,* vacant

*Sexual Violence in Conflict – Chair,* Baroness Nicholson of Winterbourne; *Clerk,* Aaron Speer

*Social Mobility – Chair,* Baroness Corston, PC; *Clerk,* Luke Hussey

*Standing Orders (Private Bills) – Chair,* Rt. Hon. Lord Laming, CBE; *Clerk,* vacant

*Joint Committees:*
*Consolidation Bills*
*Human Rights*
*National Security Strategy*
*Palace of Westminster*
*Statutory Instruments – Chair,* Derek Twigg; *Clerk,* Amelia Aspden

## THE HOUSE OF COMMONS

London SW1A 0AA
T 020-7219 3000 W www.parliament.uk

HOUSE OF COMMONS INFORMATION OFFICE
14 Tothill Street, London SW1H 9NB
T 020-7219 4272 E hcinfo@parliament.uk

The members of the House of Commons are elected by universal adult suffrage. For electoral purposes, the UK is divided into constituencies, each of which returns one member to the House of Commons, the member being the candidate who obtains the largest number of votes cast in the constituency. To ensure equitable representation, the four Boundary Commissions keep constituency boundaries under review and recommend any redistribution of seats which may seem necessary because of population movements etc. At the 2010 general election the number of seats increased from 646 to 650. Of the present 650 seats, there are 533 for England, 40 for Wales, 59 for Scotland and 18 for Northern Ireland.

NUMBER OF SEATS IN THE HOUSE OF COMMONS BY COUNTRY

|                  | 2005 | 2015 |
|------------------|------|------|
| England          | 529  | 533  |
| Wales            | 40   | 40   |
| Scotland         | 59   | 59   |
| Northern Ireland | 18   | 18   |
| *Total*          | 646  | 650  |

ELECTIONS

Elections are by secret ballot, each elector casting one vote; voting is not compulsory. When a seat becomes vacant between general elections, a by-election is held.

British subjects and citizens of the Irish Republic can stand for election as MPs provided they are 18 or over and not subject to disqualification. Those disqualified from sitting in the house include:

• undischarged bankrupts
• people sentenced to more than one year's imprisonment
• members of the House of Lords (but hereditary peers not sitting in the Lords are eligible)
• holders of certain offices listed in the House of Commons Disqualification Act 1975, eg members of the judiciary, civil service, regular armed forces, police forces, some local government officers and some members of public corporations and government commissions

A candidate does not require any party backing but his or her nomination for election must be supported by the signatures of ten people registered in the constituency. A candidate must also deposit £500 with the returning officer, which is forfeit if the candidate does not receive more than 5 per cent of the votes cast. All election expenses at a general election, except the candidate's personal expenses, are subject to a statutory limit of £8,700, plus six pence for each elector in a borough constituency or nine pence for each elector in a county constituency.

*See* pages 24–81 for an alphabetical list of MPs and results of the general election in 2015.

STATE OF THE PARTIES
*as at 1 September 2015\**

| Party | Seats |
|---|---|
| Conservative | 330 |
| Labour | 232 |
| Scottish National Party | 56 |
| Democratic Unionist Party | 8 |
| Liberal Democrats | 8 |
| Sinn Fein (have not taken their seats) | 4 |
| Plaid Cymru | 3 |
| Social Democratic & Labour Party | 3 |
| Ulster Unionist Party | 2 |
| Green | 1 |
| Independent | 1 |
| The Speaker | 1 |
| UK Independence Party | 1 |
| Total | 650 |

* Working majority of 16; 330 Conservative MPs less all other parties (exlcuding the speaker, deputy speakers and Sinn Fein)

BUSINESS
The week's business of the house is outlined each Thursday by the leader of the house, after consultation between the chief government whip and the chief opposition whip. A quarter to a third of the time will be taken up by the government's legislative programme and the rest by other business. As a rule, bills likely to raise political controversy are introduced in the Commons before going on to the Lords, and the Commons claims exclusive control in respect of national taxation and expenditure. Bills such as the finance bill, which imposes taxation, and the consolidated fund bills, which authorise expenditure, must begin in the Commons. A bill of which the financial provisions are subsidiary may begin in the Lords, and the Commons may waive its rights in regard to Lords' amendments affecting finance.

The Commons has a public register of MPs' financial and certain other interests; this is published annually as a House of Commons paper. Members must also disclose any relevant financial interest or benefit in a matter before the house when taking part in a debate, in certain other proceedings of the house, or in consultations with other MPs, with ministers or with civil servants.

MEMBERS' PAY AND ALLOWANCES
Since 1911 members of the House of Commons have received salary payments; facilities for free travel were introduced in 1924. Salary rates for the last 30 years are as follows:

| | | | |
|---|---|---|---|
| 1985 Jan | £16,904 | 2000 Apr | £48,371 |
| 1986 Jan | 17,702 | 2001 Apr | 49,822 |
| 1987 Jan | 18,500 | 2002 Apr | 55,118 |
| 1988 Jan | 22,548 | 2003 Apr | 56,358 |
| 1989 Jan | 24,107 | 2004 Apr | 57,485 |
| 1990 Jan | 26,701 | 2005 Apr | 59,095 |
| 1991 Jan | 28,970 | 2006 Apr | 59,686 |
| 1992 Jan | 30,854 | 2007 Apr | 61,181 |
| 1993 Jan | 30,854 | 2008 Apr | 63,291 |
| 1994 Jan | 31,687 | 2009 Apr | 64,766 |
| 1995 Jan | 33,189 | 2010 Apr | 65,738 |
| 1996 Jan | 34,085 | 2011 Apr | 65,738 |
| 1996 Jul | 43,000 | 2012 Apr | 65,738 |
| 1997 Apr | 43,860 | 2013 Apr | 66,396 |
| 1998 Apr | 45,066 | 2014 Apr | 67,060 |
| 1999 Apr | 47,008 | 2015 May | 74,000 |

The Independent Parliamentary Standards Authority (IPSA) was established under the Parliamentary Standards Act 2009 and is responsible for the independent regulation and administration of the MPs' Scheme of Business Costs and Expenses, as well as for paying the salaries of MPs and their staff members. Since May 2011, the IPSA has also been responsible for determining MPs' pay and setting the level of any increase to their salary.

For 2015–16, the office costs expenditure budget is £26,050 for London area MPs and £23,400 for non-London area MPs. The maximum annual staff budget for London area MPs is £147,000 and £140,000 for non-London area MPs.

Since 1972 MPs have been able to claim reimbursement for the additional cost of staying overnight away from their main residence while on parliamentary business. This is not payable to London area MPs and those MPs who reside in 'grace and favour' accommodation. Accommodation expenses for MPs claiming rental payments in the London area is capped at £20,600 a year; outside of the London area each constituency is banded according to rental values in the area and capped accordingly; annual caps range from £10,400 to £15,650 across five bands. For MPs who own their own homes, mortgage interest and associated expenses up to £8,850 are payable.

For ministerial salaries *see* Government Departments.

MEMBERS' PENSIONS
Pension arrangements for MPs were first introduced in 1964. Under the Parliamentary Contributory Pension Fund CARE (career-averaged revalued earnings) scheme, MPs receive a pension on retirement based upon accumulating proportions of pensionable earnings over each year of membership. MPs contributions are payable at a rate of 11.09 per cent of pay. Exchequer contributions are paid at a

rate recommended by the Government Actuary and meet the balance of the cost of providing MPs' retirement benefits. Pensions are normally payable upon retirement at age 65 to those who are no longer MPs. Abated pensions may be payable to members aged 55 or over. Pensions are also payable to spouses and other qualifying partners of deceased scheme members at the rate of three-eighths of the deceased member's pension. In the case of members who are in service, an enhanced spouse's or partner's pension and a lump sum equal to two times pensionable salary is payable. There are also provisions in place for dependants and MPs of any age who retire due to ill health. All pensions are CPI index-linked.

## HOUSE OF COMMONS PAY BANDS FOR SENIOR STAFF

Senior Staff are placed in the following Senior Civil Service pay bands. These pay bands apply to the most senior staff in departments and agencies.

| Pay Band 1 | £63,500–£93,380 |
| Pay Band 1A | £67,600–£105,560 |
| Pay Band 2 | £85,000–£124,845 |
| Pay Band 3 | £104,000–£139,829 |

## OFFICERS AND OFFICIALS

The House of Commons is presided over by the Speaker, who has considerable powers to maintain order. A deputy speaker, called the Chairman of Ways and Means, and two deputy chairs may preside over sittings of the House of Commons; they are elected by the house, and, like the Speaker, neither speak nor vote other than in their official capacity.

The staff of the house are employed by a commission chaired by the Speaker. The heads of the six House of Commons departments are permanent officers of the house, not MPs. The Clerk of the House is the principal adviser to the Speaker on the privileges and procedures of the house, the conduct of the business of the house, and committees. The Serjeant-at-Arms is responsible for security and ceremonial functions of the house.

*Speaker* (£142,826)*, Rt. Hon. John Bercow, MP
*Chairman of Ways and Means* (£107,108),
 Rt. Hon. Lindsay Hoyle, MP
*First Deputy Chairman of Ways and Means*
 (£102,098), Eleanor Laing, MP
*Second Deputy Chairman of Ways and Means*
 (£102,098), Natascha Engel, MP

*House of Commons Commission*, Rt, Hon. John
 Bercow, MP *(chair)*; Sir Paul Beresford, MP;
 Angela Eagle, MP; Rt. Hon. Chris Grayling, MP
*Secretary of the Commission,* Robert Twigger

 * Salaries in parentheses are the maximum available. The Speaker and Deputies have opted not to take the statutory increases awarded to them each year as office holders.

## OFFICE OF THE SPEAKER
*Speaker's Secretary,* Peter Barratt
*Assistant Secretary to the Speaker,* Ian Davies, MBE
*Trainbearer,* Jim Davey
*Speaker's Counsel,* Michael Carpenter, CB
*Chaplain to the Speaker,* Revd Rose Hudson-Wilkin

## OFFICE OF THE CLERK OF THE HOUSE
*Clerk of the House,* David Natzler
*Private Secretary,* Lloyd Owen

## PARLIAMENTARY COMMISSIONER FOR STANDARDS
*Parliamentary Commissioner for Standards,* Kathryn
 Hudson
*Registrar of Members' Financial Interests,* Heather Wood

## PARLIAMENTARY SECURITY DIRECTOR
*Parliamentary Security Director,* Paul Martin, CBE
*Deputy Parliamentary Security Director,* Emily
 Baldock

## OFFICE OF THE CHAIRMAN OF WAYS AND MEANS
*Secretary to the Chairman of Ways and Means,*
 Joanna Dodd

## GOVERNANCE OFFICE
*Head of Office,* Tom Goldsmith
*Corportate Risk Management Facilitator,* Rachel
 Harrison
*Head of Central Communications,* Marianne
 Cwynarski
*Head of Internal Audit,* Paul Dillon-Robinson
*Head of Parliamentary Programme and Project
 Assurance,* Jane Rumsam
*Strategy, Planning and Performance Manager,*
 Jane Hough

## DEPARTMENT OF CHAMBER AND COMMITTEE SERVICES
*Acting Clerk Assistant and Acting Director General,*
 Jacqy Sharpe
*Director of Departmental Services,* Elizabeth Hunt

## OVERSEAS OFFICE
*Principal Clerk,* Crispin Poyser
*Delegation Secretary,* Nick Wright
*Inward Visits Manager,* Alison Game, MBE
*National Parliament Representative (Brussels),* Alison
 Grove

COMMITTEE OFFICE
*Clerk of Committees,* Andrew Kennon
*Principal Clerk of Select Committees,* Mark Hutton;
  Colin Lee; Simon Patrick
*Business Managers,* Anita Fuki; Richard Dawson
*Operations Manager,* Karen Saunders

DEPARTMENTAL SELECT COMMITTEES
*Backbench Business – Chair,* Ian Mearns; *Clerk,* Mike
  Hennessy
*Business, Innovation and Skills – Chair,* Iain Wright;
  *Clerk,* Jessica Montgomery
*Communities and Local Government – Chair,* Clive
  Betts; *Clerk,* Dr Anna Dickson
*Culture, Media and Sport – Chair,* Jesse Norman;
  *Clerk,* Elizabeth Flood
*Defence – Chair,* Dr Julian Lewis; *Clerk,* James
  Davies
*Education – Chair,* Neil Carmichael; *Clerk,* Lynn
  Gardner
*Energy and Climate Change – Chair,* Angus Brendan
  MacNeil; *Clerk,* Dr Farrah Bhatti
*Environment, Food and Rural Affairs – Chair,* Neil
  Parish; *Clerks,* David Weir
*Foreign Affairs – Chair,* Crispin Blunt; *Clerk,*
  Kenneth Fox
*Health – Chair,* Dr Sarah Wollaston; *Clerk,* Huw
  Yardley
*High Speed Rail Bill – Chair,* Robert Syms; *Clerk,*
  Neil Caulfield
*Home Affairs – Chair,* Keith Vaz; *Clerk,* Carol
  Oxborough
*International Development – Chair,* Stephen Twigg;
  *Clerk,* Kate Emms
*Justice – Chair,* Robert Neill; *Clerk,* Nick Walker
*Northern Ireland Affairs – Chair,* Laurence
  Robertson; *Clerk,* Mike Clark
*Procedure – Chair,* Charles Walker; *Clerk,* Martyn
  Atkins
*Science and Technology – Chair,* Nicola Blackwood;
  *Clerk,* Simon Fiander
*Scottish Affairs – Chair,* Pete Wishart; *Clerk,* Jyoti
  Chandola
*Standards – Chair,* Kevin Barron; *Clerk,* Eve Samson
*Statutory Instruments – Chair,* Derek Twigg; *Clerk,*
  Amelia Aspden
*Transport – Chair,* Louise Ellman; *Clerk,* Gordon
  Clarke
*Treasury – Chair,* Andrew Tyrie; *Clerk,* James Rhys
*Welsh Affairs – Chair,* David Davies; *Clerk,* Richard
  Ward
*Women and Equalities – Chair,* Maria Miller; *Clerk,*
  Gosia McBride
*Work and Pensions – Chair,* Frank Field; *Clerk,*
  Adam Mellows-Facer

DOMESTIC COMMITTEES
*Administration – Chair,* Sir Paul Beresford; Clerks,
  Sarah Heath; Helen Wood

*Finance – Chair,* Nicholas Brown; *Clerk,* Robert
  Twigger
*Members' Expenses – Chair,* vacant; *Clerk,* Robert
  Twigger

OTHER COMMITTEES
*Environmental Audit – Chair,* Huw Irranca-Davies;
  *Clerk,* David Slater
*Liaison – Chair,* vacant; *Clerk,* Andrew Kennon
*Petitions Committee – Chair,* Helen Jones; *Clerk,*
  Anne-Marie Griffiths
*Public Accounts – Chair,* Meg Hillier; *Clerk,* Sarah
  Petit
*Public Administration and Constitutional Affairs –
  Chair,* Bernard Jenkin; *Clerks,* Dr Rebecca Davies;
  Sian Woodward
*Regulatory Reform – Chair,* vacant; *Clerk,* Jessica
  Montgomery
*European Scrutiny Committee – Chair,* Sir William
  Cash; *Clerk,* Sarah Davies

SCRUTINY UNIT
*Head of Unit,* Jessica Mulley
*Deputy Head of Unit,* Larry Honeysett

VOTE OFFICE
*Deliverer of the Vote,* Catherine Fogarty
*Deputy Deliverer of the Vote,* Owen Sweeney
*Head of Procedural Publishing,* Tom McVeagh
*Procedural Publishing Operations Manager,* Stuart
  Miller

CHAMBER BUSINESS DIRECTORATE
*Acting Clerk of Legislation,* Liam Laurence Smyth
*Principal Clerks*
  *Table Office,* Philippa Helme
  *Journals,* Paul Evans
  *Bills,* Matthew Hamlyn

OFFICIAL REPORT DIRECTORATE
*Editor,* Lorraine Sutherland
*Deputy Editor,* Alex Newton
*Director of Broadcasting,* John Angeli

SERJEANT-AT-ARMS DIRECTORATE
*Serjeant-at-Arms,* Lawrence Ward
*Deputy Serjeant-at-Arms,* Richard Latham
*Assistant Serjeant-at-Arms,* Lesley Scott

OFFICE OF SPEAKER'S COUNSEL
*Speaker's Counsel and Head of Legal Services Office,*
  Michael Carpenter, CB
*Counsel for European Legislation,* Arnold Ridout
*Assistant Counsel for European Legislation,* Joanne
  Dee
*Counsel for Domestic Legislation,* Peter Davis
*Deputy Counsel for Domestic Legislation,* Peter
  Brooksbank; Philip Davies; Daniel Greenberg
*Principal Assistant Counsel,* Helen Emes
*Legal Assistants,* Ami Cochrane; Emma Johnston

DEPARTMENT OF FACILITIES
*Director-General,* John Borley, CB
*Director of Business Management,* Della Herd
*Acting Parliamentary Director of Estates,* Brian
  Finnimore
*Director of Accommodation and Logistics Services,*
  Fiona Channon
*Director of Facilities Finance,* Philip Collins
*Executive Officer,* Katie Phelan-Molloy
*Director of Catering Services,* Richard Tapner-Evans
*Operations Manager,* Robert Gibbs
*Executive Chef,* Mark Hill

DEPARTMENT OF FINANCE
*Director of Finance,* Myfanwy Barrett
*Chief Accountant,* Alex Mills
*Head of Financial Planning,* Amanda Colledge
*Head of Financial Accounting,* Debra Shirtcliffe
*Head of Financial Services,* Sam Rao

DEPARTMENT OF HUMAN RESOURCES
AND CHANGE
*Director-General of HR and Change,* Andrew J.
  Walker
*Director of HR Services,* Alix Langley
*Occupational Health and Wellbeing Manager,* Anne
  Mossop
*Head of Safety,* Dr Marianne McDougall

DEPARTMENT OF INFORMATION SERVICES
*Director-General and Librarian,* Penny Young
*Director of Service Delivery,* John Benger
*Head of Central Support Services,* Grahame Allen
*Curator of Works of Art,* Malcolm Hay
*Head of Customer Services,* Dr Patsy Richards

PARLIAMENTARY INFORMATION AND
COMMUNICATION TECHNOLOGY (ICT)
*Director of Parliamentary Digital Service,* Rob Greig
*Director of Technology,* Steve O'Connor
*Director of Operations and Members Services,* Rob
  Sanders
*Director of Resources,* Tracey Jessup
*Director of Programmes and Projects,* Steven Mark
*Head of the Web and Intranet Service,* Tracy Green

OTHER PRINCIPAL OFFICERS
*Clerk of the Crown in Chancery,* Dame Ursula
  Brennan
*Parliamentary and Health Service Ombudsman,* Dame
  Julie Mellor

NATIONAL AUDIT OFFICE
157–197 Buckingham Palace Road, London SW1W 9SP
T 020-7798 7000
E enquiries@nao.gsi.gov.uk W www.nao.org.uk

The National Audit Office came into existence under the National Audit Act 1983 to replace and continue the work of the former Exchequer and Audit Department. The act reinforced the office's total financial and operational independence from the government and brought its head, the Comptroller and Auditor-General, into a closer relationship with parliament as an officer of the House of Commons.

The National Audit Office (NAO) scrutinises public spending on behalf of parliament, helping it to hold government departments to account and helping public service managers improve performance and service delivery. The NAO audits the financial statements of all government departments and a wide range of other public bodies. It regularly publishes 'value for money' reports on the efficiency and effectiveness of how public resources are used.
*Comptroller and Auditor-General,* Amyas Morse
*Assistant Auditors-General,* Sue Higgins; Sally
  Howes; Martin Sinclair; John Thorpe
*Chief Operating Officer,* Michael Whitehouse

## PARLIAMENTARY INFORMATION

The following is a short glossary of aspects of the work of parliament. Unless otherwise stated, references are to House of Commons procedures.

BILL – Proposed legislation is termed a bill. The stages of a public bill (for private bills, *see* below) in the House of Commons are as follows:

*First reading:* This stage introduces the legislation to the house and, for government bills, merely constitutes an order to have the bill printed.

*Second reading:* The debate on the principles of the bill.

*Committee stage:* The detailed examination of a bill, clause by clause. In most cases this takes place in a public bill committee, or the whole house may act as a committee. Public bill committees may take evidence before embarking on detailed scrutiny of the bill. Very rarely, a bill may be examined by a select committee.

*Report stage:* Detailed review of a bill as amended in committee, on the floor of the house, and an opportunity to make further changes.

*Third reading:* Final debate on the full bill in the Commons.

Public bills go through the same stages in the House of Lords, but with important differences: the committee stage is taken in committee of the whole house or in a grand committee, in which any peer may participate. There are no time limits, all amendments are debated, and further amendments can be made at third reading.

A bill may start in either house, and has to pass through both houses to become law. Both houses have to agree the final text of a bill, so that amendments made by the second house are then considered in the originating house, and if not agreed, sent back or themselves amended, until agreement is reached.

CHILTERN HUNDREDS – A nominal office of profit under the crown, the acceptance of which requires an MP to vacate his/her seat. The Manor of Northstead is similar. These are the only means by which an MP may resign.

CONSOLIDATED FUND BILL – A bill to authorise the issue of money to maintain government services. The bill is dealt with without debate.

EARLY DAY MOTION – A motion put on the notice paper by an MP without, in general, the real prospect of its being debated. Such motions are expressions of back-bench opinion.

FATHER OF THE HOUSE – The MP whose continuous service in the House of Commons is the longest. The present Father of the House is the Rt. Hon. Sir Gerald Kaufman, MP.

GRAND COMMITTEES – There are three grand committees in the House of Commons, one each for Northern Ireland, Scotland and Wales; they consider matters relating specifically to that country. In the House of Lords, bills may be sent to a grand committee instead of a committee of the whole house (see also Bill).

HOURS OF MEETING – The House of Commons normally meets on Mondays at 2.30pm, Tuesdays and Wednesdays at 11.30am, Thursdays at 9.30am and some Fridays at 9.30am. (See also Westminster Hall Sittings, below.) The House of Lords normally meets at 2.30pm Mondays and Tuesdays, 3pm on Wednesdays and at 11am on Thursdays. The House of Lords occasionally sits on Fridays at 10am.

LEADER OF THE OPPOSITION – In 1937 the office of leader of the opposition was recognised and a salary was assigned to the post. In 2015–16 this is £135,776 (including a parliamentary salary of £74,000). The present leader of the opposition is the Rt. Hon. Jeremy Corbyn, MP.

THE LORD CHANCELLOR – The office of Lord High Chancellor of Great Britain was significantly altered by the Constitutional Reform Act 2005. Previously, the Lord Chancellor was (ex officio) the Speaker of the House of Lords, and took part in debates and voted in divisions in the House of Lords. The Department for Constitutional Affairs was created in 2003, and became the Ministry of Justice in 2007, incorporating most of the responsibilities of the Lord Chancellor's department. The role of Speaker has been transferred to the post of Lord Speaker. The Constitutional Reform Act 2005 also brought to an end the Lord Chancellor's role as head of the judiciary. A Judicial Appointments Commission was created in April 2006, and a supreme court (separate from the House of Lords) was established in 2009.

THE LORD GREAT CHAMBERLAIN – The Lord Great Chamberlain is a Great Officer of State, the office being hereditary since the grant of Henry I to the family of De Vere, Earls of Oxford. It is now a joint hereditary office rotating on the death of the sovereign between the Cholmondeley, Carington and Ancaster families.

The Lord Great Chamberlain, currently the Marquess of Cholmondeley, is responsible for the royal apartments in the Palace of Westminster, the Royal Gallery, the administration of the Chapel of St Mary Undercroft and, in conjunction with the Lord Speaker and the Speaker of the House of Commons, Westminster Hall. The Lord Great Chamberlain has the right to perform specific services at a coronation and has particular responsibility for the internal administrative arrangements within the House of Lords for state openings of parliament.

THE LORD SPEAKER – The first Lord Speaker of the House of Lords, the Rt. Hon. Baroness Hayman, took up office on 4 July 2006. The Lord Speaker is independent of the government and elected by members of the House of Lords rather than appointed by the prime minister. Although the Lord Speaker's primary role is to preside over proceedings in the House of Lords, she does not have the same powers as the Speaker of the House of Commons. For example, the Lord Speaker is not responsible for maintaining order during debates, as this is the responsibility of the house as a whole. The Lord Speaker sits in the Lords on one of the woolsacks, which are couches covered in red cloth and stuffed with wool.

OPPOSITION DAY – A day on which the topic for debate is chosen by the opposition. There are 20 such days in a normal session. On 17 days, subjects are chosen by the leader of the opposition; on the remaining three days by the leader of the next largest opposition party.

PARLIAMENT ACTS 1911 AND 1949 – Under these acts, bills may become law without the consent of the Lords, though the House of Lords has the power to delay a public bill for a parliamentary session.

PRIME MINISTER'S QUESTIONS – The prime minister answers questions from 12 to 12.30pm on Wednesdays.

PRIVATE BILL – A bill promoted by a body or an individual to give powers additional to, or in conflict with, the general law, and to which a special procedure applies to enable people affected to object.

PRIVATE MEMBER'S BILL – A public bill promoted by an MP or peer who is not a member of the government.

PRIVATE NOTICE QUESTION – A question adjudged of urgent importance on submission to the Speaker (in the Lords, the Lord Speaker), answered at the end of oral questions.

PRIVILEGE – The House of Commons has rights and immunities to protect it from obstruction in carrying out its duties. These are known as parliamentary privilege and enable Members of Parliament to debate freely. The most important privilege is that of freedom of speech. MPs cannot be prosecuted for sedition or sued for libel or slander over anything said during proceedings in the house. This enables them to raise in the house questions affecting the public good which might be difficult to raise outside owing to the possibility of legal action against them. The House of Lords has similar privileges.

QUESTION TIME – Oral questions are answered by ministers in the Commons from 2.30 to 3.30pm on Mondays, 11.30am to 12.30pm on Tuesdays and Wednesdays, and 9.30 to 10.30am on Thursdays. Questions are also taken for half an hour at the start of the Lords sittings.

ROYAL ASSENT – The royal assent is signified by letters patent to such bills and measures as have passed both Houses of Parliament (or bills which have been passed under the Parliament Acts 1911 and 1949). The sovereign has not given royal assent in person since 1854. On occasion, for instance in the prorogation of parliament, royal assent may be pronounced to the two houses by Lords Commissioners. More usually royal assent is notified to each house sitting separately in accordance with the Royal Assent Act 1967. The old French formulae for royal assent are then endorsed on the acts by the Clerk of the Parliaments.

The power to withhold assent resides with the sovereign but has not been exercised in the UK since 1707.

SELECT COMMITTEES – Consisting usually of 10 to 15 members of all parties, select committees are a means used by both houses in order to investigate certain matters.

Most select committees in the House of Commons are tied to departments: each committee investigates subjects within a government department's remit. There are other select committees dealing with matters such as public accounts (ie the spending by the government of money voted by parliament) and European legislation, and also committees advising on procedures and domestic administration of the house. Major select committees usually take evidence in public; their evidence and reports are published on the parliament website and in hard copy by The Stationery Office (TSO). House of Commons select committees are reconstituted after a general election.

In the House of Lords, select committees do not mirror government departments but cover broader issues. There is a select committee on the European Union (EU), which has six sub-committees dealing with specific areas of EU policy, a select committee on science and technology, a select committee on economic affairs and also one on the constitution. There is also a select committee on delegated powers and regulatory reform and one on privileges and conduct. In addition, *ad hoc* select committees have been set up from time to time to investigate specific subjects. There are also joint committees of the two houses, eg the committees on statutory instruments and on human rights.

THE SPEAKER – The Speaker of the House of Commons is the spokesperson and chair of the Chamber. He or she is elected by the house at the beginning of each parliament or when the previous Speaker retires or dies. The Speaker neither speaks in debates nor votes in divisions except when the voting is equal.

VACANT SEATS – When a vacancy occurs in the House of Commons during a session of parliament, the writ for the by-election is moved by a whip of the party to which the member whose seat has been vacated belonged. If the house is in recess, the Speaker can issue a warrant for a writ, should two members certify to him that a seat is vacant.

WESTMINSTER HALL SITTINGS – Following a report by the Modernisation of the House of Commons Select Committee, the Commons decided in May 1999 to set up a second debating forum. It is known as 'Westminster Hall' and sittings are in the Grand Committee Room on some Mondays from 4.30pm to 7.30pm, Tuesdays and Wednesdays from 9.30am to 11.30am and from 2pm to 5pm, and Thursdays from 1.30pm to 4.30pm. Sittings are open to the public at the times indicated.

WHIPS – In order to secure the attendance of members of a particular party in parliament, particularly on the occasion of an important vote, whips (originally known as 'whippers-in') are appointed. The written appeal or circular letter issued by them is also known as a 'whip', its urgency being denoted by the number of times it is underlined. Failure to respond to a three-line whip is tantamount in the Commons to secession (at any rate temporarily) from the party. Whips are provided with office accommodation in both houses, and government and some opposition whips receive salaries from public funds.

## PARLIAMENTARY ARCHIVES

Houses of Parliament, London SW1A 0PW
T 020-7219 3074 E archives@parliament.uk
W www.parliament.uk/archives

Since 1497, the records of parliament have been kept within the Palace of Westminster. They are in the custody of the Clerk of Parliaments. In 1946 the House of Lords Record Office, which became the Parliamentary Archives in 2006, was established to supervise their preservation and their availability to the public. Some 3 million documents are preserved, including acts of parliament from 1497, journals of the House of Lords from 1510, minutes and committee proceedings from 1610, and papers laid before parliament from 1531. Among the records are the Petition of Right, the death warrant of Charles I, the Declaration of Breda, and the Bill of Rights. Records are made available through a public search room.

*Director of the Parliamentary Archives,* Adrian Brown

# GOVERNMENT OFFICE

The government is the body of ministers responsible for the administration of national affairs, determining policy and introducing into parliament any legislation necessary to give effect to government policy. The majority of ministers are members of the House of Commons but members of the House of Lords, or of neither house, may also hold ministerial responsibility. The prime minister is, by current convention, always a member of the House of Commons.

### THE PRIME MINISTER

The office of prime minister, which had been in existence for nearly 200 years, was officially recognised in 1905 and its holder was granted a place in the table of precedence. The prime minister, by tradition also First Lord of the Treasury and Minister for the Civil Service, is appointed by the sovereign and is usually the leader of the party which enjoys, or can secure, a majority in the House of Commons. Other ministers are appointed by the sovereign on the recommendation of the prime minister, who also allocates functions among ministers and has the power to dismiss ministers from their posts.

The prime minister informs the sovereign on state and political matters, advises on the dissolution of parliament, and makes recommendations for important crown appointments, ie the award of honours, etc.

As the chair of cabinet meetings and leader of a political party, the prime minister is responsible for translating party policy into government activity. As leader of the government, the prime minister is responsible to parliament and to the electorate for the policies and their implementation.

The prime minister also represents the nation in international affairs, eg summit conferences.

### THE CABINET

The cabinet developed during the 18th century as an inner committee of the Privy Council, which was the chief source of executive power until that time. The cabinet is composed of about 20 ministers chosen by the prime minister, usually the heads of government departments (generally known as secretaries of state unless they have a special title, eg Chancellor of the Exchequer), the leaders of the two houses of parliament, and the holders of various traditional offices.

The cabinet's functions are the final determination of policy, control of government and coordination of government departments. The exercise of its functions is dependent upon the incumbent party's (or parties') majority support in the House of Commons. Cabinet meetings are held in private, taking place once or twice a week during parliamentary sittings and less often during a recess. Proceedings are confidential, the members being bound by their oath as privy counsellors not to disclose information about the proceedings.

The convention of collective responsibility means that the cabinet acts unanimously even when cabinet ministers do not all agree on a subject. The policies of departmental ministers must be consistent with the policies of the government as a whole, and once the government's policy has been decided, each minister is expected to support it or resign.

The convention of ministerial responsibility holds a minister, as the political head of his or her department, accountable to parliament for the department's work. Departmental ministers usually decide all matters within their responsibility, although on matters of political importance they normally consult their colleagues collectively. A decision by a departmental minister is binding on the government as a whole.

# POLITICAL PARTIES

Before the reign of William and Mary, the principal officers of state were chosen by and were responsible to the sovereign alone, and not to parliament or the nation at large. Such officers acted sometimes in concert with one another but more often independently, and the fall of one did not, of necessity, involve that of others, although all were liable to be dismissed at any moment.

In 1693 the Earl of Sunderland recommended to William III the advisability of selecting a ministry from the political party which enjoyed a majority in the House of Commons, and the first united ministry was drawn in 1696 from the Whigs, to which party the king owed his throne. This group became known as the 'junto' and was regarded with suspicion as a novelty in the political life of the nation, being a small section meeting in secret apart from the main body of ministers. It may be regarded as the forerunner of the cabinet and in the course of time it led to the establishment of the principle of joint responsibility of ministers, so that internal disagreement caused a change of personnel or resignation of the whole body of ministers.

The accession of George I, who was unfamiliar with the English language, led to a disinclination on the part of the sovereign to preside at meetings of his ministers and caused the emergence of a prime minister, a position first acquired by Robert Walpole in 1721 and retained by him without interruption for 20 years and 326 days. The office of prime minister was formally recognised in 1905 when it was established by royal warrant.

## DEVELOPMENT OF PARTIES

In 1828 the Whigs became known as Liberals, a name originally given by opponents to imply laxity of principles, but gradually accepted by the party to indicate its claim to be pioneers and champions of political reform and progressive legislation. In 1861 a Liberal Registration Association was founded and Liberal Associations became widespread. In 1877 a National Liberal Federation was formed, with its headquarters in London. The Liberal Party was in power for long periods during the second half of the 19th century and for several years during the first quarter of the 20th century, but after a split in the party in 1931, the numbers elected remained small. In 1988 a majority of the Liberals agreed on a merger with the Social Democratic Party under the title Social and Liberal Democrats; since 1989 they have been known as the Liberal Democrats. A minority continue separately as the Liberal Party.

Soon after the change from Whig to Liberal, the Tory Party became known as Conservative, a name believed to have been invented by John Wilson Croker in 1830 and to have been generally adopted around the time of the passing of the Reform Act of 1832 – to indicate that the preservation of national institutions was the leading principle of the party. After the Home Rule crisis of 1886 the dissentient Liberals entered into a compact with the Conservatives, under which the latter undertook not to contest their seats, but a separate Liberal Unionist organisation was maintained until 1912, when it was united with the Conservatives.

Labour candidates for parliament made their first appearance at the general election of 1892, when there were 27 standing as Labour or Liberal-Labour. In 1900 the Labour Representation Committee (LRC) was set up in order to establish a distinct Labour group in parliament, with its own whips, its own policy, and a readiness to cooperate with any party which might be engaged in promoting legislation in the direct interests of labour. In 1906 the LRC became known as the Labour Party.

The Green Party was founded in 1973 and campaigns for social and environmental justice. The party began as 'People', was renamed the Ecology Party, and became the Green Party in 1985.

The UK Independence Party (UKIP) was founded in 1993 by members of the Anti-Federalist League. It is a right-wing populist party with one key policy – to leave the European Union. In the 2014 European elections, UKIP became the first party, other than the Conservatives or Labour to win a national election in over a century.

Plaid Cymru was founded in 1926 to provide an independent political voice for Wales and to campaign for self-government in Wales.

The Scottish National Party (SNP) was founded in 1934 to campaign for independence for Scotland and a referendum on the subject was held in September 2014 which culminated in a 'no' to independence result.

The Social Democratic and Labour Party (SDLP) was founded in 1970, emerging from the civil rights movement of the 1960s, with the aim of promoting reform, reconciliation and partnership across the sectarian divide in Northern Ireland, and of opposing violence from any quarter.

The Democratic Unionist Party (DUP) was founded in 1971 to resist moves by the Ulster Unionist Party which were considered a threat to the Union. Its aim is to maintain Northern Ireland as an integral part of the UK.

The Alliance Party of Northern Ireland was formed in 1970 as a non-sectarian unionist party.

Sinn Fein first emerged in the 1900s as a federation of nationalist clubs. It is a left-wing republican and labour party that seeks to end British governance in Ireland and achieve a 32-county republic.

## GOVERNMENT AND OPPOSITION

The government is formed by the party which wins the largest number of seats in the House of Commons at a general election, or which has the support of a majority of members in the House of Commons. By tradition, the leader of the majority party is asked by the sovereign to form a government, while the largest minority party becomes the official opposition with its own leader and a shadow cabinet. Leaders of the government and opposition sit on the front benches of the Commons with their supporters (the back-benchers) sitting behind them.

## FINANCIAL SUPPORT

Financial support for opposition parties in the House of Commons was introduced in 1975 and is commonly known as Short Money, after Edward Short, the leader of the house at that time, who introduced the scheme. Short Money is only payable to those parties that secured at least two seats, or one seat and more than 150,000 votes, at the previous general election and is only intended to provide assistance for parliamentary duties. The amount payable is £16,956.86 for every seat won at the most recent general election plus £33.86 for every 200 votes gained by the party. Short Money approximations for 2015–16 are:

| | |
|---|---|
| DUP | £166,000 |
| Green | £212,000 |
| Labour | £6,200,000 |
| Liberal Democrats | £450,000 |
| Plaid Cymru | £81,000 |
| SDLP | £70,000 |
| SNP | £1,200,000 |
| UKIP | £650,000 |

The sum paid to Sinn Fein and any other party that may choose not to take their seats in the House of Commons is calculated on the same basis as Short Money, but is known as Representative Money.

A specific allocation of around £777,500, for the leader of the opposition's office was introduced in April 1999.

Financial support for opposition parties in the House of Lords was introduced in 1996 and is commonly known as Cranborne Money, after former leader of the house, Viscount Cranborne.

The following list of political parties are those with at least one MP or sitting member of the House of Lords in the present parliament.

## CONSERVATIVE PARTY

Conservative Campaign Headquarters,
4 Matthew Parker Street, London SW1H 9HQ
T 020-7222 9000 W www.conservatives.com
*Parliamentary Party Leader,* Rt. Hon. David Cameron, MP
*Leader in the Lords and Lord Privy Seal,* Rt. Hon. Baroness Stowell of Beeston, MBE
*Leader in the Commons and Lord President of the Council,* Rt. Hon. Chris Grayling, MP
*Deputy Leader in the Commons,* Dr Thérèse Coffey, MP
*Chair,* Lord Feldman of Elstree
*Party Treasurer,* Michael Farmer

## GREEN PARTY

Development House, 56–64 Leonard Street,
London, EC2A 4LT
T 020-7549 0310 E office@greenparty.org.uk
W www.greenparty.org.uk
*Party Leader,* Natalie Bennett
*Deputy Leaders,* Shahrar Ali; Amelia Womack
*Chair,* Richard Mallender
*Finance Coordinator,* Michael Coffey

## LABOUR PARTY

Labour Central, Kings Manor,
Newcastle upon Tyne NE1 6PA
T 0845-092 2299 W www.labour.org.uk
*General Secretary,* Iain McNicol
*General Secretary, Welsh Labour,* Dave Hagendyk
*General Secretary, Scottish Labour Party,* Brian Roy

SHADOW CABINET *as at September 2015*
*Leader of the Opposition,* Rt. Hon. Jeremy Corbyn, MP
*Deputy Leader,* Tom Watson, MP
*Chancellor of the Exchequer,* John McDonnell, MP
*Secretary of State for Foreign Affairs,* Rt. Hon. Hilary Benn, MP
*Secretary of State for the Home Department,* Rt. Hon. Andy Burnham, MP
*First Secretary of State for Business, Innovation and Skills,* Angela Eagle, MP
*Secretary of State for Communities and Local Government and Minister for Constitutional Convention,* Jon Trickett, MP
*Secretary of State for Culture, Media and Sport,* Michael Dugher, MP
*Secretary of State for Defence,* Maria Eagle, MP
*Secretary of State for Education,* Lucy Powell, MP
*Secretary of State for Energy and Climate Change,* Lisa Nandy, MP
*Secretary of State for Environment, Food and Rural Affairs,* Kerry McCarthy, MP
*Secretary of State for Health,* Heidi Alexander, MP
*Minister for Mental Health,* Luciana Berger, MP
*Minister for Housing and Planning,* Rt. Hon. John Healey, MP
*Secretary of State for International Development,* Diane Abbott, MP
*Lord Chancellor and Secretary of State for Justice,* Rt. Hon. Lord Falconer of Thoroton, QC
*Secretary of State for Northern Ireland,* Vernon Coaker, MP
*Secretary of State for Scotland,* Ian Murray, MP
*Secretary of State for Transport,* Lilian Greenwood, MP
*Chief Secretary to the Treasury,* Seema Malhotra, MP
*Minister for Women and Equalities,* Kate Green, MP
*Secretary of State for Wales,* Nia Griffith, MP
*Secretary of State for Work and Pensions,* Owen Smith, MP
*Minister for Young People and Voter Registration,* Gloria De Piero, MP
*Leader of the House of Commons,* Chris Bryant, MP
*Leader of the House of Lords,* Rt. Hon. Baroness Smith of Basildon
*Attorney-General,* Catherine McKinnell, MP
*Minister without Portfolio,* Jonathan Ashworth, MP

LABOUR WHIPS
*Commons Chief Whip,* Rt. Hon. Rosie Winterton, MP
*Lords Chief Whip,* Rt. Hon. Lord Bassam of Brighton

## LIBERAL DEMOCRATS
8–10 Great George Street, London SW1P 3AE
T 020-7022 0988 E info@libdems.org.uk
W www.libdems.org.uk
*Parliamentary Party Leader,* Tim Farron, MP
*Deputy Party Leader,* Rt. Hon. Malcolm Bruce, MP
*Leader in the Lords,* Rt. Hon. Lord Wallace
*President,* Sarah Brinton
*Chief Executive,* Tim Gordon
*Hon. Treasurer,* Lord Wrigglesworth

## NORTHERN IRELAND DEMOCRATIC UNIONIST PARTY
91 Dundela Avenue, Belfast BT4 3BU
T 028-9047 1155
E info@mydup.com W www.mydup.com
*Parliamentary Party Leader,* Rt. Hon. Peter
  Robinson, MLA
*Deputy Leader,* Rt. Hon Nigel Dodds, OBE, MP,
  MLA
*Chair,* Lord Morrow, MLA

## PLAID CYMRU – THE PARTY OF WALES
Ty Gwynfor, Anson Court, Atlantic Wharf,
Caerdydd CF10 4AL
T 029-2047 2272 E post@plaidcymru.org
W www.partyof.wales
*Party Leader,* Leanne Wood, AM
*Hon. Party President,* Rt. Hon. Lord Wigley
*Parliamentary Group Leader,* Jonathan Edwards, MP
*Chair,* Dafydd Trystan Davies
*Chief Executive,* Rhuanedd Richards

## SCOTTISH NATIONAL PARTY
Gordon Lamb House, 3 Jackson's Entry,
Edinburgh EH8 8PJ
T 0800-633 5432 E info@snp.org W www.snp.org
*Westminster Parliamentary Party Leader,* Angus
  Robertson, MP
*Westminster Parliamentary Party Chief Whip,*
  Stewart Hosie, MP
*Scottish Parliamentary Party Leader and Leader of the
  SNP,* Rt. Hon. Nicola Sturgeon, MSP

*Deputy Leader and Deputy First Minister of Scotland,*
  Stewart Hosie, MP
*Party President,* Ian Hudghton, MEP
*National Treasurer,* Colin Beattie, MSP
*Chief Executive,* Peter Murrell

## SINN FEIN
53 Falls Road, Belfast BT12 4PD
T 028-9034 7350 E admin@sinnfein.ie
W www.sinnfein.ie
*Party President,* Gerry Adams
*Vice-President,* Mary Lou McDonald
*Chair,* Declan Kearney

## SOCIAL DEMOCRATIC AND LABOUR PARTY
121 Ormeau Road, Belfast BT7 1SH
T 028-9024 7700 E info@sdlp.ie W www.sdlp.ie
*Parliamentary Party Leader,* Dr Alisdair McDonnell,
  MP, MLA
*Deputy Leader,* Dolores Kelly, MLA
*Party Whip,* Pat Ramsey, MLA
*Chair,* Joe Byrne, MLA
*Treasurer,* Peter McEvoy

## ULSTER UNIONIST PARTY
Strandtown Hall, 2–4 Belmont Road, Belfast BT4 2AN
T 028-9047 4630
E uup@uup.org W www.uup.org
*Party Leader,* Mike Nesbitt, MLA
*Chair,* Lord Empey of Shandon, OBE
*Hon. Treasurer,* Cllr Mark Cosgrove

## UK INDEPENDENCE PARTY
Lexdrum House, King Charles Business Park,
Newton Abbot, Devon TQ12 9BG
T 01626-831290
E mail@ukip.org W www.ukip.org
*Party Leader,* Nigel Farage, MEP
*Deputy Leader,* Paul Nuttall
*Chair,* Steve Crowther
*Treasurer,* Hugh Williams
*Party Secretary,* Matt Richardson

* Denotes new MP in the 2015 parliament

**Abbott**, Diane (*b.* 1953) *Lab., Hackney North & Stoke Newington,* Maj. 24,008

**Abrahams**, Debbie (*b.* 1960) *Lab., Oldham East & Saddleworth,* Maj. 6,002

**Adams**, Nigel (*b.* 1966) *C., Selby & Ainsty,* Maj. 13,557

**Afriyie**, Adam (*b.* 1965) *C., Windsor,* Maj. 25,083

*****Ahmed-Sheikh**, Tasmina (*b.* 1970) *SNP, Ochil & Perthshire South,* Maj. 10,168

**Aldous**, Peter (*b.* 1961) *C., Waveney,* Maj. 2,408

**Alexander**, Heidi (*b.* 1975) *Lab., Lewisham East,* Maj. 14,333

**Ali**, Rushanara (*b.* 1975) *Lab., Bethnal Green & Bow,* Maj. 24,317

*****Allan**, Lucy (*b.* 1964) *C., Telford,* Maj. 730

**Allen**, Graham (*b.* 1953) *Lab., Nottingham North,* Maj. 11,860

*****Allen**, Heidi (*b.* 1975) *C., Cambridgeshire South,* Maj. 20,594

**Amess**, Sir David (*b.* 1952) *C., Southend West,* Maj. 14,021

**Anderson**, David (*b.* 1953) *Lab., Blaydon,* Maj. 14,227

**Andrew**, Stuart (*b.* 1971) *C., Pudsey,* Maj. 4,501

*****Ansell**, Caroline (*b.* 1972) *C., Eastbourne,* Maj. 733

*****Argar**, Edward (*b.* 1977) *C., Charnwood,* Maj. 16,931

*****Arkless**, Richard (*b.* 1975) *SNP, Dumfries & Galloway,* Maj. 6,514

**Ashworth**, Jonathan (*b.* 1978) *Lab. Co-op, Leicester South,* Maj. 17,865

*****Atkins**, Victoria (*b.* 1976) *C., Louth & Horncastle,* Maj. 14,977

**Austin**, Ian (*b.* 1965) *Lab., Dudley North,* Maj. 4,181

**Bacon**, Richard (*b.* 1962) *C., Norfolk South,* Maj. 20,493

**Bailey**, Adrian (*b.* 1945) *Lab. Co-op, West Bromwich West,* Maj. 7,742

**Baker**, Steve (*b.* 1971) *C., Wycombe,* Maj. 14,856

**Baldwin**, Harriett (*b.* 1960) *C., Worcestershire West,* Maj. 22,578

**Barclay**, Steve (*b.* 1972) *C., Cambridgeshire North East,* Maj. 16,874

*****Bardell**, Hannah (*b.* 1984) *SNP, Livingston,* Maj. 16,843

**Baron**, John (*b.* 1959) *C., Basildon & Billericay,* Maj. 12,482

**Barron**, Rt. Hon. Sir Kevin (*b.* 1946) *Lab., Rother Valley,* Maj. 7,297

**Barwell**, Gavin (*b.* 1972) *C., Croydon Central,* Maj. 165

**Bebb**, Guto (*b.* 1968) *C., Aberconwy,* Maj. 3,999

**Beckett**, Rt. Hon. Dame Margaret (*b.* 1943) *Lab., Derby South,* Maj. 8,828

**Bellingham**, Henry (*b.* 1955) *C., Norfolk North West,* Maj. 13,948

**Benn**, Rt. Hon. Hilary (*b.* 1953) *Lab., Leeds Central,* Maj. 16,967

**Benyon**, Richard (*b.* 1960) *C., Newbury,* Maj. 26,368

**Bercow**, Rt. Hon. John (*b.* 1963) *The Speaker, Buckingham,* Maj. 22,942

**Beresford**, Sir Paul (*b.* 1946) *C., Mole Valley,* Maj. 25,453

**Berger**, Luciana (*b.* 1981) *Lab. Co-op, Liverpool Wavertree,* Maj. 24,303

**Berry**, Jake (*b.* 1978) *C., Rossendale & Darwen,* Maj. 5,654

*****Berry**, James (*b.* 1984) *C., Kingston & Surbiton,* Maj. 2,834

**Betts**, Clive (*b.* 1950) *Lab., Sheffield South East,* Maj. 12,311

**Bingham**, Andrew (*b.* 1962) *C., High Peak,* Maj. 4,894

*****Black**, Mhairi (*b.* 1994) *SNP, Paisley & Renfrewshire South,* Maj. 5,684

*****Blackford**, Ian (*b.* 1961) *SNP, Ross, Skye & Lochaber,* Maj. 5,124

**Blackman**, Bob (*b.* 1956) *C., Harrow East,* Maj. 4,757

*****Blackman**, Kirsty (*b.* 1986) *SNP, Aberdeen North,* Maj. 13,396

**Blackman-Woods**, Dr Roberta (*b.* 1957) *Lab., Durham, City of,* Maj. 11,439

**Blackwood**, Nicola (*b.* 1979) *C., Oxford West & Abingdon,* Maj. 9,582

**Blenkinsop**, Tom (*b.* 1980) *Lab., Middlesbrough South & Cleveland East,* Maj. 2,268

**Blomfield**, Paul (*b.* 1953) *Lab., Sheffield Central,* Maj. 17,309

**Blunt**, Crispin (*b.* 1960) *C., Reigate,* Maj. 22,334

**Boles**, Nick (*b.* 1965) *C., Grantham & Stamford,* Maj. 18,989

**Bone**, Peter (*b.* 1952) *C., Wellingborough,* Maj. 16,397

*****Borwick**, Lady (Victoria) (*b.* 1956) *C., Kensington,* Maj. 7,361

*****Boswell**, Phil (*b.* 1963) *SNP, Coatbridge, Chryston & Bellshill,* Maj. 11,501

**Bottomley**, Sir Peter (*b.* 1944) *C., Worthing West,* Maj. 16,855

**Bradley**, Karen (*b.* 1970) *C., Staffordshire Moorlands,* Maj. 10,174

**Bradshaw**, Rt. Hon. Ben (*b.* 1960) *Lab., Exeter,* Maj. 7,183

**Brady**, Graham (*b.* 1967) *C., Altrincham & Sale West,* Maj. 13,290

*****Brady**, Mickey (*b.* 1950) *SF, Newry & Armagh,* Maj. 4,176

**Brake**, Rt. Hon. Tom (*b.* 1962) *LD, Carshalton & Wallington*, Maj. 1,510

**Brazier**, Julian (*b.* 1953) *C., Canterbury*, Maj. 9,798

**Brennan**, Kevin (*b.* 1959) *Lab., Cardiff West*, Maj. 6,789

**Bridgen**, Andrew (*b.* 1964) *C., Leicestershire North West*, Maj. 11,373

**Brine**, Steve (*b.* 1974) *C., Winchester*, Maj. 16,914

*****Brock**, Deidre (*b.* 1961) *SNP, Edinburgh North & Leith*, Maj. 5,597

**Brokenshire**, James (*b.* 1968) *C., Old Bexley & Sidcup*, Maj. 15,803

*****Brown**, Alan (*b.* 1970), *SNP, Kilmarnock & Loudoun*, Maj. 13,638

**Brown**, Lyn (*b.* 1960) *Lab., West Ham*, Maj. 27,986

**Brown**, Rt. Hon. Nicholas (*b.* 1950) *Lab., Newcastle upon Tyne East*, Maj. 12,494

**Bruce**, Fiona (*b.* 1957) *C., Congleton*, Maj. 16,773

**Bryant**, Chris (*b.* 1962) *Lab., Rhondda*, Maj. 7,455

**Buck**, Karen (*b.* 1958) *Lab., Westminster North*, Maj. 1,977

**Buckland**, Robert (*b.* 1968) *C., Swindon South*, Maj. 5,785

**Burden**, Richard (*b.* 1954) *Lab., Birmingham Northfield*, Maj. 2,509

*****Burgon**, Richard (*b.* 1980) *Lab., Leeds East*, Maj. 12,533

**Burnham**, Rt. Hon. Andy (*b.* 1970) *Lab., Leigh*, Maj. 14,096

**Burns**, Conor (*b.* 1972) *C., Bournemouth West*, Maj. 12,410

**Burns**, Rt. Hon. Sir Simon (*b.* 1952) *C., Chelmsford*, Maj. 18,250

**Burrowes**, David (*b.* 1969) *C., Enfield Southgate*, Maj. 4,753

**Burt**, Rt. Hon. Alistair (*b.* 1955) *C., Bedfordshire North East*, Maj. 25,644

*****Butler**, Dawn (*b.* 1969) *Lab., Brent Central*, Maj. 19,649

**Byrne**, Rt. Hon. Liam (*b.* 1970) *Lab., Birmingham Hodge Hill*, Maj. 23,362

*****Cadbury**, Ruth (*b.* 1959) *Lab., Brentford & Isleworth*, Maj. 465

**Cairns**, Alun (*b.* 1970) *C., Vale of Glamorgan*, Maj. 6,880

**Cameron**, Rt. Hon. David (*b.* 1966) *C., Witney*, Maj. 25,155

*****Cameron**, Dr Lisa (*b.* 1972) *SNP, East Kilbride, Strathaven & Lesmahagow*, Maj. 16,527

**Campbell**, Rt. Hon. Alan (*b.* 1957) *Lab., Tynemouth*, Maj. 8,240

**Campbell**, Gregory (*b.* 1953) *DUP, Londonderry East*, Maj. 7,804

**Campbell**, Ronnie (*b.* 1943) *Lab., Blyth Valley*, Maj. 9,229

**Carmichael**, Rt. Hon. Alistair (*b.* 1965) *LD, Orkney & Shetland*, Maj. 817

**Carmichael**, Neil (*b.* 1961) *C., Stroud*, Maj. 4,866

**Carswell**, Douglas (*b.* 1971) *UKIP, Clacton*, Maj. 3,437

*****Cartlidge**, James (*b.* 1974) *C., Suffolk South*, Maj. 17,545

**Cash**, Sir William (*b.* 1940) *C., Stone*, Maj. 16,250

*****Caulfield**, Maria (*b.* 1974) *C., Lewes*, Maj. 1,083

*****Chalk**, Alex (*b.* 1977) *C., Cheltenham*, Maj. 6,516

**Champion**, Sarah (*b.* 1969) *Lab., Rotherham*, Maj. 8,446

*****Chapman**, Douglas (*b.* 1955) *SNP, Dunfermline & Fife West*, Maj. 10,352

**Chapman**, Jenny (*b.* 1973) *Lab., Darlington*, Maj. 3,158

*****Cherry**, Joanna (*b.* 1966) *SNP, Edinburgh South West*, Maj. 8,135

**Chishti**, Rehman (*b.* 1978) *C., Gillingham & Rainham*, Maj. 10,530

**Chope**, Christopher (*b.* 1947) *C., Christchurch*, Maj. 18,224

*****Churchill**, Jo (*b.* 1964) *C., Bury St Edmunds*, Maj. 21,301

**Clark**, Rt. Hon. Greg (*b.* 1967) *C., Tunbridge Wells*, Maj. 22,874

**Clarke**, Rt. Hon. Kenneth (*b.* 1940) *C., Rushcliffe*, Maj. 13,829

**Clegg**, Rt. Hon. Nick (*b.* 1967) *LD, Sheffield Hallam*, Maj. 2,353

*****Cleverly**, James (*b.* 1969) *C., Braintree*, Maj. 17,610

**Clifton-Brown**, Geoffrey (*b.* 1953) *C., The Cotswolds*, Maj. 21,477

**Clwyd**, Rt. Hon. Ann (*b.* 1937) *Lab., Cynon Valley*, Maj. 9,406

**Coaker**, Vernon (*b.* 1953) *Lab., Gedling*, Maj. 2,986

**Coffey**, Ann (*b.* 1946) *Lab., Stockport*, Maj. 10,061

**Coffey**, Dr Thérèse (*b.* 1971) *C., Suffolk Coastal*, Maj. 18,842

**Collins**, Damian (*b.* 1974) *C., Folkestone & Hythe*, Maj. 13,797

**Colvile**, Oliver (*b.* 1959) *C., Plymouth Sutton & Devonport*, Maj. 523

*****Cooper**, Julie (*b.* 1960) *Lab., Burnley*, Maj. 3,244

**Cooper**, Rosie (*b.* 1950) *Lab., Lancashire West*, Maj. 8,360

**Cooper**, Rt. Hon. Yvette (*b.* 1969) *Lab., Normanton, Pontefract & Castleford*, Maj. 15,428

**Corbyn**, Jeremy (*b.* 1949) *Lab., Islington North*, Maj. 21,194

*****Costa**, Alberto (*b.* 1971) *C., Leicestershire South*, Maj. 16,824

*****Cowan**, Ronnie (*b.* 1959) *SNP, Inverclyde*, Maj. 11,063

**Cox**, Geoffrey (*b.* 1960) *C., Devon West & Torridge*, Maj. 18,403

*****Cox**, Jo (*b.* 1974) *Lab., Batley & Spen*, Maj. 6,057

*****Coyle**, Neil (*b.* 1978) *Lab., Bermondsey & Old Southwark*, Maj. 4,489

**Crabb**, Rt. Hon. Stephen (*b.* 1973) *C., Preseli Pembrokeshire,* Maj. 4,969

**Crausby**, David (*b.* 1946) *Lab., Bolton North East,* Maj. 4,377

\*Crawley, Angela (*b.* 1987) *SNP, Lanark & Hamilton East,* Maj. 10,100

**Creagh**, Mary (*b.* 1967) *Lab., Wakefield,* Maj. 2,613

**Creasy**, Stella (*b.* 1977) *Lab. Co-op, Walthamstow,* Maj. 23,195

**Crouch**, Tracey (*b.* 1975) *C., Chatham & Aylesford,* Maj. 11,455

**Cruddas**, Jon (*b.* 1965) *Lab., Dagenham & Rainham,* Maj. 4,980

**Cryer**, John (*b.* 1964) *Lab., Leyton & Wanstead,* Maj. 14,919

\*Cummins, Judith (*b.* 1967) *Lab., Bradford South,* Maj. 6,450

**Cunningham**, Alex (*b.* 1955) *Lab., Stockton North,* Maj. 8,367

**Cunningham**, Jim (*b.* 1941) *Lab., Coventry South,* Maj. 3,188

**Dakin**, Nic (*b.* 1955) *Lab., Scunthorpe,* Maj. 3,134

**Danczuk**, Simon (*b.* 1966) *Lab., Rochdale,* Maj. 12,442

**David**, Wayne (*b.* 1957) *Lab., Caerphilly,* Maj. 10,073

\*Davies, Byron (*b.* 1952) *C., Gower,* Maj. 27

\*Davies, Chris (*b.* 1967) *C., Brecon & Radnorshire,* Maj. 5,102

**Davies**, David (*b.* 1970) *C., Monmouth,* Maj. 10,982

**Davies**, Geraint (*b.* 1960) *Lab. Co-op, Swansea West,* Maj. 7,036

**Davies**, Glyn (*b.* 1944) *C., Montgomeryshire,* Maj. 5,325

\*Davies, James (*b.* 1980) *C., Vale of Clwyd,* Maj. 237

\*Davies, Mims (*b.* 1975) *C., Eastleigh,* Maj. 9,147

**Davies**, Philip (*b.* 1972) *C., Shipley,* Maj. 9,624

**Davis**, Rt. Hon. David (*b.* 1948) *C., Haltemprice & Howden,* Maj. 16,195

\*Day, Martyn (*b.* 1971) *SNP, Linlithgow & Falkirk East,* Maj. 12,934

**De Piero**, Gloria (*b.* 1972) *Lab., Ashfield,* Maj. 8,820

\*Debbonaire, Thangam (*b.* 1966) *Lab., Bristol West,* Maj. 5,673

**Dinenage**, Caroline (*b.* 1971) *C., Gosport,* Maj. 17,098

**Djanogly**, Jonathan (*b.* 1965) *C., Huntingdon,* Maj. 19,404

\*Docherty, Martin (*b.* 1971) *SNP, Dunbartonshire West,* Maj. 14,171

**Dodds**, Rt. Hon. Nigel (*b.* 1958) *DUP, Belfast North,* Maj. 5,326

**Doherty**, Pat (*b.* 1945) *SF, Tyrone West,* Maj. 10,060

**Donaldson**, Rt. Hon. Jeffrey (*b.* 1962) *DUP, Lagan Valley,* Maj. 13,000

\*Donaldson, Stuart (*b.* 1992) *SNP, Aberdeenshire West & Kincardine,* Maj. 7,033

\*Donelan, Michelle (*b.* 1984) *C., Chippenham,* Maj. 10,076

**Dorries**, Nadine (*b.* 1958) *C., Bedfordshire Mid,* Maj. 23,327

\*Double, Steve (*b.* 1966) *C., St Austell & Newquay,* Maj. 8,173

**Doughty**, Stephen (*b.* 1980) *Lab. Co-op, Cardiff South & Penarth,* Maj. 7,453

**Dowd**, Jim (*b.* 1951) *Lab., Lewisham West & Penge,* Maj. 12,714

\*Dowd, Peter (*b.* 1957) *Lab., Bootle,* Maj. 28,704

\*Dowden, Oliver (*b.* 1978) *C., Hertsmere,* Maj. 18,461

**Doyle-Price**, Jackie (*b.* 1969) *C., Thurrock,* Maj. 536

**Drax**, Richard (*b.* 1958) *C., Dorset South,* Maj. 11,994

**Dromey**, Jack (*b.* 1948) *Lab., Birmingham Erdington,* Maj. 5,129

\*Drummond, Flick (*b.* 1962) *C., Portsmouth South,* Maj. 5,241

**Duddridge**, James (*b.* 1971) *C., Rochford & Southend East,* Maj. 9,476

**Dugher**, Michael (*b.* 1975) *Lab., Barnsley East,* Maj. 12,034

**Duncan**, Rt. Hon. Sir Alan (*b.* 1957) *C., Rutland & Melton,* Maj. 21,705

**Duncan Smith**, Rt. Hon. Iain (*b.* 1954) *C., Chingford & Woodford Green,* Maj. 8,386

**Dunne**, Philip (*b.* 1958) *C., Ludlow,* Maj. 18,929

**Durkan**, Mark (*b.* 1960) *SDLP, Foyle,* Maj. 6,046

**Eagle**, Angela (*b.* 1961) *Lab., Wallasey,* Maj. 16,348

**Eagle**, Maria (*b.* 1961) *Lab., Garston & Halewood,* Maj. 27,146

**Edwards**, Jonathan (*b.* 1976) *PC, Carmarthen East & Dinefwr,* Maj. 5,599

**Efford**, Clive (*b.* 1958) *Lab., Eltham,* Maj. 2,693

**Elliott**, Julie (*b.* 1963) *Lab., Sunderland Central,* Maj. 11,179

\*Elliott, Tom (*b.* 1963) *UUP, Fermanagh & South Tyrone,* Maj. 530

**Ellis**, Michael (*b.* 1967) *C., Northampton North,* Maj. 3,245

**Ellison**, Jane (*b.* 1964) *C., Battersea,* Maj. 7,938

**Ellman**, Louise (*b.* 1945) *Lab. Co-op, Liverpool Riverside,* Maj. 24,463

**Ellwood**, Tobias (*b.* 1966) *C., Bournemouth East,* Maj. 14,612

**Elphicke**, Charlie (*b.* 1971) *C., Dover,* Maj. 6,294

**Engel**, Natascha (*b.* 1967) *Lab., Deputy Speaker, Derbyshire North East,* Maj. 1,883

**Esterson**, Bill (*b.* 1966) *Lab., Sefton Central,* Maj. 11,846

**Eustice**, George (*b.* 1971) *C., Camborne & Redruth,* Maj. 7,004

**Evans**, Chris (*b.* 1976) *Lab. Co-op, Islwyn,* Maj. 10,404

**Evans**, Graham (*b.* 1963) *C., Weaver Vale,* Maj. 806

**Evans**, Nigel (*b.* 1957) *C., Ribble Valley,* Maj. 13,606

**Evennett**, Rt. Hon. David (*b.* 1949) *C., Bexleyheath & Crayford,* Maj. 9,192

**Fabricant**, Michael (*b.* 1950) *C., Lichfield,* Maj. 18,189

**Fallon**, Rt. Hon. Michael (*b.* 1952) *C., Sevenoaks,* Maj. 19,561

**Farrelly**, Paul (*b.* 1962) *Lab., Newcastle-under-Lyme,* Maj. 650

**Farron**, Tim (*b.* 1970) *LD, Westmorland & Lonsdale,* Maj. 8,949

**\*Fellows**, Marion (*b.* 1949) *SNP, Motherwell & Wishaw,* Maj. 11,898

**\*Fernandes**, Suella (*b.* 1980) *C., Fareham,* Maj. 22,262

**\*Ferrier**, Margaret (*b.* 1960) *SNP, Rutherglen & Hamilton West,* Maj. 9,975

**Field**, Rt. Hon. Frank (*b.* 1942) *Lab., Birkenhead,* Maj. 20,652

**Field**, Rt. Hon. Mark (*b.* 1964) *C., Cities of London & Westminster,* Maj. 9,671

**Fitzpatrick**, Jim (*b.* 1952) *Lab., Poplar & Limehouse,* Maj. 16,924

**Flello**, Robert (*b.* 1966) *Lab., Stoke-on-Trent South,* Maj. 2,539

**\*Fletcher**, Colleen (*b.* 1954) *Lab., Coventry North East,* Maj. 12,274

**Flint**, Rt. Hon. Caroline (*b.* 1961) *Lab., Don Valley,* Maj. 8,885

**Flynn**, Paul (*b.* 1935) *Lab., Newport West,* Maj. 3,510

**\*Foster**, Kevin (*b.* 1978) *C., Torbay,* Maj. 3,286

**Fovargue**, Yvonne (*b.* 1956) *Lab., Makerfield,* Maj. 13,155

**Fox**, Rt. Hon. Dr Liam (*b.* 1961) *C., Somerset North,* Maj. 23,099

**\*Foxcroft**, Vicky (*b.* 1977) *Lab., Lewisham Deptford,* Maj. 21,516

**Francois**, Rt. Hon. Mark (*b.* 1965) *C., Rayleigh & Wickford,* Maj. 17,230

**\*Frazer**, Lucy (*b.* 1972) *C., Cambridgeshire South East,* Maj. 16,837

**Freeman**, George (*b.* 1967) *C., Norfolk Mid,* Maj. 17,276

**Freer**, Mike (*b.* 1960) *C., Finchley & Golders Green,* Maj. 5,662

**Fuller**, Richard (*b.* 1962) *C., Bedford,* Maj. 1,097

**\*Fysh**, Marcus (*b.* 1970) *C., Yeovil,* Maj. 5,313

**Gale**, Sir Roger (*b.* 1943) *C., Thanet North,* Maj. 10,948

**Gapes**, Mike (*b.* 1952) *Lab. Co-op, Ilford South,* Maj. 19,777

**Gardiner**, Barry (*b.* 1957) *Lab., Brent North,* Maj. 10,834

**Garnier**, Rt. Hon. Sir Edward (*b.* 1952) *C., Harborough,* Maj. 19,632

**Garnier**, Mark (*b.* 1963) *C., Wyre Forest,* Maj. 12,871

**Gauke**, David (*b.* 1971) *C., Hertfordshire South West,* Maj. 23,263

**\*Gethins**, Stephen (*b.* 1976) *SNP, Fife North East,* Maj. 4,344

**\*Ghani**, Nusrat (*b.* 1972) *C., Wealden,* Maj. 22,967

**Gibb**, Nick (*b.* 1960) *C., Bognor Regis & Littlehampton,* Maj. 13,944

**\*Gibson**, Patricia (*b.* 1968) *SNP, Ayrshire North & Arran,* Maj. 13,573

**Gillan**, Rt. Hon. Cheryl (*b.* 1952) *C., Chesham & Amersham,* Maj. 23,920

**Glass**, Pat (*b.* 1956) *Lab., Durham North West,* Maj. 10,056

**Glen**, John (*b.* 1974) *C., Salisbury,* Maj. 20,421

**Glindon**, Mary (*b.* 1957) *Lab., Tyneside North,* Maj. 17,194

**Godsiff**, Roger (*b.* 1946) *Lab., Birmingham Hall Green,* Maj. 19,818

**Goldsmith**, Zac (*b.* 1975) *C., Richmond Park,* Maj. 23,015

**Goodman**, Helen (*b.* 1958) *Lab., Bishop Auckland,* Maj. 3,508

**Goodwill**, Robert (*b.* 1956) *C., Scarborough & Whitby,* Maj. 6,200

**Gove**, Rt. Hon. Michael (*b.* 1967) *C., Surrey Heath,* Maj. 24,804

**\*Grady**, Patrick (*b.* 1980) *SNP, Glasgow North,* Maj. 9,295

**Graham**, Richard (*b.* 1958) *C., Gloucester,* Maj. 7,251

**Grant**, Helen (*b.* 1961) *C., Maidstone & The Weald,* Maj. 10,709

**\*Grant**, Peter (*b.* 1961) *SNP, Glenrothes,* Maj. 13,897

**Gray**, James (*b.* 1954) *C., Wiltshire North,* Maj. 21,046

**\*Gray**, Neil (*b.* 1986) *SNP, Airdrie & Shotts,* Maj. 8,779

**Grayling**, Rt. Hon. Chris (*b.* 1962) *C., Epsom & Ewell,* Maj. 24,443

**\*Green**, Chris (*b.* 1973) *C., Bolton West,* Maj. 801

**Green**, Rt. Hon. Damian (*b.* 1956) *C., Ashford,* Maj. 19,296

**Green**, Kate (*b.* 1960) *Lab., Stretford & Urmston,* Maj. 11,685

**Greening**, Rt. Hon. Justine (*b.* 1969) *C., Putney,* Maj. 10,180

**Greenwood**, Lilian (*b.* 1966) *Lab., Nottingham South,* Maj. 6,936

**\*Greenwood**, Margaret (*b.* 1959) *Lab., Wirral West,* Maj. 417

**Grieve**, Rt. Hon. Dominic (*b.* 1956) *C., Beaconsfield,* Maj. 26,311

**Griffith**, Nia (*b.* 1956) *Lab., Llanelli,* Maj. 7,095

**Griffiths**, Andrew (*b.* 1970) *C., Burton,* Maj. 11,252

**Gummer**, Ben (*b.* 1978) *C., Ipswich,* Maj. 3,733

**Gwynne**, Andrew (*b.* 1974) *Lab., Denton & Reddish,* Maj. 10,511

**Gyimah**, Sam (*b.* 1976) *C., Surrey East,* Maj. 22,658

**\*Haigh**, Louise (*b.* 1987) *Lab., Sheffield Heeley,* Maj. 12,954

**Halfon**, Rt. Hon. Robert (*b.* 1969) *C., Harlow,* Maj. 8,350

**\*Hall**, Luke (*b.* 1986) *C., Thornbury & Yate,* Maj. 1,495

**Hamilton**, Fabian (*b.* 1955) *Lab., Leeds North East,* Maj. 7,250

**Hammond**, Rt. Hon. Philip (*b.* 1955) *C., Runnymede & Weybridge,* Maj. 22,134

**Hammond**, Stephen (*b.* 1962) *C., Wimbledon,* Maj. 12,619

**Hancock**, Rt. Hon. Matthew (*b.* 1978) *C., Suffolk West,* Maj. 14,984

**Hands**, Rt. Hon. Greg (*b.* 1965) *C., Chelsea & Fulham,* Maj. 16,022

**Hanson**, Rt. Hon. David (*b.* 1957) *Lab., Delyn,* Maj. 2,930

**Harman**, Rt. Hon. Harriet (*b.* 1950) *Lab., Camberwell & Peckham,* Maj. 25,824

**Harper**, Rt. Hon. Mark (*b.* 1970) *C., Forest of Dean,* Maj. 10,987

**\*Harpham**, Harry (*b.* 1954) *Lab., Sheffield Brightside & Hillsborough,* Maj. 13,807

**Harrington**, Richard (*b.* 1957) *C., Watford,* Maj. 9,794

**\*Harris**, Carolyn (*b.* 1960) *Lab., Swansea East,* Maj. 12,028

**Harris**, Rebecca (*b.* 1967) *C., Castle Point,* Maj. 8,934

**Hart**, Simon (*b.* 1963) *C., Carmarthen West & Pembrokeshire South,* Maj. 6,054

**Haselhurst**, Rt. Hon. Sir Alan (*b.* 1937) *C., Saffron Walden,* Maj. 24,991

**\*Hayes**, Helen (*b.* 1974) *Lab., Dulwich & West Norwood,* Maj. 16,122

**Hayes**, Rt. Hon. John (*b.* 1958) *C., South Holland & The Deepings,* Maj. 18,567

**\*Hayman**, Sue (*b.* 1962) *Lab., Workington,* Maj. 4,686

**Heald**, Sir Oliver (*b.* 1954) *C., Hertfordshire North East,* Maj. 19,080

**Healey**, Rt. Hon. John (*b.* 1960) *Lab., Wentworth & Dearne,* Maj. 13,838

**\*Heappey**, James (*b.* 1981) *C., Wells,* Maj. 7,585

**Heaton-Harris**, Chris (*b.* 1967) *C., Daventry,* Maj. 21,059

**\*Heaton-Jones**, Peter (*b.* 1963) *C., Devon North,* Maj. 6,936

**Henderson**, Gordon (*b.* 1948) *C., Sittingbourne & Sheppey,* Maj. 12,168

**Hendrick**, Mark (*b.* 1958) *Lab. Co-op, Preston,* Maj. 12,067

**\*Hendry**, Drew (*b.* 1964) *SNP, Inverness, Nairn, Badenoch & Strathspey,* Maj. 10,809

**Hepburn**, Stephen (*b.* 1959) *Lab., Jarrow,* Maj. 13,881

**Herbert**, Rt. Hon. Nick (*b.* 1963) *C., Arundel & South Downs,* Maj. 26,177

**Hermon**, Lady (Sylvia) (*b.* 1956) *Ind., Down North,* Maj. 9,202

**Hillier**, Meg (*b.* 1969) *Lab. Co-op, Hackney South & Shoreditch,* Maj. 24,243

**Hinds**, Damian (*b.* 1969) *C., Hampshire East,* Maj. 25,147

**\*Hoare**, Simon (*b.* 1969) *C., Dorset North,* Maj. 21,118

**Hodge**, Rt. Hon. Margaret (*b.* 1944) *Lab., Barking,* Maj. 15,272

**Hodgson**, Sharon (*b.* 1966) *Lab., Washington & Sunderland West,* Maj. 13,157

**Hoey**, Kate (*b.* 1946) *Lab., Vauxhall,* Maj. 12,708

**\*Hollern**, Kate (*b.* 1955) *Lab., Blackburn,* Maj. 12,760

**Hollingbery**, George (*b.* 1963) *C., Meon Valley,* Maj. 23,913

**\*Hollinrake**, Kevin (*b.* 1963) *C., Thirsk & Malton,* Maj. 19,456

**Hollobone**, Philip (*b.* 1964) *C., Kettering,* Maj. 12,590

**Holloway**, Adam (*b.* 1965) *C., Gravesham,* Maj. 8,380

**Hopkins**, Kelvin (*b.* 1941) *Lab., Luton North,* Maj. 9,504

**Hopkins**, Kris (*b.* 1963) *C., Keighley,* Maj. 3,053

**Hosie**, Stewart (*b.* 1963) *SNP, Dundee East,* Maj. 19,162

**Howarth**, Rt. Hon. George (*b.* 1949) *Lab., Knowsley,* Maj. 34,655

**Howarth**, Sir Gerald (*b.* 1947) *C., Aldershot,* Maj. 14,901

**Howell**, John (*b.* 1955) *C., Henley,* Maj. 25,375

**\*Howlett**, Ben (*b.* 1986) *C., Bath,* Maj. 3,833

**Hoyle**, Rt. Hon. Lindsay (*b.* 1957) *Lab., Deputy Speaker, Chorley,* Maj. 4,530

**\*Huddleston**, Nigel (*b.* 1970) *C., Worcestershire Mid,* Maj. 20,532

**Hunt**, Rt. Hon. Jeremy (*b.* 1966) *C., Surrey South West,* Maj. 28,556

**Hunt**, Tristram (*b.* 1974) *Lab., Stoke-on-Trent Central,* Maj. 5,179

**\*Huq**, Rupa (*b.* 1972) *Lab., Ealing Central & Acton,* Maj. 274

**Hurd**, Nick (*b.* 1962) *C., Ruislip, Northwood & Pinner,* Maj. 20,224

**\*Hussain**, Imran (*b.* 1978) *Lab., Bradford East,* Maj. 7.084

**Irranca-Davies**, Huw (*b.* 1963) *Lab., Ogmore,* Maj. 13,043

**Jackson**, Stewart (*b.* 1965) *C., Peterborough,* Maj. 1,925

**James**, Margot (*b.* 1957) *C., Stourbridge,* Maj. 6,694

**Jarvis**, Dan (*b.* 1972) *Lab., Barnsley Central*, Maj. 12,435

**Javid**, Rt. Hon. Sajid (*b.* 1969) *C., Bromsgrove*, Maj. 16,529

\*Jayawardena, Ranil (*b.*1986) *C., Hampshire North East*, Maj. 29,916

**Jenkin**, Bernard (*b.* 1959) *C., Harwich & Essex North*, Maj. 15,174

\*Jenkyns, Andrea (*b.* 1974) *C., Morley & Outwood*, Maj. 422

**Jenrick**, Robert (*b.* 1982) *C., Newark*, Maj. 18,474

**Johnson**, Rt. Hon. Alan (*b.* 1950) *Lab., Hull West & Hessle*, Maj. 9,333

\*Johnson, Boris (*b.* 1964) *C., Uxbridge & Ruislip South*, Maj. 10,695

**Johnson**, Diana (*b.* 1966) *Lab., Hull North*, Maj. 12,899

**Johnson**, Gareth (*b.* 1969) *C., Dartford*, Maj. 12,345

**Johnson**, Joseph (*b.* 1971) *C., Orpington*, Maj. 19,979

**Jones**, Andrew (*b.* 1963) *C., Harrogate & Knaresborough*, Maj. 16,371

**Jones**, Rt. Hon. David (*b.* 1952) *C., Clwyd West*, Maj. 6,730

\*Jones, Gerald (*b.* 1970) *Lab., Merthyr Tydfil & Rhymney*, Maj. 11,513

**Jones**, Graham (*b.* 1966) *Lab., Hyndburn*, Maj. 4,400

**Jones**, Helen (*b.* 1954) *Lab., Warrington North*, Maj. 8,923

**Jones**, Kevan (*b.* 1964) *Lab., Durham North*, Maj. 13,644

**Jones**, Marcus (*b.* 1974) *C., Nuneaton*, Maj. 4,882

**Jones**, Susan (*b.* 1968) *Lab., Clwyd South*, Maj. 2,402

**Kane**, Mike (*b.* 1969) *Lab., Wythenshawe & Sale East*, Maj. 10,569

**Kaufman**, Rt. Hon. Sir Gerald (*b.* 1930) *Lab., Manchester Gorton*, Maj. 24,079

**Kawczynski**, Daniel (*b.* 1972) *C., Shrewsbury & Atcham*, Maj. 9,565

**Keeley**, Barbara (*b.* 1952) *Lab., Worsley & Eccles South*, Maj. 5,946

**Kendall**, Liz (*b.* 1971) *Lab., Leicester West*, Maj. 7,203

\*Kennedy, Seema (*b.* 1974) *C., South Ribble*, Maj. 5,945

\*Kerevan, George (*b.* 1949) *SNP, East Lothian*, Maj. 6,803

\*Kerr, Calum (*b.* 1972) *SNP, Berwickshire, Roxburgh & Selkirk*, Maj. 328

**Khan**, Rt. Hon. Sadiq (*b.* 1970) *Lab., Tooting*, Maj. 2,842

\*Kinahan, Danny (*b.*1958) *UUP, Antrim South*, Maj. 949

\*Kinnock, Stephen (*b.* 1970) *Lab., Aberavon*, Maj. 10,445

**Kirby**, Simon (*b.* 1964) *C., Brighton Kemptown*, Maj. 690

**Knight**, Rt. Hon. Sir Greg (*b.* 1949) *C., Yorkshire East*, Maj. 14,933

\*Knight, Julian (*b.* 1972) *C., Solihull*, Maj. 12,902

**Kwarteng**, Kwasi (*b.* 1975) *C., Spelthorne*, Maj. 14,152

\*Kyle, Peter (*b.* 1970) *Lab., Hove*, Maj. 1,236

**Laing**, Eleanor (*b.* 1958) *C., Deputy Speaker, Epping Forest*, Maj. 17,978

**Lamb**, Rt. Hon. Norman (*b.* 1957) *LD, Norfolk North*, Maj. 4,043

**Lammy**, Rt. Hon. David (*b.* 1972) *Lab., Tottenham*, Maj. 23,564

**Lancaster**, Mark (*b.* 1970) *C., Milton Keynes North*, Maj. 9,753

**Latham**, Pauline (*b.* 1948) *C., Derbyshire Mid*, Maj. 12,774

**Lavery**, Ian (*b.* 1962) *Lab., Wansbeck*, Maj. 10,881

\*Law, Chris (*b.* 1969) *SNP, Dundee West*, Maj. 17,092

**Leadsom**, Andrea (*b.* 1963) *C., Northamptonshire South*, Maj. 26,416

**Lee**, Dr Phillip (*b.* 1970) *C., Bracknell*, Maj. 20,650

**Lefroy**, Jeremy (*b.* 1959) *C., Stafford*, Maj. 9,177

**Leigh**, Sir Edward (*b.* 1950) *C., Gainsborough*, Maj. 15,449

**Leslie**, Charlotte (*b.* 1978) *C., Bristol North West*, Maj. 4,944

**Leslie**, Chris (*b.* 1972) *Lab. Co-op, Nottingham East*, Maj. 11,894

**Letwin**, Rt. Hon. Oliver (*b.* 1956) *C., Dorset West*, Maj. 16,130

**Lewell-Buck**, Emma (*b.* 1978) *Lab., South Shields*, Maj. 10,614

**Lewis**, Brandon (*b.* 1971) *C., Great Yarmouth*, Maj. 6,154

\*Lewis, Clive (*b.* 1971) *Lab., Norwich South*, Maj. 7,654

**Lewis**, Ivan (*b.* 1967) *Lab., Bury South*, Maj. 4,922

**Lewis**, Dr Julian (*b.* 1951) *C., New Forest East*, Maj. 19,162

**Liddell-Grainger**, Ian (*b.* 1959) *C., Bridgwater & Somerset West*, Maj. 14,583

**Lidington**, Rt. Hon. David (*b.* 1956) *C., Aylesbury*, Maj. 17,158

**Lilley**, Rt. Hon. Peter (*b.* 1943) *C., Hitchin & Harpenden*, Maj. 20,055

\*Long Bailey, Rebecca (*b.* 1979) *Lab., Salford & Eccles*, Maj. 12,541

**Lopresti**, Jack (*b.* 1969) *C., Filton & Bradley Stoke*, Maj. 9,838

**Lord**, Jonathan (*b.* 1962) *C., Woking*, Maj. 20,810

**Loughton**, Tim (*b.* 1962) *C., Worthing East & Shoreham*, Maj. 14,949

**Lucas**, Caroline (*b.* 1960) *Green, Brighton Pavilion*, Maj. 7,967

**Lucas**, Ian (*b.* 1960) *Lab., Wrexham*, Maj. 1,831

**Lumley**, Karen (*b.* 1964) *C., Redditch*, Maj. 7,054

*Lynch, Holly (b. 1986) Lab., Halifax, Maj. 428

McCabe, Steve (b. 1955) Lab., Birmingham Selly Oak, Maj. 8,447

*McCaig, Callum (b. 1985) SNP, Aberdeen South, Maj. 7,230

McCarthy, Kerry (b. 1965) Lab., Bristol East, Maj. 3,980

McCartney, Jason (b. 1968) C., Colne Valley, Maj. 5,378

McCartney, Karl (b. 1968) C., Lincoln, Maj. 1,443

McDonagh, Siobhain (b. 1960) Lab., Mitcham & Morden, Maj. 16,922

McDonald, Andy (b. 1958) Lab., Middlesbrough, Maj. 12,477

*McDonald, Stewart (b. 1986) SNP, Glasgow South, Maj. 12,269

*McDonald, Stuart (b. 1978) SNP, Cumbernauld, Kilsyth & Kirkintilloch East, Maj. 14,752

McDonnell, Dr Alasdair (b. 1949) SDLP, Belfast South, Maj. 906

McDonnell, John (b. 1951) Lab., Hayes & Harlington, Maj. 15,700

McFadden, Rt. Hon. Pat (b. 1965) Lab., Wolverhampton South East, Maj. 10,778

*McGarry, Natalie (b. 1981) SNP, Glasgow East, Maj. 10,387

*McGinn, Conor (b. 1984) Lab., St Helens North, Maj. 17,291

McGovern, Alison (b. 1980) Lab., Wirral South, Maj. 4,599

*McInnes, Liz (b. 1959) Lab., Heywood & Middleton, Maj. 5,299

*Mackinlay, Craig (b. 1967) C., Thanet South, Maj. 2,812

McKinnell, Catherine (b. 1976) Lab., Newcastle upon Tyne North, Maj. 10,153

*Mackintosh, David (b. 1979) C., Northampton South, Maj. 3,793

*McLaughlin, Anne (b. 1966) SNP, Glasgow North East, Maj. 9,222

McLoughlin, Rt. Hon. Patrick (b. 1957) C., Derbyshire Dales, Maj. 14,044

*McNally, John (b. 1951) SNP, Falkirk, Maj. 19,701

MacNeil, Angus (b. 1970) SNP, Na h-Eileanan an Iar, Maj. 4,102

McPartland, Stephen (b. 1976) C., Stevenage, Maj. 4,955

Mactaggart, Rt. Hon. Fiona (b. 1953) Lab., Slough, Maj. 7,336

*Madders, Justin (b. 1972) Lab., Ellesmere Port & Neston, Maj. 6,275

Mahmood, Khalid (b. 1961) Lab., Birmingham Perry Barr, Maj. 14,828

Mahmood, Shabana (b. 1980) Lab., Birmingham Ladywood, Maj. 21,868

Main, Anne (b. 1957) C., St Albans, Maj. 12,732

*Mak, Alan (b. 1983) C., Havant, Maj. 13,920

Malhotra, Seema (b. 1972) Lab. Co-op, Feltham & Heston, Maj. 11,463

*Malthouse, Kit (b. 1966) C., Hampshire North West, Maj. 23,943

Mann, John (b. 1960) Lab., Bassetlaw, Maj. 8,843

*Mann, Scott (b. 1977) C., Cornwall North, Maj. 6,621

*Marris, Rob (b. 1955) Lab., Wolverhampton South West, Maj. 801

Marsden, Gordon (b. 1953) Lab., Blackpool South, Maj. 2,585

*Maskell, Rachael (b. 1972) Lab., Co-op, York Central, Maj. 6,716

Maskey, Paul (b. 1967) SF, Belfast West, Maj. 12,365

*Matheson, Chris (b. 1968) Lab., Chester, City of, Maj. 93

*Mathias, Tania (b. 1964) C., Twickenham, Maj. 2,017

May, Rt. Hon. Theresa (b. 1956) C., Maidenhead, Maj. 29,059

Maynard, Paul (b. 1975) C., Blackpool North & Cleveleys, Maj. 3,340

Meacher, Rt. Hon. Michael (b. 1939) Lab., Oldham West & Royton, Maj. 14,738

Meale, Sir Alan (b. 1949) Lab., Mansfield, Maj. 5,315

Mearns, Ian (b. 1957) Lab., Gateshead, Maj. 14,784

Menzies, Mark (b. 1971) C., Fylde, Maj. 13,224

*Mercer, Johnny (b. 1981) C., Plymouth Moor View, Maj. 1,026

*Merriman, Huw (b. 1973) C., Bexhill & Battle, Maj. 20,075

Metcalfe, Stephen (b. 1966) C., Basildon South & Thurrock East, Maj. 7,691

Miliband, Rt. Hon. Edward (b. 1969) Lab., Doncaster North, Maj. 11,780

Miller, Rt. Hon. Maria (b. 1964) C., Basingstoke, Maj. 11,063

*Milling, Amanda (b. 1975) C., Cannock Chase, Maj. 4,923

Mills, Nigel (b. 1974) C., Amber Valley, Maj. 4,205

Milton, Rt. Hon. Anne (b. 1955) C., Guildford, Maj. 22,448

Mitchell, Rt. Hon. Andrew (b. 1956) C., Sutton Coldfield, Maj. 16,417

Molloy, Francie (b. 1950) SF, Ulster Mid, Maj. 13,617

*Monaghan, Carol (b. 1972) SNP, Glasgow North West, Maj. 10,364

*Monaghan, Dr Paul (b. 1966) SNP, Caithness, Sutherland & Easter Ross, Maj. 3,844

Moon, Madeleine (b. 1950) Lab., Bridgend, Maj. 1,927

Mordaunt, Penny (b. 1973) C., Portsmouth North, Maj. 10,537

Morden, Jessica (b. 1968) Lab., Newport East, Maj. 4,705

**Morgan**, Rt. Hon. Nicky (*b.* 1972) *C.,*
  *Loughborough,* Maj. 9,183
**Morris**, Anne Marie (*b.* 1957) *C., Newton Abbot,*
  Maj. 11,288
**Morris**, David (*b.* 1966) *C., Morecambe &*
  *Lunesdale,* Maj. 4,590
**Morris**, Grahame (*b.* 1961) *Lab., Easington,*
  Maj. 14,641
**Morris**, James (*b.* 1967) *C., Halesowen & Rowley*
  *Regis,* Maj. 3,082
*****Morton**, Wendy (*b.* 1967) *C., Aldridge-Brownhills,*
  Maj. 11,723
**Mowat**, David (*b.* 1957) *C., Warrington South,*
  Maj. 2,750
**Mulholland**, Greg (*b.* 1970) *LD, Leeds North West,*
  Maj. 2,907
*****Mullin**, Roger (*b.* 1948) *SNP, Kirkcaldy &*
  *Cowdenbeath,* Maj. 9,974
**Mundell**, Rt. Hon. David (*b.* 1962) *C.,*
  *Dumfriesshire, Clydesdale & Tweeddale,* Maj. 798
**Murray**, Ian (*b.* 1976) *Lab., Edinburgh South,*
  Maj. 2,637
**Murray**, Sheryll (*b.* 1956) *C., Cornwall South East,*
  Maj. 16,995
**Murrison**, Dr Andrew (*b.* 1961) *C., Wiltshire South*
  *West,* Maj. 18,168
**Nandy**, Lisa (*b.* 1979) *Lab., Wigan,* Maj. 14,236
**Neill**, Robert (*b.* 1952) *C., Bromley & Chislehurst,*
  Maj. 13,564
*****Newlands**, Gavin (*b.* 1980) *SNP, Paisley &*
  *Renfrewshire North,* Maj. 9,076
**Newton**, Sarah (*b.* 1962) *C., Truro & Falmouth,*
  Maj. 14,000
*****Nicolson**, John (*b.* 1961) *SNP, Dunbartonshire*
  *East,* Maj. 2,167
**Nokes**, Caroline (*b.* 1972) *C., Romsey &*
  *Southampton North,* Maj. 17,712
**Norman**, Jesse (*b.* 1962) *C., Hereford &*
  *Herefordshire South,* Maj. 16,890
**Nuttall**, David (*b.* 1962) *C., Bury North,* Maj. 378
**Offord**, Dr Matthew (*b.* 1969) *C., Hendon,*
  Maj. 3,724
*****O'Hara**, Brendan (*b.* 1964) *SNP, Argyll & Bute,*
  Maj. 8,473
*****Onn**, Melanie (*b.* 1979) *Lab., Great Grimsby,*
  Maj. 4,540
**Onwurah**, Chi (*b.* 1965) *Lab., Newcastle upon Tyne*
  *Central,* Maj. 12,673
**Opperman**, Guy (*b.* 1965) *C., Hexham,*
  Maj. 12,031
*****Osamor**, Kate (*b.* 1968) *Lab. Co-op, Edmonton,*
  Maj. 15,419
**Osborne**, Rt. Hon. George (*b.* 1971) *C., Tatton,*
  Maj. 18,241
*****Oswald**, Kirsten (*b.* 1972) *SNP, Renfrewshire East,*
  Maj. 3,718
**Owen**, Albert (*b.* 1960) *Lab., Ynys Mon,* Maj. 229
**Paisley**, Ian (*b.* 1966) *DUP, Antrim North,*
  Maj. 11,546

**Parish**, Neil (*b.* 1956) *C., Tiverton & Honiton,*
  Maj. 20,173
**Patel**, Rt. Hon. Priti (*b.* 1972) *C., Witham,*
  Maj. 19,554
**Paterson**, Rt. Hon. Owen (*b.* 1956) *C., Shropshire*
  *North,* Maj. 16,494
*****Paterson**, Steven (*b.* 1975) *SNP, Stirling,*
  Maj. 10,480
**Pawsey**, Mark (*b.* 1957) *C., Rugby,* Maj. 10,345
**Pearce**, Teresa (*b.* 1955) *Lab., Erith & Thamesmead,*
  Maj. 9,525
**Penning**, Rt. Hon. Mike (*b.* 1957) *C., Hemel*
  *Hempstead,* Maj. 14,420
*****Pennycook**, Matthew (*b.* 1982) *Lab., Greenwich*
  *& Woolwich,* Maj. 11,946
**Penrose**, John (*b.* 1964) *C., Weston-super-Mare,*
  Maj. 15,609
**Percy**, Andrew (*b.* 1977) *C., Brigg & Goole,*
  Maj. 11,176
**Perkins**, Toby (*b.* 1970) *Lab., Chesterfield,*
  Maj. 13,598
**Perry**, Claire (*b.* 1964) *C., Devizes,* Maj. 20,751
*****Phillips**, Jess (*b.* 1981) *Lab., Birmingham Yardley,*
  Maj. 6,595
**Phillips**, Stephen (*b.* 1970) *C., Sleaford & North*
  *Hykeham,* Maj. 24,115
**Phillipson**, Bridget (*b.* 1983) *Lab., Houghton &*
  *Sunderland South,* Maj. 12,938
*****Philp**, Chris (*b.* 1976) *C., Croydon South,*
  Maj. 17,140
**Pickles**, Rt. Hon. Sir Eric (*b.* 1952) *C., Brentwood*
  *& Ongar,* Maj. 21,810
**Pincher**, Christopher (*b.* 1969) *C., Tamworth,*
  Maj. 11,302
**Poulter**, Dr Daniel (*b.* 1978) *C., Suffolk Central &*
  *Ipswich North,* Maj. 20,144
**Pound**, Stephen (*b.* 1948) *Lab., Ealing North,*
  Maj. 12,326
*****Pow**, Rebecca (*b.* 1960) *C., Taunton Deane,*
  Maj. 15,491
**Powell**, Lucy (*b.* 1974) *Lab. Co-op, Manchester*
  *Central,* Maj. 21,639
*****Prentis**, Victoria (*b.* 1971) *C., Banbury,*
  Maj. 18,395
**Prisk**, Mark (*b.* 1962) *C., Hertford & Stortford,*
  Maj. 21,509
**Pritchard**, Mark (*b.* 1966) *C., The Wrekin,*
  Maj. 10,743
**Pugh**, Dr John (*b.* 1948) *LD, Southport,*
  Maj. 1,322
*****Pursglove**, Tom (*b.* 1988) *C., Corby,* Maj. 2,412
*****Quin**, Jeremy (*b.* 1968) *C., Horsham, Maj.* 24,658
*****Quince**, Will (*b.* 1982) *C., Colchester,* Maj. 5,575
**Qureshi**, Yasmin (*b.* 1963) *Lab., Bolton South East,*
  Maj. 10,928
**Raab**, Dominic (*b.* 1974) *C., Esher & Walton,*
  Maj. 28,616
*****Rayner**, Angela (*b.* 1980) *Lab., Ashton-under-Lyne,*
  Maj. 10,756

**Redwood**, Rt. Hon. John (b. 1951) C., Wokingham, Maj. 24,197

**Reed**, Jamie (b. 1973) Lab., Copeland, Maj. 2,564

**Reed**, Steve (b. 1963) Lab. Co-op, Croydon North, Maj. 21,364

*****Rees**, Christina (b. 1954) Lab., Neath, Maj. 9,548

**Rees-Mogg**, Jacob (b. 1969) C., Somerset North East, Maj. 12,749

**Reeves**, Rachel (b. 1979) Lab., Leeds West, Maj. 10,727

**Reynolds**, Emma (b. 1977) Lab., Wolverhampton North East, Maj. 5,495

**Reynolds**, Jonathan (b. 1980) Lab. Co-op, Stalybridge & Hyde, Maj. 6,686

*****Rimmer**, Marie (b. 1947) Lab., St Helens South & Whiston, Maj. 21,243

**Ritchie**, Margaret (b. 1958) SDLP, Down South, Maj. 5,891

**Robertson**, Angus (b. 1969) SNP, Moray, Maj. 9,065

**Robertson**, Laurence (b. 1958) C., Tewkesbury, Maj. 21,972

*****Robinson**, Gavin (b. 1985) DUP, Belfast East, Maj. 2,597

**Robinson**, Geoffrey (b. 1938) Lab., Coventry North West, Maj. 4,509

*****Robinson**, Mary (b. 1955) C., Cheadle, Maj. 6,453

**Rosindell**, Andrew (b. 1966) C., Romford, Maj. 13,859

**Rotheram**, Steve (b. 1961) Lab., Liverpool Walton, Maj. 27,777

**Rudd**, Rt. Hon. Amber (b. 1963) C., Hastings & Rye, Maj. 4,796

**Rutley**, David (b. 1961) C., Macclesfield, Maj. 14,811

*****Ryan**, Rt. Hon. Joan (b. 1955) Lab., Enfield North, Maj. 1,086

*****Salmond**, Alex (b. 1954) SNP, Gordon, Maj. 8,687

*****Sandbach**, Antoinette (b. 1969) C., Eddisbury, Maj. 12,974

*****Saville-Roberts**, Liz (b. 1964) PC, Dwyfor Meirionnydd, Maj. 5,261

*****Scully**, Paul (b. 1968) C., Sutton & Cheam, Maj. 3,921

**Selous**, Andrew (b. 1962) C., Bedfordshire South West, Maj. 17,813

*****Shah**, Naseem (b. 1973) Lab., Bradford West, Maj. 11,420

**Shannon**, Jim (b. 1955) DUP, Strangford, Maj. 10,185

**Shapps**, Rt. Hon. Grant (b. 1968) C., Welwyn Hatfield, Maj. 12,153

**Sharma**, Alok (b. 1967) C., Reading West, Maj. 6,650

**Sharma**, Virendra (b. 1947) Lab., Ealing Southall, Maj. 18,760

**Sheerman**, Barry (b. 1940) Lab. Co-op, Huddersfield, Maj. 7,345

**Shelbrooke**, Alec (b. 1976) C., Elmet & Rothwell, Maj. 8,490

*****Sheppard**, Tommy (b. 1959) SNP, Edinburgh East, Maj. 9,106

*****Sherriff**, Paula (b. 1975) Lab., Dewsbury, Maj. 1,451

**Shuker**, Gavin (b. 1981) Lab. Co-op, Luton South, Maj. 5,711

*****Siddiq**, Tulip (b. 1982) Lab., Hampstead & Kilburn, Maj. 1,138

**Simpson**, David (b. 1959) DUP, Upper Bann, Maj. 2,264

**Simpson**, Rt. Hon. Keith (b. 1949) C., Broadland, Maj. 16,838

**Skidmore**, Chris (b. 1981) C., Kingswood, Maj. 9,006

**Skinner**, Dennis (b. 1932) Lab., Bolsover, Maj. 11,778

**Slaughter**, Andy (b. 1960) Lab., Hammersmith, Maj. 6,518

*****Smeeth**, Ruth (b. 1979) Lab., Stoke-on-Trent North, Maj. 4,836

**Smith**, Rt. Hon. Andrew (b. 1951) Lab., Oxford East, Maj. 15,280

**Smith**, Angela (b. 1961) Lab., Penistone & Stocksbridge, Maj. 6,723

*****Smith**, Catherine (b. 1985) Lab., Lancaster & Fleetwood, Maj. 1,265

**Smith**, Chloe (b. 1982) C., Norwich North, Maj. 4,463

**Smith**, Henry (b. 1969) C., Crawley, Maj. 6,526

*****Smith**, Jeff (b. 1963) Lab., Manchester Withington, Maj. 14,873

**Smith**, Julian (b. 1971) C., Skipton & Ripon, Maj. 20,761

**Smith**, Nick (b. 1960) Lab., Blaenau Gwent, Maj. 12,703

**Smith**, Owen (b. 1970) Lab., Pontypridd, Maj. 8,985

*****Smith**, Royston (b. 1964) C., Southampton Itchen, Maj. 2,316

*****Smyth**, Karin (b. 1964) Lab., Bristol South, Maj. 7,128

**Soames**, Rt. Hon. Sir Nicholas (b. 1948) C., Sussex Mid, Maj. 24,286

*****Solloway**, Amanda (b. 1961) C., Derby North, Maj. 41

**Soubry**, Rt. Hon. Anna (b. 1956) C., Broxtowe, Maj. 4,287

**Spellar**, Rt. Hon. John (b. 1947) Lab., Warley, Maj. 14,702

**Spelman**, Rt. Hon. Caroline (b. 1958) C., Meriden, Maj. 18,795

**Spencer**, Mark (b. 1970) C., Sherwood, Maj. 4,647

*****Starmer**, Sir Keir (b. 1962) Lab., Holborn & St Pancras, Maj. 17,048

*****Stephens**, Christopher (b. 1973) SNP, Glasgow South West, Maj. 9,950

**Stephenson**, Andrew (b. 1981) C., Pendle, Maj. 5,453

*Stevens, Jo (b. 1966) Lab., Cardiff Central, Maj. 4,981

Stevenson, John (b. 1963) C., Carlisle, Maj. 2,774

Stewart, Bob (b. 1949) C., Beckenham, Maj. 18,471

Stewart, Iain (b. 1972) C., Milton Keynes South, Maj. 8,672

Stewart, Rory (b. 1973) C., Penrith & The Border, Maj. 19,894

Streeter, Gary (b. 1955) C., Devon South West, Maj. 20,109

*Streeting, Wes (b. 1983) Lab., Ilford North, Maj. 589

Stride, Mel (b. 1961) C., Devon Central, Maj. 21,265

Stringer, Graham (b. 1950) Lab., Blackley & Broughton, Maj. 16,874

Stuart, Gisela (b. 1955) Lab., Birmingham Edgbaston, Maj. 2,706

Stuart, Graham (b. 1962) C., Beverley & Holderness, Maj. 12,203

Sturdy, Julian (b. 1971) C., York Outer, Maj. 13,129

*Sunak, Rishi (b. 1980) C., Richmond (Yorks), Maj. 19,550

Swayne, Rt. Hon. Desmond (b. 1956) C., New Forest West, Maj. 20,604

Swire, Rt. Hon. Hugo (b. 1959) C., Devon East, Maj. 12,261

Syms, Robert (b. 1956) C., Poole, Maj. 15,789

Tami, Mark (b. 1963) Lab., Alyn & Deeside, Maj. 3,343

*Thewliss, Alison (b. 1982) SNP, Glasgow Central, Maj. 7,662

*Thomas, Derek (b. 1972) C., St Ives, Maj. 2,469

Thomas, Gareth (b. 1967) Lab. Co-op, Harrow West, Maj. 2,208

*Thomas-Symonds, Nick (b. 1980) Lab., Torfaen, Maj. 8,169

*Thompson, Owen (b. 1978) SNP, Midlothian, Maj. 9,859

*Thomson, Michelle (b. 1965) SNP, Edinburgh West, Maj. 3,210

Thornberry, Emily (b. 1960) Lab., Islington South & Finsbury, Maj. 12,708

*Throup, Maggie (b. 1957) C., Erewash, Maj. 3,584

Timms, Rt. Hon. Stephen (b. 1955) Lab., East Ham, Maj. 34,252

Timpson, Edward (b. 1973) C., Crewe & Nantwich, Maj. 3,620

*Tolhurst, Kelly (b. 1978) C., Rochester & Strood, Maj. 7,133

Tomlinson, Justin (b. 1976) C., Swindon North, Maj. 11,786

*Tomlinson, Michael (b. 1977) C., Dorset Mid & Poole North, Maj. 10,530

*Tracey, Craig (b. 1974) C., Warwickshire North, Maj. 2,973

Tredinnick, David (b. 1950) C., Bosworth, Maj. 10,988

*Trevelyan, Anne-Marie (b. 1969) C., Berwick-upon-Tweed, Maj. 4,914

Trickett, Jon (b. 1950) Lab., Hemsworth, Maj. 12,078

Truss, Rt. Hon. Elizabeth (b. 1975) C., Norfolk South West, Maj. 13,861

*Tugendhat, Tom (b. 1973) C., Tonbridge & Malling, Maj. 23,734

*Turley, Anna (b. 1978) Lab. Co-op, Redcar, Maj. 10,388

Turner, Andrew (b. 1953) C., Isle of Wight, Maj. 13,703

Turner, Karl (b. 1971) Lab., Hull East, Maj. 10,319

Twigg, Derek (b. 1959) Lab., Halton, Maj. 20,285

Twigg, Stephen (b. 1966) Lab. Co-op, Liverpool West Derby, Maj. 27,367

Tyrie, Rt. Hon. Andrew (b. 1957) C., Chichester, Maj. 24,413

Umunna, Chuka (b. 1978) Lab., Streatham, Maj. 13,934

Vaizey, Edward (b. 1969) C., Wantage, Maj. 21,749

Vara, Shailesh (b. 1960) C., Cambridgeshire North West, Maj. 19,795

Vaz, Rt. Hon. Keith (b. 1956) Lab., Leicester East, Maj. 18,352

Vaz, Valerie (b. 1954) Lab., Walsall South, Maj. 6,007

Vickers, Martin (b. 1950) C., Cleethorpes, Maj. 7,893

Villiers, Rt. Hon. Theresa (b. 1968) C., Chipping Barnet, Maj. 7,656

Walker, Charles (b. 1967) C., Broxbourne, Maj. 16,723

Walker, Robin (b. 1978) C., Worcester, Maj. 5,646

Wallace, Ben (b. 1970) C., Wyre & Preston North, Maj. 14,151

*Warburton, David (b. 1965) C., Somerton & Frome, Maj. 20,268

*Warman, Matt (b. 1981) C., Boston & Skegness, Maj. 4,336

Watkinson, Dame Angela (b. 1941) C., Hornchurch & Upminster, Maj. 13,074

Watson, Tom (b. 1967) Lab., West Bromwich East, Maj. 9,470

Weir, Mike (b. 1957) SNP, Angus, Maj. 11,230

*West, Catherine (b. 1966) Lab., Hornsey & Wood Green, Maj. 11,058

Wharton, James (b. 1984) C., Stockton South, Maj. 5,046

*Whately, Helen (b. 1976) C., Faversham & Kent Mid, Maj. 16,652

Wheeler, Heather (b. 1959) C., Derbyshire South, Maj. 11,471

White, Chris (b. 1967) C., Warwick & Leamington, Maj. 6,606

Whiteford, Dr Eilidh (b. 1969) SNP, Banff & Buchan, Maj. 14,339

Whitehead, Dr Alan (b. 1950) Lab., Southampton Test, Maj. 3,810

*Whitford, Dr Philippa (b. 1959) SNP, Ayrshire Central, Maj. 13,589

Whittaker, Craig (b. 1962) C., Calder Valley, Maj. 4,427

Whittingdale, Rt. Hon. John (b. 1959) C., Maldon, Maj. 22,070

Wiggin, Bill (b. 1966) C., Herefordshire North, Maj. 19,996

*Williams, Craig (b. 1985) C., Cardiff North, Maj. 2,137

Williams, Hywel (b. 1953) PC, Arfon, Maj. 3,668

Williams, Mark (b. 1966) LD, Ceredigion, Maj. 3,067

Williamson, Rt. Hon. Gavin (b. 1976) C., Staffordshire South, Maj. 20,371

*Wilson, Corri (b. 1963) SNP, Ayr, Carrick & Cumnock, Maj. 11,265

Wilson, Phil (b. 1959) Lab., Sedgefield, Maj. 6,843

Wilson, Rob (b. 1965) C., Reading East, Maj. 6,520

Wilson, Sammy (b. 1953) DUP, Antrim East, Maj. 5,795

Winnick, David (b. 1933) Lab., Walsall North, Maj. 1,937

Winterton, Rt. Hon. Rosie (b. 1958) Lab., Doncaster Central, Maj. 10,093

Wishart, Pete (b. 1962) SNP, Perth & Perthshire North, Maj. 9,641

Wollaston, Dr Sarah (b. 1962) C., Totnes, Maj. 18,285

*Wood, Mike (b. 1976) C., Dudley South, Maj. 4,270

Woodcock, John (b. 1978) Lab. Co-op, Barrow & Furness, Maj. 795

*Wragg, William (b. 1987) C., Hazel Grove, Maj. 6,552

Wright, Iain (b. 1972) Lab., Hartlepool, Maj. 3,024

Wright, Rt. Hon. Jeremy (b. 1972) C., Kenilworth & Southam, Maj. 21,002

Zahawi, Nadhim (b. 1967) C., Stratford-on-Avon, Maj. 22,876

*Zeichner, Daniel (b. 1956) Lab., Cambridge, Maj. 599

## BANBURY
E. 86,420 T. 58,008 (67.12%)
|  |  | C. hold |
| --- | --- | --- |
| *Victoria Prentis, C. | | 30,749 |
| Sean Woodcock, Lab. | | 12,354 |
| Dickie Bird, UKIP | | 8,050 |
| John Howson, LD | | 3,440 |
| Ian Middleton, Green | | 2,686 |
| Roseanne Edwards, NHAP | | 729 |

C. majority 18,395 (31.71%)
0.97% swing C. to Lab.
(2010: C. majority 18,227 (32.41%))

## BARKING
E. 74,004 T. 43,023 (58.14%)
|  | Lab. hold |
| --- | --- |
| Margaret Hodge, Lab. | 24,826 |
| Roger Gravett, UKIP | 9,554 |
| Mina Rahman, C. | 7,019 |
| Tony Rablen, Green | 879 |
| Peter Wilcock, LD | 562 |
| Joseph Mambuliya, TUSC | 183 |

Lab. majority 15,272 (35.50%)
7.98% swing Lab. to UKIP
(2010: Lab. majority 16,555
(36.51%))

## BARNSLEY CENTRAL
E. 64,534 T. 36,560 (56.65%)
|  | Lab. hold |
| --- | --- |
| Dan Jarvis, Lab. | 20,376 |
| Lee Hunter, UKIP | 7,941 |
| Kay Carter, C. | 5,485 |
| Michael Short, Green | 938 |
| David Ridgway, LD | 770 |
| Dave Gibson, TUSC | 573 |
| Ian Sutton, Eng. Dem. | 477 |

Lab. majority 12,435 (34.01%)
4.29% swing Lab. to UKIP
(2010: Lab. majority 11,093
(29.98%)) (2011: Lab. majority
11,771 (48.60%))

## BARNSLEY EAST
E. 69,135 T. 38,517 (55.71%)
|  | Lab. hold |
| --- | --- |
| Michael Dugher, Lab. | 21,079 |
| Robert Swiffen, UKIP | 9,045 |
| Katharine Harborne, C. | 5,622 |
| Ruth Coleman-Taylor, LD | 1,217 |
| Tony Devoy, Yorks | 647 |
| Kevin Riddiough, Eng. Dem. | 440 |
| Ralph Dyson, TUSC | 364 |
| Billy Marsden, Vapers | 103 |

Lab. majority 12,034 (31.24%)
5.65% swing Lab. to UKIP
(2010: Lab. majority 11,090
(28.89%))

## BARROW & FURNESS
E. 68,338 T. 43,275 (63.32%)
|  | Lab. Co-op hold |
| --- | --- |
| John Woodcock, Lab. Co-op | 18,320 |
| Simon Fell, C. | 17,525 |
| Nigel Cecil, UKIP | 5,070 |
| Clive Peaple, LD | 1,169 |
| Robert O'Hara, Green | 1,061 |
| Ian Jackson, Ind. | 130 |

Lab. Co-op majority 795 (1.84%)
4.98% swing Lab. Co-op to C.
(2010: Lab. Co-op majority 5,208
(11.80%))

## BASILDON & BILLERICAY
E. 68,459 T. 43,028 (62.85%)
|  | C. hold |
| --- | --- |
| John Baron, C. | 22,668 |
| Gavin Callaghan, Lab. | 10,186 |
| George Konstantinidis, UKIP | 8,538 |
| Martin Thompson, LD | 1,636 |

C. majority 12,482 (29.01%)
0.34% swing C. to Lab.
(2010: C. majority 12,338 (29.68%))

## BASILDON SOUTH & THURROCK EAST
E. 73,210 T. 45,593 (62.28%)
|  | C. hold |
| --- | --- |
| Stephen Metcalfe, C. | 19,788 |
| Ian Luder, UKIP | 12,097 |
| Mike Le-Surf, Lab. | 11,493 |
| Geoff Williams, LD | 1,356 |
| Kerry Smith, Ind. | 401 |
| None Of The Above X, ND | 253 |
| Stuart Hooper, Ind. | 205 |

C. majority 7,691 (16.87%)
10.55% swing C. to UKIP
(2010: C. majority 5,772 (12.90%))

## BASINGSTOKE
E. 79,662 T. 53,076 (66.63%)
|  | C. hold |
| --- | --- |
| Maria Miller, C. | 25,769 |
| Paul Harvey, Lab. | 14,706 |
| Alan Stone, UKIP | 8,290 |
| Janice Spalding, LD | 3,919 |
| Omar Selim, Ind. | 392 |

C. majority 11,063 (20.84%)
4.64% swing C. to Lab.
(2010: C. majority 13,176 (26.01%))

## BASSETLAW
E. 77,480 T. 49,289 (63.62%)
|  | Lab. hold |
| --- | --- |
| John Mann, Lab. | 23,965 |
| Sarah Downes, C. | 15,122 |
| David Scott, UKIP | 7,865 |
| Leon Duveen, LD | 1,331 |
| Kris Wragg, Green | 1,006 |

Lab. majority 8,843 (17.94%)
0.69% swing C. to Lab.
(2010: Lab. majority 8,215 (16.57%))

## BATH
E. 60,869 T. 47,167 (77.49%)
|  | C. gain |
| --- | --- |
| *Ben Howlett, C. | 17,833 |
| Steve Bradley, LD | 14,000 |
| Ollie Middleton, Lab. | 6,216 |
| Dominic Tristram, Green | 5,634 |
| Julian Deverell, UKIP | 2,922 |
| Loraine Morgan-Brinkhurst, Ind. | 499 |
| Jenny Knight, Eng. Dem. | 63 |

C. majority 3,833 (8.13%)
16.68% swing LD to C.
(2010: LD majority 11,883
(25.24%))

## BATLEY & SPEN
E. 78,373 T. 50,479 (64.41%)
|  | Lab. hold |
| --- | --- |
| *Jo Cox, Lab. | 21,826 |
| Imtiaz Ameen, C. | 15,769 |
| Aleks Lukic, UKIP | 9,080 |
| John Lawson, LD | 2,396 |
| Ian Bullock, Green | 1,232 |
| Dawn Wheelhouse, TUSC | 123 |
| Karl Varley, PSP | 53 |

Lab. majority 6,057 (12.00%)
1.69% swing C. to Lab.
(2010: Lab. majority 4,406 (8.62%))

## BATTERSEA
E. 76,106 T. 51,031 (67.05%)
|  | C. hold |
| --- | --- |
| Jane Ellison, C. | 26,730 |
| Will Martindale, Lab. | 18,792 |
| Luke Taylor, LD | 2,241 |
| Joe Stuart, Green | 1,682 |
| Christopher Howe, UKIP | 1,586 |

C. majority 7,938 (15.56%)
1.65% swing Lab. to C.
(2010: C. majority 5,977 (12.25%))

## BEACONSFIELD
E. 76,380 T. 53,163 (69.60%)
|  | C. hold |
| --- | --- |
| Dominic Grieve, C. | 33,621 |
| Tim Scott, UKIP | 7,310 |
| Tony Clements, Lab. | 6,074 |
| Peter Chapman, LD | 3,927 |
| Dave Hampton, Green | 2,231 |

C. majority 26,311 (49.49%)
3.31% swing C. to UKIP
(2010: C. majority 21,782 (41.50%))

## BECKENHAM
E. 67,436 T. 48,803 (72.37%)
|  | C. hold |
| --- | --- |
| Bob Stewart, C. | 27,955 |
| Marina Ahmad, Lab. | 9,484 |
| Rob Bryant, UKIP | 6,108 |
| Anuja Prashar, LD | 3,378 |
| Ruth Fabricant, Green | 1,878 |

C. majority 18,471 (37.85%)
2.78% swing C. to Lab.
(2010: C. majority 17,784 (37.29%))

**BEDFORD**
E. 69,311 T. 46,086 (66.49%)

| | C. hold |
|---|---|
| Richard Fuller, C. | 19,625 |
| Patrick Hall, Lab. | 18,528 |
| Charlie Smith, UKIP | 4,434 |
| Mahmud Henry Rogers, LD | 1,958 |
| Ben Foley, Green | 1,412 |
| Faruk Choudhury, Ind. | 129 |

C. majority 1,097 (2.38%)
0.31% swing C. to Lab.
(2010: C. majority 1,353 (3.00%))

**BEDFORDSHIRE MID**
E. 81,144 T. 58,060 (71.55%)

| | C. hold |
|---|---|
| Nadine Dorries, C. | 32,544 |
| Charlynne Pullen, Lab. | 9,217 |
| Nigel Wickens, UKIP | 8,966 |
| Linda Jack, LD | 4,193 |
| Gareth Ellis, Green | 2,462 |
| Tim Ireland, Ind. | 384 |
| Ann Kelly, Loony | 294 |

C. majority 23,327 (40.18%)
1.23% swing Lab. to C.
(2010: C. majority 15,152 (27.60%))

**BEDFORDSHIRE NORTH EAST**
E. 83,551 T. 58,672 (70.22%)

| | C. hold |
|---|---|
| Alistair Burt, C. | 34,891 |
| Saqhib Ali, Lab. | 9,247 |
| Adrianne Smyth, UKIP | 8,579 |
| Peter Morris, LD | 3,418 |
| Mark Bowler, Green | 2,537 |

C. majority 25,644 (43.71%)
2.02% swing Lab. to C.
(2010: C. majority 18,942 (34.10%))

**BEDFORDSHIRE SOUTH WEST**
E. 79,664 T. 51,304 (64.40%)

| | C. hold |
|---|---|
| Andrew Selous, C. | 28,212 |
| Daniel Scott, Lab. | 10,399 |
| John Van Weenen, UKIP | 7,941 |
| Stephen Rutherford, LD | 2,646 |
| Emily Lawrence, Green | 2,106 |

C. majority 17,813 (34.72%)
0.75% swing Lab. to C.
(2010: C. majority 16,649 (32.79%))

**BERMONDSEY & OLD SOUTHWARK**
E. 80,604 T. 51,424 (63.80%)

| | Lab. gain |
|---|---|
| *Neil Coyle, Lab. | 22,146 |
| Simon Hughes, LD | 17,657 |
| JP Floru, C. | 6,051 |
| Andrew Beadle, UKIP | 3,254 |
| William Lavin, Green | 2,023 |
| Kingsley Abrams, TUSC | 142 |
| Lucy Hall, Ind. | 72 |
| Donald Cole, AP | 59 |
| Steve Freeman, Rep. Soc. | 20 |

Lab. majority 4,489 (8.73%)
13.92% swing LD to Lab.
(2010: LD majority 8,530 (19.10%))

**BERWICK-UPON-TWEED**
E. 58,098 T. 40,423 (69.58%)

| | C. gain |
|---|---|
| *Anne-Marie Trevelyan, C. | 16,603 |
| Julie Porksen, LD | 11,689 |
| Scott Dickinson, Lab. | 6,042 |
| Nigel Coghill-Marshall, UKIP | 4,513 |
| Rachael Roberts, Green | 1,488 |
| Neil Humphrey, Eng. Dem. | 88 |

C. majority 4,914 (12.16%)
9.58% swing LD to C.
(2010: LD majority 2,690 (7.00%))

**BETHNAL GREEN & BOW**
E. 82,825 T. 52,924 (63.90%)

| | Lab. hold |
|---|---|
| Rushanara Ali, Lab. | 32,387 |
| Matt Smith, C. | 8,070 |
| Alistair Polson, Green | 4,906 |
| Paula McQueen, UKIP | 3,219 |
| Teena Lashmore, LD | 2,395 |
| Glyn Robbins, TUSC | 949 |
| M. Rowshan Ali, Community | 356 |
| Jonathan Dewey, CISTA | 303 |
| Alasdair Henderson, Whig | 203 |
| Elliot Ball, 30-50 | 78 |
| Jason Pavlou, RFAC | 58 |

Lab. majority 24,317 (45.95%)
8.47% swing C. to Lab.
(2010: Lab. majority 11,574 (22.82%))

**BEVERLEY & HOLDERNESS**
E. 80,822 T. 52,677 (65.18%)

| | C. hold |
|---|---|
| Graham Stuart, C. | 25,363 |
| Margaret Pinder, Lab. | 13,160 |
| Gary Shores, UKIP | 8,794 |
| Denis Healy, LD | 2,900 |
| Richard Howarth, Green | 1,802 |
| Lee Walton, Yorks | 658 |

C. majority 12,203 (23.17%)
1.42% swing C. to Lab.
(2010: C. majority 12,987 (24.41%))

**BEXHILL & BATTLE**
E. 78,796 T. 55,218 (70.08%)

| | C. hold |
|---|---|
| *Huw Merriman, C. | 30,245 |
| Geoffrey Bastin, UKIP | 10,170 |
| Michelle Thew, Lab. | 7,797 |
| Rachel Sadler, LD | 4,199 |
| Jonathan Kent, Green | 2,807 |

C. majority 20,075 (36.36%)
swing N/A
(2010: C. majority 12,880 (23.60%))

**BEXLEYHEATH & CRAYFORD**
E. 64,828 T. 43,685 (67.39%)

| | C. hold |
|---|---|
| David Evennett, C. | 20,643 |
| Stef Borella, Lab. | 11,451 |
| Chris Attard, UKIP | 9,182 |
| Richard Davis, LD | 1,308 |
| Stella Gardiner, Green | 950 |
| Maggi Young, Eng. Dem. | 151 |

C. majority 9,192 (21.04%)
1.46% swing C. to Lab.
(2010: C. majority 10,344 (23.95%))

**BIRKENHEAD**
E. 62,438 T. 37,680 (60.35%)

| | Lab. hold |
|---|---|
| Frank Field, Lab. | 26,468 |
| Clark Vasey, C. | 5,816 |
| Wayne Harling, UKIP | 3,838 |
| Allan Brame, LD | 1,396 |
| Kenny Peers, Green | 162 |

Lab. majority 20,652 (54.81%)
5.61% swing C. to Lab.
(2010: Lab. majority 15,395 (43.58%))

**BIRMINGHAM EDGBASTON**
E. 65,591 T. 41,293 (62.96%)

| | Lab. hold |
|---|---|
| Gisela Stuart, Lab. | 18,518 |
| Luke Evans, C. | 15,812 |
| Graham Short, UKIP | 4,154 |
| Phil Simpson, Green | 1,371 |
| Lee Dargue, LD | 1,184 |
| Gabriel Ukandu, Ch. P. | 163 |
| Henna Rai, Ind. | 91 |

Lab. majority 2,706 (6.55%)
1.74% swing C. to Lab.
(2010: Lab. majority 1,274 (3.06%))

**BIRMINGHAM ERDINGTON**
E. 65,128 T. 34,684 (53.26%)

| | Lab. hold |
|---|---|
| Jack Dromey, Lab. | 15,824 |
| Robert Alden, C. | 10,695 |
| Andrew Garcarz, UKIP | 6,040 |
| Ann Holtom, LD | 965 |
| Joe Belcher, Green | 948 |
| Ted Woodley, TUSC | 212 |

Lab. majority 5,129 (14.79%)
2.78% swing C. to Lab.
(2010: Lab. majority 3,277 (9.22%))

**BIRMINGHAM HALL GREEN**
E. 76,330 T. 47,046 (61.64%)

| | Lab. hold |
|---|---|
| Roger Godsiff, Lab. | 28,147 |
| James Bird, C. | 8,329 |
| Jerry Evans, LD | 5,459 |
| Elly Stanton, Green | 2,200 |
| Rashpal Mondair, UKIP | 2,131 |
| Shiraz Peer, Respect | 780 |

Lab. majority 19,818 (42.12%)
12.12% swing C. to Lab.
(2010: Lab. majority 3,799 (7.80%))

BIRMINGHAM HODGE HILL
E. 75,302  T. 41,039 (54.50%)

| | Lab. hold |
|---|---|
| Liam Byrne, Lab. | 28,069 |
| Kieran Mullan, C. | 4,707 |
| Albert Duffen, UKIP | 4,651 |
| Phil Bennion, LD | 2,624 |
| Chris Nash, Green | 835 |
| Andy Chaffer, Comm. | 153 |

Lab. majority 23,362 (56.93%)
8.28% swing C. to Lab.
(2010: Lab. majority 10,302
(24.26%))

BIRMINGHAM LADYWOOD
E. 68,128  T. 35,916 (52.72%)

| | Lab. hold |
|---|---|
| Shabana Mahmood, Lab. | 26,444 |
| Isabel Sigmac, C. | 4,576 |
| Clair Braund, UKIP | 1,805 |
| Margaret Okole, Green | 1,501 |
| Shazad Iqbal, LD | 1,374 |
| Timothy Burton, Lib. GB | 216 |

Lab. majority 21,868 (60.89%)
8.57% swing C. to Lab.
(2010: Lab. majority 10,105
(28.20%))

BIRMINGHAM NORTHFIELD
E. 71,428  T. 42,461 (59.45%)

| | Lab. hold |
|---|---|
| Richard Burden, Lab. | 17,673 |
| Rachel Maclean, C. | 15,164 |
| Keith Rowe, UKIP | 7,106 |
| Steven Haynes, LD | 1,349 |
| Anna Masters, Green | 1,169 |

Lab. majority 2,509 (5.91%)
0.37% swing Lab. to C.
(2010: Lab. majority 2,782 (6.65%))

BIRMINGHAM PERRY BARR
E. 69,943  T. 41,260 (58.99%)

| | Lab. hold |
|---|---|
| Khalid Mahmood, Lab. | 23,697 |
| Charlotte Hodivala, C. | 8,869 |
| Harjinder Singh, UKIP | 5,032 |
| Arjun Singh, LD | 2,001 |
| James Lovatt, Green | 1,330 |
| Robert Punton, TUSC | 331 |

Lab. majority 14,828 (35.94%)
3.48% swing C. to Lab.
(2010: Lab. majority 11,908
(28.32%))

BIRMINGHAM SELLY OAK
E. 75,092  T. 45,294 (60.32%)

| | Lab. hold |
|---|---|
| Steve McCabe, Lab. | 21,584 |
| Alex Boulter, C. | 13,137 |
| Steven Brookes, UKIP | 5,755 |
| Colin Green, LD | 2,517 |
| Clare Thomas, Green | 2,301 |

Lab. majority 8,447 (18.65%)
5.59% swing C. to Lab.
(2010: Lab. majority 3,482 (7.48%))

BIRMINGHAM YARDLEY
E. 72,146  T. 41,151 (57.04%)

| | Lab. gain |
|---|---|
| *Jess Phillips, Lab. | 17,129 |
| John Hemming, LD | 10,534 |
| Paul Clayton, UKIP | 6,637 |
| Arun Photay, C. | 5,760 |
| Grant Bishop, Green | 698 |
| Teval Stephens, Respect | 187 |
| Eamonn Flynn, TUSC | 135 |
| Peter Johnson, Soc. Dem. | 71 |

Lab. majority 6,595 (16.03%)
11.69% swing LD to Lab.
(2010: LD majority 3,002 (7.35%))

BISHOP AUCKLAND
E. 66,089  T. 39,389 (59.60%)

| | Lab. hold |
|---|---|
| Helen Goodman, Lab. | 16,307 |
| Christopher Adams, C. | 12,799 |
| Rhys Burriss, UKIP | 7,015 |
| Stephen White, LD | 1,723 |
| Thom Robinson, Green | 1,545 |

Lab. majority 3,508 (8.91%)
1.89% swing Lab. to C.
(2010: Lab. majority 5,218 (12.68%))

BLACKBURN
E. 73,265  T. 43,999 (60.05%)

| | Lab. hold |
|---|---|
| *Kate Hollern, Lab. | 24,762 |
| Bob Eastwood, C. | 12,002 |
| Dayle Taylor, UKIP | 6,280 |
| Gordon Lishman, LD | 955 |

Lab. majority 12,760 (29.00%)
3.67% swing C. to Lab.
(2010: Lab. majority 9,856 (21.66%))

BLACKLEY & BROUGHTON
E. 71,900  T. 37,112 (51.62%)

| | Lab. hold |
|---|---|
| Graham Stringer, Lab. | 22,982 |
| Martin Power, UKIP | 6,108 |
| Michelle Tanfield-Johnson, C. | 5,581 |
| David Jones, Green | 1,567 |
| Richard Gadsden, LD | 874 |

Lab. majority 16,874 (45.47%)
3.09% swing Lab. to UKIP
(2010: Lab. majority 12,303
(35.97%))

BLACKPOOL NORTH &
CLEVELEYS
E. 62,469  T. 39,393 (63.06%)

| | C. hold |
|---|---|
| Paul Maynard, C. | 17,508 |
| Sam Rushworth, Lab. | 14,168 |
| Simon Noble, UKIP | 5,823 |
| Sue Close, LD | 948 |
| John Warnock, Green | 889 |
| James Walsh, Northern | 57 |

C. majority 3,340 (8.48%)
1.59% swing Lab. to C.
(2010: C. majority 2,150 (5.30%))

BLACKPOOL SOUTH
E. 57,411  T. 32,436 (56.50%)

| | Lab. hold |
|---|---|
| Gordon Marsden, Lab. | 13,548 |
| Peter Anthony, C. | 10,963 |
| Peter Wood, UKIP | 5,613 |
| Duncan Royle, Green | 841 |
| Bill Greene, LD | 743 |
| Andy Higgins, Ind. | 655 |
| Lawrence Chard, Ind. | 73 |

Lab. majority 2,585 (7.97%)
1.35% swing C. to Lab.
(2010: Lab. majority 1,851 (5.26%))

BLAYDON
E. 67,706  T. 44,936 (66.37%)

| | Lab. hold |
|---|---|
| David Anderson, Lab. | 22,090 |
| Mark Bell, UKIP | 7,863 |
| Alison Griffiths, C. | 7,838 |
| Jonathan Wallace, LD | 5,497 |
| Paul McNally, Green | 1,648 |

Lab. majority 14,227 (31.66%)
swing N/A
(2010: Lab. majority 9,117 (20.30%))

BLYTH VALLEY
E. 63,958  T. 38,461 (60.13%)

| | Lab. hold |
|---|---|
| Ronnie Campbell, Lab. | 17,813 |
| Barry Elliott, UKIP | 8,584 |
| Greg Munro, C. | 8,346 |
| Philip Latham, LD | 2,265 |
| Dawn Furness, Green | 1,453 |

Lab. majority 9,229 (24.00%)
8.09% swing Lab. to UKIP
(2010: Lab. majority 6,668 (17.29%))

BOGNOR REGIS &
LITTLEHAMPTON
E. 73,095  T. 47,116 (64.46%)

| | C. hold |
|---|---|
| Nick Gibb, C. | 24,185 |
| Graham Jones, UKIP | 10,241 |
| Alan Butcher, Lab. | 6,508 |
| Francis Oppler, LD | 4,240 |
| Simon McDougall, Green | 1,942 |

C. majority 13,944 (29.60%)
7.67% swing C. to UKIP
(2010: C. majority 13,063 (27.88%))

BOLSOVER
E. 71,976  T. 43,998 (61.13%)

| | Lab. hold |
|---|---|
| Dennis Skinner, Lab. | 22,542 |
| Peter Bedford, C. | 10,764 |
| Ray Calladine, UKIP | 9,228 |
| David Lomax, LD | 1,464 |

Lab. majority 11,778 (26.77%)
0.67% swing C. to Lab.
(2010: Lab. majority 11,182
(25.42%))

**BOLTON NORTH EAST**
E. 67,901 T. 43,161 (63.56%)

| | Lab. hold |
|---|---|
| David Crausby, Lab. | 18,541 |
| James Daly, C. | 14,164 |
| Harry Lamb, UKIP | 8,117 |
| Stephen Rock, LD | 1,236 |
| Laura Diggle, Green | 1,103 |

Lab. majority 4,377 (10.14%)
0.35% swing C. to Lab.
(2010: Lab. majority 4,084 (9.44%))

**BOLTON SOUTH EAST**
E. 69,692 T. 40,743 (58.46%)

| | Lab. hold |
|---|---|
| Yasmin Qureshi, Lab. | 20,555 |
| Jeff Armstrong, UKIP | 9,627 |
| Mudasir Dean, C. | 8,289 |
| Alan Johnson, Green | 1,200 |
| Darren Reynolds, LD | 1,072 |

Lab. majority 10,928 (26.82%)
8.33% swing Lab. to UKIP
(2010: Lab. majority 8,634 (21.80%))

**BOLTON WEST**
E. 72,727 T. 48,592 (66.81%)

| | C. gain |
|---|---|
| *Chris Green, C. | 19,744 |
| Julie Hilling, Lab. | 18,943 |
| Bob Horsefield, UKIP | 7,428 |
| Andrew Martin, LD | 1,947 |
| Andy Smith, Ind. | 321 |
| John Vickers, TUSC | 209 |

C. majority 801 (1.65%)
0.92% swing Lab. to C.
(2010: Lab. majority 92 (0.19%))

**BOOTLE**
E. 70,137 T. 45,152 (64.38%)

| | Lab. hold |
|---|---|
| *Peter Dowd, Lab. | 33,619 |
| Paul Nuttall, UKIP | 4,915 |
| Jade Marsden, C. | 3,639 |
| Lisa Tallis, Green | 1,501 |
| David Newman, LD | 978 |
| Pete Glover, TUSC | 500 |

Lab. majority 28,704 (63.57%)
1.61% swing UKIP to Lab.
(2010: Lab. majority 21,181 (51.31%))

**BOSTON & SKEGNESS**
E. 67,834 T. 43,339 (63.89%)

| | C. hold |
|---|---|
| *Matt Warman, C. | 18,981 |
| Robin Hunter-Clarke, UKIP | 14,645 |
| Paul Kenny, Lab. | 7,142 |
| David Watts, LD | 1,015 |
| Victoria Percival, Green | 800 |
| Chris Pain, IE | 324 |
| Peter Johnson, ND | 170 |
| Lyn Luxton, Pilgrim | 143 |
| Robert West, BNP | 119 |

C. majority 4,336 (10.00%)
14.99% swing C. to UKIP
(2010: C. majority 12,426 (28.81%))

**BOSWORTH**
E. 79,742 T. 53,582 (67.19%)

| | C. hold |
|---|---|
| David Tredinnick, C. | 22,939 |
| Michael Mullaney, LD | 11,951 |
| Chris Kealey, Lab. | 9,354 |
| David Sprason, UKIP | 9,338 |

C. majority 10,988 (20.51%)
5.62% swing LD to C.
(2010: C. majority 5,032 (9.27%))

**BOURNEMOUTH EAST**
E. 71,956 T. 44,827 (62.30%)

| | C. hold |
|---|---|
| Tobias Ellwood, C. | 22,060 |
| Peter Stokes, Lab. | 7,448 |
| David Hughes, UKIP | 7,401 |
| Jon Nicholas, LD | 3,752 |
| Alasdair Keddie, Green | 3,263 |
| David Ross, Bournemouth | 903 |

C. majority 14,612 (32.60%)
1.29% swing C. to Lab.
(2010: C. majority 7,728 (17.55%))

**BOURNEMOUTH WEST**
E. 72,082 T. 41,773 (57.95%)

| | C. hold |
|---|---|
| Conor Burns, C. | 20,155 |
| Martin Houlden, UKIP | 7,745 |
| David Stokes, Lab. | 7,386 |
| Mike Plummer, LD | 3,281 |
| Elizabeth McManus, Green | 3,107 |
| Dick Franklin, Patria | 99 |

C. majority 12,410 (29.71%)
4.12% swing C. to UKIP
(2010: C. majority 5,583 (13.40%))

**BRACKNELL**
E. 78,131 T. 53,086 (67.94%)

| | C. hold |
|---|---|
| Phillip Lee, C. | 29,606 |
| James Walsh, Lab. | 8,956 |
| Richard Thomas, UKIP | 8,339 |
| Patrick Smith, LD | 3,983 |
| Derek Florey, Green | 2,202 |

C. majority 20,650 (38.90%)
1.64% swing Lab. to C.
(2010: C. majority 15,704 (30.12%))

**BRADFORD EAST**
E. 66,123 T. 41,406 (62.62%)

| | Lab. gain |
|---|---|
| *Imran Hussain, Lab. | 19,312 |
| David Ward, LD | 12,228 |
| Iftikhar Ahmed, C. | 4,682 |
| Owais Rajput, UKIP | 4,103 |
| Dave Stevens, Green | 871 |
| James Lewthwaite, Brit. Dem. | 210 |

Lab. majority 7,084 (17.11%)
9.01% swing LD to Lab.
(2010: LD majority 365 (0.90%))

**BRADFORD SOUTH**
E. 63,670 T. 37,600 (59.05%)

| | Lab. hold |
|---|---|
| *Judith Cummins, Lab. | 16,328 |
| Tanya Graham, C. | 9,878 |
| Jason Smith, UKIP | 9,057 |
| Andrew Robinson, Green | 1,243 |
| Andrew Tear, LD | 1,094 |

Lab. majority 6,450 (17.15%)
2.49% swing C. to Lab.
(2010: Lab. majority 4,622 (12.16%))

**BRADFORD WEST**
E. 63,371 T. 40,290 (63.58%)

| | Lab. gain |
|---|---|
| *Naseem Shah, Lab. | 19,977 |
| George Galloway, Respect | 8,557 |
| George Grant, C. | 6,160 |
| Harry Boota, UKIP | 3,140 |
| Alun Griffiths, LD | 1,173 |
| Celia Hickson, Green | 1,085 |
| James Kirkcaldy, Ind. | 100 |
| Therese Hirst, Eng. Dem. | 98 |

Lab. majority 11,420 (28.34%)
swing N/A
(2010: Lab. majority 5,763 (14.20%))
(2012: Respect majority 10,140 (30.90%))

**BRAINTREE**
E. 73,557 T. 50,283 (68.36%)

| | C. hold |
|---|---|
| *James Cleverly, C. | 27,071 |
| Richard Bingley, UKIP | 9,461 |
| Malcolm Fincken, Lab. | 9,296 |
| Matthew Klesel, LD | 2,488 |
| Paul Jeater, Green | 1,564 |
| Toby Pereira, Ind. | 295 |
| Paul Hooks, BNP | 108 |

C. majority 17,610 (35.02%)
6.29% swing C. to UKIP
(2010: C. majority 16,121 (32.76%))

**BRENT CENTRAL**
E. 77,038 T. 47,032 (61.05%)

| | Lab. gain |
|---|---|
| *Dawn Butler, Lab. | 29,216 |
| Alan Mendoza, C. | 9,567 |
| Lauren Keith, LD | 3,937 |
| Shahrar Ali, Green | 1,912 |
| Stephen Priestley, UKIP | 1,850 |
| John Boyle, TUSC | 235 |
| Kamran Malik, Community | 170 |
| Noel Coonan, Ind. | 145 |

Lab. majority 19,649 (41.78%)
28.36% swing LD to Lab.
(2010: LD majority 1,345 (2.97%))

**BRENT NORTH**
E. 82,196 T. 52,235 (63.55%)
Lab. hold

| | |
|---|---|
| Barry Gardiner, Lab. | 28,351 |
| Luke Parker, C. | 17,517 |
| Paul Lorber, LD | 2,607 |
| Alan Craig, UKIP | 2,024 |
| Scott Bartle, Green | 1,539 |
| Elcena Jeffers, Ind. | 197 |

Lab. majority 10,834 (20.74%)
2.70% swing C. to Lab.
(2010: Lab. majority 8,028 (15.35%))

**BRENTFORD & ISLEWORTH**
E. 84,557 T. 57,355 (67.83%)
Lab. gain

| | |
|---|---|
| *Ruth Cadbury, Lab. | 25,096 |
| Mary Macleod, C. | 24,631 |
| Richard Hendron, UKIP | 3,203 |
| Joe Bourke, LD | 2,305 |
| Daniel Goldsmith, Green | 2,120 |

Lab. majority 465 (0.81%)
2.23% swing C. to Lab.
(2010: C. majority 1,958 (3.64%))

**BRENTWOOD & ONGAR**
E. 72,461 T. 51,897 (71.62%)
C. hold

| | |
|---|---|
| Eric Pickles, C. | 30,534 |
| Michael McGough, UKIP | 8,724 |
| Liam Preston, Lab. | 6,492 |
| David Kendall, LD | 4,577 |
| Reza Hossain, Green | 1,397 |
| Robin Tilbrook, Eng. Dem. | 173 |

C. majority 21,810 (42.03%)
5.43% swing C. to UKIP
(2010: C. majority 16,921 (33.45%))

**BRIDGWATER & SOMERSET WEST**
E. 80,491 T. 54,447 (67.64%)
C. hold

| | |
|---|---|
| Ian Liddell-Grainger, C. | 25,020 |
| Stephen Fitzgerald, UKIP | 10,437 |
| Mick Lerry, Lab. | 9,589 |
| Theodore Butt Phillip, LD | 6,765 |
| Julie Harvey-Smith, Green | 2,636 |

C. majority 14,583 (26.78%)
6.86% swing C. to UKIP
(2010: C. majority 9,249 (16.97%))

**BRIGG & GOOLE**
E. 68,486 T. 43,270 (63.18%)
C. hold

| | |
|---|---|
| Andrew Percy, C. | 22,946 |
| Jacky Crawford, Lab. | 11,770 |
| David Jeffreys, UKIP | 6,694 |
| Natalie Hurst, Green | 915 |
| Liz Leffman, LD | 764 |
| Trevor Dixon, Ind. | 153 |
| Ray Spalding, IE | 28 |

C. majority 11,176 (25.83%)
7.05% swing Lab. to C.
(2010: C. majority 5,147 (11.73%))

**BRIGHTON KEMPTOWN**
E. 67,858 T. 45,306 (66.77%)
C. hold

| | |
|---|---|
| Simon Kirby, C. | 18,428 |
| Nancy Platts, Lab. | 17,738 |
| Ian Buchanan, UKIP | 4,446 |
| Davy Jones, Green | 3,187 |
| Paul Chandler, LD | 1,365 |
| Jacqueline Shodeke, SPGB | 73 |
| Matt Taylor, Ind. | 69 |

C. majority 690 (1.52%)
0.79% swing C. to Lab.
(2010: C. majority 1,328 (3.11%))

**BRIGHTON PAVILION**
E. 76,557 T. 54,676 (71.42%) Green hold

| | |
|---|---|
| Caroline Lucas, Green | 22,871 |
| Purna Sen, Lab. | 14,904 |
| Clarence Mitchell, C. | 12,448 |
| Nigel Carter, UKIP | 2,724 |
| Chris Bowers, LD | 1,525 |
| Nick Yeomans, Ind. | 116 |
| Howard Pilott, SPGB | 88 |

Green majority 7,967 (14.57%)
6.08% swing Lab. to Green
(2010: Green majority 1,252 (2.42%))

**BRISTOL EAST**
E. 71,965 T. 46,213 (64.22%)
Lab. hold

| | |
|---|---|
| Kerry McCarthy, Lab. | 18,148 |
| Theo Clarke, C. | 14,168 |
| James McMurray, UKIP | 7,152 |
| Lorraine Francis, Green | 3,827 |
| Abdul Malik, LD | 2,689 |
| Matt Gordon, TUSC | 229 |

Lab. majority 3,980 (8.61%)
0.17% swing C. to Lab.
(2010: Lab. majority 3,722 (8.27%))

**BRISTOL NORTH WEST**
E. 76,626 T. 51,805 (67.61%)
C. hold

| | |
|---|---|
| Charlotte Leslie, C. | 22,767 |
| Darren Jones, Lab. | 17,823 |
| Michael Frost, UKIP | 4,889 |
| Clare Campion-Smith, LD | 3,214 |
| Justin Quinnell, Green | 2,952 |
| Anne Lemon, TUSC | 160 |

C. majority 4,944 (9.54%)
1.24% swing C. to Lab.
(2010: C. majority 3,274 (6.50%))

**BRISTOL SOUTH**
E. 81,996 T. 50,842 (62.01%)
Lab. hold

| | |
|---|---|
| *Karin Smyth, Lab. | 19,505 |
| Isobel Grant, C. | 12,377 |
| Steve Wood, UKIP | 8,381 |
| Tony Dyer, Green | 5,861 |
| Mark Wright, LD | 4,416 |
| Tom Baldwin, TUSC | 302 |

Lab. majority 7,128 (14.02%)
0.76% swing Lab. to C.
(2010: Lab. majority 4,734 (9.79%))

**BRISTOL WEST**
E. 89,198 T. 64,218 (71.99%)
Lab. gain

| | |
|---|---|
| *Thangam Debbonaire, Lab. | 22,900 |
| Darren Hall, Green | 17,227 |
| Stephen Williams, LD | 12,103 |
| Claire Hiscott, C. | 9,752 |
| Paul Turner, UKIP | 1,940 |
| Dawn Parry, Bristol | 204 |
| Stewart Weston, LU | 92 |

Lab. majority 5,673 (8.83%)
18.67% swing LD to Lab.
(2010: LD majority 11,366 (20.54%))

**BROADLAND**
E. 74,680 T. 53,089 (71.09%)
C. hold

| | |
|---|---|
| Keith Simpson, C. | 26,808 |
| Chris Jones, Lab. | 9,970 |
| Stuart Agnew, UKIP | 8,881 |
| Steve Riley, LD | 5,178 |
| Andrew Boswell, Green | 2,252 |

C. majority 16,838 (31.72%)
0.33% swing C. to Lab.
(2010: C. majority 7,292 (13.84%))

**BROMLEY & CHISLEHURST**
E. 65,476 T. 44,066 (67.30%)
C. hold

| | |
|---|---|
| Robert Neill, C. | 23,343 |
| John Courtneidge, Lab. | 9,779 |
| Emmett Jenner, UKIP | 6,285 |
| Sam Webber, LD | 2,836 |
| Roisin Robertson, Green | 1,823 |

C. majority 13,564 (30.78%)
3.09% swing C. to Lab.
(2010: C. majority 13,900 (31.56%))

**BROMSGROVE**
E. 73,329 T. 52,245 (71.25%)
C. hold

| | |
|---|---|
| Sajid Javid, C. | 28,133 |
| Tom Ebbutt, Lab. | 11,604 |
| Stuart Cross, UKIP | 8,163 |
| Bart Ricketts, LD | 2,616 |
| Spoz Esposito, Green | 1,729 |

C. majority 16,529 (31.64%)
4.87% swing Lab. to C.
(2010: C. majority 11,308 (21.90%))

**BROXBOURNE**
E. 72,944 T. 46,024 (63.09%)
C. hold

| | |
|---|---|
| Charles Walker, C. | 25,797 |
| David Platt, UKIP | 9,074 |
| Edward Robinson, Lab. | 8,470 |
| Anthony Rowlands, LD | 1,467 |
| Russell Secker, Green | 1,216 |

C. majority 16,723 (36.34%)
9.16% swing C. to UKIP
(2010: C. majority 18,804 (41.18%))

BROXTOWE
E. 71,865 T. 53,440 (74.36%)

|  |  | C. hold |
|---|---|---|
| Anna Soubry, C. | | 24,163 |
| Nick Palmer, Lab. | | 19,876 |
| Frank Dunne, UKIP | | 5,674 |
| Stan Heptinstall, LD | | 2,120 |
| David Kirwan, Green | | 1,544 |
| Ray Barry, JMB | | 63 |

C. majority 4,287 (8.02%)
3.64% swing Lab. to C.
(2010: C. majority 389 (0.74%))

BUCKINGHAM
E. 77,572 T. 53,692 (69.22%)

|  | Speaker hold |
|---|---|
| John Bercow, Speaker | 34,617 |
| David Fowler, UKIP | 11,675 |
| Alan Francis, Green | 7,400 |

Speaker majority 22,942 (42.73%)
swing N/A
(2010: Speaker majority 12,529
(25.92%))

BURNLEY
E. 64,486 T. 39,746 (61.64%)

|  | Lab. gain |
|---|---|
| *Julie Cooper, Lab. | 14,951 |
| Gordon Birtwistle, LD | 11,707 |
| Tom Commis, UKIP | 6,864 |
| Sarah Cockburn-Price, C. | 5,374 |
| Mike Hargreaves, Green | 850 |

Lab. majority 3,244 (8.16%)
6.25% swing LD to Lab.
(2010: LD majority 1,818 (4.34%))

BURTON
E. 75,300 T. 49,334 (65.52%)

|  | C. hold |
|---|---|
| Andrew Griffiths, C. | 24,736 |
| Jon Wheale, Lab. | 13,484 |
| Mike Green, UKIP | 8,658 |
| David MacDonald, LD | 1,232 |
| Sam Patrone, Green | 1,224 |

C. majority 11,252 (22.81%)
5.08% swing Lab. to C.
(2010: C. majority 6,304 (12.65%))

BURY NORTH
E. 67,580 T. 45,230 (66.93%)

|  | C. hold |
|---|---|
| David Nuttall, C. | 18,970 |
| James Frith, Lab. | 18,592 |
| Ian Henderson, UKIP | 5,595 |
| John Southworth, Green | 1,141 |
| Richard Baum, LD | 932 |

C. majority 378 (0.84%)
2.08% swing C. to Lab.
(2010: C. majority 2,243 (4.99%))

BURY ST EDMUNDS
E. 85,993 T. 59,341 (69.01%)

|  | C. hold |
|---|---|
| *Jo Churchill, C. | 31,815 |
| Bill Edwards, Lab. | 10,514 |
| John Howlett, UKIP | 8,739 |
| Helen Geake, Green | 4,692 |
| David Chappell, LD | 3,581 |

C. majority 21,301 (35.90%)
2.52% swing Lab. to C.
(2010: C. majority 12,380 (21.08%))

BURY SOUTH
E. 73,883 T. 47,215 (63.91%)

|  | Lab. hold |
|---|---|
| Ivan Lewis, Lab. | 21,272 |
| Daniel Critchlow, C. | 16,350 |
| Seamus Martin, UKIP | 6,299 |
| Paul Ankers, LD | 1,690 |
| Glyn Heath, Green | 1,434 |
| Valerie Morris, Eng. Dem. | 170 |

Lab. majority 4,922 (10.42%)
1.80% swing C. to Lab.
(2010: Lab. majority 3,292 (6.82%))

CALDER VALLEY
E. 77,753 T. 53,541 (68.86%)

|  | C. hold |
|---|---|
| Craig Whittaker, C. | 23,354 |
| Josh Fenton-Glynn, Lab. | 18,927 |
| Paul Rogan, UKIP | 5,950 |
| Alisdair Calder McGregor, LD | 2,666 |
| Jenny Shepherd, Green | 2,090 |
| Rod Sutcliffe, Yorks | 389 |
| Joe Stead, Song | 165 |

C. majority 4,427 (8.27%)
2.08% swing C. to Lab.
(2010: C. majority 6,431 (12.42%))

CAMBERWELL & PECKHAM
E. 80,507 T. 51,561 (64.05%)

|  | Lab. hold |
|---|---|
| Harriet Harman, Lab. | 32,614 |
| Naomi Newstead, C. | 6,790 |
| Amelia Womack, Green | 5,187 |
| Yahaya Kiingi, LD | 2,580 |
| David Kurten, UKIP | 2,413 |
| Prem Goyal, AP | 829 |
| Rebecca Fox, NHAP | 466 |
| Nick Wrack, TUSC | 292 |
| Alex Robertson, CISTA | 197 |
| Joshua Ogunleye, WRP | 107 |
| Felicity Anscomb, Whig | 86 |

Lab. majority 25,824 (50.08%)
1.96% swing C. to Lab.
(2010: Lab. majority 17,187
(36.84%))

CAMBORNE & REDRUTH
E. 66,944 T. 45,868 (68.52%)

|  | C. hold |
|---|---|
| George Eustice, C. | 18,452 |
| Michael Foster, Lab. | 11,448 |
| Bob Smith, UKIP | 6,776 |
| Julia Goldsworthy, LD | 5,687 |
| Geoff Garbett, Green | 2,608 |
| Loveday Jenkin, Meb. Ker. | 897 |

C. majority 7,004 (15.27%)
2.98% swing C. to Lab.
(2010: C. majority 66 (0.16%))

CAMBRIDGE
E. 83,384 T. 51,774 (62.09%)

|  | Lab. gain |
|---|---|
| *Daniel Zeichner, Lab. | 18,646 |
| Julian Huppert, LD | 18,047 |
| Chamali Fernando, C. | 8,117 |
| Rupert Read, Green | 4,109 |
| Patrick O'Flynn, UKIP | 2,668 |
| Keith Garrett, Reboot | 187 |

Lab. majority 599 (1.16%)
8.01% swing LD to Lab.
(2010: LD majority 6,792 (13.55%))

CAMBRIDGESHIRE NORTH EAST
E. 82,990 T. 51,780 (62.39%)

|  | C. hold |
|---|---|
| Stephen Barclay, C. | 28,524 |
| Andrew Charalambous, UKIP | 11,650 |
| Ken Rustidge, Lab. | 7,476 |
| Lucy Nethsingha, LD | 2,314 |
| Helen Scott-Daniels, Green | 1,816 |

C. majority 16,874 (32.59%)
6.54% swing C. to UKIP
(2010: C. majority 16,425 (31.43%))

CAMBRIDGESHIRE NORTH
WEST
E. 91,783 T. 61,100 (66.57%)

|  | C. hold |
|---|---|
| Shailesh Vara, C. | 32,070 |
| Peter Reeve, UKIP | 12,275 |
| Nick Thulbourn, Lab. | 10,927 |
| Nicholas Sandford, LD | 3,479 |
| Nicola Day, Green | 2,159 |
| Fay Belham, CPA | 190 |

C. majority 19,795 (32.40%)
4.90% swing C. to UKIP
(2010: C. majority 16,677 (28.61%))

CAMBRIDGESHIRE SOUTH
E. 84,132 T. 61,540 (73.15%)

|  | C. hold |
|---|---|
| *Heidi Allen, C. | 31,454 |
| Dan Greef, Lab. | 10,860 |
| Sebastian Kindersley, LD | 9,368 |
| Marion Mason, UKIP | 6,010 |
| Simon Saggers, Green | 3,848 |

C. majority 20,594 (33.46%)
1.87% swing C. to Lab.
(2010: C. majority 7,838 (13.27%))

**CAMBRIDGESHIRE SOUTH EAST**
E. 84,570 T. 59,506 (70.36%)

|  |  | C. hold |
|---|---|---|
| *Lucy Frazer, C. | | 28,845 |
| Jonathan Chatfield, LD | | 12,008 |
| Huw Jones, Lab. | | 9,013 |
| Deborah Rennie, UKIP | | 6,593 |
| Clive Semmens, Green | | 3,047 |

C. majority 16,837 (28.29%)
8.99% swing LD to C.
(2010: C. majority 5,946 (10.32%))

**CANNOCK CHASE**
E. 74,531 T. 47,099 (63.19%)

|  |  | C. hold |
|---|---|---|
| *Amanda Milling, C. | | 20,811 |
| Janos Toth, Lab. | | 15,888 |
| Grahame Wiggin, UKIP | | 8,224 |
| Ian Jackson, LD | | 1,270 |
| Paul Woodhead, Green | | 906 |

C. majority 4,923 (10.45%)
1.72% swing Lab. to C.
(2010: C. majority 3,195 (7.01%))

**CANTERBURY**
E. 83,481 T. 53,465 (64.04%)

|  |  | C. hold |
|---|---|---|
| Julian Brazier, C. | | 22,918 |
| Hugh Lanning, Lab. | | 13,120 |
| Jim Gascoyne, UKIP | | 7,289 |
| James Flanagan, LD | | 6,227 |
| Stuart Jeffery, Green | | 3,746 |
| Robert Cox, SPGB | | 165 |

C. majority 9,798 (18.33%)
5.17% swing C. to Lab.
(2010: C. majority 6,048 (12.29%))

**CARLISLE**
E. 65,827 T. 42,587 (64.70%)

|  |  | C. hold |
|---|---|---|
| John Stevenson, C. | | 18,873 |
| Lee Sherriff, Lab. | | 16,099 |
| Fiona Mills, UKIP | | 5,277 |
| Helen Davison, Green | | 1,125 |
| Loraine Birchall, LD | | 1,087 |
| Alfred Okam, Ind. | | 126 |

C. majority 2,774 (6.51%)
2.25% swing Lab. to C.
(2010: C. majority 853 (2.02%))

**CARSHALTON & WALLINGTON**
E. 69,866 T. 47,613 (68.15%)   LD hold

|  |  |  |
|---|---|---|
| Tom Brake, LD | | 16,603 |
| Matthew Maxwell Scott, C. | | 15,093 |
| Siobhan Tate, Lab. | | 7,150 |
| Bill Main-Ian, UKIP | | 7,049 |
| Ross Hemingway, Green | | 1,492 |
| Ashley Dickenson, CPA | | 177 |
| Richard Edmonds, NF | | 49 |

LD majority 1,510 (3.17%)
4.14% swing LD to C.
(2010: LD majority 5,260 (11.46%))

**CASTLE POINT**
E. 68,170 T. 45,450 (66.67%)

|  |  | C. hold |
|---|---|---|
| Rebecca Harris, C. | | 23,112 |
| Jamie Huntman, UKIP | | 14,178 |
| Joe Cooke, Lab. | | 6,283 |
| Dominic Ellis, Green | | 1,076 |
| Sereena Davey, LD | | 801 |

C. majority 8,934 (19.66%)
swing N/A
(2010: C. majority 7,632 (16.95%))

**CHARNWOOD**
E. 77,269 T. 52,261 (67.64%)

|  |  | C. hold |
|---|---|---|
| *Edward Argar, C. | | 28,384 |
| Sean Kelly-Walsh, Lab. | | 11,453 |
| Lynton Yates, UKIP | | 8,330 |
| Simon Sansome, LD | | 3,605 |
| Cathy Duffy, BNP | | 489 |

C. majority 16,931 (32.40%)
1.23% swing Lab. to C.
(2010: C. majority 15,029 (28.07%))

**CHATHAM & AYLESFORD**
E. 68,625 T. 43,073 (62.77%)

|  |  | C. hold |
|---|---|---|
| Tracey Crouch, C. | | 21,614 |
| Tristan Osborne, Lab. | | 10,159 |
| Ian Wallace, UKIP | | 8,581 |
| Thomas Quinton, LD | | 1,360 |
| Luke Balnave, Green | | 1,101 |
| John-Wesley Gibson, CPA | | 133 |
| Ivor Riddell, TUSC | | 125 |

C. majority 11,455 (26.59%)
6.37% swing Lab. to C.
(2010: C. majority 6,069 (13.85%))

**CHEADLE**
E. 73,239 T. 53,095 (72.50%)

|  |  | C. gain |
|---|---|---|
| *Mary Robinson, C. | | 22,889 |
| Mark Hunter, LD | | 16,436 |
| Martin Miller, Lab. | | 8,673 |
| Shaun Hopkins, UKIP | | 4,423 |
| Matthew Torbitt, Ind. | | 390 |
| Drew Carswell, Above | | 208 |
| Helen Bashford, IE | | 76 |

C. majority 6,453 (12.15%)
9.19% swing LD to C.
(2010: LD majority 3,272 (6.23%))

**CHELMSFORD**
E. 78,580 T. 53,817 (68.49%)

|  |  | C. hold |
|---|---|---|
| Simon Burns, C. | | 27,732 |
| Chris Vince, Lab. | | 9,482 |
| Mark Gough, UKIP | | 7,652 |
| Stephen Robinson, LD | | 6,394 |
| Angela Thomson, Green | | 1,892 |
| Henry Boyle, Lib. | | 665 |

C. majority 18,250 (33.91%)
0.65% swing C. to Lab.
(2010: C. majority 5,110 (9.36%))

**CHELSEA & FULHAM**
E. 63,478 T. 40,226 (63.37%)

|  |  | C. hold |
|---|---|---|
| Greg Hands, C. | | 25,322 |
| Alexandra Sanderson, Lab. | | 9,300 |
| Simon Bailey, LD | | 2,091 |
| Adrian Noble, UKIP | | 2,039 |
| Guy Rubin, Green | | 1,474 |

C. majority 16,022 (39.83%)
1.06% swing C. to Lab.
(2010: C. majority 16,722 (41.96%))

**CHELTENHAM**
E. 77,286 T. 53,735 (69.53%)

|  |  | C. gain |
|---|---|---|
| *Alex Chalk, C. | | 24,790 |
| Martin Horwood, LD | | 18,274 |
| Paul Gilbert, Lab. | | 3,902 |
| Christina Simmonds, UKIP | | 3,808 |
| Adam Van Coevorden, Green | | 2,689 |
| Richard Lupson-Darnell, Ind. | | 272 |

C. majority 6,516 (12.13%)
10.72% swing LD to C.
(2010: LD majority 4,920 (9.32%))

**CHESHAM & AMERSHAM**
E. 73,423 T. 52,731 (71.82%)

|  |  | C. hold |
|---|---|---|
| Cheryl Gillan, C. | | 31,138 |
| Alan Stevens, UKIP | | 7,218 |
| Benjamin Davies, Lab. | | 6,712 |
| Kirsten Johnson, LD | | 4,761 |
| Gill Walker, Green | | 2,902 |

C. majority 23,920 (45.36%)
5.47% swing C. to UKIP
(2010: C. majority 16,710 (31.86%))

**CHESTER, CITY OF**
E. 72,269 T. 51,161 (70.79%)

|  |  | Lab. gain |
|---|---|---|
| *Chris Matheson, Lab. | | 22,118 |
| Stephen Mosley, C. | | 22,025 |
| Stephen Ingram, UKIP | | 4,148 |
| Bob Thompson, LD | | 2,870 |

Lab. majority 93 (0.18%)
2.85% swing C. to Lab.
(2010: C. majority 2,583 (5.52%))

**CHESTERFIELD**
E. 72,078 T. 45,567 (63.22%)

|  |  | Lab. hold |
|---|---|---|
| Toby Perkins, Lab. | | 21,829 |
| Mark Vivis, C. | | 8,231 |
| Stuart Yeowart, UKIP | | 7,523 |
| Julia Cambridge, LD | | 6,301 |
| Matthew Genn, Green | | 1,352 |
| Matt Whale, TUSC | | 202 |
| Tommy Holgate, Peace | | 129 |

Lab. majority 13,598 (29.84%)
3.27% swing C. to Lab.
(2010: Lab. majority 549 (1.20%))

CHICHESTER
E. 83,575 T. 57,139 (68.37%)

| | C. hold |
|---|---|
| Andrew Tyrie, C. | 32,953 |
| Andrew Moncreiff, UKIP | 8,540 |
| Mark Farwell, Lab. | 6,933 |
| Andrew Smith, LD | 4,865 |
| Jasper Richmond, Green | 3,742 |
| Andrew Emerson, Patria | 106 |

C. majority 24,413 (42.73%)
2.90% swing C. to UKIP
(2010: C. majority 15,877 (27.96%))

CHINGFORD & WOODFORD
GREEN
E. 66,691 T. 43,804 (65.68%)

| | C. hold |
|---|---|
| Iain Duncan Smith, C. | 20,999 |
| Bilal Mahmood, Lab. | 12,613 |
| Freddy Vachha, UKIP | 5,644 |
| Anne Crook, LD | 2,400 |
| Rebecca Tully, Green | 1,854 |
| Len Hockey, TUSC | 241 |
| Lisa McKenzie, Class War | 53 |

C. majority 8,386 (19.14%)
5.46% swing C. to Lab.
(2010: C. majority 12,963 (30.07%))

CHIPPENHAM
E. 74,225 T. 55,407 (74.65%)

| | C. gain |
|---|---|
| *Michelle Donelan, C. | 26,354 |
| Duncan Hames, LD | 16,278 |
| Julia Reid, UKIP | 5,884 |
| Andy Newman, Lab. | 4,561 |
| Tina Johnston, Green | 2,330 |

C. majority 10,076 (18.19%)
11.45% swing LD to C.
(2010: LD majority 2,470 (4.72%))

CHIPPING BARNET
E. 77,853 T. 53,013 (68.09%)

| | C. hold |
|---|---|
| Theresa Villiers, C. | 25,759 |
| Amy Trevethan, Lab. | 18,103 |
| Victor Kaye, UKIP | 4,151 |
| A Poppy, Green | 2,501 |
| Marisha Ray, LD | 2,381 |
| Mehdi Akhavan, ND | 118 |

C. majority 7,656 (14.44%)
4.56% swing C. to Lab.
(2010: C. majority 11,927 (23.57%))

CHORLEY
E. 74,679 T. 51,712 (69.25%)

| | Lab. hold |
|---|---|
| Lindsay Hoyle, Lab. | 23,322 |
| Rob Loughenbury, C. | 18,792 |
| Mark Smith, UKIP | 6,995 |
| Stephen Fenn, LD | 1,354 |
| Alistair Straw, Green | 1,111 |
| Adrian Maudsley, Ind. | 138 |

Lab. majority 4,530 (8.76%)
1.78% swing C. to Lab.
(2010: Lab. majority 2,593 (5.21%))

CHRISTCHURCH
E. 69,302 T. 49,707 (71.73%)

| | C. hold |
|---|---|
| Christopher Chope, C. | 28,887 |
| Robin Grey, UKIP | 10,663 |
| Andrew Satherley, Lab. | 4,745 |
| Andy Canning, LD | 3,263 |
| Shona Dunn, Green | 2,149 |

C. majority 18,224 (36.66%)
5.64% swing C. to UKIP
(2010: C. majority 15,410 (31.18%))

CITIES OF LONDON &
WESTMINSTER
E. 60,992 T. 36,185 (59.33%)

| | C. hold |
|---|---|
| Mark Field, C. | 19,570 |
| Nik Slingsby, Lab. | 9,899 |
| Belinda Brooks-Gordon, LD | 2,521 |
| Hugh Small, Green | 1,953 |
| Robert Stephenson, UKIP | 1,894 |
| Edouard-Henri Desforges, CISTA | 160 |
| Jill McLachlan, CPA | 129 |
| Adam Clifford, Class War | 59 |

C. majority 9,671 (26.73%)
1.63% swing C. to Lab.
(2010: C. majority 11,076 (29.99%))

CLACTON
E. 68,936 T. 44,207 (64.13%) UKIP
hold

| | |
|---|---|
| Douglas Carswell, UKIP | 19,642 |
| Giles Watling, C. | 16,205 |
| Tim Young, Lab. | 6,364 |
| Chris Southall, Green | 1,184 |
| David Grace, LD | 812 |

UKIP majority 3,437 (7.77%)
swing N/A
(2010: C. majority 12,068 (27.99%))
(2014: UKIP majority 12,404
(35.10%))

CLEETHORPES
E. 70,514 T. 45,089 (63.94%)

| | C. hold |
|---|---|
| Martin Vickers, C. | 21,026 |
| Peter Keith, Lab. | 13,133 |
| Stephen Harness, UKIP | 8,356 |
| Roy Horobin, LD | 1,346 |
| Carol Thornton, Green | 1,013 |
| Malcolm Morland, TUSC | 215 |

C. majority 7,893 (17.51%)
3.97% swing Lab. to C.
(2010: C. majority 4,298 (9.56%))

COLCHESTER
E. 74,203 T. 48,593 (65.49%)

| | C. gain |
|---|---|
| *Will Quince, C. | 18,919 |
| Bob Russell, LD | 13,344 |
| Jordan Newell, Lab. | 7,852 |
| John Pitts, UKIP | 5,870 |
| Mark Goacher, Green | 2,499 |
| Ken Scrimshaw, CPA | 109 |

C. majority 5,575 (11.47%)
13.30% swing LD to C.
(2010: LD majority 6,982 (15.13%))

COLNE VALLEY
E. 82,510 T. 56,800 (68.84%)

| | C. hold |
|---|---|
| Jason McCartney, C. | 25,246 |
| Jane East, Lab. | 19,868 |
| Melanie Roberts, UKIP | 5,734 |
| Cahal Burke, LD | 3,407 |
| Chas Ball, Green | 1,919 |
| Paul Salveson, Yorks | 572 |
| Melodie Staniforth, ND | 54 |

C. majority 5,378 (9.47%)
0.56% swing C. to Lab.
(2010: C. majority 4,837 (8.75%))

CONGLETON
E. 72,398 T. 50,976 (70.41%)

| | C. hold |
|---|---|
| Fiona Bruce, C. | 27,164 |
| Darren Price, Lab. | 10,391 |
| Lee Slaughter, UKIP | 6,922 |
| Peter Hirst, LD | 4,623 |
| Alec Heath, Green | 1,876 |

C. majority 16,773 (32.90%)
2.17% swing Lab. to C.
(2010: C. majority 7,063 (13.91%))

COPELAND
E. 62,119 T. 39,631 (63.80%)

| | Lab. hold |
|---|---|
| Jamie Reed, Lab. | 16,750 |
| Stephen Haraldsen, C. | 14,186 |
| Michael Pye, UKIP | 6,148 |
| Danny Gallagher, LD | 1,368 |
| Allan Todd, Green | 1,179 |

Lab. majority 2,564 (6.47%)
1.24% swing Lab. to C.
(2010: Lab. majority 3,833 (8.96%))

CORBY
E. 79,775 T. 56,174 (70.42%)

| | C. gain |
|---|---|
| *Tom Pursglove, C. | 24,023 |
| Andy Sawford, Lab. Co-op | 21,611 |
| Margot Parker, UKIP | 7,708 |
| Peter Harris, LD | 1,458 |
| Jonathan Hornett, Green | 1,374 |

C. majority 2,412 (4.29%)
0.40% swing Lab. to C.
(2010: C. majority 1,895 (3.49%))
(2012: Lab. majority 7,791 (21.84%))

CORNWALL NORTH
E. 67,192 T. 48,245 (71.80%)

| | C. gain |
|---|---|
| *Scott Mann, C. | 21,689 |
| Dan Rogerson, LD | 15,068 |
| Julie Lingard, UKIP | 6,121 |
| John Whitby, Lab. | 2,621 |
| Amanda Pennington, Green | 2,063 |
| Jeremy Jefferies, Meb. Ker. | 631 |
| John Allman, Restore | 52 |

C. majority 6,621 (13.72%)
10.91% swing LD to C.
(2010: LD majority 2,981 (6.36%))

CORNWALL SOUTH EAST
E. 71,071 T. 50,498 (71.05%)

| | C. hold |
|---|---|
| Sheryll Murray, C. | 25,516 |
| Phil Hutty, LD | 8,521 |
| Bradley Monk, UKIP | 7,698 |
| Declan Lloyd, Lab. | 4,692 |
| Martin Corney, Green | 2,718 |
| Andrew Long, Meb. Ker. | 1,003 |
| George Trubody, Ind. | 350 |

C. majority 16,995 (33.65%)
13.58% swing LD to C.
(2010: C. majority 3,220 (6.49%))

COTSWOLDS, THE
E. 78,292 T. 56,667 (72.38%)

| | C. hold |
|---|---|
| Geoffrey Clifton-Brown, C. | 32,045 |
| Paul Hodgkinson, LD | 10,568 |
| Chris Harlow, UKIP | 6,188 |
| Manjinder Kang, Lab. | 5,240 |
| Penny Burgess, Green | 2,626 |

C. majority 21,477 (37.90%)
7.22% swing LD to C.
(2010: C. majority 12,864 (23.46%))

COVENTRY NORTH EAST
E. 76,401 T. 42,231 (55.28%)

| | Lab. hold |
|---|---|
| *Colleen Fletcher, Lab. | 22,025 |
| Michelle Lowe, C. | 9,751 |
| Avtar Taggar, UKIP | 6,278 |
| Russell Field, LD | 2,007 |
| Matthew Handley, Green | 1,245 |
| Nicky Downes, TUSC | 633 |
| William Sidhu, Ch. M. | 292 |

Lab. majority 12,274 (29.06%)
0.96% swing C. to Lab.
(2010: Lab. majority 11,775 (27.14%))

COVENTRY NORTH WEST
E. 74,597 T. 45,246 (60.65%)

| | Lab. hold |
|---|---|
| Geoffrey Robinson, Lab. | 18,557 |
| Parvez Akhtar, C. | 14,048 |
| Harjinder Singh Sehmi, UKIP | 7,101 |
| Laura Vesty, Green | 1,961 |
| Andrew Furse, LD | 1,810 |
| Dave Nellist, TUSC | 1,769 |

Lab. majority 4,509 (9.97%)
1.77% swing Lab. to C.
(2010: Lab. majority 6,288 (13.51%))

COVENTRY SOUTH
E. 71,380 T. 43,699 (61.22%)

| | Lab. hold |
|---|---|
| Jim Cunningham, Lab. | 18,472 |
| Gary Ridley, C. | 15,284 |
| Mark Taylor, UKIP | 5,709 |
| Greg Judge, LD | 1,779 |
| Benjamin Gallaher, Green | 1,719 |
| Judy Griffiths, TUSC | 650 |
| Chris Rooney, Mainstream | 86 |

Lab. majority 3,188 (7.30%)
0.54% swing Lab. to C.
(2010: Lab. majority 3,845 (8.37%))

CRAWLEY
E. 73,940 T. 48,550 (65.66%)

| | C. hold |
|---|---|
| Henry Smith, C. | 22,829 |
| Chris Oxlade, Lab. | 16,303 |
| Chris Brown, UKIP | 6,979 |
| Sarah Osborne, LD | 1,339 |
| Guy Hudson, Green | 1,100 |

C. majority 6,526 (13.44%)
0.48% swing Lab. to C.
(2010: C. majority 5,928 (12.48%))

CREWE & NANTWICH
E. 74,039 T. 49,896 (67.39%)

| | C. hold |
|---|---|
| Edward Timpson, C. | 22,445 |
| Adrian Heald, Lab. | 18,825 |
| Richard Lee, UKIP | 7,252 |
| Roy Wood, LD | 1,374 |

C. majority 3,620 (7.26%)
2.29% swing C. to Lab.
(2010: C. majority 6,046 (11.84%))

CROYDON CENTRAL
E. 78,171 T. 52,941 (67.72%)

| | C. hold |
|---|---|
| Gavin Barwell, C. | 22,753 |
| Sarah Jones, Lab. | 22,588 |
| Peter Staveley, UKIP | 4,810 |
| Esther Sutton, Green | 1,454 |
| James Robert Fearnley, LD | 1,152 |
| April Ashley, TUSC | 127 |
| Martin Camden, UKPDP | 57 |

C. majority 165 (0.31%)
2.83% swing C. to Lab.
(2010: C. majority 2,969 (5.97%))

CROYDON NORTH
E. 85,951 T. 53,522 (62.27%)

| | Lab. Co-op hold |
|---|---|
| Steve Reed, Lab. Co-op | 33,513 |
| Vidhi Mohan, C. | 12,149 |
| Winston McKenzie, UKIP | 2,899 |
| Shasha Khan, Green | 2,515 |
| Joanna Corbin, LD | 1,919 |
| Glen Hart, TUSC | 261 |
| Lee Berks, Ind. | 141 |
| Ben Stevenson, Comm. | 125 |

Lab. Co-op majority 21,364 (39.92%)
4.01% swing C. to Lab.
(2010: Lab. majority 16,483 (31.90%)) (2012: Lab. majority 11,761 (47.87%))

CROYDON SOUTH
E. 82,010 T. 57,712 (70.37%)

| | C. hold |
|---|---|
| *Chris Philp, C. | 31,448 |
| Emily Benn, Lab. | 14,308 |
| Kathleen Garner, UKIP | 6,068 |
| Gill Hickson, LD | 3,448 |
| Peter Underwood, Green | 2,154 |
| Mark Samuel, Croydon | 221 |
| Jon Bigger, Class War | 65 |

C. majority 17,140 (29.70%)
0.59% swing C. to Lab.
(2010: C. majority 15,818 (28.08%))

DAGENHAM & RAINHAM
E. 69,049 T. 43,050 (62.35%)

| | Lab. hold |
|---|---|
| Jon Cruddas, Lab. | 17,830 |
| Peter Harris, UKIP | 12,850 |
| Julie Marson, C. | 10,492 |
| Kate Simpson, Green | 806 |
| Denise Capstick, LD | 717 |
| Tess Culnane, BNP | 151 |
| Terry London, ND | 133 |
| Kim Gandy, Eng. Dem. | 71 |

Lab. majority 4,980 (11.57%)
12.58% swing Lab. to UKIP
(2010: Lab. majority 2,630 (5.95%))

DARLINGTON
E. 65,832 T. 41,141 (62.49%)

| | Lab. hold |
|---|---|
| Jenny Chapman, Lab. | 17,637 |
| Peter Cuthbertson, C. | 14,479 |
| David Hodgson, UKIP | 5,392 |
| Anne-Marie Curry, LD | 1,966 |
| Michael Cherrington, Green | 1,444 |
| Alan Docherty, TUSC | 223 |

Lab. majority 3,158 (7.68%)
0.11% swing Lab. to C.
(2010: Lab. majority 3,388 (7.90%))

DARTFORD
E. 76,686 T. 52,418 (68.35%)

| | C. hold |
|---|---|
| Gareth Johnson, C. | 25,670 |
| Simon Thomson, Lab. | 13,325 |
| Elizabeth Jones, UKIP | 10,434 |
| Simon Beard, LD | 1,454 |
| Andy Blatchford, Green | 1,324 |
| Steve Uncles, Eng. Dem. | 211 |

C. majority 12,345 (23.55%)
1.16% swing Lab. to C.
(2010: C. majority 10,628 (21.22%))

DAVENTRY
E. 72,753 T. 52,518 (72.19%)

| | C. hold |
|---|---|
| Chris Heaton-Harris, C. | 30,550 |
| Abigail Campbell, Lab. | 9,491 |
| Michael Gerard, UKIP | 8,296 |
| Callum Delhoy, LD | 2,352 |
| Steve Whiffen, Green | 1,829 |

C. majority 21,059 (40.10%)
0.31% swing C. to Lab.
(2010: C. majority 19,188 (37.06%))

DENTON & REDDISH
E. 66,574 T. 38,681 (58.10%)

| | Lab. hold |
|---|---|
| Andrew Gwynne, Lab. | 19,661 |
| Lana Hempsall, C. | 9,150 |
| Andrew Fairfoull, UKIP | 7,225 |
| Nick Koopman, Green | 1,466 |
| Mark Jewell, LD | 957 |
| Victoria Lofas, Ind. | 222 |

Lab. majority 10,511 (27.17%)
0.53% swing C. to Lab.
(2010: Lab. majority 9,831 (26.12%))

DERBY NORTH
E. 64,739 T. 44,745 (69.12%)

|  | C. gain |
| --- | --- |
| *Amanda Solloway, C. | 16,402 |
| Chris Williamson, Lab. | 16,361 |
| Tilly Ward, UKIP | 6,532 |
| Lucy Care, LD | 3,832 |
| Alice Mason-Power, Green | 1,618 |

C. majority 41 (0.09%)
0.73% swing Lab. to C.
(2010: Lab. majority 613 (1.36%))

DERBY SOUTH
E. 70,247 T. 40,820 (58.11%)

|  | Lab. hold |
| --- | --- |
| Margaret Beckett, Lab. | 20,007 |
| Evonne Williams, C. | 11,179 |
| Victor Webb, UKIP | 6,341 |
| Joe Naitta, LD | 1,717 |
| David Foster, Green | 1,208 |
| Chris Fernandez, TUSC | 225 |
| David Gale, Brit. Ind. | 143 |

Lab. majority 8,828 (21.63%)
3.38% swing C. to Lab.
(2010: Lab. majority 6,122 (14.86%))

DERBYSHIRE DALES
E. 63,470 T. 47,361 (74.62%)

|  | C. hold |
| --- | --- |
| Patrick McLoughlin, C. | 24,805 |
| Andy Botham, Lab. | 10,761 |
| John Young, UKIP | 5,508 |
| Benjamin Fearn, LD | 3,965 |
| Ian Wood, Green | 2,173 |
| Amila Y'Mech, Humanity | 149 |

C. majority 14,044 (29.65%)
1.54% swing C. to Lab.
(2010: C. majority 13,866 (29.64%))

DERBYSHIRE MID
E. 67,576 T. 47,729 (70.63%)

|  | C. hold |
| --- | --- |
| Pauline Latham, C. | 24,908 |
| Nicola Heaton, Lab. | 12,134 |
| Martin Fitzpatrick, UKIP | 6,497 |
| Hilary Jones, LD | 2,292 |
| Sue MacFarlane, Green | 1,898 |

C. majority 12,774 (26.76%)
1.46% swing Lab. to C.
(2010: C. majority 11,292 (23.85%))

DERBYSHIRE NORTH EAST
E. 71,456 T. 47,948 (67.10%)

|  | Lab. hold |
| --- | --- |
| Natascha Engel, Lab. | 19,488 |
| Lee Rowley, C. | 17,605 |
| James Bush, UKIP | 7,631 |
| David Batey, LD | 2,004 |
| David Kesteven, Green | 1,059 |
| Rob Lane, Ind. | 161 |

Lab. majority 1,883 (3.93%)
0.64% swing Lab. to C.
(2010: Lab. majority 2,445 (5.20%))

DERBYSHIRE SOUTH
E. 74,395 T. 50,762 (68.23%)

|  | C. hold |
| --- | --- |
| Heather Wheeler, C. | 25,066 |
| Cheryl Pidgeon, Lab. | 13,595 |
| Alan Graves, UKIP | 8,998 |
| Lorraine Johnson, LD | 1,887 |
| Marianne Bamkin, Green | 1,216 |

C. majority 11,471 (22.60%)
4.23% swing Lab. to C.
(2010: C. majority 7,128 (14.14%))

DEVIZES
E. 69,211 T. 49,006 (70.81%)

|  | C. hold |
| --- | --- |
| Claire Perry, C. | 28,295 |
| David Pollitt, UKIP | 7,544 |
| Chris Watts, Lab. | 6,360 |
| Manda Rigby, LD | 3,954 |
| Emma Dawnay, Green | 2,853 |

C. majority 20,751 (42.34%)
4.12% swing C. to UKIP
(2010: C. majority 13,005 (28.06%))

DEVON CENTRAL
E. 72,737 T. 54,448 (74.86%)

|  | C. hold |
| --- | --- |
| Mel Stride, C. | 28,436 |
| John Conway, UKIP | 7,171 |
| Lynne Richards, Lab. | 6,985 |
| Alex White, LD | 6,643 |
| Andy Williamson, Green | 4,866 |
| Arthur Price, Ind. | 347 |

C. majority 21,265 (39.06%)
3.55% swing C. to UKIP
(2010: C. majority 9,230 (17.13%))

DEVON EAST
E. 74,224 T. 54,717 (73.72%)

|  | C. hold |
| --- | --- |
| Hugo Swire, C. | 25,401 |
| Claire Wright, Ind. | 13,140 |
| Andrew Chapman, UKIP | 6,870 |
| Steve Race, Lab. | 5,591 |
| Stuart Mole, LD | 3,715 |

C. majority 12,261 (22.41%)
swing N/A
(2010: C. majority 9,114 (17.17%))

DEVON NORTH
E. 74,737 T. 52,320 (70.01%)

|  | C. gain |
| --- | --- |
| *Peter Heaton-Jones, C. | 22,341 |
| Nick Harvey, LD | 15,405 |
| Steve Crowther, UKIP | 7,719 |
| Mark Cann, Lab. | 3,699 |
| Ricky Knight, Green | 3,018 |
| Gerrard Sables, Comm. | 138 |

C. majority 6,936 (13.26%)
12.30% swing LD to C.
(2010: LD majority 5,821 (11.34%))

DEVON SOUTH WEST
E. 71,035 T. 50,372 (70.91%)

|  | C. hold |
| --- | --- |
| Gary Streeter, C. | 28,500 |
| Chaz Singh, Lab. | 8,391 |
| Robin Julian, UKIP | 7,306 |
| Tom Davies, LD | 3,767 |
| Win Scutt, Green | 2,408 |

C. majority 20,109 (39.92%)
1.82% swing C. to Lab.
(2010: C. majority 15,874 (31.84%))

DEVON WEST & TORRIDGE
E. 78,582 T. 56,584 (72.01%)

|  | C. hold |
| --- | --- |
| Geoffrey Cox, C. | 28,774 |
| Derek Sargent, UKIP | 10,371 |
| Paula Dolphin, LD | 7,483 |
| Mike Sparling, Lab. | 6,015 |
| Cathrine Simmons, Green | 3,941 |

C. majority 18,403 (32.52%)
3.83% swing C. to UKIP
(2010: C. majority 2,957 (5.35%))

DEWSBURY
E. 79,765 T. 53,630 (67.24%)

|  | Lab. gain |
| --- | --- |
| *Paula Sherriff, Lab. | 22,406 |
| Simon Reevell, C. | 20,955 |
| Mark Thackray, UKIP | 6,649 |
| Ednan Hussain, LD | 1,924 |
| Adrian Cruden, Green | 1,366 |
| Richard Carter, Yorks | 236 |
| Steve Hakes, CPA | 94 |

Lab. majority 1,451 (2.71%)
2.77% swing C. to Lab.
(2010: C. majority 1,526 (2.83%))

DON VALLEY
E. 71,299 T. 42,486 (59.59%)

|  | Lab. hold |
| --- | --- |
| Caroline Flint, Lab. | 19,621 |
| Carl Jackson, C. | 10,736 |
| Guy Aston, UKIP | 9,963 |
| Rene Paterson, LD | 1,487 |
| Steve Williams, TUSC | 437 |
| Louise Dutton, Eng. Dem. | 242 |

Lab. majority 8,885 (20.91%)
6.32% swing C. to Lab.
(2010: Lab. majority 3,595 (8.28%))

DONCASTER CENTRAL
E. 71,136 T. 40,420 (56.82%)

|  | Lab. hold |
| --- | --- |
| Rosie Winterton, Lab. | 19,840 |
| Chris Hodgson, UKIP | 9,747 |
| Zoe Metcalfe, C. | 8,386 |
| John Brown, LD | 1,717 |
| Mev Akram, TUSC | 421 |
| David Burnett, Eng. Dem. | 309 |

Lab. majority 10,093 (24.97%)
5.66% swing Lab. to UKIP
(2010: Lab. majority 6,229 (14.92%))

**DONCASTER NORTH**
E. 70,898 T. 39,501 (55.72%)

| | Lab. hold |
|---|---|
| Ed Miliband, Lab. | 20,708 |
| Kim Parkinson, UKIP | 8,928 |
| Mark Fletcher, C. | 7,235 |
| Penny Baker, LD | 1,005 |
| Peter Kennedy, Green | 757 |
| David Allen, Eng. Dem. | 448 |
| Mary Jackson, TUSC | 258 |
| Nick The Flying Brick, Loony | 162 |

Lab. majority 11,780 (29.82%)
6.59% swing Lab. to UKIP
(2010: Lab. majority 10,909
(26.30%))

**DORSET MID & POOLE NORTH**
E. 68,917 T. 46,499 (67.47%)

| | C. gain |
|---|---|
| *Michael Tomlinson, C. | 23,639 |
| Vikki Slade, LD | 13,109 |
| Richard Turner, UKIP | 5,663 |
| Patrick Canavan, Lab. | 2,767 |
| Mark Chivers, Green | 1,321 |

C. majority 10,530 (22.65%)
11.61% swing LD to C.
(2010: LD majority 269 (0.57%))

**DORSET NORTH**
E. 74,576 T. 53,385 (71.58%)

| | C. hold |
|---|---|
| *Simon Hoare, C. | 30,227 |
| Steve Unwin, UKIP | 9,109 |
| Hugo Mieville, LD | 6,226 |
| Kim Fendley, Lab. | 4,785 |
| Richard Barrington, Green | 3,038 |

C. majority 21,118 (39.56%)
3.15% swing C. to UKIP
(2010: C. majority 7,625 (14.08%))

**DORSET SOUTH**
E. 71,974 T. 48,597 (67.52%)

| | C. hold |
|---|---|
| Richard Drax, C. | 23,756 |
| Simon Bowkett, Lab. | 11,762 |
| Malcolm Shakesby, UKIP | 7,304 |
| Howard Legg, LD | 2,901 |
| Jane Burnet, Green | 2,275 |
| Mervyn Stewkesbury, Ind. | 435 |
| Andy Kirkwood, Active Dem. | 164 |

C. majority 11,994 (24.68%)
4.94% swing Lab. to C.
(2010: C. majority 7,443 (14.79%))

**DORSET WEST**
E. 78,427 T. 56,458 (71.99%)

| | C. hold |
|---|---|
| Oliver Letwin, C. | 28,329 |
| Ros Kayes, LD | 12,199 |
| David Glossop, UKIP | 7,055 |
| Rachel Rogers, Lab. | 5,633 |
| Peter Barton, Green | 3,242 |

C. majority 16,130 (28.57%)
10.86% swing LD to C.
(2010: C. majority 3,923 (6.84%))

**DOVER**
E. 72,929 T. 50,224 (68.87%)

| | C. hold |
|---|---|
| Charlie Elphicke, C. | 21,737 |
| Clair Hawkins, Lab. | 15,443 |
| David Little, UKIP | 10,177 |
| Sarah Smith, LD | 1,572 |
| Jolyon Trimingham, Green | 1,295 |

C. majority 6,294 (12.53%)
1.03% swing Lab. to C.
(2010: C. majority 5,274 (10.47%))

**DUDLEY NORTH**
E. 60,718 T. 37,992 (62.57%)

| | Lab. hold |
|---|---|
| Ian Austin, Lab. | 15,885 |
| Les Jones, C. | 11,704 |
| Bill Etheridge, UKIP | 9,113 |
| Will Duckworth, Green | 517 |
| Mike Collins, LD | 478 |
| Rehan Afzal, APNI | 156 |
| Dave Pitt, TUSC | 139 |

Lab. majority 4,181 (11.00%)
4.66% swing C. to Lab.
(2010: Lab. majority 649 (1.68%))

**DUDLEY SOUTH**
E. 60,363 T. 38,210 (63.30%)

| | C. hold |
|---|---|
| *Mike Wood, C. | 16,723 |
| Natasha Millward, Lab. | 12,453 |
| Paul Brothwood, UKIP | 7,236 |
| Vicky Duckworth, Green | 970 |
| Martin Turner, LD | 828 |

C. majority 4,270 (11.18%)
0.54% swing Lab. to C.
(2010: C. majority 3,856 (10.10%))

**DULWICH & WEST NORWOOD**
E. 75,244 T. 51,362 (68.26%)

| | Lab. hold |
|---|---|
| *Helen Hayes, Lab. | 27,772 |
| Resham Kotecha, C. | 11,650 |
| James Barber, LD | 5,055 |
| Rashid Nix, Green | 4,844 |
| Rathy Alagaratnam, UKIP | 1,606 |
| Steve Nally, TUSC | 248 |
| David Lambert, Ind. | 125 |
| Amadu Kanumansa, AP | 62 |

Lab. majority 16,122 (31.39%)
3.48% swing C. to Lab.
(2010: Lab. majority 9,365 (19.42%))

**DURHAM, CITY OF**
E. 68,741 T. 45,669 (66.44%)

| | Lab. hold |
|---|---|
| Roberta Blackman-Woods, Lab. | 21,596 |
| Rebecca Coulson, C. | 10,157 |
| Liam Clark, UKIP | 5,232 |
| Craig Martin, LD | 5,153 |
| Jonathan Elmer, Green | 2,687 |
| John Marshall, Ind. | 649 |
| Jon Collings, Ind. | 195 |

Lab. majority 11,439 (25.05%)
2.99% swing Lab. to C.
(2010: Lab. majority 3,067 (6.63%))

**DURHAM NORTH**
E. 65,373 T. 40,146 (61.41%)

| | Lab. hold |
|---|---|
| Kevan Jones, Lab. | 22,047 |
| Laetitia Glossop, C. | 8,403 |
| Malcolm Bint, UKIP | 6,404 |
| Peter Maughan, LD | 2,046 |
| Vicki Nolan, Green | 1,246 |

Lab. majority 13,644 (33.99%)
2.25% swing C. to Lab.
(2010: Lab. majority 12,076
(29.48%))

**DURHAM NORTH WEST**
E. 69,817 T. 42,818 (61.33%)

| | Lab. hold |
|---|---|
| Pat Glass, Lab. | 20,074 |
| Charlotte Haitham-Taylor, C. | 10,018 |
| Bruce Reid, UKIP | 7,265 |
| Owen Temple, LD | 3,894 |
| Mark Shilcock, Green | 1,567 |

Lab. majority 10,056 (23.49%)
0.59% swing C. to Lab.
(2010: Lab. majority 7,612 (17.37%))

**EALING CENTRAL & ACTON**
E. 71,238 T. 50,894 (71.44%)

| | Lab. gain |
|---|---|
| *Rupa Huq, Lab. | 22,002 |
| Angie Bray, C. | 21,728 |
| Jon Ball, LD | 3,106 |
| Peter Florence, UKIP | 1,926 |
| Tom Sharman, Green | 1,841 |
| Jonathan Notley, Ind. | 125 |
| Scott Dore, WRP | 73 |
| Tammy Rendle, Above | 54 |
| Andrzej Rygielski, EP | 39 |

Lab. majority 274 (0.54%)
4.21% swing C. to Lab.
(2010: C. majority 3,716 (7.87%))

**EALING NORTH**
E. 73,836 T. 48,510 (65.70%)

| | Lab. hold |
|---|---|
| Stephen Pound, Lab. | 26,745 |
| Thomas O'Malley, C. | 14,419 |
| Afzal Akram, UKIP | 3,922 |
| Meena Hans, Green | 1,635 |
| Kevin McNamara, LD | 1,575 |
| David Hofman, TUSC | 214 |

Lab. majority 12,326 (25.41%)
2.95% swing C. to Lab.
(2010: Lab. majority 9,301 (19.51%))

**EALING SOUTHALL**
E. 65,495 T. 43,321 (66.14%)

| | Lab. hold |
|---|---|
| Virendra Sharma, Lab. | 28,147 |
| James Symes, C. | 9,387 |
| Jaspreet Mahal, Green | 2,007 |
| John Poynton, UKIP | 1,769 |
| Kavya Kaushik, LD | 1,550 |
| Jagdeesh Singh, Nat. Lib. | 461 |

Lab. majority 18,760 (43.30%)
10.79% swing C. to Lab.
(2010: Lab. majority 9,291 (21.73%))

EASINGTON
E. 61,675 T. 34,624 (56.14%)

| | Lab. hold |
|---|---|
| Grahame Morris, Lab. | 21,132 |
| Jonathan Arnott, UKIP | 6,491 |
| Chris Hampsheir, C. | 4,478 |
| Luke Armstrong, LD | 834 |
| Susan McDonnell, NE | 810 |
| Martie Warin, Green | 733 |
| Steve Colborn, SPGB | 146 |

Lab. majority 14,641 (42.29%)
5.99% swing Lab. to UKIP
(2010: Lab. majority 14,982
(42.91%))

EAST HAM
E. 87,378 T. 52,290 (59.84%)

| | Lab. hold |
|---|---|
| Stephen Timms, Lab. | 40,563 |
| Samir Jassal, C. | 6,311 |
| Daniel Oxley, UKIP | 2,622 |
| Tamsin Omond, Green | 1,299 |
| David Thorpe, LD | 856 |
| Mohammed Aslam, Community | 409 |
| Lois Austin, TUSC | 230 |

Lab. majority 34,252 (65.50%)
5.13% swing C. to Lab.
(2010: Lab. majority 27,826
(55.24%))

EASTBOURNE
E. 78,262 T. 52,907 (67.60%)

| | C. gain |
|---|---|
| *Caroline Ansell, C. | 20,934 |
| Stephen Lloyd, LD | 20,201 |
| Nigel Jones, UKIP | 6,139 |
| Jake Lambert, Lab. | 4,143 |
| Andrew Durling, Green | 1,351 |
| Paul Howard, Ind. | 139 |

C. majority 733 (1.39%)
3.99% swing LD to C.
(2010: LD majority 3,435 (6.59%))

EASTLEIGH
E. 79,609 T. 55,505 (69.72%)

| | C. gain |
|---|---|
| *Mims Davies, C. | 23,464 |
| Mike Thornton, LD | 14,317 |
| Patricia Culligan, UKIP | 8,783 |
| Mark Latham, Lab. | 7,181 |
| Ron Meldrum, Green | 1,513 |
| Ray Hall, Beer BS | 133 |
| Declan Clune, TUSC | 114 |

C. majority 9,147 (16.48%)
11.84% swing LD to C.
(2010: LD majority 3,864 (7.20%))
(2013: LD majority 1,771 (4.26%))

EDDISBURY
E. 68,636 T. 47,352 (68.99%)

| | C. hold |
|---|---|
| *Antoinette Sandbach, C. | 24,167 |
| James Laing, Lab. | 11,193 |
| Rob Millington, UKIP | 5,778 |
| Ian Priestner, LD | 4,289 |
| Andrew Garman, Green | 1,624 |
| George Antar, CISTA | 301 |

C. majority 12,974 (27.40%)
1.36% swing C. to Lab.
(2010: C. majority 13,255 (29.19%))

EDMONTON
E. 66,015 T. 41,338 (62.62%)

| | Lab. Co-op hold |
|---|---|
| *Kate Osamor, Lab. Co-op | 25,388 |
| Gonul Daniels, C. | 9,969 |
| Neville Watson, UKIP | 3,366 |
| Douglas Coker, Green | 1,358 |
| David Schmitz, LD | 897 |
| Lewis Peacock, TUSC | 360 |

Lab. Co-op majority 15,419 (37.30%)
6.75% swing C. to Lab.
(2010: Lab. Co-op majority 9,613
(23.81%))

ELLESMERE PORT & NESTON
E. 68,134 T. 46,727 (68.58%)

| | Lab. hold |
|---|---|
| *Justin Madders, Lab. | 22,316 |
| Katherine Fletcher, C. | 16,041 |
| Jonathan Starkey, UKIP | 5,594 |
| Trish Darraugh, LD | 1,563 |
| Michelle Palmer, Green | 990 |
| Felicity Dowling, TUSC | 192 |
| John Dyer, ND | 31 |

Lab. majority 6,275 (13.43%)
1.82% swing C. to Lab.
(2010: Lab. majority 4,331 (9.79%))

ELMET & ROTHWELL
E. 79,143 T. 57,797 (73.03%)

| | C. hold |
|---|---|
| Alec Shelbrooke, C. | 27,978 |
| Veronica King, Lab. | 19,488 |
| Paul Spivey, UKIP | 6,430 |
| Stewart Golton, LD | 2,640 |
| Dave Brooks, Green | 1,261 |

C. majority 8,490 (14.69%)
3.29% swing Lab. to C.
(2010: C. majority 4,521 (8.10%))

ELTHAM
E. 63,998 T. 43,157 (67.43%)

| | Lab. hold |
|---|---|
| Clive Efford, Lab. | 18,393 |
| Spencer Drury, C. | 15,700 |
| Peter Whittle, UKIP | 6,481 |
| Alex Cunliffe, LD | 1,308 |
| James Parker, Green | 1,275 |

Lab. majority 2,693 (6.24%)
1.14% swing C. to Lab.
(2010: Lab. majority 1,663 (3.96%))

ENFIELD NORTH
E. 68,119 T. 46,137 (67.73%)

| | Lab. gain |
|---|---|
| *Joan Ryan, Lab. | 20,172 |
| Nick de Bois, C. | 19,086 |
| Deborah Cairns, UKIP | 4,133 |
| David Flint, Green | 1,303 |
| Cara Jenkinson, LD | 1,059 |
| Yemi Awolola, CPA | 207 |
| Joe Simpson, TUSC | 177 |

Lab. majority 1,086 (2.35%)
3.08% swing C. to Lab.
(2010: C. majority 1,692 (3.81%))

ENFIELD SOUTHGATE
E. 64,938 T. 45,812 (70.55%)

| | C. hold |
|---|---|
| David Burrowes, C. | 22,624 |
| Bambos Charalambous, Lab. | 17,871 |
| David Schofield, UKIP | 2,109 |
| Jean Robertson-Molloy, Green | 1,690 |
| Paul Smith, LD | 1,518 |

C. majority 4,753 (10.38%)
3.41% swing C. to Lab.
(2010: C. majority 7,626 (17.19%))

EPPING FOREST
E. 73,545 T. 49,348 (67.10%)

| | C. hold |
|---|---|
| Eleanor Laing, C. | 27,027 |
| Andrew Smith, UKIP | 9,049 |
| Gareth Barrett, Lab. | 7,962 |
| Jon Whitehouse, LD | 3,448 |
| Anna Widdup, Green | 1,782 |
| Mark Wadsworth, Young | 80 |

C. majority 17,978 (36.43%)
6.79% swing C. to UKIP
(2010: C. majority 15,131 (32.48%))

EPSOM & EWELL
E. 78,633 T. 57,143 (72.67%)

| | C. hold |
|---|---|
| Chris Grayling, C. | 33,309 |
| Sheila Carlson, Lab. | 8,866 |
| Robert Leach, UKIP | 7,117 |
| Stephen Gee, LD | 5,002 |
| Susan McGrath, Green | 2,116 |
| Lionel Blackman, Ind. | 612 |
| Gareth Harfoot, ND | 121 |

C. majority 24,443 (42.78%)
0.75% swing C. to Lab.
(2010: C. majority 16,134 (29.36%))

EREWASH
E. 71,937 T. 48,322 (67.17%)

| | C. hold |
|---|---|
| *Maggie Throup, C. | 20,636 |
| Catherine Atkinson, Lab. | 17,052 |
| Philip Rose, UKIP | 7,792 |
| Martin Garnett, LD | 1,658 |
| Ralph Hierons, Green | 1,184 |

C. majority 3,584 (7.42%)
1.08% swing Lab. to C.
(2010: C. majority 2,501 (5.25%))

## ERITH & THAMESMEAD
E. 69,787 T. 42,617 (61.07%)

| | Lab. hold |
|---|---|
| Teresa Pearce, Lab. | 21,209 |
| Anna Firth, C. | 11,684 |
| Ronie Johnson, UKIP | 7,368 |
| Simon Waddington, LD | 972 |
| Ann Garrett, Green | 941 |
| Sidney Cordle, CPA | 255 |
| Graham Moore, Eng. Dem. | 188 |

Lab. majority 9,525 (22.35%)
4.46% swing C. to Lab.
(2010: Lab. majority 5,703 (13.43%))

## ESHER & WALTON
E. 79,894 T. 56,976 (71.31%)

| | C. hold |
|---|---|
| Dominic Raab, C. | 35,845 |
| Francis Eldergill, Lab. | 7,229 |
| Nicholas Wood, UKIP | 5,551 |
| Andrew Davis, LD | 5,372 |
| Olivia Palmer, Green | 2,355 |
| Matt Heenan, CISTA | 396 |
| Della Reynolds, Ind. | 228 |

C. majority 28,616 (50.22%)
1.00% swing Lab. to C.
(2010: C. majority 18,593 (34.09%))

## EXETER
E. 76,964 T. 54,018 (70.19%)

| | Lab. hold |
|---|---|
| Ben Bradshaw, Lab. | 25,062 |
| Dom Morris, C. | 17,879 |
| Keith Crawford, UKIP | 5,075 |
| Diana Moore, Green | 3,491 |
| Joel Mason, LD | 2,321 |
| Edmund Potts, TUSC | 190 |

Lab. majority 7,183 (13.30%)
4.04% swing C. to Lab.
(2010: Lab. majority 2,721 (5.21%))

## FAREHAM
E. 77,233 T. 54,700 (70.82%)

| | C. hold |
|---|---|
| *Suella Fernandes, C. | 30,689 |
| Malcolm Jones, UKIP | 8,427 |
| Stuart Rose, Lab. | 7,800 |
| Matt Winnington, LD | 4,814 |
| Miles Grindey, Green | 2,129 |
| Nick Gregory, Ind. | 705 |
| Harvey Hines, Ind. | 136 |

C. majority 22,262 (40.70%)
5.23% swing C. to UKIP
(2010: C. majority 17,092 (31.45%))

## FAVERSHAM & KENT MID
E. 69,523 T. 45,803 (65.88%)

| | C. hold |
|---|---|
| *Helen Whately, C. | 24,895 |
| Peter Edwards-Daem, UKIP | 8,243 |
| Michael Desmond, Lab. | 7,403 |
| David Naghi, LD | 3,039 |
| Tim Valentine, Green | 1,768 |
| Hairy Knorm Davidson, Loony | 297 |
| Gary Butler, Eng. Dem. | 158 |

C. majority 16,652 (36.36%)
8.08% swing C. to UKIP
(2010: C. majority 17,088 (36.58%))

## FELTHAM & HESTON
E. 82,328 T. 49,405 (60.01%)

| | Lab. Co-op hold |
|---|---|
| Seema Malhotra, Lab. Co-op | 25,845 |
| Simon Nayyar, C. | 14,382 |
| Peter Dul, UKIP | 6,209 |
| Roger Crouch, LD | 1,579 |
| Tony Firkins, Green | 1,390 |

Lab. Co-op majority 11,463 (23.20%)
6.80% swing C. to Lab.
(2010: Lab. Co-op majority 4,658 (9.60%)) (2011: Lab. majority 6,203 (26.71%))

## FILTON & BRADLEY STOKE
E. 70,722 T. 49,101 (69.43%)

| | C. hold |
|---|---|
| Jack Lopresti, C. | 22,920 |
| Ian Boulton, Lab. | 13,082 |
| Ben Walker, UKIP | 7,261 |
| Peter Bruce, LD | 3,581 |
| Diana Warner, Green | 2,257 |

C. majority 9,838 (20.04%)
2.86% swing Lab. to C.
(2010: C. majority 6,914 (14.31%))

## FINCHLEY & GOLDERS GREEN
E. 72,049 T. 50,759 (70.45%)

| | C. hold |
|---|---|
| Mike Freer, C. | 25,835 |
| Sarah Sackman, Lab. | 20,173 |
| Richard King, UKIP | 1,732 |
| Jonathan Davies, LD | 1,662 |
| Adele Ward, Green | 1,357 |

C. majority 5,662 (11.15%)
0.58% swing C. to Lab.
(2010: C. majority 5,809 (12.32%))

## FOLKESTONE & HYTHE
E. 83,612 T. 55,010 (65.79%)

| | C. hold |
|---|---|
| Damian Collins, C. | 26,323 |
| Harriet Yeo, UKIP | 12,526 |
| Claire Jeffrey, Lab. | 7,939 |
| Lynne Beaumont, LD | 4,882 |
| Martin Whybrow, Green | 2,956 |
| Seth Cruse, TUSC | 244 |
| Rohen Kapur, Young | 72 |
| Andy Thomas, SPGB | 68 |

C. majority 13,797 (25.08%)
9.87% swing C. to UKIP
(2010: C. majority 10,122 (19.17%))

## FOREST OF DEAN
E. 69,882 T. 49,520 (70.86%)

| | C. hold |
|---|---|
| Mark Harper, C. | 23,191 |
| Steve Parry-Hearn, Lab. | 12,204 |
| Steve Stanbury, UKIP | 8,792 |
| James Greenwood, Green | 2,703 |
| Christopher Coleman, LD | 2,630 |

C. majority 10,987 (22.19%)
0.25% swing C. to Lab.
(2010: C. majority 11,064 (22.69%))

## FYLDE
E. 65,679 T. 43,557 (66.32%)

| | C. hold |
|---|---|
| Mark Menzies, C. | 21,406 |
| Jed Sullivan, Lab. | 8,182 |
| Paul White, UKIP | 5,569 |
| Mike Hill, Ind. | 5,166 |
| Fred van Mierlo, LD | 1,623 |
| Bob Dennett, Green | 1,381 |
| Elizabeth Clarkson, Northern | 230 |

C. majority 13,224 (30.36%)
1.07% swing C. to Lab.
(2010: C. majority 13,185 (30.18%))

## GAINSBOROUGH
E. 73,212 T. 49,261 (67.29%)

| | C. hold |
|---|---|
| Edward Leigh, C. | 25,949 |
| David Prescott, Lab. | 10,500 |
| John Saxon, UKIP | 7,727 |
| Lesley Rollings, LD | 3,290 |
| Geoffrey Barnes, Green | 1,290 |
| Christopher Darcel, Lincs Ind. | 505 |

C. majority 15,449 (31.36%)
1.14% swing C. to Lab.
(2010: C. majority 10,559 (21.44%))

## GARSTON & HALEWOOD
E. 74,063 T. 48,983 (66.14%)

| | Lab. hold |
|---|---|
| Maria Eagle, Lab. | 33,839 |
| Martin Williams, C. | 6,693 |
| Carl Schears, UKIP | 4,482 |
| Anna Martin, LD | 2,279 |
| William Ward, Green | 1,690 |

Lab. majority 27,146 (55.42%)
6.01% swing C. to Lab.
(2010: Lab. majority 16,877 (39.41%))

## GATESHEAD
E. 63,910 T. 38,009 (59.47%)

| | Lab. hold |
|---|---|
| Ian Mearns, Lab. | 21,549 |
| John Tennant, UKIP | 6,765 |
| Thomas Smith, C. | 5,562 |
| Frank Hindle, LD | 2,585 |
| Andy Redfern, Green | 1,548 |

Lab. majority 14,784 (38.90%)
6.18% swing Lab. to UKIP
(2010: Lab. majority 12,549 (32.80%))

GEDLING
E. 70,046 T. 47,998 (68.52%)

|  |  | Lab. hold |
|---|---|---|
| Vernon Coaker, Lab. | | 20,307 |
| Carolyn Abbott, C. | | 17,321 |
| Lee Waters, UKIP | | 6,930 |
| Robert Swift, LD | | 1,906 |
| Jim Norris, Green | | 1,534 |

Lab. majority 2,986 (6.22%)
1.18% swing C. to Lab.
(2010: Lab. majority 1,859 (3.86%))

GILLINGHAM & RAINHAM
E. 72,609 T. 47,078 (64.84%)

|  |  | C. hold |
|---|---|---|
| Rehman Chishti, C. | | 22,590 |
| Paul Clark, Lab. | | 12,060 |
| Mark Hanson, UKIP | | 9,199 |
| Paul Chaplin, LD | | 1,707 |
| Neil Williams, Green | | 1,133 |
| Jacqui Berry, TUSC | | 273 |
| Roger Peacock, ND | | 72 |
| Mike Walters, ND | | 44 |

C. majority 10,530 (22.37%)
1.91% swing Lab. to C.
(2010: C. majority 8,680 (18.55%))

GLOUCESTER
E. 82,949 T. 52,575 (63.38%)

|  |  | C. hold |
|---|---|---|
| Richard Graham, C. | | 23,837 |
| Sophy Gardner, Lab. | | 16,586 |
| Richard Ford, UKIP | | 7,497 |
| Jeremy Hilton, LD | | 2,828 |
| Jonathan Ingleby, Green | | 1,485 |
| George Ridgeon, Loony | | 227 |
| Sue Powell, TUSC | | 115 |

C. majority 7,251 (13.79%)
4.51% swing Lab. to C.
(2010: C. majority 2,420 (4.77%))

GOSPORT
E. 73,271 T. 47,665 (65.05%)

|  |  | C. hold |
|---|---|---|
| Caroline Dinenage, C. | | 26,364 |
| Christopher Wood, UKIP | | 9,266 |
| Alan Durrant, Lab. | | 6,926 |
| Rob Hylands, LD | | 3,298 |
| Monica Cassidy, Green | | 1,707 |
| Jeffrey Roberts, ND | | 104 |

C. majority 17,098 (35.87%)
6.36% swing C. to UKIP
(2010: C. majority 14,413 (30.71%))

GRANTHAM & STAMFORD
E. 81,151 T. 53,755 (66.24%)

|  |  | C. hold |
|---|---|---|
| Nick Boles, C. | | 28,399 |
| Marietta King, UKIP | | 9,410 |
| Barrie Fairbairn, Lab. | | 9,070 |
| Harrish Bisnauthsing, LD | | 3,263 |
| Aidan Campbell, Green | | 1,872 |
| Ian Selby, Ind. | | 1,017 |
| Jan Hansen, Lincs Ind. | | 724 |

C. majority 18,989 (35.33%)
5.96% swing C. to UKIP
(2010: C. majority 14,826 (28.08%))

GRAVESHAM
E. 74,307 T. 50,149 (67.49%)

|  |  | C. hold |
|---|---|---|
| Adam Holloway, C. | | 23,484 |
| Tanmanjit Singh Dhesi, Lab. | | 15,114 |
| Sean Marriott, UKIP | | 9,306 |
| Mark Lindop, Green | | 1,124 |
| Anne-Marie Bunting, LD | | 1,111 |

C. majority 8,370 (16.71%)
1.49% swing C. to Lab.
(2010: C. majority 9,312 (19.69%))

GREAT GRIMSBY
E. 58,484 T. 33,731 (57.68%)

|  |  | Lab. hold |
|---|---|---|
| *Melanie Onn, Lab. | | 13,414 |
| Marc Jones, C. | | 8,874 |
| Victoria Ayling, UKIP | | 8,417 |
| Steve Beasant, LD | | 1,680 |
| Vicky Dunn, Green | | 783 |
| Gary Calder, Ind. | | 390 |
| Val O'Flynn, TUSC | | 173 |

Lab. majority 4,540 (13.46%)
5.65% swing C. to Lab.
(2010: Lab. majority 714 (2.17%))

GREAT YARMOUTH
E. 69,793 T. 44,469 (63.72%)

|  |  | C. hold |
|---|---|---|
| Brandon Lewis, C. | | 19,089 |
| Lara Norris, Lab. | | 12,935 |
| Alan Grey, UKIP | | 10,270 |
| James Joyce, LD | | 1,030 |
| Harry Webb, Green | | 978 |
| Samuel George Townley, CISTA | | 167 |

C. majority 6,154 (13.84%)
1.95% swing Lab. to C.
(2010: C. majority 4,276 (9.93%))

GREENWICH & WOOLWICH
E. 73,315 T. 46,716 (63.72%)

|  |  | Lab. hold |
|---|---|---|
| *Matthew Pennycook, Lab. | | 24,384 |
| Matt Hartley, C. | | 12,438 |
| Ryan Acty, UKIP | | 3,888 |
| Abideen Akinoshun, Green | | 2,991 |
| Tom Holder, LD | | 2,645 |
| Lynne Chamberlain, TUSC | | 370 |

Lab. majority 11,946 (25.57%)
0.46% swing C. to Lab.
(2010: Lab. majority 10,153 (24.65%))

GUILDFORD
E. 76,554 T. 53,986 (70.52%)

|  |  | C. hold |
|---|---|---|
| Anne Milton, C. | | 30,802 |
| Kelly-Marie Blundell, LD | | 8,354 |
| Richard Wilson, Lab. | | 6,534 |
| Harry Aldridge, UKIP | | 4,774 |
| John Pletts, Green | | 2,558 |
| Susan Parker, Guildford | | 538 |
| John Morris, Peace | | 230 |
| Gerri Smyth, CISTA | | 196 |

C. majority 22,448 (41.58%)
13.79% swing LD to C.
(2010: C. majority 7,782 (14.00%))

HACKNEY NORTH & STOKE
NEWINGTON
E. 83,195 T. 49,887 (59.96%)

|  |  | Lab. hold |
|---|---|---|
| Diane Abbott, Lab. | | 31,357 |
| Amy Gray, C. | | 7,349 |
| Heather Finlay, Green | | 7,281 |
| Simon de Deney, LD | | 2,492 |
| Keith Fraser, UKIP | | 1,085 |
| Jon Homan, AWP | | 221 |
| Jonathan Silberman, Comm. Lge | | 102 |

Lab. majority 24,008 (48.12%)
3.85% swing C. to Lab.
(2010: Lab. majority 14,461 (31.11%))

HACKNEY SOUTH &
SHOREDITCH
E. 79,962 T. 47,610 (59.54%)

|  |  | Lab. Co-op hold |
|---|---|---|
| Meg Hillier, Lab. Co-op | | 30,663 |
| Jack Tinley, C. | | 6,420 |
| Charlotte George, Green | | 5,519 |
| Ben Mathis, LD | | 2,186 |
| Angus Small, UKIP | | 1,818 |
| Brian Debus, TUSC | | 302 |
| Paul Birch, CISTA | | 297 |
| Taiwo Adewuyi, CPA | | 236 |
| Russell Higgs, Ind. | | 78 |
| Bill Rogers, WRP | | 63 |
| Gordon Shrigley, Campaign | | 28 |

Lab. Co-op majority 24,243 (50.92%)
4.36% swing C. to Lab.
(2010: Lab. majority 14,288 (33.34%))

HALESOWEN & ROWLEY REGIS
E. 74,203 T. 43,818 (59.05%)

|  |  | C. hold |
|---|---|---|
| James Morris, C. | | 18,933 |
| Stephanie Peacock, Lab. | | 15,851 |
| Dean Perks, UKIP | | 7,280 |
| Peter Tyzack, LD | | 905 |
| John Payne, Green | | 849 |

C. majority 3,082 (7.03%)
1.22% swing Lab. to C.
(2010: C. majority 2,023 (4.60%))

HALIFAX
E. 70,461 T. 43,753 (62.10%)

|  |  | Lab. hold |
|---|---|---|
| *Holly Lynch, Lab. | | 17,506 |
| Philip Allott, C. | | 17,078 |
| Liz Phillips, UKIP | | 5,621 |
| Mohammad Ilyas, LD | | 1,629 |
| Gary Scott, Green | | 1,142 |
| Asama Javed, Respect | | 465 |
| Trevor Bendrien, Ch. P. | | 312 |

Lab. majority 428 (0.98%)
1.20% swing Lab. to C.
(2010: Lab. majority 1,472 (3.38%))

## HALTEMPRICE & HOWDEN
E. 71,205 T. 48,757 (68.47%)

|  |  | C. hold |
|---|---|---|
| David Davis, C. | | 26,414 |
| Edward Hart, Lab. | | 10,219 |
| John Kitchener, UKIP | | 6,781 |
| Carl Minns, LD | | 3,055 |
| Tim Greene, Green | | 1,809 |
| Diana Wallis, Yorks | | 479 |

C. majority 16,195 (33.22%)
0.68% swing C. to Lab.
(2010: C. majority 11,602 (23.81%))

## HALTON
E. 72,818 T. 45,023 (61.83%)

|  |  | Lab. hold |
|---|---|---|
| Derek Twigg, Lab. | | 28,292 |
| Matthew Lloyd, C. | | 8,007 |
| Glyn Redican, UKIP | | 6,333 |
| Ryan Bate, LD | | 1,097 |
| David Melvin, Green | | 1,017 |
| Vic Turton, Ind. | | 277 |

Lab. majority 20,285 (45.05%)
3.77% swing C. to Lab.
(2010: Lab. majority 15,504
(37.51%))

## HAMMERSMITH
E. 72,254 T. 47,960 (66.38%)

|  |  | Lab. hold |
|---|---|---|
| Andy Slaughter, Lab. | | 23,981 |
| Charlie Dewhirst, C. | | 17,463 |
| Millicent Scott, LD | | 2,224 |
| David Akan, Green | | 2,105 |
| Richard Wood, UKIP | | 2,105 |
| Stephen Brennan, ND | | 82 |

Lab. majority 6,518 (13.59%)
3.06% swing C. to Lab.
(2010: Lab. majority 3,549 (7.48%))

## HAMPSHIRE EAST
E. 72,600 T. 51,649 (71.14%)

|  |  | C. hold |
|---|---|---|
| Damian Hinds, C. | | 31,334 |
| Peter Baillie, UKIP | | 6,187 |
| Richard Robinson, LD | | 5,732 |
| Alex Wilks, Lab. | | 5,220 |
| Peter Bisset, Green | | 3,176 |

C. majority 25,147 (48.69%)
2.61% swing C. to UKIP
(2010: C. majority 13,497 (26.30%))

## HAMPSHIRE NORTH EAST
E. 74,025 T. 54,000 (72.95%)

|  |  | C. hold |
|---|---|---|
| *Ranil Jayawardena, C. | | 35,573 |
| Graham Cockarill, LD | | 5,657 |
| Amran Hussain, Lab. | | 5,290 |
| Robert Blay, UKIP | | 4,732 |
| Andrew Johnston, Green | | 2,364 |
| Mad Max Bobetsky, Loony | | 384 |

C. majority 29,916 (55.40%)
10.14% swing LD to C.
(2010: C. majority 18,597 (35.13%))

## HAMPSHIRE NORTH WEST
E. 79,223 T. 55,195 (69.67%)

|  |  | C. hold |
|---|---|---|
| *Kit Malthouse, C. | | 32,052 |
| Sue Perkins, UKIP | | 8,109 |
| Andrew Adams, Lab. | | 7,342 |
| Alex Payton, LD | | 5,151 |
| Dan Hill, Green | | 2,541 |

C. majority 23,943 (43.38%)
4.88% swing C. to Lab.
(2010: C. majority 18,583 (34.87%))

## HAMPSTEAD & KILBURN
E. 80,241 T. 53,964 (67.25%)

|  |  | Lab. hold |
|---|---|---|
| *Tulip Siddiq, Lab. | | 23,977 |
| Simon Marcus, C. | | 22,839 |
| Maajid Nawaz, LD | | 3,039 |
| Rebecca Johnson, Green | | 2,387 |
| Magnus Nielsen, UKIP | | 1,532 |
| The Eurovisionary Carroll, Ind. | | 113 |
| Robin Ellison, U Party | | 77 |

Lab. majority 1,138 (2.11%)
1.01% swing C. to Lab.
(2010: Lab. majority 42 (0.08%))

## HARBOROUGH
E. 77,760 T. 52,471 (67.48%)

|  |  | C. hold |
|---|---|---|
| Edward Garnier, C. | | 27,675 |
| Sundip Meghani, Lab. | | 8,043 |
| Mark Hunt, UKIP | | 7,539 |
| Zuffar Haq, LD | | 7,037 |
| Darren Woodiwiss, Green | | 2,177 |

C. majority 19,632 (37.41%)
0.59% swing Lab. to C.
(2010: C. majority 9,797 (17.83%))

## HARLOW
E. 67,994 T. 44,251 (65.08%)

|  |  | C. hold |
|---|---|---|
| Robert Halfon, C. | | 21,623 |
| Suzy Stride, Lab. | | 13,273 |
| Sam Stopplecamp, UKIP | | 7,208 |
| Murray Sackwild, Green | | 954 |
| Geoff Seeff, LD | | 904 |
| David Brown, TUSC | | 174 |
| Eddy Butler, Eng. Dem. | | 115 |

C. majority 8,350 (18.87%)
3.82% swing Lab. to C.
(2010: C. majority 4,925 (11.22%))

## HARROGATE & KNARESBOROUGH
E. 77,379 T. 53,376 (68.98%)

|  |  | C. hold |
|---|---|---|
| Andrew Jones, C. | | 28,153 |
| Helen Flynn, LD | | 11,782 |
| David Simister, UKIP | | 5,681 |
| Jan Williams, Lab. | | 5,409 |
| Shan Oakes, Green | | 2,351 |

C. majority 16,371 (30.67%)
14.36% swing LD to C.
(2010: C. majority 1,039 (1.96%))

## HARROW EAST
E. 70,980 T. 49,000 (69.03%)

|  |  | C. hold |
|---|---|---|
| Bob Blackman, C. | | 24,668 |
| Uma Kumaran, Lab. | | 19,911 |
| Aidan Powlesland, UKIP | | 2,333 |
| Ross Barlow, LD | | 1,037 |
| Emma Wallace, Green | | 846 |
| Nana Asante, TUSC | | 205 |

C. majority 4,757 (9.71%)
1.31% swing Lab. to C.
(2010: C. majority 3,403 (7.09%))

## HARROW WEST
E. 69,643 T. 46,603 (66.92%)

|  |  | Lab. Co-op hold |
|---|---|---|
| Gareth Thomas, Lab. Co-op | | 21,885 |
| Hannah David, C. | | 19,677 |
| Mohammad Ali Bhatti, UKIP | | 2,047 |
| Chris Noyce, LD | | 1,567 |
| Rowan Langley, Green | | 1,310 |
| Kailash Trivedi, Ind. | | 117 |

Lab. Co-op majority 2,208 (4.74%)
1.04% swing Lab. to C.
(2010: Lab. Co-op majority 3,143 (6.82%))

## HARTLEPOOL
E. 69,516 T. 39,490 (56.81%)

|  |  | Lab. hold |
|---|---|---|
| Iain Wright, Lab. | | 14,076 |
| Phillip Broughton, UKIP | | 11,052 |
| Richard Royal, C. | | 8,256 |
| Stephen Picton, Ind. | | 2,954 |
| Michael Holt, Green | | 1,341 |
| Sandra Allison, Hospital | | 849 |
| Hilary Allen, LD | | 761 |
| John Hobbs, Ind. | | 201 |

Lab. majority 3,024 (7.66%)
13.93% swing Lab. to UKIP
(2010: Lab. majority 5,509 (14.41%))

## HARWICH & ESSEX NORTH
E. 69,289 T. 48,432 (69.90%)

|  |  | C. hold |
|---|---|---|
| Bernard Jenkin, C. | | 24,722 |
| Edward Carlsson Browne, Lab. | | 9,548 |
| Mark Hughes, UKIP | | 8,464 |
| Dominic Graham, LD | | 3,576 |
| Christopher Flossman, Green | | 2,122 |

C. majority 15,174 (31.33%)
2.17% swing Lab. to C.
(2010: C. majority 11,447 (23.36%))

## HASTINGS & RYE
E. 75,095 T. 50,927 (67.82%)

|  |  | C. hold |
|---|---|---|
| Amber Rudd, C. | | 22,686 |
| Sarah Owen, Lab. Co-op | | 17,890 |
| Andrew Michael, UKIP | | 6,786 |
| Jake Bowers, Green | | 1,951 |
| Nick Perry, LD | | 1,614 |

C. majority 4,796 (9.42%)
2.71% swing Lab. to C.
(2010: C. majority 1,993 (4.00%))

**HAVANT**

E. 70,573 T. 44,828 (63.52%)

| | C. hold |
|---|---|
| *Alan Mak, C. | 23,159 |
| John Perry, UKIP | 9,239 |
| Graham Giles, Lab. | 7,149 |
| Steve Sollitt, LD | 2,929 |
| Tim Dawes, Green | 2,352 |

C. majority 13,920 (31.05%)

7.05% swing C. to UKIP

(2010: C. majority 12,160 (27.70%))

**HAYES & HARLINGTON**

E. 74,875 T. 45,056 (60.17%)

| | Lab. hold |
|---|---|
| John McDonnell, Lab. | 26,843 |
| Pearl Lewis, C. | 11,143 |
| Cliff Dixon, UKIP | 5,388 |
| Satnam Khalsa, LD | 888 |
| Alick Munro, Green | 794 |

Lab. majority 15,700 (34.85%)

4.73% swing C. to Lab.

(2010: Lab. majority 10,824 (25.39%))

**HAZEL GROVE**

E. 63,098 T. 43,219 (68.50%)

| | C. gain |
|---|---|
| *William Wragg, C. | 17,882 |
| Lisa Smart, LD | 11,330 |
| Michael Taylor, Lab. | 7,584 |
| Darran Palmer, UKIP | 5,283 |
| Graham Reid, Green | 1,140 |

C. majority 6,552 (15.16%)

15.17% swing LD to C.

(2010: LD majority 6,371 (15.18%))

**HEMEL HEMPSTEAD**

E. 74,616 T. 49,633 (66.52%)

| | C. hold |
|---|---|
| Mike Penning, C. | 26,245 |
| Tony Breslin, Lab. | 11,825 |
| Howard Koch, UKIP | 7,249 |
| Rabi Martins, LD | 2,402 |
| Alan Borgars, Green | 1,660 |
| Brian Hall, Ind. | 252 |

C. majority 14,420 (29.05%)

0.05% swing C. to Lab.

(2010: C. majority 13,406 (27.10%))

**HEMSWORTH**

E. 72,714 T. 42,406 (58.32%)

| | Lab. hold |
|---|---|
| Jon Trickett, Lab. | 21,772 |
| Chris Pearson, C. | 9,694 |
| Steve Ashton, UKIP | 8,565 |
| Mary Macqueen, LD | 1,357 |
| Martin Roberts, Yorks | 1,018 |

Lab. majority 12,078 (28.48%)

3.01% swing C. to Lab.

(2010: Lab. majority 9,844 (22.45%))

**HENDON**

E. 74,658 T. 49,630 (66.48%)

| | C. hold |
|---|---|
| Matthew Offord, C. | 24,328 |
| Andrew Dismore, Lab. | 20,604 |
| Raymond Shamash, UKIP | 2,595 |
| Alasdair Hill, LD | 1,088 |
| Ben Samuel, Green | 1,015 |

C. majority 3,724 (7.50%)

3.64% swing Lab. to C.

(2010: C. majority 106 (0.23%))

**HENLEY**

E. 78,243 T. 55,236 (70.60%)

| | C. hold |
|---|---|
| John Howell, C. | 32,292 |
| Sam Juthani, Lab. | 6,917 |
| Susan Cooper, LD | 6,205 |
| Christopher Jones, UKIP | 6,007 |
| Mark Stevenson, Green | 3,815 |

C. majority 25,375 (45.94%)

0.34% swing Lab. to C.

(2010: C. majority 16,588 (30.99%))

**HEREFORD & HEREFORDSHIRE SOUTH**

E. 70,711 T. 47,257 (66.83%)

| | C. hold |
|---|---|
| Jesse Norman, C. | 24,844 |
| Nigel Ely, UKIP | 7,954 |
| Anna Coda, Lab. | 6,042 |
| Lucy Hurds, LD | 5,002 |
| Diana Toynbee, Green | 3,415 |

C. majority 16,890 (35.74%)

3.55% swing C. to UKIP

(2010: C. majority 2,481 (5.13%))

**HEREFORDSHIRE NORTH**

E. 66,683 T. 48,023 (72.02%)

| | C. hold |
|---|---|
| Bill Wiggin, C. | 26,716 |
| Jonathan Oakton, UKIP | 6,720 |
| Jeanie Falconer, LD | 5,768 |
| Sally Prentice, Lab. | 5,478 |
| Daisy Blench, Green | 3,341 |

C. majority 19,996 (41.64%)

2.23% swing C. to UKIP

(2010: C. majority 9,887 (20.78%))

**HERTFORD & STORTFORD**

E. 78,906 T. 56,277 (71.32%)

| | C. hold |
|---|---|
| Mark Prisk, C. | 31,593 |
| Katherine Chibah, Lab. | 10,084 |
| Adrian Baker, UKIP | 7,534 |
| Michael Green, LD | 4,385 |
| Sophie Christophy, Green | 2,681 |

C. majority 21,509 (38.22%)

0.93% swing C. to Lab.

(2010: C. majority 15,437 (27.88%))

**HERTFORDSHIRE NORTH EAST**

E. 73,944 T. 52,287 (70.71%)

| | C. hold |
|---|---|
| Oliver Heald, C. | 28,949 |
| Chris York, Lab. | 9,869 |
| William Compton, UKIP | 6,728 |
| Joe Jordan, LD | 3,952 |
| Mario May, Green | 2,789 |

C. majority 19,080 (36.49%)

0.30% swing C. to Lab.

(2010: C. majority 15,194 (30.13%))

**HERTFORDSHIRE SOUTH WEST**

E. 79,666 T. 57,267 (71.88%)

| | C. hold |
|---|---|
| David Gauke, C. | 32,608 |
| Simon Diggins, Lab. | 9,345 |
| Mark Anderson, UKIP | 6,603 |
| Nigel Quinton, LD | 5,872 |
| Charlotte Pardy, Green | 2,583 |
| Graham Cartmell, CSP | 256 |

C. majority 23,263 (40.62%)

1.05% swing C. to Lab.

(2010: C. majority 14,920 (26.29%))

**HERTSMERE**

E. 73,753 T. 50,091 (67.92%)

| | C. hold |
|---|---|
| *Oliver Dowden, C. | 29,696 |
| Richard Butler, Lab. | 11,235 |
| Frank Ward, UKIP | 6,383 |
| Sophie Bowler, LD | 2,777 |

C. majority 18,461 (36.85%)

0.19% swing C. to Lab.

(2010: C. majority 17,605 (37.24%))

**HEXHAM**

E. 60,614 T. 43,345 (71.51%)

| | C. hold |
|---|---|
| Guy Opperman, C. | 22,834 |
| Liam Carr, Lab. | 10,803 |
| David Nicholson, UKIP | 4,302 |
| Jeff Reid, LD | 2,961 |
| Lee Williscroft-Ferris, Green | 2,445 |

C. majority 12,031 (27.76%)

1.76% swing Lab. to C.

(2010: C. majority 5,788 (13.31%))

**HEYWOOD & MIDDLETON**

E. 79,989 T. 48,538 (60.68%)

| | Lab. hold |
|---|---|
| *Liz McInnes, Lab. | 20,926 |
| John Bickley, UKIP | 15,627 |
| Iain Gartside, C. | 9,268 |
| Anthony Smith, LD | 1,607 |
| Abi Jackson, Green | 1,110 |

Lab. majority 5,299 (10.92%)

13.28% swing Lab. to UKIP

(2010: Lab. majority 5,971 (12.95%))

(2014: Lab. majority 617 (2.17%))

HIGH PEAK
E. 73,336 T. 50,789 (69.26%)

|  |  |
|---|---|
|  | C. hold |
| Andrew Bingham, C. | 22,836 |
| Caitlin Bisknell, Lab. | 17,942 |
| Ian Guiver, UKIP | 5,811 |
| Stephen Worrall, LD | 2,389 |
| Charlotte Farrell, Green | 1,811 |

C. majority 4,894 (9.64%)
0.17% swing Lab. to C.
(2010: C. majority 4,677 (9.29%))

HITCHIN & HARPENDEN
E. 74,839 T. 55,375 (73.99%)

|  |  |
|---|---|
|  | C. hold |
| Peter Lilley, C. | 31,488 |
| Rachel Burgin, Lab. | 11,433 |
| John Stocker, UKIP | 4,917 |
| Pauline Pearce, LD | 4,484 |
| Richard Wise, Green | 3,053 |

C. majority 20,055 (36.22%)
2.42% swing C. to Lab.
(2010: C. majority 15,271 (27.91%))

HOLBORN & ST PANCRAS
E. 86,864 T. 54,917 (63.22%)

|  |  |
|---|---|
|  | Lab. hold |
| *Keir Starmer, Lab. | 29,062 |
| Will Blair, C. | 12,014 |
| Natalie Bennett, Green | 7,013 |
| Jill Fraser, LD | 3,555 |
| Maxine Spencer, UKIP | 2,740 |
| Shane O'Donnell, CISTA | 252 |
| Vanessa Hudson, AWP | 173 |
| David O'Sullivan, SEP | 108 |

Lab. majority 17,048 (31.04%)
2.65% swing C. to Lab.
(2010: Lab. majority 9,942 (18.19%))

HORNCHURCH & UPMINSTER
E. 79,331 T. 55,236 (69.63%)

|  |  |
|---|---|
|  | C. hold |
| Angela Watkinson, C. | 27,051 |
| Lawrence Webb, UKIP | 13,977 |
| Paul McGeary, Lab. | 11,103 |
| Jonathan Mitchell, LD | 1,501 |
| Melanie Collins, Green | 1,411 |
| Paul Borg, BNP | 193 |

C. majority 13,074 (23.67%)
11.22% swing C. to UKIP
(2010: C. majority 16,371 (30.66%))

HORNSEY & WOOD GREEN
E. 79,241 T. 57,785 (72.92%)

|  |  |
|---|---|
|  | Lab. gain |
| *Catherine West, Lab. | 29,417 |
| Lynne Featherstone, LD | 18,359 |
| Suhail Rahuja, C. | 5,347 |
| Gordon Peters, Green | 3,146 |
| Clive Morrison, UKIP | 1,271 |
| Helen Spiby-Vann, CPA | 118 |
| Frank Sweeney, WRP | 82 |
| Geoff Moseley, Hoi | 45 |

Lab. majority 11,058 (19.14%)
15.81% swing LD to Lab.
(2010: LD majority 6,875 (12.49%))

HORSHAM
E. 78,181 T. 56,925 (72.81%)

|  |  |
|---|---|
|  | C. hold |
| *Jeremy Quin, C. | 32,627 |
| Roger Arthur, UKIP | 7,969 |
| Morwen Millson, LD | 6,647 |
| Martyn Davis, Lab. | 6,499 |
| Darrin Green, Green | 2,198 |
| James Smith, S. New | 375 |
| Jim Duggan, Peace | 307 |
| Jim Rae, Ind. | 303 |

C. majority 24,658 (43.32%)
2.17% swing C. to UKIP
(2010: C. majority 11,460 (20.52%))

HOUGHTON & SUNDERLAND
SOUTH
E. 68,316 T. 38,489 (56.34%)

|  |  |
|---|---|
|  | Lab. hold |
| Bridget Phillipson, Lab. | 21,218 |
| Richard Elvin, UKIP | 8,280 |
| Stewart Hay, C. | 7,105 |
| Alan Robinson, Green | 1,095 |
| Jim Murray, LD | 791 |

Lab. majority 12,938 (33.61%)
7.01% swing Lab. to UKIP
(2010: Lab. majority 10,990 (28.91%))

HOVE
E. 73,505 T. 52,214 (71.03%)

|  |  |
|---|---|
|  | Lab. gain |
| *Peter Kyle, Lab. | 22,082 |
| Graham Cox, C. | 20,846 |
| Christopher Hawtree, Green | 3,569 |
| Kevin Smith, UKIP | 3,265 |
| Peter Lambell, LD | 1,861 |
| Jenny Barnard-Langston, Ind. | 322 |
| Dave Hill, TUSC | 144 |
| The Dame Dixon, Loony | 125 |

Lab. majority 1,236 (2.37%)
3.06% swing C. to Lab.
(2010: C. majority 1,868 (3.75%))

HUDDERSFIELD
E. 65,265 T. 40,478 (62.02%)

|  |  |
|---|---|
|  | Lab. Co-op hold |
| Barry Sheerman, Lab. Co-op | 18,186 |
| Itrat Ali, C. | 10,841 |
| Rob Butler, UKIP | 5,948 |
| Andrew Cooper, Green | 2,798 |
| Zulfiqar Ali, LD | 2,365 |
| Mike Forster, TUSC | 340 |

Lab. Co-op majority 7,345 (18.15%)
3.56% swing C. to Lab.
(2010: Lab. majority 4,472 (11.04%))

HULL EAST
E. 65,606 T. 35,144 (53.57%)

|  |  |
|---|---|
|  | Lab. hold |
| Karl Turner, Lab. | 18,180 |
| Richard Barrett, UKIP | 7,861 |
| Christine Mackay, C. | 5,593 |
| David Nolan, LD | 2,294 |
| Sarah Walpole, Green | 806 |
| Martin Clayton, Yorks | 270 |
| Mike Cooper, NF | 86 |
| Val Hoodless, Soc. Dem. | 54 |

Lab. majority 10,319 (29.36%)
5.27% swing Lab. to UKIP
(2010: Lab. majority 8,597 (25.15%))

HULL NORTH
E. 63,650 T. 35,336 (55.52%)

|  |  |
|---|---|
|  | Lab. hold |
| Diana Johnson, Lab. | 18,661 |
| Sergi Singh, UKIP | 5,762 |
| Dehenna Davison, C. | 5,306 |
| Mike Ross, LD | 3,175 |
| Martin Deane, Green | 2,066 |
| Vicky Butler, Yorks | 366 |

Lab. majority 12,899 (36.50%)
0.70% swing UKIP to Lab.
(2010: Lab. majority 641 (1.93%))

HULL WEST & HESSLE
E. 59,008 T. 31,803 (53.90%)

|  |  |
|---|---|
|  | Lab. hold |
| Alan Johnson, Lab. | 15,646 |
| Paul Salvidge, UKIP | 6,313 |
| Jo Barker, C. | 5,561 |
| Claire Thomas, LD | 3,169 |
| Angela Needham, Green | 943 |
| Paul Spooner, TUSC | 171 |

Lab. majority 9,333 (29.35%)
3.88% swing Lab. to UKIP
(2010: Lab. majority 5,742 (18.23%))

HUNTINGDON
E. 82,404 T. 55,926 (67.87%)

|  |  |
|---|---|
|  | C. hold |
| Jonathan Djanogly, C. | 29,652 |
| Nik Johnson, Lab. | 10,248 |
| Paul Bullen, UKIP | 9,473 |
| Rod Cantrill, LD | 4,375 |
| Tom MacLennan, Green | 2,178 |

C. majority 19,404 (34.70%)
1.57% swing C. to Lab.
(2010: C. majority 10,819 (19.94%))

HYNDBURN
E. 68,341 T. 42,887 (62.75%)

|  |  |
|---|---|
|  | Lab. hold |
| Graham Jones, Lab. | 18,076 |
| Kevin Horkin, C. | 13,676 |
| Janet Brown, UKIP | 9,154 |
| Kerry Gormley, Green | 1,122 |
| Alison Firth, LD | 859 |

Lab. majority 4,400 (10.26%)
1.51% swing C. to Lab.
(2010: Lab. majority 3,090 (7.24%))

### ILFORD NORTH
E. 78,162 T. 48,932 (62.60%)

| | Lab. gain |
|---|---|
| *Wes Streeting, Lab. | 21,463 |
| Lee Scott, C. | 20,874 |
| Philip Hyde, UKIP | 4,355 |
| Rich Clare, LD | 1,130 |
| David Reynolds, Green | 1,023 |
| Doris Osen, Ind. | 87 |

Lab. majority 589 (1.20%)
6.35% swing C. to Lab.
(2010: C. majority 5,404 (11.49%))

### ILFORD SOUTH
E. 95,023 T. 51,912 (54.63%)

| | Lab. Co-op hold |
|---|---|
| Mike Gapes, Lab. Co-op | 33,232 |
| Chris Chapman, C. | 13,455 |
| Amjad Khan, UKIP | 2,705 |
| RoseMary Warrington, Green | 1,506 |
| Ashburn Holder, LD | 1,014 |

Lab. Co-op majority 19,777 (38.10%)
8.02% swing C. to Lab.
(2010: Lab. Co-op majority 11,287 (22.05%))

### IPSWICH
E. 74,498 T. 48,694 (65.36%)

| | C. hold |
|---|---|
| Ben Gummer, C. | 21,794 |
| David Ellesmere, Lab. | 18,061 |
| Maria Vigneau, UKIP | 5,703 |
| Barry Broom, Green | 1,736 |
| Chika Akinwale, LD | 1,400 |

C. majority 3,733 (7.67%)
1.62% swing Lab. to C.
(2010: C. majority 2,079 (4.43%))

### ISLE OF WIGHT
E. 108,804 T. 70,300 (64.61%)

| | C. hold |
|---|---|
| Andrew Turner, C. | 28,591 |
| Iain McKie, UKIP | 14,888 |
| Vix Lowthion, Green | 9,404 |
| Stewart Blackmore, Lab. | 8,984 |
| David Goodall, LD | 5,235 |
| Ian Stephens, Ind. | 3,198 |

C. majority 13,703 (19.49%)
11.87% swing C. to UKIP
(2010: C. majority 10,527 (14.98%))

### ISLINGTON NORTH
E. 73,325 T. 49,234 (67.14%)

| | Lab. hold |
|---|---|
| Jeremy Corbyn, Lab. | 29,659 |
| Alex Burghart, C. | 8,465 |
| Caroline Russell, Green | 5,043 |
| Julian Gregory, LD | 3,984 |
| Gregory Clough, UKIP | 1,971 |
| Bill Martin, SPGB | 112 |

Lab. majority 21,194 (43.05%)
1.39% swing C. to Lab.
(2010: Lab. majority 12,401 (27.83%))

### ISLINGTON SOUTH & FINSBURY
E. 68,127 T. 44,270 (64.98%)

| | Lab. hold |
|---|---|
| Emily Thornberry, Lab. | 22,547 |
| Mark Lim, C. | 9,839 |
| Terry Stacy, LD | 4,829 |
| Pete Muswell, UKIP | 3,375 |
| Charlie Kiss, Green | 3,371 |
| Jay Kirton, CISTA | 309 |

Lab. majority 12,708 (28.71%)
2.92% swing C. to Lab.
(2010: Lab. majority 3,569 (8.19%))

### JARROW
E. 63,882 T. 38,564 (60.37%)

| | Lab. hold |
|---|---|
| Stephen Hepburn, Lab. | 21,464 |
| Steven Harrison, UKIP | 7,583 |
| Nick Mason, C. | 6,584 |
| David Herbert, Green | 1,310 |
| Stan Collins, LD | 1,238 |
| Norman Hall, TUSC | 385 |

Lab. majority 13,881 (35.99%)
swing N/A
(2010: Lab. majority 12,908 (33.28%))

### KEIGHLEY
E. 68,865 T. 49,123 (71.33%)

| | C. hold |
|---|---|
| Kris Hopkins, C. | 21,766 |
| John Grogan, Lab. | 18,713 |
| Paul Latham, UKIP | 5,662 |
| Ros Brown, Green | 1,661 |
| Gareth Epps, LD | 1,321 |

C. majority 3,053 (6.22%)
0.03% swing Lab. to C.
(2010: C. majority 2,940 (6.16%))

### KENILWORTH & SOUTHAM
E. 65,245 T. 48,791 (74.78%)

| | C. hold |
|---|---|
| Jeremy Wright, C. | 28,474 |
| Bally Singh, Lab. | 7,472 |
| Harry Cottam, UKIP | 5,467 |
| Richard Dickson, LD | 4,913 |
| Rob Ballantyne, Green | 1,956 |
| Nick Blunderbuss Green, Loony | 370 |
| Jon Foster-Smith, Digital | 139 |

C. majority 21,002 (43.04%)
1.91% swing Lab. to C.
(2010: C. majority 12,552 (25.92%))

### KENSINGTON
E. 61,333 T. 34,828 (56.79%)

| | C. gain |
|---|---|
| *Lady (Victoria) Borwick, C. | 18,199 |
| Rod Abouharb, Lab. | 10,838 |
| Robin McGhee, LD | 1,962 |
| Robina Rose, Green | 1,765 |
| Jack Bovill, UKIP | 1,557 |
| Tony Auguste, CISTA | 211 |
| Andrew Knight, AWP | 158 |
| Toby Abse, Green Soc. | 115 |
| Roland Courtenay, New IC | 23 |

C. majority 7,361 (21.14%)
1.69% swing C. to Lab.
(2010: C. majority 8,616 (24.51%))

### KETTERING
E. 70,155 T. 47,218 (67.31%)

| | C. hold |
|---|---|
| Philip Hollobone, C. | 24,467 |
| Rhea Keehn, Lab. | 11,877 |
| Jonathan Bullock, UKIP | 7,600 |
| Rob Reeves, Green | 1,633 |
| Chris McGlynn, LD | 1,490 |
| Derek Hilling, Eng. Dem. | 151 |

C. majority 12,590 (26.66%)
3.72% swing Lab. to C.
(2010: C. majority 9,094 (19.21%))

### KINGSTON & SURBITON
E. 81,277 T. 59,253 (72.90%)

| | C. gain |
|---|---|
| *James Berry, C. | 23,249 |
| Ed Davey, LD | 20,415 |
| Lee Godfrey, Lab. | 8,574 |
| Ben Roberts, UKIP | 4,321 |
| Clare Keogh, Green | 2,322 |
| Daniel Gill, CPA | 198 |
| Laurel Fogarty, TUSC | 174 |

C. majority 2,834 (4.78%)
9.01% swing LD to C.
(2010: LD majority 7,560 (13.24%))

### KINGSWOOD
E. 67,992 T. 48,125 (70.78%)

| | C. hold |
|---|---|
| Chris Skidmore, C. | 23,252 |
| Jo McCarron, Lab. | 14,246 |
| Duncan Odgers, UKIP | 7,133 |
| Adam Boyden, LD | 1,827 |
| Cezara Nanu, Green | 1,370 |
| Julie Lake, BNP | 164 |
| Richard Worth, TUSC | 84 |
| Liam Bryan, Vapers | 49 |

C. majority 9,006 (18.71%)
6.81% swing Lab. to C.
(2010: C. majority 2,445 (5.10%))

### KNOWSLEY
E. 79,109 T. 50,728 (64.12%)

| | Lab. hold |
|---|---|
| George Howarth, Lab. | 39,628 |
| Louise Bours, UKIP | 4,973 |
| Alice Bramall, C. | 3,367 |
| Carl Cashman, LD | 1,490 |
| Vikki Gregorich, Green | 1,270 |

Lab. majority 34,655 (68.32%)
swing N/A
(2010: Lab. majority 25,686 (57.52%))

### LANCASHIRE WEST
E. 70,945 T. 49,676 (70.02%)

| | Lab. hold |
|---|---|
| Rosie Cooper, Lab. | 24,474 |
| Paul Greenall, C. | 16,114 |
| Jack Sen, UKIP | 6,058 |
| Ben Basson, Green | 1,582 |
| Daniel Lewis, LD | 1,298 |
| David Braid, WVPTFP | 150 |

Lab. majority 8,360 (16.83%)
3.93% swing C. to Lab.
(2010: Lab. majority 4,343 (8.96%))

## LANCASTER & FLEETWOOD
E. 60,883  T. 41,738 (68.55%)

|  | Lab. gain |
|---|---|
| *Cat Smith, Lab. | 17,643 |
| Eric Ollerenshaw, C. | 16,378 |
| Matthew Atkins, UKIP | 4,060 |
| Chris Coates, Green | 2,093 |
| Robin Long, LD | 1,390 |
| Harold Elletson, Northern | 174 |

Lab. majority 1,265 (3.03%)
1.91% swing C. to Lab.
(2010: C. majority 333 (0.78%))

## LEEDS CENTRAL
E. 81,799  T. 45,048 (55.07%)

|  | Lab. hold |
|---|---|
| Hilary Benn, Lab. | 24,758 |
| Nicola Wilson, C. | 7,791 |
| Luke Senior, UKIP | 7,082 |
| Michael Hayton, Green | 3,558 |
| Emma Spriggs, LD | 1,529 |
| Liz Kitching, TUSC | 330 |

Lab. majority 16,967 (37.66%)
4.27% swing C. to Lab.
(2010: Lab. majority 10,645
(28.47%))

## LEEDS EAST
E. 64,754  T. 38,196 (58.99%)

|  | Lab. hold |
|---|---|
| *Richard Burgon, Lab. | 20,530 |
| Ryan Stephenson, C. | 7,997 |
| Mark Maniatt, UKIP | 7,256 |
| Ed Sanderson, LD | 1,296 |
| Kate Bisson, Green | 1,117 |

Lab. majority 12,533 (32.81%)
2.80% swing C. to Lab.
(2010: Lab. majority 10,293
(27.22%))

## LEEDS NORTH EAST
E. 69,097  T. 48,291 (69.89%)

|  | Lab. hold |
|---|---|
| Fabian Hamilton, Lab. | 23,137 |
| Simon Wilson, C. | 15,887 |
| Warren Hendon, UKIP | 3,706 |
| Aqila Choudhry, LD | 2,569 |
| Emma Carter, Green | 2,541 |
| Celia Foote, Green Soc. | 451 |

Lab. majority 7,250 (15.01%)
2.73% swing C. to Lab.
(2010: Lab. majority 4,545 (9.56%))

## LEEDS NORTH WEST
E. 61,974  T. 43,357 (69.96%)   LD
hold

| Greg Mulholland, LD | 15,948 |
|---|---|
| Alex Sobel, Lab. | 13,041 |
| Alex Story, C. | 8,083 |
| Tim Goodall, Green | 3,042 |
| Julian Metcalfe, UKIP | 2,997 |
| Bob Buxton, Yorks | 143 |
| Mike Davies, Green Soc. | 79 |
| Mark Flanagan, Above | 24 |

LD majority 2,907 (6.70%)
9.90% swing LD to Lab.
(2010: LD majority 9,103 (20.93%))

## LEEDS WEST
E. 64,950  T. 38,423 (59.16%)

|  | Lab. hold |
|---|---|
| Rachel Reeves, Lab. | 18,456 |
| Alex Pierre-Traves, C. | 7,729 |
| Anne Murgatroyd, UKIP | 7,104 |
| Andrew Pointon, Green | 3,217 |
| Laura Coyle, LD | 1,495 |
| Matthew West, CISTA | 217 |
| Ben Mayor, TUSC | 205 |

Lab. majority 10,727 (27.92%)
2.67% swing C. to Lab.
(2010: Lab. majority 7,016 (18.10%))

## LEICESTER EAST
E. 75,430  T. 48,068 (63.73%)

|  | Lab. hold |
|---|---|
| Keith Vaz, Lab. | 29,386 |
| Kishan Devani, C. | 11,034 |
| Susanna Steptoe, UKIP | 4,290 |
| Nimit Jethwa, Green | 1,468 |
| Dave Raval, LD | 1,233 |
| Michael Barker, TUSC | 540 |
| Tom Darwood, ND | 117 |

Lab. majority 18,352 (38.18%)
4.42% swing C. to Lab.
(2010: Lab. majority 14,082
(29.34%))

## LEICESTER SOUTH
E. 73,518  T. 45,962 (62.52%)

|  | Lab. Co-op hold |
|---|---|
| Jon Ashworth, Lab. Co-op | 27,473 |
| Leon Hadji-Nikolaou, C. | 9,628 |
| Peter Stone, UKIP | 3,832 |
| Gabby Garcia, Green | 2,533 |
| Anita Prabhakar, LD | 2,127 |
| Andrew Walton, TUSC | 349 |

Lab. Co-op majority 17,845 (38.87%)
7.32% swing C. to Lab.
(2010: Lab. majority 8,808 (18.69%))
(2011: Lab. majority 12,078 (35.34%))

## LEICESTER WEST
E. 63,204  T. 34,522 (54.62%)

|  | Lab. hold |
|---|---|
| Liz Kendall, Lab. | 16,051 |
| Paul Bessant, C. | 8,848 |
| Stuart Young, UKIP | 5,950 |
| Peter Hague, Green | 1,878 |
| Ian Bradwell, LD | 1,507 |
| Heather Rawling, TUSC | 288 |

Lab. majority 7,203 (20.86%)
4.83% swing C. to Lab.
(2010: Lab. majority 4,017 (11.21%))

## LEICESTERSHIRE NORTH WEST
E. 72,194  T. 51,548 (71.40%)

|  | C. hold |
|---|---|
| Andrew Bridgen, C. | 25,505 |
| Jamie McMahon, Lab. Co-op | 14,132 |
| Andy McWilliam, UKIP | 8,704 |
| Mark Argent, LD | 2,033 |
| Benjamin Gravestock, Green | 1,174 |

C. majority 11,373 (22.06%)
3.80% swing Lab. to C.
(2010: C. majority 7,511 (14.46%))

## LEICESTERSHIRE SOUTH
E. 76,877  T. 53,926 (70.15%)

|  | C. hold |
|---|---|
| *Alberto Costa, C. | 28,700 |
| Amanda Hack, Lab. | 11,876 |
| Barry Mahoney, UKIP | 9,363 |
| Geoffrey Welsh, LD | 3,987 |

C. majority 16,824 (31.20%)
1.30% swing Lab. to C.
(2010: C. majority 15,524 (28.44%))

## LEIGH
E. 75,974  T. 45,123 (59.39%)

|  | Lab. hold |
|---|---|
| Andy Burnham, Lab. | 24,312 |
| Louisa Townson, C. | 10,216 |
| Les Leggett, UKIP | 8,903 |
| Bill Winlow, LD | 1,150 |
| Stephen Hall, TUSC | 542 |

Lab. majority 14,096 (31.24%)
2.07% swing C. to Lab.
(2010: Lab. majority 12,011
(27.09%))

## LEWES
E. 69,481  T. 50,540 (72.74%)

|  | C. gain |
|---|---|
| *Maria Caulfield, C. | 19,206 |
| Norman Baker, LD | 18,123 |
| Ray Finch, UKIP | 5,427 |
| Lloyd Russell-Moyle, Lab. | 5,000 |
| Alfie Stirling, Green | 2,784 |

C. majority 1,083 (2.14%)
8.70% swing LD to C.
(2010: LD majority 7,647 (15.27%))

## LEWISHAM DEPTFORD
E. 73,426  T. 47,426 (64.59%)

|  | Lab. hold |
|---|---|
| *Vicky Foxcroft, Lab. | 28,572 |
| Bim Afolami, C. | 7,056 |
| John Coughlin, Green | 5,932 |
| Michael Bukola, LD | 2,497 |
| Massimo Dimambro, UKIP | 2,013 |
| Helen Mercer, PBP | 666 |
| Malcolm Martin, CPA | 300 |
| Chris Flood, TUSC | 286 |
| Phillip Badger, Dem. Ref. | 74 |
| David Harvey, ND | 30 |

Lab. majority 21,516 (45.37%)
2.57% swing C. to Lab.
(2010: Lab. majority 12,499
(30.32%))

## LEWISHAM EAST
E. 73,428  T. 42,923 (58.46%)

|  | Lab. hold |
|---|---|
| Heidi Alexander, Lab. | 23,907 |
| Peter Fortune, C. | 9,574 |
| Anne Marie Waters, UKIP | 3,886 |
| Julia Fletcher, LD | 2,455 |
| Storm Poorun, Green | 2,429 |
| Nick Long, PBP | 390 |
| Maureen Martin, CPA | 282 |

Lab. majority 14,333 (33.39%)
6.97% swing C. to Lab.
(2010: Lab. majority 6,216 (14.90%))

## LEWISHAM WEST & PENGE
E. 72,289 T. 48,125 (66.57%)

| | | Lab. hold |
|---|---|---|
| Jim Dowd, Lab. | | 24,347 |
| Russell Jackson, C. | | 11,633 |
| Tom Chance, Green | | 4,077 |
| Gary Harding, UKIP | | 3,764 |
| Alex Feakes, LD | | 3,709 |
| Martin Powell-Davies, TUSC | | 391 |
| David Hansom, Ind. | | 160 |
| George Whale, Lib. GB | | 44 |

Lab. majority 12,714 (26.42%)
5.42% swing C. to Lab.
(2010: Lab. majority 5,828 (12.94%))

## LEYTON & WANSTEAD
E. 64,746 T. 40,705 (62.87%)

| | | Lab. hold |
|---|---|---|
| John Cryer, Lab. | | 23,858 |
| Matthew Scott, C. | | 8,939 |
| Ashley Gunstock, Green | | 2,974 |
| Rosamund Beattie, UKIP | | 2,341 |
| Carl Quilliam, LD | | 2,304 |
| Mahtab Aziz, Ind. | | 289 |

Lab. majority 14,919 (36.65%)
7.64% swing C. to Lab.
(2010: Lab. majority 6,416 (15.98%))

## LICHFIELD
E. 83,339 T. 51,467 (61.76%)

| | | C. hold |
|---|---|---|
| Michael Fabricant, C. | | 28,389 |
| Chris Worsey, Lab. | | 10,200 |
| John Rackham, UKIP | | 8,082 |
| Paul Ray, LD | | 2,700 |
| Robert Pass, Green | | 1,976 |
| Andy Bennetts, Class War | | 120 |

C. majority 18,189 (35.34%)
0.39% swing Lab. to C.
(2010: C. majority 17,683 (34.29%))

## LINCOLN
E. 74,121 T. 46,852 (63.21%)

| | | C. hold |
|---|---|---|
| Karl McCartney, C. | | 19,976 |
| Lucy Rigby, Lab. | | 18,533 |
| Nick Smith, UKIP | | 5,721 |
| Ross Pepper, LD | | 1,992 |
| Elaine Smith, TUSC | | 344 |
| Helen Powell, Lincs Ind. | | 286 |

C. majority 1,443 (3.08%)
0.38% swing Lab. to C.
(2010: C. majority 1,058 (2.31%))

## LIVERPOOL RIVERSIDE
E. 70,950 T. 44,263 (62.39%)

| | | Lab. Co-op hold |
|---|---|---|
| Louise Ellman, Lab. Co-op | | 29,835 |
| Martin Dobson, Green | | 5,372 |
| Jackson Ng, C. | | 4,245 |
| Joe Chiffers, UKIP | | 2,510 |
| Paul Childs, LD | | 1,719 |
| Tony Mulhearn, TUSC | | 582 |

Lab. Co-op majority 24,463 (55.27%)
0.26% swing Lab. to Green
(2010: Lab. majority 14,173 (36.53%))

## LIVERPOOL WALTON
E. 62,868 T. 38,403 (61.09%)

| | | Lab. hold |
|---|---|---|
| Steve Rotheram, Lab. | | 31,222 |
| Steve Flatman, UKIP | | 3,445 |
| Norsheen Bhatti, C. | | 1,802 |
| Jonathan Clatworthy, Green | | 956 |
| Pat Moloney, LD | | 899 |
| Alexander Karran, Ind. | | 56 |
| Jonathan Dzon, Plural | | 23 |

Lab. majority 27,777 (72.33%)
1.49% swing UKIP to Lab.
(2010: Lab. majority 19,818 (57.72%))

## LIVERPOOL WAVERTREE
E. 61,731 T. 40,974 (66.38%)

| | | Lab. Co-op hold |
|---|---|---|
| Luciana Berger, Lab. Co-op | | 28,401 |
| James Pearson, C. | | 4,098 |
| Adam Heatherington, UKIP | | 3,375 |
| Leo Evans, LD | | 2,454 |
| Peter Cranie, Green | | 2,140 |
| Dave Walsh, TUSC | | 362 |
| Niamh McCarthy, Ind. | | 144 |

Lab. Co-op majority 24,303 (59.31%)
6.84% swing C. to Lab.
(2010: Lab. Co-op majority 7,167 (18.90%))

## LIVERPOOL WEST DERBY
E. 63,875 T. 41,031 (64.24%)

| | | Lab. Co-op hold |
|---|---|---|
| Stephen Twigg, Lab. Co-op | | 30,842 |
| Neil Miney, UKIP | | 3,475 |
| Ed McRandal, C. | | 2,710 |
| Steve Radford, Lib. | | 2,049 |
| Rebecca Lawson, Green | | 996 |
| Paul Twigger, LD | | 959 |

Lab. Co-op majority 27,367 (66.70%)
2.80% swing UKIP to Lab.
(2010: Lab. Co-op majority 18,467 (51.61%))

## LOUGHBOROUGH
E. 72,644 T. 52,020 (71.61%)

| | | C. hold |
|---|---|---|
| Nicky Morgan, C. | | 25,762 |
| Matthew O'Callaghan, Lab. | | 16,579 |
| Bill Piper, UKIP | | 5,704 |
| Steve Coltman, LD | | 2,130 |
| Matt Sisson, Green | | 1,845 |

C. majority 9,183 (17.65%)
5.28% swing Lab. to C.
(2010: C. majority 3,744 (7.09%))

## LOUTH & HORNCASTLE
E. 74,280 T. 50,336 (67.77%)

| | | C. hold |
|---|---|---|
| *Victoria Atkins, C. | | 25,755 |
| Colin Mair, UKIP | | 10,778 |
| Matthew Brown, Lab. | | 9,077 |
| Lisa Gabriel, LD | | 2,255 |
| Romy Rayner, Green | | 1,549 |
| Daniel Simpson, Lincs Ind. | | 659 |
| Peter Hill, Loony | | 263 |

C. majority 14,977 (29.75%)
7.78% swing C. to UKIP
(2010: C. majority 13,871 (27.47%))

## LUDLOW
E. 66,423 T. 48,063 (72.36%)

| | | C. hold |
|---|---|---|
| Philip Dunne, C. | | 26,093 |
| David Kelly, UKIP | | 7,164 |
| Charlotte Barnes, LD | | 6,469 |
| Simon Slater, Lab. | | 5,902 |
| Janet Phillips, Green | | 2,435 |

C. majority 18,929 (39.38%)
4.52% swing C. to UKIP
(2010: C. majority 9,749 (20.01%))

## LUTON NORTH
E. 66,533 T. 42,571 (63.98%)

| | | Lab. hold |
|---|---|---|
| Kelvin Hopkins, Lab. | | 22,243 |
| Dean Russell, C. | | 12,739 |
| Allan White, UKIP | | 5,318 |
| Aroosa Ulzaman, LD | | 1,299 |
| Sofiya Ahmed, Green | | 972 |

Lab. majority 9,504 (22.33%)
2.42% swing C. to Lab.
(2010: Lab. majority 7,520 (17.48%))

## LUTON SOUTH
E. 67,234 T. 42,216 (62.79%)

| | | Lab. Co-op hold |
|---|---|---|
| Gavin Shuker, Lab. Co-op | | 18,660 |
| Katie Redmond, C. | | 12,949 |
| Yasin Rehman, UKIP | | 5,129 |
| Ashuk Ahmed, LD | | 3,183 |
| Simon Hall, Green | | 1,237 |
| Attiq Malik, Ind. | | 900 |
| Paul Weston, Lib. GB | | 158 |

Lab. Co-op majority 5,711 (13.53%)
4.01% swing C. to Lab.
(2010: Lab. Co-op majority 2,329 (5.52%))

## MACCLESFIELD
E. 71,580 T. 49,598 (69.29%)

| | | C. hold |
|---|---|---|
| David Rutley, C. | | 26,063 |
| Tim Roca, Lab. | | 11,252 |
| Adrian Howard, UKIP | | 6,037 |
| Neil Christian, LD | | 3,842 |
| Joan Plimmer, Green | | 2,404 |

C. majority 14,811 (29.86%)
1.61% swing Lab. to C.
(2010: C. majority 11,959 (23.89%))

## MAIDENHEAD
E. 74,963 T. 53,855 (71.84%)

| | | C. hold |
|---|---|---|
| Theresa May, C. | | 35,453 |
| Charles Smith, Lab. | | 6,394 |
| Tony Hill, LD | | 5,337 |
| Herbie Crossman, UKIP | | 4,539 |
| Emily Blyth, Green | | 1,915 |
| Ian Taplin, Ind. | | 162 |
| Joe Wilcox, Class War | | 55 |

C. majority 29,059 (53.96%)
0.79% swing Lab. to C.
(2010: C. majority 16,769 (31.22%))

## MAIDSTONE & THE WEALD
E. 73,181 T. 50,010 (68.34%)

|  |  | C. hold |
|---|---|---|
| Helen Grant, C. | | 22,745 |
| Jasper Gerard, LD | | 12,036 |
| Eddie Powell, UKIP | | 7,930 |
| Allen Simpson, Lab. | | 5,268 |
| Hannah Patton, Green | | 1,396 |
| Paul Hobday, NHAP | | 583 |
| Robin Kinrade, Ind. | | 52 |

C. majority 10,709 (21.41%)
4.69% swing LD to C.
(2010: C. majority 5,889 (12.04%))

## MAKERFIELD
E. 74,370 T. 44,788 (60.22%)

|  | Lab. hold |
|---|---|
| Yvonne Fovargue, Lab. | 23,208 |
| Andrew Collinson, UKIP | 10,053 |
| Zehra Zaidi, C. | 8,752 |
| John Skipworth, LD | 1,639 |
| Philip Mitchell, Green | 1,136 |

Lab. majority 13,155 (29.37%)
swing N/A
(2010: Lab. majority 12,490
(28.53%))

## MALDON
E. 69,455 T. 48,045 (69.17%)

|  | C. hold |
|---|---|
| John Whittingdale, C. | 29,112 |
| Beverley Acevedo, UKIP | 7,042 |
| Peter Edwards, Lab. | 5,690 |
| Ken Martin, Ind. | 2,424 |
| Zoe O'Connell, LD | 2,157 |
| Robert Graves, Green | 1,504 |
| John Marett, TSPP | 116 |

C. majority 22,070 (45.94%)
4.40% swing C. to UKIP
(2010: C. majority 19,407 (40.52%))

## MANCHESTER CENTRAL
E. 98,435 T. 45,331 (46.05%)

|  | Lab. Co-op hold |
|---|---|
| Lucy Powell, Lab. Co-op | 27,772 |
| Xingang Wang, C. | 6,133 |
| Myles Power, UKIP | 5,033 |
| Kieran Turner-Dave, Green | 3,838 |
| John Reid, LD | 1,867 |
| Loz Kaye, Pirate | 346 |
| Alex Davidson, TUSC | 270 |
| Paul Davies, Comm. Lge | 72 |

Lab. Co-op majority 21,639 (47.74%)
3.39% swing C. to Lab.
(2010: Lab. majority 10,439
(26.15%)) (2012: Lab. majority 9,936
(59.68%))

## MANCHESTER GORTON
E. 72,959 T. 42,019 (57.59%)

|  | Lab. hold |
|---|---|
| Gerald Kaufman, Lab. | 28,187 |
| Laura Bannister, Green | 4,108 |
| Mo Afzal, C. | 4,063 |
| Phil Eckersley, UKIP | 3,434 |
| Dave Page, LD | 1,782 |
| Simon Hickman, TUSC | 264 |
| Cris Chesha, Pirate | 181 |

Lab. majority 24,079 (57.31%)
4.96% swing Green to Lab.
(2010: Lab. majority 6,703 (17.49%))

## MANCHESTER WITHINGTON
E. 80,590 T. 49,966 (62.00%)

|  | Lab. gain |
|---|---|
| *Jeff Smith, Lab. | 26,843 |
| John Leech, LD | 11,970 |
| Robert Manning, C. | 4,872 |
| Lucy Bannister, Green | 4,048 |
| Mark Davies, UKIP | 2,172 |
| Marcus Farmer, Ind. | 61 |

Lab. majority 14,873 (29.77%)
16.99% swing LD to Lab.
(2010: LD majority 1,894 (4.21%))

## MANSFIELD
E. 77,534 T. 47,193 (60.87%)

|  | Lab. hold |
|---|---|
| Sir Alan Meale, Lab. | 18,603 |
| Andrea Clarke, C. | 13,288 |
| Sid Pepper, UKIP | 11,850 |
| Tony Rogers, LD | 1,642 |
| Paul Frost, Green | 1,486 |
| Karen Seymour, TUSC | 324 |

Lab. majority 5,315 (11.26%)
0.58% swing Lab. to C.
(2010: Lab. majority 6,012 (12.42%))

## MEON VALLEY
E. 72,738 T. 51,717 (71.10%)

|  | C. hold |
|---|---|
| George Hollingbery, C. | 31,578 |
| Dave Alexander, UKIP | 7,665 |
| Gemma McKenna, Lab. | 5,656 |
| Chris Carrigan, LD | 4,987 |
| Diana Korchien, Green | 1,831 |

C. majority 23,913 (46.24%)
3.55% swing C. to UKIP
(2010: C. majority 12,125 (23.66%))

## MERIDEN
E. 81,079 T. 52,603 (64.88%)

|  | C. hold |
|---|---|
| Caroline Spelman, C. | 28,791 |
| Tom McNeil, Lab. | 9,996 |
| Mick Gee, UKIP | 8,908 |
| Ade Adeyemo, LD | 2,638 |
| Alison Gavin, Green | 2,170 |
| Chris Booth, IE | 100 |

C. majority 18,795 (35.73%)
2.29% swing Lab. to C.
(2010: C. majority 16,253 (31.16%))

## MIDDLESBROUGH
E. 61,868 T. 32,706 (52.86%)

|  | Lab. hold |
|---|---|
| Andy McDonald, Lab. | 18,584 |
| Nigel Baker, UKIP | 6,107 |
| Simon Clarke, C. | 5,388 |
| Hannah Graham, Green | 1,407 |
| Richard Kilpatrick, LD | 1,220 |

Lab. majority 12,477 (38.15%)
2.02% swing Lab. to UKIP
(2010: Lab. majority 8,689 (25.97%))
(2012: Lab. majority 8,211 (47.7%))

## MIDDLESBROUGH SOUTH & CLEVELAND EAST
E. 71,153 T. 45,677 (64.20%)

|  | Lab. hold |
|---|---|
| Tom Blenkinsop, Lab. | 19,193 |
| Will Goodhand, C. | 16,925 |
| Steve Turner, UKIP | 6,935 |
| Ben Gibson, LD | 1,564 |
| Martin Brampton, Green | 1,060 |

Lab. majority 2,268 (4.97%)
0.67% swing C. to Lab.
(2010: Lab. majority 1,677 (3.63%))

## MILTON KEYNES NORTH
E. 84,892 T. 57,692 (67.96%)

|  | C. hold |
|---|---|
| Mark Lancaster, C. | 27,244 |
| Emily Darlington, Lab. | 17,491 |
| David Reilly, UKIP | 6,852 |
| Paul Graham, LD | 3,575 |
| Jennifer Marklew, Green | 2,255 |
| Katie Simpson, TUSC | 163 |
| David Mortimer, Ind. | 112 |

C. majority 9,753 (16.91%)
0.14% swing Lab. to C.
(2010: C. majority 8,961 (16.63%))

## MILTON KEYNES SOUTH
E. 87,968 T. 59,019 (67.09%)

|  | C. hold |
|---|---|
| Iain Stewart, C. | 27,671 |
| Andrew Pakes, Lab. Co-op | 18,929 |
| Vince Peddle, UKIP | 7,803 |
| Lisa Smith, LD | 2,309 |
| Samantha Pancheri, Green | 1,936 |
| Stephen Fulton, Ind. | 255 |
| Matthew Gibson, Real | 116 |

C. majority 8,742 (14.81%)
2.71% swing Lab. to C.
(2010: C. majority 5,201 (9.40%))

## MITCHAM & MORDEN
E. 68,474 T. 45,142 (65.93%)

|  | Lab. hold |
|---|---|
| Siobhain McDonagh, Lab. | 27,380 |
| Paul Holmes, C. | 10,458 |
| Richard Hilton, UKIP | 4,287 |
| Mason Redding, Green | 1,422 |
| Diana Coman, LD | 1,378 |
| Des Coke, CPA | 217 |

Lab. majority 16,922 (37.49%)
3.14% swing C. to Lab.
(2010: Lab. majority 13,666
(31.20%))

MOLE VALLEY
E. 74,317 T. 55,140 (74.20%)

|  |  |
|---|---|
|  | C. hold |
| Paul Beresford, C. | 33,434 |
| Paul Kennedy, LD | 7,981 |
| Paul Oakley, UKIP | 6,181 |
| Len Amos, Lab. | 4,565 |
| Jacquetta Fewster, Green | 2,979 |

C. majority 25,453 (46.16%)
8.67% swing LD to C.
(2010: C. majority 15,653 (28.81%))

MORECAMBE & LUNESDALE
E. 66,476 T. 43,242 (65.05%)

|  |  |
|---|---|
|  | C. hold |
| David Morris, C. | 19,691 |
| Amina Lone, Lab. | 15,101 |
| Steve Ogden, UKIP | 5,358 |
| Matthew Severn, LD | 1,612 |
| Phil Chandler, Green | 1,395 |
| Michael Dawson, ND | 85 |

C. majority 4,590 (10.61%)
4.31% swing Lab. to C.
(2010: C. majority 866 (1.99%))

MORLEY & OUTWOOD
E. 76,179 T. 48,250 (63.34%)

|  |  |
|---|---|
|  | C. gain |
| *Andrea Jenkyns, C. | 18,776 |
| Ed Balls, Lab. Co-op | 18,354 |
| David Dews, UKIP | 7,951 |
| Rebecca Taylor, LD | 1,426 |
| Martin Hemingway, Green | 1,264 |
| Arnie Craven, Yorks | 479 |

C. majority 422 (0.87%)
1.56% swing Lab. to C.
(2010: Lab. Co-op majority 1,101
(2.25%))

NEW FOREST EAST
E. 72,720 T. 49,447 (68.00%)

|  |  |
|---|---|
|  | C. hold |
| Julian Lewis, C. | 27,819 |
| Roy Swales, UKIP | 8,657 |
| Andrew Pope, Lab. | 6,018 |
| Bruce Tennent, LD | 4,626 |
| Sally May, Green | 2,327 |

C. majority 19,162 (38.75%)
4.53% swing C. to UKIP
(2010: C. majority 11,307 (22.60%))

NEW FOREST WEST
E. 68,465 T. 47,410 (69.25%)

|  |  |
|---|---|
|  | C. hold |
| Desmond Swayne, C. | 28,420 |
| Paul Bailey, UKIP | 7,816 |
| Lena Samuels, Lab. | 5,133 |
| Imogen Shepherd-DuBey, LD | 3,293 |
| Janet Richards, Green | 2,748 |

C. majority 20,604 (43.46%)
4.75% swing C. to UKIP
(2010: C. majority 16,896 (35.52%))

NEWARK
E. 73,724 T. 52,302 (70.94%)

|  |  |
|---|---|
|  | C. hold |
| Robert Jenrick, C. | 29,834 |
| Michael Payne, Lab. | 11,360 |
| Brian Mapletoft, UKIP | 6,294 |
| David Dobbie, LD | 2,385 |
| Elayne Forster, Green | 1,792 |
| Helen Tyrer, Consensus | 637 |

C. majority 18,474 (35.32%)
1.90% swing Lab. to C.
(2010: C. majority 16,152 (31.53%))
(2014: C. majority 7,403 (19.13%))

NEWBURY
E. 79,058 T. 57,300 (72.48%)

|  |  |
|---|---|
|  | C. hold |
| Richard Benyon, C. | 34,973 |
| Judith Bunting, LD | 8,605 |
| Catherine Anderson, UKIP | 6,195 |
| Jonny Roberts, Lab. | 4,837 |
| Paul Field, Green | 2,324 |
| Peter Norman, AD | 228 |
| Barrie Singleton, Ind. | 85 |
| Andrew Stott, PSP | 53 |

C. majority 26,368 (46.02%)
12.56% swing LD to C.
(2010: C. majority 12,248 (20.90%))

NEWCASTLE-UNDER-LYME
E. 66,752 T. 42,997 (64.41%)

|  |  |
|---|---|
|  | Lab. hold |
| Paul Farrelly, Lab. | 16,520 |
| Tony Cox, C. | 15,870 |
| Phil Wood, UKIP | 7,252 |
| Ian Wilkes, LD | 1,826 |
| Sam Gibbons, Green | 1,246 |
| David Nixon, Ind. | 283 |

Lab. majority 650 (1.51%)
1.04% swing Lab. to C.
(2010: Lab. majority 1,552 (3.59%))

NEWCASTLE UPON TYNE
CENTRAL
E. 61,061 T. 35,085 (57.46%)

|  |  |
|---|---|
|  | Lab. hold |
| Chi Onwurah, Lab. | 19,301 |
| Simon Kitchen, C. | 6,628 |
| Daniel Thompson, UKIP | 5,214 |
| Nick Cott, LD | 2,218 |
| Alexander Johnson, Green | 1,724 |

Lab. majority 12,673 (36.12%)
4.76% swing C. to Lab.
(2010: Lab. majority 7,466 (21.86%))

NEWCASTLE UPON TYNE EAST
E. 74,112 T. 39,222 (52.92%)

|  |  |
|---|---|
|  | Lab. hold |
| Nick Brown, Lab. | 19,378 |
| Duncan Crute, C. | 6,884 |
| David Robinson-Young, UKIP | 4,910 |
| Wendy Taylor, LD | 4,332 |
| Andrew Gray, Green | 3,426 |
| Paul Phillips, TUSC | 170 |
| Mollie Stevenson, Comm. | 122 |

Lab. majority 12,494 (31.85%)
1.43% swing C. to Lab.
(2010: Lab. majority 4,453 (11.77%))

NEWCASTLE UPON TYNE
NORTH
E. 67,267 T. 44,891 (66.74%)

|  |  |
|---|---|
|  | Lab. hold |
| Catherine McKinnell, Lab. | 20,689 |
| Stephen Bates, C. | 10,536 |
| Tim Marron, UKIP | 7,447 |
| Anita Lower, LD | 4,366 |
| Alison Whalley, Green | 1,515 |
| Violet Rook, NE | 338 |

Lab. majority 10,153 (22.62%)
0.05% swing Lab. to C.
(2010: Lab. majority 3,414 (7.77%))

NEWTON ABBOT
E. 69,743 T. 48,199 (69.11%)

|  |  |
|---|---|
|  | C. hold |
| Anne Marie Morris, C. | 22,794 |
| Richard Younger-Ross, LD | 11,506 |
| Rod Peers, UKIP | 6,726 |
| Roy Freer, Lab. | 4,736 |
| Steven Smyth-Bonfield, Green | 2,216 |
| Sean Brogan, TUSC | 221 |

C. majority 11,288 (23.42%)
11.17% swing LD to C.
(2010: C. majority 523 (1.08%))

NORFOLK MID
E. 76,975 T. 52,212 (67.83%)

|  |  |
|---|---|
|  | C. hold |
| George Freeman, C. | 27,206 |
| Anna Coke, UKIP | 9,930 |
| Harry Clarke, Lab. | 9,585 |
| Paul Speed, LD | 3,300 |
| Simeon Jackson, Green | 2,191 |

C. majority 17,276 (33.09%)
5.44% swing C. to UKIP
(2010: C. majority 13,856 (27.29%))

NORFOLK NORTH
E. 68,958 T. 49,414 (71.66%)    LD
hold

|  |  |
|---|---|
| Norman Lamb, LD | 19,299 |
| Ann Steward, C. | 15,256 |
| Michael Baker, UKIP | 8,328 |
| Denise Burke, Lab. | 5,043 |
| Michael Macartney-Filgate, Green | 1,488 |

LD majority 4,043 (8.18%)
7.61% swing LD to C.
(2010: LD majority 11,626
(23.41%))

NORFOLK NORTH WEST
E. 72,400 T. 47,371 (65.43%)

|  |  |
|---|---|
|  | C. hold |
| Henry Bellingham, C. | 24,727 |
| Jo Rust, Lab. | 10,779 |
| Toby Coke, UKIP | 8,412 |
| Michael de Whalley, Green | 1,780 |
| Hugh Lanham, LD | 1,673 |

C. majority 13,948 (29.44%)
5.74% swing C. to Lab.
(2010: C. majority 14,810 (30.98%))

## NORFOLK SOUTH
E. 78,885 T. 57,123 (72.41%)

| | | |
|---|---|---|
| | | C. hold |
| Richard Bacon, C. | | 30,995 |
| Deborah Sacks, Lab. | | 10,502 |
| Barry Cameron, UKIP | | 7,847 |
| Jacqueline Howe, LD | | 4,689 |
| Catherine Rowett, Green | | 3,090 |

C. majority 20,493 (35.88%)
0.14% swing C. to Lab.
(2010: C. majority 10,940 (19.89%))

## NORFOLK SOUTH WEST
E. 76,970 T. 50,110 (65.10%)

| | | |
|---|---|---|
| | | C. hold |
| Elizabeth Truss, C. | | 25,515 |
| Paul Smyth, UKIP | | 11,654 |
| Peter Smith, Lab. | | 8,649 |
| Rupert Moss-Eccardt, LD | | 2,217 |
| Sandra Walmsley, Green | | 2,075 |

C. majority 13,861 (27.66%)
7.22% swing C. to UKIP
(2010: C. majority 13,140 (26.73%))

## NORMANTON, PONTEFRACT & CASTLEFORD
E. 82,592 T. 45,897 (55.57%)

| | | |
|---|---|---|
| | | Lab. hold |
| Yvette Cooper, Lab. | | 25,213 |
| Nathan Garbutt, UKIP | | 9,785 |
| Beth Prescott, C. | | 9,569 |
| Edward McMillan-Scott, LD | | 1,330 |

Lab. majority 15,428 (33.61%)
swing N/A
(2010: Lab. majority 10,979 (23.74%))

## NORTHAMPTON NORTH
E. 59,147 T. 39,411 (66.63%)

| | | |
|---|---|---|
| | | C. hold |
| Michael Ellis, C. | | 16,699 |
| Sally Keeble, Lab. | | 13,454 |
| Tom Rubython, UKIP | | 6,354 |
| Tony Clarke, Green | | 1,503 |
| Angela Paterson, LD | | 1,401 |

C. majority 3,245 (8.23%)
1.71% swing Lab. to C.
(2010: C. majority 1,936 (4.81%))

## NORTHAMPTON SOUTH
E. 61,284 T. 38,884 (63.45%)

| | | |
|---|---|---|
| | | C. hold |
| *David Mackintosh, C. | | 16,163 |
| Kevin McKeever, Lab. | | 12,370 |
| Rose Gibbins, UKIP | | 7,114 |
| Sadik Chaudhury, LD | | 1,673 |
| Julie Hawkins, Green | | 1,403 |
| Kevin Willsher, Ind. | | 161 |

C. majority 3,793 (9.75%)
2.82% swing C. to Lab.
(2010: C. majority 6,004 (15.40%))

## NORTHAMPTONSHIRE SOUTH
E. 85,092 T. 60,862 (71.52%)

| | | |
|---|---|---|
| | | C. hold |
| Andrea Leadsom, C. | | 36,607 |
| Lucy Mills, Lab. | | 10,191 |
| Roger Clark, UKIP | | 8,204 |
| Tom Snowdon, LD | | 3,613 |
| Damon Boughen, Green | | 2,247 |

C. majority 26,416 (43.40%)
2.75% swing Lab. to C.
(2010: C. majority 20,478 (34.19%))

## NORWICH NORTH
E. 65,136 T. 43,592 (66.92%)

| | | |
|---|---|---|
| | | C. hold |
| Chloe Smith, C. | | 19,052 |
| Jessica Asato, Lab. | | 14,589 |
| Glenn Tingle, UKIP | | 5,986 |
| Adrian Holmes, Green | | 1,939 |
| James Wright, LD | | 1,894 |
| Mick Hardy, Ind. | | 132 |

C. majority 4,463 (10.24%)
0.54% swing Lab. to C.
(2010: C. majority 3,901 (9.16%))

## NORWICH SOUTH
E. 74,875 T. 48,463 (64.73%)

| | | |
|---|---|---|
| | | Lab. gain |
| *Clive Lewis, Lab. | | 19,033 |
| Lisa Townsend, C. | | 11,379 |
| Lesley Grahame, Green | | 6,749 |
| Simon Wright, LD | | 6,607 |
| Steve Emmens, UKIP | | 4,539 |
| David Peel, Class War | | 96 |
| Cengiz Ceker, Ind. | | 60 |

Lab. majority 7,654 (15.79%)
13.15% swing LD to Lab.
(2010: LD majority 310 (0.65%))

## NOTTINGHAM EAST
E. 60,464 T. 35,209 (58.23%)

| | | |
|---|---|---|
| | | Lab. Co-op hold |
| Chris Leslie, Lab. Co-op | | 19,208 |
| Garry Hickton, C. | | 7,314 |
| Fran Loi, UKIP | | 3,501 |
| Antonia Zenkevitch, Green | | 3,473 |
| Tadeusz Jones, LD | | 1,475 |
| Seb Soar, Ind. | | 141 |
| James Stephenson, Ind. | | 97 |

Lab. Co-op majority 11,894 (33.78%)
6.05% swing C. to Lab.
(2010: Lab. Co-op majority 6,969 (21.05%))

## NOTTINGHAM NORTH
E. 65,918 T. 35,343 (53.62%)

| | | |
|---|---|---|
| | | Lab. hold |
| Graham Allen, Lab. | | 19,283 |
| Louise Burfitt-Dons, C. | | 7,423 |
| Stephen Crosby, UKIP | | 6,542 |
| Katharina Boettge, Green | | 1,088 |
| Tony Sutton, LD | | 847 |
| Cathy Meadows, TUSC | | 160 |

Lab. majority 11,860 (33.56%)
4.91% swing C. to Lab.
(2010: Lab. majority 8,138 (23.74%))

## NOTTINGHAM SOUTH
E. 68,987 T. 43,465 (63.00%)

| | | |
|---|---|---|
| | | Lab. hold |
| Lilian Greenwood, Lab. | | 20,697 |
| Jane Hunt, C. | | 13,761 |
| David Hollas, UKIP | | 4,900 |
| Adam McGregor, Green | | 2,345 |
| Deborah Newton-Cook, LD | | 1,532 |
| Andrew Clayworth, TUSC | | 230 |

Lab. majority 6,936 (15.96%)
5.81% swing C. to Lab.
(2010: Lab. majority 1,772 (4.34%))

## NUNEATON
E. 68,032 T. 45,749 (67.25%)

| | | |
|---|---|---|
| | | C. hold |
| Marcus Jones, C. | | 20,827 |
| Vicky Fowler, Lab. | | 15,945 |
| Alwyn Waine, UKIP | | 6,582 |
| Keith Kondakor, Green | | 1,281 |
| Christina Jebb, LD | | 816 |
| Paul Reilly, TUSC | | 194 |
| Stephen Paxton, Eng. Dem. | | 104 |

C. majority 4,882 (10.67%)
3.02% swing Lab. to C.
(2010: C. majority 2,069 (4.63%))

## OLD BEXLEY & SIDCUP
E. 66,035 T. 46,748 (70.79%)

| | | |
|---|---|---|
| | | C. hold |
| James Brokenshire, C. | | 24,682 |
| Ibrahim Mehmet, Lab. | | 8,879 |
| Catherine Reilly, UKIP | | 8,528 |
| Jennifer Keen, LD | | 1,644 |
| Derek Moran, Green | | 1,336 |
| Bob Gill, NHAP | | 1,216 |
| Laurence Williams, Ch. P. | | 245 |
| Nicola Finch, BNP | | 218 |

C. majority 15,803 (33.80%)
0.53% swing C. to Lab.
(2010: C. majority 15,857 (34.86%))

## OLDHAM EAST & SADDLEWORTH
E. 72,005 T. 44,483 (61.78%)

| | | |
|---|---|---|
| | | Lab. hold |
| Debbie Abrahams, Lab. | | 17,529 |
| Sajjad Hussain, C. | | 11,527 |
| Peter Klonowski, UKIP | | 8,557 |
| Richard Marbrow, LD | | 5,718 |
| Miranda Meadowcroft, Green | | 1,152 |

Lab. majority 6,002 (13.49%)
4.04% swing C. to Lab.
(2010: Lab. majority 103 (0.23%))
(2011: Lab. majority 3,558 (10.23%))

## OLDHAM WEST & ROYTON
E. 72,341 T. 43,137 (59.63%)

| | | |
|---|---|---|
| | | Lab. hold |
| Michael Meacher, Lab. | | 23,630 |
| Francis Arbour, UKIP | | 8,892 |
| Kamran Ghafoor, C. | | 8,187 |
| Garth Harkness, LD | | 1,589 |
| Simeon Hart, Green | | 839 |

Lab. majority 14,738 (34.17%)
4.03% swing Lab. to UKIP
(2010: Lab. majority 9,352 (21.79%))

ORPINGTON
E. 68,129 T. 49,032 (71.97%)

|  |  |
|---|---|
|  | C. hold |
| Joseph Johnson, C. | 28,152 |
| Idham Ramadi, UKIP | 8,173 |
| Nigel de Gruchy, Lab. | 7,645 |
| Peter Brooks, LD | 3,330 |
| Tamara Galloway, Green | 1,732 |

C. majority 19,979 (40.75%)
8.09% swing C. to UKIP
(2010: C. majority 17,200 (35.17%))

OXFORD EAST
E. 78,974 T. 50,689 (64.18%)

|  |  |
|---|---|
|  | Lab. hold |
| Andrew Smith, Lab. | 25,356 |
| Melanie Magee, C. | 10,076 |
| Ann Duncan, Green | 5,890 |
| Alasdair Murray, LD | 5,453 |
| Ian Macdonald, UKIP | 3,451 |
| Chaka Artwell, Ind. | 160 |
| Mad Hatter, Loony | 145 |
| James Morbin, TUSC | 108 |
| Kevin Parkin, SPGB | 50 |

Lab. majority 15,280 (30.14%)
3.25% swing C. to Lab.
(2010: Lab. majority 4,581 (8.87%))

OXFORD WEST & ABINGDON
E. 79,767 T. 57,247 (71.77%)

|  |  |
|---|---|
|  | C. hold |
| Nicola Blackwood, C. | 26,153 |
| Layla Moran, LD | 16,571 |
| Sally Copley, Lab. | 7,274 |
| Alan Harris, UKIP | 3,963 |
| Larry Sanders, Green | 2,497 |
| Helen Salisbury, NHAP | 723 |
| Mike Foster, SPGB | 66 |

C. majority 9,582 (16.74%)
8.21% swing LD to C.
(2010: C. majority 176 (0.31%))

PENDLE
E. 64,657 T. 44,448 (68.74%)

|  |  |
|---|---|
|  | C. hold |
| Andrew Stephenson, C. | 20,978 |
| Azhar Ali, Lab. | 15,525 |
| Mick Waddington, UKIP | 5,415 |
| Graham Roach, LD | 1,487 |
| Laura Fisk, Green | 1,043 |

C. majority 5,453 (12.27%)
2.15% swing Lab. to C.
(2010: C. majority 3,585 (7.96%))

PENISTONE & STOCKSBRIDGE
E. 71,048 T. 46,854 (65.95%)

|  |  |
|---|---|
|  | Lab. hold |
| Angela Smith, Lab. | 19,691 |
| Steven Jackson, C. | 12,968 |
| Graeme Waddicar, UKIP | 10,738 |
| Rosalyn Gordon, LD | 2,957 |
| Colin Porter, Eng. Dem. | 500 |

Lab. majority 6,723 (14.35%)
3.90% swing C. to Lab.
(2010: Lab. majority 3,049 (6.55%))

PENRITH & THE BORDER
E. 65,209 T. 43,921 (67.35%)

|  |  |
|---|---|
|  | C. hold |
| Rory Stewart, C. | 26,202 |
| Lee Rushworth, Lab. | 6,308 |
| John Stanyer, UKIP | 5,353 |
| Neil Hughes, LD | 3,745 |
| Bryan Burrow, Green | 2,313 |

C. majority 19,894 (45.29%)
2.42% swing Lab. to C.
(2010: C. majority 11,241 (24.93%))

PETERBOROUGH
E. 72,521 T. 47,075 (64.91%)

|  |  |
|---|---|
|  | C. hold |
| Stewart Jackson, C. | 18,684 |
| Lisa Forbes, Lab. | 16,759 |
| Mary Herdman, UKIP | 7,485 |
| Darren Fower, LD | 1,774 |
| Darren Bisby-Boyd, Green | 1,218 |
| Chris Ash, Lib. | 639 |
| John Fox, Ind. | 516 |

C. majority 1,925 (4.09%)
3.37% swing C. to Lab.
(2010: C. majority 4,861 (10.82%))

PLYMOUTH MOOR VIEW
E. 69,146 T. 42,606 (61.62%)

|  |  |
|---|---|
|  | C. gain |
| *Johnny Mercer, C. | 16,020 |
| Alison Seabeck, Lab. | 14,994 |
| Penny Mills, UKIP | 9,152 |
| Stuart Bonar, LD | 1,265 |
| Ben Osborn, Green | 1,023 |
| Louise Parker, TUSC | 152 |

C. majority 1,026 (2.41%)
3.12% swing Lab. to C.
(2010: Lab. majority 1,588 (3.82%))

PLYMOUTH SUTTON &
DEVONPORT
E. 69,146 T. 47,963 (69.36%)

|  |  |
|---|---|
|  | C. hold |
| Oliver Colvile, C. | 18,120 |
| Luke Pollard, Lab. Co-op | 17,597 |
| Roy Kettle, UKIP | 6,731 |
| Libby Brown, Green | 3,401 |
| Graham Reed, LD | 2,008 |
| Laura-Jane Rossington, Comm. | 106 |

C. majority 523 (1.09%)
0.76% swing C. to Lab.
(2010: C. majority 1,149 (2.62%))

POOLE
E. 72,557 T. 47,393 (65.32%)

|  |  |
|---|---|
|  | C. hold |
| Robert Syms, C. | 23,745 |
| David Young, UKIP | 7,956 |
| Helen Rosser, Lab. | 6,102 |
| Philip Eades, LD | 5,572 |
| Adrian Oliver, Green | 2,198 |
| Mark Howell, Poole | 1,766 |
| Ian Northover, ND | 54 |

C. majority 15,789 (33.32%)
4.45% swing C. to UKIP
(2010: C. majority 7,541 (15.90%))

POPLAR & LIMEHOUSE
E. 82,076 T. 51,044 (62.19%)

|  |  |
|---|---|
|  | Lab. hold |
| Jim Fitzpatrick, Lab. | 29,886 |
| Christopher Wilford, C. | 12,962 |
| Nicholas McQueen, UKIP | 3,128 |
| Maureen Childs, Green | 2,463 |
| Elaine Bagshaw, LD | 2,149 |
| Hugo Pierre, TUSC | 367 |
| Rene Mugenzi, RFAC | 89 |

Lab. majority 16,924 (33.16%)
10.12% swing C. to Lab.
(2010: Lab. majority 6,030 (12.91%))

PORTSMOUTH NORTH
E. 73,105 T. 45,390 (62.09%)

|  |  |
|---|---|
|  | C. hold |
| Penny Mordaunt, C. | 21,343 |
| John Ferrett, Lab. | 10,806 |
| Mike Fitzgerald, UKIP | 8,660 |
| Darren Sanders, LD | 2,828 |
| Gavin Ellis, Green | 1,450 |
| Jon Woods, TUSC | 231 |
| Steven George, JACP | 72 |

C. majority 10,537 (23.21%)
3.35% swing Lab. to C.
(2010: C. majority 7,289 (16.52%))

PORTSMOUTH SOUTH
E. 71,639 T. 41,903 (58.49%)

|  |  |
|---|---|
|  | C. gain |
| *Flick Drummond, C. | 14,585 |
| Gerald Vernon-Jackson, LD | 9,344 |
| Sue Castillon, Lab. | 8,184 |
| Steve Harris, UKIP | 5,595 |
| Ian McCulloch, Green | 3,145 |
| Mike Hancock, Ind. | 716 |
| Sean Hoyle, TUSC | 235 |
| Don Jerrard, JACP | 99 |

C. majority 5,241 (12.51%)
12.55% swing LD to C.
(2010: LD majority 5,200 (12.60%))

PRESTON
E. 59,981 T. 33,469 (55.80%)

|  |  |
|---|---|
|  | Lab. Co-op hold |
| Mark Hendrick, Lab. Co-op | 18,755 |
| Richard Holden, C. | 6,688 |
| James Barker, UKIP | 5,139 |
| Gemma Christie, Green | 1,643 |
| Jo Barton, LD | 1,244 |

Lab. Co-op majority 12,067 (36.05%)
4.79% swing C. to Lab.
(2010: Lab. Co-op majority 7,733
(23.79%))

PUDSEY
E. 70,533 T. 50,927 (72.20%)

|  |  |
|---|---|
|  | C. hold |
| Stuart Andrew, C. | 23,637 |
| Jamie Hanley, Lab. | 19,136 |
| Roger Tattersall, UKIP | 4,689 |
| Ryk Downes, LD | 1,926 |
| Claire Allen, Green | 1,539 |

C. majority 4,501 (8.84%)
2.73% swing Lab. to C.
(2010: C. majority 1,659 (3.38%))

## PUTNEY
E. 63,918 T. 42,813 (66.98%)

| | C. hold |
|---|---|
| Justine Greening, C. | 23,018 |
| Sheila Boswell, Lab. | 12,838 |
| Andy Hallett, LD | 2,717 |
| Chris Poole, Green | 2,067 |
| Tricia Ward, UKIP | 1,989 |
| Guy Dessoy, AWP | 184 |

C. majority 10,180 (23.78%)
0.44% swing C. to Lab.
(2010: C. majority 10,053 (24.65%))

## RAYLEIGH & WICKFORD
E. 77,870 T. 53,220 (68.34%)

| | C. hold |
|---|---|
| Mark Francois, C. | 29,088 |
| John Hayter, UKIP | 11,858 |
| David Hough, Lab. | 6,705 |
| Linda Kendall, Ind. | 2,418 |
| Mike Pitt, LD | 1,622 |
| Sarah Yapp, Green | 1,529 |

C. majority 17,230 (32.38%)
10.60% swing C. to UKIP
(2010: C. majority 22,338 (42.68%))

## READING EAST
E. 74,651 T. 50,494 (67.64%)

| | C. hold |
|---|---|
| Rob Wilson, C. | 23,217 |
| Matt Rodda, Lab. | 16,697 |
| Jenny Woods, LD | 3,719 |
| Christine Forrester, UKIP | 3,647 |
| Rob White, Green | 3,214 |

C. majority 6,520 (12.91%)
2.09% swing C. to Lab.
(2010: C. majority 7,605 (15.21%))

## READING WEST
E. 72,302 T. 48,404 (66.95%)

| | C. hold |
|---|---|
| Alok Sharma, C. | 23,082 |
| Victoria Groulef, Lab. | 16,432 |
| Malik Azam, UKIP | 4,826 |
| Meri O'Connell, LD | 2,355 |
| Miriam Kennet, Green | 1,406 |
| Suzie Ferguson, Ind. | 156 |
| Neil Adams, TUSC | 83 |
| Philip West, Roman | 64 |

C. majority 6,650 (13.74%)
0.55% swing Lab. to C.
(2010: C. majority 6,004 (12.63%))

## REDCAR
E. 64,825 T. 40,919 (63.12%)

| | Lab. Co-op gain |
|---|---|
| *Anna Turley, Lab. Co-op | 17,946 |
| Josh Mason, LD | 7,558 |
| Chris Gallacher, UKIP | 7,516 |
| Jacob Young, C. | 6,630 |
| Peter Pinkney, Green | 880 |
| Philip Lockey, NE | 389 |

Lab. Co-op majority 10,388 (25.39%)
18.91% swing LD to Lab.
(2010: LD majority 5,214 (12.43%))

## REDDITCH
E. 65,529 T. 44,098 (67.30%)

| | C. hold |
|---|---|
| Karen Lumley, C. | 20,771 |
| Rebecca Blake, Lab. | 13,717 |
| Peter Jewell, UKIP | 7,133 |
| Hilary Myers, LD | 1,349 |
| Kevin White, Green | 960 |
| Seth Colton, Ind. | 168 |

C. majority 7,054 (16.00%)
1.39% swing Lab. to C.
(2010: C. majority 5,821 (13.22%))

## REIGATE
E. 73,429 T. 51,349 (69.93%)

| | C. hold |
|---|---|
| Crispin Blunt, C. | 29,151 |
| Joseph Fox, UKIP | 6,817 |
| Ali Aklakul, Lab. | 6,578 |
| Anna Tarrant, LD | 5,369 |
| Jonathan Essex, Green | 3,434 |

C. majority 22,334 (43.49%)
2.86% swing C. to UKIP
(2010: C. majority 13,591 (27.19%))

## RIBBLE VALLEY
E. 77,873 T. 52,243 (67.09%)

| | C. hold |
|---|---|
| Nigel Evans, C. | 25,404 |
| David Hinder, Lab. | 11,798 |
| Shirley Parkinson, UKIP | 8,250 |
| Jackie Pearcey, LD | 2,756 |
| Graham Sowter, Green | 2,193 |
| David Brass, Ind. | 1,498 |
| Grace Astley, Ind. | 288 |
| Tony Johnson, IPAP | 56 |

C. majority 13,606 (26.04%)
1.10% swing C. to Lab.
(2010: C. majority 14,769 (28.25%))

## RICHMOND (YORKS)
E. 83,451 T. 53,999 (64.71%)

| | C. hold |
|---|---|
| *Rishi Sunak, C. | 27,744 |
| Matthew Cooke, UKIP | 8,194 |
| Mike Hill, Lab. | 7,124 |
| John Harris, LD | 3,465 |
| John Blackie, Ind. | 3,348 |
| Leslie Rowe, Green | 2,313 |
| Robin Scott, Ind. | 1,811 |

C. majority 19,550 (36.20%)
swing N/A
(2010: C. majority 23,336 (43.69%))

## RICHMOND PARK
E. 77,297 T. 59,101 (76.46%)

| | C. hold |
|---|---|
| Zac Goldsmith, C. | 34,404 |
| Robin Meltzer, LD | 11,389 |
| Sachin Patel, Lab. | 7,296 |
| Andree Frieze, Green | 3,548 |
| Sam Naz, UKIP | 2,464 |

C. majority 23,015 (38.94%)
16.02% swing LD to C.
(2010: C. majority 4,091 (6.90%))

## ROCHDALE
E. 79,170 T. 45,430 (57.38%)

| | Lab. hold |
|---|---|
| Simon Danczuk, Lab. | 20,961 |
| Mohammed Masud, UKIP | 8,519 |
| Azi Ahmed, C. | 7,742 |
| Andy Kelly, LD | 4,667 |
| Farooq Ahmed, Rochdale | 1,535 |
| Mark Hollinrake, Green | 1,382 |
| Kevin Bryan, NF | 433 |
| Mohammed Salim, IZB | 191 |

Lab. majority 12,442 (27.39%)
2.32% swing Lab. to UKIP
(2010: Lab. majority 889 (1.94%))

## ROCHESTER & STROOD
E. 79,000 T. 52,516 (66.48%)

| | C. gain |
|---|---|
| *Kelly Tolhurst, C. | 23,142 |
| Mark Reckless, UKIP | 16,009 |
| Naushabah Khan, Lab. | 10,396 |
| Clive Gregory, Green | 1,516 |
| Prue Bray, LD | 1,251 |
| Dan Burn, TUSC | 202 |

C. majority 7,133 (13.58%)
swing N/A
(2010: C. majority 9,953 (20.75%))
(2014: UKIP majority 2,920 (7.29%))

## ROCHFORD & SOUTHEND EAST
E. 71,935 T. 43,608 (60.62%)

| | C. hold |
|---|---|
| James Duddridge, C. | 20,241 |
| Ian Gilbert, Lab. | 10,765 |
| Floyd Waterworth, UKIP | 8,948 |
| Simon Cross, Green | 2,195 |
| Peter Gwizdala, LD | 1,459 |

C. majority 9,476 (21.73%)
2.41% swing C. to Lab.
(2010: C. majority 11,050 (26.54%))

## ROMFORD
E. 72,594 T. 49,178 (67.74%)

| | C. hold |
|---|---|
| Andrew Rosindell, C. | 25,067 |
| Gerard Batten, UKIP | 11,208 |
| Sam Gould, Lab. | 10,268 |
| Ian Sanderson, LD | 1,413 |
| Lorna Tooley, Green | 1,222 |

C. majority 13,859 (28.18%)
11.71% swing C. to UKIP
(2010: C. majority 16,954 (36.48%))

## ROMSEY & SOUTHAMPTON NORTH
E. 66,519 T. 48,398 (72.76%)

| | C. hold |
|---|---|
| Caroline Nokes, C. | 26,285 |
| Ben Nicholls, LD | 8,573 |
| Darren Paffey, Lab. | 5,749 |
| Sandra James, UKIP | 5,511 |
| Ian Callaghan, Green | 2,280 |

C. majority 17,712 (36.60%)
14.05% swing LD to C.
(2010: C. majority 4,156 (8.49%))

## ROSSENDALE & DARWEN
E. 84,011 T. 49,024 (58.35%)

|  |  |
|---|---|
|  | C. hold |
| Jake Berry, C. | 22,847 |
| Will Straw, Lab. | 17,193 |
| Clive Balchin, UKIP | 6,862 |
| Karen Pollard-Rylance, Green | 1,046 |
| Afzal Anwar, LD | 806 |
| Kevin Scranage, Ind. | 122 |
| Simon Thomas, TUSC | 103 |
| Shaun Hargreaves, Northern | 45 |

C. majority 5,654 (11.53%)
1.00% swing Lab. to C.
(2010: C. majority 4,493 (9.53%))

## ROTHER VALLEY
E. 74,275 T. 47,019 (63.30%)

|  |  |
|---|---|
|  | Lab. hold |
| Kevin Barron, Lab. | 20,501 |
| Allen Cowles, UKIP | 13,204 |
| Gareth Streeter, C. | 10,945 |
| Robert Teal, LD | 1,992 |
| Sharon Pilling, Eng. Dem. | 377 |

Lab. majority 7,297 (15.52%)
9.92% swing Lab. to UKIP
(2010: Lab. majority 5,866 (12.55%))

## ROTHERHAM
E. 63,698 T. 37,823 (59.38%)

|  |  |
|---|---|
|  | Lab. hold |
| Sarah Champion, Lab. | 19,860 |
| Jane Collins, UKIP | 11,414 |
| Sebastian Lowe, C. | 4,656 |
| Janice Middleton, LD | 1,093 |
| Pat McLaughlin, TUSC | 409 |
| Adam Walker, BNP | 225 |
| Dean Walker, Eng. Dem. | 166 |

Lab. majority 8,446 (22.33%)
8.19% swing Lab. to UKIP
(2010: Lab. majority 10,462
(27.89%)) (2012: Lab. majority 5,318
(24.79%))

## RUGBY
E. 79,557 T. 49,006 (61.60%)

|  |  |
|---|---|
|  | C. hold |
| Mark Pawsey, C. | 24,040 |
| Claire Edwards, Lab. | 13,695 |
| Gordon Davies, UKIP | 6,855 |
| Ed Goncalves, LD | 2,776 |
| Terence White, Green | 1,415 |
| Pete McLaren, TUSC | 225 |

C. majority 10,345 (21.11%)
4.23% swing Lab. to C.
(2010: C. majority 6,000 (12.64%))

## RUISLIP, NORTHWOOD & PINNER
E. 73,219 T. 51,222 (69.96%)

|  |  |
|---|---|
|  | C. hold |
| Nick Hurd, C. | 30,521 |
| Michael Borio, Lab. | 10,297 |
| Gerard Barry, UKIP | 5,598 |
| Joshua Dixon, LD | 2,537 |
| Karen Pillai, Green | 1,801 |
| Wally Kennedy, TUSC | 302 |
| Sockalingam Yogalingam, Nat. Lib. | 166 |

C. majority 20,224 (39.48%)
0.76% swing Lab. to C.
(2010: C. majority 19,060 (37.96%))

## RUNNYMEDE & WEYBRIDGE
E. 73,744 T. 50,052 (67.87%)

|  |  |
|---|---|
|  | C. hold |
| Philip Hammond, C. | 29,901 |
| Arran Neathey, Lab. | 7,767 |
| Joe Branco, UKIP | 6,951 |
| John Vincent, LD | 3,362 |
| Rustam Majainah, Green | 2,071 |

C. majority 22,134 (44.22%)
0.86% swing Lab. to C.
(2010: C. majority 16,509 (34.29%))

## RUSHCLIFFE
E. 73,294 T. 55,164 (75.26%)

|  |  |
|---|---|
|  | C. hold |
| Kenneth Clarke, C. | 28,354 |
| David Mellen, Lab. | 14,525 |
| Matthew Faithfull, UKIP | 5,943 |
| Richard Mallender, Green | 3,559 |
| Bob Johnston, LD | 2,783 |

C. majority 13,829 (25.07%)
2.69% swing C. to Lab.
(2010: C. majority 15,811 (29.45%))

## RUTLAND & MELTON
E. 79,789 T. 54,603 (68.43%)

|  |  |
|---|---|
|  | C. hold |
| Alan Duncan, C. | 30,383 |
| Richard Billington, UKIP | 8,678 |
| James Moore, Lab. | 8,383 |
| Ed Reynolds, LD | 4,407 |
| Alastair McQuillan, Green | 2,325 |
| Marilyn Gordon, Ind. | 427 |

C. majority 21,705 (39.75%)
3.40% swing C. to UKIP
(2010: C. majority 14,000 (25.35%))

## SAFFRON WALDEN
E. 80,615 T. 57,563 (71.40%)

|  |  |
|---|---|
|  | C. hold |
| Sir Alan Haselhurst, C. | 32,926 |
| Peter Day, UKIP | 7,935 |
| Jane Berney, Lab. | 6,791 |
| Mike Hibbs, LD | 6,079 |
| Karmel Stannard, Green | 2,174 |
| Heather Asker, Uttlesford | 1,658 |

C. majority 24,991 (43.42%)
3.98% swing C. to UKIP
(2010: C. majority 15,242 (28.03%))

## ST ALBANS
E. 72,507 T. 54,433 (75.07%)

|  |  |
|---|---|
|  | C. hold |
| Anne Main, C. | 25,392 |
| Kerry Pollard, Lab. | 12,660 |
| Sandy Walkington, LD | 10,076 |
| Chris Wright, UKIP | 4,271 |
| Jack Easton, Green | 2,034 |

C. majority 12,732 (23.39%)
0.11% swing Lab. to C.
(2010: C. majority 2,305 (4.36%))

## ST AUSTELL & NEWQUAY
E. 76,607 T. 50,361 (65.74%)

|  |  |
|---|---|
|  | C. gain |
| *Stephen Double, C. | 20,250 |
| Stephen Gilbert, LD | 12,077 |
| David Mathews, UKIP | 8,503 |
| Deborah Hopkins, Lab. | 5,150 |
| Steve Slade, Green | 2,318 |
| Dick Cole, Meb. Ker. | 2,063 |

C. majority 8,173 (16.23%)
9.50% swing LD to C.
(2010: LD majority 1,312 (2.78%))

## ST HELENS NORTH
E. 75,262 T. 46,256 (61.46%)

|  |  |
|---|---|
|  | Lab. hold |
| *Conor McGinn, Lab. | 26,378 |
| Paul Richardson, C. | 9,087 |
| Ian Smith, UKIP | 6,983 |
| Denise Aspinall, LD | 2,046 |
| Elizabeth Ward, Green | 1,762 |

Lab. majority 17,291 (37.38%)
3.99% swing C. to Lab.
(2010: Lab. majority 13,101
(29.40%))

## ST HELENS SOUTH & WHISTON
E. 77,720 T. 48,397 (62.27%)

|  |  |
|---|---|
|  | Lab. hold |
| *Marie Rimmer, Lab. | 28,950 |
| Gillian Keegan, C. | 7,707 |
| John Beirne, UKIP | 6,766 |
| Brian Spencer, LD | 2,737 |
| James Chan, Green | 2,237 |

Lab. majority 21,243 (43.89%)
4.42% swing C. to Lab.
(2010: Lab. majority 14,122
(30.65%))

## ST IVES
E. 65,570 T. 48,312 (73.68%)

|  |  |
|---|---|
|  | C. gain |
| *Derek Thomas, C. | 18,491 |
| Andrew George, LD | 16,022 |
| Graham Calderwood, UKIP | 5,720 |
| Cornelius Olivier, Lab. | 4,510 |
| Tim Andrewes, Green | 3,051 |
| Rob Simmons, Meb. Ker. | 518 |

C. majority 2,469 (5.11%)
4.43% swing LD to C.
(2010: LD majority 1,719 (3.74%))

## SALFORD & ECCLES
E. 74,290 T. 43,261 (58.23%)

| | | Lab. hold |
|---|---|---|
| *Rebecca Long Bailey, Lab. | | 21,364 |
| Greg Downes, C. | | 8,823 |
| Paul Doyle, UKIP | | 7,806 |
| Emma Van Dyke, Green | | 2,251 |
| Charlie Briggs, LD | | 1,614 |
| Bez Berry, Reality | | 703 |
| Noreen Bailey, TUSC | | 517 |
| Sam Clark, Pirate | | 183 |

Lab. majority 12,541 (28.99%)
4.67% swing C. to Lab.
(2010: Lab. majority 5,725 (13.78%))

## SALISBURY
E. 69,590 T. 50,705 (72.86%)

| | | C. hold |
|---|---|---|
| John Glen, C. | | 28,192 |
| Tom Corbin, Lab. | | 7,771 |
| Paul Martin, UKIP | | 6,152 |
| Reetendra Nath Banerji, LD | | 5,099 |
| Alison Craig, Green | | 2,762 |
| King Arthur Pendragon, Ind. | | 729 |

C. majority 20,421 (40.27%)
0.66% swing C. to Lab.
(2010: C. majority 5,966 (12.31%))

## SCARBOROUGH & WHITBY
E. 73,511 T. 47,739 (64.94%)

| | | C. hold |
|---|---|---|
| Robert Goodwill, C. | | 20,613 |
| Ian McInnes, Lab. | | 14,413 |
| Samuel Cross, UKIP | | 8,162 |
| David Malone, Green | | 2,185 |
| Michael Beckett, LD | | 2,159 |
| Juliet Boddington, Green Soc. | | 207 |

C. majority 6,200 (12.99%)
1.75% swing C. to Lab.
(2010: C. majority 8,130 (16.50%))

## SCUNTHORPE
E. 64,010 T. 36,941 (57.71%)

| | | Lab. hold |
|---|---|---|
| Nic Dakin, Lab. | | 15,393 |
| Jo Gideon, C. | | 12,259 |
| Stephen Howd, UKIP | | 6,329 |
| Des Comerford, Ind. | | 1,097 |
| Martin Dwyer, Green | | 887 |
| Simon Dodd, LD | | 770 |
| Paul Elsom, Ind. | | 206 |

Lab. majority 3,134 (8.48%)
0.80% swing C. to Lab.
(2010: Lab. majority 2,549 (6.88%))

## SEDGEFIELD
E. 62,860 T. 38,716 (61.59%)

| | | Lab. hold |
|---|---|---|
| Phil Wilson, Lab. | | 18,275 |
| Scott Wood, C. | | 11,432 |
| John Leathley, UKIP | | 6,426 |
| Stephen Glenn, LD | | 1,370 |
| Greg Robinson, Green | | 1,213 |

Lab. majority 6,843 (17.67%)
1.97% swing Lab. to C.
(2010: Lab. majority 8,696 (21.62%))

## SEFTON CENTRAL
E. 67,746 T. 49,021 (72.36%)

| | | Lab. hold |
|---|---|---|
| Bill Esterson, Lab. | | 26,359 |
| Valerie Allen, C. | | 14,513 |
| Tim Power, UKIP | | 4,879 |
| Paula Keaveney, LD | | 2,086 |
| Lindsay Melia, Green | | 1,184 |

Lab. majority 11,846 (24.17%)
8.10% swing C. to Lab.
(2010: Lab. majority 3,862 (7.97%))

## SELBY & AINSTY
E. 76,082 T. 52,804 (69.40%)

| | | C. hold |
|---|---|---|
| Nigel Adams, C. | | 27,725 |
| Mark Hayes, Lab. | | 14,168 |
| Colin Heath, UKIP | | 7,389 |
| Nicola Turner, LD | | 1,920 |
| Ian Richards, Green | | 1,465 |
| Ian Wilson, TUSC | | 137 |

C. majority 13,557 (25.67%)
0.98% swing Lab. to C.
(2010: C. majority 12,265 (23.71%))

## SEVENOAKS
E. 70,741 T. 50,124 (70.86%)

| | | C. hold |
|---|---|---|
| Michael Fallon, C. | | 28,531 |
| Steve Lindsay, UKIP | | 8,970 |
| Chris Clark, Lab. | | 6,448 |
| Alan Bullion, LD | | 3,937 |
| Amelie Boleyn, Green | | 2,238 |

C. majority 19,561 (39.03%)
7.10% swing C. to UKIP
(2010: C. majority 17,515 (35.45%))

## SHEFFIELD BRIGHTSIDE & HILLSBOROUGH
E. 73,090 T. 40,053 (54.80%)

| | | Lab. hold |
|---|---|---|
| *Harry Harpham, Lab. | | 22,663 |
| John Booker, UKIP | | 8,856 |
| Elise Dunweber, C. | | 4,407 |
| Jonathan Harston, LD | | 1,802 |
| Christine Gilligan Kubu, Green | | 1,712 |
| Maxine Bowler, TUSC | | 442 |
| Justin Saxton, Eng. Dem. | | 171 |

Lab. majority 13,807 (34.47%)
8.21% swing Lab. to UKIP
(2010: Lab. majority 13,632 (35.03%))

## SHEFFIELD CENTRAL
E. 77,014 T. 44,173 (57.36%)

| | | Lab. hold |
|---|---|---|
| Paul Blomfield, Lab. | | 24,308 |
| Jillian Creasy, Green | | 6,999 |
| Stephanie Roe, C. | | 4,917 |
| Joe Otten, LD | | 4,278 |
| Dominic Cook, UKIP | | 3,296 |
| Steve Andrew, Comm. | | 119 |
| Andy Halsall, Pirate | | 113 |
| Elizabeth Breed, Eng. Dem. | | 68 |
| Thom Brown, Above | | 42 |
| Michael Driver, WRP | | 33 |

Lab. majority 17,309 (39.18%)
swing N/A
(2010: Lab. majority 165 (0.40%))

## SHEFFIELD HALLAM
E. 73,658 T. 55,481 (75.32%)   LD hold

| | | |
|---|---|---|
| Nick Clegg, LD | | 22,215 |
| Oliver Coppard, Lab. | | 19,862 |
| Ian Walker, C. | | 7,544 |
| Joseph Jenkins, UKIP | | 3,575 |
| Peter Garbutt, Green | | 1,772 |
| Carlton Reeve, Ind. | | 249 |
| Steven Clegg, Eng. Dem. | | 167 |
| Jim Stop the fiasco Wild, Ind. | | 97 |

LD majority 2,353 (4.24%)
16.55% swing LD to Lab.
(2010: LD majority 15,284 (29.89%))

## SHEFFIELD HEELEY
E. 69,265 T. 42,048 (60.71%)

| | | Lab. hold |
|---|---|---|
| *Louise Haigh, Lab. | | 20,269 |
| Howard Denby, UKIP | | 7,315 |
| Stephen Castens, C. | | 6,792 |
| Simon Clement-Jones, LD | | 4,746 |
| Rita Wilcock, Green | | 2,566 |
| Alan Munro, TUSC | | 238 |
| David Haslett, Eng. Dem. | | 122 |

Lab. majority 12,954 (30.81%)
4.02% swing Lab. to UKIP
(2010: Lab. majority 5,807 (14.21%))

## SHEFFIELD SOUTH EAST
E. 70,422 T. 41,685 (59.19%)

| | | Lab. hold |
|---|---|---|
| Clive Betts, Lab. | | 21,439 |
| Steve Winstone, UKIP | | 9,128 |
| Matt Sleat, C. | | 7,242 |
| Gail Smith, LD | | 2,226 |
| Linda Duckenfield, Green | | 1,117 |
| Jen Battersby, CISTA | | 207 |
| Ian Whitehouse, TUSC | | 185 |
| Matthew Roberts, Eng. Dem. | | 141 |

Lab. majority 12,311 (29.53%)
7.31% swing Lab. to UKIP
(2010: Lab. majority 10,505 (25.37%))

SHERWOOD
E. 73,334 T. 50,698 (69.13%)

|  | C. hold |
|---|---|
| Mark Spencer, C. | 22,833 |
| Leonie Mathers, Lab. | 18,186 |
| Sally Chadd, UKIP | 7,399 |
| Lydia Davies-Bright, Green | 1,108 |
| Dan Mosley, LD | 1,094 |
| Dave Perkins, Class War | 78 |

C. majority 4,647 (9.17%)
4.36% swing Lab. to C.
(2010: C. majority 214 (0.44%))

SHIPLEY
E. 70,466 T. 50,542 (71.73%)

|  | C. hold |
|---|---|
| Philip Davies, C. | 25,269 |
| Steve Clapcote, Lab. | 15,645 |
| Waqas Khan, UKIP | 4,479 |
| Kevin Warnes, Green | 2,657 |
| Andrew Martin, LD | 1,949 |
| Darren Hill, Yorks | 543 |

C. majority 9,624 (19.04%)
0.54% swing C. to Lab.
(2010: C. majority 9,944 (20.12%))

SHREWSBURY & ATCHAM
E. 76,460 T. 54,102 (70.76%)

|  | C. hold |
|---|---|
| Daniel Kawczynski, C. | 24,628 |
| Laura Davies, Lab. | 15,063 |
| Suzanne Evans, UKIP | 7,813 |
| Christine Tinker, LD | 4,268 |
| Emma Bullard, Green | 2,247 |
| Stirling McNeillie, Atom | 83 |

C. majority 9,565 (17.68%)
2.85% swing C. to Lab.
(2010: C. majority 7,944 (14.98%))

SHROPSHIRE NORTH
E. 78,910 T. 52,573 (66.62%)

|  | C. hold |
|---|---|
| Owen Paterson, C. | 27,041 |
| Graeme Currie, Lab. | 10,547 |
| Andrea Allen, UKIP | 9,262 |
| Tom Thornhill, LD | 3,148 |
| Duncan Kerr, Green | 2,575 |

C. majority 16,494 (31.37%)
0.98% swing C. to Lab.
(2010: C. majority 15,828 (30.52%))

SITTINGBOURNE & SHEPPEY
E. 76,018 T. 49,378 (64.96%)

|  | C. hold |
|---|---|
| Gordon Henderson, C. | 24,425 |
| Richard Palmer, UKIP | 12,257 |
| Guy Nicholson, Lab. | 9,673 |
| Keith Nevols, LD | 1,563 |
| Gary Miller, Green | 1,185 |
| Mad Mike Young, Loony | 275 |

C. majority 12,168 (24.64%)
10.02% swing C. to UKIP
(2010: C. majority 12,383 (25.49%))

SKIPTON & RIPON
E. 76,243 T. 54,559 (71.56%)

|  | C. hold |
|---|---|
| Julian Smith, C. | 30,248 |
| Malcolm Birks, Lab. | 9,487 |
| Alan Henderson, UKIP | 7,651 |
| Jacquie Bell, LD | 4,057 |
| Andy Brown, Green | 3,116 |

C. majority 20,761 (38.05%)
1.25% swing C. to Lab.
(2010: C. majority 9,950 (18.18%))

SLEAFORD & NORTH HYKEHAM
E. 88,188 T. 61,944 (70.24%)

|  | C. hold |
|---|---|
| Stephen Phillips, C. | 34,805 |
| Jason Pandya-Wood, Lab. | 10,690 |
| Steven Hopkins, UKIP | 9,716 |
| Matthew Holden, LD | 3,500 |
| Marianne Overton, Lincs Ind. | 3,233 |

C. majority 24,115 (38.93%)
2.11% swing Lab. to C.
(2010: C. majority 19,905 (33.44%))

SLOUGH
E. 86,366 T. 48,275 (55.90%)

|  | Lab. hold |
|---|---|
| Fiona Mactaggart, Lab. | 23,421 |
| Gurcharan Singh, C. | 16,085 |
| Diana Coad, UKIP | 6,274 |
| Tom McCann, LD | 1,275 |
| Julian Edmonds, Green | 1,220 |

Lab. majority 7,336 (15.20%)
1.81% swing C. to Lab.
(2010: Lab. majority 5,523 (11.57%))

SOLIHULL
E. 77,251 T. 54,779 (70.91%)

|  | C. gain |
|---|---|
| *Julian Knight, C. | 26,956 |
| Lorely Burt, LD | 14,054 |
| Phil Henrick, UKIP | 6,361 |
| Nigel Knowles, Lab. | 5,693 |
| Howard Allen, Green | 1,632 |
| Mike Nattrass, IE | 50 |
| Matthew Ward, DP | 33 |

C. majority 12,902 (23.55%)
11.94% swing LD to C.
(2010: LD majority 175 (0.32%))

SOMERSET NORTH
E. 80,115 T. 58,942 (73.57%)

|  | C. hold |
|---|---|
| Liam Fox, C. | 31,540 |
| Greg Chambers, Lab. | 8,441 |
| Ian Kealey, UKIP | 7,669 |
| Marcus Kravis, LD | 7,486 |
| David Derbyshire, Green | 3,806 |

C. majority 23,099 (39.19%)
0.52% swing Lab. to C.
(2010: C. majority 7,862 (13.57%))

SOMERSET NORTH EAST
E. 69,380 T. 51,110 (73.67%)

|  | C. hold |
|---|---|
| Jacob Rees-Mogg, C. | 25,439 |
| Todd Foreman, Lab. | 12,690 |
| Ernie Blaber, UKIP | 6,150 |
| Wera Hobhouse, LD | 4,029 |
| Katy Boyce, Green | 2,802 |

C. majority 12,749 (24.94%)
7.67% swing Lab. to C.
(2010: C. majority 4,914 (9.60%))

SOMERTON & FROME
E. 83,527 T. 60,309 (72.20%)

|  | C. gain |
|---|---|
| *David Warburton, C. | 31,960 |
| David Rendel, LD | 11,692 |
| Alan Dimmick, UKIP | 6,439 |
| Theo Simon, Green | 5,434 |
| David Oakensen, Lab. | 4,419 |
| Ian Angell, Ind. | 365 |

C. majority 20,268 (33.61%)
18.30% swing LD to C.
(2010: LD majority 1,817 (3.00%))

SOUTH HOLLAND & THE
DEEPINGS
E. 77,015 T. 49,207 (63.89%)

|  | C. hold |
|---|---|
| John Hayes, C. | 29,303 |
| David Parsons, UKIP | 10,736 |
| Matthew Mahabadi, Lab. | 6,122 |
| Daniel Wilshire, Green | 1,580 |
| George Smid, LD | 1,466 |

C. majority 18,567 (37.73%)
7.43% swing C. to UKIP
(2010: C. majority 21,880 (43.60%))

SOUTH RIBBLE
E. 76,489 T. 52,370 (68.47%)

|  | C. hold |
|---|---|
| *Seema Kennedy, C. | 24,313 |
| Veronica Bennett, Lab. | 18,368 |
| David Gallagher, UKIP | 7,377 |
| Sue McGuire, LD | 2,312 |

C. majority 5,945 (11.35%)
0.28% swing Lab. to C.
(2010: C. majority 5,554 (10.79%))

SOUTH SHIELDS
E. 62,730 T. 36,265 (57.81%)

|  | Lab. hold |
|---|---|
| Emma Lewell-Buck, Lab. | 18,589 |
| Norman Dennis, UKIP | 7,975 |
| Robert Oliver, C. | 6,021 |
| Shirley Ford, Green | 1,614 |
| Lisa Nightingale, Ind. | 1,427 |
| Gita Gordon, LD | 639 |

Lab. majority 10,614 (29.27%)
swing N/A
(2010: Lab. majority 11,109
(30.42%)) (2013: Lab. majority 6,505
(26.30%))

## SOUTHAMPTON ITCHEN
E. 72,309 T. 44,710 (61.83%)

|  |  | C. gain |
| --- | --- | --- |
| *Royston Smith, C. | | 18,656 |
| Rowenna Davis, Lab. Co-op | | 16,340 |
| Kim Rose, UKIP | | 6,010 |
| John Spottiswoode, Green | | 1,876 |
| Eleanor Bell, LD | | 1,595 |
| Sue Atkins, TUSC | | 233 |

C. majority 2,316 (5.18%)
2.81% swing Lab. to C.
(2010: Lab. majority 192 (0.43%))

## SOUTHAMPTON TEST
E. 70,285 T. 43,652 (62.11%)

|  |  | Lab. hold |
| --- | --- | --- |
| Alan Whitehead, Lab. | | 18,017 |
| Jeremy Moulton, C. | | 14,207 |
| Pearline Hingston, UKIP | | 5,566 |
| Angela Mawle, Green | | 2,568 |
| Adrian Ford, LD | | 2,121 |
| Chris Davis, Ind. | | 770 |
| Nick Chaffey, TUSC | | 403 |

Lab. majority 3,810 (8.73%)
1.63% swing C. to Lab.
(2010: Lab. majority 2,413 (5.46%))

## SOUTHEND WEST
E. 66,876 T. 44,509 (66.55%)

|  |  | C. hold |
| --- | --- | --- |
| David Amess, C. | | 22,175 |
| Julian Ware-Lane, Lab. | | 8,154 |
| Brian Otridge, UKIP | | 7,803 |
| Paul Collins, LD | | 4,129 |
| Jonathan Fuller, Green | | 2,083 |
| Jeremy Moss, Eng. Dem. | | 165 |

C. majority 14,021 (31.50%)
0.57% swing C. to Lab.
(2010: C. majority 7,270 (16.67%))

## SOUTHPORT
E. 67,328 T. 44,101 (65.50%)   LD
hold

| John Pugh, LD | | 13,652 |
| --- | --- | --- |
| Damien Moore, C. | | 12,330 |
| Liz Savage, Lab. | | 8,468 |
| Terry Durrance, UKIP | | 7,429 |
| Laurence Rankin, Green | | 1,230 |
| Jacqueline Barlow, Southport | | 992 |

LD majority 1,322 (3.00%)
5.38% swing LD to C.
(2010: LD majority 6,024 (13.77%))

## SPELTHORNE
E. 71,592 T. 49,079 (68.55%)

|  |  | C. hold |
| --- | --- | --- |
| Kwasi Kwarteng, C. | | 24,386 |
| Redvers Cunningham, UKIP | | 10,234 |
| Rebecca Geach, Lab. | | 9,114 |
| Rosie Shimell, LD | | 3,163 |
| Paul Jacobs, Green | | 1,724 |
| Juliet Griffith, ND | | 230 |
| Paul Couchman, TUSC | | 228 |

C. majority 14,152 (28.84%)
4.87% swing C. to UKIP
(2010: C. majority 10,019 (21.18%))

## STAFFORD
E. 68,705 T. 48,767 (70.98%)

|  |  | C. hold |
| --- | --- | --- |
| Jeremy Lefroy, C. | | 23,606 |
| Kate Godfrey, Lab. | | 14,429 |
| Edward Whitfield, UKIP | | 6,293 |
| Karen Howell, NHAP | | 1,701 |
| Mike Shone, Green | | 1,390 |
| Keith Miller, LD | | 1,348 |

C. majority 9,177 (18.82%)
3.98% swing Lab. to C.
(2010: C. majority 5,460 (10.87%))

## STAFFORDSHIRE MOORLANDS
E. 63,104 T. 42,587 (67.49%)

|  |  | C. hold |
| --- | --- | --- |
| Karen Bradley, C. | | 21,770 |
| Trudie McGuinness, Lab. | | 11,596 |
| George Langley-Poole, UKIP | | 6,236 |
| John Redfern, LD | | 1,759 |
| Brian Smith, Green | | 1,226 |

C. majority 10,174 (23.89%)
4.31% swing Lab. to C.
(2010: C. majority 6,689 (15.27%))

## STAFFORDSHIRE SOUTH
E. 84,243 T. 49,598 (58.87%)

|  |  | C. hold |
| --- | --- | --- |
| Gavin Williamson, C. | | 29,478 |
| Kevin McElduff, Lab. | | 9,107 |
| Lyndon Jones, UKIP | | 8,267 |
| Robert Woodthorpe Browne, LD | | 1,448 |
| Claire McIlvenna, Green | | 1,298 |

C. majority 20,371 (41.07%)
4.09% swing Lab. to C.
(2010: C. majority 16,590 (32.89%))

## STALYBRIDGE & HYDE
E. 69,081 T. 41,034 (59.40%)

|  |  | Lab. Co-op hold |
| --- | --- | --- |
| Jonathan Reynolds, Lab. Co-op | | 18,447 |
| Martin Riley, C. | | 11,761 |
| Angela McManus, UKIP | | 7,720 |
| Jenny Ross, Green | | 1,850 |
| Pete Flynn, LD | | 1,256 |

Lab. Co-op majority 6,686 (16.29%)
4.79% swing C. to Lab.
(2010: Lab. majority 2,744 (6.71%))

## STEVENAGE
E. 70,597 T. 47,799 (67.71%)

|  |  | C. hold |
| --- | --- | --- |
| Stephen McPartland, C. | | 21,291 |
| Sharon Taylor, Lab. Co-op | | 16,336 |
| David Collins, UKIP | | 6,864 |
| Susan Van De Ven, LD | | 1,582 |
| Graham White, Green | | 1,369 |
| Trevor Palmer, TUSC | | 175 |
| Charles Vickers, Eng. Dem. | | 115 |
| David Cox, Ind. | | 67 |

C. majority 4,955 (10.37%)
1.18% swing Lab. to C.
(2010: C. majority 3,578 (8.01%))

## STOCKPORT
E. 63,931 T. 39,649 (62.02%)

|  |  | Lab. hold |
| --- | --- | --- |
| Ann Coffey, Lab. | | 19,771 |
| Daniel Hamilton, C. | | 9,710 |
| Steven Woolfe, UKIP | | 5,206 |
| Daniel Hawthorne, LD | | 3,034 |
| Gary Lawson, Green | | 1,753 |
| John Pearson, LU | | 175 |

Lab. majority 10,061 (25.38%)
4.02% swing C. to Lab.
(2010: Lab. majority 6,784 (17.34%))

## STOCKTON NORTH
E. 66,126 T. 39,571 (59.84%)

|  |  | Lab. hold |
| --- | --- | --- |
| Alex Cunningham, Lab. | | 19,436 |
| Chris Daniels, C. | | 11,069 |
| Mandy Boylett, UKIP | | 7,581 |
| Anthony Sycamore, LD | | 884 |
| John Tait, NE | | 601 |

Lab. majority 8,367 (21.14%)
2.12% swing C. to Lab.
(2010: Lab. majority 6,676 (16.90%))

## STOCKTON SOUTH
E. 75,109 T. 51,797 (68.96%)

|  |  | C. hold |
| --- | --- | --- |
| James Wharton, C. | | 24,221 |
| Louise Baldock, Lab. Co-op | | 19,175 |
| Ted Strike, UKIP | | 5,480 |
| Drew Durning, LD | | 1,366 |
| Jacqui Lovell, Green | | 952 |
| Steve Walmsley, IASI | | 603 |

C. majority 5,046 (9.74%)
4.54% swing C. to Lab.
(2010: C. majority 332 (0.66%))

## STOKE-ON-TRENT CENTRAL
E. 62,250 T. 31,084 (49.93%)

|  |  | Lab. hold |
| --- | --- | --- |
| Tristram Hunt, Lab. | | 12,220 |
| Mick Harold, UKIP | | 7,041 |
| Liam Ascough, C. | | 7,008 |
| Mark Breeze, Ind. | | 2,120 |
| Zulfiqar Ali, LD | | 1,296 |
| Jan Zablocki, Green | | 1,123 |
| Ali Majid, CISTA | | 244 |
| Paul Toussaint, Ubuntu | | 32 |

Lab. majority 5,179 (16.66%)
8.92% swing Lab. to UKIP
(2010: Lab. majority 5,566 (17.14%))

## STOKE-ON-TRENT NORTH
E. 72,689 T. 38,654 (53.18%)

|  |  | Lab. hold |
| --- | --- | --- |
| *Ruth Smeeth, Lab. | | 15,429 |
| Ben Adams, C. | | 10,593 |
| Geoffrey Locke, UKIP | | 9,542 |
| Paul Roberts, LD | | 1,137 |
| Sean Adam, Green | | 1,091 |
| John Millward, Ind. | | 508 |
| Craig Pond, Ind. | | 354 |

Lab. majority 4,836 (12.51%)
3.99% swing Lab. to C.
(2010: Lab. majority 8,235 (20.49%))

## STOKE-ON-TRENT SOUTH
E. 68,788 T. 39,107 (56.85%)

| | Lab. hold |
|---|---|
| Rob Flello, Lab. | 15,319 |
| Joe Rich, C. | 12,780 |
| Tariq Mahmood, UKIP | 8,298 |
| Peter Andras, LD | 1,309 |
| Luke Bellamy, Green | 1,029 |
| Matt Wright, TUSC | 372 |

Lab. majority 2,539 (6.49%)
1.94% swing Lab. to C.
(2010: Lab. majority 4,130 (10.36%))

## STONE
E. 67,339 T. 47,031 (69.84%)

| | C. hold |
|---|---|
| Bill Cash, C. | 25,733 |
| Sam Hale, Lab. | 9,483 |
| Andrew Illsley, UKIP | 7,620 |
| Martin Lewis, LD | 2,473 |
| Wenslie Naylon, Green | 1,191 |
| John Coutouvidis, Ind. | 531 |

C. majority 16,250 (34.55%)
2.33% swing Lab. to C.
(2010: C. majority 13,292 (28.14%))

## STOURBRIDGE
E. 69,077 T. 46,029 (66.63%)

| | C. hold |
|---|---|
| Margot James, C. | 21,195 |
| Pete Lowe, Lab. | 14,501 |
| James Carver, UKIP | 7,774 |
| Chris Bramall, LD | 1,538 |
| Christian Kiever, Green | 1,021 |

C. majority 6,694 (14.54%)
1.81% swing Lab. to C.
(2010: C. majority 5,164 (10.93%))

## STRATFORD-ON-AVON
E. 70,914 T. 51,459 (72.57%)

| | C. hold |
|---|---|
| Nadhim Zahawi, C. | 29,674 |
| Edward Fila, UKIP | 6,798 |
| Jeff Kenner, Lab. | 6,677 |
| Elizabeth Adams, LD | 6,182 |
| Dominic Giles, Green | 2,128 |

C. majority 22,876 (44.45%)
1.72% swing C. to UKIP
(2010: C. majority 11,346 (22.45%))

## STREATHAM
E. 78,673 T. 49,933 (63.47%)

| | Lab. hold |
|---|---|
| Chuka Umunna, Lab. | 26,474 |
| Kim Caddy, C. | 12,540 |
| Amna Ahmad, LD | 4,491 |
| Jonathan Bartley, Green | 4,421 |
| Bruce Machan, UKIP | 1,602 |
| Artificial Beast, CISTA | 192 |
| Unjum Mirza, TUSC | 164 |
| Deon Gayle, WRP | 49 |

Lab. majority 13,934 (27.91%)
1.72% swing C. to Lab.
(2010: Lab. majority 3,259 (6.96%))

## STRETFORD & URMSTON
E. 69,490 T. 46,386 (66.75%)

| | Lab. hold |
|---|---|
| Kate Green, Lab. | 24,601 |
| Lisa Cooke, C. | 12,916 |
| Kalvin Chapman, UKIP | 5,068 |
| Geraldine Coggins, Green | 2,187 |
| Louise Ankers, LD | 1,362 |
| Paul Bradley-Law, Whig | 169 |
| Paul Carson, PP UK | 83 |

Lab. majority 11,685 (25.19%)
2.65% swing C. to Lab.
(2010: Lab. majority 8,935 (19.90%))

## STROUD
E. 80,522 T. 60,819 (75.53%)

| | C. hold |
|---|---|
| Neil Carmichael, C. | 27,813 |
| David Drew, Lab. Co-op | 22,947 |
| Caroline Stephens, UKIP | 4,848 |
| Sarah Lunnon, Green | 2,779 |
| Adrian Walker-Smith, LD | 2,086 |
| Rich Wilson, Ind. | 246 |
| David Michael, FPT | 100 |

C. majority 4,866 (8.00%)
2.88% swing Lab. to C.
(2010: C. majority 1,299 (2.24%))

## SUFFOLK CENTRAL & IPSWICH NORTH
E. 78,782 T. 54,089 (68.66%)

| | C. hold |
|---|---|
| Daniel Poulter, C. | 30,317 |
| Jack Abbott, Lab. | 10,173 |
| Mark Cole, UKIP | 7,459 |
| Jon Neal, LD | 3,314 |
| Rhodri Griffiths, Green | 2,664 |
| Tony Holyoak, Eng. Dem. | 162 |

C. majority 20,144 (37.24%)
1.32% swing Lab. to C.
(2010: C. majority 13,786 (25.81%))

## SUFFOLK COASTAL
E. 78,782 T. 55,594 (70.57%)

| | C. hold |
|---|---|
| Therese Coffey, C. | 28,855 |
| Russell Whiting, Lab. | 10,013 |
| Daryll Pitcher, UKIP | 8,655 |
| James Sandbach, LD | 4,777 |
| Rachel Smith-Lyte, Green | 3,294 |

C. majority 18,842 (33.89%)
1.77% swing Lab. to C.
(2010: C. majority 9,128 (16.63%))

## SUFFOLK SOUTH
E. 73,220 T. 51,907 (70.89%)

| | C. hold |
|---|---|
| *James Cartlidge, C. | 27,546 |
| Jane Basham, Lab. | 10,001 |
| Steven Whalley, UKIP | 7,897 |
| Grace Weaver, LD | 4,044 |
| Robert Lindsay, Green | 2,253 |
| Stephen Todd, CPA | 166 |

C. majority 17,545 (33.80%)
0.19% swing Lab. to C.
(2010: C. majority 8,689 (16.90%))

## SUFFOLK WEST
E. 76,197 T. 49,232 (64.61%)

| | C. hold |
|---|---|
| Matthew Hancock, C. | 25,684 |
| Julian Flood, UKIP | 10,700 |
| Michael Jefferys, Lab. | 8,604 |
| Elfreda Tealby-Watson, LD | 2,465 |
| Niall Pettitt, Green | 1,779 |

C. majority 14,984 (30.44%)
6.85% swing C. to UKIP
(2010: C. majority 13,050 (27.14%))

## SUNDERLAND CENTRAL
E. 72,933 T. 41,762 (57.26%)

| | Lab. hold |
|---|---|
| Julie Elliott, Lab. | 20,959 |
| Jeffrey Townsend, C. | 9,780 |
| Bryan Foster, UKIP | 7,997 |
| Rachel Featherstone, Green | 1,706 |
| Adrian Page, LD | 1,105 |
| Joseph Young, ND | 215 |

Lab. majority 11,179 (26.77%)
5.47% swing C. to Lab.
(2010: Lab. majority 6,725 (15.84%))

## SURREY EAST
E. 79,654 T. 56,103 (70.43%)

| | C. hold |
|---|---|
| Sam Gyimah, C. | 32,211 |
| Helena Windsor, UKIP | 9,553 |
| Matt Wilson, Lab. | 6,627 |
| David Lee, LD | 5,189 |
| Nicky Dodgson, Green | 2,159 |
| Sandy Pratt, Ind. | 364 |

C. majority 22,658 (40.39%)
4.73% swing C. to UKIP
(2010: C. majority 16,874 (30.88%))

## SURREY HEATH
E. 79,515 T. 54,431 (68.45%)

| | C. hold |
|---|---|
| Michael Gove, C. | 32,582 |
| Paul Chapman, UKIP | 7,778 |
| Laween Atroshi, Lab. | 6,100 |
| Ann-Marie Barker, LD | 4,937 |
| Kimberley Lawson, Green | 2,400 |
| Juliana Brimicombe, Ch. P. | 361 |
| Bob Smith, Ind. | 273 |

C. majority 24,804 (45.57%)
2.88% swing C. to UKIP
(2010: C. majority 17,289 (31.81%))

## SURREY SOUTH WEST
E. 77,050 T. 57,119 (74.13%)

| | C. hold |
|---|---|
| Jeremy Hunt, C. | 34,199 |
| Mark Webber, UKIP | 5,643 |
| Howard Kaye, Lab. | 5,415 |
| Louise Irvine, NHAP | 4,851 |
| Patrick Haveron, LD | 3,586 |
| Susan Ryland, Green | 3,105 |
| Paul Robinson, S. New | 320 |

C. majority 28,556 (49.99%)
3.05% swing C. to UKIP
(2010: C. majority 16,318 (28.50%))

SUSSEX MID
E. 79,520 T. 57,492 (72.30%)

|  |  | C. hold |
|---|---|---|
| Nicholas Soames, C. |  | 32,268 |
| Greg Mountain, Lab. |  | 7,982 |
| Toby Brothers, UKIP |  | 6,898 |
| Daisy Cooper, LD |  | 6,604 |
| Miranda Diboll, Green |  | 2,453 |
| Beki Adam, Ind. |  | 958 |
| Baron Von Thunderclap, Loony |  | 329 |

C. majority 24,286 (42.24%)
0.94% swing C. to Lab.
(2010: C. majority 7,402 (13.25%))

SUTTON & CHEAM
E. 69,160 T. 49,905 (72.16%)

|  |  | C. gain |
|---|---|---|
| *Paul Scully, C. |  | 20,732 |
| Paul Burstow, LD |  | 16,811 |
| Emily Brothers, Lab. |  | 5,546 |
| Angus Dalgleish, UKIP |  | 5,341 |
| Maeve Tomlinson, Green |  | 1,051 |
| Dave Ash, NHAP |  | 345 |
| Pauline Gorman, TUSC |  | 79 |

C. majority 3,921 (7.86%)
5.59% swing LD to C.
(2010: LD majority 1,608 (3.31%))

SUTTON COLDFIELD
E. 74,956 T. 50,854 (67.85%)

|  |  | C. hold |
|---|---|---|
| Andrew Mitchell, C. |  | 27,782 |
| Rob Pocock, Lab. |  | 11,365 |
| Marcus Brown, UKIP |  | 7,489 |
| Richard Brighton-Knight, LD |  | 2,627 |
| David Ratcliff, Green |  | 1,426 |
| Mark Sleigh, Ubuntu |  | 165 |

C. majority 16,417 (32.28%)
0.67% swing C. to Lab.
(2010: C. majority 17,005 (33.61%))

SWINDON NORTH
E. 81,005 T. 52,242 (64.49%)

|  |  | C. hold |
|---|---|---|
| Justin Tomlinson, C. |  | 26,295 |
| Mark Dempsey, Lab. |  | 14,509 |
| James Faulkner, UKIP |  | 8,011 |
| Poppy Hebden-Leeder, Green |  | 1,723 |
| Janet Ellard, LD |  | 1,704 |

C. majority 11,786 (22.56%)
4.26% swing Lab. to C.
(2010: C. majority 7,060 (14.04%))

SWINDON SOUTH
E. 73,956 T. 49,263 (66.61%)

|  |  | C. hold |
|---|---|---|
| Robert Buckland, C. |  | 22,777 |
| Anne Snelgrove, Lab. |  | 16,992 |
| John Short, UKIP |  | 5,920 |
| Damon Hooton, LD |  | 1,817 |
| Talis Kimberley-Fairbourn, Green |  | 1,757 |

C. majority 5,785 (11.74%)
2.11% swing Lab. to C.
(2010: C. majority 3,544 (7.52%))

TAMWORTH
E. 71,912 T. 47,174 (65.60%)

|  |  | C. hold |
|---|---|---|
| Christopher Pincher, C. |  | 23,606 |
| Carol Dean, Lab. |  | 12,304 |
| Jan Higgins, UKIP |  | 8,727 |
| Jenny Pinkett, LD |  | 1,427 |
| Nicola Holmes, Green |  | 1,110 |

C. majority 11,302 (23.96%)
5.42% swing Lab. to C.
(2010: C. majority 6,090 (13.13%))

TATTON
E. 64,512 T. 45,298 (70.22%)

|  |  | C. hold |
|---|---|---|
| George Osborne, C. |  | 26,552 |
| David Pinto-Duschinsky, Lab. |  | 8,311 |
| Stuart Hutton, UKIP |  | 4,871 |
| Gareth Wilson, LD |  | 3,850 |
| Tina Louise Rothery, Green |  | 1,714 |

C. majority 18,241 (40.27%)
1.47% swing Lab. to C.
(2010: C. majority 14,487 (32.03%))

TAUNTON DEANE
E. 81,830 T. 57,887 (70.74%)

|  |  | C. gain |
|---|---|---|
| *Rebecca Pow, C. |  | 27,849 |
| Rachel Gilmour, LD |  | 12,358 |
| Laura Bailhache, UKIP |  | 6,921 |
| Neil Guild, Lab. |  | 5,347 |
| Clive Martin, Green |  | 2,630 |
| Mike Rigby, Ind. |  | 2,568 |
| Stephen German, TUSC |  | 118 |
| Bruce Gauld, Ind. |  | 96 |

C. majority 15,491 (26.76%)
16.81% swing LD to C.
(2010: LD majority 3,993 (6.87%))

TELFORD
E. 66,166 T. 40,645 (61.43%)

|  |  | C. gain |
|---|---|---|
| *Lucy Allan, C. |  | 16,094 |
| David Wright, Lab. |  | 15,364 |
| Denis Allen, UKIP |  | 7,330 |
| Peter Hawkins, Green |  | 930 |
| Ian Croll, LD |  | 927 |

C. majority 730 (1.80%)
2.08% swing Lab. to C.
(2010: Lab. majority 978 (2.37%))

TEWKESBURY
E. 78,500 T. 55,344 (70.50%)

|  |  | C. hold |
|---|---|---|
| Laurence Robertson, C. |  | 30,176 |
| Ed Buxton, Lab. |  | 8,204 |
| Alistair Cameron, LD |  | 7,629 |
| Stuart Adair, UKIP |  | 7,128 |
| Jemma Clarke, Green |  | 2,207 |

C. majority 21,972 (39.70%)
2.04% swing Lab. to C.
(2010: C. majority 6,310 (11.69%))

THANET NORTH
E. 70,504 T. 47,053 (66.74%)

|  |  | C. hold |
|---|---|---|
| Roger Gale, C. |  | 23,045 |
| Piers Wauchope, UKIP |  | 12,097 |
| Frances Rehal, Lab. |  | 8,411 |
| Ed Targett, Green |  | 1,719 |
| George Cunningham, LD |  | 1,645 |
| Cemanthe McKenzie, Thanet |  | 136 |

C. majority 10,948 (23.27%)
11.45% swing C. to UKIP
(2010: C. majority 13,528 (31.21%))

THANET SOUTH
E. 70,182 T. 49,401 (70.39%)

|  |  | C. hold |
|---|---|---|
| *Craig Mackinlay, C. |  | 18,838 |
| Nigel Farage, UKIP |  | 16,026 |
| Will Scobie, Lab. |  | 11,740 |
| Ian Driver, Green |  | 1,076 |
| Russ Timpson, LD |  | 932 |
| Al Murray, FUKP |  | 318 |
| Ruth Bailey, Manston |  | 191 |
| Nigel Askew, Reality |  | 126 |
| Grahame Birchall, Thanet |  | 63 |
| Dean McCastree, Ind. |  | 61 |
| Zebadiah Abu-Obadiah, Zeb |  | 30 |

C. majority 2,812 (5.69%)
18.40% swing C. to UKIP
(2010: C. majority 7,617 (16.58%))

THIRSK & MALTON
E. 77,451 T. 52,365 (67.61%)

|  |  | C. hold |
|---|---|---|
| *Kevin Hollinrake, C. |  | 27,545 |
| Alan Avery, Lab. |  | 8,089 |
| Toby Horton, UKIP |  | 7,805 |
| Dinah Keal, LD |  | 4,703 |
| Chris Newsam, Green |  | 2,404 |
| John Clark, Lib. |  | 1,127 |
| Philip Tate, Ind. |  | 692 |

C. majority 19,456 (37.15%)
1.08% swing C. to Lab.
(2010: C. majority 11,281 (29.58%))

THORNBURY & YATE
E. 65,884 T. 48,570 (73.72%)

|  |  | C. gain |
|---|---|---|
| *Luke Hall, C. |  | 19,924 |
| Steve Webb, LD |  | 18,429 |
| Russ Martin, UKIP |  | 5,126 |
| Hadleigh Roberts, Lab. |  | 3,775 |
| Iain Hamilton, Green |  | 1,316 |

C. majority 1,495 (3.08%)
8.92% swing LD to C.
(2010: LD majority 7,116 (14.76%))

THURROCK
E. 77,569 T. 49,564 (63.90%)

|  |  | C. hold |
|---|---|---|
| Jackie Doyle-Price, C. | | 16,692 |
| Polly Billington, Lab. | | 16,156 |
| Tim Aker, UKIP | | 15,718 |
| Rhodri Jamieson-Ball, LD | | 644 |
| Jamie Barnes, CISTA | | 244 |
| Daniel Munyambu, ND | | 79 |
| Aba Kristilolu, AP | | 31 |

C. majority 536 (1.08%)
0.44% swing Lab. to C.
(2010: C. majority 92 (0.20%))

TIVERTON & HONITON
E. 76,270 T. 53,763 (70.49%)

|  |  | C. hold |
|---|---|---|
| Neil Parish, C. | | 29,030 |
| Graham Smith, UKIP | | 8,857 |
| Caroline Kolek, Lab. | | 6,835 |
| Stephen Kearney, LD | | 5,626 |
| Paul Edwards, Green | | 3,415 |

C. majority 20,173 (37.52%)
3.41% swing C. to UKIP
(2010: C. majority 9,320 (16.98%))

TONBRIDGE & MALLING
E. 74,877 T. 53,670 (71.68%)

|  |  | C. hold |
|---|---|---|
| *Thomas Tugendhat, C. | | 31,887 |
| Robert Izzard, UKIP | | 8,153 |
| Claire Leigh, Lab. | | 7,604 |
| Mary Varrall, LD | | 3,660 |
| Howard Porter, Green | | 2,366 |

C. majority 23,734 (44.22%)
4.99% swing C. to UKIP
(2010: C. majority 18,178 (35.43%))

TOOTING
E. 76,778 T. 53,529 (69.72%)

|  |  | Lab. hold |
|---|---|---|
| Sadiq Khan, Lab. | | 25,263 |
| Dan Watkins, C. | | 22,421 |
| Esther Obiri-Darko, Green | | 2,201 |
| Philip Ling, LD | | 2,107 |
| Przemek Skwirczynski, UKIP | | 1,537 |

Lab. majority 2,842 (5.31%)
0.16% swing C. to Lab.
(2010: Lab. majority 2,524 (4.98%))

TORBAY
E. 76,259 T. 48,079 (63.05%)

|  |  | C. gain |
|---|---|---|
| *Kevin Foster, C. | | 19,551 |
| Adrian Sanders, LD | | 16,265 |
| Tony McIntyre, UKIP | | 6,540 |
| Su Maddock, Lab. | | 4,166 |
| Paula Hermes, Green | | 1,557 |

C. majority 3,286 (6.83%)
7.56% swing LD to C.
(2010: LD majority 4,078 (8.29%))

TOTNES
E. 68,630 T. 47,097 (68.62%)

|  |  | C. hold |
|---|---|---|
| Sarah Wollaston, C. | | 24,941 |
| Justin Haque, UKIP | | 6,656 |
| Nicky Williams, Lab. | | 5,988 |
| Gill Coombs, Green | | 4,845 |
| Julian Brazil, LD | | 4,667 |

C. majority 18,285 (38.82%)
0.50% swing C. to UKIP
(2010: C. majority 4,927 (10.30%))

TOTTENHAM
E. 70,809 T. 42,558 (60.10%)

|  |  | Lab. hold |
|---|---|---|
| David Lammy, Lab. | | 28,654 |
| Stefan Mrozinski, C. | | 5,090 |
| Dee Searle, Green | | 3,931 |
| Turhan Ozen, LD | | 1,756 |
| Tariq Saeed, UKIP | | 1,512 |
| Jenny Sutton, TUSC | | 1,324 |
| Tania Mahmood, Peace | | 291 |

Lab. majority 23,564 (55.37%)
5.49% swing C. to Lab.
(2010: Lab. majority 16,931 (41.61%))

TRURO & FALMOUTH
E. 73,601 T. 51,544 (70.03%)

|  |  | C. hold |
|---|---|---|
| Sarah Newton, C. | | 22,681 |
| Simon Rix, LD | | 8,681 |
| Stuart Roden, Lab. | | 7,814 |
| John Hyslop, UKIP | | 5,967 |
| Karen Westbrook, Green | | 4,483 |
| Loic Rich, Ind. | | 792 |
| Stephen Richardson, Meb. Ker. | | 563 |
| Rik Evans, NHAP | | 526 |
| Stanley Guffogg, PPP | | 37 |

C. majority 14,000 (27.16%)
13.13% swing LD to C.
(2010: C. majority 435 (0.89%))

TUNBRIDGE WELLS
E. 73,429 T. 51,428 (70.04%)

|  |  | C. hold |
|---|---|---|
| Greg Clark, C. | | 30,181 |
| Kevin Kerrigan, Lab. | | 7,307 |
| Colin Nicholson, UKIP | | 6,481 |
| James MacCleary, LD | | 4,342 |
| Marie Jones, Green | | 2,659 |
| Graham Naismith, Ind. | | 458 |

C. majority 22,874 (44.48%)
0.47% swing C. to Lab.
(2010: C. majority 15,576 (30.95%))

TWICKENHAM
E. 80,242 T. 62,004 (77.27%)

|  |  | C. gain |
|---|---|---|
| *Tania Mathias, C. | | 25,580 |
| Vince Cable, LD | | 23,563 |
| Nick Grant, Lab. | | 7,129 |
| Barry Edwards, UKIP | | 3,069 |
| Tanya Williams, Green | | 2,463 |
| Dominic Stockford, Ch. P. | | 174 |
| David Wedgwood, MC | | 26 |

C. majority 2,017 (3.25%)
11.79% swing LD to C.
(2010: LD majority 12,140 (20.33%))

TYNEMOUTH
E. 77,523 T. 53,495 (69.01%)

|  |  | Lab. hold |
|---|---|---|
| Alan Campbell, Lab. | | 25,791 |
| Glenn Hall, C. | | 17,551 |
| Gary Legg, UKIP | | 6,541 |
| Julia Erskine, Green | | 2,017 |
| John Paton-Day, LD | | 1,595 |

Lab. majority 8,240 (15.40%)
2.25% swing C. to Lab.
(2010: Lab. majority 5,739 (10.90%))

TYNESIDE NORTH
E. 79,286 T. 46,818 (59.05%)

|  |  | Lab. hold |
|---|---|---|
| Mary Glindon, Lab. | | 26,191 |
| Martin McGann, C. | | 8,997 |
| Scott Hartley, UKIP | | 7,618 |
| John Appleby, LD | | 2,075 |
| Martin Collins, Green | | 1,442 |
| Tim Wall, TUSC | | 304 |
| Bob Batten, NF | | 191 |

Lab. majority 17,194 (36.73%)
2.21% swing C. to Lab.
(2010: Lab. majority 12,884 (27.76%))

UXBRIDGE & RUISLIP SOUTH
E. 70,634 T. 44,811 (63.44%)

|  |  | C. hold |
|---|---|---|
| *Boris Johnson, C. | | 22,511 |
| Chris Summers, Lab. | | 11,816 |
| Jack Duffin, UKIP | | 6,346 |
| Mike Cox, LD | | 2,215 |
| Graham Lee, Green | | 1,414 |
| Gary Harbord, TUSC | | 180 |
| Jenny Thompson, Ind. | | 84 |
| Howling Laud Hope, Loony | | 72 |
| Sabrina Moosun, Community | | 52 |
| Lord Toby Jug, Eccentric | | 50 |
| Michael Doherty, Ind. | | 39 |
| Jane Lawrence, Realist | | 18 |
| James Jackson, ND | | 14 |

C. majority 10,695 (23.87%)
0.51% swing C. to Lab.
(2010: C. majority 11,216 (24.88%))

## VAUXHALL
E. 81,698 T. 47,941 (58.68%)

| | | Lab. hold |
|---|---|---|
| Kate Hoey, Lab. | | 25,778 |
| James Bellis, C. | | 13,070 |
| Gulnar Hasnain, Green | | 3,658 |
| Adrian Hyyrylainen-Trett, LD | | 3,312 |
| Ace Nnorom, UKIP | | 1,385 |
| Mark Chapman, Pirate | | 201 |
| Simon Hardy, LU | | 188 |
| Louis Jensen, CISTA | | 164 |
| Waleed Salman Ghani, Whig | | 103 |
| Danny Lambert, SPGB | | 82 |

Lab. majority 12,708 (26.51%)
0.87% swing Lab. to C.
(2010: Lab. majority 10,651 (24.66%))

## WAKEFIELD
E. 70,521 T. 42,973 (60.94%)

| | | Lab. hold |
|---|---|---|
| Mary Creagh, Lab. | | 17,301 |
| Antony Calvert, C. | | 14,688 |
| Alan Hazelhurst, UKIP | | 7,862 |
| Finbarr Cronin, LD | | 1,483 |
| Rebecca Thackray, Green | | 1,069 |
| Mick Griffiths, TUSC | | 287 |
| Elliot Barr, CISTA | | 283 |

Lab. majority 2,613 (6.08%)
1.23% swing C. to Lab.
(2010: Lab. majority 1,613 (3.63%))

## WALLASEY
E. 65,495 T. 43,366 (66.21%)

| | | Lab. hold |
|---|---|---|
| Angela Eagle, Lab. | | 26,176 |
| Chris Clarkson, C. | | 9,828 |
| Geoff Caton, UKIP | | 5,063 |
| Julian Pratt, Green | | 1,288 |
| Kris Brown, LD | | 1,011 |

Lab. majority 16,348 (37.70%)
8.64% swing C. to Lab.
(2010: Lab. majority 8,507 (20.42%))

## WALSALL NORTH
E. 67,080 T. 36,883 (54.98%)

| | | Lab. hold |
|---|---|---|
| David Winnick, Lab. | | 14,392 |
| Douglas Hansen-Luke, C. | | 12,455 |
| Liz Hazell, UKIP | | 8,122 |
| Nigel Jones, LD | | 840 |
| Pete Smith, TUSC | | 545 |
| Mike Harrison, Green | | 529 |

Lab. majority 1,937 (5.25%)
1.26% swing C. to Lab.
(2010: Lab. majority 990 (2.74%))

## WALSALL SOUTH
E. 67,743 T. 41,838 (61.76%)

| | | Lab. hold |
|---|---|---|
| Valerie Vaz, Lab. | | 19,740 |
| Sue Arnold, C. | | 13,733 |
| Derek Bennett, UKIP | | 6,540 |
| Charlotte Fletcher, Green | | 1,149 |
| Joel Kenrick, LD | | 676 |

Lab. majority 6,007 (14.36%)
5.03% swing C. to Lab.
(2010: Lab. majority 1,755 (4.29%))

## WALTHAMSTOW
E. 67,289 T. 41,796 (62.11%)

| | | Lab. Co-op hold |
|---|---|---|
| Stella Creasy, Lab. Co-op | | 28,779 |
| Molly Samuel-Leport, C. | | 5,584 |
| Michael Gold, Green | | 2,661 |
| Paul Hillman, UKIP | | 2,507 |
| Steven Cheung, LD | | 1,661 |
| Nancy Taaffe, TUSC | | 394 |
| Ellie Merton, ND | | 129 |
| Jonty Leff, WRP | | 81 |

Lab. Co-op majority 23,195 (55.50%)
8.82% swing C. to Lab.
(2010: Lab. majority 9,478 (23.12%))

## WANSBECK
E. 63,273 T. 38,528 (60.89%)

| | | Lab. hold |
|---|---|---|
| Ian Lavery, Lab. | | 19,267 |
| Chris Galley, C. | | 8,386 |
| Melanie Hurst, UKIP | | 7,014 |
| Tom Hancock, LD | | 2,407 |
| Christopher Hedley, Green | | 1,454 |

Lab. majority 10,881 (28.24%)
0.03% swing Lab. to C.
(2010: Lab. majority 7,031 (18.37%))

## WANTAGE
E. 83,516 T. 58,320 (69.83%)

| | | C. hold |
|---|---|---|
| Ed Vaizey, C. | | 31,092 |
| Stephen Webb, Lab. | | 9,343 |
| Alex Meredith, LD | | 7,611 |
| Lee Upcraft, UKIP | | 7,288 |
| Kate Prendergast, Green | | 2,986 |

C. majority 21,749 (37.29%)
0.37% swing C. to Lab.
(2010: C. majority 13,547 (24.04%))

## WARLEY
E. 63,740 T. 37,829 (59.35%)

| | | Lab. hold |
|---|---|---|
| John Spellar, Lab. | | 22,012 |
| Tom Williams, C. | | 7,310 |
| Pete Durnell, UKIP | | 6,237 |
| Robert Buckman, Green | | 1,465 |
| Catherine Smith, LD | | 805 |

Lab. majority 14,702 (38.86%)
5.38% swing C. to Lab.
(2010: Lab. majority 10,756 (28.11%))

## WARRINGTON NORTH
E. 72,632 T. 45,419 (62.53%)

| | | Lab. hold |
|---|---|---|
| Helen Jones, Lab. | | 21,720 |
| Richard Short, C. | | 12,797 |
| Trevor Nicholls, UKIP | | 7,757 |
| Stefan Krizanac, LD | | 1,881 |
| Sarah Hayes, Green | | 1,264 |

Lab. majority 8,923 (19.65%)
2.17% swing C. to Lab.
(2010: Lab. majority 6,771 (15.32%))

## WARRINGTON SOUTH
E. 85,566 T. 59,353 (69.37%)

| | | C. hold |
|---|---|---|
| David Mowat, C. | | 25,928 |
| Nick Bent, Lab. | | 23,178 |
| Malcolm Lingley, UKIP | | 4,909 |
| Bob Barr, LD | | 3,335 |
| Stephanie Davies, Green | | 1,765 |
| Kevin Bennett, TUSC | | 238 |

C. majority 2,750 (4.63%)
0.90% swing Lab. to C.
(2010: C. majority 1,553 (2.83%))

## WARWICK & LEAMINGTON
E. 71,570 T. 50,581 (70.67%)

| | | C. hold |
|---|---|---|
| Chris White, C. | | 24,249 |
| Lynnette Kelly, Lab. | | 17,643 |
| Alastair MacBrayne, UKIP | | 4,183 |
| Haseeb Arif, LD | | 2,512 |
| Azzees Minott, Green | | 1,994 |

C. majority 6,606 (13.06%)
2.95% swing Lab. to C.
(2010: C. majority 3,513 (7.16%))

## WARWICKSHIRE NORTH
E. 70,152 T. 47,377 (67.53%)

| | | C. hold |
|---|---|---|
| *Craig Tracey, C. | | 20,042 |
| Mike O'Brien, Lab. | | 17,069 |
| William Cash, UKIP | | 8,256 |
| Alan Beddow, LD | | 978 |
| Ian Bonner, Green | | 894 |
| Eileen Hunter, TUSC | | 138 |

C. majority 2,973 (6.28%)
3.08% swing Lab. to C.
(2010: C. majority 54 (0.11%))

## WASHINGTON & SUNDERLAND WEST
E. 68,188 T. 37,257 (54.64%)

| | | Lab. hold |
|---|---|---|
| Sharon Hodgson, Lab. | | 20,478 |
| Aileen Casey, UKIP | | 7,321 |
| Bob Dhillon, C. | | 7,033 |
| Anthony Murphy, Green | | 1,091 |
| Dominic Haney, LD | | 993 |
| Gary Duncan, TUSC | | 341 |

Lab. majority 13,157 (35.31%)
6.92% swing Lab. to UKIP
(2010: Lab. majority 11,458 (30.69%))

## WATFORD
E. 84,270 T. 56,149 (66.63%)

| | | C. hold |
|---|---|---|
| Richard Harrington, C. | | 24,400 |
| Matt Turmaine, Lab. | | 14,606 |
| Dorothy Thornhill, LD | | 10,152 |
| Nick Lincoln, UKIP | | 5,481 |
| Aidan Cottrell-Boyce, Green | | 1,332 |
| Mark O'Connor, TUSC | | 178 |

C. majority 9,794 (17.44%)
4.61% swing Lab. to C.
(2010: C. majority 1,425 (2.58%))

**WAVENEY**
E. 80,171 T. 52,196 (65.11%)

| | C. hold |
|---|---|
| Peter Aldous, C. | 22,104 |
| Bob Blizzard, Lab. | 19,696 |
| Simon Tobin, UKIP | 7,580 |
| Graham Elliott, Green | 1,761 |
| Steve Gordon, LD | 1,055 |

C. majority 2,408 (4.61%)
1.55% swing Lab. to C.
(2010: C. majority 769 (1.50%))

**WEALDEN**
E. 80,252 T. 57,017 (71.05%)

| | C. hold |
|---|---|
| *Nus Ghani, C. | 32,508 |
| Peter Griffiths, UKIP | 9,541 |
| Solomon Curtis, Lab. | 6,165 |
| Giles Goodall, LD | 5,180 |
| Mark Smith, Green | 3,623 |

C. majority 22,967 (40.28%)
5.12% swing C. to UKIP
(2010: C. majority 17,179 (31.25%))

**WEAVER VALE**
E. 68,407 T. 46,867 (68.51%)

| | C. hold |
|---|---|
| Graham Evans, C. | 20,227 |
| Julia Tickridge, Lab. | 19,421 |
| Amos Wright, UKIP | 4,547 |
| Mary Di Mauro, LD | 1,395 |
| Chris Copeman, Green | 1,183 |
| Joseph Whyte, TUSC | 94 |

C. majority 806 (1.72%)
0.27% swing C. to Lab.
(2010: C. majority 991 (2.25%))

**WELLINGBOROUGH**
E. 77,127 T. 50,430 (65.39%)

| | C. hold |
|---|---|
| Peter Bone, C. | 26,265 |
| Jonathan Munday, UKIP | 9,868 |
| Richard Garvie, Lab. | 9,839 |
| Chris Nelson, LD | 2,240 |
| Marion Turner-Hawes, Green | 2,218 |

C. majority 16,397 (32.51%)
6.28% swing C. to UKIP
(2010: C. majority 11,787 (22.82%))

**WELLS**
E. 79,405 T. 56,904 (71.66%)

| | C. gain |
|---|---|
| *James Heappey, C. | 26,247 |
| Tessa Munt, LD | 18,662 |
| Helen Hims, UKIP | 5,644 |
| Chris Inchley, Lab. | 3,780 |
| Jon Cousins, Green | 2,331 |
| Paul Arnold, ND | 83 |
| Dave Dobbs, Birthday | 81 |
| Gypsy Watkins, Ind. | 76 |

C. majority 7,585 (13.33%)
7.38% swing LD to C.
(2010: LD majority 800 (1.43%))

**WELWYN HATFIELD**
E. 73,264 T. 50,205 (68.53%)

| | C. hold |
|---|---|
| Grant Shapps, C. | 25,281 |
| Anawar Miah, Lab. | 13,128 |
| Arthur Stevens, UKIP | 6,556 |
| Hugh Annand, LD | 3,140 |
| Marc Scheimann, Green | 1,742 |
| Michael Green, Ind. | 216 |
| Richard Shattock, TUSC | 142 |

C. majority 12,153 (24.21%)
5.69% swing C. to Lab.
(2010: C. majority 17,423 (35.58%))

**WENTWORTH & DEARNE**
E. 74,283 T. 43,189 (58.14%)

| | Lab. hold |
|---|---|
| John Healey, Lab. | 24,571 |
| Mike Hookem, UKIP | 10,733 |
| Michael Naughton, C. | 6,441 |
| Edwin Simpson, LD | 1,135 |
| Alan England, Eng. Dem. | 309 |

Lab. majority 13,838 (32.04%)
5.23% swing Lab. to UKIP
(2010: Lab. majority 13,920 (33.06%))

**WEST BROMWICH EAST**
E. 63,641 T. 37,492 (58.91%)

| | Lab. hold |
|---|---|
| Tom Watson, Lab. | 18,817 |
| Olivia Seccombe, C. | 9,347 |
| Steve Latham, UKIP | 7,949 |
| Flo Clucas, LD | 751 |
| Barry Lim, Green | 628 |

Lab. majority 9,470 (25.26%)
3.81% swing C. to Lab.
(2010: Lab. majority 6,696 (17.64%))

**WEST BROMWICH WEST**
E. 65,533 T. 35,026 (53.45%)

| | Lab. Co-op hold |
|---|---|
| Adrian Bailey, Lab. Co-op | 16,578 |
| Graham Eardley, UKIP | 8,836 |
| Paul Ratner, C. | 8,365 |
| Mark Redding, Green | 697 |
| Karen Trench, LD | 550 |

Lab. Co-op majority 7,742 (22.10%)
9.26% swing Lab. to UKIP
(2010: Lab. majority 5,651 (15.62%))

**WEST HAM**
E. 90,634 T. 52,793 (58.25%)

| | Lab. hold |
|---|---|
| Lyn Brown, Lab. | 36,132 |
| Festus Akinbusoye, C. | 8,146 |
| Jamie McKenzie, UKIP | 3,950 |
| Rachel Collinson, Green | 2,651 |
| Paul Reynolds, LD | 1,430 |
| Andy Uzoka, CPA | 369 |
| Cydatty Bogie, Community | 115 |

Lab. majority 27,986 (53.01%)
2.51% swing C. to Lab.
(2010: Lab. majority 22,534 (47.99%))

**WESTMINSTER NORTH**
E. 62,346 T. 39,514 (63.38%)

| | Lab. hold |
|---|---|
| Karen Buck, Lab. | 18,504 |
| Lindsey Hall, C. | 16,527 |
| Nigel Sussman, UKIP | 1,489 |
| Kirsty Allan, LD | 1,457 |
| Jennifer Nadel, Green | 1,322 |
| Gabriela Fajardo, Ch. P. | 152 |
| Nicholas Ward, Ind. | 63 |

Lab. majority 1,977 (5.00%)
0.18% swing Lab. to C.
(2010: Lab. majority 2,126 (5.37%))

**WESTMORLAND & LONSDALE**
E. 65,857 T. 48,929 (74.30%)   LD hold

| | |
|---|---|
| Tim Farron, LD | 25,194 |
| Ann Myatt, C. | 16,245 |
| Alan Piper, UKIP | 3,031 |
| John Bateson, Lab. | 2,661 |
| Chris Loynes, Green | 1,798 |

LD majority 8,949 (18.29%)
2.76% swing LD to C.
(2010: LD majority 12,264 (23.82%))

**WESTON-SUPER-MARE**
E. 79,493 T. 52,552 (66.11%)

| | C. hold |
|---|---|
| John Penrose, C. | 25,203 |
| Tim Taylor, Lab. | 9,594 |
| Ernie Warrender, UKIP | 9,366 |
| John Munro, LD | 5,486 |
| Richard Lawson, Green | 2,592 |
| Ronald Lavelle, Eng. Dem. | 311 |

C. majority 15,609 (29.70%)
1.83% swing C. to Lab.
(2010: C. majority 2,691 (5.10%))

**WIGAN**
E. 76,068 T. 45,293 (59.54%)

| | Lab. hold |
|---|---|
| Lisa Nandy, Lab. | 23,625 |
| Caroline Kerswell, C. | 9,389 |
| Mark Bradley, UKIP | 8,818 |
| Will Patterson, Green | 1,273 |
| Mark Clayton, LD | 1,255 |
| Gareth Fairhurst, Wigan | 768 |
| Brian Parr, Ind. | 165 |

Lab. majority 14,236 (31.43%)
3.84% swing C. to Lab.
(2010: Lab. majority 10,487 (23.76%))

**WILTSHIRE NORTH**
E. 67,858 T. 50,556 (74.50%)

| | C. hold |
|---|---|
| James Gray, C. | 28,938 |
| Brian Mathew, LD | 7,892 |
| Patricia Bryant, UKIP | 5,813 |
| Peter Baldrey, Lab. | 4,930 |
| Phil Chamberlain, Green | 2,350 |
| Simon Killane, Ind. | 390 |
| Giles Wareham, Ind. | 243 |

C. majority 21,046 (41.63%)
13.13% swing LD to C.
(2010: C. majority 7,483 (15.37%))

WILTSHIRE SOUTH WEST
E. 73,030 T. 51,643 (70.71%)

| | C. hold |
|---|---|
| Andrew Murrison, C. | 27,198 |
| Matthew Brown, UKIP | 9,030 |
| George Aylett, Lab. | 6,948 |
| Trevor Carbin, LD | 5,482 |
| Phil Randle, Green | 2,985 |

C. majority 18,168 (35.18%)
5.50% swing C. to UKIP
(2010: C. majority 10,367 (21.15%))

WIMBLEDON
E. 65,853 T. 48,422 (73.53%)

| | C. hold |
|---|---|
| Stephen Hammond, C. | 25,225 |
| Andrew Judge, Lab. | 12,606 |
| Shas Sheehan, LD | 6,129 |
| Peter Bucklitsch, UKIP | 2,476 |
| Charles Barraball, Green | 1,986 |

C. majority 12,619 (26.06%)
0.38% swing C. to Lab.
(2010: C. majority 11,408 (24.07%))

WINCHESTER
E. 74,119 T. 55,316 (74.63%)

| | C. hold |
|---|---|
| Steve Brine, C. | 30,425 |
| Jackie Porter, LD | 13,511 |
| Mark Chaloner, Lab. | 4,613 |
| Martin Lyon, UKIP | 4,122 |
| Michael Wilks, Green | 2,645 |

C. majority 16,914 (30.58%)
12.56% swing LD to C.
(2010: C. majority 3,048 (5.45%))

WINDSOR
E. 74,119 T. 50,160 (67.67%)

| | C. hold |
|---|---|
| Adam Afriyie, C. | 31,797 |
| Fiona Dent, Lab. | 6,714 |
| Tariq Malik, UKIP | 4,992 |
| George Fussey, LD | 4,323 |
| Derek Wall, Green | 1,834 |
| Wisdom Da Costa, Ind. | 500 |

C. majority 25,083 (50.01%)
0.47% swing C. to Lab.
(2010: C. majority 19,054 (38.42%))

WIRRAL SOUTH
E. 56,956 T. 41,837 (73.45%)

| | Lab. hold |
|---|---|
| Alison McGovern, Lab. | 20,165 |
| John Bell, C. | 15,566 |
| David Scott, UKIP | 3,737 |
| Elizabeth Jewkes, LD | 1,474 |
| Paul Cartlidge, Green | 895 |

Lab. majority 4,599 (10.99%)
4.83% swing C. to Lab.
(2010: Lab. majority 531 (1.33%))

WIRRAL WEST
E. 55,377 T. 41,858 (75.59%)

| | Lab. gain |
|---|---|
| *Margaret Greenwood, Lab. | 18,898 |
| Esther McVey, C. | 18,481 |
| Hilary Jones, UKIP | 2,772 |
| Peter Reisdorf, LD | 1,433 |
| David James, ND | 274 |

Lab. majority 417 (1.00%)
3.59% swing C. to Lab.
(2010: C. majority 2,436 (6.19%))

WITHAM
E. 67,090 T. 47,168 (70.31%)

| | C. hold |
|---|---|
| Priti Patel, C. | 27,123 |
| Garry Cockrill, UKIP | 7,569 |
| John Clarke, Lab. | 7,467 |
| Jo Hayes, LD | 2,891 |
| James Abbott, Green | 2,038 |
| Doreen Scrimshaw, CPA | 80 |

C. majority 19,554 (41.46%)
2.11% swing C. to UKIP
(2010: C. majority 15,196 (32.45%))

WITNEY
E. 79,767 T. 58,482 (73.32%)

| | C. hold |
|---|---|
| David Cameron, C. | 35,201 |
| Duncan Enright, Lab. | 10,046 |
| Simon Strutt, UKIP | 5,352 |
| Andrew Graham, LD | 3,953 |
| Stuart Macdonald, Green | 2,970 |
| Clive Peedell, NHAP | 616 |
| Colin Bex, Wessex Reg. | 110 |
| Chris Tompson, Ind. | 94 |
| Vivien Saunders, VAT | 56 |
| Bobby Smith, Elmo | 37 |
| Deek Jackson, LP | 35 |
| Nathan Handley, ND | 12 |

C. majority 25,155 (43.01%)
1.40% swing C. to Lab.
(2010: C. majority 22,740 (39.36%))

WOKING
E. 74,287 T. 51,964 (69.95%)

| | C. hold |
|---|---|
| Jonathan Lord, C. | 29,199 |
| Jill Rawling, Lab. | 8,389 |
| Chris Took, LD | 6,047 |
| Rob Burberry, UKIP | 5,873 |
| Martin Robson, Green | 2,109 |
| Declan Wade, CISTA | 229 |
| Ruth Temple, Magna Carta | 77 |
| Angela Woolford, TEP | 41 |

C. majority 20,810 (40.05%)
1.10% swing C. to Lab.
(2010: C. majority 6,807 (12.90%))

WOKINGHAM
E. 77,881 T. 55,999 (71.90%)

| | C. hold |
|---|---|
| John Redwood, C. | 32,329 |
| Andy Croy, Lab. | 8,132 |
| Clive Jones, LD | 7,572 |
| Philip Cunnington, UKIP | 5,516 |
| Adrian Windisch, Green | 2,092 |
| Kaz Lokuciewski, Ind. | 358 |

C. majority 24,197 (43.21%)
0.30% swing Lab. to C.
(2010: C. majority 13,492 (24.74%))

WOLVERHAMPTON NORTH
EAST
E. 61,073 T. 34,003 (55.68%)

| | Lab. hold |
|---|---|
| Emma Reynolds, Lab. | 15,669 |
| Darren Henry, C. | 10,174 |
| Star Etheridge, UKIP | 6,524 |
| Ian Jenkins, LD | 935 |
| Becky Cooper, Green | 701 |

Lab. majority 5,495 (16.16%)
4.52% swing C. to Lab.
(2010: Lab. majority 2,484 (7.12%))

WOLVERHAMPTON SOUTH
EAST
E. 62,561 T. 34,764 (55.57%)

| | Lab. hold |
|---|---|
| Pat McFadden, Lab. | 18,539 |
| Suria Photay, C. | 7,761 |
| Barry Hodgson, UKIP | 7,061 |
| Ian Griffiths, LD | 798 |
| Geeta Kauldhar, Green | 605 |

Lab. majority 10,778 (31.00%)
6.00% swing C. to Lab.
(2010: Lab. majority 6,593 (19.00%))

WOLVERHAMPTON SOUTH
WEST
E. 60,375 T. 40,209 (66.60%)

| | Lab. gain |
|---|---|
| *Rob Marris, Lab. | 17,374 |
| Paul Uppal, C. | 16,573 |
| David Everett, UKIP | 4,310 |
| Andrea Cantrill, Green | 1,058 |
| Neale Upstone, LD | 845 |
| Brian Booth, Ind. | 49 |

Lab. majority 801 (1.99%)
1.86% swing C. to Lab.
(2010: C. majority 691 (1.72%))

WORCESTER
E. 71,003 T. 49,723 (70.03%)

| | C. hold |
|---|---|
| Robin Walker, C. | 22,534 |
| Joy Squires, Lab. | 16,888 |
| James Goad, UKIP | 6,378 |
| Louis Stephen, Green | 2,024 |
| Federica Smith, LD | 1,677 |
| Pete McNally, TUSC | 153 |
| Mark Shuker, Ind. | 69 |

C. majority 5,646 (11.35%)
2.63% swing Lab. to C.
(2010: C. majority 2,982 (6.09%))

**WORCESTERSHIRE MID**
E. 73,069 T. 52,225 (71.47%)

| | | C. hold |
|---|---|---|
| *Nigel Huddleston, C. | | 29,763 |
| Richard Keel, UKIP | | 9,231 |
| Robin Lunn, Lab. | | 7,548 |
| Margaret Rowley, LD | | 3,750 |
| Neil Franks, Green | | 1,933 |

C. majority 20,532 (39.31%)
4.61% swing C. to UKIP
(2010: C. majority 15,864 (31.15%))

**WORCESTERSHIRE WEST**
E. 73,415 T. 54,100 (73.69%)

| | | C. hold |
|---|---|---|
| Harriett Baldwin, C. | | 30,342 |
| Richard Chamings, UKIP | | 7,764 |
| Daniel Walton, Lab. | | 7,244 |
| Dennis Wharton, LD | | 5,245 |
| Julian Roskams, Green | | 3,505 |

C. majority 22,578 (41.73%)
2.33% swing C. to UKIP
(2010: C. majority 6,754 (12.49%))

**WORKINGTON**
E. 58,672 T. 38,463 (65.56%)

| | | Lab. hold |
|---|---|---|
| *Sue Hayman, Lab. | | 16,282 |
| Rozila Kana, C. | | 11,596 |
| Mark Jenkinson, UKIP | | 7,538 |
| Phill Roberts, LD | | 1,708 |
| Jill Perry, Green | | 1,149 |
| Roy Ivinson, ND | | 190 |

Lab. majority 4,686 (12.18%)
0.26% swing C. to Lab.
(2010: Lab. majority 4,575 (11.65%))

**WORSLEY & ECCLES SOUTH**
E. 72,174 T. 42,048 (58.26%)

| | | Lab. hold |
|---|---|---|
| Barbara Keeley, Lab. | | 18,600 |
| Iain Lindley, C. | | 12,654 |
| Owen Hammond, UKIP | | 7,688 |
| Christopher Bertenshaw, Green | | 1,242 |
| Kate Clarkson, LD | | 1,100 |
| Steve North, TUSC | | 380 |
| Mags McNally, Reality | | 200 |
| Geoffrey Berg, Ind. | | 184 |

Lab. majority 5,946 (14.14%)
1.87% swing C. to Lab.
(2010: Lab. majority 4,337 (10.40%))

**WORTHING EAST & SHOREHAM**
E. 74,272 T. 49,898 (67.18%)

| | | C. hold |
|---|---|---|
| Tim Loughton, C. | | 24,686 |
| Tim Macpherson, Lab. | | 9,737 |
| Mike Glennon, UKIP | | 8,267 |
| Bob Smytherman, LD | | 3,360 |
| James Doyle, Green | | 2,605 |
| Carl Walker, NHAP | | 1,243 |

C. majority 14,949 (29.96%)
0.90% swing C. to Lab.
(2010: C. majority 11,105 (22.95%))

**WORTHING WEST**
E. 75,617 T. 50,763 (67.13%)

| | | C. hold |
|---|---|---|
| Peter Bottomley, C. | | 26,124 |
| Tim Cross, UKIP | | 9,269 |
| Jim Deen, Lab. | | 7,955 |
| Hazel Thorpe, LD | | 4,477 |
| David Aherne, Green | | 2,938 |

C. majority 16,855 (33.20%)
6.29% swing C. to UKIP
(2010: C. majority 11,729 (23.88%))

**WREKIN, THE**
E. 65,942 T. 45,437 (68.90%)

| | | C. hold |
|---|---|---|
| Mark Pritchard, C. | | 22,579 |
| Katrina Gilman, Lab. | | 11,836 |
| Jill Seymour, UKIP | | 7,620 |
| Rod Keyes, LD | | 1,959 |
| Cath Edwards, Green | | 1,443 |

C. majority 10,743 (23.64%)
1.54% swing Lab. to C.
(2010: C. majority 9,450 (20.56%))

**WYCOMBE**
E. 76,371 T. 51,439 (67.35%)

| | | C. hold |
|---|---|---|
| Steven Baker, C. | | 26,444 |
| David Williams, Lab. | | 11,588 |
| David Meacock, UKIP | | 5,198 |
| Steve Guy, LD | | 4,546 |
| Jem Bailey, Green | | 3,086 |
| David Fitton, Ind. | | 577 |

C. majority 14,856 (28.88%)
1.24% swing C. to Lab.
(2010: C. majority 9,560 (19.85%))

**WYRE & PRESTON NORTH**
E. 70,697 T. 49,893 (70.57%)

| | | C. hold |
|---|---|---|
| Ben Wallace, C. | | 26,528 |
| Ben Whittingham, Lab. | | 12,377 |
| Kate Walsh, UKIP | | 6,577 |
| John Potter, LD | | 2,712 |
| Anne Power, Green | | 1,699 |

C. majority 14,151 (28.36%)
1.36% swing C. to Lab.
(2010: C. majority 15,844 (30.88%))

**WYRE FOREST**
E. 77,451 T. 49,440 (63.83%)

| | | C. hold |
|---|---|---|
| Mark Garnier, C. | | 22,394 |
| Matt Lamb, Lab. | | 9,523 |
| Michael Wrench, UKIP | | 7,967 |
| Richard Taylor, Ind. CHC | | 7,211 |
| Andy Crick, LD | | 1,228 |
| Natalie McVey, Green | | 1,117 |

C. majority 12,871 (26.03%)
1.72% swing Lab. to C.
(2010: C. majority 2,643 (5.19%))

**WYTHENSHAWE & SALE EAST**
E. 75,980 T. 43,263 (56.94%)

| | | Lab. hold |
|---|---|---|
| Mike Kane, Lab. | | 21,693 |
| Fiona Green, C. | | 11,124 |
| Lee Clayton, UKIP | | 6,354 |
| Victor Chamberlain, LD | | 1,927 |
| Jess Mayo, Green | | 1,658 |
| Johnny Disco, Loony | | 292 |
| Lynn Worthington, TUSC | | 215 |

Lab. majority 10,569 (24.43%)
2.92% swing C. to Lab.
(2010: Lab. majority 7,575 (18.59%))
(2014: Lab. majority 8,960 (37.54%))

**YEOVIL**
E. 82,446 T. 56,933 (69.05%)

| | | C. gain |
|---|---|---|
| *Marcus Fysh, C. | | 24,178 |
| David Laws, LD | | 18,865 |
| Simon Smedley, UKIP | | 7,646 |
| Sheena King, Lab. | | 4,053 |
| Emily McIvor, Green | | 2,191 |

C. majority 5,313 (9.33%)
16.07% swing LD to C.
(2010: LD majority 13,036 (22.81%))

**YORK CENTRAL**
E. 75,351 T. 47,677 (63.27%)

| | | Lab. Co-op hold |
|---|---|---|
| *Rachael Maskell, Lab. Co-op | | 20,212 |
| Robert McIlveen, C. | | 13,496 |
| Ken Guest, UKIP | | 4,795 |
| Jonathan Tyler, Green | | 4,791 |
| Nick Love, LD | | 3,804 |
| Chris Whitwood, Yorks | | 291 |
| Megan Ollerhead, TUSC | | 288 |

Lab. Co-op majority 6,716 (14.09%)
0.10% swing C. to Lab.
(2010: Lab. majority 6,451 (13.88%))

**YORK OUTER**
E. 78,561 T. 53,903 (68.61%)

| | | C. hold |
|---|---|---|
| Julian Sturdy, C. | | 26,477 |
| Joe Riches, Lab. | | 13,348 |
| James Blanchard, LD | | 6,269 |
| Paul Abbott, UKIP | | 5,251 |
| Ginnie Shaw, Green | | 2,558 |

C. majority 13,129 (24.36%)
0.77% swing C. to Lab.
(2010: C. majority 3,688 (6.92%))

**YORKSHIRE EAST**
E. 81,030 T. 49,991 (61.69%)

| | | C. hold |
|---|---|---|
| Greg Knight, C. | | 25,276 |
| Kevin Hickson, Lab. | | 10,343 |
| Stephanie Todd, UKIP | | 8,955 |
| Robert Adamson, LD | | 2,966 |
| Mark Maloney, Green | | 1,731 |
| Stewart Arnold, Yorks | | 720 |

C. majority 14,933 (29.87%)
1.35% swing Lab. to C.
(2010: C. majority 13,486 (26.31%))

# WALES

## ABERAVON
E. 49,821 T. 31,523 (63.27%)

| | | Lab. hold |
|---|---|---|
| *Stephen Kinnock, Lab. | | 15,416 |
| Peter Bush, UKIP | | 4,971 |
| Edward Yi He, C. | | 3,742 |
| Duncan Higgitt, PC | | 3,663 |
| Helen Ceri Clarke, LD | | 1,397 |
| Captain Beany, Ind. | | 1,137 |
| Jonathan Tier, Green | | 711 |
| Andrew Jordan, Soc. Lab. | | 352 |
| Owen Herbert, TUSC | | 134 |

Lab. majority 10,445 (33.13%)
8.60% swing Lab. to UKIP
(2010: Lab. majority 11,039 (35.66%))

## ABERCONWY
E. 45,540 T. 30,148 (66.20%)

| | | C. hold |
|---|---|---|
| Guto Bebb, C. | | 12,513 |
| Mary Wimbury, Lab. | | 8,514 |
| Dafydd Meurig, PC | | 3,536 |
| Andrew Haigh, UKIP | | 3,467 |
| Victor Babu, LD | | 1,391 |
| Petra Haig, Green | | 727 |

C. majority 3,999 (13.26%)
0.96% swing Lab. to C.
(2010: C. majority 3,398 (11.34%))

## ALYN & DEESIDE
E. 62,016 T. 41,314 (66.62%)

| | | Lab. hold |
|---|---|---|
| Mark Tami, Lab. | | 16,540 |
| Laura Knightly, C. | | 13,197 |
| Blair Smillie, UKIP | | 7,260 |
| Tudor Jones, LD | | 1,733 |
| Jacqueline Hurst, PC | | 1,608 |
| Alasdair Ibbotson, Green | | 976 |

Lab. majority 3,343 (8.09%)
0.39% swing C. to Lab.
(2010: Lab. majority 2,919 (7.31%))

## ARFON
E. 40,492 T. 26,837 (66.28%)  PC hold

| | | |
|---|---|---|
| Hywel Williams, PC | | 11,790 |
| Alun Pugh, Lab. | | 8,122 |
| Anwen Barry, C. | | 3,521 |
| Simon Wall, UKIP | | 2,277 |
| Mohammed Shultan, LD | | 718 |
| Kathrine Jones, Soc. Lab. | | 409 |

PC majority 3,668 (13.67%)
4.04% swing Lab. to PC
(2010: PC majority 1,455 (5.58%))

## BLAENAU GWENT
E. 51,332 T. 31,683 (61.72%)

| | | Lab. hold |
|---|---|---|
| Nick Smith, Lab. | | 18,380 |
| Susan Boucher, UKIP | | 5,677 |
| Tracey West, C. | | 3,419 |
| Steffan Lewis, PC | | 2,849 |
| Mark Pond, Green | | 738 |
| Sam Rees, LD | | 620 |

Lab. majority 12,703 (40.09%)
5.40% swing Lab. to UKIP
(2010: Lab. majority 10,516 (32.46%))

## BRECON & RADNORSHIRE
E. 54,311 T. 40,074 (73.79%)

| | | C. gain |
|---|---|---|
| *Chris Davies, C. | | 16,453 |
| Roger Williams, LD | | 11,351 |
| Matthew Dorrance, Lab. | | 5,904 |
| Darran Thomas, UKIP | | 3,338 |
| Freddy Greaves, PC | | 1,767 |
| Chris Carmichael, Green | | 1,261 |

C. majority 5,102 (12.73%)
11.19% swing LD to C.
(2010: LD majority 3,747 (9.65%))

## BRIDGEND
E. 59,998 T. 39,453 (65.76%)

| | | Lab. hold |
|---|---|---|
| Madeleine Moon, Lab. | | 14,624 |
| Meirion Jenkins, C. | | 12,697 |
| Caroline Jones, UKIP | | 5,911 |
| James Radcliffe, PC | | 2,784 |
| Anita Davies, LD | | 1,648 |
| Les Tallon-Morris, Ind. | | 763 |
| Tony White, Green | | 736 |
| Aaron David, TUSC | | 118 |
| David Elston, Pirate | | 106 |
| Adam Lloyd, NF | | 66 |

Lab. majority 1,927 (4.88%)
0.51% swing Lab. to C.
(2010: Lab. majority 2,263 (5.90%))

## CAERPHILLY
E. 62,793 T. 40,283 (64.15%)

| | | Lab. hold |
|---|---|---|
| Wayne David, Lab. | | 17,864 |
| Sam Gould, UKIP | | 7,791 |
| Leo Docherty, C. | | 6,683 |
| Beci Newton, PC | | 5,895 |
| Katy Beddoe, Green | | 937 |
| Aladdin Ayesh, LD | | 935 |
| Jaime Davies, TUSC | | 178 |

Lab. majority 10,073 (25.01%)
8.61% swing Lab. to UKIP
(2010: Lab. majority 10,755 (27.58%))

## CARDIFF CENTRAL
E. 57,454 T. 38,646 (67.26%)

| | | Lab. gain |
|---|---|---|
| *Jo Stevens, Lab. | | 15,462 |
| Jenny Willott, LD | | 10,481 |
| Richard Hopkin, C. | | 5,674 |
| Anthony Raybould, UKIP | | 2,499 |
| Christopher von Ruhland, Green | | 2,461 |
| Martin Pollard, PC | | 1,925 |
| Steve Williams, TUSC | | 110 |
| Kazimir Hubert, Ind. | | 34 |

Lab. majority 4,981 (12.89%)
12.77% swing LD to Lab.
(2010: LD majority 4,576 (12.66%))

## CARDIFF NORTH
E. 67,193 T. 51,151 (76.13%)

| | | C. hold |
|---|---|---|
| *Craig Williams, C. | | 21,709 |
| Mari Williams, Lab. | | 19,572 |
| Ethan Wilkinson, UKIP | | 3,953 |
| Elin Walker Jones, PC | | 2,301 |
| Elizabeth Clark, LD | | 1,953 |
| Ruth Osner, Green | | 1,254 |
| Jeff Green, Ch. P. | | 331 |
| Shaun Jenkins, Change | | 78 |

C. majority 2,137 (4.18%)
1.89% swing Lab. to C.
(2010: C. majority 194 (0.41%))

## CARDIFF SOUTH & PENARTH
E. 75,714 T. 46,667 (61.64%)

| | | Lab. Co-op hold |
|---|---|---|
| Stephen Doughty, Lab. Co-op | | 19,966 |
| Emma Warman, C. | | 12,513 |
| John Rees-Evans, UKIP | | 6,423 |
| Ben Foday, PC | | 3,443 |
| Nigel Howells, LD | | 2,318 |
| Anthony Slaughter, Green | | 1,746 |
| Ross Saunders, TUSC | | 258 |

Lab. Co-op majority 7,453 (15.97%)
2.68% swing C. to Lab.
(2010: Lab. Co-op majority 4,710 (10.62%)) (2012: Lab. majority 5,334 (27.44%))

## CARDIFF WEST
E. 66,758 43,792 (65.60%) Lab. hold

| | | |
|---|---|---|
| Kevin Brennan, Lab. | | 17,803 |
| James Taghdissian, C. | | 11,014 |
| Neil McEvoy, PC | | 6,096 |
| Brian Morris, UKIP | | 4,923 |
| Cadan ap Tomos, LD | | 2,069 |
| Ken Barker, Green | | 1,704 |
| Helen Jones, TUSC | | 183 |

Lab. majority 6,789 (15.50%)
1.95% swing C. to Lab.
(2010: Lab. majority 4,750 (11.60%))

### CARMARTHEN EAST & DINEFWR
E. 55,750 T. 39,399 (70.67%) PC hold

| | |
|---|---|
| Jonathan Edwards, PC | 15,140 |
| Calum Higgins, Lab. | 9,541 |
| Matthew Paul, C. | 8,336 |
| Norma Woodward, UKIP | 4,363 |
| Ben Rice, Green | 1,091 |
| Sara Lloyd-Williams, LD | 928 |

PC majority 5,599 (14.21%)
2.53% swing Lab. to PC
(2010: PC majority 3,481 (9.16%))

### CARMARTHEN WEST & PEMBROKESHIRE SOUTH
E. 57,755 T. 40,350 (69.86%) C. hold

| | |
|---|---|
| Simon Hart, C. | 17,626 |
| Delyth Evans, Lab. | 11,572 |
| John Atkinson, UKIP | 4,698 |
| Elwyn Williams, PC | 4,201 |
| Gary Tapley, Green | 1,290 |
| Selwyn Runnett, LD | 963 |

C. majority 6,054 (15.00%)
3.28% swing Lab. to C.
(2010: C. majority 3,423 (8.45%))

### CEREDIGION
E. 54,215 T. 37,416 (69.01%) LD hold

| | |
|---|---|
| Mark Williams, LD | 13,414 |
| Mike Parker, PC | 10,347 |
| Henrietta Hensher, C. | 4,123 |
| Gethin James, UKIP | 3,829 |
| Huw Thomas, Lab. | 3,615 |
| Daniel Thompson, Green | 2,088 |

LD majority 3,067 (8.20%)
6.78% swing LD to PC
(2010: LD majority 8,324 (21.76%))

### CLWYD SOUTH
E. 54,996 T. 35,064 (63.76%) Lab. hold

| | |
|---|---|
| Susan Elan Jones, Lab. | 13,051 |
| David Nicholls, C. | 10,649 |
| Mandy Jones, UKIP | 5,480 |
| Mabon ap Gwynfor, PC | 3,620 |
| Bruce Roberts, LD | 1,349 |
| Duncan Rees, Green | 915 |

Lab. majority 2,402 (6.85%)
0.66% swing Lab. to C.
(2010: Lab. majority 2,834 (8.17%))

### CLWYD WEST
E. 58,657 T. 38,028 (64.83%) C. hold

| | |
|---|---|
| David Jones, C. | 16,463 |
| Gareth Thomas, Lab. | 9,733 |
| Warwick Nicholson, UKIP | 4,988 |
| Marc Jones, PC | 4,651 |
| Sarah Lesiter-Burgess, LD | 1,387 |
| Bob English, Soc. Lab. | 612 |
| Rory Jepson, Above | 194 |

C. majority 6,730 (17.70%)
0.43% swing Lab. to C.
(2010: C. majority 6,419 (16.84%))

### CYNON VALLEY
E. 51,421 T. 30,472 (59.26%) Lab. hold

| | |
|---|---|
| Ann Clwyd, Lab. | 14,532 |
| Cerith Griffiths, PC | 5,126 |
| Rebecca Rees-Evans, UKIP | 4,976 |
| Keith Dewhurst, C. | 3,676 |
| Angharad Jones, LD | 830 |
| John Matthews, Green | 799 |
| Chris Beggs, Soc. Lab. | 533 |

Lab. majority 9,406 (30.87%)
0.66% swing Lab. to PC
(2010: Lab. majority 9,617 (32.19%))

### DELYN
E. 53,639 T. 37,457 (69.83%) Lab. hold

| | |
|---|---|
| David Hanson, Lab. | 15,187 |
| Mark Isherwood, C. | 12,257 |
| Nigel Williams, UKIP | 6,150 |
| Paul Rowlinson, PC | 1,803 |
| Tom Rippeth, LD | 1,380 |
| Kay Roney, Green | 680 |

Lab. majority 2,930 (7.82%)
0.84% swing C. to Lab.
(2010: Lab. majority 2,272 (6.14%))

### DWYFOR MEIRIONNYDD
E. 44,395 T. 28,913 (65.13%) PC hold

| | |
|---|---|
| *Liz Saville-Roberts, PC | 11,811 |
| Neil Fairlamb, C. | 6,550 |
| Mary Griffiths Clarke, Lab. | 3,904 |
| Christopher Gillibrand, UKIP | 3,126 |
| Louise Hughes, Ind. | 1,388 |
| Steve Churchman, LD | 1,153 |
| Marc Fothergill, Green | 981 |

PC majority 5,261 (18.20%)
1.92% swing PC to C.
(2010: PC majority 6,367 (22.03%))

### GOWER
E. 61,820 T. 42,758 (69.17%) C. gain

| | |
|---|---|
| *Byron Davies, C. | 15,862 |
| Liz Evans, Lab. | 15,835 |
| Colin Beckett, UKIP | 4,773 |
| Darren Thomas, PC | 3,051 |
| Mike Sheehan, LD | 1,552 |
| Julia Marshall, Green | 1,161 |
| Baron Barnes Von Claptrap, Loony | 253 |
| Steve Roberts, Ind. | 168 |
| Mark Evans, TUSC | 103 |

C. majority 27 (0.06%)
3.25% swing Lab. to C.
(2010: Lab. majority 2,683 (6.44%))

### ISLWYN
E. 55,075 T. 35,401 (64.28%) Lab. Co-op hold

| | |
|---|---|
| Chris Evans, Lab. Co-op | 17,336 |
| Joe Smyth, UKIP | 6,932 |
| Laura Jones, C. | 5,366 |
| Lyn Ackerman, PC | 3,794 |
| Brendan D'Cruz, LD | 950 |
| Peter Varley, Green | 659 |
| Baron Von Magpie, Loony | 213 |
| Josh Rawcliffe, TUSC | 151 |

Lab. Co-op majority 10,404 (29.39%)
8.56% swing Lab. to UKIP
(2010: Lab. Co-op majority 12,215 (35.21%))

### LLANELLI
E. 59,314 T. 38,574 (65.03%) Lab. hold

| | |
|---|---|
| Nia Griffith, Lab. | 15,948 |
| Vaughan Williams, PC | 8,853 |
| Ken Rees, UKIP | 6,269 |
| Selaine Saxby, C. | 5,534 |
| Cen Phillips, LD | 751 |
| Guy Smith, Green | 689 |
| Sian Caiach, PF | 407 |
| Scott Jones, TUSC | 123 |

Lab. majority 7,095 (18.39%)
2.92% swing PC to Lab.
(2010: Lab. majority 4,701 (12.55%))

### MERTHYR TYDFIL & RHYMNEY
E. 61,719 T. 32,715 (53.01%) Lab. hold

| | |
|---|---|
| *Gerald Jones, Lab. | 17,619 |
| David Rowlands, UKIP | 6,106 |
| Bill Rees, C. | 3,292 |
| Rhayna Mann, PC | 3,099 |
| Bob Griffin, LD | 1,351 |
| Elspeth Parris, Green | 603 |
| Eddy Blanche, Ind. | 459 |
| Robert Griffiths, Comm. | 186 |

Lab. majority 11,513 (35.19%)
2.88% swing Lab. to UKIP
(2010: Lab. majority 4,056 (12.64%))

**MONMOUTH**
E. 65,706 T. 47,462 (72.23%)

| | C. hold |
|---|---|
| David Davies, C. | 23,701 |
| Ruth Jones, Lab. | 12,719 |
| Gareth Dunn, UKIP | 4,942 |
| Veronica German, LD | 2,496 |
| Jonathan Clark, PC | 1,875 |
| Christopher Were, Green | 1,629 |
| Stephen Morris, Eng. Dem. | 100 |

C. majority 10,982 (23.14%)
0.36% swing Lab. to C.
(2010: C. majority 10,425 (22.41%))

**MONTGOMERYSHIRE**
E. 48,491 T. 33,757 (69.61%)

| | C. hold |
|---|---|
| Glyn Davies, C. | 15,204 |
| Jane Dodds, LD | 9,879 |
| Des Parkinson, UKIP | 3,769 |
| Martyn Singleton, Lab. | 1,900 |
| Ann Griffith, PC | 1,745 |
| Richard Chaloner, Green | 1,260 |

C. majority 5,325 (15.77%)
6.14% swing LD to C.
(2010: C. majority 1,184 (3.50%))

**NEATH**
E. 56,099 T. 37,135 (66.20%)

| | Lab. hold |
|---|---|
| *Christina Rees, Lab. | 16,270 |
| Daniel Thomas, PC | 6,722 |
| Richard Pritchard, UKIP | 6,094 |
| Ed Hastie, C. | 5,691 |
| Catrin Brock, Green | 1,185 |
| Clare Bentley, LD | 1,173 |

Lab. majority 9,548 (25.71%)
0.31% swing Lab. to PC
(2010: Lab. majority 9,775 (26.33%))

**NEWPORT EAST**
E. 56,018 T. 35,108 (62.67%)

| | Lab. hold |
|---|---|
| Jessica Morden, Lab. | 14,290 |
| Natasha Asghar, C. | 9,585 |
| David Stock, UKIP | 6,466 |
| Paul Halliday, LD | 2,251 |
| Tony Salkeld, PC | 1,231 |
| David Mclean, Green | 887 |
| Shangara Singh Bhatoe, Soc. Lab. | 398 |

Lab. majority 4,705 (13.40%)
0.30% swing Lab. to C.
(2010: Lab. majority 1,650 (4.79%))

**NEWPORT WEST**
E. 62,145 T. 40,347 (64.92%)

| | Lab. hold |
|---|---|
| Paul Flynn, Lab. | 16,633 |
| Nick Webb, C. | 13,123 |
| Gordon Norrie, UKIP | 6,134 |
| Simon Coopey, PC | 1,604 |
| Ed Townsend, LD | 1,581 |
| Pippa Bartolotti, Green | 1,272 |

Lab. majority 3,510 (8.70%)
0.11% swing Lab. to C.
(2010: Lab. majority 3,544 (8.92%))

**OGMORE**
E. 55,320 T. 35,250 (63.72%)

| | Lab. hold |
|---|---|
| Huw Irranca-Davies, Lab. | 18,663 |
| Jane March, C. | 5,620 |
| Glenda Davies, UKIP | 5,420 |
| Tim Thomas, PC | 3,556 |
| Gerald Francis, LD | 1,072 |
| Laurie Brophy, Green | 754 |
| Emma Saunders, TUSC | 165 |

Lab. majority 13,043 (37.00%)
0.61% swing Lab. to C.
(2010: Lab. majority 13,246 (38.23%))

**PONTYPRIDD**
E. 58,929 T. 37,882 (64.28%)

| | Lab. hold |
|---|---|
| Owen Smith, Lab. | 15,554 |
| Ann-Marie Mason, C. | 6,569 |
| Andrew Tomkinson, UKIP | 5,085 |
| Mike Powell, LD | 4,904 |
| Osian Lewis, PC | 4,348 |
| Katy Clay, Green | 992 |
| Damien Biggs, Soc. Lab. | 332 |
| Esther Pearson, TUSC | 98 |

Lab. majority 8,985 (23.72%)
0.56% swing C. to Lab.
(2010: Lab. majority 2,785 (7.59%))

**PRESELI PEMBROKESHIRE**
E. 57,291 T. 40,556 (70.79%)

| | C. hold |
|---|---|
| Stephen Crabb, C. | 16,383 |
| Paul Miller, Lab. | 11,414 |
| Howard Lillyman, UKIP | 4,257 |
| Chris Overton, ISWSL | 3,729 |
| John Osmond, PC | 2,518 |
| Frances Bryant, Green | 1,452 |
| Nick Tregoning, LD | 780 |
| Rodney Maile, Worth | 23 |

C. majority 4,969 (12.25%)
0.31% swing Lab. to C.
(2010: C. majority 4,605 (11.63%))

**RHONDDA**
E. 51,809 T. 31,538 (60.87%)

| | Lab. hold |
|---|---|
| Chris Bryant, Lab. | 15,976 |
| Shelley Rees-Owen, PC | 8,521 |
| Ron Hughes, UKIP | 3,998 |
| Lyn Hudson, C. | 2,116 |
| George Summers, LD | 474 |
| Lisa Rapado, Green | 453 |

Lab. majority 7,455 (23.64%)
6.77% swing Lab. to PC
(2010: Lab. majority 11,553 (37.18%))

**SWANSEA EAST**
E. 58,011 T. 33,618 (57.95%)

| | Lab. hold |
|---|---|
| *Carolyn Harris, Lab. | 17,807 |
| Cliff Johnson, UKIP | 5,779 |
| Altaf Hussain, C. | 5,142 |
| Dic Jones, PC | 3,498 |
| Amina Jamal, LD | 1,392 |

Lab. majority 12,028 (35.78%)
6.56% swing Lab. to UKIP
(2010: Lab. majority 10,838 (33.17%))

**SWANSEA WEST**
E. 58,776 T. 35,156 (59.81%)

| | Lab. Co-op hold |
|---|---|
| Geraint Davies, Lab. Co-op | 14,967 |
| Emma Lane, C. | 7,931 |
| Martyn Ford, UKIP | 4,744 |
| Chris Holley, LD | 3,178 |
| Harri Roberts, PC | 2,266 |
| Ashley Wakeling, Green | 1,784 |
| Ronnie Job, TUSC | 159 |
| Maxwell Rosser, Ind. | 78 |
| Brian Johnson, SPGB | 49 |

Lab. Co-op majority 7,036 (20.01%)
3.08% swing C. to Lab.
(2010: Lab. majority 504 (1.42%))

**TORFAEN**
E. 61,896 T. 37,937 (61.29%)

| | Lab. hold |
|---|---|
| *Nick Thomas-Symonds, Lab. | 16,938 |
| Graham Smith, C. | 8,769 |
| Ken Beswick, UKIP | 7,203 |
| Boydd Hackley-Green, PC | 2,169 |
| Alison Willott, LD | 1,271 |
| Matt Cooke, Green | 746 |
| John Cox, Soc. Lab. | 697 |
| Mark Griffiths, Comm. | 144 |

Lab. majority 8,169 (21.53%)
1.60% swing Lab. to C.
(2010: Lab. majority 9,306 (24.72%))

**VALE OF CLWYD**
E. 56,505 T. 35,261 (62.40%)

| | C. gain |
|---|---|
| *James Davies, C. | 13,760 |
| Chris Ruane, Lab. | 13,523 |
| Paul Davies-Cooke, UKIP | 4,577 |
| Mair Rowlands, PC | 2,486 |
| Gwyn Williams, LD | 915 |

C. majority 237 (0.67%)
3.87% swing Lab. to C.
(2010: Lab. majority 2,509 (7.06%))

**VALE OF GLAMORGAN**
E. 72,187 T. 51,293 (71.06%)

| | C. hold |
|---|---|
| Alun Cairns, C. | 23,607 |
| Chris Elmore, Lab. | 16,727 |
| Kevin Mahoney, UKIP | 5,489 |
| Ian Johnson, PC | 2,869 |
| David Morgan, LD | 1,309 |
| Alan Armstrong, Green | 1,054 |
| Steve Reed, CISTA | 238 |

C. majority 6,880 (13.41%)
2.28% swing Lab. to C.
(2010: C. majority 4,307 (8.85%))

**WREXHAM**
E. 50,992 T. 32,719 (64.16%)

| | Lab. hold |
|---|---|
| Ian Lucas, Lab. | 12,181 |
| Andrew Atkinson, C. | 10,350 |
| Niall Plevin-Kelly, UKIP | 5,072 |
| Carrie Harper, PC | 2,501 |
| Rob Walsh, LD | 1,735 |
| David Munnerley, Green | 669 |
| Brian Edwards, Ind. | 211 |

Lab. majority 1,831 (5.60%)
2.94% swing Lab. to C.
(2010: Lab. majority 3,658 (11.09%))

**YNYS MON**
E. 49,944 T. 34,926 (69.93%)

| | Lab. hold |
|---|---|
| Albert Owen, Lab. | 10,871 |
| John Rowlands, PC | 10,642 |
| Michelle Willis, C. | 7,393 |
| Nathan Gill, UKIP | 5,121 |
| Mark Rosenthal, LD | 751 |
| Liz Screen, Soc. Lab. | 148 |

Lab. majority 229 (0.66%)
3.24% swing Lab. to PC
(2010: Lab. majority 2,461 (7.14%))

---

# SCOTLAND

**ABERDEEN NORTH**
E. 67,745 T. 43,936 (64.85%)

| | SNP gain |
|---|---|
| *Kirsty Blackman, SNP | 24,793 |
| Richard Baker, Lab. Co-op | 11,397 |
| Sanjoy Sen, C. | 5,304 |
| Euan Davidson, LD | 2,050 |
| Tyrinne Rutherford, TUSC | 206 |
| Christopher Willett, NF | 186 |

SNP majority 13,396 (30.49%)
26.33% swing Lab. to SNP
(2010: Lab. majority 8,361 (22.18%))

**ABERDEEN SOUTH**
E. 68,056 T. 48,551 (71.34%)

| | SNP gain |
|---|---|
| *Callum McCaig, SNP | 20,221 |
| Anne Begg, Lab. | 12,991 |
| Ross Thomson, C. | 11,087 |
| Denis Rixon, LD | 2,252 |
| Dan Yeats, Scot. Green | 964 |
| Sandra Skinner, UKIP | 897 |
| Christopher Gray, Ind. | 139 |

SNP majority 7,230 (14.89%)
19.78% swing Lab. to SNP
(2010: Lab. majority 3,506 (8.15%))

**ABERDEENSHIRE WEST &
KINCARDINE**
E. 73,445 T. 55,196 (75.15%)

| | SNP gain |
|---|---|
| *Stuart Donaldson, SNP | 22,949 |
| Alexander Burnett, C. | 15,916 |
| Robert Smith, LD | 11,812 |
| Barry Black, Lab. | 2,487 |
| David Lansdell, UKIP | 1,006 |
| Richard Openshaw, Scot. Green | 885 |
| Graham Reid, Ind. | 141 |

SNP majority 7,033 (12.74%)
21.46% swing LD to SNP
(2010: LD majority 3,684 (8.15%))

**AIRDRIE & SHOTTS**
E. 66,715 T. 44,286 (66.38%)

| | SNP gain |
|---|---|
| *Neil Gray, SNP | 23,887 |
| Pamela Nash, Lab. | 15,108 |
| Eric Holford, C. | 3,389 |
| Matt Williams, UKIP | 1,088 |
| John Love, LD | 678 |
| Deryck Beaumont, Ind. | 136 |

SNP majority 8,779 (19.82%)
27.22% swing Lab. to SNP
(2010: Lab. majority 12,408
(34.61%))

**ANGUS**
E. 65,792 T. 44,485 (67.61%)

| | SNP hold |
|---|---|
| Mike Weir, SNP | 24,130 |
| Derek Wann, C. | 12,900 |
| Gerard McMahon, Lab. | 3,919 |
| Calum Walker, UKIP | 1,355 |
| Sanjay Samani, LD | 1,216 |
| David Mumford, Scot. Green | 965 |

SNP majority 11,230 (25.24%)
8.30% swing C. to SNP
(2010: SNP majority 3,282 (8.65%))

**ARGYLL & BUTE**
E. 68,875 T. 51,883 (75.33%)

| | SNP gain |
|---|---|
| *Brendan O'Hara, SNP | 22,959 |
| Alan Reid, LD | 14,486 |
| Alastair Redman, C. | 7,733 |
| Mary Galbraith, Lab. | 5,394 |
| Caroline Santos, UKIP | 1,311 |

SNP majority 8,473 (16.33%)
14.50% swing LD to SNP
(2010: LD majority 3,431 (7.59%))

**AYR, CARRICK & CUMNOCK**
E. 72,985 T. 52,209 (71.53%)

| | SNP gain |
|---|---|
| *Corri Wilson, SNP | 25,492 |
| Sandra Osborne, Lab. | 14,227 |
| Lee Lyons, C. | 10,355 |
| Joseph Adam-Smith, UKIP | 1,280 |
| Richard Brodie, LD | 855 |

SNP majority 11,265 (21.58%)
25.34% swing Lab. to SNP
(2010: Lab. majority 9,911 (21.60%))

**AYRSHIRE CENTRAL**
E. 69,982 T. 50,774 (72.55%)

| | SNP gain |
|---|---|
| *Philippa Whitford, SNP | 26,999 |
| Brian Donohoe, Lab. | 13,410 |
| Marc Hope, C. | 8,803 |
| Gordon Bain, LD | 917 |
| Veronika Tudhope, Scot. Green | 645 |

SNP majority 13,589 (26.76%)
27.71% swing Lab. to SNP
(2010: Lab. majority 12,007
(27.34%))

**AYRSHIRE NORTH & ARRAN**
E. 75,772 T. 53,869 (71.09%)

| | SNP gain |
|---|---|
| *Patricia Gibson, SNP | 28,641 |
| Katy Clark, Lab. | 15,068 |
| Jamie Greene, C. | 7,968 |
| Sharon McGonigal, UKIP | 1,296 |
| Ruby Kirkwood, LD | 896 |

SNP majority 13,573 (25.20%)
23.33% swing Lab. to SNP
(2010: Lab. majority 9,895 (21.46%))

**BANFF & BUCHAN**
E. 68,609 T. 45,629 (66.51%)

| | SNP hold |
|---|---|
| Eilidh Whiteford, SNP | 27,487 |
| Alex Johnstone, C. | 13,148 |
| Sumon Hoque, Lab. | 2,647 |
| David Evans, LD | 2,347 |

SNP majority 14,339 (31.43%)
10.48% swing C. to SNP
(2010: SNP majority 4,027
(10.47%))

**BERWICKSHIRE, ROXBURGH &
SELKIRK**
E. 74,179 T. 55,038 (74.20%)

| | SNP gain |
|---|---|
| *Calum Kerr, SNP | 20,145 |
| John Lamont, C. | 19,817 |
| Michael Moore, LD | 10,294 |
| Kenryck Lloyd-Jones, Lab. | 2,700 |
| Peter Neilson, UKIP | 1,316 |
| Pauline Stewart, Scot. Green | 631 |
| Jesse Rae, Ind. | 135 |

SNP majority 328 (0.60%)
27.04% swing LD to SNP
(2010: LD majority 5,675 (11.58%))

## CAITHNESS, SUTHERLAND & EASTER ROSS
E. 47,558 T. 34,186 (71.88%)

|  |  | SNP gain |
|---|---|---|
| *Paul Monaghan, SNP | | 15,831 |
| John Thurso, LD | | 11,987 |
| John Erskine, Lab. | | 3,061 |
| Alastair Graham, C. | | 2,326 |
| Ann Therese Murray, UKIP | | 981 |

SNP majority 3,844 (11.24%)
16.73% swing LD to SNP
(2010: LD majority 4,826 (16.78%))

## COATBRIDGE, CHRYSTON & BELLSHILL
E. 73,813 T. 50,698 (68.68%)   SNP gain

| | |
|---|---|
| *Phil Boswell, SNP | 28,696 |
| Tom Clarke, Lab. | 17,195 |
| Mhairi Fraser, C. | 3,209 |
| Scott Cairns, UKIP | 1,049 |
| Robert Simpson, LD | 549 |

SNP majority 11,501 (22.69%)
36.22% swing Lab. to SNP
(2010: Lab. majority 20,714 (49.75%))

## CUMBERNAULD, KILSYTH & KIRKINTILLOCH EAST
E. 67,009 T. 49,382 (73.69%)

| |  | SNP gain |
|---|---|---|
| *Stuart McDonald, SNP | | 29,572 |
| Gregg McClymont, Lab. | | 14,820 |
| Malcolm Mackay, C. | | 3,891 |
| John Duncan, LD | | 1,099 |

SNP majority 14,752 (29.87%)
31.65% swing Lab. to SNP
(2010: Lab. majority 13,755 (33.43%))

## DUMFRIES & GALLOWAY
E. 75,249 T. 56,602 (75.22%)

| |  | SNP gain |
|---|---|---|
| *Richard Arkless, SNP | | 23,440 |
| Finlay Carson, C. | | 16,926 |
| Russell Brown, Lab. | | 13,982 |
| Geoff Siddall, UKIP | | 1,301 |
| Andrew Metcalf, LD | | 953 |

SNP majority 6,514 (11.51%)
25.16% swing Lab. to SNP
(2010: Lab. majority 7,449 (14.28%))

## DUMFRIESSHIRE, CLYDESDALE & TWEEDDALE
E. 68,483 T. 52,134 (76.13%)

| |  | C. hold |
|---|---|---|
| David Mundell, C. | | 20,759 |
| Emma Harper, SNP | | 19,961 |
| Archie Dryburgh, Lab. | | 7,711 |
| Kevin Newton, UKIP | | 1,472 |
| Amanda Kubie, LD | | 1,392 |
| Jody Jamieson, Scot. Green | | 839 |

C. majority 798 (1.53%)
12.87% swing C. to SNP
(2010: C. majority 4,194 (9.14%))

## DUNBARTONSHIRE EAST
E. 66,966 T. 54,871 (81.94%)

| |  | SNP gain |
|---|---|---|
| *John Nicolson, SNP | | 22,093 |
| Jo Swinson, LD | | 19,926 |
| Amanjit Jhund, Lab. | | 6,754 |
| Andrew Polson, C. | | 4,727 |
| Ross Greer, Scot. Green | | 804 |
| Wilfred Arasaratnam, UKIP | | 567 |

SNP majority 2,167 (3.95%)
16.05% swing LD to SNP
(2010: LD majority 2,184 (4.55%))

## DUNBARTONSHIRE WEST
E. 69,193 T. 51,141 (73.91%)

| |  | SNP gain |
|---|---|---|
| *Martin Docherty, SNP | | 30,198 |
| Gemma Doyle, Lab. Co-op | | 16,027 |
| Maurice Corry, C. | | 3,597 |
| Aileen Morton, LD | | 816 |
| Claire Muir, Ind. | | 503 |

SNP majority 14,171 (27.71%)
34.45% swing Lab. to SNP
(2010: Lab. Co-op majority 17,408 (41.19%))

## DUNDEE EAST
E. 66,960 T. 48,185 (71.96%)

| |  | SNP hold |
|---|---|---|
| Stewart Hosie, SNP | | 28,765 |
| Lesley Brennan, Lab. | | 9,603 |
| Bill Bowman, C. | | 7,206 |
| Craig Duncan, LD | | 1,387 |
| Helen Grayshan, Scot. Green | | 895 |
| Lesley Parker-Hamilton, CISTA | | 225 |
| Carlo Morelli, TUSC | | 104 |

SNP majority 19,162 (39.77%)
17.64% swing Lab. to SNP
(2010: SNP majority 1,821 (4.49%))

## DUNDEE WEST
E. 66,287 T. 44,714 (67.46%)

| |  | SNP gain |
|---|---|---|
| *Chris Law, SNP | | 27,684 |
| Michael Marra, Lab. | | 10,592 |
| Nicola Ross, C. | | 3,852 |
| Pauline Hinchion, Scot. Green | | 1,225 |
| Daniel Coleman, LD | | 1,057 |
| Jim McFarlane, TUSC | | 304 |

SNP majority 17,092 (38.23%)
28.91% swing Lab. to SNP
(2010: Lab. majority 7,278 (19.60%))

## DUNFERMLINE & FIFE WEST
E. 78,037 T. 55,890 (71.62%)

| |  | SNP gain |
|---|---|---|
| *Douglas Chapman, SNP | | 28,096 |
| Thomas Docherty, Lab. | | 17,744 |
| James Reekie, C. | | 6,623 |
| Gillian Cole-Hamilton, LD | | 2,232 |
| Lewis Campbell, Scot. Green | | 1,195 |

SNP majority 10,352 (18.52%)
27.07% swing Lab. to SNP
(2010: Lab. majority 5,470 (11.18%))

## EAST KILBRIDE, STRATHAVEN & LESMAHAGOW
E. 83,071 T. 60,539 (72.88%)

| |  | SNP gain |
|---|---|---|
| *Lisa Cameron, SNP | | 33,678 |
| Michael McCann, Lab. | | 17,151 |
| Graham Simpson, C. | | 7,129 |
| Robert Sale, UKIP | | 1,221 |
| Paul McGarry, LD | | 1,042 |
| John Houston, Ind. | | 318 |

SNP majority 16,527 (27.30%)
27.88% swing Lab. to SNP
(2010: Lab. majority 14,503 (28.47%))

## EAST LOTHIAN
E. 79,481 T. 59,014 (74.25%)

| |  | SNP gain |
|---|---|---|
| *George Kerevan, SNP | | 25,104 |
| Fiona O'Donnell, Lab. | | 18,301 |
| David Roach, C. | | 11,511 |
| Ettie Spencer, LD | | 1,517 |
| Jason Rose, Scot. Green | | 1,245 |
| Oluf Marshall, UKIP | | 1,178 |
| Mike Allan, Ind. | | 158 |

SNP majority 6,803 (11.53%)
20.04% swing Lab. to SNP
(2010: Lab. majority 12,258 (24.93%))

## EDINBURGH EAST
E. 66,178 T. 47,089 (71.16%)

| |  | SNP gain |
|---|---|---|
| *Tommy Sheppard, SNP | | 23,188 |
| Sheila Gilmore, Lab. | | 14,082 |
| James McMordie, C. | | 4,670 |
| Peter McColl, Scot. Green | | 2,809 |
| Karen Utting, LD | | 1,325 |
| Oliver Corbishley, UKIP | | 898 |
| Ayesha Saleem, TUSC | | 117 |

SNP majority 9,106 (19.34%)
21.18% swing Lab. to SNP
(2010: Lab. majority 9,181 (23.03%))

## EDINBURGH NORTH & LEITH
E. 80,978 T. 58,008 (71.63%)

| |  | SNP gain |
|---|---|---|
| *Deidre Brock, SNP | | 23,742 |
| Mark Lazarowicz, Lab. Co-op | | 18,145 |
| Iain McGill, C. | | 9,378 |
| Sarah Beattie-Smith, Scot. Green | | 3,140 |
| Martin Veart, LD | | 2,634 |
| Alan Melville, UKIP | | 847 |
| Bruce Whitehead, TUSC | | 122 |

SNP majority 5,597 (9.65%)
18.73% swing Lab. to SNP
(2010: Lab. Co-op majority 1,724 (3.64%))

EDINBURGH SOUTH
E. 65,846 T. 49,286 (74.85%)

|  | Lab. hold |
|---|---|
| Ian Murray, Lab. | 19,293 |
| Neil Hay, SNP | 16,656 |
| Miles Briggs, C. | 8,626 |
| Phyl Meyer, Scot. Green | 2,090 |
| Pramod Subbaraman, LD | 1,823 |
| Paul Marshall, UKIP | 601 |
| Colin Fox, SSP | 197 |

Lab. majority 2,637 (5.35%)
swing N/A
(2010: Lab. majority 316 (0.72%))

EDINBURGH SOUTH WEST
E. 72,178 T. 51,602 (71.49%)

|  | SNP gain |
|---|---|
| *Joanna Cherry, SNP | 22,168 |
| Ricky Henderson, Lab. | 14,033 |
| Gordon Lindhurst, C. | 10,444 |
| Alan Doherty, Scot. Green | 1,965 |
| Daniel Farthing-Sykes, LD | 1,920 |
| Richard Lucas, UKIP | 1,072 |

SNP majority 8,135 (15.76%)
23.22% swing Lab. to SNP
(2010: Lab. majority 8,447 (18.58%))

EDINBURGH WEST
E. 71,749 T. 54,858 (76.46%)

|  | SNP gain |
|---|---|
| *Michelle Thomson, SNP | 21,378 |
| Michael Crockart, LD | 18,168 |
| Lindsay Paterson, C. | 6,732 |
| Cammy Day, Lab. | 6,425 |
| Pat Black, Scot. Green | 1,140 |
| Otto Inglis, UKIP | 1,015 |

SNP majority 3,210 (5.85%)
14.30% swing LD to SNP
(2010: LD majority 3,803 (8.19%))

FALKIRK
E. 83,380 T. 60,340 (72.37%)

|  | SNP gain |
|---|---|
| *John McNally, SNP | 34,831 |
| Karen Whitefield, Lab. | 15,130 |
| Alison Harris, C. | 7,325 |
| David Coburn, UKIP | 1,829 |
| Galen Milne, LD | 1,225 |

SNP majority 19,701 (32.65%)
24.05% swing Lab. to SNP
(2010: Lab. majority 7,843 (15.45%))

FIFE NORTH EAST
E. 62,003 T. 45,263 (73.00%)

|  | SNP gain |
|---|---|
| *Stephen Gethins, SNP | 18,523 |
| Tim Brett, LD | 14,179 |
| Huw Bell, C. | 7,373 |
| Brian Thomson, Lab. | 3,476 |
| Andy Collins, Scot. Green | 1,387 |
| Mike Scott-Hayward, Ind. | 325 |

SNP majority 4,344 (9.60%)
19.87% swing LD to SNP
(2010: LD majority 9,048 (22.58%))

GLASGOW CENTRAL
E. 70,945 T. 39,318 (55.42%)

|  | SNP gain |
|---|---|
| *Alison Thewliss, SNP | 20,658 |
| Anas Sarwar, Lab. | 12,996 |
| Simon Bone, C. | 2,359 |
| Cass MacGregor, Scot. Green | 1,559 |
| Stuart Maskell, UKIP | 786 |
| Chris Young, LD | 612 |
| James Marris, CISTA | 171 |
| Andrew Elliott, TUSC | 119 |
| Katie Rhodes, SEP | 58 |

SNP majority 7,662 (19.49%)
27.00% swing Lab. to SNP
(2010: Lab. majority 10,551
(34.50%))

GLASGOW EAST
E. 70,378 T. 42,417 (60.27%)

|  | SNP gain |
|---|---|
| *Natalie McGarry, SNP | 24,116 |
| Margaret Curran, Lab. | 13,729 |
| Andy Morrison, C. | 2,544 |
| Arthur Thackeray, UKIP | 1,105 |
| Kim Long, Scot. Green | 381 |
| Gary McLelland, LD | 318 |
| Liam McLaughlan, SSP | 224 |

SNP majority 10,387 (24.49%)
30.65% swing Lab. to SNP
(2010: Lab. majority 11,840
(36.81%))

GLASGOW NORTH
E. 58,875 T. 36,922 (62.71%)

|  | SNP gain |
|---|---|
| *Patrick Grady, SNP | 19,610 |
| Ann McKechin, Lab. | 10,315 |
| Lauren Hankinson, C. | 2,901 |
| Martin Bartos, Scot. Green | 2,284 |
| Jade O'Neil, LD | 1,012 |
| Jamie Robertson, UKIP | 486 |
| Angela McCormick, TUSC | 160 |
| Russell Benson, CISTA | 154 |

SNP majority 9,295 (25.17%)
28.88% swing Lab. to SNP
(2010: Lab. majority 3,898 (13.16%))

GLASGOW NORTH EAST
E. 66,678 T. 37,857 (56.78%)

|  | SNP gain |
|---|---|
| *Anne McLaughlin, SNP | 21,976 |
| Willie Bain, Lab. | 12,754 |
| Annie Wells, C. | 1,769 |
| Zara Kitson, Scot. Green | 615 |
| Eileen Baxendale, LD | 300 |
| Geoff Johnson, CISTA | 225 |
| Jamie Cocozza, TUSC | 218 |

SNP majority 9,222 (24.36%)
39.28% swing Lab. to SNP
(2010: Lab. majority 15,942
(54.21%))

GLASGOW NORTH WEST
E. 68,418 T. 43,854 (64.10%)

|  | SNP gain |
|---|---|
| *Carol Monaghan, SNP | 23,908 |
| John Robertson, Lab. | 13,544 |
| Roger Lewis, C. | 3,692 |
| James Harrison, LD | 1,194 |
| Moira Crawford, Scot. Green | 1,167 |
| Chris MacKenzie, CISTA | 213 |
| Zoe Streatfield, Comm. | 136 |

SNP majority 10,364 (23.63%)
31.21% swing Lab. to SNP
(2010: Lab. majority 13,611
(38.25%))

GLASGOW SOUTH
E. 74,051 T. 48,778 (65.87%)

|  | SNP gain |
|---|---|
| *Stewart McDonald, SNP | 26,773 |
| Tom Harris, Lab. | 14,504 |
| Kyle Thornton, C. | 4,752 |
| Alastair Whitelaw, Scot. Green | 1,431 |
| Ewan Hoyle, LD | 1,019 |
| Brian Smith, TUSC | 299 |

SNP majority 12,269 (25.15%)
28.36% swing Lab. to SNP
(2010: Lab. majority 12,658
(31.57%))

GLASGOW SOUTH WEST
E. 66,209 T. 40,921 (61.81%)

|  | SNP gain |
|---|---|
| *Christopher Stephens, SNP | 23,388 |
| Ian Davidson, Lab. Co-op | 13,438 |
| Gordon McCaskill, C. | 2,036 |
| Sarah Hemy, UKIP | 970 |
| Sean Templeton, Scot. Green | 507 |
| Isabel Nelson, LD | 406 |
| Bill Bonnar, SSP | 176 |

SNP majority 9,950 (24.32%)
35.24% swing Lab. to SNP
(2010: Lab. Co-op majority 14,671
(46.16%))

GLENROTHES
E. 69,781 T. 47,598 (68.21%)

|  | SNP gain |
|---|---|
| *Peter Grant, SNP | 28,459 |
| Melanie Ward, Lab. Co-op | 14,562 |
| Alex Stewart-Clark, C. | 3,685 |
| Jane Ann Liston, LD | 892 |

SNP majority 13,897 (29.20%)
34.90% swing Lab. to SNP
(2010: Lab. majority 16,448 (40.61%))

GORDON
E. 79,393 T. 58,161 (73.26%)

|  | SNP gain |
|---|---|
| *Alex Salmond, SNP | 27,717 |
| Christine Jardine, LD | 19,030 |
| Colin Clark, C. | 6,807 |
| Braden Davy, Lab. | 3,441 |
| Emily Santos, UKIP | 1,166 |

SNP majority 8,687 (14.94%)
14.39% swing LD to SNP
(2010: LD majority 6,748 (13.83%))

INVERCLYDE
E. 59,350 T. 44,607 (75.16%)

|  | SNP gain |
|---|---|
| *Ronnie Cowan, SNP | 24,585 |
| Iain McKenzie, Lab. | 13,522 |
| George Jabbour, C. | 4,446 |
| John Watson, LD | 1,106 |
| Michael Burrows, UKIP | 715 |
| Craig Hamilton, CISTA | 233 |

SNP majority 11,063 (24.80%)
31.63% swing Lab. to SNP
(2010: Lab. majority 14,426
(38.47%)) (2011: Lab. majority 5,838
(20.78%))

INVERNESS, NAIRN, BADENOCH
& STRATHSPEY
E. 77,268 T. 57,613 (74.56%)

|  | SNP gain |
|---|---|
| *Drew Hendry, SNP | 28,838 |
| Danny Alexander, LD | 18,029 |
| Mike Robb, Lab. | 4,311 |
| Edward Mountain, C. | 3,410 |
| Isla O'Reilly, Scot. Green | 1,367 |
| Les Durance, UKIP | 1,236 |
| Donald Boyd, SCP | 422 |

SNP majority 10,809 (18.76%)
20.39% swing LD to SNP
(2010: LD majority 8,765 (18.61%))

KILMARNOCK & LOUDOUN
E. 75,233 T. 53,903 (71.65%)

|  | SNP gain |
|---|---|
| *Alan Brown, SNP | 30,000 |
| Cathy Jamieson, Lab. Co-op | 16,362 |
| Brian Whittle, C. | 6,752 |
| Rod Ackland, LD | 789 |

SNP majority 13,638 (25.30%)
25.95% swing Lab. to SNP
(2010: Lab. Co-op majority 12,378
(26.59%))

KIRKCALDY & COWDENBEATH
E. 75,941 T. 52,892 (69.65%)

|  | SNP gain |
|---|---|
| *Roger Mullin, SNP | 27,628 |
| Kenny Selbie, Lab. Co-op | 17,654 |
| Dave Dempsey, C. | 5,223 |
| Jack Neill, UKIP | 1,237 |
| Callum Leslie, LD | 1,150 |

SNP majority 9,974 (18.86%)
34.55% swing Lab. to SNP
(2010: Lab. majority 23,009
(50.24%))

LANARK & HAMILTON EAST
E. 78,846 T. 55,258 (70.08%)

|  | SNP gain |
|---|---|
| *Angela Crawley, SNP | 26,976 |
| Jim Hood, Lab. | 16,876 |
| Alex Allison, C. | 8,772 |
| Donald MacKay, UKIP | 1,431 |
| Gregg Cullen, LD | 1,203 |

SNP majority 10,100 (18.28%)
23.61% swing Lab. to SNP
(2010: Lab. majority 13,478
(28.95%))

LINLITHGOW & FALKIRK EAST
E. 86,955 T. 61,597 (70.84%)

|  | SNP gain |
|---|---|
| *Martyn Day, SNP | 32,055 |
| Michael Connarty, Lab. | 19,121 |
| Sandy Batho, C. | 7,384 |
| Alistair Forrest, UKIP | 1,682 |
| Emma Farthing-Sykes, LD | 1,252 |
| Neil McIvor, NF | 103 |

SNP majority 12,934 (21.00%)
22.70% swing Lab. to SNP
(2010: Lab. majority 12,553 (24.40%))

LIVINGSTON
E. 82,373 T. 57,547 (69.86%)

|  | SNP gain |
|---|---|
| *Hannah Bardell, SNP | 32,736 |
| Graeme Morrice, Lab. | 15,893 |
| Chris Donnelly, C. | 5,929 |
| Nathan Somerville, UKIP | 1,757 |
| Charles Dundas, LD | 1,232 |

SNP majority 16,843 (29.27%)
25.90% swing Lab. to SNP
(2010: Lab. majority 10,791
(22.52%))

MIDLOTHIAN
E. 67,875 T. 48,331 (71.21%)

|  | SNP gain |
|---|---|
| *Owen Thompson, SNP | 24,453 |
| Kenny Young, Lab. | 14,594 |
| Michelle Ballantyne, C. | 5,760 |
| Ian Baxter, Scot. Green | 1,219 |
| Gordon Norrie, UKIP | 1,173 |
| Aisha Mir, LD | 1,132 |

SNP majority 9,859 (20.40%)
23.39% swing Lab. to SNP
(2010: Lab. majority 10,349 (26.37%))

MORAY
E. 71,685 T. 49,280 (68.75%)

|  | SNP hold |
|---|---|
| Angus Robertson, SNP | 24,384 |
| Douglas Ross, C. | 15,319 |
| Sean Morton, Lab. | 4,898 |
| Robert Scorer, UKIP | 1,939 |
| Jamie Paterson, LD | 1,395 |
| James MacKessack-Leitch, Scot. Green | 1,345 |

SNP majority 9,065 (18.39%)
swing N/A
(2010: SNP majority 5,590
(13.63%))

MOTHERWELL & WISHAW
E. 70,269 T. 48,237 (68.65%)

|  | SNP gain |
|---|---|
| *Marion Fellows, SNP | 27,275 |
| Frank Roy, Lab. | 15,377 |
| Meghan Gallacher, C. | 3,695 |
| Neil Wilson, UKIP | 1,289 |
| Ross Laird, LD | 601 |

SNP majority 11,898 (24.67%)
33.81% swing Lab. to SNP
(2010: Lab. majority 16,806
(42.96%))

NA H-EILEANAN AN IAR
E. 21,744 T. 15,938 (73.30%)

|  | SNP hold |
|---|---|
| Angus MacNeil, SNP | 8,662 |
| Alasdair Morrison, Lab. | 4,560 |
| Mark Brown, C. | 1,215 |
| John Cormack, SCP | 1,045 |
| Ruaraidh Ferguson, LD | 456 |

SNP majority 4,102 (25.74%)
6.46% swing Lab. to SNP
(2010: SNP majority 1,885
(12.81%))

OCHIL & PERTHSHIRE SOUTH
E. 77,370 T. 57,871 (74.80%)

|  | SNP gain |
|---|---|
| *Tasmina Ahmed-Sheikh, SNP | 26,620 |
| Gordon Banks, Lab. | 16,452 |
| Luke Graham, C. | 11,987 |
| Iliyan Stefanov, LD | 1,481 |
| Martin Gray, UKIP | 1,331 |

SNP majority 10,168 (17.57%)
13.92% swing Lab. to SNP
(2010: Lab. majority 5,187 (10.28%))

ORKNEY & SHETLAND
E. 34,551 T. 22,728 (65.78%)

|  | LD hold |
|---|---|
| Alistair Carmichael, LD | 9,407 |
| Danus Skene, SNP | 8,590 |
| Donald Cameron, C. | 2,025 |
| Gerry McGarvey, Lab. | 1,624 |
| Robert Smith, UKIP | 1,082 |

LD majority 817 (3.59%)
23.91% swing LD to SNP
(2010: LD majority 9,928 (51.32%))

PAISLEY & RENFREWSHIRE
NORTH
E. 66,206 T. 50,462 (76.22%)

|  | SNP gain |
|---|---|
| *Gavin Newlands, SNP | 25,601 |
| Jim Sheridan, Lab. | 16,525 |
| John Anderson, C. | 6,183 |
| James Speirs, LD | 1,055 |
| Ryan Morrison, Scot. Green | 703 |
| Andy Doyle, CISTA | 202 |
| Jim Halfpenny, TUSC | 193 |

SNP majority 9,076 (17.99%)
26.47% swing Lab. to SNP
(2010: Lab. majority 15,280
(34.96%))

PAISLEY & RENFREWSHIRE
SOUTH
E. 61,281 T. 46,226 (75.43%)

|  | SNP gain |
|---|---|
| *Mhairi Black, SNP | 23,548 |
| Douglas Alexander, Lab. | 17,864 |
| Fraser Galloway, C. | 3,526 |
| Eileen McCartin, LD | 1,010 |
| Sandra Webster, SSP | 278 |

SNP majority 5,684 (12.30%)
26.92% swing Lab. to SNP
(2010: Lab. majority 16,614
(41.54%))

**PERTH & PERTHSHIRE NORTH**
E. 72,447 T. 54,200 (74.81%)

| | SNP hold |
|---|---|
| Pete Wishart, SNP | 27,379 |
| Alexander Stewart, C. | 17,738 |
| Scott Nicholson, Lab. | 4,413 |
| Peter Barrett, LD | 2,059 |
| Louise Ramsay, Scot. Green | 1,146 |
| John Myles, UKIP | 1,110 |
| Xander McDade, Ind. | 355 |

SNP majority 9,641 (17.79%)
4.36% swing C. to SNP
(2010: SNP majority 4,379 (9.07%))

**RENFREWSHIRE EAST**
E. 69,982 T. 56,730 (81.06%)

| | SNP gain |
|---|---|
| *Kirsten Oswald, SNP | 23,013 |
| Jim Murphy, Lab. | 19,295 |
| David Montgomery, C. | 12,465 |
| Graeme Cowie, LD | 1,069 |
| Robert Malyn, UKIP | 888 |

SNP majority 3,718 (6.55%)
24.23% swing Lab. to SNP
(2010: Lab. majority 10,420 (20.36%))

**ROSS, SKYE & LOCHABER**
E. 54,169 T. 41,811 (77.19%)

| | SNP gain |
|---|---|
| *Ian Blackford, SNP | 20,119 |
| Charles Kennedy, LD | 14,995 |
| Lindsay McCallum, C. | 2,598 |
| Chris Conniff, Lab. | 2,043 |
| Anne Thomas, Scot. Green | 1,051 |
| Philip Anderson, UKIP | 814 |
| Ronnie Campbell, Ind. | 191 |

SNP majority 5,124 (12.26%)
24.89% swing LD to SNP
(2010: LD majority 13,070 (37.52%))

**RUTHERGLEN & HAMILTON WEST**
E. 82,701 T. 57,615 (69.67%)

| | SNP gain |
|---|---|
| *Margaret Ferrier, SNP | 30,279 |
| Tom Greatrex, Lab. Co-op | 20,304 |
| Taylor Muir, C. | 4,350 |
| Janice MacKay, UKIP | 1,301 |
| Tony Hughes, LD | 1,045 |
| Yvonne Maclean, CISTA | 336 |

SNP majority 9,975 (17.31%)
31.01% swing Lab. to SNP
(2010: Lab. Co-op majority 21,002 (44.70%))

**STIRLING**
E. 67,236 T. 52,135 (77.54%)

| | SNP gain |
|---|---|
| *Steven Paterson, SNP | 23,783 |
| Johanna Boyd, Lab. | 13,303 |
| Stephen Kerr, C. | 12,051 |
| Mark Ruskell, Scot. Green | 1,606 |
| Elisabeth Wilson, LD | 1,392 |

SNP majority 10,480 (20.10%)
22.30% swing Lab. to SNP
(2010: Lab. majority 8,354 (17.85%))

# NORTHERN IRELAND

**ANTRIM EAST**
E. 62,810 T. 33,497 (53.33%)

| | DUP hold |
|---|---|
| Sammy Wilson, DUP | 12,103 |
| Roy Beggs, UUP | 6,308 |
| Stewart Dickson, Alliance | 5,021 |
| Noel Jordan, UKIP | 3,660 |
| Oliver McMullan, SF | 2,314 |
| Ruth Wilson, TUV | 1,903 |
| Margaret Anne McKillop, SDLP | 1,639 |
| Alex Wilson, C. | 549 |

DUP majority 5,795 (17.30%)
swing N/A
(2010: DUP majority 6,770 (22.20%))

**ANTRIM NORTH**
E. 75,874 T. 41,907 (55.23%)

| | DUP hold |
|---|---|
| Ian Paisley, DUP | 18,107 |
| Timothy Gaston, TUV | 6,561 |
| Daithi McKay, SF | 5,143 |
| Robin Swann, UUP | 5,054 |
| Declan O'Loan, SDLP | 2,925 |
| Jayne Dunlop, Alliance | 2,351 |
| Robert Hill, UKIP | 1,341 |
| Carol Freeman, C. | 368 |
| Thomas Palmer, Ind. | 57 |

DUP majority 11,546 (27.55%)
1.03% swing DUP to TUV
(2010: DUP majority 12,558 (29.62%))

**ANTRIM SOUTH**
E. 67,423 T. 36,523 (54.17%)

| | UUP gain |
|---|---|
| *Danny Kinahan, UUP | 11,942 |
| William McCrea, DUP | 10,993 |
| Declan Kearney, SF | 4,699 |
| Neil Kelly, Alliance | 3,576 |
| Roisin Lynch, SDLP | 2,990 |
| Richard Cairns, TUV | 1,908 |
| Alan Dunlop, C. | 415 |

UUP majority 949 (2.60%)
swing N/A
(2010: DUP majority 1,183 (3.48%))

**BELFAST EAST**
E. 63,154 T. 39,682 (62.83%)

| | DUP gain |
|---|---|
| *Gavin Robinson, DUP | 19,575 |
| Naomi Long, Alliance | 16,978 |
| Neil Wilson, C. | 1,121 |
| Ross Brown, Green | 1,058 |
| Niall O Donnghaile, SF | 823 |
| Mary Muldoon, SDLP | 127 |

DUP majority 2,597 (6.54%)
5.49% swing Alliance to DUP
(2010: Alliance majority 1,533 (4.45%))

**BELFAST NORTH**
E. 68,552 T. 40,593 (59.21%)

| | DUP hold |
|---|---|
| Nigel Dodds, DUP | 19,096 |
| Gerry Kelly, SF | 13,770 |
| Alban Maginness, SDLP | 3,338 |
| Jason O'Neill, Alliance | 2,941 |
| Gemma Weir, WP | 919 |
| Fra Hughes, Ind. | 529 |

DUP majority 5,326 (13.12%)
3.55% swing SF to DUP
(2010: DUP majority 2,224 (6.01%))

**BELFAST SOUTH**
E. 64,912 T. 38,957 (60.02%)

| | SDLP hold |
|---|---|
| Alasdair McDonnell, SDLP | 9,560 |
| Jonathan Bell, DUP | 8,654 |
| Paula Bradshaw, Alliance | 6,711 |
| Mairtin O Muilleoir, SF | 5,402 |
| Rodney McCune, UUP | 3,549 |
| Clare Bailey, Green | 2,238 |
| Bob Stoker, UKIP | 1,900 |
| Ben Manton, C. | 582 |
| Lily Kerr, WP | 361 |

SDLP majority 906 (2.33%)
7.50% swing SDLP to DUP
(2010: SDLP majority 5,926 (17.33%))

**BELFAST WEST**
E. 62,685 T. 35,329 (56.36%)   SF
hold

| | |
|---|---:|
| Paul Maskey, SF | 19,163 |
| Gerry Carroll, PBP | 6,798 |
| Alex Attwood, SDLP | 3,475 |
| Frank McCoubrey, DUP | 2,773 |
| Bill Manwaring, UUP | 1,088 |
| Brian Higginson, UKIP | 765 |
| Gerard Catney, Alliance | 636 |
| John Lowry, WP | 597 |
| Paul Shea, C. | 34 |

SF majority 12,365 (35.00%)
swing N/A
(2010: SF majority 17,579 (54.71%))
(2011: SF majority 13,123 (50.6%))

**DOWN NORTH**
E. 64,207 T. 35,947 (55.99%)
Ind. hold

| | |
|---|---:|
| Lady (Sylvia) Hermon, Ind. | 17,689 |
| Alex Easton, DUP | 8,487 |
| Andrew Muir, Alliance | 3,086 |
| Steven Agnew, Green | 1,958 |
| Mark Brotherston, C. | 1,593 |
| Jonny Lavery, UKIP | 1,482 |
| William Cudworth, TUV | 686 |
| Tom Woolley, SDLP | 355 |
| Glenn Donnelly, CISTA | 338 |
| Therese McCartney, SF | 273 |

Ind. majority 9,202 (25.60%)
swing N/A
(2010: Ind. majority 14,364
(42.90%))

**DOWN SOUTH**
E. 75,215 T. 42,697 (56.77%)
SDLP hold

| | |
|---|---:|
| Margaret Ritchie, SDLP | 18,077 |
| Chris Hazzard, SF | 12,186 |
| Harold McKee, UUP | 3,964 |
| Jim Wells, DUP | 3,486 |
| Henry Reilly, UKIP | 3,044 |
| Martyn Todd, Alliance | 1,622 |
| Felicity Buchan, C. | 318 |

SDLP majority 5,891 (13.80%)
2.98% swing SDLP to SF
(2010: SDLP majority 8,412
(19.75%))

**FERMANAGH & SOUTH TYRONE**
E. 70,106 T. 50,864 (72.55%)
UUP gain

| | |
|---|---:|
| *Tom Elliott, UUP | 23,608 |
| Michelle Gildernew, SF | 23,078 |
| John Coyle, SDLP | 2,732 |
| Tanya Jones, Green | 788 |
| Hannah Su, Alliance | 658 |

UUP majority 530 (1.04%)
swing N/A
(2010: SF majority 4 (0.01%))

**FOYLE**
E. 70,035 T. 37,002 (52.83%)
SDLP hold

| | |
|---|---:|
| Mark Durkan, SDLP | 17,725 |
| Gearoid O hEara, SF | 11,679 |
| Gary Middleton, DUP | 4,573 |
| Julia Kee, UUP | 1,226 |
| David Hawthorne, Alliance | 835 |
| Kyle Thompson, UKIP | 832 |
| Hamish Badenoch, C. | 132 |

SDLP majority 6,046 (16.34%)
1.80% swing SF to SDLP
(2010: SDLP majority 4,824
(12.73%))

**LAGAN VALLEY**
E. 71,140 T. 39,795 (55.94%)
DUP hold

| | |
|---|---:|
| Jeffrey Donaldson, DUP | 19,055 |
| Alex Redpath, UUP | 6,055 |
| Trevor Lunn, Alliance | 5,544 |
| Pat Catney, SDLP | 2,500 |
| Alan Love, UKIP | 2,200 |
| Samuel Morrison, TUV | 1,887 |
| Jacqui McGeough, SF | 1,144 |
| Jonny Orr, Ind. | 756 |
| Helen Osborne, C. | 654 |

DUP majority 13,000 (32.67%)
swing N/A
(2010: DUP majority 10,486
(28.70%))

**LONDONDERRY EAST**
E. 66,925 T. 34,714 (51.87%)
DUP hold

| | |
|---|---:|
| Gregory Campbell, DUP | 14,663 |
| Caoimhe Archibald, SF | 6,859 |
| William McCandless, UUP | 5,333 |
| Gerry Mullan, SDLP | 4,268 |
| Yvonne Boyle, Alliance | 2,642 |
| Neil Paine, CISTA | 527 |
| Liz St Clair-Legge, C. | 422 |

DUP majority 7,804 (22.48%)
3.58% swing SF to DUP
(2010: DUP majority 5,355
(15.32%))

**NEWRY & ARMAGH**
E. 77,622 T. 49,877 (64.26%)
SF hold

| | |
|---|---:|
| *Mickey Brady, SF | 20,488 |
| Danny Kennedy, UUP | 16,312 |
| Justin McNulty, SDLP | 12,026 |
| Kate Nicholl, Alliance | 841 |
| Robert Rigby, C. | 210 |

SF majority 4,176 (8.37%)
swing N/A
(2010: SF majority 8,331 (18.55%))

**STRANGFORD**
E. 64,286 T. 33,924 (52.77%)
DUP hold

| | |
|---|---:|
| Jim Shannon, DUP | 15,053 |
| Robert Burgess, UUP | 4,868 |
| Kellie Armstrong, Alliance | 4,687 |
| Joe Boyle, SDLP | 2,335 |
| Joe Jordan, UKIP | 2,237 |
| Johnny Andrews, C. | 2,167 |
| Stephen Cooper, TUV | 1,701 |
| Sheila Bailie, SF | 876 |

DUP majority 10,185 (30.02%)
swing N/A
(2010: DUP majority 5,876
(18.08%))

**TYRONE WEST**
E. 63,854 T. 38,654 (60.53%)
SF hold

| | |
|---|---:|
| Pat Doherty, SF | 16,807 |
| Tom Buchanan, DUP | 6,747 |
| Daniel McCrossan, SDLP | 6,444 |
| Ross Hussey, UUP | 6,144 |
| Stephen Donnelly, Alliance | 869 |
| Ciaran McClean, Green | 780 |
| Barry Brown, CISTA | 528 |
| Claire-Louise Leyland, C. | 169 |
| Susan-Anne White, Ind. | 166 |

SF majority 10,060 (26.03%)
1.32% swing SF to DUP
(2010: SF majority 10,685 (28.67%))

**ULSTER MID**
E. 67,831 T. 40,922 (60.33%)
SF hold

| | |
|---|---:|
| Francie Molloy, SF | 19,935 |
| Sandra Overend, UUP | 6,318 |
| Ian McCrea, DUP | 5,465 |
| Malachy Quinn, SDLP | 5,055 |
| Gareth Ferguson, TUV | 1,892 |
| Alan Day, UKIP | 863 |
| Eric Bullick, Alliance | 778 |
| Hugh Scullion, WP | 496 |
| Lucille Nicholson, C. | 120 |

SF majority 13,617 (33.28%)
swing N/A
(2010: SF majority 15,363 (37.62%))
(2013: SF majority 4,681 (12.58%))

**UPPER BANN**
E. 80,052 T. 47,219 (58.99%)
DUP hold

| | |
|---|---:|
| David Simpson, DUP | 15,430 |
| Jo-Anne Dobson, UUP | 13,166 |
| Catherine Seeley, SF | 11,593 |
| Dolores Kelly, SDLP | 4,238 |
| Peter Lavery, Alliance | 1,780 |
| Martin Kelly, CISTA | 460 |
| Damien Harte, WP | 351 |
| Amandeep Singh Bhogal, C. | 201 |

DUP majority 2,264 (4.79%)
swing N/A
(2010: DUP majority 3,361 (8.12%))

# MANIFESTO COMMITMENTS

## THE CONSERVATIVE PARTY MANIFESTO 2015

Below are selected key commitments made by the Conservative Party in their 2015 manifesto.

### ECONOMY AND TAXATION
- Increase the income tax personal allowance to £12,500
- Increase the higher rate income tax threshold to £50,000
- Freeze income tax, national insurance and VAT rates for the duration of the next parliament
- Reduce government spending by 1 per cent in real terms for the first two years of the next parliament
- Increase annual tax charges paid by those with non-domiciled status
- Invest in infrastructure and devolve power to support industry growth and jobs in the English regions

### HEALTH
- Provide an additional £8bn of real terms funding to NHS England over the five years to 2020
- Ensure everyone can access a GP and necessary hospital care seven days a week by 2020
- Guarantee same-day GP appointments for those aged 75 and over if they need one
- Continue to invest in the Cancer Drugs Fund and deliver earlier detection and diagnosis, and better treatment and care for cancer and dementia patients
- Increase funding for mental health care and enforce new access and waiting time standards for those with mental ill-health

### EDUCATION
- Train an extra 17,500 maths and physics teachers over the next five years
- Create 3 million new apprenticeships
- Ensure there is no cap on university places
- Turn every 'failing' secondary school into an academy
- Support the delivery of free schools for parents and communities that want them

### LAW AND ORDER
- Replace the Human Rights Act with a British Bill of Rights; curtailing the role of the European Court of Human Rights and making the UK Supreme Court arbiter of human rights matters in the UK
- Develop the role of Police and Crime Commissioners

- Prioritise victim support
- Deploy new technology to monitor offenders in the community and to bring persistent offenders to justice quickly
- Continue to reform the police and prison systems

### SOCIETY
- Support museums, libraries, media, press freedom, creative industries and tourism
- Introduce three days a year paid volunteering leave for those in the public sector and with big companies
- Guarantee a place on the National Citizen Service scheme for every 16 and 17-year-old who wants one
- Build 200,000 new starter homes for first-time buyers aged under 40
- Increase the state pension by at least 2.5 per cent, in line with inflation, or in line with earnings – whichever is higher

### IMMIGRATION
- Continue to work towards the goal of reducing annual net migration to under 100,000 a year*
- Maintain an annual cap of 20,700 on the number of skilled migrants who can come to the UK from outside the EU
- Reform welfare rules so that EU migrants have to be resident in the UK for at least four years before they can claim certain benefits or social housing
- End the provision of out of work benefits for all EU migrants
- Migrants will be required to leave the UK if they have not found a job within six months
- Enhance border security and strengthen the enforcement of immigration rules

* For the year ending December 2014 net migration stood at 318,000 (*Source:* ONS)

### POLITICAL REFORM
- Maintain the Westminster Parliament as the UKs law-making body
- Give English MPs a veto over matters only affecting England
- Introduce a Scotland bill, to ensure that more than 50 per cent of the Scottish parliament's budget is funded from revenues raised in Scotland and also devolve further powers in welfare, taxation and spending to the Scottish parliament
- Devolve new powers to the Welsh Assembly, including control over its name, size, assembly electoral system and voting age
- Fully implement the Stormont House Agreement in Northern Ireland

ENVIRONMENT
• Establishing a new 'Blue Belt' category to protect marine habitats
• Spend £3bn over this parliament enhancing England's countryside
• Build 1,400 new flood defence schemes to protect 300,000 homes
• Work with the natural capital committee on a 25-year plan to restore the UK's biodiversity
• Phase-out public subsidies for new onshore wind farms

DEFENCE AND FOREIGN AFFAIRS
• Give the UK people a say in whether we should remain in the EU, with an 'in-out' referendum by 2017
• Work for peace and stability in Iraq and Syria; pursuing a comprehensive political and military strategy to defeat IS
• Uphold the sovereignty of Ukraine by continuing to reject Russia's illegal annexation of Crimea
• Invest at least £160bn in new military equipment over the next decade
• Spend 0.7 per cent of GNI on international development

# POLITICAL PARTIES' KEY PLEDGES

Includes the political parties which are represented by at least one MP in the current parliament (see State of the Parties, page 14). The parties are ordered by number of seats held and then alphabetical order if tied.

CONSERVATIVES
• Eliminate the deficit and be running a surplus by the end of the parliament
• Provide an extra £8bn above inflation for the NHS by 2020
• Extend the right-to-buy scheme to housing association tenants in England
• Introduce legislation so that those working 30 hours a week on the minimum wage are not eligible for tax
• 30 hours of free childcare a week for working parents of all three- and four-year-olds
• Referendum on the UK's EU membership

LABOUR
• Cut the deficit every year; balance the books as soon as possible in next parliament
• An extra £2.5bn for the NHS, largely paid for by a mansion tax on properties valued at over £2m
• Increase the hourly minimum wage to more than £8 by 2019
• No increases in VAT, national insurance or basic and higher rates of income tax

• Access to childcare from 8am to 6pm for parents of primary school children
• A freeze on energy bills until 2017 and new powers to the energy regulator to reduce bills for winter 2015

SCOTTISH NATIONAL PARTY
• Increase government spending by 0.5 per cent a year to enable £140bn extra investment in the economy and public services
• Annual UK target of 100,000 affordable homes
• Increase the hourly minimum wage to £8.70 by 2020
• Restore the 50 per cent income tax rate for those earning over £150,000
• Build an alliance against the renewal of the Trident nuclear weapons system
• Retain the triple lock on pensions and protect the winter fuel allowance

DEMOCRATIC UNIONIST PARTY
• Grow the Northern Ireland economy by making the region an attractive option for foreign investment
• Deliver world class public services
• Create a society based on fairness and opportunity for everyone
• Make politics and government work better in Northern Ireland and enhance British identity

LIBERAL DEMOCRATS
• Balance the budget fairly through a mixture of cuts and taxes on higher earners
• Increase the tax-free allowance to £12,500
• Guarantee education funding for all from nursery age to 19 years and ensure every school-aged child is taught by a qualified teacher
• Invest £8bn in the NHS and bring mental health care in line with that provided for physical health
• Five new laws to protect the natural environment and fight climate change

SINN FEIN
• End austerity – negotiate an extra £1.5bn for job creation and strong public services in Northern Ireland
• Return economic powers for a fair recovery, including full control over income tax
• Fully implement the welfare protection outlined in the Stormont House Agreement
• Continue to campaign for a referendum on Irish unity

PLAID CYMRU
• Living wage for all employees by 2020
• Extra 1,000 doctors for Wales NHS
• Devolve control of the criminal justice system – including policing – to Wales

- Oppose renewal of the Trident nuclear weapons system
- Wales to get the same devolved powers and similar funding to Scotland – an additional £1.2bn a year

## SOCIAL DEMOCRATIC AND LABOUR PARTY
- A Scottish-style commission on devolving fiscal powers to Northern Ireland
- A prosperity process rather than continued austerity
- VAT in the hospitality and tourism industry reduced to 5 per cent
- Opposition to further welfare spending cuts

## ULSTER UNIONIST PARTY
- Reduce the rate of corporation tax in Northern Ireland to encourage economic growth and create tens of thousands of new jobs
- An integrated education system in Northern Ireland where children mix from age four to ensure against sectarianism
- Benchmark the performance of the NHS in Northern Ireland against the best performing aspects of the NHS in other parts of the UK
- Improve mental health and wellbeing

## GREEN
- End austerity and restore the public sector, creating jobs that pay at least a living wage
- End privatisation of the NHS and re-nationalise the railways
- Work with other countries on climate change to ensure global temperature increases do not exceed 2°C
- Invest £85bn in a public programme of renewable fuel generation, flood defences and building insulation
- Provide 500,000 social homes for rent by 2020 and introduce rent caps

## UK INDEPENDENCE PARTY
- Hold a referendum on the UK's membership of the European Union
- Limit immigration to 50,000 skilled workers a year and implement a five-year ban on unskilled immigration
- Provide an additional £3bn a year of funding for the NHS in England
- No tax on the minimum wage
- Meet the NATO target of spending 2 per cent of GDP on defence, and look to increase this target substantially

# THE GOVERNMENT

*as at 1 September 2015*

## THE CABINET

*Prime Minister, First Lord of the Treasury and Minister for the Civil Service*
Rt. Hon. David Cameron, MP
*Chancellor of the Exchequer and First Secretary of State*
Rt. Hon. George Osborne, MP
*Secretary of State for Foreign and Commonwealth Affairs*
Rt. Hon. Philip Hammond, MP
*Secretary of State for the Home Department*
Rt. Hon. Theresa May, MP
*Lord Chancellor and Secretary of State for Justice*
Rt. Hon. Michael Gove, MP
*Secretary of State for Defence*
Rt. Hon. Michael Fallon, MP
*Secretary of State for Work and Pensions*
Rt. Hon. Iain Duncan Smith, MP
*Secretary of State for Health*
Rt. Hon. Jeremy Hunt, MP
*Lord President of the Council and Leader of the House of Commons*
Rt. Hon. Chris Grayling, MP
*Secretary of State for International Development*
Rt. Hon. Justine Greening, MP
*Secretary of State for Education and Minister for Women and Equalities*
Rt. Hon. Nicky Morgan, MP
*Lord Privy Seal and Leader of the House of Lords*
Rt. Hon. Baroness Stowell of Beeston, MBE
*Secretary of State for Transport*
Rt. Hon. Patrick McLoughlin, MP
*Secretary of State for Business, Innovation and Skills and President of the Board of Trade*
Rt. Hon. Sajid Javid, MP
*Secretary of State for Northern Ireland*
Rt. Hon. Theresa Villiers, MP
*Secretary of State for Environment, Food and Rural Affairs*
Rt. Hon. Elizabeth Truss, MP
*Secretary of State for Communities and Local Government*
Rt. Hon. Greg Clark, MP
*Secretary of State for Wales*
Rt. Hon. Stephen Crabb, MP
*Chancellor of the Duchy of Lancaster*
Rt. Hon. Oliver Letwin, MP
*Secretary of State for Culture, Media and Sport*
Rt. Hon. John Whittingdale, MP
*Secretary of State for Scotland*
David Mundell, MP

*Secretary of State for Energy and Climate Change*
Rt. Hon. Amber Rudd, MP

## ALSO ATTENDING CABINET MEETINGS
*Attorney-General*
Rt. Hon. Jeremy Wright, QC, MP
*Minister for the Cabinet Office and Paymaster General*
Rt. Hon. Matthew Hancock, MP
*Chief Secretary to the Treasury*
Rt. Hon. Greg Hands, MP
*Minister for Small Business, Industry and Enterprise*
Rt. Hon. Anna Soubry, MP
*Minister without Portfolio*
Rt. Hon. Robert Halfon, MP
*Parliamentary Secretary to the Treasury and Chief Whip*
Rt. Hon. Mark Harper, MP
*Minister of State at the Foreign and Commonwealth Office*
Rt. Hon. Baroness Anelay of St Johns, DBE
*Minister of State for Employment*
Rt. Hon. Priti Patel, MP

## LAW OFFICERS

*Attorney-General*
Rt. Hon. Jeremy Wright, QC, MP
*Solicitor-General*
Robert Buckland, QC, MP
*Advocate-General for Scotland*
Rt. Hon. Lord Keen of Elie, QC

## MINISTERS OF STATE

*Business, Innovation and Skills*
Jo Johnson, MP
*Ed Vaizey, MP
†Rt. Hon. Lord Maude of Horsham
‡Nick Boles, MP
*Communities and Local Government*
Rt. Hon. Mark Francois, MP
Brandon Lewis, MP
*Culture, Media and Sport*
§Ed Vaizey, MP
*Defence*
Philip Dunne, MP
Penny Mordaunt, MP
Rt. Hon. Earl Howe
*Education*
§Nick Boles, MP
Nick Gibb, MP
Edward Timpson, MP

*Energy and Climate Change*
Andrea Leadsom, MP
*Enivronment, Food and Rural Affairs*
George Eustice, MP
*Foreign and Commonwealth Office*
Rt. Hon. David Lidington, MP
Rt. Hon. Hugo Swire, MP
§Rt. Hon. Lord Maude of Horsham
Rt. Hon. Baroness Anelay of St Johns, DBE
Rt. Hon. Grant Shapps, MP
*Health*
Rt. Hon. Alistair Burt, MP
*Home Office*
Rt. Hon. Mike Penning, MP
Rt. Hon. John Hayes, MP
James Brokenshire, MP
Rt. Hon. Lord Bates
*Justice*
Rt. Hon. Mike Penning, MP
Rt. Hon. Lord Faulks, QC
*International Development*
Rt. Hon. Grant Shapps, MP
Rt. Hon. Desmond Swayne, TD, MP
*Work and Pensions*
Rt. Hon. Priti Patel, MP
Rt. Hon. Lord Freud
Baroness Altmann, CBE
*UK Export Finance*
\*\*Lord Maude of Horsham

\* position held jointly with the Department for Culture, Media and Sport
† position held jointly with the Foreign and Commonwealth Office (FCO)
‡ position held jointly with the Department for Education
§ position held jointly with the Department for Business, Innovation and Skills (BIS)
\*\* position held jointly with the the FCO and the BIS

## UNDER-SECRETARIES OF STATE

*Business, Innovation and Skills*
\*George Freeman, MP
Baroness Neville-Rolfe, DBE, CMG
*Communities and Local Government*
Marcus Jones, MP
*Culture, Media and Sport*
Richard Harrington, MP
Baroness Neville-Rolfe, DBE, CMG
Tracey Crouch, MP
Baroness Shields, OBE
*Defence*
Mark Lancaster, TD, MP
Julian Brazier, MP
*Education*
Caroline Dinenage, MP
Sam Gyimah, MP
Lord Nash

*Energy and Climate Change*
Lord Bourne of Aberystwyth
*Environment, Food and Rural Affairs*
Rory Stewart, MP
*Foreign and Commonwealth Office*
Tobias Ellwood, MP
*Health*
Ben Gummer, MP
Jane Ellison, MP
†George Freeman, MP
Lord Prior of Brampton
*Home Office*
Karen Bradley, MP
Lord Ahmad of Wimbledon
Richard Harrington, MP
*International Development*
Baroness Verma
Richard Harrington, MP
*Justice*
Caroline Dinenage, MP
Dominic Raab, MP
Andrew Selous, MP
Shailesh Vara, MP
*Northern Ireland Office*
Ben Wallace, MP
*Scotland Office*
Lord Dunlop
*Transport*
Robert Goodwill, MP
Claire Perry, MP
Andrew Jones, MP
Lord Ahmad of Wimbledon
*Wales Office*
Alun Cairns, MP
Lord Bourne of Aberystwyth
*Work and Pensions*
Justin Tomlinson, MP
Shailesh Vara, MP

\* Jointly with the Department for Health
† Jointly with BIS

## OTHER MINISTERS

*Cabinet Office*
Rob Wilson, MP *(Parliamentary Secretary)*
John Penrose, MP *(Parliamentary Secretary)*
Lord Bridges of Headley *(Parliamentary Secretary)*
James Wharton, MP
Baroness Williams of Trafford
*Office of the Leader of the House of Commons*
Thérèse Coffey, MP
*(Parliamentary Secretary and Deputy Leader of the Commons)*
*Office of the Leader of the House of Lords*
Rt. Hon. Earl Howe *(Deputy Leader of the House of Lords)*

*Treasury*
Damian Hinds, MP *(Exchequer Secretary)*
David Gauke, MP *(Financial Secretary)*
Harriet Baldwin, MP *(Economic Secretary)*
Lord O'Neill of Gatley *(Commercial Secretary)*

## GOVERNMENT WHIPS

## HOUSE OF LORDS
*Lords Chief Whip and Captain of the Honourable*
*Corps of Gentlemen-at-Arms*
Lord Taylor of Holbeach, CBE
*Deputy Chief Whip and Captain of the Queen's*
*Bodyguard of the Yeomen of the Guard*
Lord Gardiner of Kimble
*Lords-in-Waiting*
Lord Ashton of Hyde
Lord Bourne of Aberystwyth
Viscount Young of Leckie
Earl of Courtown
*Baronesses-in-Waiting*
Baroness Chisholm of Owlpen
Baroness Evans of Bowes Park

## HOUSE OF COMMONS
*Chief Whip and Parliamentary Secretary to the*
*Treasury*
Rt. Hon. Mark Harper, MP
*Deputy Chief Whip and Treasurer of HM Household*
Anne Milton, MP
*Deputy Chief Whip and Comptroller of HM*
*Household*
Gavin Barwell, MP
*Government Whip and Vice-Chamberlain of HM*
*Household*
Kris Hopkins, MP
*Lords Commissioners of HM Treasury (Whips)*
David Evennett, MP; John Penrose, *Alun Cairns,
MP; Charlie Elphicke, MP; Mel Stride, MP;
George Hollignberry, MP
*Assistant Whips* Guy Opperman, MP; Julian Smith,
MP; Margot James, MP; Sarah Newton, MP;
Stephen Barclay, MP; Simon Kirby, MP; Jackie
Doyle-Price, MP

* alongside role as Under-Secretary of State at the Wales
Office

# GOVERNMENT DEPARTMENTS

## THE CIVIL SERVICE

The civil service helps the government develop and deliver its policies as effectively as possible. It works in three types of organisations – departments, executive agencies, and non-departmental government bodies (NDPBs). Under the Next Steps programme, launched in 1988, many semi-autonomous executive agencies were established to carry out much of the work of the civil service. Executive agencies operate within a framework set by the responsible minister which specifies policies, objectives and available resources. All executive agencies are set annual performance targets by their minister. Each agency has a chief executive, who is responsible for the day-to-day operations of the agency and who is accountable to the minister for the use of resources and for meeting the agency's targets. The minister accounts to parliament for the work of the agency.

There are currently 412,000 civil servants on a full-time equivalent (FTE) basis and 447,000 on a headcount basis. FTE is a measure that counts staff according to the proportion of full-time hours that they work. Almost three-quarters of all civil servants work outside London and the south-east. All government departments and executive agencies are responsible for their own pay and grading systems for civil servants outside the senior civil service.

## SALARIES 2015–16

### MINISTERIAL SALARIES *from 31 July 2015 until May 2020*

Ministers who are members of the House of Commons receive a parliamentary salary of £74,000 in addition to their ministerial salary.

| | |
|---|---|
| Prime minister | £75,440 |
| Cabinet minister (Commons) | £67,505 |
| Cabinet minister (Lords) | £101,038 |
| Minister of state (Commons) | £31,680 |
| Minister of state (Lords) | £78,891 |
| Parliamentary under-secretary (Commons) | £22,375 |
| Parliamentary under-secretary (Lords) | £68,710 |

SPECIAL ADVISERS' SALARIES *from 1 April 2015*
Special advisers to government ministers are paid out of public funds; their salaries are negotiated individually, but are usually in the range of £40,352 to £106,864.

### CIVIL SERVICE SALARIES *from 1 April 2015*

| Senior Civil Servants | |
|---|---|
| Permanent secretary | £142,000–£200,000 |
| Band 3 | £105,000–£208,100 |
| Band 2 | £86,000–£162,500 |
| Band 1 | £63,000–£117,800 |

Staff are placed in pay bands according to their level of responsibility and taking account of other factors such as experience and marketability. Movement within and between bands is based on performance. Following the delegation of responsibility for pay and grading to government departments and agencies from 1 April 1996, it is no longer possible to show service-wide pay rates for staff outside the Senior Civil Service.

## GOVERNMENT DEPARTMENTS

For more information on government departments, *see* W www.gov.uk/government/ministers

### ATTORNEY-GENERAL'S OFFICE

Attorney-General's Office, 20 Victoria Street, London SW1H 0NF
T 020-7271 2492
E correspondence@attorneygeneral.gsi.gov.uk
W www.gov.uk/government/organisations/attorney-generals-office

The law officers of the crown for England and Wales are the Attorney-General and the Solicitor-General. The Attorney-General, assisted by the Solicitor-General, is the chief legal adviser to the government and is also ultimately responsible for all crown litigation. He has overall responsibility for the work of the Law Officers' Departments (the Treasury Solicitor's Department, the Crown Prosecution Service – incorporating the Revenue and Customs Prosecutions Office – and the Serious Fraud Office, and HM Crown Prosecution Service Inspectorate). The Attorney-General also oversees the armed forces' prosecuting authority and the government legal service. He has a specific statutory duty to superintend the discharge of their duties by the Director of Public Prosecutions (who heads the Crown Prosecution Service) and the Director of the Serious Fraud Office. The Attorney-General has specific responsibilities for the enforcement of the criminal law and also performs certain public interest functions, eg protecting charities and appealing unduly lenient sentences. He also deals with questions of law arising in bills and with issues of legal policy.

Following the devolution of power to the Northern Ireland Assembly on 12 April 2010, the assembly now appoints the Attorney-General for Northern Ireland. The Attorney-General for England and Wales holds the office of Advocate-General for Northern Ireland, with significantly reduced responsibilities in Northern Ireland.

*Attorney-General,* Rt. Hon. Jeremy Wright, QC, MP
*Parliamentary Private Secretary,* Rehman Chishti, MP
*Solicitor-General,* Robert Buckland, QC, MP
*Director-General,* Rowena Collins Rice

## DEPARTMENT FOR BUSINESS, INNOVATION AND SKILLS

1 Victoria Street, London SW1H 0ET
T 020-7215 5000
W www.gov.uk/government/organisations/department-for-business-innovation-skills

The Department for Business, Innovation and Skills (BIS) was established in June 2009 by merging the Department for Business, Enterprise and Regulatory Reform and the Department for Innovation, Universities and Skills. BIS is the department for economic growth which invests in skills and education to promote trade, boost innovation and help people to start and grow a business. BIS also protects consumers and reduces the impact of regulation.

*Secretary of State for Business, Innovation and Skills and President of the Board of Trade,*
  Rt. Hon. Sajid Javid, MP*
*Parliamentary Private Secretary,* John Glen, MP
*Principal Private Secretary,* Emma Squire
*Senior Private Secretary,* Emily Shirtcliff
*Special Advisers,* Nick King; Salma Shah; Daniel Gilbert
*Minister of State,* Jo Johnson, MP *(Universities and Science)*
*Parliamentary Private Secretary,* Anne Marie Morris, MP
*Senior Private Secretary,* Hannah Nicholls
*Minister of State,* Rt. Hon. Lord Maude of Horsham *(Trade and Investment)*\*
*Senior Private Secretary,* John Frew
*Special Adviser,* Simone Finn
*Minister of State,* Rt. Hon. Anna Soubry, MP *(Small Business, Industry and Enterprise)*
*Parliamentary Private Secretary,* Mark Pawsey, MP
*Senior Private Secretary,* Claire Rannard
*Special Adviser,* Elliott Burton
*Minister of State,* Ed Vaizey, MP *(Culture and the Digital Economy)*†
*Parliamentary Private Secretary,* Sheryll Murray, MP
*Private Secretary,* Jack Hindley
*Minister of State,* Nick Boles, MP *(Skills)*‡
*Parliamentary Private Secretary,* Anne Marie Morris, MP

*Senior Private Secretary,* Rose McNamee
*Parliamentary Under-Secretary of State,* George Freeman, MP *(Life Sciences)*§
*Senior Private Secretary,* Rebecca Molyneux
*Parliamentary Under-Secretary of State (Minister for Intellectual Property),* Baroness Neville-Rolfe, DBE, CMG†
*Private Secretary,* Harriet Smith
*Permanent Secretary,* Martin Donnelly
*Senior Private Secretary,* Casey Malynn
*Head of Parliamentary Unit,* Georgina Holme-Skelton

\* Jointly with UK Export Finance
† Jointly with the Department for Culture, Media and Sport
‡ Jointly with the Department for Education
§ Jointly with the Department of Health

DEPARTMENTAL BOARD
*Chair,* Rt. Hon. Sajid Javid, MP *(Secretary of State)*
*Members,* Sam Beckett *(Economics and Markets);* Gareth Davies *(Knowledge and Innovation);* Martin Donnelly *(Permanent Secretary);* Dominic Jermey *(Chief Executive, UK Trade and Investment);* Bernadette Kelly *(Business and Local Growth);* Philippa Lloyd *(People and Strategy);* Howard Orme *(Finance and Commercial);* Mark Russell *(Chief Executive, Shareholder Executive);* Rachel Sandby-Thomas, CB *(Enterprise and Skills and Legal)*
*Non-Executive Members,* Stephen Bligh; Allan Cook *(Lead);* Prof. Dame Ann Dowling, DBE; Juergen Maier; Dale Murray; Dalton Philips; Prof. Wendy Purcell

BETTER REGULATION EXECUTIVE
1 Victoria Street, London SW1
T 020-7215 5000 E betterregulation@bis.gsi.gov.uk
W www.gov.uk/government/policy-teams/better-regulation-executive

The Better Regulation Executive (BRE) is a joint BIS/Cabinet Office unit which leads on delivering the government's manifesto commitment to reduce the overall burden on business, in order to increase growth and create jobs. Each government department is however responsible for delivering its part of the deregulation agenda within the framework put in place by the BRE.

*Non-Executive Chair,* Lord Curry of Kirkharle, CBE
*Chief Executive,* Graham Turnock

SHAREHOLDER EXECUTIVE
1 Victoria Street, London SW1H 0ET
T 020-7215 5000
W www.shareholderexecutive.gov.uk

The Shareholder Executive was set up in September 2003 to work with other departments in government to improve the government's capabilities and performance as a shareholder, and to offer corporate finance expertise and advice across government. Its goal is to create a climate of ownership that, while challenging, is genuinely supportive and provides the framework for the 23 businesses under its remit to be successful. In addition, the Shareholder Executive's Government Property Unit is responsible for maximising value from the state's property portfolio.

*Chair*, Robert Swannell
*Chief Executive*, Mark Russell

# CABINET OFFICE

70 Whitehall, London SW1A 2AS
T 020-7276 1234
W www.gov.uk/government/organisations/cabinet-office

The Cabinet Office, alongside the Treasury, sits at the centre of the government, with an overarching purpose of making government work better. It supports the prime minister and the cabinet, helping to ensure effective development, co-ordination and implementation of policy and operations across all government departments. The Cabinet Office also leads work to ensure that the Civil Service provides the most effective and efficient support to the government to meet its objectives. The department is headed by the Minister for the Cabinet Office.

*Prime Minister, First Lord of the Treasury and Minister for the Civil Service*, Rt. Hon. David Cameron, MP
*Parliamentary Private Secretary*, Gavin Williamson, MP
*Principal Private Secretary*, Chris Martin
*Chancellor of the Duchy of Lancaster*, Rt. Hon. Oliver Letwin, MP
*Parliamentary Private Secretary*, Alok Sharma, MP
*Minister for the Cabinet Office and Paymaster General*, Rt. Hon. Matthew Hancock, MP
*Parliamentary Private Secretary*, Gareth Johnson, MP
*Principal Private Secretary*, Athith Shetty
*Private Secretaries*, Helen Devanny, Miriam Laurance, Joe Taylor
*Lord President of the Council*, Rt. Hon. Chris Grayling, MP
*Parliamentary Private Secretary*, Mike Freer, MP
*Minister for Civil Society*, Rob Wilson, MP
*Private Secretary*, Elizabeth Jacobs
*Minister for Constitutional Reform*, John Penrose, MP
*Parliamentary Secretary*, Lord Bridges of Headley
*Private Secretary*, Luke Montague
*Minister without Portfolio*, Rt. Hon. Robert Halfon, MP
*Parliamentary Private Secretary*, Andrew Stephenson, MP

*Head of the Civil Service and Cabinet Secretary*, Sir Jeremy Heywood, KCB, CVO
*Chief Executive of the Civil Service*, John Manzoni
*Permanent Secretary and First Parliamentary Counsel*, Richard Heaton, CB
*Chair of the Joint Intelligence Committee*, Jon Day
*National Security Adviser*, Sir Kim Darroch
*Head of European and Global Issues*, Tom Scholar

## MANAGEMENT BOARD

*Chair*, Rt. Hon. Francis Maude, MP
*Board Members*, Melanie Dawes *(Director-General, Economic and Domestic Affairs Secretariat)*; Sue Gray *(Director-General, Propriety and Ethics Team, and Head of Private Offices Group)*; Richard Heaton, CB *(Permanent Secretary and First Parliamentary Counsel)*; Sir Jeremy Heywood, KCB, CVO *(Cabinet Secretary)*; Nick Hurd, MP *(Minister for Civil Society)*; Bruce Mann, CB *(Finance Director)*
*Non-Executive Directors*, Lord Browne of Madingley; Ian Davis; Rona Fairhead; Dame Barbara Stocking, DBE

## HONOURS AND APPOINTMENTS SECRETARIAT

Room G-39, Horse Guards Road, London SW1A 2HQ
T 020-7276 2777
*Head*, Richard Tilbrook

## OFFICE OF THE LEADER OF THE HOUSE OF COMMONS

1 Horse Guards Road, London SW1A 2HQ
T 020-7276 1005
E commonsleader@cabinetoffice.gov.uk
W www.gov.uk/government/organisations/the-office-of-the-leader-of-the-house-of-commons

The Office of the Leader of the House of Commons is responsible for the arrangement of government business in the House of Commons and for planning and supervising the government's legislative programme. The Leader of the House of Commons upholds the rights and privileges of the house and acts as a spokesperson for the government as a whole.

The leader reports regularly to the cabinet on parliamentary business and the legislative programme. In his capacity as leader of the house, he is a member of the House of Commons Commission. He also chairs the cabinet committee on the legislative programme. As Lord President of the Council, he is a member of the cabinet and in charge of the Office of the Privy Council.

The Deputy Leader of the House of Commons supports the leader in handling the government's business in the house. He is responsible for monitoring MPs' and peers' correspondence.

*Leader of the House of Commons and Lord Privy Seal,*
Rt. Hon. Chris Grayling, MP
*Parliamentary Private Secretary,* Mike Freer, MP
*Head of Office,* Mike Winter
*Deputy Head of Office,* Christine Hill
*Assistant Private Secretaries,* James Waddington
*(Parliamentary Business);* Mark Fernandes
*(Parliamentary Reform)*
*Deputy Leader of the House of Commons,* Dr Thérèse
Coffey, MP
*Private Secretary,* Mark Fernandes

## OFFICE OF THE LEADER OF THE HOUSE OF LORDS

House of Lords, London SW1A 0PW
**T** 020-7219 3200 **E** pslseaderofthelords@cabinet-
office.x.gsi.gov.uk
**W** www.gov.uk/government/organisations/office-of-the-
leader-of-the-house-of-lords

The Office of the Leader of the House of Lords
provides support to the leader in their parliamentary and ministerial duties, which include
leading the government benches in the House of
Lords; the delivery of the government's business in
the Lords; taking part in formal ceremonies such
as the state opening of parliament; and giving
guidance to the House of Lords on matters of
procedure and order.
*Lord Privy Seal, Leader of the House of Lords,*
Rt. Hon. Baroness Stowell of Beeston, MBE
*Parliamentary Private Secretary,* Kwasi Kwarteng, MP
*Deputy Leader of the House of Lords,* Rt. Hon. Earl
Howe

## GOVERNMENT POLICY
## PRIME MINISTER'S OFFICE

10 Downing Street, London SW1A 2AA
**T** 020-7930 4433
**W** www.number-10.gov.uk
*Prime Minister,* Rt. Hon. David Cameron, MP
*Parliamentary Private Secretary,* Gavin Williamson,
MP
*Principal Private Secretary,* Chris Martin
*Private Secretaries,* Nigel Casey *(Foreign Affairs);*
Kate Joseph *(Home Affairs);* Ed Whiting *(Foreign
Affairs and Development)*
*Speech Writer to the Prime Minister,* Tim Kiddell
*Director of Communications,* Craig Oliver
*Director of External Relations,* Gabby Bertin
*Director of Operations and Campaigns,* Liz Sugg
*Director of Strategy,* Ameet Gill
*Prime Minister's Official Spokesman,* Helen Bower
*Chief of Staff*, Ed Llewellyn
*Deputy Chief of Staff*, Catherine Fall
*Press Secretary to the Prime Minister,* Graeme Wilson
*Head of Policy Unit,* Camilla Cavendish
*Head of Implementation Unit,* Antonia Romeo
*Head of Corporate Services,* Helen Lederer

## CIVIL SERVICE REFORM
*Director-General,* Oliver Robbins, CB

## ECONOMIC AND DOMESTIC AFFAIRS SECRETARIAT
*Director-General,* Antonia Romeo

## IMPLEMENTATION GROUP
*Executive Director,* Simon Case

## PRIVATE OFFICES GROUP
*Director-General, Propriety and Ethics and Head of
Private Offices Group,* Sue Gray

## UK GOVERNANCE GROUP
*Second Permanent Secretary and Head of UK
Governance Group,* Philip Rycroft

## CABINET OFFICE CORPORATE SERVICES
*Executive Director, Government Communications,*
Alex Aiken
*Finance Director,* Guy Lester
*Human Resources Directors,* Crystal Akass; Ruth
Bailey

## NATIONAL SECURITY
Comprises the National Security Secretariat and the
Joint Intelligence Organisation. The National
Security Secretariat is responsible for providing
policy advice to the National Security Council,
where ministers discuss national security issues at a
strategic level; coordinating and developing foreign
and defence policy across government; coordinating
policy, ethical and legal issues across the
intelligence community, managing its funding and
priorities, and dealing with the Intelligence and
Security Committee which calls it to account;
developing effective protective security policies and
capabilities for government; improving the UK's
resilience to respond to and recover from
emergencies, and maintaining facilities for the
effective coordination of government response to
crises; and providing strategic leadership for cyber
security in the UK, in line with the National Cyber
Security Strategy.

## NATIONAL SECURITY SECRETARIAT
*National Security Adviser,* Sir Mark Lyall Grant
*Deputy National Security Adviser,* Julian Miller, CB

## JOINT INTELLIGENCE ORGANISATION
*Chair, Joint Intelligence Committee,* Jon Day

## EFFICIENCY AND REFORM GROUP
*Chief Procurement Officer,* Bill Crothers, CB
*Deputy Chief Procurement Officer,* Sally Collier

INDEPENDENT OFFICES

## CIVIL SERVICE COMMISSION
1 Horse Guards Road, London SW1A 2HQ
T 020-7271 0831
W http://civilservicecommission.independent.gov.uk

The Civil Service Commission regulates the requirement that selection for appointment to the Civil Service must be on merit on the basis of fair and open competition; the commission publishes its recruitment principles and audit departments and agencies' performance against these. Commissioners personally chair competitions for the most senior jobs in the civil service. In addition, the commission hears complaints from civil servants under the Civil Service Code.

The commission was established as a statutory body in November 2010 under the provisions of the Constitutional Reform and Governance Act 2010.

*First Commissioner (part-time),* Sir David
    Normington, GCB
*Commissioners,* Jonathan Baume; Kathryn Bishop;
    Andrew Flanagan; Dame Moira Gibb, DBE;
    Wanda Goldwag; Angela Sarkis, CBE

## THE COMMISSIONER FOR PUBLIC APPOINTMENTS
G/8, 1 Horse Guards Road, London SW1A 2HQ
T 020-7271 0831 E publicappointments@csc.gsi.gov.uk
W http://publicappointmentscommissioner.
independent.gov.uk

The Commissioner for Public Appointments is responsible for monitoring, regulating and reporting on ministerial appointments (including those made by Welsh government ministers) to public bodies. The commissioner can investigate complaints about the way in which appointments were made.

*Commissioner for Public Appointments,* Sir David
    Normington, GCB
*Chief Executive Commission Secretariat,* Clare Salters

## OFFICE OF THE PARLIAMENTARY COUNSEL
1 Horse Guards Road, London SW1A 2HQ
T 02-7276 6586 E goodlaw@cabinet-office.gsi.gov.ukk
W www.gov.uk/government/organisations/office-of-the-
parliamentary-counsel

The Office of the Parliamentary Counsel is a group of government lawyers who specialise in drafting government bills; advising departments on the rules and procedures of Parliament; reviewing orders and regulations which amend Acts of Parliament; and assisting the government on a range of legal and constitutional issues.

*First Parliamentary Counsel,* Richard Heaton, CB
*Chief Executive,* Jim Barron, CBE

## DEPARTMENT FOR COMMUNITIES AND LOCAL GOVERNMENT
2 Marsham Street, London SW1P 4DF
T 0303-444 0000
W www.gov.uk/government/organisations/department-
for-communities-and-local-government

The Department for Communities and Local Government was formed in May 2006 with a remit to promote community cohesion and prevent extremism, and was given responsibility for housing, urban regeneration and planning. It unites the communities and civil renewal functions previously undertaken by the Home Office, with responsibility for regeneration, neighbourhood renewal and local government (previously held by the Office of the Deputy Prime Minister, which was abolished following a cabinet reshuffle in May 2006). The department ensures that the Fire and Rescue services have the resources they need to reduce the number of deaths from fire, promote fire prevention activity and respond swiftly to national emergencies. The department also has responsibility for equality policy on race and faith (functions that were previously split between several government departments).

*Secretary of State for Communities and Local
    Government and Minister for Faith,* Rt. Hon. Greg
    Clark, MP
*Parliamentary Private Secretary,* Henry Smith, MP
*Principal Private Secretary,* Alex Williams
*Special Advisers,* Megan Powell-Chandler; Jacob
    Willmer
*Minister of State,* Brandon Lewis, MP *(Housing and
    Planning)*
*Parliamentary Private Secretary,* Andrew Griffiths,
    MP
*Private Secretary,* Ruth Long
*Minister of State,* Rt. Hon. Mark Francois, MP
    *(Communities and Resilience)*
*Parliamentary Private Secretary,* Andrew Griffiths, MP
*Private Secretary,* Lucy Yates
*Parliamentary Under-Secretary of State,* Marcus Jones,
    MP *(Local Government)*
*Private Secretary,* Peter Fenn
*Parliamentary Under-Secretary of State,* James
    Wharton, MP *(Local Growth and the Northern
    Powerhouse)*
*Private Secretary,* Kerr McKendrick
*Parliamentary Under-Secretary of State,* Baroness
    Williams of Trafford
*Private Secretary,* Shamila Meadows

MANAGEMENT BOARD
*Permanent Secretary,* Melanie Dawes, CB
*Members,* Stephen Aldridge, CB; Dawn Brodrick,
    CB; Andrew Campbell, CB; Louise Casey, CB;
    Helen Edwards, CBE; David Hill; Jacinda
    Humphry; Peter Schofield

*Non-Executive Members,* Stephen Hay; Nick
 Markham; Grenville Turner; Sara Weller *(Lead)*

## DEPARTMENT FOR CULTURE, MEDIA AND SPORT

100 Parliament Street, London SW1A 2BQ
T 020-7211 6000 E enquiries@culture.gov.uk
W www.gov.uk/government/organisations/department-
for-culture-media-sport

The Department for Culture, Media and Sport
(DCMS) was established in July 1997 and aims to
improve the quality of life for all those in the UK
through cultural and sporting activities while
championing the tourism, creative and leisure
industries. It is responsible for government policy
relating to the arts, sport, the National Lottery,
tourism, libraries, museums and galleries,
broadcasting, creative industries – including film
and the music industry – press freedom and
regulation, licensing, gambling, the historic
environment, telecommunications and online and
media ownership and mergers.

   The department is also responsible for 41
agencies and public bodies that help deliver the
department's strategic aims and objectives, the
listing of historic buildings and scheduling of
ancient monuments, the export licensing of cultural
goods, and the management of the Government Art
Collection and the Royal Parks (its sole executive
agency). It has the responsibility for humanitarian
assistance in the event of a disaster, as well as for
the organisation of the annual Remembrance Day
ceremony at the Cenotaph. In September 2012,
the Government Equalities Office became part of
DCMS, having previously been part of the Home
Office.

*Secretary of State for Culture, Media and Sport,*
 Rt. Hon. John Whittingdale, MP
*Parliamentary Private Secretary,* Heather Wheeler,
 MP
*Principal Private Secretary,* Ben Dean
*Minister of State,* Ed Vaizey, MP *(Culture and the
 Digital Economy)\**
*Parliamentary Private Secretary,* Sheryll Murray, MP
*Private Secretary,* Jack Hindley
*Parliamentary Under-Secretary of State,* Tracey
 Crouch, MP *(Sport, Tourism and Heritage)*
*Private Secretary,* Philip Bland
*Parliamentary Under-Secretary of State,* Baroness
 Neville-Rolfe, DBE, CMG *(Minister for
 Intellectual Property)\**
*Private Secretary,* Lizzie Glithero-West
*Parliamentary Under-Secretary of State,* Baroness
 Shields *(Internet Safety and Security)*
*Private Secretary,* Saskia Bradbury

\*Jointly with the Department for Business, Innovation
and Skills

MANAGEMENT BOARD
*Permanent Secretary,* Sue Owen
*Members,* Hugh Harris; Sarah Healey; Clare
 Pillman; Alison Pritchard; David Rossington;
 Chris Townsend; Andrea Young
*Non-Executive Members,* Ajay Chowdhury; Dr Tracy
 Long; Ruby McGregor-Smith, CBE; Sir David
 Verey

GOVERNMENT EQUALITIES OFFICE (GEO)
100 Parliament Street, London SW1A 2BQ
T 020-7211 6000 E enquiries@culture.gsi.gov.uk
W www.gov.uk/government/organisations/government-
equalities-office

The GEO is responsible for the government's
overall strategy on equality. Its work includes
leading the development of a more integrated
approach on equality across government with the
aim of improving equality and reducing
discrimination and disadvantage for all. The office
is also responsible for leading policy on gender
equality, sexual orientation and transgender
equality matters.
*Minister for Women and Equality,* Rt. Hon. Nicky
 Morgan, MP
*Parliamentary Under-Secretary of State,* Caroline
 Dinenage, MP *(Women, Equalities and Family
 Justice)*
*Director,* Alison Pritchard

## MINISTRY OF DEFENCE

Main Building, Whitehall, London SW1A 2HB
T 020-7218 9000 W www.gov.uk/government/
organisations/ministry-of-defence

*Secretary of State for Defence,* Rt. Hon. Michael
 Fallon, MP
*Parliamentary Private Secretary,* Graham Evans, MP
*Private Secretary,* Luke Dearden
*Special Advisers,* Ben Mascall; James Wild
*Minister of State (Defence Procurement),* Philip
 Dunne, MP
*Parliamentary Private Secretary,* Oliver Colville,
 MP
*Minister of State (Armed Forces),* Penny Mordaunt,
 MP
*Parliamentary Private Secretary,* Oliver Colville, MP
*Parliamentary Under-Secretary of State and Minister
 for Defence, Personnel and Veterans,* Mark
 Lancaster, TD, MP
*Parliamentary Under-Secretary of State and Minister
 for Reserves,* Julian Brazier, MP
*Private Secretary,* Emma Frost
*Parliamentary Under-Secretary of State and Lords
 Spokesman,* Rt. Hon. Earl Howe

CHIEFS OF STAFF
*Chief of the Defence Staff,* Gen. Sir Nicholas
 Houghton, GCB, CBE, ADC

*Vice Chief of the Defence Staff,* Air Chief Marshal Sir
   Stuart Peach, KCB, CBE, ADC
*Chief of the Naval Staff and First Sea Lord,* Adm. Sir
   George Zambellas, KCB, DSC, ADC
*Second Sea Lord,* Rear-Adm. (Simon) Jonathan
   Woodcock, OBE
*Chief of the General Staff,* Gen. Sir Nicholas Carter,
   KCB, CBE, DSO, ADC
*Assistant Chief of the General Staff,* Maj.-Gen. David
   Cullen, OBE
*Chief of the Air Staff,* Air Chief Marshal Sir Andrew
   Pulford, KCB, CBE, ADC
*Assistant Chief of the Air Staff,* Air Vice-Marshal
   Richard Knighton

SENIOR OFFICIALS
*Permanent Under-Secretary of State,* Jon Thompson
*Chief of Defence Materiel,* Sir Bernard Gray
*Chief Scientific Adviser,* Prof. Vernon Gibson, FRS
*Director-General Finance,* Louise Tulett

THE DEFENCE COUNCIL
The Defence Council is chaired by the Secretary
of State, and comprises the other ministers, the
Permanent Under-Secretary, the Chief of Defence
Staff and senior service officers and officials who
head the armed services and the department's major
corporate functions. It provides the formal legal
basis for the conduct of UK defence through a range
of powers vested in it by statute and letters patent.

THE DEFENCE BOARD
Chaired by the Secretary of State, the Defence
Board is the main corporate board of the MoD,
providing senior level leadership and strategic
management of defence. The current membership
of the Defence Board is: the Secretary of State; the
Minister of State for Defence Procurement; the
Permanent Secretary (the most senior civilian in
the MoD); the Chief of Defence Staff (the professional head of the armed forces); the Vice-Chief
of the Defence Staff (the chief operating officer
for the armed forces element of defence business);
the Chief of Defence Materiel (the head of Defence
Equipment and Support); the Director-General
Finance; and three non-executive members.

CENTRAL STAFF
*Vice-Chief of the Defence Staff,* Air Chief Marshal Sir
   Stuart Peach, KCB, CBE, ADC

JOINT FORCES COMMAND
*Commander Joint Forces Command,* Gen. Sir Richard
   Barrons, KCB, CBE, ADC
*Chief of Joint Operations,* Lt.-Gen. John Lorimer,
   MBE, DSO
*Chief of Staff (Operations),* Air Vice-Marshal Stuart
   Atha, DSO
*Chief of Staff HQ,* Rear-Adm. Paul Bennett, OBE

FLEET COMMAND
*First Sea Lord,* Adm. Sir George Zambellas, KCB,
   DSC, ADC
*Fleet Commander and Deputy Chief of Naval Staff,*
   Vice-Adm. Sir Philip Jones, KCB

NAVAL HOME COMMAND
*Second Sea Lord,* Rear-Adm. (Simon) Jonathan
   Woodcock, OBE

LAND FORCES
*Commander Land Forces,* Lt.-Gen. James Everard,
   CBE
*Chief of Staff Land Forces,* Maj.-Gen. Timothy
   Robinson, CBE

AIR COMMAND
*Deputy Commander Operations,* Air Marshal Greg
   Bagwell, CB, CBE
*Deputy Commander Capability and Air Member for
   Personnel and Capability,* Air Marshal Sir Barry
   North, OBE

DEFENCE EQUIPMENT AND SUPPORT
*Chief of Defence Materiel,* Sir Bernard Gray
*Chief of Materiel (Fleet),* Vice-Adm. Simon Lister,
   CB, OBE
*Chief of Materiel (Land),* Lt.-Gen. Sir Christopher
   Deverell, KCB, MBE
*Chief of Materiel (Air),* Air Marshal Simon Bollom,
   CB

# DEPARTMENT FOR EDUCATION
Piccadilly Gate, Store Street, Manchester M1 2WD
T 0370-000 2288
W www.gov.uk/government/organisations/department-
for-education

The Department for Education (DfE) was
established in May 2010 in place of the
Department for Children, Schools and Families
(DCSF), in order to refocus the department on its
core purpose of supporting teaching and learning.
The department is responsible for education and
children's services, while the Department for
Business, Innovation and Skills is responsible for
higher education. The DfE is supported by nine
executive agencies and public bodies.
   The department's objectives include the expansion
of the academies programme, to allow schools to
apply to become independent of their local authority,
and the introduction of the free schools programme,
to allow any suitable proposers, such as parents,
businesses or charities, to set up their own school.
*Secretary of State for Education and Minister for
   Women and Equalities,* Rt. Hon. Nicky Morgan,
   MP
*Parliamentary Private Secretary,* Robin Walker, MP
*Principal Private Secretary,* Rose Pennells

*Special Advisers,* Lee Davis; George Looker; Luke Tryl
*Minister of State,* Nick Boles, MP *(Skills)**
*Parliamentary Private Secretary,* Anne Marie Morris, MP
*Senior Private Secretary,* Rose McNamee
*Minister of State,* Nick Gibb, MP *(Schools)*
*Parliamentary Private Secretary,* Stephen Metcalfe, MP
*Private Secretary,* Huw Leslie
*Minister of State,* Edward Timpson, MP *(Children and Families)*
*Parliamentary Private Secretary,* Stephen Metcalfe, MP
*Private Secretary,* Holly Jones
*Parliamentary Under-Secretary of State,* Lord Nash *(Schools)*
*Private Secretary,* Bonnie Wang
*Parliamentary Under-Secretary of State,* Caroline Dinenage, MP *(Women, Equalities and Family Justice)†*
*Private Secretary,* Ben Charnock
*Parliamentary Under-Secretary of State,* Sam Gyimah, MP *(Childcare and Education)*
*Private Secretary,* Hannah Maher

* Jointly with the Department for Business, Innovation and Skills
†Jointly with the Ministry of Justice

MANAGEMENT BOARD
*Permanent Secretary,* Chris Wormald
*Members,* Shona Dunn; Simon Fryer; Simon Judge; Paul Kissack; Peter Lauener; Andrew McCully; Tom Shinner
*Non-Executive Members,* Paul Marshall *(Lead);* David Meller; Marion Plant, OBE

## DEPARTMENT OF ENERGY AND CLIMATE CHANGE
3 Whitehall Place, London SW1A 2AW
T 0300-060 4000 E correspondence@decc.gsi.gov.uk
W www.gov.uk/government/organisations/department-of-energy-climate-change

The Department of Energy and Climate Change (DECC) was formed in 2008 to ensure that the UK has secure, clean, affordable energy supplies and to promote international action to mitigate climate change. It is supported by nine agencies and public bodies.
*Secretary of State for the Department of Energy and Climate Change,* Rt. Hon. Amber Rudd, MP
*Parliamentary Private Secretary,* Paul Maynard, MP
*Private Secretary,* Tim Lord
*Minister of State,* Andrea Leadsom, MP
*Parliamentary Private Secretary,* Sheryll Murray, MP
*Private Secretary,* Stephen Burke

*Parliamentary Under-Secretary of State,* Lord Bourne of Aberystwyth*
*Private Secretary,* Edward Hogg

*Jointly with the Wales Office

MANAGEMENT BOARD
*Permanent Secretary,* Stephen Lovegrove
*Members,* Prof. John Loughhead *(Chief Scientific Adviser);* Clive Maxwell *(Director-General, Consumers and Households);* Angie Ridgwell *(Director-General, Finance and Corporate Services);* Jeremy Pocklington *(Director-General, Markets and Infrastructure);* Katrina Williams *(Director-General, International, Science and Resilience)*

## DEPARTMENT FOR ENVIRONMENT, FOOD AND RURAL AFFAIRS
Nobel House, 17 Smith Square, London SW1P 3JR
T 03459-335577
E defra.helpline@defra.gsi.gov.uk
W www.gov.uk/government/organisations/department-for-environment-food-rural-affairs

The Department for Environment, Food and Rural Affairs (DEFRA) is responsible for government policy on the environment, rural matters and farming and food production. In association with the agriculture departments of the Scottish government, the National Assembly for Wales and the Northern Ireland Office, the department is responsible for negotiations in the EU on the common agricultural and fisheries policies, and for single European market questions relating to its responsibilities. Its remit includes international agricultural and food trade policy.

The department's five strategic priorities are climate change adaptation; sustainable consumption and production; the protection of natural resources and the countryside; sustainable rural communities; and sustainable farming and food, including animal health and welfare. DEFRA, which is supported by 34 executive agencies and public bodies, is also the lead government department for emergencies in animal and plant diseases, flooding, food and water supply, dealing with the consequences of a chemical, biological, radiological or nuclear incident, and other threats to the environment.
*Secretary of State for Environment, Food and Rural Affairs,* Rt. Hon. Elizabeth Truss, MP
*Parliamentary Private Secretary,* Mark Spencer, MP
*Principal Private Secretary,* Dr Jeremy Marlow
*Senior Private Secretary,* Stuart Colville
*Private Secretaries,* Emma Southard; Adam Stevens
*Parliamentary Under-Secretary of State,* Rory Stewart, MP *(Natural Environment, Floods and Water, Resource and Environmental Management, Rural Affairs, Lead responsibility for the Environment Agency, Natural England and the Forestry Commission and Deputy for the Secretary of State on Environment Council)*

*Senior Private Secretary,* Suzie Pinkett
*Minister of State,* George Eustice, MP *(Farming, Food and the Marine Environment)*
*Parliamentary Private Secretary,* Matthew Offord
*Senior Private Secretary,* Matthew Sabourin
*Private Secretaries,* Yasmin Hussain; James Turner; David How
*Spokesman in the House of Lords,* Lord Gardiner of Kimble
*Permanent Secretary,* Bronwyn Hill, CBE
*Private Secretary,* Linda Kiff

SUPERVISORY BOARD
*Chair,* Bronwyn Hill *(Permanent Secretary)*
*Members,* Betsy Bassis *(Chief Operating Officer);* Prof Ian Boyd *(Chief Scientific Adviser);* Alastair Bridges *(Finance);* Nick Joicey *(Strategy, International and Biosecurity);* Sonia Phippard *(Policy Delivery)*
*Non-Executive Members,* Catherine Doran; Iain Ferguson; Sir Tony Hawkhead, CBE; Paul Rew

# FOREIGN AND COMMONWEALTH OFFICE

King Charles Street, London SW1A 2AH
T 020-7008 1500 E fcocorrespondence@fco.gov.uk
W www.gov.uk/government/organisations/foreign-commonwealth-office

The Foreign and Commonwealth Office (FCO) provides the means of communication between the British government and other governments – and international governmental organisations – on all matters falling within the field of international relations. The FCO employs over 14,000 people in nearly 270 places across the world through a network of embassies and consulates, which help to protect and promote national interests. FCO diplomats are skilled in understanding and influencing what is happening abroad, supporting British citizens who are travelling and living overseas, helping to manage migration into Britain, promoting British trade and other interests abroad and encouraging foreign investment in the UK. The FCO is supported by 11 executive agencies and public bodies.

*Secretary of State for Foreign and Commonwealth Affairs,* Rt. Hon. Philip Hammond, MP
*Parliamentary Private Secretary,* Christopher Pincher, MP
*Principal Private Secretary,* Martin Reynolds
*Special Advisers,* Graham Hook; Hayden Allan; Duncan McCourt
*Minister of State,* Rt. Hon. David Lidington, MP *(Europe)*
*Parliamentary Private Secretary,* James Morris, MP
*Private Secretary,* Jennifer MacNaughton
*Minister of State,* Rt. Hon. Hugo Swire, MP
*Parliamentary Private Secretary,* Pauline Latham, MP

*Private Secretary,* Fergus Eckersley
*Minister of State,* Rt. Hon. Lord Maude of Horsham *(Trade and Investment)\**
*Private Secretary,* Nick Whittingham
*Minister of State,* Rt. Hon. Baroness Anelay of St Johns, DBE
*Private Secretary,* Kate English
*Minister of State,* Rt. Hon. Grant Shapps, MP†
*Private Secretary,* Iain Griffiths
*Parliamentary Under-Secretary of State,* Tobias Ellwood, MP
*Private Secretary,* Sharon Wilkins
*Special Representatives,* Rt. Hon. Baroness Anelay of St Johns, DBE *(Prime Minister's Special Representative on Preventing Sexual Violence in Conflict);* Sir Andrew Burns *(Post-Holocaust Issues);* Rt. Hon. Sir Alan Duncan, MP *(Special Envoy to Oman and Yemen);* Owen Jenkins *(Afghanistan and Pakistan);* Matthew Cannell *(Sudan and South Sudan);* Sir David King *(Climate Change)*

\* Jointly with the Department for Business, Innovation and Skills and UK Export Finance
† Jointly with the Department for International Development

BOARD
*Permanent Under-Secretary and Head of the Diplomatic Service,* Sir Simon Fraser, KCMG
*Members,* Deborah Bronnert; Sir Simon Gass *(Political);* Dominic Jermey, OBE *(Chief Executive, UK Trade and Investment);* Julian King, KCVO, CMG *(Economic and Consular);* Sara Mackintosh *(Defence and Intelligence)*
*Non-Executive Members,* Julia Bond; Prof. Robin Grimes; Sir Richard Lambert *(Lead);* Rudy Markham

# DEPARTMENT OF HEALTH

Richmond House, 79 Whitehall, London SW1A 2NS
T 020-7210 4850
W https://www.gov.uk/government/organisations/department-of-health

The Department of Health (DH) leads, shapes and funds health and care in England, making sure people have the support, care and treatment they need and that this is delivered in a compassionate, respectful and dignified manner.

The DH leads across health and care by creating national policies and legislation to meet current and future challenges. It provides funding, assures the delivery and continuity of services and accounts to parliament in a way that represents the best interests of the patient, public and taxpayer. 26 executive agencies and public bodies support the DH.

*Secretary of State for Health,* Rt. Hon. Jeremy Hunt, MP

*Parliamentary Private Secretary,* Steve Brine, MP
*Principal Private Secretary,* Kristen McLeod
*Private Secretary,* Andrew Edmunds
*Minister of State,* Rt. Hon. Alistair Burt, MP
  *(Community and Social Care)*
*Parliamentary Private Secretary,* Karen Lumley
*Private Secretary,* Claire McAvinchey
*Parliamentary Under-Secretary of State,* Ben Gummer,
  MP *(Care Quality)*
*Private Secretary,* Alex Wallace
*Parliamentary Under-Secretary of State,* Jane Ellison,
  MP *(Public Health)*
*Private Secretary,* Kirsty Bell
*Parliamentary Under-Secretary of State,* Lord Prior of
  Brampton *(NHS Productivity)*
*Private Secretary,* Ilaria Regondi
*Parliamentary Under-Secretary of State,* George
  Freeman, MP *(Life Sciences)**
*Private Secretary,* Rebecca Molyneux

* Jointly with the Department for Business, Innovation
and Skills

DEPARTMENTAL BOARD
*Chair,* Rt. Hon. Jeremy Hunt, MP
*Members,* Rt. Hon. Alistair Burt MP; Will Cavendish
  *(Innovation, Growth and Technology);* Prof. Dame
  Sally Davies, DBE *(Chief Medical Officer);* Jane
  Ellison, MP; Tamara Finkelstein *(Chief Operating
  Officer);* Ben Gummer, MP; Felicity Harvey, CBE
  *(Public Health);* Charlie Massey *(Strategy and
  External Relations);* Dame Una O'Brien, DCB
  *(Permanent Secretary);* Dr Daniel Poulter, MP;
  Lord Prior; Jon Rouse *(Social Care, Local
  Government and Care Partnerships);* David
  Williams *(Finance and NHS)*
*Non-Executive Members,* Dr Catherine Bell; Gerry
  Murphy; Chris Pilling; Peter Sands *(Lead)*

## HOME OFFICE

2 Marsham Street, London SW1P 4DF
T 020-7035 4848
E public.enquiries@homeoffice.gsi.gov.uk
W www.gov.uk/government/organisations/home-office

The Home Office deals with those internal affairs in
England and Wales which have not been assigned
to other government departments. The Secretary of
State for the Home Department is the link between
the Queen and the public, and exercises certain
powers on her behalf, including that of the royal
pardon.
  The Home Office aims to build a safe, just and
tolerant society and to maintain and enhance public
security and protection; to support and mobilise
communities so that they are able to shape policy
and improvement for their locality, overcome
nuisance and anti-social behaviour, maintain and
enhance social cohesion and enjoy their homes and

public spaces peacefully; to deliver departmental
policies and responsibilities fairly, effectively and
efficiently; and to make the best use of resources.
These objectives reflect the priorities of the
government and the home secretary in areas of
crime, citizenship and communities, namely to
work on the problems caused by illegal drug use;
shape the alcohol strategy, policy and licensing
conditions; keep the UK safe from the threat of
terrorism; reduce and prevent crime, and ensure
people feel safe in their homes and communities;
secure the UK border and control immigration;
consider applications to enter and stay in the
UK; issue passports and visas; and to support
visible, responsible and accountable policing by
empowering the public and freeing up the police to
fight crime.
  The Home Office delivers these aims through
the immigration services, its 29 executive agencies
and non-departmental public bodies, and by
working with partners in private, public and
voluntary sectors, individuals and communities. The
home secretary is also the link between the UK
government and the governments of the Channel
Islands and the Isle of Man.
*Secretary of State for the Home Department,*
  Rt. Hon. Theresa May, MP
*Parliamentary Private Secretary,* Michael Ellis, MP
*Principal Private Secretary,* Andrew Scurry
*Special Advisers,* Alex Dawson; Stephen Parkinson;
  Liz Sanderson
*Minister of State,* Mike Penning, MP *(Policing, Crime
  and Criminal Justice and Victims)**
*Principal Private Secretary,* Chris White
*Private Secretary,* Sarah Phillips
*Minister of State,* Rt. Hon. John Hayes, MP
  *(Security)*
*Minister of State,* James Brokenshire, MP
  *(Immigration)*
*Parliamentary Private Secretary,* Craig Whittaker, MP
*Private Secretary,* Jon Rosenorn-Lanng
*Minister of State,* Rt. Hon. Lord Bates
*Private Secretary,* Moore Flannery
*Parliamentary Under-Secretary of State,* Karen
  Bradley, MP *(Preventing Abuse and Exploitation)*
*Parliamentary Under-Secretary of State,* Lord Ahmad
  of Wimbledon *(Countering Extremism)*

*Jointly with the Ministry of Justice

MANAGEMENT BOARD
*Permanent Secretary,* Mark Sedwill
*Members,* Mary Calam *(Crime and Policing Group);*
  Mandie Campbell *(Immigration Enforcement);*
  Charles Farr *(Office for Security and Counter
  Terrorism);* Peter Fish *(Legal);* Sir Charles
  Montgomery *(Border Force);* Mike Parsons *(Chief
  Operating Officer, Home Office);* Sarah Rapson
  *(UK Visas and Immigration);* Prof. Bernard

Silverman *(Chief Scientific Adviser)*; Peter Storr *(International and Immigration Policy)*; Julie Taylor *(Transformation)*; Mark Thomson *(HM Passport Office)*; Kevin White, CB *(Human Resources)*; Simon Wren *(Communications)*

# DEPARTMENT FOR INTERNATIONAL DEVELOPMENT

22 Whitehall, London SW1A 2EG **T** 020-7023 0000
Abercrombie House, Eaglesham Road, East Kilbride,
Glasgow G75 8EA **T** 01355-844000
**Public Enquiries** 0845-300 4100
**E** enquiry@dfid.gov.uk
**W** www.gov.uk/government/organisations/department-for-international-development

The Department for International Development (DFID) is responsible for promoting sustainable development and reducing poverty. The central focus of the government's policy, based on the 1997, 2000, 2006 and 2009 white papers on international development, is a commitment to the internationally agreed Millennium Development Goals, to be achieved by 2015. These seek to eradicate extreme poverty and hunger; achieve universal primary education; promote gender equality and empower women; reduce child mortality; improve maternal health; combat HIV/AIDS, malaria and other diseases; improve sanitation and access to clean water; ensure environmental sustainability; and encourage a global partnership for development.

DFID's assistance is concentrated in the poorest countries of sub-Saharan Africa and Asia, but also contributes to poverty reduction and sustainable development in middle-income countries, including those in Latin America and Eastern Europe. It also responds to overseas emergencies. The department works in partnership with governments of developing countries, charities, non-governmental organisations and businesses. It also works with multilateral institutions, including the World Bank, United Nations agencies and the European Commission. The department, which is supported by two executive agencies and public bodies, has headquarters in London and East Kilbride, offices in many developing countries, and staff based in British embassies and high commissions around the world.

*Secretary of State for International Development,*
Rt. Hon. Justine Greening, MP
*Parliamentary Private Secretary,* Andrew Bingham, MP
*Principal Private Secretary,* Jonathan Baxter
*Special Advisers,* Simon Bishop; Aline Nassif
*Minister of State,* Rt. Hon. Grant Shapps, MP\*
*Parliamentary Private Secretary,* Charlotte Leslie, MP
*Private Secretary,* Vicky Seymour
*Minister of State,* Rt. Hon. Desmond Swayne, TD, MP

*Parliamentary Private Secretary,* Charlotte Leslie, MP
*Private Secretary,* Heather Opie
*Parliamentary Under-Secretary of State,* Baroness Verma
*Private Secretary,* Zoe Ware

\*Jointly with the Foreign and Commonwealth Office

MANAGEMENT BOARD
*Chair,* Rt. Hon. Justine Greening, MP
*Members,* Richard Calvert *(Finance and Corporate Performance)*; Nick Dyer *(acting Policy and Global Programmes)*; Joy Hutcheon *(Country Programmes)*; David Kennedy *(Economic Development)*; Mark Lowcock *(Permanent Secretary)*; Rt. Hon. Grant Shapps, MP; Rt. Hon. Desmond Swayne, TD, MP; Baroness Verma
*Non-Executive Members,* Vivienne Cox *(Lead)*; Richard Keys; Tim Robinson; Eric Salama

CDC GROUP
123 Victoria Street, London SW1E 6DE
**T** 020-7963 4700 **E** enquiries@cdcgroup.com
**W** www.cdcgroup.com

Founded in 1948, CDC is the UK's Development Finance Institution wholly owned by the UK government. It invests to create jobs and build businesses in developing countries in Africa and South Asia. In 2014 CDC made 19 new investment commitments which totalled £296.8m across these regions. CDC is a public limited company with net assets of £3,369m.
*Chair,* Graham Wrigley
*Chief Executive,* Diana Noble

# MINISTRY OF JUSTICE
102 Petty France, London SW1H 9AJ
**T** 020-3334 3555 **E** general.queries@justice.gsi.gov.uk
**W** www.gov.uk/government/organisations/ministry-of-justice

The Ministry of Justice (MoJ) was established in May 2007. MoJ is headed by the Lord Chancellor and Secretary of State for Justice who is responsible for improvements to the justice system so that it better serves the public. He is also responsible for some areas of constitutional policy (those not covered by the Deputy Prime Minister).

The MoJ established five key priorities for 2014. These were to reduce reoffending by using the skills of the public, private and voluntary sectors; reduce youth crime by putting education at the centre of youth justice; build a prison system that delivers maximum value for money; reduce the cost of legal aid and ensure it helps those cases that genuinely require it; and to improve the way the courts are run and put the needs of victims first. The MoJ has a budget of around £9bn and is supported by 38 executive agencies and public bodies to achieve its targets.

The Lord Chancellor and Secretary of State for Justice is the government minister responsible to parliament for the judiciary, the court system and prisons and probation. The Lord Chief Justice has been the head of the judiciary since 2006.

MoJ incorporates the National Offender Management Service; HM Prison Service and the National Probation Service; Her Majesty's Courts and Tribunals Service; the Legal Aid Agency; and the Youth Justice Board.

MoJ has several associated departments, non-departmental public bodies and executive agencies, including the National Archives and the Office of the Public Guardian.

*Lord Chancellor and Secretary of State for Justice,* Rt. Hon. Michael Gove, MP
*Parliamentary Private Secretary,* Robert Jenrick, MP
*Principal Private Secretary,* Amy Rees
*Minister of State,* Rt. Hon. Mike Penning, MP *(Policing, Crime and Criminal Justice and Victims)**
*Parliamentary Private Secretary,* Chris White, MP
*Private Secretary,* Marc Attwell
*Minister of State,* Lord Edward Faulks, QC *(Civil Justice)*
*Private Secretary,* Elaine Cobb
*Parliamentary Under-Secretary of State,* Shailesh Vara, MP *(Courts and Legal Aid)*
*Private Secretary,* Stephen Doney
*Parliamentary Under-Secretary of State,* Andrew Selous, MP *(Prisons, Probation, Rehabilitation and Sentencing)*
*Private Secretary,* Catherine Bennion
*Parliamentary Under-Secretary of State,* Caroline Dinenage, MP *(Women, Equalities and Family Justice)†*
*Private Secretary,* Ben Charnock
*Parliamentary Under-Secretary of State,* Dominic Raab, MP *(Human Rights)*
*Private Secretary,* Mary Jones

*Jointly with the Home Office
†Jointly with the Department for Education

MANAGEMENT BOARD
*Permanent Secretary,* Ursula Brennan
*Members,* Ann Beasley *(Director-General, Finance);* Matthew Coats *(Director-General, Legal Aid Agency and Corporate Services Group);* Catherine Lee *(Director-General, Law and Access to Justice Group);* Michael Spurr *(Chief Executive, National Offender Management Service)*
*Non-Executive Member,* Sir Theodore Agnew

## NORTHERN IRELAND OFFICE
1 Horse Guards Road, London SW1A 2HQ
Stormont House, Stormont Estate, Belfast BT4 3SH
T 028-9052 0700 E nioweb.editor@nio.x.gsi.gov.uk
W www.gov.uk/government/organisations/northern-ireland-office

The Northern Ireland Office was established in 1972, when the Northern Ireland (Temporary Provisions) Act transferred the legislative and executive powers of the Northern Ireland parliament and government to the UK parliament and a secretary of state. Under the terms of the 1998 Good Friday Agreement, power was devolved to the Northern Ireland Assembly in 1999. The assembly took on responsibility for the relevant areas of work previously undertaken by the departments of the Northern Ireland Office, covering agriculture and rural development, the environment, regional development, social development, education, higher education, training and employment, enterprise, trade and investment, culture, arts and leisure, health, social services, public safety and finance and personnel. In October 2002 the Northern Ireland Assembly was suspended and Northern Ireland returned to direct rule, but despite repeated setbacks, devolution was restored on 8 May 2007.

The Northern Ireland Office is supported by three executive agencies and public bodies and is currently responsible for overseeing the devolution settlement; representing Northern Ireland interests within the UK government and similarly representing the UK government in Northern Ireland; working in partnership with the Northern Ireland Executive for a stable, prosperous Northern Ireland; and supporting and implementing political agreements to increase stability.

*Secretary of State for Northern Ireland,* Rt. Hon. Theresa Villiers, MP
*Parliamentary Private Secretary,* Rebecca Harris, MP
*Parliamentary Under-Secretary of State,* Ben Wallace, MP
*Private Secretary,* Andy Monaghan
*Permanent Secretary,* Sir Jonathan Stephens

## OFFICE OF THE ADVOCATE-GENERAL FOR SCOTLAND
Dover House, Whitehall, London SW1A 2AU
T 020-7270 6770
Office of the Solicitor to the Advocate-General, Victoria Quay, Edinburgh EH6 6QQ
T 0131-244 0359
E enquiries@advocategeneral.gsi.gov.uk
W www.gov.uk/government/organisations/office-of-the-advocate-general-for-scotland

The Advocate-General for Scotland is one of the three law officers of the crown, alongside the Attorney-General and the Solicitor-General for England and Wales. He is the legal adviser to the UK government on Scottish law and is supported by staff in the Office of the Advocate-General for Scotland. The office is divided into the Legal Secretariat, based mainly in London, and the Office of the Solicitor to the Advocate-General, based in Edinburgh.

The post was created as a consequence of the constitutional changes set out in the Scotland Act 1998, which created a devolved Scottish parliament. The Lord Advocate and the Solicitor-General for Scotland then became part of the Scottish government and the Advocate-General took over their previous role as legal adviser to the UK government on Scots law.

*Advocate-General for Scotland,* Lord Keen of Elie, QC
*Private Secretary,* Craig Chalcraft

MANAGEMENT BOARD
*Direcor and Solicitor,* Michael Chalmers
*Members,* Jim Logie; Ruraidh Macniven; Fiona Robertson; Neil Taylor

## SCOTLAND OFFICE
Dover House, Whitehall, London SW1A 2AU
1 Melville Crescent, Edinburgh EH3 7HW
T 0131-244 9010  E enquiries@scotlandoffice.gsi.gov.uk
W www.gov.uk/government/organisations/scotland-office

The Scotland Office is the department of the Secretary of State for Scotland which represents Scottish interests within the UK government in matters reserved to the UK parliament. The Secretary of State for Scotland maintains the stability of the devolution settlement for Scotland; delivers secondary legislation under the Scotland Act 1998; is responsible for the conduct and funding of the Scottish parliament elections; manages the Scottish vote provision and authorises the monthly payment of funds from the UK consolidated fund to the Scottish consolidated fund; and publishes regular information on the state of the Scottish economy.

Matters reserved to the UK parliament include the constitution, foreign affairs, defence, international development, the civil service, financial and economic matters, national security, immigration and nationality, misuse of drugs, trade and industry, various aspects of energy regulation (eg coal, electricity, oil, gas and nuclear energy), various aspects of transport, social security, employment, abortion, genetics, surrogacy, medicines, broadcasting and equal opportunities. Devolved matters include health and social work, education and training, local government and housing, justice and police, agriculture, forestry, fisheries, the environment, tourism, sports, heritage, economic development and internal transport.

*Secretary of State for Scotland,* Rt. Hon. David Mundell, MP

*Parliamentary Private Secretary,* Iain Stewart, MP
*Principal Private Secretary,* Chris Flatt
*Parliamentary Under-Secretary of State,* Lord Dunlop
*Private Secretary,* Stephanie Sandison

MANAGEMENT BOARD
*Director,* Francesca Osowska, OBE
*Members,* Colin Faulkner; Chris Flatt; Helena Gray; Glenn Preston

## DEPARTMENT FOR TRANSPORT
Great Minster House, 33 Horseferry Road, London SW1P 4DR
T 0300-330 3000
W www.gov.uk/government/organisations/department-for-transport

The Department for Transport (DfT) works with its agencies and partners to support the transport network that helps the UK's businessees and gets people and goods travelling around the country. The DfT plans and invests in transport infrastructure to keep the UK on the move. DFT is supported by 19 executive agencies and public bodies.

*Secretary of State for Transport,* Rt. Hon. Patrick McLoughlin, MP
*Parliamentary Private Secretary,* Stuart Andrew, MP
*Principal Private Secretary,* Phil West
*Parliamentary Under-Secretary of State,* Robert Goodwill, MP
*Private Secretary,* Alex Philpott
*Parliamentary Under-Secretary of State,* Andrew Jones, MP
*Private Secretary,* Rory Sedgley
*Parliamentary Under-Secretary of State,* Claire Perry, MP
*Private Secretary,* Matthew Eglinton
*Parliamentary Under-Secretary of State,* Lord Ahmad of Wimbledon
*Private Secretary,* Fiona Douglas
*Permanent Secretary,* Philip Rutnam
*Private Secretary,* Natalie Golding

MANAGEMENT BOARD
*Chair,* Rt. Hon. Patrick McLoughlin, MP *(Secretary of State)*
*Members,* Lord Ahmad of Wimbledon; Lucy Chadwick *(Director-General, International, Security and Environment);* John Dowie *(Director-General, Roads, Traffic and Local);* Robert Goodwill, MP; Andrew Jones, MP; Jonathan Moor, CBE *(Director-General, Resources and Strategy);* Clare Moriarty *(Director-General, Rail Executive);* Nick Olley *(General Counsel);* Claire Perry, MP; David Prout *(Director-General, High Speed 2);* Philip Rutnam *(Permanent Secretary)*

# HM TREASURY

1 Horse Guards Road, London SW1A 2HQ
T 020-7270 5000
E public.enquiries@hmtreasury.gsi.gov.uk
W www.gov.uk/government/organisations/hm-treasury

HM Treasury is the country's economics and finance ministry, and is responsible for formulating and implementing the government's financial and economic policy. It aims to raise the rate of sustainable growth, boost prosperity, and provide the conditions necessary for universal economic and employment opportunities. The Office of the Lord High Treasurer has been continuously in commission for over 200 years. The Lord High Commissioners of HM Treasury are the First Lord of the Treasury (who is also the prime minister), the Chancellor of the Exchequer and five junior lords. This board of commissioners is assisted at present by the chief secretary, the parliamentary secretary (who is also the government chief whip in the House of Commons), the financial secretary, the economic secretary, the exchequer secretary and the commercial secretary. The prime minister as first lord is not primarily concerned with the day-to-day aspects of Treasury business; neither are the parliamentary secretary and the junior lords as government whips. Treasury business is managed by the Chancellor of the Exchequer and the other Treasury ministers, assisted by the permanent secretary.

The chief secretary is responsible for public expenditure, including spending reviews and strategic planning; in-year control; public-sector pay and pensions; Annually Managed Expenditure and welfare reform; efficiency in public services; procurement and capital investment. He also has responsibility for the Treasury's interest in devolution.

The financial secretary has responsibility for financial services policy including banking and financial services reform and regulation; financial stability; city competitiveness; wholesale and retail markets in the UK, Europe and internationally; and the Financial Services Authority. His other responsibilities include banking support; bank lending; UK Financial Investments; Equitable Life; and personal savings and pensions policy. He also provides support to the chancellor on EU and wider international finance issues.

The exchequer secretary is a title only used occasionally, normally when the post of paymaster-general is allocated to a minister outside of the Treasury (as it is at present; the Rt. Hon. Matthew Hancock, MP was appointed paymaster-general and minister of the Cabinet Office in May 2015). The exchequer secretary's responsibilities include strategic oversight of the UK tax system; corporate and small business taxation, with input from the commercial secretary; departmental minister for HM Revenue and Customs and the Valuation Office

Agency; and lead minister on European and international tax issues.

The economic secretary's responsibilities include environmental issues such as taxation of transport, international climate change and energy; North Sea oil taxation; tax credits and child poverty; assisting the chief secretary on welfare reform; charities and the voluntary sector; excise duties and gambling; stamp duty land tax; EU Budget; the Royal Mint; and departmental minister for HM Treasury Group.

The role of commercial secretary was created in 2010. Responsibilities include enterprise and productivity; corporate finance; assisting the financial secretary on financial services, banking policy promoting the government's financial services policies and the competitiveness of the UK; asset freezing and financial crime; foreign exchange reserves and debt management policy; National Savings and Investments; and the Debt Management Office. The commercial secretary is also the treasury spokesperson in the House of Lords.

*Prime Minister and First Lord of the Treasury,*
    Rt. Hon. David Cameron, MP
*Chancellor of the Exchequer,* Rt. Hon. George
    Osborne, MP
*Parliamentary Private Secretary,* Chris Skidmore, MP
*Principal Private Secretary,* Clare Lombardelli
*Private Secretary,* Melanie Pitt
*Special Advisers to the Chancellor of the Exchequer,*
    James Chapman; Matt Cook; Thea Rogers
*Council of Economic Advisers,* Lisa Buckland;
    Richard Davies; Simon Glasson; Neil O'Brien;
    Eleanor Wolfson
*Chief Secretary to the Treasury,* Rt. Hon. Greg Hands,
    MP
*Parliamentary Private Secretary,* Jake Berry, MP
*Private Secretary,* Alex Furse
*Special Adviser to the Chief Secretary,* Jennifer
    Donnellan
*Financial Secretary to the Treasury,* David Gauke, MP
*Parliamentary Private Secretary,* Conor Burns, MP
*Exchequer Secretary to the Treasury,* Damian Hinds,
    MP
*Private Secretary,* David Pares
*Economic Secretary to the Treasury,* Harriet Baldwin,
    MP
*Private Secretary,* Luke Seaman
*Commercial Secretary to the Treasury,* Lord O'Neill of
    Gatley
*Private Secretary,* Zoe McNulty
*Lords Commissioners of HM Treasury (Whips),* Alun
    Cairns, MP; Charlie Elphicke, MP; David
    Evennett, MP; George Hollingberry, MP; John
    Penrose, MP; Mel Stride, MP
*Assistant Whips,* Stephen Barclay, MP; Jackie Doyle-
    Price, MP; Margot James, MP; Simon Kirby, MP;
    Sarah Newton, MP; Guy Opperman, MP; Julian
    Smith, MP

MANAGEMENT BOARD

*Chair,* Sir Nicholas Macpherson, GCB *(Permanent Secretary)*

*Executive Members,* Mark Bowman *(Director-General, International and EU);* James Bowler *(Director-General, Tax and Welfare);* Julian Kelly *(Public Spending and Finance);* John Kingman *(Second Permanent Secretary);* Sir Dave Ramsden, CBE *(Chief Economic Adviser);* Charles Roxburgh *(Director-General, Financial Services)*

## ROYAL MINT LTD

PO Box 500, Llantrisant, Pontyclun CF72 8YT
T 01443-222111 W www.royalmint.com

From 1975 the Royal Mint operated as a trading fund and was established as an executive agency in 1990. Since 2010 it has operated as Royal Mint Ltd, a company 100 per cent owned by HM Treasury, with an exclusive contract to supply all coinage for the UK.

The Royal Mint actively competes in world markets for a share of the available circulating coin business and about half of the coins and blanks it produces annually are exported. It is the leading export mint, accounting for around 15 per cent of the world market. The Royal Mint also manufactures special proof and uncirculated quality coins in gold, silver and other metals; military and civil decorations and medals; commemorative and prize medals; and royal and official seals.

*Master of the Mint,* Chancellor of the Exchequer *(ex officio)*
*Chair,* Peter Warry
*Chief Executive,* Adam Lawrence

## UK EXPORT FINANCE

1 Horse Guards Road, London SW1A 2HQ
T 020-7271 8000 E contact-us@ukef.gsi.gov.uk
W www.gov.uk/government/organisations/uk-export-finance

UK Export Finance is the UK's export credit agency. It helps UK exporters by providing insurance to them and guarantees to banks to share the risks of providing export finance. Additionally, it can make loans to overseas buyers of goods and services from the UK. UK Export Finance is the operating name of the Export Credits Guarantee Department.

The priorities of UK Export Finance are to fulfil its statutory remit to support exports; operate within the policy and financial objectives established by the government, which includes international obligations; and to recover the maximum amount of debt in respect of claims paid, taking account of the government's policy on debt forgiveness. It is supported by the Export Guarantees Advisory Council.

*Secretary of State for Business, Innovation and Skills and President of the Board of Trade,* Rt. Hon. Sajid Javid, MP*
*Senior Private Secretary,* Emily Shirtcliffe
*Minister of State,* Rt. Hon. Lord Maude of Horsham *(Trade and Investment)*†
*Private Secretary,* Nick Whittingham

*Jointly with the Department for Business, Innovation, and Skills
†Jointly with the Foreign and Commonwealth Office

MANAGEMENT BOARD

*Members,* Steve Dodgson *(Business Group);* Cameron Fox *(Finance);* David Godfrey *(Chief Executive);* David Havelock *(Credit Risk Group);* Lucy Wylde *(General Counsel)*
*Non-Executive Members,* Guy Beringer; Roger Lowe; Amin Mawji, OBE; Jane Owen; Sir Eric Peacock

## WALES OFFICE

Gwydyr House, Whitehall, London SW1A 2NP
T 029-2092 4220
E correspondence@walesoffice.gsi.gov.uk
W www.gov.uk/wales-office

The Wales Office was established in 1999 when most of the powers of the Welsh Office were handed over to the National Assembly for Wales. It is the department of the Secretary of State for Wales, who is the key government figure liaising with the devolved government in Wales and who represents Welsh interests in the cabinet and parliament. The secretary of state has the right to attend and speak at sessions of the National Assembly (and must consult the assembly on the government's legislative programme).

*Secretary of State for Wales,* Rt. Hon. Stephen Crabb, MP
*Parliamentary Private Secretary,* David Morris, MP
*Special Adviser,* Emily Poole
*Parliamentary Under-Secretary of State,* Alun Cairns, MP
*Private Secretary,* Elizabeth Allen
*Parliamentary Under-Secretary of State,* Lord Bourne of Aberystwyth*
*Private Secretary,* Elizabeth Allen
*Director of Office,* Glynne Jones

*Jointly with the Department of Energy and Climate Change

## DEPARTMENT FOR WORK AND PENSIONS

Caxton House, Tothill Street, London SW1H 9NA
T 020-7340 4000 E ministers@dwp.gsi.gov.uk
W www.gov.uk/government/organisations/department-for-work-pensions

The Department for Work and Pensions was formed in June 2001 from parts of the former Department of Social Security, the Department for Education and Employment and the Employment Service. The department helps unemployed people of working age into work, helps employers to fill their vacancies and provides financial support to people unable to help themselves, through back-to-work programmes. The department also administers the child support system, social security benefits and the social fund. In addition, the department has reciprocal social security arrangements with other countries.

*Secretary of State for Work and Pensions,* Rt. Hon. Iain Duncan Smith, MP
*Parliamentary Private Secretary,* David Rutley, MP
*Principal Private Secretary,* Paul McComb
*Private Secretaries,* Rob Cook; David Slovak
*Minister of State,* Rt. Hon. Priti Patel, MP *(Employment)*
*Parliamentary Private Secretary,* Alec Shelbrooke, MP
*Private Secretary,* Mike Maynard
*Assistant Private Secretaries,* Tia Priest; Nicholas Slim; Sam Gilbert
*Minister of State,* Baroness Altmann, CBE *(Pensions)*
*Private Secretary,* Michael Dynan-Oakley
*Assistant Private Secretaries,* Yasna Reynolds; Victoria Olipliant; Ella Taylor
*Parliamentary Under-Secretary,* Justin Tomlinson, MP *(Disabled People)*
*Private Secretary,* Jack Goodwin
*Assistant Private Secretaries,* Heather Lockley; Frank Shields; Joanna Ziff
*Minister of State,* Lord Freud *(Welfare Reform)*
*Private Secretary,* Becky Richards
*Assistant Private Secretaries,* Gemma Alcorn; Chris Ramm; Sarah Gaskell
*Permanent Secretary,* Robert Devereux

MANAGEMENT BOARD
*Permanent Secretary and Head of Department,* Robert Devereux
*Members,* Debbie Alder *(Director-General, Human Resources)*; Neil Couling, CBE *(Director-General, Universal Credit)*; Kevin Cunnington *(Director-General, Digital Transformation)*; Mike Driver *(Director-General, Finance)*; Jeremy Moore *(Director-General, Strategy, Policy and Analysis)*; Mayank Prakash *(Director-General, Technology)*; Noel Shanahan, CB *(Director-General, Operations)*

# EXECUTIVE AGENCIES

Executive agencies are well-defined business units that carry out services with a clear focus on delivering specific outputs within a framework of accountability to ministers. They can be set up or disbanded without legislation, and they are organisationally independent from the department they are answerable to. In the following list the agencies are shown in the accounts of their sponsor departments. Legally they act on behalf of the relevant secretary of state. Their chief executives also perform the role of accounting officers, which means they are responsible for the money spent by their organisations. Staff employed by agencies are civil servants.

## DEPARTMENT FOR BUSINESS, INNOVATION AND SKILLS

### COMPANIES HOUSE
Crown Way, Cardiff CF14 3UZ
T 0303-123 4500
E enquiries@companies-house.gov.uk
W www.companies-house.gov.uk

Companies House incorporates and dissolves companies, examines and stores company information delivered under the Companies Act and related legislation; and makes this information available to the public.
*Registrar of Companies for England and Wales and Chief Executive,* Tim Moss
*Registrar of Companies for Scotland,* Aoife Ann Martin
*Registrar of Companies for Northern Ireland,* Helen Shilliday

### THE INSOLVENCY SERVICE
4 Abbey Orchard Street, London SW1P 2HT
T 020-7637 1110
E redundancyclaims@insolvency.gsi.gov.uk
W www.bis.gov.uk/insolvency

The role of the service includes administration and investigation of the affairs of bankrupts, individuals subject to debt relief orders, partnerships and companies in compulsory liquidation; dealing with the disqualification of directors in all corporate failures; authorising and regulating the insolvency profession; providing banking and investment services for bankruptcy and liquidation estate funds; assessing and paying statutory entitlement to redundancy payments when an employer cannot, or will not, pay its employees; and advising ministers on insolvency, redundancy and related issues. The service has around 1,700 staff, operating from 21 locations across Great Britain.
*Inspector-General and Chief Executive,* Sarah Albon
*Deputy Chief Executive,* Graham Horne

### INTELLECTUAL PROPERTY OFFICE
Concept House, Cardiff Road, Newport NP10 8QQ
T 0300-300 2000 E information@ipo.gov.uk
W www.gov.uk/government/organisations/intellectual-property-office

The Intellectual Property Office (an operating name of the Patent Office) was set up in 1852 to act as the UK's sole office for the granting of patents. It

was established as an executive agency in 1990 and became a trading fund in 1991. The office is responsible for the granting of intellectual property (IP) rights which include patents, trade marks, designs and copyright.
*Comptroller-General and Chief Executive,* John Alty

## MET OFFICE
FitzRoy Road, Exeter, Devon EX1 3PB
T 01392-885680 E enquiries@metoffice.gov.uk
W www.metoffice.gov.uk

The Met Office is the UK's National Weather Service, operating as an executive agency of BIS, having transferred from the MoD in July 2011. It is a world leader in providing weather and climate services, using over 10 million weather observations a day, and employs more than 1,700 people at 60 locations throughout the world.
*Chief Executive,* Rob Varley
*Chief Scientist,* Prof. Julia Slingo, OBE

## NATIONAL MEASUREMENT AND REGULATION OFFICE
Stanton Avenue, Teddington, Middx TW11 0JZ
T 020-8943 7272 E info@nmro.gov.uk
W www.gov.uk/nmro

The National Measurement and Regulation Office (NMRO), formerly the National Measurement Office, aims to simplify technical regulation for the benefit of British business. The work of the NMRO should reduce unnecessary costs and give businesses greater confidence to invest and grow.
*Chief Executive (acting),* Richard Sanders

## SKILLS FUNDING AGENCY
Cheylesmore House, Quinton Road, Coventry CV1 2WT
T 0345-377 5000 E info@skillsfundingagency.bis.gov.uk
W www.gov.uk/sfa

The Skills Funding Agency (SFA) funds skills training for further education (FE) in England, including traineeships and apprenticeships. The SFA supports over 1,000 colleges, private training organisations and employers with more than £4bn of funding annually. It is responsible for giving colleges, training organisations and employers the right funding to help adults, young people, the unemployed and those with low skill levels the opportunity to obtain the skills they require for employment.
*Chief Executive,* Peter Lauener

## UK SPACE AGENCY
Polaris House, North Star Avenue, Swindon, Wiltshire SN2 1SZ
T 020-7215 5000 E info@ukspaceagency.bis.gsi.gov.uk
W www.gov.uk/uk-space-agency

The UK Space Agency was established on 23 March 2010 and became an executive agency on 1 April 2011. It was created to provide a single voice for UK space ambitions, and is responsible for all strategic decisions on the UK civil space programme. Responsibilities of the UK Space Agency include coordinating UK civil space activity; supporting academic research; nurturing the UK space industry; raising the profile of UK space activities at home and abroad; working to increase understanding of space science and its practical benefits; and inspiring the next generation of UK scientists and engineers. It aims to capture 10 per cent of the global market for space by 2030.
*Chief Executive,* Dr David Parker

# CABINET OFFICE

## CROWN COMMERCIAL SERVICE
Floor 9, The Capital Building, Old Hall Street, Liverpool L3 9PP
T 0345-410 2222 E info@crowncommercial.gov.uk
W www.gov.uk/government/organisations/crown-commercial-service

The Crown Commercial Service (CCS) is an executive agency of the Cabinet Office, bringing together policy, advice and direct buying; providing commercial services to the public sector and saving money for the taxpayer. The CCS works with over 1,400 organisations in the public sector.
*Chair,* Ed Smith
*Chief Executive,* Sally Collier

# DEPARTMENT FOR COMMUNITIES AND LOCAL GOVERNMENT

## PLANNING INSPECTORATE
Temple Quay House, 2 The Square, Temple Quay, Bristol BS1 6PN
T 0303-444 5000 E enquiries@pins.gsi.gov.uk
W www.gov.uk/government/organisations/planning-inspectorate; www.planningportal.gov.uk/planning/planninginspectorate

The main work of the inspectorate consists of national infrastructure planning under the Planning Act 2008 as amended by the Localism Act 2011, the processing of planning and enforcement appeals, and holding examinations into development plan documents. It also deals with listed building consent appeals; advertisement appeals; rights of way cases; cases arising from the Environmental Protection and Water acts, the Transport and Works Act 1992 and other highways legislation; and reporting on planning applications called in for decision by the Department for Communities and Local Government and the Welsh government.
*Chief Executive,* Simon Ridley

## THE QUEEN ELIZABETH II CONFERENCE CENTRE
Broad Sanctuary, London SW1P 3EE
T 020-7798 4000 W www.qeiicentre.london

The centre provides secure conference facilities for national and international government and private sector use.
*Chief Executive,* Mark Taylor

# DEPARTMENT FOR CULTURE, MEDIA AND SPORT
## THE ROYAL PARKS
The Old Police House, Hyde Park, London W2 2UH
T 0300-061 2000 E hq@royalparks.gsi.gov.uk
W www.royalparks.org.uk

Royal Parks is responsible for maintaining and developing over 2,000 hectares (5,000 acres) of urban parkland contained within the eight royal parks in London: Bushy Park (with the Longford river); Green Park; Greenwich Park; Hyde Park; Kensington Gardens; Regent's Park (with Primrose Hill); Richmond Park and St James's Park.
*Chief Executive,* Andrew Scattergood

# MINISTRY OF DEFENCE

## DEFENCE ELECTRONICS AND COMPONENTS AGENCY
Welsh Road, Deeside, Flintshire CH5 2LS
T 01244-847745
E decainfo@deca.mod.uk
W www.gov.uk/government/organisations/defence-electronics-and-components-agency

The Defence Electronics and Components Agency (DECA) provides avionics, electronics, components and general engineering capability to support the MoD.
*Director Support Services,* Ian Doughty

## DEFENCE SCIENCE AND TECHNOLOGY LABORATORY
Porton Down, Salisbury, Wiltshire SP4 0JQ
T 01980-613000 E centralenquiries@dstl.gov.uk
W www.gov.uk/government/organisations/defence-science-and-technology-laboratory

The Defence Science and Technology Laboratory supplies specialist science and technology services to the MoD and wider government.
*Chief Executive,* Jonathan Lyle

## UK HYDROGRAPHIC OFFICE
Admiralty Way, Taunton, Somerset TA1 2DN
T 01823-337900
E customerservices@ukho.gov.uk
W www.gov.uk/government/organisations/uk-hydrographic-office

The UK Hydrographic Office (UKHO) produces nautical publications and services for the Royal Navy and merchant shipping, to protect lives at sea.
*Chief Executive,* John Humphrey

# DEPARTMENT FOR EDUCATION

## THE EDUCATION FUNDING AGENCY
Sanctuary Buildings, 20 Great Smith Street, London SW1P 3BT
T 0370-000 2288
W www.gov.uk/government/organisations/education-funding-agency

Formed on 1 April 2012, the Education Funding Agency (EFA) is the DFE's delivery agency for funding and compliance. It manages £54m of funding each year to support all state-provided education for 8 million children aged 3 to 16, and 1.6 million young people aged 16 to 19. The EFA also supports the delivery of building and maintenance programmes for schools, academies, free schools and sixth-form colleges.
*Chief Executive,* Peter Lauener

## NATIONAL COLLEGE FOR TEACHING AND LEADERSHIP
Piccadilly Gate, Store Street, Manchester M1 2WD
T 0370-000 2288 E enquiries@nationalcollege.org.uk
W www.gov.uk/government/organisations/national-college-for-teaching-and-leadership

On 1 April 2013 the National College merged with the Teaching Agency to become the National College for Teaching and Leadership. It has two key aims: improving the quality of the workforce; and helping schools to help each other to improve. It is also the awarding body for Qualified Teacher Status (QTS).
*Chief Executive,* Charlie Taylor

## STANDARDS AND TESTING AGENCY
53–55 Butts Road, Earlsdon Park, Coventry CV1 3BH
T 0300-303 3013 E assessments@education.gov.uk
W www.gov.uk/government/organisations/standards-and-testing-agency

The Standards and Testing Agency (STA) opened on 1 October 2011 and is responsible for the development and delivery of all statutory assessments from early years to the end of Key Stage 2.
*Chief Executive,* Claire Burton

## DEPARTMENT FOR ENVIRONMENT, FOOD AND RURAL AFFAIRS

### ANIMAL AND PLANT HEALTH AGENCY
Woodham Lane, New Haw, Addlestone, Surrey KT15 3NB
T 01932-341 111
E apha.corporate_centre@apha.gsi.gov.uk
W www.gov.uk/government/organisations/animal-and-plant-health-agency

The Animal and Plant Health Agency (APHA) was launched on 1 October 2014. It merged the former Animal Health and Veterinary Laboratories Agency with parts of the Food and Environment Research Agency responsible for plant and bee health to create a single agency responsible for animal, plant and bee health.

APHA is responsible for identifying and controlling endemic and exotic diseases and pests in animals, plants and bees, and surveillance of new and emerging pests and diseases; scientific research in areas such as bacterial, viral, prion and parasitic diseases, vaccines and food safety and act as an international reference laboratory for many farm animal diseases; facilitating international trade in animals, products of animal origin, and plants; protecting endangered wildlife through licensing and registration; managing a programme of apiary inspections, diagnostics, research and development, training and advice; and regulating the safe disposal of animal by-products to reduce the risk of potentially dangerous substances entering the food chain.

The agency provides all or some of these services to DEFRA and the Scottish and Welsh governments.
*Chief Executive,* Chris Hadkiss

### CENTRE FOR ENVIRONMENT, FISHERIES AND AQUACULTURE SCIENCE (CEFAS)
Pakefield Road, Lowestoft, Suffolk NR33 0HT
T 01502-562244 W www.cefas.gov.uk

Established in April 1997, the agency provides research and consultancy services in fisheries science and management, aquaculture, fish health and hygiene, environmental impact assessment, and environmental quality assessment.
*Chief Executive,* Tom Karsten

### RURAL PAYMENTS AGENCY
PO Box 69, Reading RG1 3YD
T 0300-0200 301 E ruralpayments@defra.gsi.gov.uk
W www.gov.uk/government/organisations/rural-payments-agency

The RPA was established in 2001. It pays out over £2bn each year to support the farming and food sector and is responsible for Common Agricultural Policy (CAP) schemes in England. In addition it manages over 40 other rural economy and community schemes. It is also responsible for operating cattle tracing services across Great Britain; conducting inspections of farms, processing plants and fresh produce markets in England; and managing the Rural Land Register.
*Chief Executive,* Mark Grimshaw

### VETERINARY MEDICINES DIRECTORATE
Woodham Lane, New Haw, Addlestone, Surrey KT15 3LS
T 01932-336911 E postmaster@vmd.defra.gsi.gov.uk
W www.gov.uk/government/organisations/veterinary-medicines-directorate

The Veterinary Medicines Directorate is responsible for all aspects of the authorisation and control of veterinary medicines, including post-authorisation surveillance of residues in animals and animal products. It is also responsible for the development and enforcement of legislation concerning veterinary medicines and the provision of policy advice to ministers.
*Chief Executive,* Prof. Pete Borriello

## FOREIGN AND COMMONWEALTH OFFICE

### FCO SERVICES
Hanslope Park, Milton Keynes MK19 7BH
T 01908-515 789
E fcoservices.customercontactcentre@fco.gov.uk
W www.fcoservices.gov.uk

FCO Services was established as an executive agency in April 2006 and became a trading fund in April 2008. It operates as the service delivery arm of the FCO, keeping their people, assets and information across the globe safe and secure from the threats they face. FCO Services also works with central government departments, law enforcement, HM government abroad, local government and the UK's critical national infrastructure.
*Chief Executive,* Danny Payne

### WILTON PARK CONFERENCE CENTRE
Wiston House, Steyning, W. Sussex BN44 3DZ
T 01903-815020 W www.wiltonpark.org.uk

Wilton Park organises international affairs conferences and is hired out to government departments and commercial users.
*Chair,* Iain Ferguson
*Chief Executive,* Richard Burge

# DEPARTMENT OF HEALTH

## MEDICINES AND HEALTHCARE PRODUCTS REGULATORY AGENCY (MHRA)
151 Buckingham Palace Road, London SW1W 9SZ
E info@mhra.gsi.gov.uk
W www.gov.uk/government/organisations/medicines-and-healthcare-products-regulatory-agency

The MHRA is a centre of the Medicines and Healthcare Products Regulatory Agency which also includes the National Institute for Biological Standards and Control (NIBSC) and the Clinical Practice Research Datalink (CPRD). The MHRA is responsible for regulating all medicines and medical devices in the UK by ensuring they work and are acceptably safe.
*Chair,* Sir Michael Rawlins
*Chief Executive,* Dr Ian Hudson

## PUBLIC HEALTH ENGLAND
Wellington House, 133–155 Waterloo Road, London SE1 8UG
T 020-7654 8000 E enquiries@phe.gov.uk
W www.gov.uk/government/organisations/public-health-england

Public Health England (PHE) began operating on 1 April 2013 with a remit to protect and improve the health and wellbeing of people within the UK, and reducing health inequalities. PHE employs 5,000 staff who are mostly scientists, researchers and public health professionals. It has 15 local centres and four regions in England and works closely with public health profesionals in Wales, Scotland, Northern Ireland and internationally.
*Chair,* Prof. David Heymann, CBE
*Chief Executive,* Duncan Selbie

# MINISTRY OF JUSTICE

## CRIMINAL INJURIES COMPENSATION AUTHORITY (CICA)
Tay House, 300 Bath Street, Glasgow G2 4LN
T 0300-003 3601
W www.gov.uk/goverment/organisations/criminal-injuries-compensation-authority

CICA is the executive agency responsible for administering the Criminal Injuries Compensation Scheme in England, Scotland and Wales (separate arrangements apply in Northern Ireland). CICA handles up to 40,000 applications for compensation each year, covering every aspect of compensation under the 1996, 2001 and 2008 Criminal Injuries Compensation Schemes. Appeals against decisions made by CICA can be put to the First-tier Tribunal (Criminal Injuries Compensation).
*Chief Executive,* Carole Oatway

## HER MAJESTY'S COURTS AND TRIBUNALS SERVICE
102 Petty France, London SW1H 9AJ
W www.gov.uk/government/organisations/hm-courts-and-tribunals-service

HM Courts Service and the Tribunals Service merged on 1 April 2011 to form HM Courts and Tribunals Service, an integrated agency providing support for the administration of justice in courts and tribunals. As an agency within the MoJ it operates as a partnership between the Lord Chancellor, the Lord Chief Justice and the Senior President of Tribunals. It is responsible for the administration of the criminal, civil and family courts and tribunals in England and Wales and non-devolved tribunals in Scotland and Northern Ireland. The agency's work is overseen by a board headed by an independent chair working with non-executive, executive and judicial members.
*Chief Executive,* Natalie Ceeney, CBE

## LEGAL AID AGENCY
Berkley Way, Viking Business Park, Jarrow, South Tyneside NE31 1SF
T 0300-200 2020 E contactcivil@legalaid.gsi.gov.uk
W www.gov.uk/government/organisations/legal-aid-agency

The Legal Aid Agency provides civil and criminal legal aid and advice in England and Wales. Formed on 1 April 2013 as part of the Legal Aid, Sentencing and Punishment of Offenders Act 2012, the agency replaces the Legal Services Commission, a non-departmental public body of the MoJ.
*Chief Executive,* Matthew Coats

## NATIONAL OFFENDER MANAGEMENT SERVICE
Clive House, 70 Petty France, London SW1H 9EX
T 0300-047 6325 E public.enquiries@noms.gsi.gov.uk
W www.gov.uk/government/organisations/national-offender-management-service

HM Prison Service became part of the National Offender Management Service (NOMS) on 1 April 2008 as part of the reorganisation of the MoJ. Through HM Prison Service NOMS is responsible for managing public sector prisons in England and Wales and is also responsible for overseeing probation delivery in England and Wales through the National Probation Service and community rehabilitation companies.
*Chief Executive,* Michael Spurr

## OFFICE OF THE PUBLIC GUARDIAN

PO Box 16185, Birmingham B2 2WH
T 0300-456 0300
E customerservices@publicguardian.gsi.gov.uk
W www.gov.uk/government/organisations/office-of-the-public-guardian

The Office of the Public Guardian (OPG) works within the Mental Capacity Act 2005 to support and protect those who lack the mental capacity to make decisions for themselves. It supports the Public Guardian in the registration of Enduring Powers of Attorney (EPA) and Lasting Powers of Attorney (LPA), and the supervision of deputies appointed by the Court of Protection. The OPG also has responsibility for investigating and acting on allegations of abuse by attorneys and deputies. The OPG's responsibility extends across England and Wales.
*Chief Executive and Public Guardian,* Alan Eccles, CBE

## DEPARTMENT FOR TRANSPORT

### DRIVER AND VEHICLE LICENSING AGENCY (DVLA)

Longview Road, Swansea SA6 7JL
W www.gov.uk/government/organisations/driver-and-vehicle-licensing-agency

The DVLA, established as an executive agency in 1990, maintains registers of drivers and vehicles in Great Britain. The information collated by the DVLA helps to improve road safety, reduce vehicle related crime, support environmental initiatives and limit vehicle tax evasion. The DVLA maintains over 45 million driver records and over 38 million vehicle records and collects over £6bn a year in vehicle tax.
*Chief Executive,* Oliver Morley

### DRIVER AND VEHICLE STANDARDS AGENCY

Berkeley House, Croydon Street, Bristol BS5 0DA
T 0300-123 9000 E inform@vosa.gov.uk
W www.gov.uk/government/organisations/driver-and-vehicle-standards-agency

Formed by the merger of the Driving Standards Agency and the Vehicle and Operator Services Agency in 2014, the Driver and Vehicle Standards Agency (DVSA) is responsible for improving road safety in the UK by setting standards for driving and motorcycling, and ensuring drivers, vehicle operators and MOT garages understand and comply with roadworthiness standards. It additionally provides a range of licensing, testing, education and enforcement services.
*Chief Executive,* Alastair Peoples

## MARITIME AND COASTGUARD AGENCY

Spring Place, 105 Commercial Road, Southampton SO15 1EG
T 023-8032 9100
W www.gov.uk/government/organisations/maritime-and-coastguard-agency

The agency's aims are to prevent loss of life, continuously improve maritime safety and protect the marine environment.
*Chief Executive,* Sir Alan Massey
*Chief Coastguard,* Keith Oliver

## VEHICLE CERTIFICATION AGENCY

1 Eastgate Office Centre, Eastgate Road, Bristol BS5 6XX
T 0300-330 5797 E enquiries@vca.gov.uk
W www.dft.gov.uk/vca

The agency is the UK authority responsible for ensuring that new road vehicles, agricultural tractors, off-road vehicles and vehicle parts have been designed and constructed to meet internationally agreed standards of safety and environmental protection.
*Chief Executive,* Paul Markwick

## HM TREASURY

### UK DEBT MANAGEMENT OFFICE

Eastcheap Court, 11 Philpot Lane, London EC3M 8UD
T 020-7862 6500
W www.gov.uk/government/organisations/uk-debt-management-office

The UK Debt Management Office (DMO) was launched as an executive agency of HM Treasury in April 1998. The Chancellor of the Exchequer determines the policy and financial framework within which the DMO operates, but delegates operational decisions on debt and cash management and the day-to-day running of the office to the chief executive. The DMO's remit is to carry out the government's debt management policy of minimising financing costs over the long term, and to minimise the cost of offsetting the government's net cash flows over time, while operating at a level of risk approved by ministers in both cases. The DMO is also responsible for providing loans to local authorities through the Public Works Loan Board, and for managing the assets of certain public-sector bodies through the Commissioners for the Reduction of the National Debt.
*Chief Executive,* Robert Stheeman

## NON-MINISTERIAL GOVERNMENT DEPARTMENTS

Non-ministerial government departments are part of central government but are not headed by a minister and are not funded by a sponsor department. They are created to implement specific legislation, but do not have the ability to change it. Departments may have links to a minister, but the minister is not responsible for the department's overall performance. Staff employed by non-ministerial departments are civil servants.

## CHARITY COMMISSION

PO Box 1227, Liverpool L69 3UG **T** 0845-300 0218
**W** www.gov.uk/government/organisations/charity-commission

The Charity Commission is established by law as the independent regulator and registrar of charities in England and Wales. Its aim is to provide the best possible regulation of these charities in order to ensure their legal compliance and increase their efficiency, accountability and effectiveness, as well as to encourage public trust and confidence in them. The commission maintains a register of over 160,000 charities. It is accountable to both parliament and the First-tier Tribunal (Charity), and the chamber of the Upper Tribunal or high court for decisions made in exercising the commission's legal powers. The Charity Commission has offices in London, Liverpool, Taunton and Newport.
*Chair,* William Shawcross, CVO
*Chief Executive,* Paula Sussex

## COMPETITION AND MARKETS AUTHORITY

Victoria House, Southampton Row, London WC1B 4AD
**T** 020-3738 6000 **E** general.enquiries@cma.gsi.gov.uk
**W** www.gov.uk/cma

The Competition and Markets Authority (CMA) is the UK's primary competition and consumer authority. It is an independent non-ministerial government department with responsibility for carrying out investigations into mergers, markets and the regulated industries and enforcing competition and consumer law. From 1 April 2014 it took over the functions of the Competition Commission and the competition and certain consumer functions of the Office of Fair Trading under the Enterprise Act 2002, as amended by the Enterprise and Regulatory Reform Act 2013.
*Chair,* David Currie
*Chief Executive,* Alex Chisholm

## CROWN PROSECUTION SERVICE

Rose Court, 2 Southwark Bridge Road, London SE1 9HS
**T** 020-3357 0000 **E** enquiries@cps.gsi.gov.uk
**W** www.cps.gov.uk

The Crown Prosecution Service (CPS) is the independent body responsible for prosecuting people in England and Wales. The CPS was established as a result of the Prosecution of Offences Act 1985. It works closely with the police to advise on lines of inquiry and to decide on

appropriate charges and other disposals in all but minor cases. *See also* Law Courts and Offices.
*Director of Public Prosecutions,* Alison Saunders, CB
*Chief Executive,* Peter Lewis, CB

## FOOD STANDARDS AGENCY

Aviation House, 125 Kingsway, London WC2B 6NH
**T** 020-7276 8829 **E** helpline@foodstandards.gsi.gov.uk
**W** www.food.gov.uk

Established in April 2000, the FSA is a UK-wide non-ministerial government body responsible for food safety and hygiene. The agency has the general function of developing policy in these areas and provides information and advice to the government, other public bodies and consumers. The FSA also works with local authorities to enforce food safety regulations and has staff working in UK meat plants to check that the requirements of the regulations are being met.
*Chair,* Tim Bennett
*Chief Executive,* Catherine Brown

FOOD STANDARDS AGENCY NORTHERN IRELAND, 10C Clarendon Road, Belfast BT1 3BG
**T** 028-9041 7700
**E** infofsani@foodstandards.gsi.gov.uk
FOOD STANDARDS AGENCY WALES, 11th Floor, South Gate House, Wood Street, Cardiff CF10 1EW
**T** 029-2067 8999 **E** wales@foodstandards.gsi.gov.uk

## FORESTRY COMMISSION

Silvan House, 231 Corstorphine Road, Edinburgh EH12 7AT
**T** 0300-067 4321 **E** enquiries@forestry.gsi.gov.uk
**W** www.forestry.gov.uk

The Forestry Commission is the government department responsible for forestry policy in England and Scotland. It is divided into Forestry Commission England and Forestry Commission Scotland, which report to forestry ministers (the Secretary of State for Environment, Food & Rural Affairs in the UK government, and to ministers in the Scottish government), to whom it is responsible for advice on and implementation of forestry policy. It has an agency, Forest Research, which carries out scientific research and technical development relevant to forestry. The public forests are managed through two additional executive agencies, known as Forest Enterprise England and Forest Enterprise Scotland.

On 1 April 2013 the functions of its Welsh division, Forestry Commission Wales, were subsumed into Natural Resources Wales, a new body established by the Welsh government to regulate and manage natural resources in Wales.

The commission's principal objectives are to protect and expand England's and Scotland's forests and woodlands; enhance the economic value of forest resources; conserve and improve the biodiversity, landscape and cultural heritage of forests and woodlands; develop opportunities for woodland recreation; and increase public understanding of, and community participation in, forestry. It does this by managing public forests in its care to implement these objectives; by supporting other woodland owners with grants, regulation, advice and tree felling licences; and, through its Forest Research agency, by carrying out scientific research and technical development in support of these objectives.

*Chair (2014–17),* Sir Harry Studholme, Bt.
*Deputy Chair and Director, England,* Ian Gambles
*Forestry Commissioner, Scotland,* Dr Bob McIntosh
FORESTRY COMMISSION ENGLAND, 620 Bristol Business Park, Coldharbour Lane, Bristol BS16 1EJ
T 0117-906 6000
FORESTRY COMMISSION SCOTLAND, Silvan House, 231 Corstorphine Road, Edinburgh EH12 7AT
T 0845-367 3787

## GOVERNMENT ACTUARY'S DEPARTMENT

Finlaison House, 15–17 Furnival Street,
London EC4A 1AB
T 020-7211 2601
Belford House, 59 Belford Road, Edinburgh EH4 3UE
T 0131-467 0324
E enquiries@gad.gov.uk W www.gov.uk/gad

The Government Actuary's Department (GAD) was established in 1919 and provides actuarial advice to the public sector in the UK and overseas, and also to the private sector, where consistent with government policy. The GAD provides advice on occupational pension schemes, social security and National Insurance, investment and strategic risk management, insurance analysis and advice, financial risk management, and healthcare financing.

*Government Actuary,* Martin Clarke
*Deputy Government Actuaries,* George Russell; Colin Wilson
*Chief Actuaries,* Sandra Bell; Ian Boonin; Tracey Cutler; Adrian Hale; Stephen Humphrey; Ken Kneller; Ian Rogers; Aidan Smith; Sue Vivian; Matt Wood

## GOVERNMENT LEGAL DEPARTMENT

1 Kemble Street, London WC2B 4TS
T 020-7210 3000
E thetreasurysolicitor@governmentlegal.gov.uk
W www.gov.uk/gld

The Treasury Solicitor's Department became the Government Legal Department (GLD) on 1 April 2015. The department provides legal advice to government on the development, design and implementation of government policies and decisions, and represents the government in court.

It is superintended by the Attorney-General. The permanent secretary of the GLD, the Treasury Solicitor, is also the Queen's Proctor, and is responsible for collecting ownerless goods *(bona vacantia)* on behalf of the crown.

*HM Procurator-General and Treasury Solicitor,* Jonathan Jones
*Directors-General,* Stephen Braviner-Roman; Peter Fish; Claire Johnston
*Head of Bona Vacantia,* Mayur Patel

## HM REVENUE AND CUSTOMS (HMRC)

100 Parliament Street, London SW1A 2BQ
Income Tax Enquiries 0300-200 3300
National Insurance Enquiries 0300-200 3500
VAT Enquiries 0300-200 3700
W www.gov.uk/government/organisations/hm-revenue-customs

HMRC was formed following the integration of the Inland Revenue and HM Customs and Excise, which was made formal by parliament in April 2005. It collects and administers direct taxes (capital gains tax, corporation tax, income tax, inheritance tax and national insurance contributions) and indirect taxes (excise duties, insurance premium tax, petroleum revenue tax, stamp duty, stamp duty land tax, stamp duty reserve tax and value-added tax). HMRC also pays and administers child benefit, tax credits and the Child Trust Fund, in addition to being responsible for environmental taxes, national minimum wage enforcement, recovery of student loans, the climate change levy and landfill tax. HMRC also administers the Government Banking Service.

*Chief Executive and Permanent Secretary,* Lin Homer
*Tax Assurance Commissioner and Second Permanent Secretary,* Edward Troup

## VALUATION OFFICE AGENCY

Wingate House, 93–107 Shaftesbury Avenue,
London W1D 5BU
T 0300-050 0385 W www.voa.gov.uk

Established in 1991, the Valuation Office is an executive agency of HM Revenue and Customs. It is responsible for compiling and maintaining the business rating and council tax valuation lists for England and Wales; valuing property throughout Great Britain for the purposes of taxes administered by HMRC; providing statutory and non-statutory property valuation services in England, Wales and Scotland; and giving policy advice to ministers on property valuation matters. In April 2009 the VOA assumed responsibility for the functions of The Rent Service, which provided a rental valuation service to local authorities in England, and fair rent determinations for landlords and tenants.

*Chief Executive,* Penny Ciniewicz

## LAND REGISTRY

Trafalgar House, 1 Bedford Park, Croydon CR0 2AQ
**T** 0300-006 0411
**W** www.gov.uk/government/organisations/land-registry

A government department and trading fund of BIS, Land Registry maintains the Land Register – the definitive source of information for more than 24 million property titles in England and Wales. The Land Register has been open to public inspection since 1990.

*Chief Land Registrar and Chief Executive,* Graham Farrant

## NATIONAL ARCHIVES

NATIONAL ARCHIVES
Kew, Richmond, Surrey TW9 4DU
**T** 020-8876 3444 **W** www.nationalarchives.gov.uk

The National Archives is a non-ministerial government department of the Ministry of Justice. It incorporates the Public Record Office, Historical Manuscripts Commission, Office of Public Sector Information and Her Majesty's Stationery Office. As the official archive of the UK government, it preserves, protects and makes accessible the historical collection of official records.

The National Archives also manages digital information including the UK government web archive which contains over one billion digital documents, and devises solutions for keeping government records readable now and in the future.

The organisation administers the UK's public records system under the Public Records Acts of 1958 and 1967. The records it holds span 1,000 years – from the Domesday Book to the latest government papers to be released – and fill more than 167km (104 miles) of shelving.

*Chief Executive and Keeper,* Jeff James

## NATIONAL CRIME AGENCY

Units 1–6 Citadel Place, Tinworth Street, London SE11 5EF
**T** 0370-496 7622 **E** communication@nca.x.gsi.gov.uk
**W** www.nationalcrimeagency.gov.uk

The National Crime Agency (NCA) is an operational crime fighting agency introduced under the Crime and Courts Act 2013, which became fully operational in October 2013. The NCA's remit is to fight organised crime, strengthen UK borders, tackle fraud and cyber crime and protect children and young people. The agency employs over 4,000 officers and provides leadership through its organised crime, border policing, economic crime and Child Exploitation and Online Protection Centre commands, the National Cyber Crime Unit and specialist capability teams.

Chair, Keith Bristow, QPM

## NATIONAL SAVINGS AND INVESTMENTS

Glasgow G58 1SB
**T** 0500-007 007 **W** www.nsandi.com

NS&I (National Savings and Investments) came into being in 1861 when the Palmerston government set up the Post Office Savings Bank, a savings scheme which aimed to encourage ordinary wage earners 'to provide for themselves against adversity and ill health'. NS&I was established as a government department in 1969. It is responsible for the design, marketing and administration of savings and investment products for personal savers and investors. It has over 25 million customers and more than £110bn invested.

*Chief Executive,* Jane Platt, CBE

## OFFICE OF GAS AND ELECTRICITY MARKETS (OFGEM)

9 Millbank, London SW1P 3GE
**T** 020-7901 7295 **W** www.ofgem.gov.uk

OFGEM is the regulator for Britain's gas and electricity industries. Its role is to protect and advance the interests of consumers by promoting competition where possible, and through regulation only where necessary. OFGEM operates under the direction and governance of the Gas and Electricity Markets Authority, which makes all major decisions and sets policy priorities for OFGEM. OFGEM's powers are provided for under the Gas Act 1986 and the Electricity Act 1989, as amended by the Utilities Act 2000. It also has enforcement powers under the Competition Act 1998 and the Enterprise Act 2002.

*Chair,* David Gray
*Chief Executive,* Dermot Nolan

## OFFICE OF QUALIFICATIONS AND EXAMINATIONS REGULATION (OFQUAL)

Spring Place, Herald Avenue, Coventry CV5 6UB
**T** 0300-303 3344 **E** public.enquiries@ofqual.gov.uk
**W** www.gov.uk/government/organisations/ofqual

OFQUAL became the independent regulator of qualifications, examinations and assessments on 1 April 2010. It is responsible for maintaining standards, improving confidence and distributing information about qualifications and examinations, as well as regulating general and vocational qualifications in England and vocational qualifications in Northern Ireland.

*Chief Executive,* Glenys Stacey

## OFFICE OF RAIL REGULATION
1 Kemble Street, London WC2B 4AN
T 020-7282 2000 E contact.cct@orr.gsi.gov.uk
W www.orr.gov.uk

The Office of the Rail and Road (ORR) is the operating name of the Office of Rail Regulation. The Office of Rail Regulation was established on 5 July 2004 under the Railways and Transport Safety Act 2003. It replaced the Office of the Rail Regulator.

On 1 April 2006, ORR assumed new responsibilities as a combined safety and economic regulator under the Railways Act 2005. It also has concurrent jurisdiction with the Competition and Market Authority under the Competition Act 1998 as the competition authority for the railways.

As the railway industry's independent health and safety and econimic regulator, its principal functions are to: ensure that Network Rail and HS1 manage the national network efficiently and in a way that meets the needs of its users; encourage continuous health and safety performance; secure compliance with relevant health and safety law, including taking enforcement action as necessary; develop policy and enhance relevant railway health and safety legislation; and license operators of railway assets, setting the terms for access by operators to the network and other railway facilities, and enforce competition and consumer law in the rail sector.

On 1 April 2015, under the Infrastructure Act 2015, ORR assumed responsibility for monitoring Highways England's management and development of the strategic road network – the motorways and main 'A' roads in England. In this role ORR ensures that the network is managed efficiently, safely and sustainably, for the benefit of road users and the public.

On 16 March 2015, ORR signed an agreement with the French rail regulator ARAF to establish a collaborative regulatory approach for consistent independent regulation across the Channel tunnel network.

ORR is led by a board appointed by the Secretary of State for Transport.
*Chair,* Anna Walker

## OFFICE FOR STANDARDS IN EDUCATION, CHILDREN'S SERVICES AND SKILLS (OFSTED)
Piccadilly Gate, Store Street, Manchester M1 2WD
T 0300-123 1231 E enquiries@ofsted.gov.uk
W www.gov.uk/government/organisations/ofsted

Ofsted was established under the Education (Schools Act) 1992 and was relaunched on 1 April 2007 with a wider remit, bringing together four formerly separate inspectorates. It works to raise standards in services through the inspection and regulation of care for children and young people,

and inspects education and training for children of all ages.
*HM Chief Inspector,* Sir Michael Wilshaw
*Chair,* David Hoare

## ORDNANCE SURVEY
Adanac Drive, Southampton SO16 0AS
T 0845-605 0505
E customerservices@os.uk
W www.ordnancesurvey.co.uk

Ordnance Survey is the national mapping agency for Great Britain. It is a government department and executive agency operating as a trading fund since 1999.
*Director-General and Chief Executive,* Nigel Clifford

## SERIOUS FRAUD OFFICE
2–4 Cockspur Street, London SW1Y 5BS
T 020-7239 7272 E public.enquiries@sfo.gsi.gov.uk
W www.sfo.gov.uk

The Serious Fraud Office is an independent government department that investigates and, where appropriate, prosecutes serious or complex fraud, bribery and corruption. It is part of the UK criminal justice system with jurisdiction over England, Wales and Northern Ireland but not Scotland, the Isle of Man or the Channel Islands. The office is headed by a director who is superintended by the Attorney-General.
*Director,* David Green, CB, QC

## SUPREME COURT OF THE UNITED KINGDOM
Parliament Square, London SW1P 3BD
T 020-7960 1900 E enquiries@supremecourt.uk
W www.supremecourt.uk

The Supreme Court of the United Kingdom is the highest domestic judicial authority; it replaced the appellate committee of the House of Lords (the house functioning in its judicial capacity) on 1 October 2009. It is the final court of appeal for cases heard in Great Britain and Northern Ireland (except for criminal cases from Scotland). Cases concerning the interpretation and application of European Union law, including preliminary rulings requested by British courts and tribunals, are decided by the Court of Justice of the European Union (CJEU), and the supreme court can make a reference to the CJEU in appropriate cases. Additionally, in giving effect to rights contained in the European Convention on Human Rights, the supreme court must take account of any decision of the European Court of Human Rights.

The supreme court also assumed jurisdiction in relation to devolution matters under the Scotland Act 1998 (now partly superseded by the Scotland Act 2012), the Northern Ireland Act 1988 and the

Government of Wales Act 2006; these powers were transferred from the Judicial Committee of the Privy Council. Ten of the 12 Lords of Appeal in Ordinary (Law Lords) from the House of Lords transferred to the 12-member supreme court when it came into operation (at the same time one law lord retired and another was appointed Master of the Rolls). All new justices of the supreme court are now appointed by an independent selection commission, and, although styled Rt. Hon. Lord, are not members of the House of Lords. Peers who are members of the judiciary are disqualified from sitting or voting in the House of Lords until they retire from their judicial office.

*Chief Executive,* Mark Ormerod, CB

## UK STATISTICS AUTHORITY

1 Drummond Gate, London SW1V 2QQ
T 0845-604 1857
E authority.enquiries@statistics.gsi.gov.uk
W www.statisticsauthority.gov.uk

The UK Statistics Authority was established on 1 April 2008 by the Statistics and Registration Service Act 2007 as an independent body operating at arm's length from government, reporting to the UK parliament and the devolved legislatures. Its overall objective is to promote and safeguard the production and publication of official statistics and ensure their quality and comprehensiveness. The authority's main functions are the oversight of the Office for National Statistics (ONS); monitoring and reporting on all UK official statistics, which includes around 30 central government departments and the devolved administrations; and the production of a code of practice for statistics and the assessment of official statistics against the code.

### BOARD

*Chair,* Sir Andrew Dilnot, CBE
*Board Members,* Dr Dame Colette Bowe, DBE; Carolyn Fairbairn; Dame Moira Gibb, DBE; Prof. David Hand; Ed Humpherson *(Director-General, Regulation);* Dr David Levy; John Pullinger *(National Statistician);* Prof. Sir Adrian Smith, FRS *(Deputy Chair, ONS);* Glen Watson *(Deputy National Statistician)*

### OFFICE FOR NATIONAL STATISTICS (ONS)

Cardiff Road, Newport NP10 8XG
T 0845-601 3034 E info@statistics.gov.uk
W www.ons.gov.uk

The ONS was created in 1996 by the merger of the Central Statistical Office and the Office of Population Censuses and Surveys. On 1 April 2008

it became the executive office of the UK Statistics Authority. As part of these changes, the office's responsibility for the General Register Office transferred to HM Passport Office of the Home Office.

The ONS is responsible for preparing, interpreting and publishing key statistics on the government, economy and society of the UK. Its key responsibilities include designing, managing and running the Census and providing statistics on health and other demographic matters in England and Wales; the production of the UK National Accounts and other economic indicators; the organisation of population censuses in England and Wales and surveys for government departments and public bodies.

*National Statistician,* John Pullinger
*Director-Generals,* Jonathan Athow; Heather Savory; Glen Watson

## UK TRADE AND INVESTMENT

1 Victoria Street, London SW1H 0ET
T 020-7215 5000 E enquiries@ukti.gsi.gov.uk
W www.gov.uk/government/organisations/uk-trade-investment

UK Trade and Investment is a government organisation that helps UK-based companies succeed in international markets. It assists overseas companies to bring high quality investment to the UK economy.

*Chief Executive,* Dominic Jermey, OBE, CVO

## WATER SERVICES REGULATION AUTHORITY (OFWAT)

Centre City Tower, 7 Hill Street, Birmingham B5 4UA
T 0121-644 7500 E mailbox@ofwat.gsi.gov.uk
W www.ofwat.gov.uk

OFWAT is the independent economic regulator of the water and sewerage companies in England and Wales. It is responsible for ensuring that the water industry in England and Wales provides household and business customers with a good quality service and value for money. This is done by ensuring that the companies provide customers with a good quality, efficient service at a fair price; limiting the prices companies can charge; monitoring the companies' performance and taking action, including enforcement, to protect customers' interests; settting the companies efficiency targets; making sure the companies deliver the best for consumers and the environment in the long term; and encouraging competition where it benefits consumers.

*Chair,* Jonson Cox
*Chief Executive,* Cathryn Ross

# PARLIAMENT: THE YEAR IN REVIEW

*Patrick Robathan*

The final session of the 2010 parliament saw the coalition government defeated on a further ten occasions in the House of Lords, mainly on the criminal justice and courts bill. By agreeing to so many urgent questions, the total that the Speaker, John Bercow, granted over the whole parliament rose to an unprecedented 159, meaning a relevant minister had to come to the Commons to answer for the government, with no prior notice. The coalition remained united until the end of the session – although the presentation of what many saw as an alternative budget by the Liberal Democrat chief secretary to the Treasury put this under some strain – and most of their legislative programme was approved. The session ended with the defeat of what many MPs saw as an attempt by the government to prevent the re-election of the incumbent Speaker following the general election.

When MPs returned to Westminster on 13 October 2014, health secretary Jeremy Hunt updated MPs on the government's response to the ebola epidemic in west Africa. Scotland secretary Alistair Carmichael made a statement about the position of Scotland within the UK, following the referendum on Scottish independence, publishing a factual summary of the proposals for further devolution from each of the three pro-UK parties and promising to 'reach an agreement that will provide the enhanced powers to the people of Scotland and accountability for the Scottish parliament while retaining the strength and benefits of being part of the United Kingdom.' Labour MP Grahame Morris introduced a debate calling for the recognition of the state of Palestine alongside the state of Israel, which, although not binding on the government, was passed by 274 votes to 12. On 16 October, the minister for business and enterprise, Matthew Hancock, responded to an urgent question on the proposal for Tata Steel to sell its long products division. Foreign secretary Philip Hammond made a statement on Iraq and Syria following the killing of Alan Henning, David Haines and two American hostages.

On 22 October the home secretary, Theresa May, responded to an urgent question from her Labour shadow Yvette Cooper about the removal of foreign national offenders. On 23 October Jeremy Hunt replied to an urgent question from his Labour shadow, Andy Burnham, on the Five Year Forward View for the NHS.

On 27 October, the day after British forces concluded their combat mission in Afghanistan,

prime minister David Cameron reported back on the European Council. The Labour work and pensions spokesperson, Kate Green, moved a motion calling for welfare reform minister Lord Freud to be dismissed following his reported remark that the work of disabled people was not worth the minimum wage; it was defeated by 302 votes to 243. On 30 October, immigration minister James Brokenshire responded to an urgent question about why the government had decided not to support search and rescue operations for refugees and migrants in the Mediterranean.

On 3 November, Theresa May made a statement on the independent inquiry into child abuse, following the resignation of the panel's chair, Fiona Woolf. On 4 November, communities and local government secretary Eric Pickles made a statement about the London borough of Tower Hamlets and his decision to put in place a team of three commissioners to oversee certain functions of the council until 31 March 2017. On 5 November, Matthew Hancock replied to an urgent question about the government's response to the 2,600 job cuts announced by Rolls-Royce (Aerospace Group). On 6 November, energy and climate change secretary Edward Davey delivered the government's annual energy statement.

On 10 November, the chancellor, George Osborne, responded to an urgent question clarifying his agreement on the European Union budget surcharge. On 11 November Theresa May replied to an urgent question on the Wanless review into how the Home Office had acted on information it received in the 1980s about child abuse. Justice secretary Chris Grayling made a statement on possible recording of telephone calls between prisoners and their constituency MPs.

On 17 November, defence minister Julian Brazier replied to an urgent question on army reserve recruitment. David Cameron reported on the G20 summit in Brisbane and the murder of American aid worker Peter Kassig. Environment secretary Elizabeth Truss made a statement on a confirmed case of avian flu at a duck-breeding farm in east Yorkshire: 'the risk to public health is very low'.

On 25 November the prime minister made a statement on the publication of the intelligence and security committee report into the murder of Fusilier Lee Rigby. Philip Hammond made a statement on the negotiations between the E3+3 and Iran regarding the future of Iran's nuclear programme. Work and pensions secretary Iain Duncan Smith made a statement about the roll-out of the next part of universal credit. On 27 November, Alistair Carmichael made a statement on further devolution in Scotland and the publication of the heads of agreement resulting from Lord Smith's five-party talks, which would lead to draft legislation in January. Defence secretary Michael Fallon made the quarterly statement on Afghanistan: 'the campaign was long, but it was worthwhile, and we believe that we have given Afghanistan the best chance of a safer future'.

On 1 December, Patrick McLoughlin made a statement about plans to invest £15bn in England's strategic road network. Jeremy Hunt made a statement on the implementation of the NHS Five Year Forward View: 'a long-term plan for the economy; a long-term plan for the NHS'. On 2 December the Speaker granted an emergency debate to the Conservative chair of the foreign affairs committee on the ban by China on that committee visiting Hong Kong.

AUTUMN STATEMENT

Chancellor George Osborne delivered the final Autumn Statement of the 2010 parliament on 3 December. The main points were:

- the UK's is the fastest growing G7 economy
- 3 per cent growth forecast for 2014 and 2.4 per cent growth for 2015
- unemployment forecast to fall to 5.4 per cent in 2015
- inflation predicted to be 1.5 per cent in 2014, falling to 1.2 per cent in 2015
- reform of stamp duty on residential property
- borrowing forecast to fall from £97.5bn in 2013–14 to £91.3bn in 2014–15
- deficit projected to fall to £75.9bn in 2015–6
- fuel duty to be frozen
- personal tax allowance to increase to £10,600 in April 2015
- higher rate income tax threshold to rise to £42,385 in 2015
- new £90,000 charge for non-domiciled residents who have lived in the UK for 17 of the past 20 years
- £2bn extra for the NHS every year until 2020
- corporation tax to be devolved to Northern Ireland if the Stormont executive can manage the 'financial implications'
- income tax to be devolved in full to the Scottish parliament

The chancellor said: 'Four-and-a-half years ago, our economy was in crisis. People questioned whether Britain could remain among the front-rank economic nations of the world, but we set a course to restore stability, to get on top of our debts and to show that Britain was not going to be counted out. Now Britain is on course for surplus, on course for lower taxes, on course for more jobs, on course for

higher growth and on course for a truly national recovery – a long-term economic plan on course to prosperity.' Shadow chancellor Ed Balls countered: 'We need a recovery for the many, not just a few. We need to balance the books fairly. We need a long-term plan to save our NHS. That is the autumn statement that we needed. It will take a Labour government to deliver it.'

On 4 December, pensions minister Steve Webb announced the annual pensions and benefits uprating for 2015–16, with the basic state pension increasing by 2.5 per cent.

On 8 December, Foreign Office minister Tobias Ellwood replied to an urgent question from the Labour chair of the home affairs committee, Keith Vaz, on the death of Luke Somers and the safety of British citizens in Yemen. On 10 December James Brokenshire responded to an urgent question about the resettlement of vulnerable Syria refugees. Education secretary Nicky Morgan made a statement on the next phase of the government's plan for education, preparing young people for the world of work.

On 15 December Michael Fallon replied to an urgent question from his Labour shadow Vernon Coaker on the role of UK armed forces in Iraq. Northern Ireland secretary Theresa Villiers responded to an urgent question from her Labour shadow Ivan Lewis on the talks process in Northern Ireland following the prime minister's visit: 'ultimately, whether an overall agreement is reached will be down to Northern Ireland's political leaders. They have the chance to show that, once again, they can move Northern Ireland forward towards a better future in which politics works, the economy grows and society is stronger and more united. That is the prize on offer.' On 16 December the Leader of the Commons, William Hague, made a statement on the implications of devolution for England: 'whichever option is ultimately decided upon must be clear, decisive and effective in producing fairness for the whole United Kingdom'. For Labour, Sadiq Khan said: 'we must consider the unintended consequences of our actions and think through the way changes are interrelated and interdependent. There should be no more backroom stitch-ups.' On 17 December Michael Fallon made a statement on the report into the al-Sweady inquiry into allegations that British forces tortured and executed up to 20 Iraqi men and mistreated nine others in 2004: 'it is now beyond doubt that those allegations were without foundation'. On 18 December Jeremy Hunt replied to an urgent question on plans to help accident and emergency (A&E) departments and ambulance services cope with winter pressures. Matthew Hancock responded to an urgent question on the publication of the government's anti-corruption plan. Local government minister Kris Hopkins made a statement on funding for local authorities in England in 2015: 'we have kept the overall reduction to 1.8 per cent – lower than last year, and one of the lowest levels of reduction under this government.'

On 5 January 2015, Patrick McLoughlin replied to an urgent question on the major disruptions to Britain's rail network over the Christmas period, which he described as 'totally unacceptable'. Jeremy Hunt made a statement about the UK's Ebola preparedness and the care being given to Pauline Cafferkey, an NHS nurse being treated for Ebola at the Royal Free Hospital in London. On 7 January Jeremy Hunt replied to an urgent question on the major incidents declared at a number of hospitals and on A&E performance in England. Theresa Villiers made a statement on the political talks in Northern Ireland culminating in the Stormont House agreement on 23 December: 'this agreement gives the five parties in the devolved executive the chance to refocus and work together with renewed confidence for a more prosperous, more stable, more united and more secure future'.

On 12 January Foreign Office minister Hugo Swire replied to an urgent question on the situation in Nigeria. On 13 January Edward Davey responded to an urgent question on the Nuclear Decommissioning Authority announcement of a change to its commercial model at Sellafield. On 14 January Theresa May made a statement about the terrorist attacks in Paris, and the threat from terrorism in the UK.

On 21 January Tobias Ellwood replied to an urgent question on clashes between the Houthis and Yemeni security forces in Yemen. On 22 January Theresa May responded to an urgent question on the child abuse inquiry; the second nominee to chair the inquiry had, like the first, resigned after it became apparent that they did not command the full confidence of victims. Scottish Office minister David Mundell made a statement about the further devolution process in Scotland and the publication of draft clauses to implement the Smith commission agreement.

On 27 January Theresa Villiers replied to an urgent question from Democratic Unionist MP Ian Paisley about recent developments relating to the 'on-the-run' letters: 'there is no amnesty, immunity or exemption from prosecution . . . if the evidence is sufficient to warrant prosecution, they will be prosecuted.' On 28 January Jeremy Hunt replied to an urgent question about guidance issued by NHS England on declaring a major incident: 'the Opposition have tried to spin as part of their policy to "weaponise the NHS" – this government will support NHS workers, not try to turn their efforts into a political football'. On 29 January Nicky Morgan updated the Commons on progress in implementing the recommendations contained in Peter Clarke's report on Birmingham schools. The

minister for universities, science and cities, Greg Clark, made a statement about growth deals, 'which will fuel the resurgence of our local economies'. MPs passed without division a motion moved by David Davis (C.) that 'this House regrets that the Iraq inquiry has decided to defer publication of its report until after 7 May 2015'.

On 2 February the care services minister Norman Lamb answered an urgent question on the availability of child and adolescent mental health in-patient beds. On 4 February Theresa May announced the appointment of Justice Lowell Goddard, a judge of the High Court of New Zealand, as the chairman of the independent inquiry into child sexual abuse. She had also decided to set up a new statutory inquiry under the 2005 Act with a new panel. Eric Pickles made a statement on Louise Casey's inspection of Rotherham council, which had revealed the council's failure to accept, understand or combat the crimes of child sexual exploitation, proposing an intervention package to restore good local governance.

On 9 February the financial secretary to the Treasury, David Gauke, answered an urgent question on tax avoidance and evasion by HSBC. On 10 February Philip Hammond made a statement on the situation in Ukraine: 'civilised nations do not behave in the way Russia under Putin has behaved towards Ukraine'. On 11 February Jeremy Hunt made a statement on the government's response to Sir Robert Francis' report on NHS whistleblowing and on progress in implementing previous recommendations from the public inquiry into the failures of care at Mid Staffordshire NHS Foundation Trust: 'today is about tackling that culture challenge head on so that we build an NHS that supports staff to deliver the highest standards of safe and compassionate care and that avoids the mistakes that have led to both unacceptable waste and unspeakable tragedy.'

On 23 February George Osborne replied to an urgent question on the HSBC tax avoidance scandal: 'unlike the previous government, this government are taking action now and will do so again at the Budget'. David Cameron reported back on the European Council meeting. On 25 February Michael Fallon responded to an urgent question on the deployment of UK personnel to train Ukrainian forces: 'where we can help a friend with non-lethal equipment, we should do so'. On 26 February Jeremy Hunt updated the Commons on the NHS investigations into Jimmy Savile, publishing a further 16 investigations into his activities, including the main report from Stoke Mandeville hospital: 'we must show by our deeds as well as our words that we have learned the necessary lessons'.

On 2 March Theresa May responded to an urgent question on the government's counter-terrorism policy and the implications for individuals travelling to the Iraq/Syria conflict zones: 'tackling the extremist threat needs everyone to play their part. It requires educational institutions, social media companies, communities, religious leaders and families to help to protect people vulnerable to radicalisation and to confront this poisonous ideology.' On 3 March Nicky Morgan answered an urgent question on the serious case review into child sexual exploitation in Oxfordshire. Jeremy Hunt made a statement on the investigation into the care of mothers and babies at the University Hospitals of Morecambe Bay NHS Foundation Trust: 'despite many challenges, NHS staff have made excellent progress recently in improving the quality of care, with the highest ever ratings from the public for safety and compassionate care. The tragedy must strengthen our resolve to deliver real and lasting culture change so that these mistakes are never repeated.' Local government minister Brandon Lewis updated the Commons on the government's ambition to create a new garden city at Ebbsfleet.

On 9 March the Speaker made a statement on the serious breach of security over the weekend in the Palace of Westminster. On 10 March Eric Pickles made a statement on the troubled families programme. The minister for the Cabinet Office, Francis Maude, made a statement on trade unions in the civil service, eight departments having notified trade unions that they intend to end the practice of deducting union subscriptions from salaries. On 12 March the international development secretary Justine Greening updated the Commons on the Ebola outbreak in west Africa.

### THE BUDGET AND FINANCE BILL 2015

Chancellor George Osborne delivered his sixth budget on 18 March. The main points included:

- the UK economy grew 2.6 per cent in 2014, faster than any other advanced economy but lower than the 3 per cent predicted in December 2014; 2.5 per cent growth forecast in 2015
- inflation projected to fall to 0.2 per cent in 2015
- borrowing forecast to fall from £97.5bn in 2013–14 to £90.2bn in 2014–15
- debt as a share of GDP to fall from 80.4 per cent in 2014 to 80.2 per cent in 2015–16
- the public spending squeeze to end in 2019–20, a year earlier than planned
- duty on beer cut by 1p a pint and on cider by 2p; 2 per cent cut in duty on spirits; duty on wine frozen
- no changes to gambling taxes
- tobacco duties set to rise by 2 per cent above inflation
- a new 'horse racing betting right' to replace the horse race betting levy
- petrol duty to be frozen; September's planned increase cancelled
- annual tax returns on paper to be replaced by digital accounts

- a new 'help to buy' ISA for first-time buyers to allow the government to add £50 to every £200 saved for a house deposit
- a review of business rates
- mental health services to get £1.25bn in extra funding
- Greater Manchester councils to be allowed to keep 100 per cent of growth in business rates
- a new intercity rail franchise for south-west England

Mr Osborne said: 'I present the Budget of an economy that is stronger in every way than the one we inherited – the Budget of an economy taking another big step from austerity to prosperity. We cut the deficit, and confidence is returning. We limited spending, made work pay and backed business, and growth is returning. We gave people control over their savings and helped people own their own homes, and optimism is returning. We have provided clear and decisive economic leadership, and from the depths Britain is returning . . . This is the Budget for Britain, the come-back country.' The leader of the Opposition, Ed Miliband, responded, 'never has the gap between the chancellor's rhetoric and the reality of people's lives been greater . . . This is a Budget that people will not believe from a government who are not on their side.' After three days of debate the Budget was approved by 334 votes to 250. All stages of a much reduced finance bill were taken in the Commons on 25 March, with the third reading being passed by 307 votes to 226.

On 19 March the chief secretary to the Treasury, Danny Alexander, made a statement on fiscal responsibility and fairness, widely derided as the alternative Liberal Democrat budget statement: 'combining fiscal responsibility with fairness – that is the approach that we as Liberal Democrats have brought to the coalition government . . . That is the approach that will deliver a stronger economy and a fairer society.' His Labour shadow Chris Leslie thought, 'what a farce! Why has he been allowed to use the government dispatch box for his party political pleading?'

On 23 March the Speaker announced that the present acting Clerk of the House, David Natzler, should be recommended for appointment as Clerk of the House. David Cameron reported on the outcome of the European Council meeting. Francis Maude made a statement on government savings from efficiency and reform: 'we have shown that we can get more and better for less'. On 24 March, environment minister George Eustice replied to an urgent question on the delivery of the digital-only system for processing the basic payment scheme via the Rural Payments Agency. Francis Maude made a statement on the government's national cyber-security programme: 'we want Britain to benefit from the best digital economy in the world –

effective cyber-security is central to that success.' On 26 March, the final day of the 2010 parliament, police minister Mike Penning replied to an urgent question about Lord Justice Pitchford's public inquiry into undercover policing; the inquiry would review and publish the terms of reference for the inquiry by the end of July. Public health minister Jane Ellison responded to an urgent question on the publication of the Penrose inquiry. The final act of the parliament was to debate a motion moved by William Hague to allow for a secret ballot to elect the Speaker in the new parliament, as recommended by the procedure committee; this was defeated by 228 votes to 202. In the Lords, the finance bill was approved and all outstanding bills received royal assent. Parliament was then prorogued for the general election on 7 May 2015, which produced a result that few people foresaw: a majority of 12 for the Conservative party.

## STATE OPENING OF PARLIAMENT AND THE QUEEN'S SPEECH

The Queen's Speech on 27 May, the first Conservative Queen's Speech in nearly two decades, contained details of 26 bills. David Cameron called it a programme 'for working people, from a one-nation government that will bring our country together. We have a clear mandate from the British people, a long-term economic plan that is working, a detailed and compelling manifesto, and we will not waste a single moment in getting on with the task.' The acting Labour leader Harriet Harman felt, 'we fear that the reality of this Queen's Speech will be very different from the rhetoric. At a time when our economy, our constitution and our public services are fragile, we fear that this Tory government will make things worse.' For the Scottish National Party – now officially the third party in the Commons – Angus Robertson thought 'the problem with the Queen's Speech is that there is no recognition in it of the fact that Scotland completely rejected the Tory agenda ... At a time when people are suffering from the impact of austerity, the Tories are focused on the wrong issues.' After six days of debate a SNP motion of regret was defeated by 318 votes to 60 and the Queen's Speech was approved by 326 votes to 279.

On 28 May the Speaker ruled in response to a point of order from Alex Salmond (SNP) about whether the changes to standing orders the government proposed to bring forward on English votes for English laws (EVEL) would breach the principle that all members of the Commons were equal before the chair: 'I would not accept the motion if it breached the rules of the House, but it is not for the chair to judge the merits of a proposal. It is for the House to decide whether to agree to the government's proposal.' The new culture secretary,

John Whittingdale, responded to an urgent question on indictments against FIFA officials: 'this is merely the latest sorry episode to suggest that FIFA is a deeply flawed and corrupt organisation'. On 1 June John Whittingdale returned to the subject following the election of Sepp Blatter as president of FIFA: 'for the good of the game, we must work together to bring about change ... it is time for Sepp Blatter to go'. On 3 June the Commons paid tribute to the former Liberal Democrat leader Charles Kennedy. On 4 June, health minister Ben Gummer replied to an urgent question on the NHS Success Regime.

On 8 June James Brokenshire replied to an urgent question on the discovery and detention of 68 migrants by the Border Force at Harwich international port, stressing that 'the government are clear that the EU's approach to migratory flows must include the proper management of the external border, the prompt return of those not in genuine need of protection and action to tackle the efforts of the smugglers and traffickers who profit from human misery'. This was followed by the second reading of the Scotland bill, which David Mundell felt represented 'the fulfilment of a promise to the people of Scotland that a no vote in the referendum was not a vote for no change and it delivers on the all-party Smith commission agreement'. Angus Robertson was sceptical: 'in the weeks ahead, the House of Commons will debate amendments that can strengthen the bill. I hope that the government will deliver on their vow, accept the verdict of the electorate and ensure that the bill does deliver what the Scottish people require.' The bill was in committee of the whole house on 15, 29 and 30 June and 6 July. Although some 500 amendments were tabled, none were passed; Tommy Sheppard (SNP) expressing frustration that Mr Mundell appeared to be resisting any amendment which was contrary to his point of view. On 9 June the European Union referendum bill had its second reading. Foreign secretary Philip Hammond suggested that 'this bill delivers the simple in/out referendum that we promised'. It was passed by 544 votes to 53 (all SNP). The bill was in committee of the whole house on 16 and 18 June. On 10 June David Cameron reported on the G7 meeting in Germany. On 11 June home secretary Theresa May made a statement on the publication of the Anderson Report and parliamentary consideration of investigatory powers, reiterating that the government intended to bring forward legislation. The economic secretary to the Treasury, Harriett Baldwin, made a statement on plans to sell the government's stake in Royal Bank of Scotland and on the sale of half of the government's remaining stake in Royal Mail, stressing that the government would dispose of all their shares in Royal Mail during this parliament.

On 22 June, energy and climate change secretary Amber Rudd made a statement on ending new subsidies for onshore wind: 'an important part of our current and future low-carbon energy mix, but we are reaching the limits of what is affordable and what the public are prepared to accept'. On 24 June Theresa May replied to an urgent question on the management of the border in Calais, where striking French workers had caused significant disruption: 'the most important step to resolving the situation in the Mediterranean is breaking the link between migrants making this dangerous journey and achieving settlement in Europe'. On 25 June transport secretary Patrick McLoughlin made a statement on Network Rail and the chairman stepping down to be replaced by the current transport commissioner in London, Sir Peter Hendy; electrification of Midland Main Line and the trans-Pennine route between Leeds and Manchester would be paused; commuter rail fares would continue to be capped in real terms for the whole of this parliament.

On 29 June David Cameron made a statement on the killing of British nationals in Tunisia, announcing a national one-minute silence the following Friday and pledging that 'we must step up our own efforts to support our agencies in tracking vital online communications, and we will bring forward a draft bill to achieve this'. On the outcome of the European Council, he said: 'we will put the Common Market back at the heart of our membership, get off the treadmill to ever-closer union, address the issue of migration to Britain from the rest of the EU and protect Britain's place in the single market for the long term'. George Osborne made a statement on developments in the financial crisis in Greece and how they might affect British citizens. On 1 July Patrick McLoughlin made a statement on the publication of the final Davies commission report on runway capacity in south-east England, which had concluded that 'Heathrow offers a stronger solution to the UK's aviation capacity and connectivity needs than a second runway at Gatwick', and said he would come back to parliament in autumn 2015 to provide a clear direction on the government's plans. Work and pensions secretary Iain Duncan Smith announced that he would bring forward legislation to remove the existing measures and targets in the Child Poverty Act 2010 but introduce a statutory duty to report on measures of worklessness and educational attainment: 'we need to move from a low wage, high tax, high welfare society to a higher wage, lower tax, lower welfare society'. On 2 July the leader of the Commons, Chris Grayling, made a statement setting out proposals on EVEL – 'we are committed to delivering a balanced and fair constitutional settlement for all the people of the United Kingdom' – and promising to lay draft orders 'in the next few days' for full debate and decision shortly before the summer recess. His Labour shadow Angela Eagle felt: 'It is hard not to conclude that the proposals are not an attempt to address the West Lothian question, but rather a cynical attempt by a government with an overall majority of just 12 to use procedural trickery to manufacture themselves a very much larger one.' The SNP chief whip Pete Wishart called it 'a lot of constitutional bilge and unworkable garbage!'

On 6 July John Whittingdale answered an urgent question on government proposals on concessionary television licences: 'the BBC will take on the cost of providing free television licences for those households with over-75s, phased in from 2018–19, with the BBC taking on the full costs from 2020–21'. George Osborne updated the Commons on the situation in Greece following the referendum there rejecting the creditors' terms: 'the situation risks going from bad to worse, and Britain will be affected the longer the Greek crisis lasts and the worse it gets'. On 7 July the Speaker granted Alistair Carmichael (Liberal Democrat) an emergency debate on EVEL.

THE SECOND 2015 BUDGET
On 8 July George Osborne presented the first Conservative Budget for 18 years. The key points were:

• a new national living wage of over £9 an hour by 2020
• the government to run a surplus in 2019–20
• the personal tax allowance to increase to £11,000 in April 2016 and the higher rate threshold to £43,000 in 2016–17
• defence spending to be protected
• the family home to be taken out of inheritance tax
• corporation Tax to be cut to 19 per cent in 2017 and 18 per cent in 2020
• insurance premium tax to increase to 9.5 per cent
• permanent non-domiciled status to be ended
• £30m of funding for transport for northern England
• 30 hours of free childcare for three- and four-year-olds
• student maintenance grants to be replaced with loans
• public sector pay to increase by 1 per cent

The chancellor said: 'A Budget that puts security first: the economic security of a country that lives within its means; the financial security of lower taxes and a new national living wage; the national security of a Britain that defends itself and its values. One purpose, one policy, one nation.' Harriet Harman felt 'it does not put working people first; it ducks the big decisions on infrastructure and fails to give businesses the productivity boost they need. He says that he stands up for working people;

what he does is make them worse off.' For the SNP, Stewart Hosie said 'it was less of a plan to boost productivity and more a sermon from the high priest of an austerity cult ... This was not the Budget the country needed and it was not the Budget that those who have suffered most over the past five years should have had to endure.' After five days of debate the Budget was approved by 320 votes to 290. The finance bill was introduced on 14 July and received its second reading on 21 July by 301 votes to 75.

On 13 July the government was defeated in the House of Lords when a motion for a delay to the enactment of the 'waiting days' amendment to universal credit regulations was passed by 11 votes, and they suffered three defeats on amendments to the cities and local government devolution bill. On 14 July Theresa May updated the Commons on action to tackle illegal immigration: 'we are continuing our close collaboration with the French authorities to bolster the security of the ports in northern France; working closely with them to mitigate the consequences of irresponsible French strikers; providing the assistance our hard-working hauliers and the travelling public deserve; and leading the international efforts to tackle this problem in the longer term'. Chris Grayling announced that the government had decided not to press ahead with a motion on relaxing the rules on hunting with dogs, which Pete Wishart described as 'an utter and absolute shambles'. In the Lords the government proposal in the psychoactive substances bill to make supplying new psychoactive substances in prisons an aggravating offence was defeated by 38 votes. On 15 July Philip Hammond made a statement on the outcome of the nuclear negotiations with Iran: 'we now have a common responsibility to ensure that the wider potential benefits of this deal for the region and for the international community as a whole are delivered.' Theresa May made a statement on her decision not to authorise water cannon for use by the police in England and Wales. The Commons began the first of two days of debate on EVEL (the second was scheduled for September, when the substantive motions would be put and debated). In the Lords the government were defeated when an amendment to the cities and local government devolution bill to insert a clause lowering the age for voting in local government elections from 18 to 16 was passed by 67 votes. On 16 July Jeremy Hunt made a statement on measures to improve the safety culture in the NHS, strengthening its transition to a modern, patient-centric healthcare system and the publication of Lord Rose's report 'Better leadership for tomorrow'. John Whittingdale published his consultation paper on the BBC charter review.

On 20 July Ben Gummer replied to an urgent question on the support available to recipients of contaminated blood. The welfare reform and work bill passed its second reading by 308 votes to 124, but some 48 Labour MPs defied their leadership to vote against. In the Lords an amendment to the charities (protection and social investment) bill to insert a clause ensuring that charities are able to dispose of their assets in a way consistent with their charitable purposes was passed by 83 votes, against the wishes of the government. On 21 July, employment minister Priti Patel answered an urgent question on Department for Work and Pensions data on the number of people in receipt of benefit who have died since November 2011: 'the government intend to publish mortality statistics, but before doing so the statistics need to meet the high standards expected of official statistics. Once we have completed that important work, we will publish them.' The Commons then rose for the summer recess. The government suffered their ninth and tenth defeats in the Lords in the first eight weeks of the new parliament when an amendment to the cities and local government devolution bill to prevent the transfer of regulatory functions for the health service to devolved bodies was passed against their wishes by 65 votes, and a proposal to appoint a joint committee to produce a report on the constitutional implications of the government's revised proposals on EVEL by 30 March 2016 was passed by 181 votes. The House of Lords rose for the summer recess on 22 July.

On 7 September David Cameron updated MPs on the situation in the Middle East, confirming that he had authorised an RAF drone strike in Syria which had killed two British IS fighters, and on the refugee crisis in Europe, pledging that the UK would take 20,000 refugees from the camps in the Middle East over the next five years. He also experienced the first defeat for his government in the Commons when 37 Conservative MPs voted against government plans to amend the European Union referendum bill to change the rules limiting government activity during the campaign period, leading to a defeat by 312 votes to 285. On 8 September Theresa Villliers told MPs that despite a request from the DUP, the government did not think the time was right to suspend Northern Ireland's devolved institutions, but that if circumstances changed, the government would review its options. On 11 September Labour MP Rob Marris' private members bill on assisted dying was defeated on a free vote at second reading by 330 votes to 118.

# WHO'S WHO

List of Abbreviations Used

**BIOGRAPHIES A–Z**
Members of Parliament and Lords who are Ministers of State

# ABBREVIATIONS USED IN THIS BOOK

Some of the designatory letters in this list are used merely for economy of space
and do not necessarily imply any professional or other qualification.

| | | | |
|---|---|---|---|
| **AA** | Anti-aircraft; Automobile Association; Architectural Association; Augustinians of the Assumption; Associate in Arts | **ARICS** | Professional Associate, Royal Institution of Chartered Surveyors (*now* MRICS) |
| **A and SH** | Argyll and Sutherland Highlanders | **AS** | Anglo-Saxon |
| **AB** | Bachelor of Arts (US); able-bodied seaman; airborne; Alberta (postal) | **ASEAN** | Association of South East Asian Nations |
| **ABC** | Australian Broadcasting Commission; American Broadcasting Companies; Amateur Boxing Club; Associate, Birmingham Conservatoire; Accredited Business Communicator | **ASLEF** | Associated Society of Locomotive Engineers and Firemen |
| | | **Asst** | Assistant |
| | | **ASTMS** | Association of Scientific, Technical and Managerial Staffs (subsequently part of MSF) |
| **ACA** | Associate, Institute of Chartered Accountants | **ATC** | Air Training Corps; Art Teachers Certificate |
| **Acad.** | Academy | **BA** | Bachelor of Arts |
| **ACEVO** | Association of Chief Executives of Voluntary Organisations | **BAO** | Bachelor of Art of Obstetrics |
| **ACI** | Airports Council International (Europe) | **BAOR** | British Army of the Rhine (*formerly* on the Rhine) |
| **ACIB** | Associate, Chartered Institute of Bankers | **BASW** | British Association of Social Workers |
| **ACII** | Associate, Chartered Insurance Institute | **BBC** | British Broadcasting Corporation |
| | | **BC** | Before Christ; British Columbia; Borough Council |
| **ACTT** | Association of Cinematograph, Television and Allied Technicians | **BCh** or **Bchir** | Bachelor of Surgery |
| **ADC** | Aide-de-camp; Association of District Councils | **BCL** | Bachelor of Civil Law |
| | | **BCom** | Bachelor of Commerce |
| **Adjt** | Adjutant | **Bd** | Board |
| **Adm.** | Admiral | **Bde** | Brigade |
| **Adv.** | Advisory; Advocate | **BEd** | Bachelor of Education |
| **AEEU** | Amalgamated Engineering and Electrical Union | **Beds** | Bedfordshire |
| | | **BEng** | Bachelor of Engineering |
| **AEI** | Associated Electrical Industries | **Berks** | Berkshire |
| **AEU** | Amalgamated Engineering Union (later AEEU) | **BERR** | Department for Business, Enterprise and Regulatory Reform |
| **AFC** | Air Force Cross; Association Football Club | **BFI** | British Film Institute |
| | | **BHF** | British Heart Foundation |
| **AG** | Attorney-General | **BIS** | Bank for International Settlements; British Interplanetary Society; Department for Business, Innovation and Skills |
| **AIB** | Associate, Institute of Bankers (*now* ACIB) | | |
| **AKC** | Associate, Kings College London | **BITC** | Business in the Community |
| **ALA** | Associate, Library Association; Association of London Authorities | **BM** | British Museum; Bachelor of Medicine; Brigade Major; British Monomark |
| **AMA** | Association of Metropolitan Authorities; Assistant Masters Association; Associate, Museums Association; Australian Medical Association | **Bn** | Battalion |
| | | **BNFL** | British Nuclear Fuels Ltd |
| | | **BoT** | Board of Trade |
| | | **BR** | British Rail |
| | | **Br.** | Branch |
| **AMP** | Advanced Management Program; Air Member for Personnel | **Brig.** | Brigadier |
| | | **BRNC** | Britannia Royal Naval College |
| **APEX** | Association of Professional, Executive, Clerical and Computer Staff | **BS** | Bachelor of Surgery; Bachelor of Science; British Standard |
| **ARAgS** | Associate, Royal Agricultural Societies (*ie* of England, Scotland and Wales) | **BSc** | Bachelor of Science |
| | | **BSC** | British Steel Corporation; Bengal Staff Corps |
| **ARCM** | Associate, Royal College of Music | **BScEcon** | Bachelor of Science in Economics |

| | |
|---|---|
| **BSocSc** | Bachelor of Social Science |
| **Bt** | Baronet; Brevet |
| **BT** | Bachelor of Teaching; British Telecommunications |
| **BTEC** | Business and Technology (*formerly* Technician) Education Council |
| **Bucks** | Buckinghamshire |
| **BUPA** | British United Provident Association |
| **BVC** | Bar Vocational Course |
| **BVI** | British Virgin Islands |
| **c** | child; cousin; *circa* (about) |
| **C** | Conservative; 100 |
| **CA** | Central America; County Alderman; Chartered Accountant (Scotland and Canada); California (postal) |
| **CAB** | Citizens Advice Bureau; Centre for Agricultural and Biosciences (*formerly* Commonwealth Agricultural Bureau) |
| **CAF** | Charities Aid Foundation |
| **Calif** | California |
| **Cambs** | Cambridgeshire |
| **C&G** | City and Guilds of London Institute |
| **Capt.** | Captain |
| **CB** | Companion, Order of the Bath; County Borough |
| **CBC** | County Borough Council |
| **CBE** | Commander, Order of the British Empire |
| **CBI** | Confederation of British Industry |
| **CC** | Companion, Order of Canada; City Council; County Council; Cricket Club; Cycling Club; County Court |
| **CCC** | Corpus Christi College; Central Criminal Court; County Cricket Club |
| **CCETSW** | Central Council for Education and Training in Social Work |
| **CCS** | Casualty Clearing Station; Ceylon Civil Service; Countryside Commission for Scotland |
| **CDS** | Chief of the Defence Staff |
| **CEng** | Chartered Engineer |
| **CEO** | Chief Executive Officer |
| **Cert Ed** | Certificate of Education |
| **CH** | Companion of Honour |
| **ChB** | Bachelor of Surgery |
| **CHC** | Community Health Council |
| **Chm.** | Chairman or Chairwoman |
| **CIM** | China Inland Mission; Chartered Institute of Marketing |
| **CIPD** | Companion, Institute of Personnel and Development; Chartered Institute of Personnel and Development |
| **CISI** | Chartered Institute for Securities & Investment |
| **cl** | *cum laude* |
| **Cl.** | Class |
| **CLA** | Country Land & Business Association (*formerly* Country Landowners Association) |
| **CLP** | Constituency Labour Party |
| **CMA** | Canadian Medical Association; Cost and Management Accountant (NZ); Competition and Markets Authority |
| **CMG** | Companion, Order of St Michael and St George |
| **CMS** | Church Mission (*formerly* Church Missionary) Society; Certificate in Management Studies |
| **CNAA** | Council for National Academic Awards |
| **CND** | Campaign for Nuclear Disarmament |
| **CO** | Commanding Officer; Commonwealth Office (after Aug. 1966) (*now* FCO); Colonial Office (before Aug. 1966); Conscientious Objector; Colorado (postal); Congregation of the Oratory |
| **Co.** | County; Company |
| **C of E** | Church of England |
| **C of S** | Chief of Staff; Church of Scotland |
| **Col** | Colonel |
| **Coll.** | College; Collegiate |
| **Comdr** | Commander |
| **Commn** | Commission |
| **Commnd** | Commissioned |
| **Comr** | Commissioner |
| **Co-op.** | Co-operative |
| **Corp.** | Corporation; Corporal |
| **COS** | Chief of Staff; Charity Organization Society |
| **COSLA** | Convention of Scottish Local Authorities |
| **CPA** | Commonwealth Parliamentary Association; Chartered Patent Agent; Certified Public Accountant (USA) |
| **CPE** | Common Professional Examination; Clinical Pastoral Education |
| **CPLS** | Certificate of Professional Legal Studies |
| **CPRE** | Campaign to Protect Rural England (*formerly* Council for the Protection of Rural England) |
| **CPS** | Crown Prosecution Service; Certificate in Pastoral Studies |
| **CQSW** | Certificate of Qualification in Social Work |
| **CRAeS** | Companion, Royal Aeronautical Society |
| **CS** | Civil Service; Clerk to the Signet; Companion, Order of Samoa |
| **CSA** | Confederate States of America; Child Support Agency |
| **CSG** | Companion, Order of the Star of Ghana; Company of the Servants of God |
| **CSM** | Civil Service Medal (Fiji); Companion, Star of Merit (Federation of Saint Kitts and Nevis); Companion, Star of Melanesia (Papua New Guinea) |
| **CSV** | Community Service Volunteers |

| | |
|---|---|
| CTA | Chaplain Territorial Army; Chartered Tax Adviser |
| CWU | Communication Workers Union |
| D | Duke |
| DBE | Dame Commander, Order of the British Empire |
| DC | District Council; District of Columbia |
| DCA | Doctor of Creative Arts; Department for Constitutional Affairs |
| DCL | Doctor of Civil Law; Dr of Canon Law |
| DCLG | Department for Communities and Local Government |
| DCMS | Department for Culture, Media and Sport |
| DCSF | Department for Children, Schools and Families |
| DECC | Department of Energy and Climate Change |
| decd | deceased |
| DEd | Doctor of Education |
| DEFRA | Department for Environment, Food and Rural Affairs |
| (DemU) | Democratic Unionist |
| Dep. | Deputy |
| DES | Department of Education and Science (later DFE); Dr in Environmental Studies |
| DETR | Department of the Environment, Transport and the Regions |
| DFC | Distinguished Flying Cross |
| DFE | Department for Education |
| DfEE or DFEE | Department for Education and Employment (later DFES) |
| DfES or DFES | Department for Education and Skills |
| DFID | Department for International Development |
| DfT | Department for Transport |
| DHA | District Health Authority |
| DHSS | Department of Health and Social Security |
| Dio. | Diocese |
| DipLaw | Diploma in Law |
| DipLib | Diploma of Librarianship |
| DipLP | Diploma in Legal Practice |
| DipM | Diploma in Marketing |
| DipSW | Diploma in Social Work |
| DipTh | Diploma in Theology |
| DIUS | Department for Innovation, Universities and Skills |
| Div. | Division; Divorced |
| DL | Deputy Lieutenant; Democratie Libérale |
| DLaws | Doctor of Laws |
| DLitt | Doctor of Literature; Doctor of Letters |
| DM | Doctor of Medicine |
| DoE | Department of the Environment |
| DoH | Department of Health |
| DoI | Department of Industry |
| DPH | Diploma in Public Health |
| DPhil | Doctor of Philosophy |
| Dr | Doctor |

| | |
|---|---|
| DRCOG | Diploma of Royal College of Obstetricians and Gynaecologists |
| Dr jur | Doctor of Laws |
| DSA | Diploma in Social Administration |
| DSc | Doctor of Science |
| DSG | Dame, Order of St Gregory the Great |
| DSO | Companion of the Distinguished Service Order |
| DSocSc | Doctor of Social Science |
| DSS | Department of Social Security; Doctor of Sacred Scripture |
| DTI | Department of Trade and Industry |
| DTLR | Department for Transport, Local Government and the Regions |
| Dunelm | *Dunelmensis* (of Durham) |
| DUniv | Honorary Doctor of the University |
| DUP | Democratic Unionist Party; Docteur de lUniversité de Paris |
| DWP | Department for Work and Pensions |
| E | East; Earl; England; E-mail |
| Ebor | *Eboracensis* (of York) |
| EBRD | European Bank for Reconstruction and Development |
| EC | Etoile du Courage (Canada); European Community; European Commission; Emergency Commission |
| ed | edited |
| Educn | Education |
| EEC | European Economic Community (*now* EC); Commission of the European Communities |
| EMEA | European Medicines Agency (formerly European Agency for the Evaluation of Medical Products); Europe, Middle East and Africa |
| EMU | European Monetary Union |
| Eng. | England |
| Engr | Engineer |
| EOC | Equal Opportunities Commission |
| EP | European Parliament |
| ESRC | Economic and Social Research Council; Electricity Supply Research Council |
| ESU | English–Speaking Union |
| EU | European Union |
| Ext | Extinct; external |
| FA | Football Association |
| FACE | Fellow, Australian College of Educators (*formerly* of Education) |
| F and GP | Finance and General Purposes |
| FC | Football Club |
| FCA | Fellow, Institute of Chartered Accountants; Fellow, Institute of Chartered Accountants in Australia; Fellow, New Zealand Society of Accountants; Federation of Canadian Artists |
| FCGI | Fellow, City and Guilds of London Institute |
| FCIArb | Fellow, Chartered Institute of Arbitrators |
| FCIHort | Fellow, Chartered Institute of Horticulture |

| | |
|---|---|
| **FCIM** | Fellow, Chartered Institute of Marketing; Fellow, Institute of Corporate Managers (Australia) |
| **FCIOB** | Fellow, Chartered Institute of Building |
| **FCIPD** | Fellow, Chartered Institute of Personnel and Development |
| **FCIS** | Fellow, Institute of Chartered Secretaries and Administrators (*formerly* Chartered Institute of Secretaries) |
| **FCMI** | Fellow, Chartered Management Institute |
| **FCO** | Foreign and Commonwealth Office |
| **FCS** | Federation of Conservative Students |
| **FCS** | Fellow, Chemical Society (now absorbed into Royal Society of Chemistry) |
| **FCSI** | Fellow, Chartered Institute for Securities & Investment |
| **FE** | Far East; Further Education |
| **FFPH** | Fellow, Faculty of Public Health |
| **FIET** | Fédération Internationale des Employés, Techniciens et Cadres; Fellow, Institution of Engineering and Technology |
| **FInstLM** | Fellow, Institute of Leadership and Management |
| **FInstPet** | Fellow, Institute of Petroleum |
| **FM** | Field-Marshal |
| **For.** | Foreign |
| **FRAME** | Fund for the Replacement of Animals in Medical Experiments |
| **FRCP** | Fellow, Royal College of Physicians, London |
| **FRCS** | Fellow, Royal College of Surgeons of England |
| **FRCSGlas** | Fellow, Royal College of Physicians and Surgeons of Glasgow |
| **FRCSI** | Fellow, Royal College of Surgeons in Ireland |
| **FRGS** | Fellow, Royal Geographical Society |
| **FRHistS** | Fellow, Royal Historical Society |
| **FRIBA** | Fellow, Royal Institute of British Architects |
| **FRICS** | Fellow, Royal Institution of Chartered Surveyors |
| **FRS** | Fellow, Royal Society |
| **FRSA** | Fellow, Royal Society of Arts |
| **FRSL** | Fellow, Royal Society of Literature |
| **FSA** | Fellow, Society of Antiquaries; Financial Services Authority |
| **FSI** | Fellow, Chartered Surveyors Institution (*now* FRICS); Fellow, Securities Institute (later Securities & Investment Institute, *now* FCSI) |
| **GAP** | Gap Activity Projects |
| **GB** | Great Britain |
| **GCB** | Knight or Dame Grand Cross, Order of the Bath |
| **GCMG** | Knight or Dame Grand Cross, Order of St Michael and St George |
| **GCVO** | Knight or Dame Grand Cross, Royal Victorian Order |
| **Gen.** | General |
| **GLA** | Greater London Authority |
| **GLC** | Greater London Council |
| **Glos** | Gloucestershire |
| **GM** | George Medal; Grand Medal (Ghana); genetically modified |
| **GMB** | (Union for) General, Municipal, Boilermakers |
| **GMBATU** | General, Municipal, Boilermakers and Allied Trades Union (*now* GMB) |
| **GMC** | General Medical Council; Guild of Memorial Craftsmen; General Management Course (Henley) |
| **GMWU** | General and Municipal Workers Union (later GMBATU; *now* GMB) |
| **GOC** | General Officer Commanding |
| **Gov.** | Governor |
| **Govt** | Government |
| **Gp** | Group |
| **GP** | General Practitioner; Grand Prix |
| **GPMU** | Graphical, Paper and Media Union |
| **GPO** | General Post Office |
| **GS** | General Staff; Grammar School |
| **GSM** | General Service Medal; (Member of) Guildhall School of Music and Drama |
| **HA** | Historical Association; Health Authority |
| **HAC** | Honourable Artillery Company |
| **Hants** | Hampshire |
| **HEFCE** | Higher Education Funding Council for England |
| **Herts** | Hertfordshire |
| **HIV** | Human Immunodeficiency Virus |
| **HM** | His (or Her) Majesty, or Majestys |
| **HMS** | His (or Her) Majestys Ship |
| **HNC** | Higher National Certificate |
| **HND** | Higher National Diploma |
| **H of C** | House of Commons |
| **H of L** | House of Lords |
| **Hon.** | Honourable; Honorary |
| **HPk** | Hilal-e-Pakistan |
| **HQ** | Headquarters |
| **HR** | Human Resources |
| **HSC** | Health and Safety Commission; Higher School Certificate |
| **Hum.** | Humanity; Humanities (Classics) |
| **I** | Island; Ireland |
| **IBRD** | International Bank for Reconstruction and Development (World Bank) |
| **i/c** | in charge; in command |
| **ICAEW** | Institute of Chartered Accountants in England and Wales |
| **ICAS** | Institute of Chartered Accountants of Scotland |
| **ICI** | Imperial Chemical Industries |
| **ICL** | International Computers Ltd |
| **ICRF** | Imperial Cancer Research Fund |
| **IEA** | Institute of Economic Affairs |
| **IISS** | International Institute of Strategic Studies |
| **ILEA** | Inner London Education Authority |

| | |
|---|---|
| ILO | International Labour Office; International Labour Organisation |
| IMC | Instrument Meteorological Conditions |
| Inc. | Incorporated |
| Ind. | Independent |
| Inf. | Infantry |
| INSEAD | Institut Européen dAdministration des Affaires |
| Inst. | Institute |
| Instn | Institution |
| IoW | Isle of Wight |
| IPPR | Institute for Public Policy Research |
| IPSO | Independent Press Standards Organisation |
| IPU | Inter-Parliamentary Union |
| Is | Island(s) |
| ISC | Imperial Service College, Haileybury; Indian Staff Corps; Independent Schools Council |
| IT | Information Technology; Indian Territory (US) |
| ITN | Independent Television News |
| ITV | Independent Television |
| JCR | Junior Common Room |
| JP | Justice of the Peace |
| JSDC | Joint Service Defence College |
| JSSC | Joint Services Staff College |
| jtly | joint, jointly |
| Jun. | Junior |
| KCB | Knight Commander, Order of the Bath |
| KCL | Kings College London |
| KCMG | Knight Commander, Order of St Michael and St George |
| KCVO | Knight Commander, Royal Victorian Order |
| KG | Knight, Order of the Garter |
| KStJ | Knight, Most Venerable Order of the Hospital of St John of Jerusalem |
| Kt | Knight |
| KT | Knight, Order of the Thistle |
| L | Liberal |
| La | Louisiana |
| LA | Los Angeles; Library Association; Liverpool Academy; Louisiana (postal) |
| Lab | Labour |
| LACSAB | Local Authorities Conditions of Service Advisory Board |
| Lancs | Lancashire |
| LBC | London Broadcasting Company; London Borough Council |
| LCCI | London Chamber of Commerce and Industry |
| LCD | Lord Chancellors Department |
| Ldr | Leader |
| LG | Lady Companion, Order of the Garter |
| LGA | Local Government Association |
| LGSM | Licentiate, Guildhall School of Music and Drama |
| Lib Dem | Liberal Democrat |
| Lieut | Lieutenant |
| Lincs | Lincolnshire |
| Lit. | Literature; Literary |
| LLB | Bachelor of Laws |
| LLD | Doctor of Laws |
| LLM | Master of Laws |
| LLP | Limited Liability Partnership |
| LP | Limited Partnership |
| LSE | London School of Economics and Political Science |
| Lt | Lieutenant; Light |
| Lt Col | Lieutenant Colonel |
| Lt Gen. | Lieutenant General |
| LVO | Lieutenant, Royal Victorian Order (*formerly* MVO (Fourth Class)) |
| M | Marquess; Member; Monsieur |
| MA | Master of Arts; Military Assistant; Massachusetts (postal) |
| MAFF | Ministry of Agriculture, Fisheries and Food |
| Maj. Gen. | Major General |
| Man | Manitoba |
| Mass | Massachusetts |
| MB | Medal of Bravery (Canada); Bachelor of Medicine; Manitoba (postal) |
| MBA | Master of Business Administration |
| MBC | Metropolitan/Municipal Borough Council |
| MBE | Member, Order of the British Empire |
| MBPsS | Graduate Member, British Psychological Society |
| MC | Military Cross; Missionaries of Charity |
| MCC | Marylebone Cricket Club; Metropolitan County Council |
| MCIM | Member, Chartered Institute of Marketing |
| MCIPD | Member, Charted Institute of Personnel and Development |
| MCSI | Member, Chartered Institute for Securities & Investment |
| MD | Doctor of Medicine; Military District; Maryland (postal) |
| MDC | Metropolitan District Council |
| ME | Mining Engineer; Middle East; Master of Engineering; Maine (postal); Myalgic Encephalomyelitis |
| MEd | Master of Education |
| Med. | Medical |
| MEP | Member of the European Parliament |
| MFOM | Member, Faculty of Occupational Medicine |
| Mgr | Monsignor |
| MIFF | Member, Institute of Freight Forwarders |
| MIH | Member, Institute of Housing; Member, Institute of Hospitality |
| MIHort | Member, Institute of Horticulture |
| Mil. | Military |
| MILog | Member, Institute of Logistics |
| Min. | Ministry |
| MInstD | Member, Institute of Directors |
| MInstRE | Member, Institution of Royal Engineers |
| MInstTA | Member, Institute of Transport Administration |

| | |
|---|---|
| **MIPD** | Member, Institute of Personnel and Development (*now* MCIPD) |
| **MLA** | Member of Legislative Assembly; Modern Language Association; Master in Landscape Architecture; Museums, Libraries and Archives Council |
| **MLitt** | Master of Letters |
| **MMus** | Master of Music |
| **MO** | Medical Officer; Military Operations; Missouri (postal) |
| **MoD** | Ministry of Defence |
| **MoJ** | Ministry of Justice |
| **Most Rev.** | Most Reverend |
| **MP** | Member of Parliament |
| **MPhil** | Master of Philosophy |
| **MPhys** | Master of Physics |
| **MPP** | Member, Provincial Parliament; Master in Public Policy (Harvard) |
| **MRCGP** | Member, Royal College of General Practitioners |
| **MRICS** | Member, Royal Institution of Chartered Surveyors |
| **MRTPI** | Member, Royal Town Planning Institute |
| **MS** | Master of Surgery; Master of Science (US); Mississippi (postal); Multiple Sclerosis; Motor Ship |
| **MS** | Manuscript, Manuscripts |
| **MSc** | Master of Science |
| **MSF** | (Union for) Manufacturing, Science, Finance |
| **MSI** | Member, Securities Institute (later Securities & Investment Institute, *now* MCSI) |
| **MSP** | Member, Scottish Parliament; Managing Successful Programmes |
| **MSSc** | Master of Social Sciences |
| **MSt** | Master of Studies |
| **MSW** | Master of Social Work |
| **Mt** | Mount; Mountain |
| **MTh** | Master of Theology |
| **N** | Nationalist; Navigating Duties; North |
| **NACRO** | National Association for the Care and Resettlement of Offenders |
| **NALGO** | National and Local Government Officers Association |
| **NATO** | North Atlantic Treaty Organisation |
| **NCA** | National Certificate of Agriculture |
| **NCB** | National Coal Board |
| **NCCL** | National Council for Civil Liberties |
| **NCOPF** | National Council for One Parent Families |
| **NCTJ** | National Council for the Training of Journalists |
| **NCVO** | National Council for Voluntary Organisations |
| **NE** | North-east |
| **NEC** | National Executive Committee |
| **NESTA** | National Endowment for Science, Technology and the Arts |
| **NFU** | National Farmers Union |
| **NHS** | National Health Service |
| **NI** | Northern Ireland; Native Infantry |
| **Northants** | Northamptonshire |

| | |
|---|---|
| **Notts** | Nottinghamshire |
| **NP** | Notary Public |
| **NPG** | National Portrait Gallery |
| **NPQH** | National Professional Qualification for Headship |
| **NSPCC** | National Society for Prevention of Cruelty to Children |
| **NSW** | New South Wales |
| **NUJ** | National Union of Journalists |
| **NUM** | National Union of Mineworkers |
| **NUPE** | National Union of Public Employees |
| **NUS** | National Union of Students; National University of Singapore |
| **NUT** | National Union of Teachers |
| **NW** | North-west |
| **NY** | New York |
| **NYC** | New York City |
| **NZ** | New Zealand |
| **OBE** | Officer, Order of the British Empire |
| **ODPM** | Office of the Deputy Prime Minister |
| **Ofcom** | Office of Communications |
| **OSCE** | Organisation for Security and Co-operation in Europe |
| **OU** | Oxford University; Open University |
| **Oxon** | Oxfordshire; *Oxoniensis* (of Oxford) |
| **PA** | Pakistan Army; Personal Assistant; Pennsylvania (postal) |
| **P&O** | Peninsular and Oriental Steamship Co. |
| **PBS** | Public Broadcasting Service |
| **PC** | Privy Counsellor; Police Constable; Perpetual Curate; Peace Commissioner (Ireland); Progressive Conservative (Canada) |
| **PCC** | Parochial Church Council; Protected Cell Company (Guernsey); Private Cell Company |
| **PCS** | Parti Chrétien-Social; Public and Commercial Services Union |
| **PCT** | Primary Care Trust |
| **Penn** | Pennsylvania |
| **PGCE** | Post Graduate Certificate of Education |
| **PhD** | Doctor of Philosophy |
| **Phil.** | Philology; Philological; Philosophy; Philosophical |
| **PLC or plc** | public limited company |
| **PLP** | Parliamentary Labour Party; Progressive Liberal Party (Bahamas) |
| **PO** | Post Office |
| **PPE** | Philosophy, Politics and Economics |
| **PPS** | Parliamentary Private Secretary |
| **PR** | Public Relations; Parti républicain |
| **Prep.** | Preparatory |
| **Pres.** | President |
| **Prin.** | Principal |
| **Prof.** | Professor; Professional |
| **Pty** | Proprietary |
| **QC** | Queens Counsel; Quebec (postal) |
| **Qly** | Quarterly |
| **QMC** | Queen Mary College, London |
| **QPM** | Queens Police Medal |
| **QUB** | Queens University, Belfast |

| | |
|---|---|
| **RA** | Royal Academician; Royal Academy; Royal (Regiment of) Artillery |
| **RAC** | Royal Automobile Club; Royal Agricultural College; Royal Armoured Corps |
| **RAEC** | Royal Army Educational Corps |
| **RAF** | Royal Air Force |
| **RAFA** | Royal Air Forces Association |
| **RAFVR** | Royal Air Force Volunteer Reserve |
| **RAMC** | Royal Army Medical Corps |
| **R&D** | Research and Development |
| **RBK&C** | Royal Borough of Kensington and Chelsea |
| **RBL** | Royal British Legion |
| **RBS** | Royal Society of British Sculptors |
| **RC** | Roman Catholic |
| **rcds** | completed a course at, or served for a year on the Staff of, the Royal College of Defence Studies |
| **RCDS** | Royal College of Defence Studies |
| **RCM** | (Member of) Royal College of Music |
| **RCN** | Royal Canadian Navy; Royal College of Nursing |
| **Rd** | Road |
| **RD** | Rural Dean; Royal Naval and Royal Marine Forces Reserve Decoration |
| **RE** | Royal Engineers; Fellow, Royal Society of Painter-Printmakers (*formerly* of Painter-Etchers and Engravers); Religious Education |
| **Rear Adm.** | Rear Admiral |
| **Regt** | Regiment |
| **Res.** | Resigned; Reserve; Resident; Research |
| **Rev.** | Reverend; Review |
| **RFC** | Royal Flying Corps (*now* RAF); Rugby Football Club |
| **RGJ** | Royal Green Jackets |
| **RGN** | Registered General Nurse |
| **RHA** | Royal Hibernian Academy; Royal Horse Artillery; Regional Health Authority |
| **RICS** | (Member of) Royal Institution of Chartered Surveyors |
| **RIIA** | Royal Institute of International Affairs |
| **RLFC** | Rugby League Football Club |
| **RM** | Royal Marines; Resident Magistrate; Registered Midwife |
| **RMA** | Royal Marine Artillery; Royal Military Academy Sandhurst (*now* incorporating Royal Military Academy, Woolwich) |
| **RMT** | National Union of Rail, Maritime and Transport Workers; Registered Massage Therapist |
| **RN** | Royal Navy; Royal Naval; Registered Nurse |
| **RNLI** | Royal National Life-boat Institution |
| **RNR** | Royal Naval Reserve |
| **RRF** | Royal Regiment of Fusiliers |
| **RSGS** | Royal Scottish Geographical Society |
| **RSH** | Royal Society for the Promotion of Health (*now* RSPH) |
| **RSL** | Royal Society of Literature; Returned Services League of Australia |
| **RSPCA** | Royal Society for Prevention of Cruelty to Animals |
| **RSPH** | Royal Society for Public Health |
| **RSRE** | Royal Signals and Radar Establishment |
| **Rt Hon.** | Right Honourable |
| **RTR** | Royal Tank Regiment |
| **Rt Rev.** | Right Reverend |
| **RUSI** | Royal United Services Institute for Defence and Security Studies (*formerly* Royal United Service Institution) |
| **s** | son |
| **S** | Succeeded; South; Saint |
| **SAS** | Special Air Service |
| **Sch.** | School |
| **SCM** | State Certified Midwife; Student Christian Movement |
| **Scot.** | Scotland |
| **SDLP** | Social Democratic and Labour Party |
| **SE** | South-east |
| **Sec.** | Secretary |
| **SEEDA** | South East England Development Agency |
| **SEN** | State Enrolled Nurse; Special Educational Needs |
| **SERC** | Science and Engineering Research Council |
| **SF** | Sinn Féin |
| **SHAPE** | Supreme Headquarters, Allied Powers, Europe |
| **SMO** | Senior Medical Officer; Sovereign Military Order |
| **SNP** | Scottish National Party |
| **SO** | Staff Officer; Scientific Officer; Symphony Orchestra |
| **SOAS** | School of Oriental and African Studies |
| **Soc.** | Society; Socialist (France, Belgium) |
| **SPR** | Society for Psychical Research |
| **Sqdn** or **Sqn** | Squadron |
| **SS** | Saints; Straits Settlements; Steamship |
| **SSAFA** | Soldiers, Sailors, Airmen and Families Association (*formerly* Soldiers, Sailors, and Airmens Families Association, then Soldiers, Sailors, Airmen and Families Association Forces Help) |
| **St** | Street; Saint |
| **STC** | Senior Training Corps |
| **STV** | Scottish Television |
| **Surg.** | Surgeon |
| **SW** | South-west |
| **T** | Telephone; Territorial |
| **TA** | Telegraphic Address; Territorial Army |

| | |
|---|---|
| TD | Territorial Efficiency Decoration; Efficiency Decoration (T) (since April 1967); Teachta Dala (Member of the Dáil, Eire) |
| TEC | Technician Education Council (later BTEC); Training and Enterprise Council |
| TES | Times Educational Supplement |
| TGWU | Transport and General Workers Union |
| THES | Times Higher Education Supplement |
| TSB | Trustee Savings Bank |
| TUC | Trades Union Congress |
| TV | Television |
| UC | University College |
| UCH | University College Hospital (London) |
| UCL | University College London |
| UCNW | University College of North Wales |
| UCW | University College of Wales; Union of Communication Workers (*now* CWU) |
| UDC | Urban District Council; Urban Development Corporation |
| UDR | Ulster Defence Regiment; Union des Démocrates pour la V$^{ème}$ République |
| UK | United Kingdom |
| UKIAS | United Kingdom Immigrants Advisory Service |
| UKTI | UK Trade & Investment |
| UN | United Nations |
| UNA | United Nations Association |
| UNDP | United Nations Development Programme |
| UNESCO | United Nations Educational, Scientific and Cultural Organisation |
| UNFAO | United Nations Food and Agriculture Organisation |
| UNFICYP | United Nations Force in Cyprus |
| UNICEF | United Nations Childrens Fund (*formerly* United Nations International Childrens Emergency Fund) |
| UNIDO | United Nations Industrial Development Organisation |
| Univ. | University |
| UNRWA | United Nations Relief and Works Agency |
| US | United States |
| USA | United States of America |
| USDAW | Union of Shop Distributive and Allied Workers |
| USPG | United Society for the Propagation of the Gospel |
| UU | Ulster Unionist |
| V | Five (Roman numerals); Version; Vicar; Viscount; Vice |
| VCT | Venture Capital Trust |
| Vet. | Veterinary |
| Vice Adm. | Vice Admiral |
| Vol. | Volume; Voluntary; Volunteers |
| VRD | Royal Naval Volunteer Reserve Officers Decoration |
| VSO | Voluntary Service Overseas |

| | |
|---|---|
| W | West; Website |
| WA | Western Australia; Washington (postal) |
| WEA | Workers Educational Association; Royal West of England Academy |
| WEF | World Economic Forum |
| WEU | Western European Union |
| Wilts | Wiltshire |
| Wm | William |
| Worcs | Worcestershire |
| WS | Writer to the Signet |
| WTO | World Trade Organisation |
| y | youngest |
| YC | Young Conservative |
| Yeo. | Yeomanry |
| Yorks | Yorkshire |
| yr | younger |
| yrs | years |
| YTS | Youth Training Scheme |

# OUR GOVERNMENT: WHO'S WHO

**ABBOTT, Diane Julie;** MP (Lab) Hackney North and Stoke Newington, since 1987; *b* 27 Sept. 1953; *d* of late Reginald and Julia Abbott; *m* 1991, David Thompson (marr. diss. 1993); one *s*. *Educ:* Harrow County Girls' Grammar Sch.; Newnham Coll., Cambridge. Formerly: Admin. Trainee, Home Office; Race Relations Officer, NCCL; Researcher, Thames Television; Reporter, TV-am; Equality Officer, ACTT; Press and PR Officer, GLC; Principal Press Officer, Lambeth Borough Council. Joined Labour Party, 1971; Mem., NEC, 1994–97. Mem., Westminster City Council, 1982–86. Mem. resp. for equality and women's issues, Mayor of London's Cabinet, 2000–08. Shadow Minister for Public Health, 2010–13; Shadow Sec. of State for Internat. Develt, 2015–. *Address:* House of Commons, SW1A 0AA.

**ABRAHAMS, Deborah Angela Elspeth;** MP (Lab) Oldham East and Saddleworth, since Jan. 2011; *b* Sheffield, 1960; *m* John Abrahams; two *d*. *Educ:* Univ. of Salford; Univ. of Liverpool. FFPH 2012. Hd, Healthy Cities for Knowsley, 1992–2000; Sen. Res. Fellow, Univ. of Liverpool, full time, 2000–02, pt time, 2002–06; Chm., Rochdale PCT, 2002–06; Dir, Internat. Health Impact Assessment Consortium, Univ. of Liverpool, 2006–10. Mem. Bd, Bury and Rochdale HA, 1998–2002. Contested (Lab) Colne Valley, 2010. Mem., Work and Pensions Select Cttee, 2011–. *Address:* House of Commons, SW1A 0AA.

**ADAMS, Nigel;** MP (C) Selby and Ainsty, since 2010; *b* Goole, E Yorks, 30 Nov. 1966; *s* of Derek Adams and late Isabella Adams; *m* 1992, Claire Robson; one *s* three *d*. *Educ:* Selby Grammar Sch.; Selby High Sch. Sales and mktg roles in advertising and telecommunications industry, 1985–93; Founder and Man. Dir, Advanced Digital Telecom Ltd, 1993–99; Dir, JWE Telecom plc, 1999–2000; non-exec. Chm., Pareto Law plc, 2001–02; Director: Ebor Events Ltd, 2003–05; Yorks Tourist Bd, 2005–06; NGC Networks Ltd, 2006–; NGC Network Services Ltd, 2007–. Hon. Sec., All Party Parly Cricket Gp, 2010–. *Recreations:* cricket, playing and watching (Member: Yorks CCC; Carlton Club CC; Hovingham CC; Sec., Lords and Commons CC). *Address:* House of Commons, SW1A 0AA. *E:* nigel.adams.mp@parliament.uk; 17 High Street, Tadcaster, N Yorks LS24 9AP. *Club:* Carlton.

**AFRIYIE, Adam;** MP (C) Windsor, since 2005; *b* 4 Aug. 1965. *Educ:* Addey and Stanhope Sch., New Cross; Imperial Coll., London (BSc 1987). Man. Dir, then non-exec. Chm., Connect Support Services, 1993–; Exec. Chm.,

DeHavilland Inf. Services, 1998–2005; non-exec. Chm., Axonn Media Ltd (formerly Adfero), 2005–. Shadow Minister for Sci. and Innovation, 2007–10. Chairman: Parly Space Cttee, 2010–; Parly Office of Sci. and Technol., 2010–; Members' Expenses Cttee, 2011–15. Mem. Bd, Policy Exchange, 2003–05. Gov., Mus. of London, 1999–2005. *Address:* (office) 87 St Leonards Road, Windsor SL4 3BZ; House of Commons, SW1A 0AA.

**AHMAD OF WIMBLEDON,** Baron *cr* 2011 (Life Peer), of Wimbledon in the London Borough of Merton; **Tariq Mahmood Ahmad;** Parliamentary Under-Secretary of State, Home Office and Department for Transport, since 2015; *b* London, 3 April 1968; *s* of Chaudhry Mansoor Ahmad, BT and Amtul Matin Ahmad (*née* Mir); *m* 2011, Siddiquea Masud; two *s* one *d*. *Educ:* Rutlish Sch.; London South Bank Univ. (BA Hons Business 1990); City Univ. (ACIB 1996). Mgt roles in corporate banking and Hd Office, NatWest Gp, 1991–2000; Vice Pres., and Dir, Marketing, Alliance Berstein, 2000–03; Dir, Strategy and Marketing, Sucden Financial Ltd, 2004–12. Mem. (C) Merton LBC, 2002–12 (Mem. Cabinet for Envmt, 2006–08, for Community Safety and Policing, 2008–09). A Lord in Waiting (Govt Whip), 2012–14; Parly Under-Sec. of State, DCLG, 2014–15. Contested (C) Croydon N, 2005. Vice Chm., Conservative Party, 2008–10. MInstD. *Recreations:* charity work, various sports, charity runs. *Address:* House of Lords, SW1A 0PW. *E:* ahmadt@parliament.uk.

**AHMED-SHEIKH, Tasmina,** OBE 2014; MP (SNP) Ochil and South Perthshire, since 2015; *b* Chelsea; *m* Zulfikar Sheikh; two *s* two *d*. *Educ:* Univ. of Edinburgh (MA 1991); Strathclyde Univ. (LLB 1995; Postgrad. DipLaw 1996). NP; WS 2009. Mem., Faculty of Procurators, 1996; admitted as solicitor, 1997; Partner, 2005–10, Equity Partner, 2010–15, Hamilton Burns, WS. Columnist, The National. City of Glasgow College: Chm., Internat. and Commercial Develt Cttee, 2011–; Mem. Bd, Remuneration and Nominations Cttee, 2011–. Mem., Adv. Bd, Yes Scotland Campaign, Yes Scotland Ltd, 2012–14. Scottish National Party: Mem. Bd, Finance and Audit Cttee, 2012–; Nat. Women's and Equalities Officer, 2012–. Founder and Chair, Scottish Asian Women's Assoc., 2012–. *Address:* House of Commons, SW1A 0AA.

**ALDOUS, Peter;** MP (C) Waveney, since 2010; *b* Ipswich, 26 Aug. 1961. *Educ:* Harrow Sch.; Reading Univ. (BSc Land Mgt 1982). Chartered Surveyor, in private practice, Norwich and Ipswich, 1983–2010. Member (C): Waveney DC,

1999–2002; Suffolk CC, 2001–05 (Dep. Leader, Cons. Gp, 2002–05). *Recreations:* cricket, squash, football, horse racing. *Address:* House of Commons, SW1A 0AA. *E:* peter.aldous.mp@parliament.uk.

**ALEXANDER, Heidi;** MP (Lab) Lewisham East, since 2010; *b* Swindon, 17 April 1975; *d* of Malcolm and Elaine Alexander; *m* 2011, Martin Ballantyne. *Educ:* Churchfields Secondary Sch., Swindon; Durham Univ. (BA Geog. 1996; MA Eur. Urban and Regl Change 1999). Researcher to Joan Ruddock, MP, 1999–2005; Campaign Manager, Clothes Aid, 2006. Dir and Chair, Gtr London Enterprise, 2007–09; Dir, Lewisham Schs for the Future Local Educn Partnership, 2007–09. Mem. (Lab) Lewisham LBC, 2004–10 (Dep. Mayor, 2006–10; Cabinet Mem. for Regeneration, 2006–10). Shadow Health Sec., 2015–. *Address:* House of Commons, SW1A 0AA.

**ALI, Rushanara;** MP (Lab) Bethnal Green and Bow, since 2010; *b* Bangladesh, 14 March 1975. *Educ:* Mulberry Sch. for Girls; Tower Hamlets Coll.; St John's Coll., Oxford (BA PPE). Res. asst to Lord Young of Dartington on estabt of Tower Hamlets Summer Univ., 1995; helped to develop Language Line; Parly Asst to Oona King MP, 1997–99; FCO, 2000–01; Communities Directorate, Home Office, 2002–05; Associate Dir, Young Foundn, 2005–10. Res. Fellow, IPPR, 1999–2002. Shadow Minister: for Internat. Develt, 2010–14; for Educn, 2013–14. Mem., Treasury Select Cttee, 2014–15. Chair, UpRising Leadership Prog. *Address:* House of Commons, SW1A 0AA.

**ALLAN, Lucy;** MP (C) Telford, since 2015; *b* Cheltenham, 2 Oct. 1964; *m* Robin; one *s. Educ:* Durham Univ. (BA Hons Anthropol. 1986); Kingston Univ. (LLM Employment Law 2006). CA 1992. Insolvency Manager, Price Waterhouse, 1987–94; Mercury Asset Mgt plc, 1994–95; De La Rue plc, 1995–97; Hd, Investment Trusts, Gartmore Investment, 1997–2001; Dir, Investment Trust Team, UBS Warburg, 2001–02; Hd, Investment Trusts, First State Investment, 2002–04; freelance employment law advr, Workplacelaw Ltd, 2004–. Mem. (C) Wandsworth LBC, 2006–12. *Address:* House of Commons, SW1A 0AA.

**ALLEN, Graham William;** MP (Lab) Nottingham North, since 1987; *b* 11 Jan. 1953; *s* of William and Edna Allen. *Educ:* Robert Shaw Primary Sch.; Forest Fields Grammar Sch.; City of London Polytechnic; Leeds Univ. Warehouseman, Nottingham, 1971–72; Labour Party Res. Officer, 1978–83; Local Govt Officer, GLC, 1983–84; Trades Union National Co-ordinator, Political Fund Ballots Campaign, 1984–86; Regional Res. and Educn Officer, GMBATU, 1986–87. Opposition front bench spokesman on social security, 1991–92, on democracy and the constitution, 1992–94, on the

media, 1994, on transport, 1995, on environment, 1996–97; a Lord Comr of HM Treasury (Govt Whip), 1997–98; Vice Chamberlain of HM Household, 1998–2001. Member: Public Accounts Cttee, 1988–91; Procedure Cttee, 1989–91; 1990 Financial Bill Cttee. Chm., PLP Treasury Cttee, 1990–91. Chm., One Nottingham, 2005–10. *Publications:* Reinventing Democracy, 1995; The Last Prime Minister: being honest about the UK Presidency, 2002; (jtly) Early Intervention: good parents, great kids, better citizens, 2009. *Recreations:* cricket, golf, painting, cooking. *Address:* House of Commons, SW1A 0AA. *T:* (020) 7219 4343. *Clubs:* Strelley Social, Beechdale Community Centre, Bulwell Community Centre, Basford Hall Miners Welfare (Nottingham).

**ALLEN, Heidi Suzanne;** MP (C) South Cambridgeshire, since 2015; *b* Notton, Yorks; *m* Phil Allen. *Educ:* University Coll. London (BSc Hons Astrophysics 1996); London Business Sch. (Exxon Develt prog.); BPP London (DipLaw 2007). *Address:* House of Commons, SW1A 0AA.

**ALTMANN,** Baroness *cr* 2015 (Life Peer), of Tottenham in the London Borough of Haringey; **Rosalind Miriam Altmann,** CBE 2014; PhD; Minister of State (Minister for Pensions), Department for Work and Pensions, since 2015; *b* 8 April 1956; *d* of Leo and Renate Altmann; *m* 1982, Paul Richer; one *s* two *d. Educ:* University Coll. London (BSc Econ 1st Cl. Hons); Harvard Univ. (Kennedy Schol.); London Sch. of Econs (PhD 1981). Investment Mgt Cert. Fund Manager, Prudential Assce, London, 1981–84; Hd, Internat. Equities, Chase Manhattan Bank, 1984–89; Director: Rothschild Asset Mgt, 1989–91; Natwest Investment Mgt, 1991–93; ind. policy advr on pensions, investment, savings and retirement, 1993–2015; Dir-Gen., Saga Gp, 2010–13. Consultant to HM Treasury on Pension Fund Investment, 2000; Mem., Lord Chancellor's Strategic Investment Bd, 2004–; Policy Advr to Number 10 Policy Unit on pensions, investments and savings, 2000–05. Non-exec. Mem., Court Funds Office, 2004–15; Mem. Bd, IPSO, 2014–15. Gov., 1989–, and non-exec. Dir, 2004–, LSE. Life Gov., Nightingale House for the Elderly, 1985. MCSI (MSI 1992); MInstD 2000. Hon. DLitt Westminster, 2009. *Publications:* articles in newspapers, jls and industry magazines, incl. Financial Times, The Times, Pensions Week, Financial Advr, Money Mktg, Pensions World, Wall St Jl, Professional Investor, Global Finance, Instnl Investor. *Recreations:* charity fund-raising, swimming, walking, table tennis. *E:* altmannr@parliament.uk.

**AMESS, Sir David (Anthony Andrew),** Kt 2015; MP (C) Southend West, since 1997 (Basildon, 1983–97); *b* Plaistow, 26 March 1952; *s* of late James Henry Valentine Amess and of Maud Ethel Martin; *m* 1983, Julia Monica Margaret Arnold; one *s* four *d. Educ:* St Bonaventure's Grammar Sch.; Bournemouth

Coll. of Technol. (BScEcon Hons 2.2, special subject Govt). Teacher, St John the Baptist Jun. Mixed Sch., Bethnal Green, 1970–71; Jun. Underwriter, Leslie & Godwin Agencies, 1974–76; Sen. Manager, Accountancy Personnel, 1976–79; Senior Consultant: Executemps Co. Agency, 1979–81; AA Recruitment Co., 1981–87; Chairman and Chief Executive: Accountancy Solutions, 1987–90; Accountancy Gp, 1990–96. Mem., Redbridge Council, 1982–86 (Vice Chm., Housing Cttee, 1982–85). Contested (C) Newham NW, 1979. Parliamentary Private Secretary: to Parly Under-Secs of State (Health), DHSS, 1987–88; to Minister of State and Parly Under-Sec. of State, Dept of Transport, 1988–90; to Minister of State, DoE, 1990–92; to Chief Sec. to the Treasury, 1992–94; to Sec. of State for Employment, 1994–95; to Sec. of State for Defence, 1995–97. Member: Broadcasting Select Cttee, 1994–97; Health Select Cttee, 1998–2007; Chairman's Panel, 2001–. All-Party Groups: Chairman: Solvent Abuse, 2000; Fire Safety and Rescue, 2001–; Rheumatoid Arthritis, 2002; Hepatology, 2004–; Holy See, 2006; FRAME, 2006; Maldives, 2009–; Democracy in Bahrain, 2013; Maternity, 2013–; Jt Chm., Scouts, 1997; Vice-Chairman: Guides, 2000; Hungary, 2003–; Obesity, 2003; Deep Vein Thrombosis Awareness, 2003–; Asthma, 2003; Funerals and Bereavement, 2005–; Bermuda, 2005–; Warm Homes, 2005; Thrombosis, 2006–; Lions Club Internat., 2006; Mauritius, 2010–; MS, 2010–; Sec., Eye Health and Visual Impairment, 2003; Treasurer: ME (Myalgic Encephalomyelitis), 2001; N Korea, 2004–; Zoos and Aquariums, 2010–; Cardiac Risk in the Young, 2011–. Chm., Cons. Back Bench Health Cttee, 1999–; Member: Backbench Business Cttee, 2012–15; Admin Cttee, 2015–. Mem. Exec., 1922 Cttee, 2004–12. Vice Pres., Nat. Lotteries Council, 1998. Chm. Trustees, Industry and Parlt Trust, 2014–. Dir, Parly Broadcasting Unit Ltd, 1997–99. Chm., 1912 Club, 1996–; Vice Chm., Assoc. of Cons. Clubs, 1997–. Hon. Sec., Cons. Friends of Israel, 1998–. Fellow, Industry and Parliament Trust, 1994 (Chm., Fellowship Cttee, 2007–). Publications: The Road to Basildon, 1993; Basildon Experience: Conservatives fight back, 1994; Against All Odds, 2012; Party of Opportunity, 2014, 2nd edn 2015; contrib. magazines and pamphlets. Recreations: gardening, music, sport, animals, theatre, travel. Address: c/o House of Commons, SW1A 0AA.

**ANDERSON, David;** MP (Lab) Blaydon, since 2005; b 2 Dec. 1953; s of Cyril and Janet Anderson; m 1973, Elizabeth Eva Jago. Educ: Doncaster and Durham Tech. Colls; Durham Univ. (DipSocSc); Moscow Higher Trade Union Sch. Colliery mechanic, 1969–89; care worker, 1989–2005. PPS to Minister of State, DIUS, 2007–08, FCO, 2008–09, MoD, 2009–10; an Opposition Whip, 2010–11. Chm., All-Party

Parly Gp on Third World Solidarity, on Muscular Dystrophy, on Coalfield Communities, on Industrial Heritage; Sec., All-Party Parly Gp on Kurdistan. Trade Union Lay Official: NUM, 1978–89; UNISON, 1989–2005; Pres., UNISON, 2003–04; Mem., TUC Gen. Council, 2000–05. Recreations: walking, travel, music, caravanning. Address: House of Commons, SW1A 0AA. T: (020) 7219 4348. E: andersonda@parliament.uk.

**ANDREW, Stuart James;** MP (C) Pudsey, since 2010; b Bangor, N Wales, 25 Nov. 1971; s of James Edward and Maureen Catherine Andrew; partner, 2001, Robin Rogers. Educ: Ysgol David Hughes, Menai Bridge. Fundraiser: BHF, 1994–98; Hope House Children's Hospice, 1998–2000; Hd of Fundraising, E Lancs Hospice, 2000–03. Mem. (C) Leeds CC, 2003–. PPS to Minister for Cabinet Office and Paymaster Gen., 2012–. Treas., All Party Parly Gp on Hospice and Palliative Care, 2010–. Recreations: walking Yorkshire Dales, attending gym, socialising. Address: House of Commons, SW1A 0AA. T: (020) 7219 7130. E: stuart. andrew.mp@parliament.uk.

**ANELAY OF ST JOHNS,** Baroness cr 1996 (Life Peer), of St Johns in the county of Surrey; **Joyce Anne Anelay,** DBE 1995 (OBE 1990); PC 2009; JP; Minister of State, Foreign and Commonwealth Office, since 2014; Prime Minister's Special Representative on Preventing Sexual Violence in Conflict, since 2015; b 17 July 1947; d of late Stanley Charles Clarke and of Annette Marjorie Clarke; m 1970, Richard Alfred Anelay, QC. Educ: Merryhills Primary Sch., Enfield; Enfield Co. Sch.; Bristol Univ. (BA Hons Hist.); London Univ. Inst. of Educn (Cert Ed); Brunel Univ. (MA Public and Social Admin). Teacher, St David's Sch., Ashford, Middx, 1969–74; Voluntary Advr, Woking CAB, 1976–85 (Chm., 1988–93; Pres., 1996–). Member: Social Security Appeal Tribunal, 1983–96; Social Security Adv. Cttee for GB and NI, 1989–96. Opposition spokesman on agriculture, 1997–98, on culture, media and sport, 1998–2002, on Home Affairs, 2002–07; an Opposition Whip, 1997–98, Opposition Chief Whip, 2007–10, H of L; Captain of the Honourable Corps of Gentlemen at Arms (Govt Chief Whip in H of L), 2010–14. Mem., Procedure Cttee, 1997–2000, 2007–. Conservative Women's Committee: Chm., SE Area, 1987–90; Vice-Chm., SE Area Exec. Cttee, 1990–93; Chm., Nat. Cttee, 1993–96; Member: Nat. Union of Cons. Party, 1987–97 (Vice-Pres., 1996–97); Women's Nat. Commission, 1990–93. Trustee: UNICEF UK, 2004–07; Just a Drop, 2004–06. JP NW Surrey, 1985–97. Chm. Govs, Hermitage First and Middle Schs, 1981–88. FRSA 1991. Hon. DSocSc Brunel, 1997. Recreations: golf, reading. Address: House of Lords, SW1A 0PW. Club: Woking Golf.

**ANSELL, Caroline Julie Porte;** MP (C) Eastbourne, since 2015; *b* 1971; *m* 1997, Nicholas Ansell; three *s. Educ:* Royal Holloway Coll., Univ. of London (BA French); MEd 2001. NPQH. Teacher; Schs Inspector. Mem. (C) Eastbourne BC, 2012–15. *Address:* House of Commons, SW1A 0AA.

**ARGAR, Edward John Comport;** MP (C) Charnwood, since 2015; *b* Ashford, Kent, 9 Dec. 1977; *s* of Edward Henry Argar and Patricia Joan Argar. *Educ:* Harvey Grammar Sch., Folkestone; Oriel Coll., Oxford (BA; MSt). Political Advr to Shadow Foreign Sec., 2001–05; Mgt Consultant, Hedra plc, then Mouchel, 2005–11; Hd, Public Affairs, UK and Europe, Serco Gp plc, 2011–14. Non-exec. Mem. Bd, NHS Westminster PCT, 2008–10. Trustee, Groundwork London, 2010–15. Mem., Westminster CC, 2006–15. *Recreations:* reading, ski-ing, tennis, cricket, gardening. *Address:* House of Commons, SW1A 0AA. *T:* (020) 7219 8140. *E:* edward.argar.mp@parliament.uk. *Club:* Travellers.

**ARKLESS, Richard Lambert Thomas;** MP (SNP) Dumfries and Galloway, since 2015; *b* Stranraer, 1975; *m* Anne; two *c. Educ:* Glasgow Caledonian Univ. (BA Hons Financial Services); Strathclyde Univ. (LLB); Glasgow Grad. Sch. of Law (DipLP). Solicitor trainee, Edinburgh incl. secondment to RBS; solicitor, specialising in consumer litigation, Cheshire, until 2013; set up small online business, 2013. *Address:* House of Commons, SW1A 0AA.

**ASHTON OF HYDE,** 4th Baron *cr* 1911; **Thomas Henry Ashton;** a Lord in Waiting (Government Whip), since 2014; *b* 18 July 1958; *s* of 3rd Baron Ashton of Hyde and Pauline Trewlove Ashton (*née* Brackenbury); *S* father, 2008; *m* 1987, Emma Louise, *d* of C. N. G. Allinson and Mrs J. R. W. Palmer; four *d. Educ:* Eton; Trinity Coll., Oxford (MA). Late Lt Royal Hussars (PWO), Royal Wessex Yeo. Vice Pres., Guy Carpenter & Co., Inc., 1990–92; Director: C. T. Bowring Reinsurance Ltd, 1992–93; D. P. Mann Ltd, 1996–99; Chief Executive Officer: Faraday Underwriting Ltd, 2005–13 (Dir, 1999–2013); Faraday Reinsurance Co. Ltd, 2005–13 (Dir, 2002–13). Member: Council of Lloyd's, 2010–13; Adv. Council, Century Capital LLP, Boston, 2006–14. Elected Mem., H of L, 2011. Mem., RCDS, 2013–14. Jt Master, Heythrop Hunt, 2007–09. *Heir: b* Hon. John, (Jack), Edward Ashton, *b* 30 Jan. 1966. *Address:* Broadwell Hill, Moreton-in-Marsh, Glos GL56 0UD. *Club:* Boodle's.

**ASHWORTH, Jonathan Michael Graham;** MP (Lab) Leicester South, since May 2011; *b* Salford, 14 Oct. 1978; *m* 2010, Emilie Oldknow; one *d. Educ:* Philips High Sch.; Bury Coll.; Durham Univ. (BA Hons Politics and Philosophy). Pol Res. Officer, 2001, Econs and Welfare Policy Officer, 2002–03, Labour Party; Special Advr, HM Treasury, 2003–07; Dep.

Political Sec. to Prime Minister, 2007–10; Political Sec. to Acting Leader, Labour Party, 2010; Hd, Labour Party Relns for Rt Hon. Edward Miliband, MP, 2010–11. Shadow Cabinet Office Minister, 2013–15; Shadow Minister without Portfolio, 2015–. *Address:* House of Commons, SW1A 0AA.

**ATKINS, Victoria Mary;** MP (C) Louth and Horncastle, since 2015; *d* of Rt Hon. Sir Robert (James) Atkins; *m* Paul; one *s. Educ:* Univ. of Cambridge (Law). Called to the Bar, 1998; in practice as barrister, specialising in serious organised crime, 1998–. *Address:* House of Commons, SW1A 0AA.

**AUSTIN, Ian;** MP (Lab) Dudley North, since 2005; *b* 6 March 1965; *s* of Alfred and Margaret Austin; *m* 1993, Catherine Miles; two *s* one *d. Educ:* Dudley Sch.; Univ. of Essex (BA Hons Govt). Communications Manager, Focus Housing, 1989–94; Press Officer, Labour Party, 1995–98; Dep. Dir of Communications, Scottish Labour Party, 1998–99; political advr to Chancellor of Exchequer, 1999–2005. Mem. (Lab) Dudley MBC, 1991–95. PPS to Prime Minister, 2007–08; an Asst Govt Whip, 2008–09; Minister for the W Midlands, 2008–10; Parly Under-Sec. of State, DCLG, 2009–10. *Recreations:* reading, watching football, cycling. *Address:* House of Commons, SW1A 0AA. *T:* (020) 7219 8012, *Fax:* (020) 7219 4408; Turner House, 157/185 Wrens Nest Road, Dudley DY1 3RU. *T:* (01384) 342503/4, *Fax:* (01384) 342523.

**BACON, Richard Michael;** MP (C) South Norfolk, since 2001; *b* 3 Dec. 1962; *s* of Michael Edward Bacon and Sheila Margaret Bacon (*née* Taylor, now Campbell); *m* 2006, Victoria Louise Panton; two *s. Educ:* King's Sch., Worcester; LSE (BSc 1st cl. Hons 1986); Goethe Inst., Berlin. Investment banker, Barclays de Zoete Wedd Ltd, 1986–89; financial journalist, principally with Euromoney Publications, 1993–94; Dep. Dir, Mgt Consultancies Assoc., 1994–96; Associate Partner, Brunswick Public Relations, 1996–99; Founder, English Word Factory, 1999–. Member: Public Accounts Cttee, H of C, 2001–; European Scrutiny Cttee, 2003–07; Public Accounts Commn, 2005–. Chm., Hammersmith Cons. Assoc., 1995–96. Co-founder, Cons. Party Geneva project, 2000. Contested (C) Vauxhall, 1997. *Publications:* (with Christopher Hope) Conundrum, 2013. *Recreation:* playing the bongos. *Address:* House of Commons, SW1A 0AA. *T:* (constituency office) (01379) 643728. *Club:* Ronnie Scott's.

**BAILEY, Adrian Edward;** MP (Lab and Co-op) West Bromwich West, since Nov. 2000; *b* 11 Dec. 1945; *s* of Edward Arthur Bailey and Sylvia Alice Bailey; *m* 1989, Jill Patricia Millard (*née* Hunscott); one step *s. Educ:* Cheltenham Grammar Sch.; Univ. of Exeter (BA Hons Econ. Hist.); Loughborough Coll. of Librarianship (Post

Grad. DipLib). Librarian, Cheshire CC, 1971–82; Pol Organiser, Co-op Party, 1982–2000. Mem. (Lab), Sandwell MBC, 1991–2000 (Dep. Leader, 1997–2000). Contested (Lab): S Worcs, 1970; Nantwich, Feb. and Oct. 1974; Wirral, March 1976; Cheshire W, EP, 1979. *Recreations:* supporting Cheltenham Town FC, cricket, dog walking. *Address:* House of Commons, SW1A 0AA; 181 Oakham Road, Tividale, Oldbury, W Midlands B69 1PZ.

**BAKER, Steven John;** MP (C) Wycombe, since 2010; *b* St Austell, 6 June 1971; *s* of Michael Baker and Diane Vivienne Baker (*née* Brimble); *m* 1996, Julia Elizabeth Perks. *Educ:* Poltair Comp. Sch., St Austell; St Austell Sixth Form Coll.; Univ. of Southampton (BEng Aerospace Systems Engrg 1992); St Cross Coll., Oxford (MSc Computation (Computer Sci.) 2000). CEng 1999. Engr Officer (Aerosystems), RAF, 1989–99; Hd, Consulting and Product Manager, DecisionSoft Ltd, Oxford, 2000–01; Chief Technol. Officer, BASDA Ltd, Great Missenden, 2002–07; Dir, Product Develt, CoreFiling Ltd, Oxford, 2005–06; Chief Architect, Global Financing and Asset Servicing Platforms, Lehman Brothers, 2006–08. Principal, Ambriel Consulting Ltd, 2001–10. Associate Consultant, Centre for Social Justice, 2008–10; Corporate Affairs Dir, 2009–10, Trustee, 2010–, Cobden Centre. Dir, Thermal Engineering Ltd, 2013. Trustee, GB Job Clubs, 2010–13. FRSA 2012. *Recreations:* skydiving, sailing, ski-ing, motorcycling, driving. *Address:* (office) 150A West Wycombe Road, High Wycombe HP12 3AE. *T:* (01494) 448408. *Club:* Royal Air Force.

**BALDWIN, Harriett Mary Morison;** MP (C) West Worcestershire, since 2010; Economic Secretary, HM Treasury, since 2015; *b* Watford, 2 May 1960; *d* of Anthony Francis Eggleston, OBE; *m* 2004, James Stanley Baldwin; two step *d*; one *s* by a previous marriage. *Educ:* Friends' Sch., Saffron Walden; Marlborough Coll.; Lady Margaret Hall, Oxford (BA French and Russian 1982); McGill Univ. (MBA 1985). J. P. Morgan, 1986–2008, Man. Dir, 1998–2008; Vice Chm., Social Investment Business, 2008–12. PPS to Minister for Employment, 2012–14; an Asst Govt Whip, 2014; a Lord Comr of HM Treasury (Govt Whip), 2014–15. Contested (C) Stockton N, 2005. *Recreations:* family, walking, swimming, travel. *Address:* House of Commons, SW1A 0AA. *T:* (020) 7219 7187. *E:* harriett.baldwin.mp@parliament.uk. *Club:* Carlton.

**BARCLAY, Stephen Paul;** MP (C) North East Cambridgeshire, since 2010; an Assistant Government Whip, since 2015; *b* Lytham, Lancs, 1972; *s* of Robert and Janice Barclay; *m* Karen; one *s* one *d*. *Educ:* King Edward VII Sch., Lancs; Peterhouse, Cambridge (BA Hist. 1994); Coll. of Law, Chester. 2nd Lieut, RRF, 1991. Trainee solicitor, Lawrence Graham, Solicitors, 1996–98; admitted as solicitor, 1998; Solicitor, Axa Insce, 1998–2001; FSA, 2002–06; Dir, Regulatory Affairs, then Hd, Anti-money Laundering and

Sanction, Barclays UK Retail Bank, 2006–10. Contested (C): Manchester Blackley, 1997; Lancaster and Wyre, 2001. *Address:* House of Commons, SW1A 0AA.

**BARDELL, Hannah Mary;** MP (SNP) Livingston, since 2015; *b* Craigshill, Livingston. *Educ:* Broxburn Acad.; Univ. of Stirling (BA Hons Film and Media, Politics and English 2005). Researcher, then Asst Producer, GMTV, 2005–07; Office Manager, Rt Hon. Alex Salmond, MSP, 2007–10; Protocol Exec. and Events Manager, American Consulate, Edinburgh, 2010–12; Communications Manager, Subsea 7, 2012; Hd, Communications and Mktg (UK and Africa), Stork Tech. Services, 2013–15. *Address:* House of Commons, SW1A 0AA.

**BARON, John Charles;** MP (C) Basildon and Billericay, since 2010 (Billericay, 2001–10); *b* 21 June 1959; *s* of Raymond Arthur Ernest Baron and Kathleen Ruby Baron; *m* 1992, Thalia Anne Mayson Laird; two *d. Educ:* Jesus Coll., Cambridge (MA). Capt., RRF, 1984–88. Director: Henderson Private Investors, 1988–99; Rothschild Asset Mgt, 1999–2001. Contested (C) Basildon, 1997. Shadow Health Minister, 2002–03; an Opposition Whip, 2007–10. *Recreations:* financial journalism, gardening. *Address:* c/o House of Commons, SW1A 0AA. *T:* (constituency office) (01268) 520765.

**BARRON, Rt Hon. Sir Kevin (John);** Kt 2014; PC 2001; MP (Lab) Rother Valley, since 1983; *b* 26 Oct. 1946; *s* of Richard Barron; *m* 1969 (*d* 2008); one *s* two *d. Educ:* Maltby Hall Secondary Modern Sch.; Ruskin Coll., Oxford. NCB, 1962–83. PPS to Leader of the Opposition, 1985–87; Opposition spokesman on energy, 1988–92, on employment, 1993–95, on health, 1995–97. Member: Select Cttee on Energy, 1983–85; Select Cttee on Environmental Affairs, 1992–93; Parly Intelligence and Security Cttee, 1997–2005; Liaison Cttee, 2005–15; Chairman: Select Cttee on Health, 2005–10; Standards and Privileges Cttee, 2010– (Mem., 2005–10). Chm., Yorkshire Labour MPs, 1987–. Pres., Rotherham and Dist TUC, 1982–83. Trustee and Dir, Nat. Coal Mining Mus. for England. Vice Pres., RSPH (formerly RSH, then RIPH), 2007–. Hon. FRCP 2008. *Address:* House of Commons, SW1A 0AA.

**BARWELL, Gavin Laurence;** MP (C) Croydon Central, since 2010; Comptroller of HM Treasury (Government Whip), since 2015; *b* Cuckfield, W Sussex, 23 Jan. 1972; *s* of David and Jennifer Barwell; *m* 2001, Karen McKenzie; three *s. Educ:* Trinity Sch. of John Whitgift, Croydon; Trinity Coll., Cambridge (BA Natural Scis 1993). Conservative Party: Envmt Desk Officer, 1993–95; Special Advr to Sec. of State for Envmt, 1995–97; Press Officer, 1997; Hd of Pol Sect., 1997–98; Hd of Local Govt Dept, 1998–2003, Cons. Campaign HQ; Chief Operating Officer, Cons. Party, 2003–06; consultant, 2006–10. PPS to Minister of State, DCLG, 2012–13; an Asst Govt Whip. 2013–14; a Lord Comr of HM Treasury (Govt Whip), 2014–15. Mem. (C) Croydon LBC, 1998–2010 (Cons. Chief Whip, 2006–07; Cabinet Mem. for Resources and Customer Services, 2007–08, for Community Safety and Cohesion, 2008–10). Mem., Sci. and Technol. Select Cttee, 2010–12. Mem. Exec., 1922 Cttee, 2010–12. Chm. Govs, Trinity Sch. Cons. Backbencher of the Year, Asian Voice, 2011. *Recreations:* sport, particularly football and tennis, military history, travel. *Address:* House of Commons, SW1A 0AA. *E:* gavin.barwell.mp@ parliament.uk.

**BATES,** Baron *cr* 2008 (Life Peer), of Langbaurgh in the County of North Yorkshire; **Michael Walton Bates;** PC 2015; Minister of State, Home Office, since 2015; *b* 26 May 1961; *s* of John Bates and Ruth Walton; *m* 1st, 1983, Carole Whitfield (marr. diss. 2008); two *s*; 2nd, 2012, Xuelin Li. *Educ:* Heathfield Sen. High Sch.; Gateshead Coll.; Wadham Coll., Oxford (MBA 1998). Young Conservatives: Mem., Nat. Adv. Cttee, 1984–87; Chm., Northern Area, 1984–87. Sen. Vice-Pres., later Dir of Consultancy and Res., 1998–2006, Sen. Advr, 2006–07, Oxford Analytica Inc.; Man. Dir, Walton Bates Associates Ltd, 2006–11. Director: estandardsforum.com Inc., 2001–07; Financial Standards Foundn (Bermuda) Ltd, 2001–03; non-executive Director: Congregational & General plc, 2001–06; Vardy Gp of Cos, 2006–10; non-exec. Chm., Scholes & Brown Asset Management, 2008–11. Assoc. Chm., Northern Area Develt Initiative, 1990–92. Contested (C): Tyne Bridge, 1987; Langbaurgh, Nov. 1991. MP (C) Langbaurgh, 1992–97; contested (C) Middlesbrough South and Cleveland East, 1997. PPS to Minister of State, DSS, 1992–93, NI Office, 1994; an Asst Govt Whip, 1994–95; a Lord Comr, HM Treasury, 1995–96; HM Paymaster Gen., 1996–97. Shadow Minister for Cabinet Office, Communities and Local Govt, Energy and Climate Change, Children, Schs and Families, 2009–10; Dep. Speaker, H of L, 2013; a Lord in Waiting (Govt Whip), 2013–14; Parly Under-Sec. of State, Home Office, 2014–15. Member: Select Cttee on Social Security, 1992; Select Cttee on Health, 1994. Dep. Chm., Cons. Party (North), 2007–10. Shell Fellow, Industry and Parlt Trust, 1997–. Mem., RIIA, 1998–2005. Member: Business Adv. Forum, Saïd Business Sch. (formerly Mem. Council, Sch. of Mgt Studies), Oxford Univ., 2000–10; Caux Round Table, 2001– (Trustee, 2006–08; Fellow, 2008–); European Ideas Network, 2002–05. Vice Chairman: Emmanuel Schs Foundn, 2009–10; Emmanuel Coll., 2008–10; King's Acad., 2008–10; Trinity Acad., 2008–10; Bede Acad., 2008–10. *Address:* House of Lords, SW1A 0PW. *E:* batesm@parliament.uk.

**BEBB, Guto ap Owain;** MP (C) Aberconwy, since 2010; *b* Wrexham, 9 Oct. 1968; *s* of Owain Bebb and Helen Gwyn; *m* 1993, Esyllt Penri;

three *s* two *d* (incl. twin *s*). *Educ:* Univ. of Wales, Aberystwyth (BA Hist. 1990). Founder, Partneriaeth Egin Partnership, econ. develt consultancy, 1993–2010. Business Develt Dir, Innovas Wales. Contested (C): Ogmore, Feb. 2002; Conwy, 2005. *Recreations:* reading, music. *Address:* House of Commons, SW1A 0AA. *T:* (020) 7219 7002. *E:* guto.bebb.mp@ parliament.uk.

**BECKETT, Rt Hon. Dame Margaret (Mary),** DBE 2013; PC 1993; MP (Lab) Derby South, since 1983; *b* 15 Jan. 1943; *d* of late Cyril and Winifred Jackson; *m* 1979, Lionel A. Beckett; two step *s*. *Educ:* Notre Dame High Sch., Norwich; Manchester Coll. of Sci. and Technol. Formerly: engrg apprentice (metallurgy), AEI, Manchester; exptl officer, Manchester Univ.; Labour Party res. asst, 1970–74; political adviser, Minister for Overseas Develt, 1974; Principal Researcher, Granada TV, 1979–83. Contested (Lab) Lincoln, Feb. 1974; MP (Lab) Lincoln, Oct. 1974–1979; PPS to Minister for Overseas Develt, 1974–75; Asst Govt Whip, 1975–76; Parly Under-Sec. of State, DES, 1976–79; Opposition front bench spokesman on health and social security, 1984–89; Mem., Shadow Cabinet, 1989–97; Shadow Chief Sec. to the Treasury, 1989–92; Shadow Leader, H of C, 1992–94; Campaigns Co-ordinator and Dep. Leader, Lab Party, 1992–94; Actg Leader, Lab Party, May–July 1994; opposition front bench spokesman on health, 1994–95, on trade and industry, 1995–97; Pres., BoT, and Sec. of State for Trade and Industry, 1997–98; Pres. of the Council and Leader, H of C, 1998–2001; Secretary of State: for Envmt, Food and Rural Affairs, 2001–06; for Foreign and Commonwealth Affairs, 2006–07; Minister of State (Minister for Housing and Planning), DCLG, 2008–09. Chair: Intelligence and Security Cttee, 2008; Jt Cttee on Nat. Security Strategy, 2011–. Mem. NEC, Labour Party, 1980–81, 1985–86, 1988–97. *Recreations:* cooking, reading, caravanning. *Address:* c/o House of Commons, SW1A 0AA.

**BELLINGHAM, Henry Campbell;** MP (C) North West Norfolk, 1983–97 and since 2001; *b* 29 March 1955; *s* of late Henry Bellingham; *m* 1993, Emma, *o d* of P. J. H. Whiteley and Lady Angela Whiteley. *Educ:* Eton; Magdalene Coll., Cambridge (BA 1977). Called to the Bar, Middle Temple, 1978; in practice as barrister, 1978–88. Dir of and consultant to companies, 1998–2010. Contested (C) Norfolk North West, 1997. PPS to Sec. of State for Transport, 1990–92, for Defence, 1992–95, for Foreign and Commonwealth Affairs, 1995–97; Opposition spokesman on Trade and Industry, and Shadow Minister for Small Businesses and Employment, 2002–05; Opposition Whip, 2005–06; Shadow Minister for Justice and Legal Services, 2006–10; Parly Under-Sec. of State (Minister for Africa, UN and Overseas Territories), FCO, 2010–12. Member: Select Cttee on the Environment, 1987–90; NI Select Cttee, 2001–02; Trade and Industry Select

Cttee, 2003–04. Chm., Cons. Council on Eastern Europe, 1989–94; officer, Cons. back bench cttees, 1983–90. *Address:* c/o House of Commons, SW1A 0AA. *Club:* White's.

**BENN, Rt Hon. Hilary (James Wedgwood);** PC 2003; MP (Lab) Leeds Central, since June 1999; *b* 26 Nov. 1953; *s* of Rt Hon. Tony Benn, PC; *m* 1st, 1973, Rosalind Caroline Retey (*d* 1979); 2nd, 1982, Sally Christina Clark; three *s* one *d*. *Educ:* Holland Park Comprehensive Sch.; Sussex Univ. (BA Hons Russian and East European Studies). Res. Asst, Nat. Referendum Campaign, 1975; Res. Officer, 1975–93, Head of Res., 1993–96, Head of Policy and Communications, 1996–97, ASTMS, then MSF; Jt Sec., Finance Panel, Labour Party Commn of Inquiry, on secondment, 1980; Special Advr to Sec. of State for Educn and Employment, 1997–99. MSF Rep., Labour Party Nat. Policy Forum, 1994–97; Chair: Educn Cttee, ALA, 1988–90; Unions 21, 1995–99; Member: Educn Cttee, AMA, 1986–90; Envmt Policy Commn, Labour Party, 1994–97; Party into Power Task Force on Labour Party's Democracy, 1996–97. Parliamentary Under-Secretary of State: DFID, 2001–02; Home Office, 2002–03; Minister of State, DFID, 2003; Secretary of State: for Internat. Develt, 2003–07; for Envmt, Food and Rural Affairs, 2007–10; Shadow Sec. of State for Envmt, Food and Rural Affairs, 2010; Shadow Leader, H of C, 2010–11; Shadow Sec. of State for Communities and Local Govt, 2011–15; Shadow Foreign Sec., 2015–. Member: Envmt, Transport and the Regions Select Cttee, 1999–2001; H of C Commn, 2010–11. Vice-Chair, PLP Educn and Employment Cttee, 2000–01; Mem., Sustainable Communities Policy Commn, Labour Party, 2007–; Pres., Acton CLP, 1979–82. Mem. (Lab) Ealing LBC, 1979–99 (Dep. Leader, 1986–90; Chair, Educn Cttee, 1986–90; Dep. Leader, Labour Gp, 1984–94). Vice-Chm., Commn for Africa, 2004–05. Contested (Lab) Ealing N, 1983, 1987. *Publications:* (contrib.) Beyond 2002: long-term policies for Labour, 1999; (contrib.) Men Who Made Labour, 2006. *Recreations:* watching sport, gardening. *Address:* House of Commons, SW1A 0AA.

**BENYON, Richard Henry Ronald;** MP (C) Newbury, since 2005; *b* 21 Oct. 1960; *s* of Sir William Richard Benyon; *m* 2004, Zoe Robinson; two *s*, and three *s* from previous marriage. *Educ:* Bradfield Coll.; Royal Agricl Coll. MRICS. Served Army, 1980–84: commnd RGJ; served NI and Far East. Land Agent, 1987–90; farmer, Englefield, Berks, 1990–; Chm., Englefield Estate Trust Corp. Ltd (Rural and Urban Land Hldgs), 2001–10. Parly Under Sec. of State, DEFRA, 2010–13. *Recreations:* walking, conservation, shooting, cooking. *Address:* House of Commons, SW1A 0AA. *Club:* Beefsteak.

**BERCOW, Rt Hon. John (Simon);** PC 2009; MP Buckingham; Speaker of the House of Commons, since June 2009; *b* 19 Jan. 1963; *s* of

late Charles Bercow and of Brenda Bercow (*née* Bailey); *m* 2002, Sally Illman; two *s* one *d*. *Educ:* Finchley Manorhill Sch.; Univ. of Essex (BA 1st Cl. Hons Govt 1985). Nat. Chm., Fedn of Cons. Students, 1986–87; Credit Analyst, Hambros Bank, 1987–88; Public Affairs Consultant, Sallingbury Casey, later Rowland Sallingbury Casey, 1988–95; Dir, Rowland Co., 1994–95; Special Adviser to: Chief Sec. to Treasury, 1995; Sec. of State for Nat. Heritage, 1995–96; free-lance consultant, 1996–97. Councillor (C), Lambeth BC, 1986–90 (Dep. Leader, Opposition Gp, 1987–89). Vice-Chm., Cons. Collegiate Forum, 1987. MP Buckingham, 1997– ((C) 1997–June 2009, when elected Speaker). Opposition spokesman: on educn and employment, 1999–2000; on home affairs, 2000–01; Shadow Chief Sec. to HM Treasury, 2001–02; Shadow Minister for Work and Pensions, 2002; Shadow Sec. of State for Internat. Develt, 2003–04. Member: Trade and Industry Select Cttee, 1998–99; Internat. Develt Select Cttee, 2004–09; Chairmen's Panel, 2005–09. Chair: (ex officio) H of C Commn, 2009–; Speaker's Cttee on Electoral Commn, 2009–; Speaker's Cttee for indep. Parly Standards Authy, 2009–; Speaker's Commn on Digital Democracy, 2014–. President: All-Party Parly Gp for America, 2009–; All-Party Parly Gp for Internet and Communications Technol., 2011–. Contested (C): Motherwell S, 1987; Bristol S, 1992. Leader, Review of Services for Children and Young People with Speech, Language and Communication Needs, 2007–08 (report published 2008). Pres., UK Br., CPA, 2009–; Hon. President: Hansard Soc. for Parly Govt, 2009–; IPU British Gp, 2009–. Co-Dir, Advanced Speaking and Campaigning Course, 1989–97. Chancellor, Bedfordshire Univ., 2014–. DUniv Essex, 2010; Hon. Dr of Laws: Buckingham, 2013; De Montfort, 2014; DSc City, 2014. Backbencher to Watch, Spectator Mag., 1998; Opposition MP of the Year, C4/Hansard Soc. Political Awards, 2005; Backbencher of the Year, House Mag., 2005; ePolitix/Dods Health Champion, 2006, Disability Champion, 2007, Internat. Champion, 2007; Politician of the Year, Stonewall Awards, 2010. *Publications:* Tennis Maestros, 2014. *Recreations:* tennis, swimming, reading, cinema. *Address:* Speaker's House, Westminster, SW1A 0AA.

**BERESFORD, Sir (Alexander) Paul,** Kt 1990; dental surgeon; MP (C) Mole Valley, since 1997 (Croydon Central, 1992–97); *b* 6 April 1946; *s* of Raymond and Joan Beresford; *m* Julie Haynes; three *s* one *d*. *Educ:* Richmond Primary Sch., Richmond, Nelson, NZ; Waimea Coll., Richmond; Otago Univ., Dunedin. Mem. (C), Wandsworth BC, 1978–94 (Leader of Council, 1983–92). Mem., Audit Commn, 1991–92. Parly Under-Sec. of State, DoE, 1994–97. *Address:* c/o House of Commons, SW1A 0AA.

**BERGER, Luciana Clare;** MP (Lab Co-op) Liverpool, Wavertree, since 2010; *b* Wembley, 13 May 1981. *Educ:* Haberdashers' Aske's Sch. for Girls, Elstree; Univ. of Birmingham (BCom); Birkbeck Coll., Univ. of London (MSc Govt). Govt Strategy Unit, Accenture, 2005–06; Govt and Parly Manager, NHS Confedn, 2006–07. Shadow Minister: for Energy and Climate Change, 2010–13; of Public Health, 2013–15; for Mental Health, 2015–. Dir, Labour Friends of Israel, 2007–10. FRSA. *Address:* House of Commons, SW1A 0AA.

**BERRY, James Jacob Gilchrist, (Jake);** MP (C) Rossendale and Darwen, since 2010; *b* Liverpool, 29 Dec. 1978; *s* of John David Gilchrist Berry and Ann Elizabeth Berry (*née* Curtis); *m* 2009, Charlotte Piroska Alexa. *Educ:* Liverpool Coll.; Sheffield Univ. (BA Hons); Coll. of Law, Chester. Admitted solicitor, 2003; Solicitor: Bremner Sons and Corlett, 2001–02; City Law Partnership, 2002–04; DWF Solicitors, 2004–07; Halliwells, 2007–10. PPS to Minister of State for Housing and Local Govt, 2010–12, to Minister without Portfolio, Cabinet Office, 2012–15, to Chief Secretary to the Treasury, 2015–. Mem., Downing Street Policy Unit, 2013–. Consultant Solicitor, Squire Sanders (UK) LLP, 2011–. *Recreations:* sailing, ski-ing, fishing. *Address:* House of Commons, SW1A 0AA. *E:* jake.berry.mp@parliament.uk. *Clubs:* Carlton; St James's (Manchester); Rawtenstall Conservative.

**BERRY, (Michael) James (Ellwood);** MP (C) Kingston and Surbiton, since 2015; *b* Canterbury, 4 Aug. 1983; *s* of Dr Michael Berry and Margaret Berry; *m* 2013, Nehali Shah. *Educ:* King's Sch., Canterbury; University Coll. London (LLB 1st Cl. Hons 2005); Harvard Law Sch. (LLM 2007). Called to the Bar, Lincoln's Inn, 2006; barrister, specialising in healthcare and police law. Associate, Coll. of Policing, 2014–. *Recreations:* walking, cooking. *Address:* House of Commons, SW1A 0AA. *E:* james.berry.mp@parliament.uk.

**BETTS, Clive James Charles;** MP (Lab) Sheffield South East, since 2010 (Sheffield Attercliffe, 1992–2010); *b* 13 Jan. 1950; *s* of late Harold and Nellie Betts. *Educ:* Longley Sch., Sheffield; King Edward VII Sch., Sheffield; Pembroke Coll., Cambridge (BA Econ). Sheffield City Council: Councillor (Lab), 1976–92; Chm., Housing Cttee, 1980–86; Chm., Finance Cttee, 1986–88; Dep. Leader, 1986–87; Leader, 1987–92. Chm., S Yorks Pension Authority, 1989–92; Dep. Chm., AMA, 1988–91 (Chm., Housing Cttee, 1985–89). An Asst Government Whip, 1997–98; a Lord Comr of HM Treasury (Govt Whip), 1998–2001. Member, Select Committee on: HM Treasury, 1995–96; Selection, 1997–2001; Transport, Local Govt and the Regions, 2001–02; DCLG (formerly ODPM), 2002– (Chm., 2010–); Finance and Services, 2005–. Member: Parly Contributory Pension Fund, 2005–; H of C Members' Fund, 2005–. Chm., 1995–96, Sec., 1995–97, Labour's

Treasury Deptl Cttee; Labour Ldr's Campaign Team, 1995–96. *Recreations:* Sheffield Wednesday FC, football, squash, walking, real ale. *Address:* House of Commons, SW1A 0AA.

**BINGHAM, Andrew Russell;** MP (C) High Peak, since 2010; *b* Buxton, 23 June 1962; *s* of late Anthony Russell Bingham and of Mary Dorothea Bingham; *m* 1986, Jayne Elizabeth Dranfield. *Educ:* Long Lane Sec. Sch., Chapel-en-le-Frith; High Peak Coll. of Further Educn. Company Dir, A.R.B. Sales Ltd, 1983–2004. Mem. (C) High Peak BC, 1999– (Chm., Social Inclusion Cttee, 2003–07). Contested (C) High Peak, 2005. *Recreations:* cricket, football, cooking. *Address:* House of Commons, SW1A 0AA. *T:* (020) 7219 7086. *E:* andrew.bingham.mp@parliament.uk.

**BLACK, Mhairi;** MP (SNP) Paisley and Renfrewshire South, since 2015; *b* Paisley, 1994; *d* of Alan Black. *Educ:* Univ. of Glasgow (BA 1st Cl. Hons Politics 2015). *Address:* House of Commons, SW1A 0AA.

**BLACKFORD, Ian;** MP (SNP) Ross, Skye and Lochaber, since 2015; *b* Edinburgh, 1961; *m* Ann. *Educ:* Royal High Sch., Edinburgh. Dir, UBS Philips and Drew, 1989–93; Man. Dir, Nat West Mkts, 1993–99; Man. Dir, Deutsche Bank, 1999–2003; Man. Dir, First Seer, 2003–; Hd, Investor Relns, CSM, 2005–12. Non-executive Director: Edinburgh Bicycle Cooperative, 2008–13; Commsworld, 2006– (Chm., 2014–). Chm., NW Skye Recreational Assoc. Dir, Cuillin FM (community radio stn). Mem. Bd, Golden Charter Trust, 2008–. Contested (SNP): Ayr, 1997; Paisley, Nov. 1997. *Address:* House of Commons, SW1A 0AA.

**BLACKMAN, Kirsty;** MP (SNP) Aberdeen North, since 2015; *b* Aberdeen; *m* Luke Blackman; one *s* one *d*. *Educ:* Robert Gordon's Coll. Adminr, Planning Dept, Aberdeen Council. Mem. (SNP) Aberdeen CC, 2007–15. *Address:* House of Commons, SW1A 0AA.

**BLACKMAN, Robert;** MP (C) Harrow East, since 2010; *b* 26 April 1956; *m* 1988, Nicola Jennings. *Educ:* Univ. of Liverpool (BSc). Sales trng, 1991–98, Regulatory Compliance Manager, 1998–2010, BT. Mem. (C) Brent BC, 1986–2010 (Leader, 1991–96; Dep. Leader, 2006–10). Mem. (C) Brent and Harrow, London Assembly, GLA, 2004–08. Contested (C): Brent S, 1992; Bedford, 1997; Brent N, 2005. *Address:* House of Commons, SW1A 0AA.

**BLACKMAN-WOODS, Roberta C.,** PhD; MP (Lab) City of Durham, since 2005; *b* 16 Aug. 1957; *d* of Charles and Eleanor Woods; *m* Prof. Timothy J. Blackman; one *d*. *Educ:* Univ. of Ulster (BSc Combined Soc. Scis 1979; PhD 1989). Welfare Rights Officer, Newcastle CC, 1982–85; Lectr in Social Policy, Univ. of Ulster, then Univ. of Newcastle upon Tyne, 1985–95; Dean of Social and Labour Studies, Ruskin Coll., Oxford, 1995–2000; Prof. of Social Policy and

Dep. Dean, Sch. of Arts and Social Scis, Univ. of Northumbria, 2000–05. Mem., Child Poverty Action Gp. PPS to Minister of State for Innovation, Univs and Skills, 2008–10; Asst Regl Minister for NE; Shadow Minister: Cabinet Office, 2010–11; BIS, 2010–11; DCLG, 2011–15. Chair, Parly Gp, 2011–; Vice Chair, All Party Parly Gp on Sch. Food, 2010–. *Recreation:* music. *Address:* (office) The Miners' Hall, Redhills, Durham DH1 4BD. *T:* (0191) 374 1915, *Fax:* (0191) 374 1916. *E:* mail@roberta.org.uk; House of Commons, SW1A 0AA.

**BLACKWOOD, Nicola;** MP (C) Oxford West and Abingdon, since 2010; *b* Johannesburg, 1979. *Educ:* home schooled; Trinity Coll. of Music; St Anne's Coll., Oxford (BA 1st Cl. Music); Emmanuel Coll., Cambridge (MPhil Musicology). Political Unit, Cons. Res. Dept, Gen. Election, 2005; Parly researcher to Andrew Mitchell, MP, 2007; PPS to Minister for Skills and Enterprise, 2013–14, for Energy, 2014–15. Mem., Home Affairs Select Cttee, 2010–15; Chm., Sci. and Technol. Select Cttee, 2015–; Chair, All Party Gp on Women, Peace and Security, 2010–. Vice Chm., Cons. Party, 2010–13. *Address:* House of Commons, SW1A 0AA.

**BLENKINSOP, Thomas Francis;** MP (Lab) Middlesbrough South and East Cleveland, since 2010; *b* Middlesbrough, 14 Aug. 1980; *s* of William Blenkinsop and Barbara Blenkinsop; *m* 2007, Victoria Emtage. *Educ:* Teesside Univ. (BSc PPE); Warwick Univ. (MA Continental Philos.). Constituency Researcher for Dr Ashok Kumar, MP, 2002–08; full-time Regl Official, Community Trade Union, 2008–10. An Opposition Whip, 2011–. *Recreation:* football (playing and watching Middlesbrough Football Club). *Address:* (office) Harry Tout House, 8 Wilson Street, Guisborough TS14 6NA. *T:* (01287) 610878. *E:* info@tomblenkinsop.com.

**BLOMFIELD, Paul;** MP (Lab) Sheffield Central, since 2010; *b* Chatham, Kent, 25 Aug. 1953; *s* of Henry and Mabel Blomfield; *m* 2000, Linda McAvan; one *s* by a previous marriage. *Educ:* Abbeydale Boys' Grammar Sch.; Tadcaster Grammar Sch.; St John's Coll., York (Cert Ed). Mem., NEC and Vice-Pres., NUS, 1976–78. Various roles, Sheffield Univ., 1978–2003; Gen. Manager, Sheffield Univ. Students' Union, 2003–10. Mem. Bd, Sheffield City Trust, 1994–2008 (Chair, 1997–2008). Gov., Sheffield City Poly., 1982–92. Chm., Sheffield Lab Party, 1993–2008. Mem., Exec. Cttee, Anti-Apartheid Movement, 1978–94. *Recreations:* walking, cycling, watching Sheffield United. *Address:* House of Commons, SW1A 0AA. *E:* paul.blomfield.mp@parliament.uk; Unit 4, Edmund Road Business Centre, 135 Edmund Road, Sheffield S2 4ED. *T:* (0114) 272 2882, *Fax:* (0114) 272 2442.

**BLUNT, Crispin Jeremy Rupert;** MP (C) Reigate, since 1997; *b* 15 July 1960; *s* of Maj. Gen. Peter Blunt, CB, MBE, GM and Adrienne (*née* Richardson); *m* 1990, Victoria Ainsley Jenkins (separated 2010); one *s* one *d*. *Educ:* Wellington Coll.; RMA, Sandhurst; Durham Univ. (BA 1984); Cranfield Inst. of Technology (MBA 1991). Commnd, 13th/18th Royal Hussars (QMO), 1980; Troop Leader: UK and Cyprus, 1980–81; BAOR, 1984–85; Regtl Signals Officer/Ops Officer, BAOR/UK, 1985–87; Sqn Leader, 2IC UK, 1987–89; resigned commn, 1990; Rep., Forum of Private Business, 1991–92; Consultant, Politics Internat., 1993; Special Advr to Sec. of State for Defence, 1993–95, to Foreign Sec., 1995–97. Opposition spokesman on NI, 2001–02, on trade, energy and science, 2002–03; on security and counter terrorism, 2009–10; Opposition Whip, 2004–09; Parly Under-Sec. of State, MoJ, 2010–12. Member: Select Cttee on Defence, 1997–2000, 2003–04; Select Cttee on Envmt, Transport and the Regions, 2000–01; Chm., Select Cttee on Foreign Affairs, 2015–. Sec., Cons. Foreign and Commonwealth Affairs Cttee, 1997–2001; Chm., Cons. Middle East Council, 2004–08. Co-Chm., Council for Advancement of Arab-British Understanding, 2004–09. *Recreations:* cricket, skiing, bridge, gardening. *Address:* House of Commons, SW1A 0AA. *T:* (020) 7219 2254. *Clubs:* MCC; Reigate Priory Cricket.

**BOLES, Nicholas Edward Coleridge;** MP (C) Grantham and Stamford, since 2010; Minister of State, Department for Business, Innovation and Skills and Department for Education, since 2014; *b* 2 Nov. 1965; *s* of Sir John Dennis, (Sir Jack), Boles, MBE. *Educ:* Winchester; Magdalen Coll., Oxford (BA PPE); John F. Kennedy Sch. of Govt, Harvard Univ. (MPP 1989). Founder, 1995, Chief Exec., 1995–2000, non-exec. Chm., 2000–08, Longwall Hldgs Ltd. Founder and Dir, Policy Exchange, 2002–07; COS to Mayor of London, 2008. Mem. (C) Westminster CC, 1998–2002 (Chm., Housing Cttee, 1999–2001). Contested (C) Hove, 2005. PPS to Minister of State, DfE, 2010–12; Parly Under-Sec. of State (Minister for Planning), DCLG, 2012–14. Sen. Fellow, Inst. for Govt, 2010–12. *Publications:* Which Way's Up?: the future for coalition Britain and how to get there, 2010. *Address:* House of Commons, SW1A 0AA.

**BONE, Peter William,** FCA; MP (C) Wellingborough, since 2005; *b* 19 Oct. 1952; *m* 1981, Jeanette Sweeney; two *s* one *d*. *Educ:* Westcliff-on-Sea Grammar Sch. FCA 1976. Financial Dir, Essex Electronics and Precision Engrg Gp, 1977–83; Chief Exec., High Tech Electronics Co., 1983–90; Man. Dir, Palm Travel (West) Ltd, 1990–2002. Mem. (C), Southend-on-Sea BC, 1977–86. Contested (C): Islwyn, 1992; Pudsey, 1997; Wellingborough, 2001. *Address:* House of Commons, SW1A 0AA; (office) 21 High Street, Wellingborough, Northants NN8 4JZ.

**BORWICK, Lady; Victoria Lorne Peta Borwick;** MP (C) Kensington, since 2015; Member (C), London Assembly, Greater London Authority, since 2008; *b* London, 26 April 1956; *d* of late R. Dennis and Peta Poore; *m* 1981, Geoffrey Robert James Borwick (Baron Borwick); three *s* one *d*. *Educ:* Wispers Sch. Dir, Clarion Events, 1976–2002; Dir, Treasurer's Dept, Conservative Central Office, 2002–04; Commercial Dir, ACI, 2004–06; Mem., Adv. Council, Open Europe, 2007–. Mem. (C), RBK&C Council, 2002–. Greater London Authority: Member: Transport Cttee, 2008–; Police and Crime Cttee, 2012–; Chm., Health Cttee, 2011–12; Dep. Mayor of London, 2012–15; Chm., Civil Liberties Panel, Metropolitan Police Authy, 2009–12. Gov., Golborne Children's Centre (formerly Ainsworth Nursery Sch.), 1990–. Trustee, Federated Foundn, 1985–. FRSA 1989. Freeman, City of London, 1999; Liveryman, Clockmakers' Co., 2000. *Publications:* The Cost of the London Mayor, 2007; Streets Ahead: relieving congestion on Oxford Street, Regent Street and Bond Street, 2010; Responding to G20, 2010. *Recreations:* making fudge, ski-ing, tennis. *Address:* 33 Phillimore Gardens, W8 7QG. *T:* (020) 7376 9262, *Fax:* (020) 7937 2656; House of Commons, SW1A 0AA. *E:* cllr.borwick@rbkc.gov.uk.

**BOSWELL, Philip John;** MP (SNP) Coatbridge, Chryston and Bellshill, since 2015; *b* Bellshill, 23 July 1963; *s* of Peter and Joan Boswell; *m* Anne; one *s* two *d*. *Educ:* Glasgow Caledonian Univ. (BSc Quantity Surveying 1989); Univ. of Reading (Dip. Arbitration 2007). FCIArb 2007. Sen. Contracts Engr, Qatar Petroleum, 2003–06; Sen. Contracts Engr and Project Services Engr, 2006–08, Lead Contracts Engr, 2008–11, BP; Contracts and Procurement Specialist, Shell, 2011–14; Contracts Engr, Premier Oil, 2014–15. *Recreations:* family, music, cycling, walking, reading. *Address:* House of Commons, SW1A 0AA. *E:* phil.boswell.mp@parliament.uk.

**BOTTOMLEY, Sir Peter (James),** Kt 2011; MP (C) Worthing West, since 1997 (Greenwich, Woolwich West, June 1975–1983, Eltham, 1983–97); *b* 30 July 1944; *er s* of Sir James Reginald Alfred Bottomley, KCMG; *m* 1967, Virginia Garnett (Baroness Bottomley of Nettlestone); one *s* two *d*. *Educ:* comprehensive sch.; Westminster Sch.; Trinity Coll., Cambridge (MA). Driving, industrial sales, industrial relations, industrial economics. Contested (C) GLC elect., Vauxhall, 1973; (C) Woolwich West, gen. elecns, 1974. PPS to Minister of State, FCO, 1982–83, to Sec. of State for Social Services, 1983–84, to Sec. of State for NI, 1990; Parly Under Sec. of State, Dept of Employment, 1984–86, Dept of Transport, 1986–89, NI Office, 1989–90. Member: Transport Cttee, 1992–97; Ecclesiastical Cttee, 2002–05, 2010–15; Select Cttee on HS2. Sec., Cons. Parly For. and Commonwealth Cttee, 1979–81; Leader, UK Delegn to Parly Assembly, OSCE, 2010–. Pres.,

Cons. Trade Unionists, 1978–80; Vice-Pres., Fedn of Cons. Students, 1980–82. Chairman: British Union of Family Orgns, 1973–80; Family Forum, 1980–82; Church of England Children's Soc., 1983–84. Member Council: MIND, 1981–82; NACRO, 1997–2004; Trustee, Christian Aid, 1978–84. Parly Swimming Champion, 1980–81, 1984–86; Captain, Parly Football Team; occasional Parly Dinghy Sailing Champion; Parly Warden, St Margaret's Church, Westminster, 2010–. Mem., Ct of Assts, Drapers' Co. Castrol/Inst. of Motor Industry Road Safety Gold Medal, 1988. *Recreations:* children, book reviewing, canoeing. *Address:* House of Commons, SW1A 0AA. *E:* bottomleyp@parliament.uk.

**BOURNE OF ABERYSTWYTH, Baron** *cr* 2013 (Life Peer), of Aberystwyth in the County of Ceredigion and of Wethersfield in the County of Essex; **Nicholas Henry Bourne;** a Lord in Waiting (Government Whip), since 2014; Parliamentary Under-Secretary of State, Department for Energy and Climate Change and Wales Office, since 2015; *b* 1 Jan. 1952; *s* of late John Morgan Bourne and Joan Edith Mary Bourne. *Educ:* King Edward VI Sch., Chelmsford; UCW, Aberystwyth (LLB 1st Cl. Hons; LLM 1976); Trinity Coll., Cambridge (LLM). Called to the Bar, Gray's Inn, 1976. Supervisor in Law: Corpus Christi Coll., Cambridge, 1974–80; St Catharine's Coll., Cambridge, 1974–82; LSE, 1975–77; Principal, Chart Univ. Tutors Ltd, 1979–88; Co. Sec. and Dir, Chart Foulks Lynch plc, 1984–88; Dir, Holborn Gp Ltd, 1988–91; Swansea Institute: Prof. of Law, 1991–96; Dean of Law, 1992–96; Asst Principal, 1996–98. Lectr in Co. Law, Univ. of London Ext. Degree Prog. at UCL, 1991–96; Sen. Lectr in Law, South Bank Univ., 1991–92; Vis. Lectr, Hong Kong Univ., 1996–2008. Member: Editl Bd, Malaysian Law News, 1991–2008; Editl Adv. Bd, Business Law Rev., 1991–. Member: NE Thames RHA, 1990–92; W Glamorgan HA, 1994–97; Doctors' and Dentists' Review Body, 1998–99. Mem. (C) Mid and W Wales, and Leader of Conservatives, Nat. Assembly for Wales, 1999–2011; contested (C) same seat, 2011. Mem., Delegated Powers and Regulatory Reform Cttee, H of L, 2014. *Publications:* Duties and Responsibilities of British Company Directors, 1982; British Company Law and Practice, 1983; Business Law for Accountants, 1987; Lecture Notes for Company Law, 1993, 3rd edn 1998; Essential Company Law, 1994, 2nd edn 1997; Business Law and Practice, 1994; (with B. Pillans) Scottish Company Law, 1996, 2nd edn 1999; Bourne on Company Law, 1993, 6th edn 2013; contrib. to business and co. law jls. *Recreations:* walking, tennis, badminton, squash, theatre, cricket, travel, cinema. *Address:* House of Lords, SW1A 0PW. *Club:* Oxford and Cambridge.

**BRADLEY, Karen Anne;** MP (C) Staffordshire Moorlands, since 2010; Parliamentary Under-Secretary of State, Home Office, since 2014; *b*

Newcastle-under-Lyme, 12 March 1970; *d* of Kenneth and Olive Howarth; *m* 2001, Neil Austin Bradley; two *s. Educ:* Buxton Girls' Sch., Derbys; Imperial Coll., London (BSc Hons Maths). Tax Manager, Deloitte & Touche (formerly Touche Ross), 1991–98; Sen. Tax Manager, KPMG, 1998–2004; self-employed fiscal and economic consultant, 2004–07; Sen. Tax Manager, KPMG, 2007–10. An Asst Govt Whip, 2012–13; a Lord Comr of HM Treasury (Govt Whip), 2013–14. Associate Mem., ICAEW, 1995; Mem., Chartered Inst. of Taxation, 1996. *Recreations:* travel, wine tasting, cooking, puzzles. *Address:* House of Commons, SW1A 0AA. *T:* (020) 7219 7215. *E:* karen.bradley.mp@parliament.uk.

**BRADSHAW, Rt Hon. Benjamin (Peter James);** PC 2009; MP (Lab) Exeter, since 1997; *b* 30 Aug. 1960; *s* of late Canon Peter Bradshaw and Daphne Bradshaw (*née* Murphy); civil partnership 2006, Neal Thomas Dalgleish. *Educ:* Thorpe St Andrew Sch., Norwich; Univ. of Sussex (BA Hons). Reporter: Express and Echo, Exeter, 1984–85; Eastern Daily Press, Norwich, 1985–86; BBC Radio Devon, Exeter, 1986–89; BBC Radio Corresp., Berlin, 1989–91; reporter, World At One and World This Weekend, BBC Radio 4, 1991–97. Parly Under-Sec. of State, FCO, 2001–02; Parly Sec., Privy Council Office, 2002–03; Parly Under-Sec. of State, 2003–06; Minister of State, 2006–07, DEFRA; Minister of State, DoH, 2007–09; Minister for the SW, 2007–09; Sec. of State for Culture, Media and Sport, 2009–10; Shadow Sec. of State for Culture, Media and Sport, 2010. Member: European Legislation Select Cttee, 1997–2001; Ecclesiastical Cttee, 1997–2001, 2010–15; Culture, Media and Sport Select Cttee, 2012–15. Member: Christians on the Left (formerly Christian Socialist Movement), 1997–; Lab. Campaign for Electoral Reform, 1997–. Mem., Inst. of Internat. and Foreign Affairs. Consumer Journalist of Year, Argos, 1988; Journalist of Year, Anglo-German Foundn, 1990; Sony News Reporter Award, 1993. *Recreations:* cycling, walking in Devon, classical music, cooking, gardening. *Address:* House of Commons, SW1A 0AA. *T:* (020) 7219 6597, (constituency office) (01392) 424464. *Club:* Whipton Labour (Exeter).

**BRADY, Graham Stuart;** MP (C) Altrincham and Sale West, since 1997; *b* 20 May 1967; *s* of John Brady and Maureen Brady (*née* Birch); *m* 1992, Victoria Anne Lowther; one *s* one *d. Educ:* Altrincham Grammar Sch.; Univ. of Durham (BA Hons Law 1989); Chm., Durham Univ. Cons. Assoc., 1987; Chm., Northern Area Cons. Collegiate Forum, 1987–89. Shandwick plc, 1989–90; Centre for Policy Studies, 1990–92; Public Affairs Dir, Waterfront Partnership, 1992–97; PPS to Chm. Cons. Party, 1999–2000; an Opposition Whip, 2000; Opposition frontbench spokesman on educn and employment, 2000–01, on educn, 2001–03; PPS to Leader of the Opposition, 2003–04; Shadow

Minister for Europe, 2004–07. Member: Educn and Employment Select Cttee, 1997–2001; Treasury Select Cttee, 2007–10; Select Cttee on Parly Reform, 2009–10; Jt Chm., All Party Railfreight Gp, 1998–99; Vice-Chm., All Party Gp on Advertising, 1999–2008. Sec., Cons. backbench Educn and Employment Cttee, 1997–2000; Chm., 1922 Cttee, 2010– (Mem. Exec., 1998–2000, 2007–10). Vice-Chm., E Berks Cons. Assoc., 1992–95. Patron, Counselling and Family Centre (formerly Family Contact Line), 2006–; Vice Patron, Friends of Rosie, 1997–; Trustee, Jubilee Centre, 2008–. Associate: GMC, 2011–12; Medical Practitioners' Tribunal Service, 2012–. Vice Pres., Gtr Altrincham Chamber of Commerce, 1997–. Ind. Gov., Manchester Metropolitan Univ., 2008–11. *Recreations:* family, friends, garden. *Address:* House of Commons, SW1A 0AA.

**BRADY, Mickey;** MP (SF) Newry and Armagh, since 2015; *b* Ballybot, Newry. Project Manager and worker, Newry Welfare Rights Centre. Mem. (SF) Newry and Armagh, NI Assembly, 2007–15. Mem. Bd, Confederation of Community Gps. Gov., Abbey Primary Sch. *Address:* (office) 1 Kilmorey Terrace, Patrick Street, Ballinlare, Newry BT35 8DW.

**BRAKE, Rt Hon. Thomas (Anthony);** PC 2011; MP (Lib Dem) Carshalton and Wallington, since 1997; *b* 6 May 1962; *s* of Michael and Judy Brake; *m* 1998, Candida Goulden; one *s* one *d. Educ:* Imperial Coll., London (BSc Hons Physics); Lycée International, France (Internat. Baccalauréat). Formerly Principal Consultant, Cap Gemini, (IT services). Lib Dem spokesman: on envmt, 1997–2001; on transport, local govt and the regions, 2001–02; on transport and London, 2002–03; on internat. develt, 2003–05; on transport, 2005–06; on local govt, 2006–07; on the Olympics, 2007–10; on London, 2007–10; on foreign affairs, 2015–; a Lib Dem Whip, 2000–01; Parly Sec. (Dep. Leader), Office of the Leader of the H of C, 2012–15; an Asst Govt Whip, 2014–15; Lib Dem Chief Whip, 2015–. Mem., Select Cttee on Transport, 2002–03. Mem., Accommodation and Works Cttee, H of C, 2001–02; Co-Chair, Lib Dem backbench cttee on Home Affairs, Justice and Equalities, 2010– (Lib Dem spokesman on home affairs, 2008–10). *Publications:* (jtly) Costing the Earth, 1991. *Recreations:* running, swimming, cycling. *Address:* House of Commons, SW1A 0AA.

**BRAZIER, Julian William Hendy,** TD; MP (C) Canterbury, since 1987; Parliamentary Under-Secretary of State, Ministry of Defence, since 2014; *b* 24 July 1953; *s* of Lt-Col P. H. Brazier; *m* 1984, Katharine Elizabeth, *d* of Brig. P. M. Blagden; three *s* (incl. twins). *Educ:* Wellington Coll.; Brasenose Coll., Oxford (schol. in maths; MA); London Business Sch. Chm., Oxford Univ. Cons. Assoc., 1974. Charter Consolidated, 1975–84, Sec., Exec. Cttee of Bd, 1981–84; management consultant to industry, H.

B. Maynard, internat. management consultants, 1984–87. Contested (C) Berwick-upon-Tweed, 1983. PPS to Minister of State, HM Treasury, 1990–92, to Sec. of State for Employment, 1992–93; an Opposition Whip, 2001–02; Opposition front bench spokesman: for work and pensions, 2002–03; for internat. develt and overseas trade, 2004–05; for transport (aviation and shipping), 2005–10. Mem., Defence Select Cttee, 1997–2001 and 2010–14; Chm.; All-Party Reserves and Cadets Gp, 2008–14; Co-Chm., All-Party Ports and Maritime Gp, 2010–14; Vice Chm., Cons. Backbench Defence Cttee, 1993–97; Sec., Cons. Backbench Finance Cttee, 1990. Vice-Chm., Ind. Commn on Reserve Forces, 2010–11. Served 13 yrs as an officer in TA, incl. 5 yrs with 21 SAS. *Publications:* pamphlets on defence, economic policy, social security and family issues. *Recreations:* science, philosophy, cross-country running. *Address:* House of Commons, SW1A 0AA.

**BRENNAN, Kevin Denis;** MP (Lab) Cardiff West, since 2001; *b* 16 Oct. 1959; *s* of Michael John Brennan and Beryl Marie Brennan (*née* Evans); *m* 1988, Amy Lynn Wack; one *d*. *Educ:* St Alban's RC Comprehensive Sch., Pontypool; Pembroke Coll., Oxford (BA); UC, Cardiff (PGCE); Univ. of Glamorgan (MSc). Volunteer organiser/news ed., Cwmbran Community Press, 1982–84; Hd, Econs and Business Studies, Radyr Comprehensive Sch., 1985–94; Res. Officer for Rhodri Morgan, MP, 1995–2000; Special Advr to First Minister, Nat. Assembly for Wales, 2000. An Asst Govt Whip, 2005–06; a Lord Comr of HM Treasury (Govt Whip), 2006–07; Parly Under-Sec. of State, DCSF, 2007–08; Parly Sec. and Minister for the Third Sector, Cabinet Office, 2008–09; Minister for E Midlands, 2008–10; Minister of State, BIS and DCSF, 2009–10. *Recreations:* Rugby (watching now), music (Mem., parly rock gp MP4). *Address:* House of Commons, SW1A 0AA; 33–35 Cathedral Road, Riverside, Cardiff CF11 9HB. *Club:* Canton Labour (Cardiff).

**BRIDGEN, Andrew;** MP (C) North West Leicestershire, since 2010; *b* Burton upon Trent, Staffs, 28 Oct. 1964; *s* of Alan and Ann Bridgen; *m* 2000, Jacqueline Cremin (marr. diss. 2014); two *s*. *Educ:* Pingle Sch., Swadlincote; Nottingham Univ. (BSc Biol Scis 1986). Officer trng, RM, 1987–88; Officer, Staffords (TA), 1989–91. Non-exec. Chm., AB Produce plc, 2010–14 (Man. Dir, 1988–2010). Business Mem., E Midlands Regl Assembly, 1999–2000. Mem., Regulatory Reform Select Cttee, 2010–15. *Address:* House of Commons, SW1A 0AA.

**BRIDGES OF HEADLEY,** Baron *cr* 2015 (Life Peer), of Headley Heath in the County of Surrey; **James George Robert Bridges,** MBE 1997; Parliamentary Secretary, Cabinet Office, since 2015; *b* Wimbledon, 15 July 1970; *s* of late Hon. Robert Oliver Bridges, *s* of 1st Baron Bridges, and

of (Rosamund) Theresa Bridges; *m* 2007, Alice Mary Hickman; one *s* two *d* (incl. twin *s* and *d*). *Educ:* Eton Coll.; Exeter Coll., Oxford (Stapledon Schol.; MA 1st cl. Hist.); Fels Center of Govt, Univ. of Pennsylvania (Thouron Schol.). Cons. Res. Dept, 1992–93; Asst Pol Sec. to Prime Minister, 1994–97; Dir of Communications, British Digital Broadcasting, 1997–98; leader writer, The Times, 1998–2000; Consultant, Quiller Consultants, 2000–04; Chm., Cons. Res. Dept, 2004–05; Campaign Dir, Cons. Party, 2006–07; Consultant, Quiller Consultants, 2007–09; Campaign Co-ordinator, Cons. Party, 2010; Chief Exec., Quiller Consultants, 2010–13; Sen. Advr to Gp Exec. Chm., Santander, 2014–15. Mem. Bd, Centre for Policy Studies, 2007–. Trustee, Foundation Years Trust, 2014–. *Recreations:* family, walking, history. *Clubs:* Beefsteak, White's.

**BRINE, Stephen Charles;** MP (C) Winchester, since 2010; *b* 28 Jan. 1974; *s* of Clive Charles Brine and late Gloria Elizabeth Brine; *m* 2003, Susie Toulson; one *s* one *d*. *Educ:* Bohunt Comprehensive Sch.; Highbury Coll., Portsmouth; Liverpool Hope UC (BA Hist. Liverpool Univ. 1997). Journalist: BBC Radio Surrey; BBC Southern Counties Radio; WGN Radio, Chicago; work in consultancy firm specialising in customer care; former Dir, Azalea Gp. Area Campaign Dir, Hants and IoW, Cons. Party, 2001–05. *Address:* House of Commons, SW1A 0AA.

**BROCK, Deidre Leanne;** MP (SNP) Edinburgh North and Leith, since 2015; *b* Western Australia; partner, Dougie; two *d*. *Educ:* John Curtin Univ. (BA English); WA Acad. of Performing Arts. Manager, office of Rob Gibson, MSP. Mem. (SNP) Edinburgh CC, 2007–15; Depute Lord Provost of Edinburgh, until 2015. Member, Board: Edinburgh Internat. Fest. Council; Centre for the Moving Image; Creative Edinburgh. *Address:* House of Commons, SW1A 0AA.

**BROKENSHIRE, Rt Hon. James (Peter);** PC 2015; MP (C) Old Bexley and Sidcup, since 2010 (Hornchurch, 2005–10); Minister of State (Minister for Immigration), Home Office, since 2014; *b* 8 Jan. 1968; *m* 1999, Cathrine Anne Mamelok; one *s* two *d*. *Educ:* Davenant Foundn Grammar Sch.; Cambridge Centre for Sixth Form Studies; Univ. of Exeter (LLB). Solicitor with Jones Day Gouldens, 1991–2005. Opposition front bench spokesman on home affairs, 2006–10. Parly Under-Sec. of State, Home Office, 2010–14. *Address:* House of Commons, SW1A 0AA.

**BROWN, Alan;** MP (SNP) Kilmarnock and Loudoun, since 2015; *b* Newmilns, 12 Aug. 1970; *s* of Eric and Irene Brown; *m* 2007, Cyndi Aukerman; two *s*. *Educ:* Loudoun Acad.; Glasgow Univ. (BEng Hons). Engineer: West of Scotland Water, then Strathclyde Regl Council, later

Scottish Water, 1993–2007; Grontmij, 2007–15. Mem. (SNP), E Ayrshire Council, 2007–15. *Address:* House of Commons, SW1A 0AA.

**BROWN, Lyn Carol;** MP (Lab) West Ham, since 2005; *b* 13 April 1960; *m* 2008, John Cullen. *Educ:* Univ. of London (BA). Residential Social Worker, Ealing, 1984–85, Newham, 1985–87, Waltham Forest, 1988–2005. Mem. (Lab) Newham BC, 1988–2005. Founder and Chm., London Libraries Develt Agency, 2000–06. Contested (Lab) Wanstead and Woodford, 1992. An Asst Govt Whip, 2009–10; an Opposition Whip, 2010–13; Shadow Fire and Communities Minister, 2013–15. *Address:* House of Commons, SW1A 0AA.

**BROWN, Rt Hon. Nicholas (Hugh);** PC 1997; MP (Lab) Newcastle upon Tyne East, since 2010 (Newcastle upon Tyne East, 1983–97; Newcastle upon Tyne East and Wallsend, 1997–2010); *b* 13 June 1950; *s* of late R. C. Brown and G. K. Brown (*née* Tester). *Educ:* Swattenden Secondary Modern Sch.; Tunbridge Wells Tech. High Sch.; Manchester Univ. (BA 1971). Trade Union Officer, GMWU Northern Region, 1978–83. Mem., Newcastle upon Tyne City Council, 1980–84. Opposition front-bench spokesman: on legal affairs, 1984–87; on Treasury affairs, 1987–94; on health, 1994–95; Dep. Chief Opposition Whip, 1995–97; Parly Sec. to HM Treasury (Govt Chief Whip), 1997–98 and 2008–10; Minister, Agriculture, Fisheries and Food, 1998–2001; Minister of State (Minister for Work), DWP, 2001–03; Treasurer of HM Household (Dep. Chief Whip), 2007–08; Minister for NE of England, 2007–10; Shadow Parly Sec. to HM Treasury (Govt Chief Whip), 2010. Freeman, City of Newcastle, 2001. *Address:* House of Commons, SW1A 0AA. *Clubs:* Shieldfield Working Men's, West Walker Social, Newcastle Labour (Newcastle); Lindisfarne (Wallsend).

**BRUCE, Fiona Claire;** MP (C) Congleton, since 2010; *b* Wick, 26 March 1957; *d* of Allan Stewart Riley and late Greta Riley (*née* Scott); *m* 1990, Richard John Bruce; two *s. Educ:* Burnley High Sch.; Howell's Sch., Llandaff; Manchester Univ. (LLB); Chester Law Coll. (LLB). Admitted solicitor, 1981; Founder and Sen. Partner, Fiona Bruce & Co. LLP, 1988–. Mem. (C) Warrington BC, 2004–10 (Exec. Mem. for Value for Money and Finance, 2006–09). Contested (C) Warrington S, 2005. Mem., Internat. Develt Select Cttee, 2012–; Vice Chm., All Party Parly Dying Well Gp, 2012–15; Chairman: All Party Parly ProLife Gp, 2013–; All Party Parly Gp Supporting Couple Relationships, 2014–; All Party Parly Gp on Alcohol Harm, 2015–; Cons. Party Human Rights Commn, 2015–; Co-Chm., All Party Gp on N Korea, 2013– (Vice Chm., 2012–13). Mem. Bd, Lawyers' Christian Fellowship, 1996–2004; Pres., Warrington Law Soc., 2009. *Publications:* (contrib.) There is Such a

Thing as Society, 2002. *Recreations:* family, countryside. *Address:* House of Commons, SW1A 0AA.

**BRYANT, Christopher John;** MP (Lab) Rhondda, since 2001; *b* 11 Jan. 1962; *s* of Rees Bryant and Anne Gracie Bryant (*née* Goodwin). *Educ:* Cheltenham Coll.; Mansfield Coll., Oxford (MA); Ripon Coll., Cuddesdon (MA, DipTh). Ordained deacon, 1986, priest, 1987; Asst Curate, All Saints, High Wycombe, 1986–89; Youth Chaplain, Dio. Peterborough, 1989–91; Organiser, Holborn & St Pancras Lab. Party, 1991–93; Local Govt Develt Officer, Lab. Party, 1993–94. London Manager, Common Purpose, 1994–96; freelance writer, 1996–98; Hd, Eur. Affairs, BBC, 1998–2000. Dep. Leader, H of C, 2008–09; Parly Under-Sec. of State (Minister for Europe and Latin America), FCO, 2009–10; Shadow Minister for Immigration, 2011–13, for Welfare Reform, 2013–14, for Culture, Media and Sport, 2014–15; Shadow Sec. of State for Culture, Media and Sport, 2015; Shadow Leader, H of C, 2015–. *Publications:* (ed) Reclaiming the Ground, 1993; (ed) John Smith: an appreciation, 1995; Possible Dreams, 1996; Stafford Cripps: the first modern Chancellor, 1997; Glenda Jackson: the biography, 1998; Parliament: the biography, 2 vols, 2014. *Recreations:* theatre, modern art, Spain. *Address:* House of Commons, SW1A 0AA. *T:* (020) 7219 8315. *E:* bryantc@parliament.uk. *Club:* Ferndale Rugby Football (Vice-Pres.) (Rhondda).

**BUCK, Karen Patricia;** MP (Lab) Westminster North, since 2010 (Regent's Park and Kensington North, 1997–2010); *b* 30 Aug. 1958; partner, Barrie Taylor; one *s. Educ:* Chelmsford High Sch.; LSE (BSc, MSc, MA). R&D worker, Outset, 1979–83; London Borough of Hackney: Specialist Officer, Developing Services and Employment for Disabled People, 1983–86; Public Health Officer, 1986–87; Lab. Party Policy Directorate (Health), 1987–92; Co-ordinator, Lab. Party Campaign Strategy, 1992–96. Parly Under-Sec. of State, DfT, 2005–06; PPS to Leader of the Opposition, 2013–. Member: Social Security Select Cttee, 1997–2001; Work and Pensions Select Cttee, 2001–05; Home Affairs Select Cttee, 2006–09. Chm., London Gp of Labour MPs, 1998–2005. *Address:* House of Commons, SW1A 0AA.

**BUCKLAND, Robert James;** QC 2014; MP (C) South Swindon, since 2010; Solicitor General, since 2014; *b* Llanelli, 22 Sept. 1968; *s* of Roger Buckland and Barbara Buckland; *m* 1997, Sian Reed; one *s* one *d* (twins). *Educ:* St Michael's Sch., Bryn; Durham Univ. (BA Hons Law 1990). Called to the Bar, Inner Temple, 1991, Bencher, 2015; in practice as a barrister, 1992–; a Recorder, 2009–. Mem. (C) Dyfed CC, 1993–96. Contested (C): Islwyn, Feb. 1995; Preseli Pembrokeshire, 1997; S Swindon, 2005. Member: Justice Select Cttee, 2010–13 and 2014; Cttee on Standards, 2012–14; Cttee on Privileges,

2012–14; Jt Cttee on Human Rights, 2013–15; Chairman: Autism All Party Parly Gp, 2011–14; Cons. Party Human Rights Commn, 2011–14; Vice Pres., Tory Reform Gp, 2010–; Jt Sec., 1922 Cttee, 2012–14; Chm. Exec. Cttee, Soc. of Cons. Lawyers, 2013–14. Mem., Funding Review Panel for Wales, Legal Services Commn, 2000–09. Gov., Ridgeway Sch., Wroughton, 2005–09; Co-ordinator, Swindon Special Educnl Needs Network, 2006–. *Recreations:* music, food, wine, trying to keep up with my family, political and military history, churches, cathedrals, towers, domes and temples. *Address:* House of Commons, SW1A 0AA. *T:* (020) 7219 7168. *E:* robert.buckland.mp@parliament.uk. *Clubs:* Carlton; Llanelli Conservative; Swindon Conservative; Crawshays Welsh Rugby Football.

**BURDEN, Richard Haines;** MP (Lab) Birmingham Northfield, since 1992; *b* 1 Sept. 1954; *s* of late Kenneth Rodney Burden and Pauline Langan Burden (*née* Ronnan). *Educ:* Wallasey Technical Grammar Sch.; Bramhall Comprehensive Sch.; St John's Coll. of Further Educn, Manchester; York Univ. (BA Politics); Warwick Univ. (MA Indust. Relns). Pres., York Univ. Students' Union, 1976–77. Br. Organiser, 1979–81, Dist Officer, 1979–92, NALGO; whilst working for NALGO led Midlands campaign against water privatisation. Founder and Sec., Joint Action for Water Services, 1985–90. Contested (Lab) Meriden, 1987. PPS to Minister of State: MAFF, 1997–99; DSS, 1999–2001; Shadow Minister for Transport, 2013–15. Member: Trade and Industry Select Cttee, 2001–05; Internat. Develt Select Cttee, 2005–13; Cttee on Arms Exports, 2005–; Parly Advr to Sports Minister on Motor Sports, 2002–10. Secretary: All Party Parly Water Gp, 1994–97; PLP Trade and Industry Cttee, 1996–97 (Vice-Chm., 1995–96); Chm., Birmingham Gp of Labour MPs, 2001–11 (Sec., 1997–2001); Chairman: All Party Parly Gp on Electoral Reform, 1997–2011; All Party Parly Motor Gp, 1998–; Britain-Palestine All Party Parly Gp, 2001–; Jordan All Party Parly Gp, 2010–13; W Midlands Regl Select Cttee, 2009–10. Chm., Labour Campaign for Electoral Reform, 1996–98 (Vice-Chm., 1998–99). Mem., Austin Br., RBL. *Publications:* Tap Dancing: water, the environment and privatisation, 1988; contribs to Tribune, Chartist and other jls. *Recreations:* motor racing, cinema, reading, food. *Address:* House of Commons, SW1A 0AA. *T:* (020) 7219 2318, (0121) 477 7746. *W:* www.richardburden.com. *Clubs:* Austin Sports and Social, Kingshurst Labour, 750 Motor.

**BURGON, Richard;** MP (Lab) Leeds East, since 2015; *b* Leeds. *Educ:* Cardinal Heenan RC High Sch.; Univ. of Cambridge. Admitted as solicitor, 2006; trade union lawyer, Thompsons Solicitors, Leeds. *Address:* House of Commons, SW1A 0AA.

**BURNHAM, Rt Hon. Andrew (Murray);** PC 2007; MP (Lab) Leigh, since 2001; *b* Liverpool, 7 Jan. 1970; *s* of Kenneth Roy Burnham and Eileen Mary (*née* Murray); *m* 2000, Marie-France van Heel; one *s* two *d. Educ:* St Aelred's RC High Sch., Merseyside; Fitzwilliam Coll., Cambridge (MA Hons Eng.). Researcher to Tessa Jowell, MP, and Labour Health Team, 1994–97; Parly Officer, NHS Confedn, 1997; Advr to Football Task Force, 1997–98; Special Advr to Rt Hon. Chris Smith, MP, DCMS, 1998–2001. PPS to Sec. of State for Home Dept, 2003–05; Parly Under-Sec. of State, Home Office, 2005–06; Minister of State, DoH, 2006–07; Chief Sec. to HM Treasury, 2007–08; Sec. of State for Culture, Media and Sport, 2008–09, for Health, 2009–10; Shadow Sec. of State for Health, 2010, for Educn and Election Coordinator, 2010–11, for Health, 2011–15; Shadow Home Sec., 2015–. Mem., Health Select Cttee, 2001–03. Chm., Supporters Direct, 2002–05. *Recreations:* football (Everton FC), Rugby league (Leigh RLC), cricket. *Address:* House of Commons, SW1A 0AA. *T:* (020) 7219 8250; (constituency office) 10 Market Street, Leigh WN7 1DS. *T:* (01942) 682353. *Clubs:* Lowton, Hindley, Wigan Road and Leigh Labour; Leigh Catholic.

**BURNS, Conor;** MP (C) Bournemouth West, since 2010; *b* Belfast, 24 Sept. 1972; *s* of Thomas Burns and Kathleen Burns (*née* Kennedy). *Educ:* St Columba's Coll., St Albans; Southampton Univ. (BA Hons Modern Hist. and Politics 1994). Co. Sec., De Havilland Global Knowledge Distribution plc, 1998–2003; Regl Sales Manager, Zurich Advice Network, 2003–04; self-employed, 2004–08; Associate Dir, PLMR, 2008–10. Mem. (C) Southampton CC, 1999–2002. Contested (C) Eastleigh, 2001, 2005. PPS to Minister of State in NI Office, 2010–11, to Sec. of State for NI, 2011–12. Member: Educn Select Cttee, 2010; Culture, Media and Sport Select Cttee, 2012–15. *Recreations:* swimming, cooking, watching snooker, collecting political biography. *Address:* House of Commons, SW1A 0AA. *T:* (020) 7219 2071. *E:* conor.burns.mp@parliament.uk, cb@conorburns.com. *Clubs:* Southern Parishes Conservative (Life Mem.) (Southampton); Westbourne Conservative, Kinson Conservative (Bournemouth).

**BURNS, Rt Hon. Sir Simon (Hugh McGuigan),** Kt 2015; PC 2011; MP (C) Chelmsford, 1987–97 and since 2010 (Chelmsford West, 1997–2010); *b* 6 Sept. 1952; *s* of late Brian Stanley Burns, MC, and of Shelagh Mary Nash; *m* 1982, Emma Mary Clifford (marr. diss. 2000); one *s* one *d. Educ:* Christ the King Sch., Accra, Ghana; Stamford Sch.; Worcester Coll., Oxford (BA Hons Modern History). Political Adviser to Rt Hon. Sally Oppenheim, 1975–81; Dir, What to Buy Ltd, 1981–83; Policy Exec., Inst. of Dirs, 1983–87. PPS to Minister of State: Dept of Employment, 1989–90; Dept of Educn, 1990–92; DTI, 1992–93; PPS to Minister of Agric., Fisheries and Food, 1993–94; an Asst Govt Whip, 1994–95; a Lord Comr of HM Treasury (Govt Whip), 1995–96; Parly Under-Sec. of State, DoH, 1996–97; Opposition spokesman on: social security, 1997–98; envmt, housing and planning, 1998–99; health, 2001–05; an Opposition Whip, 2005–10; Minister of State: DoH, 2010–12; DfT, 2012–13. Mem., Health Select Cttee, 1999–2005. Treas., 1922 Cttee, 1999–2001 (Mem. Exec., 1999). *Recreations:* American politics, reading, swimming, travelling. *Address:* House of Commons, SW1A 0AA. *T:* (020) 7219 3000. *Clubs:* Essex, Chelmsford Conservative (Patron).

**BURROWES, David John Barrington;** MP (C) Enfield Southgate, since 2005; *b* 12 June 1969; *m* 1996, Janet; four *s* two *d* (of whom one *s* one *d* are twins). *Educ:* Highgate Sch.; Univ. of Exeter (LLB 1991). Asst Solicitor, 1995–2005, Consultant, 2005–, Shepherd Harris and Co., Enfield. Mem. (C), Enfield BC, 1994–2006 (Cabinet Mem. for voluntary and community develt, 2003–04). Parliamentary Private Secretary: to Minister for Cabinet Office and Minister for Policy, 2010; to Minister for Policy, 2010–12; to Sec. of State for Envmt, Food and Rural Affairs, 2012–14. Contested (C) Edmonton, 2001. *Publications:* (jtly) Moral Basis of Conservatism, 1995; Such a Thing as Society: Maggie's children and volunteering, 2006. *Recreations:* sports, particularly football and cricket. *Address:* (office) 1c Chaseville Parade, Chaseville Park Road, Winchmore Hill, N21 1PG. *T:* (020) 8360 0234. *E:* david@davidburrowes.com; House of Commons, SW1A 0AA. *T:* (020) 7219 8144.

**BURT, Rt Hon. Alistair (James Hendrie);** PC 2013; MP (C) North East Bedfordshire, since 2001; Minister of State, Department of Health, since 2015; *b* 25 May 1955; *s* of James Hendrie Burt, med. practitioner and Mina Christie Robertson; *m* 1983, Eve Alexandra Twite; one *s* one *d*. *Educ:* Bury Grammar Sch.; St John's Coll., Oxford (BA Hons Jurisprudence 1977). Pres., OU Law Soc., Michaelmas term, 1976. Articled Slater Heelis & Co., Manchester, 1978–80; solicitor, Watts, Vallance & Vallance, 1980–92; Consultant, Teeman, Levine and Co. (Solicitors), Leeds, 1992. Councillor, Archway Ward, London Bor. of Haringey, 1982–84. MP (C) Bury North, 1983–97; contested (C) same seat, 1997. Parliamentary Private Secretary: to Sec. of State for the Environment, 1985–86; to Sec. of State for Educn and Science, 1986–89; to Chancellor of Duchy of Lancaster and Chm. of Cons. Party, 1989–90; Parly Under-Sec. of State, DSS, 1992–95; Minister of State (Minister for Disabled People), DSS, 1995–97; Opposition frontbench spokesman on Higher and Further Educn, 2001–02; PPS to Leader of the Opposition, 2002–05; Shadow Minister for Communities and Regeneration, 2005–08; Dep. Chm., Cons. Party, 2007–10; Asst Opposition Chief Whip, 2008–10; Parly Under-Sec. of State, FCO, 2010–13. Vice-Chm., 1985–88, Vice Pres.,

2003–, Tory Reform Gp. Secretary: NW Cons. MPs Group, 1984–88; Parly Christian Fellowship, 1984–97 (Chm., 2003–06). Consultant, Whitehead Mann plc, 1997–2001. Chm., Enterprise Forum, 1998–2002. *Recreations:* reading left-wing publications, sport, modern art, marathon running, gardening. *Address:* c/o House of Commons, SW1A 0AA. *W:* www.alistair-burt.co.uk.

**BUTLER, Dawn;** MP (Lab) Brent Central, since 2015; training and development executive, since 2010; bespoke training designer and developer, since 2010; *b* 3 Nov. 1969; *d* of Milo and Ambrozene Butler. *Educ:* Tom Hood Sch.; Waltham Forest Coll. Associate CIPD 1993. Systems analyst, Johnson Matthey, 1989–92; Exec. Officer, Employment Service, 1993–97; Union Officer and Race Audit Co-ordinator, GMB, 1997–2005. Voluntary work, incl. at African Caribbean Centre; mentor; fund-raising co-ordinator. MP (Lab) Brent South, 2005–10; contested (Lab) Brent Central, 2010. PPS to Minister of State, Dept of Health, 2005–06; an Asst Govt Whip, 2008–10; Minister for Young Citizens and Youth Engagement, Cabinet Office, 2009–10. Chm., All Party Parly Gp on Youth Affairs, 2006–10. Political commentator, leadership mentor, and consultant on diversity and policy. Founder: Bernie's List, 2008–; Labour Friends of the Caribbean, 2009–. Patron: W Indian Self Effort, Brent; Mathematics, Brent; Black Women's Mental Health Project, Brent; Hindu Forum Britain; City Mission Community Project; Sister Circle; Sickle Cell Soc.; Betterdays Cancer Care; London Young Labour. *Recreations:* salsa, mentoring. *Address:* House of Commons, SW1A 0AA. *E:* dawn@dawnbutler.org.uk.

**BYRNE, Rt Hon. Liam (Dominic);** PC 2008; MP (Lab) Birmingham, Hodge Hill, since July 2004; *b* 2 Oct. 1970; *s* of Dermot and Ruth Byrne; *m* 1998, Sarah; two *s* one *d*. *Educ:* Manchester Univ. (BA Hons); Harvard Business Sch. (Fulbright Schol.; MBA). Leader, Manchester Univ. Students' Union, 1992–93; Sen. Business Analyst, Strategic Services, Andersen Consulting, 1993–96; Advr on Reinventing Govt, then Dir, Business Liaison, Office of the Leader of the Labour Party, 1996–97; Exec., N. M. Rothschild & Sons Ltd, 1997–99; Co-Founder, EGS Gp Ltd, 2000–04. Associate Fellow, Social Market Foundn, 2001–05. Parly Under-Sec. of State, DoH, 2005–06; Minister of State, Home Office, 2006–08; Minister for the W Midlands, 2007–08; Chancellor of the Duchy of Lancaster and Minister for the Cabinet Office, 2008–09; Chief Sec. to the Treasury, 2009–10; Shadow Chief Sec. to the Treasury, 2010; Shadow Minister for the Cabinet Office, 2010–11; Shadow Sec. of State for Work and Pensions, 2011–13; Shadow Minister for Univs, Sci. and Skills, 2013–15. *Publications:* Local Government Transformed, 1996; Information Age Government, 1998; Cities of Enterprise: new strategies for full employment,

2002; Britain in 2020, 2003; Reinventing Government Again, 2004; Turning to Face the East; how Britain can prosper in the Asian century, 2013; contribs to Parly Affairs and Progress mag. *Recreation:* spending time with family. *Address:* House of Commons, SW1A 0AA. *T:* (020) 7219 3000.

**CADBURY, Ruth;** MP (Lab) Brentford and Isleworth, since 2015; *m* Nick; two *s. Educ:* Mount Sch., York; Bourneville FE Coll.; Univ. of Salford (BSc Hons 1981). Planning Advr, Planning Aid for London, 1989–96; Policy Planner, Richmond upon Thames LBC, 1996–2001; freelance consultant, 2006–10. Mem. (Lab), Hounslow LBC, 1986–94 and 1998– (Dep. Leader, 2010–12; Cabinet Mem., 2010–13). Trustee, Barrow Cadbury Trust. *Address:* House of Commons, SW1A 0AA.

**CAIRNS, Alun Hugh;** MP (C) Vale of Glamorgan, since 2010; Parliamentary Under-Secretary of State, Wales Office, since 2014; a Lord Commissioner of HM Treasury (Government Whip), since 2014; *b* 30 July 1970; *s* of Hewitt and Margaret Cairns; *m* 1996, Emma Elizabeth Turner; one *s. Educ:* Ysgol Gyfun Ddwyieithog Ystalyfera; MBA Wales 2001. Joined Lloyds Bank Gp, 1989; Business Develt Consultant, 1992–98, Field Manager, 1998–99, Lloyds TSB (formerly Lloyds Bank). Mem. (C) S Wales W, Nat. Assembly for Wales, 1999–2011; econ. spokesman, 1997–2007; educn spokesman, 2007–08. Contested (C): Gower, 1997; Vale of Glamorgan, 2005. Joined Conservative Party, 1987. *Address:* House of Commons, SW1A 0AA.

**CAMERON, Rt Hon. David William Donald;** PC 2005; MP (C) Witney, since 2001; Prime Minister and First Lord of the Treasury, since 2010; Leader of the Conservative Party, since 2005; *b* 9 Oct. 1966; *s* of late Ian Donald Cameron and of Mary Fleur Cameron; *m* 1996, Samantha Gwendoline, *e d* of Sir Reginald Sheffield, Bt; one *s* two *d* (and one *s* decd). *Educ:* Eton Coll.; Brasenose Coll., Oxford (BA 1st Cl. Hons PPE; Hon. Fellow, 2006). Cons. Res. Dept, 1988–92; Special Adviser: HM Treasury, 1992–93; Home Office, 1993–94; Hd, Corporate Affairs, Carlton Communications plc, 1994–2001. Shadow Sec. of State for Educn and Skills, 2005; Leader of the Opposition, 2005–10. Mem., Select Cttee on Home Affairs, 2001–05. Dep. Chm., Cons. Party, 2003–04. *Publications:* (with Dylan Jones) Cameron on Cameron: conversations with Dylan Jones, 2008. *Recreations:* tennis, cooking. *Address:* 10 Downing Street, SW1A 2AA. *T:* (020) 7930 4433.

**CAMERON, Dr Lisa;** MP (SNP) East Kilbride, Strathaven and Lesmahagow, since 2015; *b* Glasgow, 8 April 1972; *d* of Campbell McCulloch and Sandra Cameron; *m* 2009, Mark Hersham; two *d. Educ:* Univ. of Strathclyde (BA Hons); Univ. of Stirling (MSc Psychol. and Health); Univ. of Glasgow (DClinPsy). NHS Greater

Glasgow, 1999–2001; Clin. Psychologist, NHS Lanarks, 2001–04; Consultant Clin. Psychologist, State Hosp., 2004–06; Consultant Forensic and Clin. Psychologist, NHS Greater Glasgow and Clyde, 2006–15. Accredited Risk Assessor, Risk Mgt Authy Scotland, 2012–15. *Recreations:* gym, swimming, travel. *Address:* House of Commons, Room 510, 1 Parliament Street, Westminster, SW1A 0AA. *E:* lisa.cameron.mp@parliament.uk. *Club:* Rotary (Lanark).

**CAMPBELL, Rt Hon. Alan;** PC 2014; MP (Lab) Tynemouth, since 1997; *b* 8 July 1957; *s* of Albert Campbell and Marian Campbell (*née* Hewitt); *m* 1991, Jayne Lamont; one *s* one *d. Educ:* Univ. of Lancaster (BA Hons); Univ. of Leeds (PGCE); Newcastle Poly. (MA). Teacher: Whitley Bay High Sch., 1980–89; Hirst High Sch., Ashington, 1989–97. An Asst Govt Whip, 2005–06; a Lord Comr of HM Treasury (Govt Whip), 2006–08; Parly Under-Sec. of State, Home Office, 2008–10; Dep. Opposition Chief Whip, 2010–. *Address:* House of Commons, SW1A 0AA; (office) 99 Howard Street, North Shields NE30 1NA.

**CAMPBELL, Gregory Lloyd;** MP (DemU) Londonderry East, since 2001; Member (DemU) East Londonderry, Northern Ireland Assembly, since 1998; *b* 15 Feb. 1953; *m* Frances; one *s* three *d. Educ:* Ebrington Primary Sch.; Londonderry Tech. Coll.; Magee Coll. Civil Servant, 1972–82 and 1986–94; businessman, 1994–. Mem. (DemU) Londonderry CC, 1981–. Mem. (DemU), NI Assembly, 1982–86; Mem., NI Forum for Political Dialogue, 1996–98. Minister for Regl Develt, 2000–01, for Culture, Arts and Leisure, 2008–09, NI. Contested (DemU): Foyle, 1992; E Londonderry, 1997. *Publications:* Discrimination: the truth, 1987; Discrimination: where now?, 1993; Ulster's Verdict on the Joint Declaration, 1994; Working Toward 2000, 1998. *Recreations:* soccer, music, reading. *Address:* (office) 25 Bushmills Road, Coleraine, Co. Londonderry, Northern Ireland BT52 2BP; 6–8 Catherine Street, Limavady BT49 9DB.

**CAMPBELL, Ronald, (Ronnie);** MP (Lab) Blyth Valley, since 1987; *b* 14 Aug. 1943; *m* 1967, Deirdre (*née* McHale); five *s* one *d. Educ:* Ridley High Sch., Blyth. Miner, 1958–86. Member: Blyth Borough Council, 1969–74; Blyth Valley Council, 1974–88 (Chm., Environmental Health Cttee; Vice-Chm., Housing Cttee). Mem., NUM. *Address:* 82 Middleton Street, Blyth, Northumberland NE24 2LX; House of Commons, SW1A 0AA.

**CARMICHAEL, Rt Hon. Alexander Morrison, (Rt Hon. Alistair);** PC 2010; MP (Lib Dem) Orkney and Shetland, since 2001; *b* 15 July 1965; *s* of Alexander C. Carmichael and Mina Neil McKay or Carmichael; *m* 1987, Kathryn Jane Eastham; two *s. Educ:* Port Ellen Primary Sch.; Islay High Sch.; Aberdeen Univ. (LLB 1992; DipLP 1993). Hotel Manager, Glasgow and

Orkney, 1984–89; Procurator Fiscal Depute, Crown Office, Edinburgh and Aberdeen, 1993–96; solicitor in private practice, Aberdeen and Macduff, 1996–2001. Comptroller of HM Household (Dep. Chief Whip), 2010–13; Sec. of State for Scotland, 2013–15. *Recreations:* music, theatre. *Address:* House of Commons, SW1A 0AA. *T:* (020) 7219 8181; The Old Manse, Evie, Orkney KW17 2PH. *T:* (01856) 751343.

**CARMICHAEL, (William) Neil;** MP (C) Stroud, since 2010; *b* Northumberland, 15 April 1961; *m* 1995, Laurence Jagodzinski; one *s* two *d*. *Educ:* St Peter's Sch., York; Nottingham Univ. (BA Politics 1982). Farmer, 1982–2001; land mgt, 2001–; Business Consultant, 2001–10. Vis. Lectr in British Political Hist. and Rural Econs in Europe, Sunderland and De Montfort Univs, 1996–99. Mem. (C) Northumberland CC, 1989–93. Contested (C): Leeds E, 1992; Stroud, 2001, 2005. Member: Educn Select Cttee, 2010– (Chm., 2015–); Envmtl Select Cttee, 2010–15. Chair: All-Party Parly Gp for Educn Leadership and Governance, 2011–; All-Party Parly Gp for Vascular Disease, 2012–; Sec., All-Party Health Gp, 2010–. Chair, Cons. Europe Gp, 2014–. Dir, Modern Europe, 2013–. Chm., Northumbria Daybreak, 1992–99. Chm. Govs, Marling Sch., 2008–09; Governor: Kirkley Hall Coll. of Agric., 1989–93; Stroud Coll., 2001–10 (Vice-Chm., 2007–08). *Address:* House of Commons, SW1A 0AA.

**CARSWELL, (John) Douglas (Wilson);** MP (UK Ind) Clacton, since Oct. 2014 (MP (C) Harwich, 2005–10, Clacton, 2010–Aug. 2014); *b* 3 May 1971; *s* of John Wilson Carswell, OBE, FRCS and Margaret Carswell (*née* Clark); *m* 2008, Clementine Bailey; one *d*. *Educ:* Charterhouse; Univ. of E Anglia (BA Hons 1993); King's Coll. London (MA). Corporate Develt Manager, Orbit Television, Rome, 1997–99; Chief Project Officer, Invesco Continental Europe, 1999–2003. Mem., Cons. Party Policy Unit, 2004–05. Member: Commons Select Cttee on Educn, 2006–10; Public Accounts Cttee, 2009–10. Founder, www.direct-democracy. co.uk, 2006–09. *Publications:* (jtly) Direct Democracy: an agenda for a new model party, 2005; (with Daniel Hannan) The Plan: 12 months to renew Britain, 2008; The End of Politics and the birth of iDemocracy, 2012; pamphlets. *Recreations:* blogs each day at www. TalkCarswell.com, keen swimmer, occasional rider, passionate gardener. *Address:* House of Commons, SW1A 0AA. *E:* douglas@ douglascarswell.com. *W:* www. TalkCarswell. com, www. douglascarswell.com.

**CARTLIDGE, James Roger;** MP (C) South Suffolk, since 2015; *m* Emily, *d* of Sir (James) Gerald (Douglas) Howarth, *qv*; four *c* (incl. twins). *Educ:* Univ. of Manchester. Researcher for Cons. Party; leader writer, Daily Telegraph; Founder,

Share to Buy Ltd, 2004. Mem. (C) Babergh DC, 2013–15. Contested (C) Lewisham Deptford, 2005. *Address:* House of Commons, SW1A 0AA.

**CASH, Sir William (Nigel Paul),** Kt 2014; MP (C) Stone, since 1997 (Stafford, 1984–97); *b* 10 May 1940; *s* of Paul Trevor Cash, MC (killed in action Normandy, July 13, 1944) and Moyra Roberts (*née* Morrison); *m* 1965, Bridget Mary Lee; two *s* one *d*. *Educ:* Stonyhurst Coll.; Lincoln Coll., Oxford (MA History). Qualified as Solicitor, 1967; William Cash & Co. (constitutional and administrative lawyer), 1979–. Shadow Attorney-General, 2001–03; Shadow Sec. of State for Constitutional Affairs, 2003. Chm., European Scrutiny Cttee (formerly Select Cttee on European Legislation), 2010– (Mem., 1985–); Chairman: Cons. Backbench Cttee on European Affairs, 1989–91; All Party Cttee on Uganda (formerly on E Africa), 1988–, on Kenya, 2007–; All Party Gp, Jubilee 2000, 1997–2003; All Party Cttee, Malaysia, 2006–; All Party Cttee, Sanitation and Water, 2007–; Jt Chm., All Party Jazz Gp, 1991–2000; Mem., Jt Cttee on Privileges, 2012–15. Founder, and Chm., European Foundn, 1993–. Vice Pres., Cons. Small Business Bureau, 1986–2000. KStJ. *Publications:* Against a Federal Europe—The Battle for Britain, 1991; Europe: the crunch, 1992; John Bright—Statesman, Orator, Agitator, 2011. *Recreations:* history, cricket, jazz. *Address:* The Tithe Barn, Upton Cressett, near Bridgnorth, Shropshire WV16 6UH. *T:* (01746) 714307. *E:* bcash@me.com. *Clubs:* Garrick, Carlton; Vincent's (Oxford).

**CAULFIELD, Maria Colette;** MP (C) Lewes, since 2015. Nurse and Research Sister, Royal Marsden Hosp. An owner and shareholder, Lewes FC. Non-exec. Dir, BHT Sussex. Mem. (C) Brighton and Hove CC, 2007–11. Contested (C) Caerphilly, 2010. *Address:* House of Commons, SW1A 0AA.

**CHALK, Alexander John Gervase;** MP (C) Cheltenham, since 2015; *b* 8 Aug. 1976; *s* of Gilbert Chalk and Gillian Miller (*née* Blois); *m* 2011, Sarah Beslee; two *d*. *Educ:* Winchester Coll.; Magdalen Coll., Oxford (BA Mod. Hist. 1998); City Univ. (DipLaw Dist. 2000). Called to the Bar, Middle Temple, 2001; barrister, 6 King's Bench Walk, then 6KBW College Hill, 2001–. Mem. (C), Hammersmith and Fulham Council, 2006–14. *Recreations:* cycling, playing guitar, reading, family. *Address:* House of Commons, SW1A 0AA. *E:* alex.chalk.mp@parliament.uk. *Club:* MCC.

**CHAMPION, Sarah Deborah;** MP (Lab) Rotherham, since Nov. 2012; *b* Maldon, Essex, 10 July 1969. *Educ:* Prince William Sch., Oundle; Sheffield Univ. (BA Hons Psychol. 1991). Manager, Rotherham Arts Centre, Rotherham MBC, 1992–94; Arts Officer, Ashfield DC, 1994–96; CEO, Chinese Arts Centre, Manchester, 1996–2008; Chief Exec., Bluebell

Wood Children's Hospice, 2008–12. *Publications:* Representing the People, 1999; Made in China, 2001; Vital: international artists of Chinese descent, 2008; (jtly) 21: discussions with artists of Chinese descent in the UK, 2009. *Recreations:* gardening, food, travel, wine, endurance horse riding, pets. *Address:* House of Commons, SW1A 0AA. *T:* (constituency office) (01709) 331035. *E:* sarah.champion.mp@parliament.uk.

**CHAPMAN, Douglas;** MP (SNP) Dunfermline and West Fife, since 2015; *b* Edinburgh, 1955; *m*; two *c. Educ:* W Calder High Sch.; Napier Coll. Branch banking, then personnel mgt, TSB Scotland; work for Bruce Crawford, MSP, 1999–2005; Campaign Manager, SNP, 2006–07. Mem. (SNP) Fife Council, 1997–98 and 2007– (Chm., Educn and Children's Services Cttee, 2007–12). Educn spokesman, COSLA, 2012–. Contested (SNP): Dunfermline and W Fife, 2005, Feb. 2006; Kirkcaldy and Cowdenbeath, 2010. *Address:* House of Commons, SW1A 0AA.

**CHAPMAN, Jennifer;** MP (Lab) Darlington, since 2010; *b* 25 Sept. 1973; *m* 2014, Nicholas Desmond John Smith, *qv*; two *s* by a previous marriage. *Educ:* Hummersknott Sch., Darlington; Queen Elizabeth Sixth Form Coll., Darlington; Brunel Univ. (BSc Psychol. 1996); Durham Univ. (MA Medieval Archaeol. 2004). Sen. Parly researcher to Alan Milburn, MP, 1997–2005. Mem. (Lab) Darlington BC, 2007–10. *Address:* House of Commons, SW1A 0AA.

**CHERRY, Joanna Catherine;** QC (Scot.) 2009; MP (SNP) Edinburgh South West, since 2015; *b* Edinburgh, 18 March 1966; *d* of Thomas Alastair Cherry and Mary Margaret Cherry (*née* Haslette). *Educ:* Holy Cross Sch., Edinburgh; St Margaret's Convent Sch. for Girls, Edinburgh; Univ. of Edinburgh (LLB Hons 1988; LLM 1989; DipLP 1990). Called to the Bar, 1995; Standing Jun. to Scottish Govt, 2003–09; Advocate Depute, 2008–11. *Recreations:* travel, reading, swimming. *Address:* Advocates Library, Parliament House, Edinburgh EH1 1RF. *T:* (0131) 466 4429, 07710 769081. *E:* joanna.cherry@advocates.org.uk.

**CHISHOLM OF OWLPEN,** Baroness *cr* 2014 (Life Peer), of Owlpen in the County of Gloucestershire; **Hon. Caroline Elizabeth Chisholm;** a Baroness in Waiting (Government Whip), since 2015; *b* 23 Dec. 1951; *d* of 1st Baron Egremont, MBE; *m* 1976, Colin Chisholm; two *s* one *d*. Co-Chm., Conservatives Candidates Committee. Trustee, Nat. Osteoporosis Soc.

**CHISHTI, Rehman;** MP (C) Gillingham and Rainham, since 2010; *b* Muzaffarabad, Pakistan, 4 Oct. 1978; *s* of Abdul Rehman Chishti and Zarina Chishti. *Educ:* Fort Luton High Sch. for Boys; Chatham Grammar Sch. for Girls; University of Wales, Aberystwyth (LLB Hons 2000). Called to the Bar, Lincoln's Inn, 2001; in practice as a barrister, Goldsmith Chambers, 2003–09. Special Adviser: to Benazir Bhutto, 1999–2007; to Rt Hon. Francis Maude, MP, 2006–07. Mem.,

Medway Council, 2003– (Lab, 2003–06, C, 2006–) (Mem. Cabinet, 2007–10). Contested (Lab) Horsham, 2005. *Recreations:* running, cricket, tennis, football, theatre, cinema. *Address:* House of Commons, SW1A 0AA. *T:* (020) 7219 3000. *E:* rehman.chishti.mp@parliament.uk.

**CHOPE, Christopher Robert,** OBE 1982; MP (C) Christchurch, since 1997; barrister; *b* 19 May 1947; *s* of late His Honour Robert Charles Chope and Pamela Durell; *m* 1987, Christo Hutchinson; one *s* one *d. Educ:* St Andrew's Sch., Eastbourne; Marlborough Coll.; St Andrews Univ. (LLB Hons). Called to the Bar, Inner Temple, 1972. Mem., Wandsworth Borough Council, 1974–83; Chm., Housing Cttee, 1978–79; Leader of Council, 1979–83. Consultant, Ernst & Young, 1992–98. MP (C) Southampton, Itchen, 1983–92; contested (C) Southampton, Itchen, 1992. PPS to Minister of State, HM Treasury, 1986; Parly Under-Sec. of State, DoE, 1986–90; Parly Under-Sec. of State (Minister for Roads and Traffic), Dept of Transport, 1990–92; front bench spokesman on trade and industry, 1998–99, on Treasury, 2001–02, on Transport, 2002–05. Jt Sec., Cons. Backbench Environment Cttee, 1983–86; Member: Select Cttee on Procedure, 1984–86, 2005–10; Select Cttee on Trade and Industry, 1999–2001; H of C Admin Cttee, 2006–10; Speaker's Panel of Chairmen, 2005–; Select Cttee on: Constitutional and Political Reform, 2010–15; Standards Cttee, 2013–15; Privileges Cttee, 2013–15; Scottish Affairs, 2015–. Member: Exec., 1922 Cttee, 2005–12 (Jt Sec., 2006–12); Delegn, Council of Europe, 2005– (Vice Chm., Legal Affairs and Human Rights Cttee, 2012–). Chm., Cons. Parly Candidates Assoc., 1995–97. A Vice Chm., Cons. Party, 1997–98. Chm., Cons. Way Forward, 2002–09. Member: HSC, 1993–97; Local Govt Commn for England, 1994–95; Vice-Pres., LGA, 2000. Mem. Exec. Cttee, Soc. of Cons. Lawyers, 1983–86. *Address:* House of Commons, SW1A 0AA. *T:* (020) 7219 5808. *Clubs:* Royal Southampton Yacht; Christchurch Conservative.

**CHURCHILL, Johanna Peta;** MP (C) Bury St Edmunds, since 2015; *m* 1992, Peter Ian Churchill; four *d. Educ:* Dame Alice Harper Sch., Bedford; Univ. of Lincoln (BSc); Univ. of Nottingham (MSc). Retail work for regl and global brands, then site develt and building industry; manager of contracting cos, 1994–2015. Mem. (C) Lincs CC, 2013–15. *Address:* House of Commons, SW1A 0AA.

**CLARK, Rt Hon. Greg(ory David);** PC 2010; PhD; MP (C) Tunbridge Wells, since 2005; Secretary of State for Communities and Local Government, since 2015; *b* 28 Aug. 1967; *s* of John and Patricia Clark; *m* 1999, Helen Fillingham; one *s* two *d. Educ:* St Peter's Comprehensive Sch., S Bank, Middlesbrough; Magdalene Coll., Cambridge (MA Econs); LSE (PhD 1992). Consultant, Boston Consulting Gp, 1991–94; res. and teaching, LSE and Open Univ.

Business Sch., 1994–96; Special Advr to Sec. of State for Trade and Industry, 1996–97; Chief Advr, 1997–99, Controller, 1999–2001, Commercial Policy, BBC; Dir of Policy, 2001–03, of Policy and Res., 2003–05, Cons. Party. Shadow Minister: for Charities, Social Enterprise and Volunteering, 2006–08; for Cabinet Office, 2007–08; Shadow Energy and Climate Change Sec., 2008–10; Minister of State: DCLG, 2010–12; BIS, 2011–12; Financial Sec., HM Treasury, 2012–13; Minister of State, Cabinet Office, 2013–15; Minister of State (Minister for Univs and Sci.), BIS, 2014–15. Mem. (C) Westminster CC, 2002–05 (Cabinet Mem., 2003–05). Vis. Fellow, Nuffield Coll., Oxford, 2007–. *Address:* House of Commons, SW1A 0AA.

**CLARKE, Rt Hon. Kenneth Harry;** CH 2014; PC 1984; QC 1980; MP (C) Rushcliffe, since 1970; *b* 2 July 1940; *e c* of Kenneth Clarke and Doris (*née* Smith), Nottingham; *m* 1964, Gillian Mary Edwards (*d* 2015); one *s* one *d. Educ:* Nottingham High Sch.; Gonville and Caius Coll., Cambridge (BA, LLB; Hon. Fellow, 1997). Chm., Cambridge Univ. Conservative Assoc., 1961; Pres., Cambridge Union, 1963; Chm., Fedn Conservative Students, 1963. Called to Bar, Gray's Inn 1963, Hon. Bencher, 1989, Bencher, 1998; Mem., Midland Circuit. Research Sec., Birmingham Bow Group, 1965–66. Contested Mansfield, 1964 and 1966. PPS to Solicitor General, 1971–72; an Asst Govt Whip, 1972–74 (Govt Whip for Europe, 1973–74); a Lord Comr, HM Treasury, 1974; Parly Sec., DoT, later Parly Under Sec. of State for Transport, 1979–82; Minister of State (Minister for Health), DHSS, 1982–85; entered Cabinet as Paymaster General and Minister for Employment, 1985–87; Chancellor of Duchy of Lancaster and Minister for Trade and Industry (with addnl responsibility to co-ordinate Govt policy on Inner Cities), 1987–88; Secretary of State: for Health, 1988–90; for Educn and Science, 1990–92; for the Home Dept, 1992–93; Chancellor of the Exchequer, 1993–97; Minister of State (Minister without Portfolio), 2012–14. Mem., Parly delegn to Council of Europe and WEU, 1973–74; Sec., Cons. Parly Health and Social Security Cttee, 1974; Opposition Spokesman on: Social Services, 1974–76; Industry, 1976–79; Shadow Sec. of State for Business (formerly Business, Enterprise and Regulatory Reform), 2009–10; Lord Chancellor and Sec. of State for Justice, 2010–12. Liveryman, Clockmakers' Co., 2001–. Hon. LLD: Nottingham, 1989; Huddersfield, 1993; DUniv Nottingham Trent, 1996. *Publications:* New Hope for the Regions, 1969; pamphlets published by Bow Group, 1964–. *Recreations:* modern jazz music; watching Association Football and cricket, bird-watching. *Address:* House of Commons, SW1A 0AA. *Clubs:* Garrick; Nottinghamshire CC (Pres., 2002–04).

**CLEGG, Rt Hon. Nicholas (William Peter);** PC 2008; MP (Lib Dem) Sheffield, Hallam, since 2005; *b* 7 Jan. 1967; *s* of Nicholas P. Clegg and Hermance Eulalie van den Wall Bake; *m* 2000, Miriam Gonzalez Durantez; three *s. Educ:* Westminster Sch.; Robinson Coll., Cambridge (MA Anthropol.); Univ. of Minnesota (post grad. res., Political Theory); Coll. of Europe, Bruges (MA European Studies). Trainee journalist, The Nation mag., NY, 1990; Consultant, GJW Govt Relns, London, 1992–93; Official, Relns with New Independent States, EC, 1994–96; Mem. of Cabinet, Office of Sir Leon Brittan, EC, 1996–99; MEP (Lib Dem) E Midlands, 1999–2004. Lib Dem Home Affairs spokesman, 2006–07; Leader, Liberal Democrats, 2007–15; Dep. Prime Minister and Lord President of the Council, 2010–15. Political Columnist, Guardian Unlimited, 2000–05. Pt-time Lectr, Sheffield Univ., 2004–05. Trustee, NPG, 2012–. David Thomas Prize, Financial Times, 1993. *Recreations:* outdoors, arts. *Address:* (office) 85 Nethergreen Road, Sheffield S11 7EH. *T:* (0114) 230 9002. *Club:* National Liberal.

**CLEVERLY, James Spencer,** TD; MP (C) Braintree, since 2015; Member (C) Bexley and Bromley, London Assembly, Greater London Authority, since 2008; *b* Lewisham, 4 Sept. 1969; *s* of James Philip Cleverly and Evelyn Suna Cleverly; *m* 2000, Susannah Janet Temple Sparks; two *s. Educ:* Colfe's Sch. for Boys; Thames Valley Univ. (BA Hons Hospitality Mgt). Sales Manager, VNU, 1996–2002; Internat. Advertising Manager, Informa, 2002–04; mobilised service, British Army, 2004; Gp Advertising Manager, Crimson Publishing, 2005–06; Online Commercial Manager, Caspian Publishing, 2006–07; Dir, Point & Fire Media Ltd, 2007–11. Mem. Bd, London Develt Agency, 2008–12; Chairman: London Waste and Recycling Bd, 2010–12; London Fire and Emergency Planning Authy, 2012–15; London Local Resilience Forum, 2012–15. Served Army Reserves (formerly TA), 1989–. *Recreations:* Rugby, triathlon, spending time with my family. *Address:* House of Commons, SW1A 0AA. *T:* (020) 7219 3000. *E:* james.cleverly.mp@parliament.uk; Greater London Authority, City Hall, The Queen's Walk, SE1 2AA. *T:* (020) 7983 6571. *E:* james.cleverly@london.gov.uk. *Club:* Carlton.

**CLIFTON-BROWN, Geoffrey Robert;** MP (C) The Cotswolds, since 2010 (Cirencester and Tewkesbury, 1992–97, Cotswold, 1997–2010); chartered surveyor and farmer; *b* 23 March 1953; *s* of Robert and late Elizabeth Clifton-Brown; *m* 1979, Alexandra Peto-Shepherd (marr. diss. 2004); one *s* one *d. Educ:* Tormore Sch., Kent; Eton Coll.; RAC, Cirencester. FRICS 2002. Chm., N Norfolk Cons. Assoc., 1986–91. PPS to Minister of Agric., Fisheries and Food, 1995–97; an Opposition Whip, 1999–2001, 2003, Opposition Asst Chief Whip, 2005; Opposition front bench spokesman on local and devolved govt, 2003–04; Shadow Minister: for Foreign

Affairs and Trade, 2005–07; for Internat. Develt and Trade, 2007–10. Member: Envmt Select Cttee, 1992–95; Public Accounts Commn, 1997–99; Public Accounts Cttee, 1997–99. Vice Chm., Euro Atlantic Gp, 1996–. Freeman, City of London, 1981; Liveryman, Farmers' Co., 1984. *Recreations:* fishing, all country pursuits. *Address:* House of Commons, SW1A 0AA. *T:* (020) 7219 3000. *Clubs:* Carlton, Farmers.

**CLWYD, Rt Hon. Ann;** PC 2004; MP (Lab) Cynon Valley, since May 1984; journalist and broadcaster; *b* 21 March 1937; *d* of Gwilym Henri Lewis and Elizabeth Ann Lewis; *m* 1963, Owen Dryhurst Roberts (*d* 2012), TV director and producer. *Educ:* Halkyn Primary Sch.; Holywell Grammar Sch.; The Queen's Sch., Chester; University Coll., Bangor. Former: Student-teacher, Hope Sch., Flintshire; BBC Studio Manager; freelance reporter, producer; Welsh corresp., The Guardian and The Observer, 1964–79; Vice-Chm., Welsh Arts Council, 1975–79. Member: Welsh Hospital Board, 1970–74; Cardiff Community Health Council, 1975–79; Royal Commn on NHS, 1976–79; Working Party, report, Organisation of Out-Patient Care, for Welsh Hosp. Bd; Working Party, Bilingualism in the Hospital Service; Labour Party Study Gp, People and the Media; Arts Council of Gt Britain, 1975–80; Labour Party NEC, 1983–84; PLP Exec., 1997–2006 (Vice Chm., 2001–05; Chm., 2005–06); Chm., Cardiff Anti-Racialism Cttee, 1978–80. Chm., Labour back bench cttee on Health and Social Security, 1985–87; Vice-Chm., Labour back bench cttee on Defence, 1985–87; Opposition front bench spokesperson on women, 1987–88, on educn, 1987–88, on overseas develt and co-operation, 1989–92, on Wales, 1992, on Nat. Heritage, 1992–93, on employment, 1993–94, on foreign affairs, 1994–95. Member: Shadow Cabinet, 1989–93; Select Cttee on Internat. Develt, 1997–2005, on Foreign Affairs, 2010–. Chm., All Party Gp on Human Rights, 1997–; Special Envoy to the Prime Minister on Human Rights in Iraq, 2003–10; apptd by the Prime Minister to lead review into NHS, 2013–. Chair, Indict, 2003–. Member: NUJ; TGWU. Contested (Lab): Denbigh, 1970; Gloucester, Oct. 1974; Mem. (Lab) Mid and West Wales, European Parlt, 1979–84. Hon. Fellow: Univ. of Wales, Bangor; N Wales Inst. of Higher Educn. Hon. Dr Wales; Hon. LLD Trinity Coll., Carmarthen. White Robe, Gorsedd of Bards, Nat. Eisteddfod of Wales, 1991. Backbencher of the Year, House Magazine and Spectator Parly Awards, 2003; Campaigning MP of the Year, Channel 4 Political Awards, 2003. *Address:* (office) 4th Floor, Crown Buildings, Aberdare, Mid Glam CF44 7HU. *T:* (01685) 871394.

**COAKER, Vernon Rodney;** MP (Lab) Gedling, since 1997; *b* 17 June 1953; *s* of Edwin Coaker; *m* 1978, Jacqueline Heaton; one *s* one *d*. *Educ:* Drayton Manor Grammar Sch., London; Warwick Univ. (BA Hons); Trent Poly. (PGCE).

Hist. Teacher, Manvers Pierrepont Sch., 1976–82; Hd of Dept, Arnold Hill Sch., 1982–88; Sen. Teacher, Bramcote Pk Sch., 1989–95; Dep. Headteacher, Big Wood Sch., 1995–97. Mem., Rushcliffe BC, 1983–97 (Leader, 1987–97). PPS to Minister of State for Social Security, 1999, to Financial Sec. to HM Treasury, 1999–2001, to Minister of State (Minister for School Standards), DfES, 2001–02, to Sec. of State for Culture, Media and Sport, 2002–03; an Asst Govt Whip, 2003–05; a Lord Comr of HM Treasury (Govt Whip), 2005–06; Parly Under-Sec. of State, 2006–08, Minister of State, 2008–09, Home Office; Minister of State (Minister for Schs and Learners), DCSF, 2009–10; Shadow Sec. of State for NI, 2011–13, 2015–, for Defence, 2013–15. Contested (Lab): Rushcliffe, 1983; Gedling, 1987, 1992. *Address:* House of Commons, SW1A 0AA.

**COFFEY, (Margaret) Ann;** MP (Lab) Stockport, since 1992; *b* 31 Aug. 1946; *d* of late John Brown, MBE, and of Marie Brown; *m* 1973 (marr. diss. 1989); one *d*; *m* 1998, Peter Saraga. *Educ:* Poly. of South Bank (BSc); Manchester Univ. (MSc). Trainee Social Worker, Walsall Social Services Dept, 1971–72; Social Worker: Birmingham, 1972–73; Gwynedd, 1973–74; Wolverhampton, 1974–75; Stockport, 1977–82; Cheshire, 1982–88; Team Leader, Fostering, Oldham Social Services Dept, 1988–92. Mem. (Lab) Stockport MBC, 1984–92 (Leader, Labour Group, 1988–92). Contested (Lab) Cheadle, 1987. An Opposition Whip, 1995–96; Opposition spokeswoman on health, 1996–97; PPS to Prime Minister, 1997–98, to Sec. of State for Social Security, 1998–2001, to Sec. of State for Work and Pensions, 2001–02, to Sec. of State for Transport, 2002–06, to Sec. of State for Trade and Industry, 2006–07, to Chancellor of the Exchequer, 2007–10. Mem., Trade and Industry Select Cttee, 1993–95. *Address:* House of Commons, SW1A 0AA.

**COFFEY, Dr Therese Anne;** MP (C) Suffolk Coastal, since 2010; Parliamentary Secretary (Deputy Leader), Office of the Leader of the House of Commons, since 2015; *b* Billinge, 18 Nov. 1971; *d* of late Tom Coffey and of Sally Coffey. *Educ:* St Mary's Coll., Crosby; St Edward's Coll., Liverpool; University Coll., London (BSc 1993; PhD Chem. 1997). Mgt Accountant. Various posts with Mars UK Ltd, 1997–2007; Finance Dir, Mars Drinks UK, 2007–09; Property Finance Manager, BBC, 2009–10. Mem. (C) Whitchurch Town Council, 1999–2003. An Asst Govt Whip, 2014–15. Contested (C): SE England, EP, 2004, 2009; Wrexham, 2005. *Recreations:* dog walking, sudoku, pub quizzes, live music. *Address:* House of Commons, SW1A 0AA. *T:* (020) 7219 7164. *E:* therese.coffey.mp@parliament.uk.

**COLLINS, Damian Noel Thomas;** MP (C) Folkestone and Hythe, since 2010; *b* Northampton, 4 Feb. 1974; *s* of Fearghal and Diane Collins; *m* 2004, Sarah Richardson; one *s* one d. *Educ:* St Mary's High Sch., Herefordshire; Belmont Abbey Sch., Hereford; St Benet's Hall, Oxford (BA Hons Modern Hist.). Cons. Res. Dept and Press Officer, 1996–99; Dir, M & C Saatchi, 1999–2008; Sen. Counsel, Lexington Communications, 2008–10. PPS to Sec. of State for NI, 2012–14, to Foreign Sec., 2014–. Mem., H of C Select Cttee on Culture, Media and Sport, 2010–12. Pres., Oxford Univ. Cons. Assoc., 1995. *Publications:* (contrib.) Conservative Revival, 2006; (contrib.) The New Blue, 2008. *Recreations:* cricket, football, Rugby (watching), walking in Kent, cooking with Jamie Oliver. *Address:* House of Commons, SW1A 0AA. *T:* (020) 7219 7072. *E:* damian.collins.mp@ parliament.uk. *Clubs:* Lord's Taverners, MCC; Manchester United.

**COLVILE, Oliver Newton;** MP (C) Plymouth, Sutton and Devonport, since 2010; *b* 26 Aug. 1959. *Educ:* Stowe Sch. Agent, Cons. Party, 1981–93; Account Dir, Rowland Sallingbury Casey, 1993, 1995–96; Dir, PR co., 1993–95; Proprietor, Oliver Colvile and Associates, 1996–2010. Dir, Polity Communications, 2005–10. Mem., NI Select Cttee, 2010–; Chm., All Party Parly Gp for Excellence in the Built Envmt, 2012– (Vice Chm., 2010–12); Vice Chairman: All Party Parly Gp: for the Armed Forces (RM), 2010–; on Pharmacy, 2010–; for Zambia and Malawi, 2011–; for Zimbabwe; Sec., All Party Parly Gp on Integrated Health, 2010–. Contested (C) Plymouth Sutton, 2001, 2005. *Address:* House of Commons, SW1A 0AA.

**COOPER, Julie Elizabeth;** MP (Lab) Burnley, since 2015; *b* 20 June 1960; *d* of Robert Calder and Teresa Fletcher; *m* 1984, Brian Cooper; one *s* one d. *Educ:* Colne Park High Sch., Colne; Edge Hill Coll., Ormskirk (BA Hons Eng. Lang. and Lit.). English teacher, Birkdale High Sch., Dewsbury, 1982–84; Librarian, Hagergham High Sch., Burnley, 1990–92; Dir, Coopers Chemist, Burnley, 1992–2010. Mem. (Lab), Burnley BC, 2005– (Leader, 2012–14). *Recreations:* travel, film, music, reading. *Address:* House of Commons, SW1A 0AA. *T:* (01282) 425744.

**COOPER, Rosemary Elizabeth;** MP (Lab) West Lancashire, since 2005; *b* 5 Sept. 1950; *d* of William and Rose Cooper. *Educ:* Bellerive Convent GS; Liverpool Univ. W. Cooper Ltd, 1973–80; Littlewoods Organisation: merchandiser, 1980–92; PR Manager, Littlewoods Internat., 1994–95; Gp Corporate Communications Manager, 1995–2001; EOC, 1999–2000. Mem. and Vice-Chm., Liverpool HA, 1994–96; Chm., Liverpool Women's Hosp. NHS Trust, 1996–2005. Mem. (Lib Dem, then Lab), Liverpool CC, 1973–2000; Lord Mayor of Liverpool, 1992–93. Contested (Lib Dem): Knowsley N, Nov. 1986, 1987; Liverpool Garston, 1983; Liverpool Broadgreen, 1992; contested (Lab) NW Reg., EP elecns, 2004.

Former Director: Merseyside Centre for Deaf People; Roy Castle Foundn. *Address:* House of Commons, SW1A 0AA.

**COOPER, Rt Hon. Yvette;** PC 2007; MP (Lab) Normanton, Pontefract and Castleford, since 2010 (Pontefract and Castleford, 1997–2010); *b* 20 March 1969; *d* of (Derek) Anthony Cooper and June Cooper (*née* Iley); *m* 1998, Rt Hon. Edward Michael Balls; one *s* two d. *Educ:* Eggars Comprehensive Sch., Hants; Balliol Coll., Oxford (BA 1st Cl. Hons PPE 1990); Harvard Univ.; London Sch. of Econs (MSc Econs 1995). Economic researcher for Rt Hon. John Smith, MP, 1991–92; Domestic Policy specialist, Clinton Presidential Campaign, Arkansas, 1992; Policy Advr to Labour's Treasury Team, 1992–95; leader writer and economic columnist, The Independent, 1995–97. Parliamentary Under-Secretary of State: for Public Health, DoH, 1999–2002; Lord Chancellor's Dept, 2002–03; (Social Exclusion Minister), ODPM, 2003–05; Minister of State (Minister for Housing and Planning), ODPM, later DCLG, 2005–07; Minister for Housing, DCLG, 2007–08; Chief Sec. to HM Treasury, 2008–09; Sec. of State for Work and Pensions, 2009–10; Shadow Sec. of State for Work and Pensions, 2010; Shadow Minister for Women and Equalities, 2010–13; Shadow Sec. of State for Foreign and Commonwealth Affairs, 2010–11, for the Home Dept, 2011–15. Member: Select Cttee on Educn and Employment, 1997–99; Intelligence and Security Cttee, 1997–99. *Address:* House of Commons, SW1A 0AA. *T:* (020) 7219 5080.

**CORBYN, Rt Hon. Jeremy (Bernard);** PC 2015; MP (Lab) Islington North, since 1983; Leader of the Labour Party and Leader of the Opposition, since 2015; *b* 26 May 1949; *s* of David Benjamin Corbyn. *Educ:* Adams Grammar Sch., Newport, Shropshire. NUPE Official, 1975–83; sponsored NUPE, then UNISON, MP. Mem., Haringey Borough Council, 1974–84 (Chm., Community Develt Cttee 1975–78, Public Works 1978–79, Planning Cttee 1980–81, 1982–83). Member: Select Cttee on Social Security, 1990–97; Justice Select Cttee, 2011–15; Chair, London Gp of Lab MPs, 1993–96 (Vice-Chair, 1985–93); All Party Parliamentary Groups: Chair, Mexico, Chagos Islands; Jt Vice Chair, Human Rights; Vice Chair, Latin America, African Great Lakes; Sec., Bolivia, Dalits; Mem., traveller law reform, cycling; Member, Parliamentary Groups: RMT; CWU; Justice Unions; Socialist Campaign; CND (Chair). Chair: Liberation; Stop the War Coalition; Vice Chair, Nat. Council, CND. Trustee: Highbury Vale Blackstock Trust; Dalit Solidarity Campaign. Patron, Mitford Under Fives. *Address:* House of Commons, SW1A 0AA. *T:* (020) 7219 3545.

**COSTA, Alberto Castrenze;** MP (C) South Leicestershire, since 2015.

**COURTOWN,** 9th Earl of, *cr* 1762; **James Patrick Montagu Burgoyne Winthrop Stopford;** Baron Courtown (Ire.), 1758; Viscount Stopford, 1762; Baron Saltersford (GB), 1796; a Lord in Waiting (Government Whip), since 2015; *b* 19 March 1954; *s* of 8th Earl of Courtown, OBE, TD, DL, and Patricia, 3rd *d* of Harry S. Winthrop, Auckland, NZ; *S* father, 1975; *m* 1985, Elisabeth, *yr d* of I. R. Dunnett, Broad Campden, Glos; one *s* two *d*. *Educ:* Eton College; Berkshire Coll. of Agriculture; RAC, Cirencester. A Lord in Waiting (Govt Whip), 1995–97; an Opposition Whip, 1997–2000; elected Mem., H of L, 1999. *Heir: s* Viscount Stopford. *Address:* House of Lords, SW1A 0PW.

**COWAN, Ronald Jack;** MP (SNP) Inverclyde, since 2015; *b* Greenock, 6 Sept. 1959; *s* of James Clews Cowan and May Harper Cowan; one *s* two *d*. *Educ:* Greenock Acad. Systems Analyst, Playtex, 1978–86; IT Consultant, Campbell Lee Computer Services, 1986–2001; Man. Dir, Ronnie Cowan Solutions, 2001–15. *Recreations:* art (appreciation), sport (watching), sleeping (with optional snoring). *Address:* House of Commons, SW1A 0AA. *E:* ronnie.cowan.mp@parliament.uk. *Club:* Greenock Wanderers Rugby Football.

**COX, (Charles) Geoffrey;** QC 2003; MP (C) Torridge and West Devon, since 2005; *b* 30 April 1960; *s* of Michael and Diane Cox; *m* 1985, Jeanie (*née* McDonald); two *s* one *d*. *Educ:* Downing Coll., Cambridge (BA). Called to the Bar, Middle Temple, 1982; in practice, specialising in criminal law, human rights, constitutional, commercial and defamation law; Hd of Chambers, Thomas More Chambers, 2003–. Contested (C) Torridge and W Devon, 2001. *Recreations:* walking, swimming, theatre, literature, political history, enjoying rural life. *Address:* Thomas More Chambers, 7 Lincoln's Inn Fields, WC2A 3BP. *T:* (020) 7404 7000, *Fax:* (020) 7831 4606. *E:* clerks@thomasmore.co.uk; House of Commons, SW1A 0AA.

**COX, Helen Joanne, (Jo);** MP (Lab) Batley and Spen, since 2015; *b* Batley; *m* Brendan Cox; two *c*. *Educ:* Heckmondwike Grammar Sch.; Pembroke Coll., Cambridge (BA Social and Pol Studies 1995); London Sch. of Econs and Pol Sci. Pol Advr, Joan Walley, MP, 1995–97; Hd, Key Campaigns, Britain in Europe, 1998–99; Pol Advr, Glenys Kinnock, MEP, 2000–02; Head, EU Office, 2002–05; Policy and Advocacy, 2005–07; Humanitarian Campaigning, 2007–09; Oxfam; Dir, Maternal Mortality Campaign, 2009–11; Strategy Consultant: Save the Children, 2012; NSPCC, 2012; Dir of Strategy, White Ribbon Alliance for Safe Motherhood, 2012; CEO and Founder, UK Women, 2013–14; Strategic Adviser: Freedom Fund, 2014; Bill and Melinda Gates Foundn, 2014–15. Chair, Labour Women's Network, 2010–14. *Address:* House of Commons, SW1A 0AA.

**COYLE, Neil;** MP (Lab) Bermondsey and Old Southwark, since 2015; *b* Luton, Dec. 1978; *s* of Alan Coyle and Mary Coyle (*née* Wesson); *m* 2014, Sarah Lindars. *Educ:* Hull Univ. (BA Hons). Lived in China, 2001–03; Disability Rights Commn, 2003–07, latterly as Policy Manager for health and social care; Hd of Policy, Nat. Centre for Ind. Living, 2007–09; Dir of Policy, Disability Alliance, 2009–12; Dir of Policy and Campaigns, DRUK, 2012–13. Mem. (Lab), Southwark LBC, 2010–15; Dep. Mayor of Southwark, 2014–15. Vice Chm., Walworth Community Council, 2010–11. Trustee, N Southwark Envmt Trust. *Address:* House of Commons, SW1A 0AA.

**CRABB, Rt Hon. Stephen;** PC 2014; MP (C) Preseli Pembrokeshire, since 2005; Secretary of State for Wales, since 2014; *b* 20 Jan. 1973; *m* 1996, Béatrice Alice Claude Odile Monnier; one *s* one *d*. *Educ:* Bristol Univ. (BSc Hons 1995); London Business Sch. (MBA 2004). Res. Asst to Andrew Rowe, MP, 1995–96; Parly Officer, Nat. Council for Voluntary Youth Services, 1996–98; Policy and Campaigns Manager, LCCI, 1998–2002; mktg consultant, 2003–05. An Opposition Whip, 2009–10; an Asst Govt Whip, 2010–12; a Lord Comr of HM Treasury (Govt Whip), 2012–14; Parly Under-Sec. of State, Wales Office, 2012–14. *Recreations:* Rugby, cooking, spending time with family. *Address:* House of Commons, SW1A 0AA. *T:* (020) 7219 3000. *E:* crabbs@parliament.uk. *Clubs:* Balfour, Haverfordwest Co. Assoc. Football (Haverfordwest).

**CRAUSBY, David Anthony;** MP (Lab) Bolton North East, since 1997; *b* 17 June 1946; *s* of Thomas Crausby and Kathleen Lavin; *m* 1965, Enid Anne Noon; two *s*. *Educ:* Derby Grammar Sch., Bury. Apprentice centre lathe turner, 1962, skilled turner, 1967; Works Convenor, AEEU (formerly AEU), 1978–97. Mem (Lab) Bury MDC, 1979–92. Contested (Lab): Bury N, 1987; Bolton NE, 1992. *Recreations:* football, walking, cinema. *Address:* (office) 426 Blackburn Road, Bolton BL1 8NL. *T:* (01204) 303340.

**CRAWLEY, Angela;** MP (SNP) Lanark and Hamilton East, since 2015; *b* Hamilton, 3 June 1987. *Educ:* John Ogilvie High Sch.; Stirling Univ. (BA Hons Politics 2009); Univ. of Glasgow (LLB 2015). Parly Asst, Scottish Parlt, 2007–09; Tour Co-ordinator and Sen. Gp Leader, Educn Travel Gp, 2009–11; Parly Asst and Researcher, Scottish Parlt, 2011–13; Legal Asst, Aamer Anwar & Co., Solicitors, 2014. Mem. (SNP), S Lanarkshire Council, 2012–15. SNP spokesperson for Equalities, Women and Children, 2015–. Nat. Convenor, Young Scots for Independence, 2014–. *Address:* House of Commons, SW1A 0AA.

**CREAGH, Mary Helen;** MP (Lab) Wakefield, since 2005; *b* 2 Dec. 1967; *d* of Thomas and Elizabeth Creagh; *m* 2001, Adrian Pulham; one *s* one *d*. *Educ:* Pembroke Coll., Oxford (BA Jt Hons

---

Modern Langs (French and Italian)); London Sch. of Econs (MSc Eur. Studies). Press Officer: Youth Forum of EU, 1991–95; London Enterprise Agency, 1995–97; Lectr in Entrepreneurship, Cranfield Sch. of Mgt, 1997–2005. Mem. (Lab) Islington BC, 1998–2005 (Leader, Labour Gp, 2000–04). An Asst Govt Whip, 2009–10; Shadow Sec. of State for Envmt, Food and Rural Affairs, 2010–13, for Transport, 2013–14, for Internat. Develt, 2014–15. Trustee, Rathbone Trng, 1997–2004. *Recreations:* cycling, cooking, theatre, friends and family, pop music. *Address:* House of Commons, SW1A 0AA. *T:* (020) 7219 6984. *E:* mary@marycreagh.co.uk. *Club:* Red Shed (Wakefield).

**CREASY, Dr Stella Judith;** MP (Lab Co-op) Walthamstow, since 2010; *b* 1977. *Educ:* Colchester High Sch.; Magdalene Coll., Cambridge; London Sch. of Econs (PhD Social Psychol.). Formerly: researcher to Douglas Alexander, MP, Charles Clarke, MP and Ross Cranston, MP; Dep. Dir, Involve think tank; Hd, Public Affairs and Campaigns, Scout Assoc. Formerly Mem. (Lab Co-op) Waltham Forest LBC (Dep. Mayor, then Mayor). Shadow Minister: for Home Affairs, 2011–13; BIS, 2013–15. *Address:* House of Commons, SW1A 0AA.

**CROUCH, Tracey Elizabeth Anne;** MP (C) Chatham and Aylesford, since 2010; Parliamentary Under-Secretary of State for Sport and Tourism, Department for Culture, Media and Sport, since 2015; *b* Ashford, Kent, 24 July 1975; *d* of Kenneth Allen Crouch and Sallyanne Crouch (*née* French). *Educ:* Folkestone Sch. for Girls; Hull Univ. (BA Jt Hons Law and Pols 1996). Parly Researcher, 1996–98; Sen. Public Affairs Manager, Harcourt Public Affairs, 1999–2000; Westminster Strategy, 2000–03; COS to Shadow Educn Sec., then Shadow Transport Sec., 2003; COS to Shadow Home Sec., 2003–05; Hd, Public Affairs, Aviva, 2005–10. Mem., Culture, Media and Sport Select Cttee, 2012–15. Chm., All Party Parly Gp on Alcohol Misuse, 2011–14 (Vice Chm., 2010–11); Vice Chm., All Party Parly Gp on Athletics, 2010–, on Dementia, 2010–; Sec., All Party Parly Gp on Insce and Financial Services, 2010–11. Mem., British delegn, OSCE, 2010–; Parly Ambassador, Us Girls, 2011–. Mem., Exec., 1922 Cttee, 2010–12. Trustee, Women's Sport and Fitness Foundn, 2013. Pres., RSPCA Medway, 2010–; Chm., Pet Adv. Cttee, 2011–; Patron: Chatham Town FC, 2011–; Nat. Osteoporosis Soc. Hon. MInstRE 2011. *Recreations:* sport, travel, manager of Meridian Girls FC. *Address:* House of Commons, SW1A 0AA. *E:* tracey. crouch.mp@parliament.uk.

**CRUDDAS, Jon,** PhD; MP (Lab) Dagenham and Rainham, since 2010 (Dagenham, 2001–10); *b* 7 April 1962; *s* of John and Pat Cruddas; *m* 1992, Anna Mary Healy (Baroness Healy of Primrose

Hill); one *s. Educ:* Oaklands RC Comprehensive Sch., Waterlooville; Warwick Univ. (BSc, MA; PhD 1991). Labour Party: Policy Officer, 1989–94; Chief Asst to Gen. Sec., 1994–97; Dep. Political Sec., Prime Minister's Office, 1997–2001. Policy Rev. Co-ordinator, Labour Party, 2012–15. Mem., White Hart Angling Soc., 2000–. Mem., Dagenham Royal Naval Assoc., 2000–. *Publications:* Blue Labour: forging a new politics, 2015. *Recreations:* golf, angling. *Address:* House of Commons, SW1A 0AA. *Club:* Dagenham Working Men's.

**CRYER, John Robert;** MP (Lab) Leyton and Wanstead, since 2010; *b* 11 April 1964; *s* of late (George) Robert Cryer, MP and of Ann Cryer; *m* 1994, Narinder Bains (marr. diss. 2012), *d* of Shiv Singh Bains and Bakhshish Bains; two *s* one *d*; *m* 2012, Ellie Reeves. *Educ:* Oakbank Sch., Keighley; Hatfield Poly. (BA). Underwriter, 1986–88; Journalist, Morning Star, 1989–92; Editor, Labour Briefing, 1992–93; Journalist: GPMU Jl, 1992–93; Tribune, 1993–96; Lloyd's of London Pubns, 1996–97; Pol Officer, ASLEF, 2005–06; Nat. Pol Officer, T&G section of Unite – the union (formerly TGWU), 2006–10. MP (Lab) Hornchurch, 1997–2005; contested (Lab) same seat, 2005. Mem., Treasury Select Cttee, 2010–11. Chm., Parly Labour Party, 2015–. Chm., Labour Against the Superstate. Trustee, Thames Chase Community Forest. Mem., Editl Bd, Tribune. *Publications:* (jtly) Boldness be My Friend: remembering Bob Cryer, 1997. *Recreations:* most sports, reading, cinema, old cars. *Address:* House of Commons, SW1A 0AA.

**CUMMINS, Judith;** MP (Lab) Bradford South, since 2015; *b* W Yorks; one *s* one *d*. *Educ:* Ruskin Coll.; Univ. of Leeds. Former Mem. (Lab) Bradford MDC; Mem. (Lab), Leeds CC, 2012–. *Address:* House of Commons, SW1A 0AA. *T:* (020) 7219 8607. *E:* judith.cummins.mp @parliament.uk.

**CUNNINGHAM, Alex;** MP (Lab) Stockton North, since 2010; *b* 1 May 1955; *s* of John and Jean Cunningham; *m* 1977, Evaline; two *s. Educ:* Branksome Comprehensive Sch., Darlington; Queen Elizabeth Sixth Form Coll., Darlington; Darlington Coll. of Technol. (Cert. Journalism 1976). Journalist: Darlington and Stockton Times, 1974–76; The Mail, Hartlepool, 1976–77; Radio Tees, 1977–79; Radio Clyde, 1979; Evening Gazette, 1979–84; PR officer, British Gas, 1984–89; Transco: communications advr, 1995–2000; Hd of Communications, 2000–02; Man. Dir, Tees Valley Communicators, 2002–10. Chm., NE Mus. and Libraries Council, 1993–99; Member: NE Regl Bd, Arts Council England, 1992–2000; Bd, One North East, 2008–10; non-exec. Dir, N Tees and Hartlepool NHS Foundn Trust, 2008–10. PPS to Shadow Lord Chancellor and Sec. of State for Justice, 2010–. Member (Lab): Cleveland CC, 1989–96; Stockton on Tees BC, 1999–2010. Mem. Council, MLA, 2008–09.

*Address:* House of Commons, SW1A 0AA; Unit 142, Stockton Business Centre, 70–74 Brunswick Street, Stockton on Tees TS18 1DW.

**CUNNINGHAM, James Dolan;** MP (Lab) Coventry South, since 1997 (Coventry South East, 1992–97); *b* Coatbridge, 4 Feb. 1941; *s* of Adam and Elizabeth Cunningham; *m* 1985, Marion Douglas; one *s* one *d* and one step *s* one step *d*. *Educ:* St Columba High Sch., Coatbridge. Trade Union Diplomas in Industrial Law and Social Sciences. Engineer, 1964–88. Mem. (Lab) Coventry CC, 1972–92 (Leader, 1988–92; formerly Dep. Leader, Chief Whip, Chm. and Vice Chm. of Cttees). Chm., W Midlands Jt Cttee of Local Authority, 1990–92; Sec., AMA, 1991–92. PPS to Solicitor Gen., 2005–07, to Minister of State, DWP, 2007–10. Chm., HM Treasury Back Bench Cttee, 1997–2010. Chm., W Midland Gp of MPs, 2005–10. Mem., MSF. *Address:* House of Commons, SW1A 0AA.

**DAKIN, Nicholas;** MP (Lab) Scunthorpe, since 2010; an Opposition Whip, since 2011; *b* 10 July 1955; *m* Audrey; three *c. Educ:* Longslade Upper Sch., Birstall, Leics; Hull Univ.; King's Coll. London. English teacher: Greatfield High Sch., Hull; Gävle, Sweden; John Leggott College, Scunthorpe: English teacher, then Vice Principal; Principal, 2007–10. Mem. (Lab) N Lincs Council, 1996–2007 (Leader, 1997–2003; Leader, Lab Gp, 2003–07). Mem., Select Cttee on Educn, 2010–11, on Procedure, 2011–. *Address:* House of Commons, SW1A 0AA.

**DANCZUK, Simon Christopher;** MP (Lab) Rochdale, since 2010; *b* 24 Oct. 1966; *m* 1st (marr. diss.); one *s* one *d*; 2nd, 2012, Karen Burke; two *s. Educ:* Gawthorpe Comprehensive Sch., Padiham; Lancaster Univ. (BA Econs and Sociol. 1991). Prodn worker, Main Gas, Padiham, 1982–86; labourer, ICI factory, Darwen, 1986–88; barman, ICI Sports and Social Club, Darwen, 1988–91; res. asst, Sociol. Dept, Lancaster Univ., 1991–93; Res. Officer, Bolton Bury TEC, 1993–95; res. consultant, Opinion Res. Corp. Internat., 1995–97; Res. Co-ordinator, 1997–98, Media and PR Officer, 1998–99, Big Issue in N Trust; Co-founder and Dir, Vision Twentyone, 1999–2011. Mem. (Lab) Blackburn with Darwen BC, 1993–2001. *Publications:* (jtly) Smile for the Camera: the double life of Cyril Smith, 2014. *Address:* House of Commons, SW1A 0AA.

**DAVID, Wayne;** MP (Lab) Caerphilly, since 2001; *b* 1 July 1957; *s* of late D. Haydn David and of Edna A. David; *m* 1991, Catherine Thomas (marr. diss. 2008). *Educ:* Cynffig Comprehensive Sch.; University Coll., Cardiff (BA Hons History; PGCE); University Coll., Swansea. History teacher, Brynteg Comprehensive Sch., Bridgend, 1983–85; Mid Glam Tutor Organiser, S Wales Dist, WEA, 1985–89. Policy Advr, Wales Youth Agency, 1999–2001. MEP (Lab) S Wales, 1989–94, S Wales Central, 1994–99. Treas.,

1989–91, Leader, 1994–98, European Parly Labour Party (formerly British Labour Gp); 1st Vice-Pres., Regl Policy and Planning Cttee, Eur. Parlt, 1992–94; Sec., Tribune Gp of MEPs, 1992–94. Mem., Labour Party NEC, 1994–98. PPS to Minister of State for Armed Forces, 2005–06; an Asst Govt Whip, 2007–08; Parly Under-Sec. of State, Wales Office, 2008–10; Shadow Minister: for Europe, 2010–11; for Political and Constitutional Reform, 2011–13; PPS to Leader of the Opposition, 2013–15. Mem., European Scrutiny Select Cttee, 2001–07; Chm., All Party Parly Gp on EU, 2006–07. Sec., DWP Gp, 2002–07; Wales Gp, 2003–07, PLP; Sec., Labour Movt for Europe, 2003–07. Bd Mem., European Movt, 2002–07; Pres., Wales Council, European Movt, 2006–. Pres., Council for Wales of Voluntary Youth Services, 2001–; Vice-Pres., City of Cardiff Br., UNA, 1989–; Mem., Cefn Cribwr Community Council, 1985–91. President: Aber Valley Male Voice Choir, 2001–; Caerphilly Local Hist. Soc., 2006–; Lab Heritage, 2015–. Fellow, Univ. of Wales Coll. of Cardiff, 1995. *Publications:* (contrib.) Oxford Companion to the Literature of Wales, 1986; Remaining True: a biography of Ness Edwards, 2006; three pamphlets; contrib. Llafur—Jl of Welsh Labour History, Gelligaer Hist. Soc. Jl. *Recreations:* music, reading. *Address:* c/o House of Commons, SW1A 0AA. *T:* (020) 7219 8152. *Club:* Bargoed Bowls (Pres., 2005–).

**DAVIES, Christopher Paul;** MP (C) Brecon and Radnorshire, since 2015; *b* Swansea, 18 Aug. 1967; *s* of T. V. S. Davies and late M. G. Davies (*née* Morgan); *m* 2006, Elizabeth Mary Dwyer; two *d. Educ:* Morriston Sch., Swansea. Rural auctioneer and estate agent; Manager, Hay Vet. Gp, Hay-on-Wye, 2008–14. Mem., Brecon Beacons Nat. Park Authy, 2012–15. Asst Hon. Dir, Royal Welsh Show, 2014–. Mem. (C) Powys CC, 2012–15. Contested (C) Brecon and Radnorshire, Welsh Assembly, 2011. Gov., Gwernyfed High Sch., 2012–. *Recreation:* countryside activities. *Address:* Ty Gwyn, Brookside, Glasbury-on-Wye, Powys HR3 5NF. *T:* (01982) 559180. *E:* chris.davies.mp@ parliament.uk.

**DAVIES, David Thomas Charles;** MP (C) Monmouth, since 2005; *b* 26 June 1970; *s* of Peter Hugh Charles Davies and Kathleen Diane Davies (*née* Elton); *m* 2003, Aliz Harnisföger; one *s* two *d. Educ:* Clytha Sch., Newport; Bassaleg Sch., Newport. MInstTA; MILog; MIFF. BSC, 1988–89; Australia, 1989–91; Gen. Manager, Tea Importing and Shipping Co. (family business), 1991–99. Chm., Welsh Affairs Select Cttee, 2010–. Mem. (C) Monmouth, Nat. Assembly for Wales, 1999–2007. Contested (C) Bridgend, 1997. *Recreations:* running, surfing, white collar boxing (incl. charity bouts as 'The Tory Tornado'), salsa dancing, debunking climate change alarmism. *Address:* (constituency office) The Grange, 16 Maryport Street, Usk, Monmouthshire NP15 1AB; House of

Commons, SW1A 0AA. *Clubs:* Abergavenny Conservative; Chepstow Conservative; Monmouth Conservative; Usk Conservative.

**DAVIES, Geraint Richard;** MP (Lab and Co-op) Swansea West, since 2010; *b* 3 May 1960; *s* of David Thomas Morgan Davies and Betty Ferrer Davies; *m* 1991, Dr Vanessa Catherine Fry; three *d. Educ:* Llanishen Comp. Sch., Cardiff; Jesus Coll., Oxford (JCR Pres.; BA Hons PPE, MA). Joined Brooke Bond Oxo as sales and mkting trainee, 1982; subseq. Gp Product Manager, Unilever; Marketing Manager, Colgate Palmolive Ltd; Founder, and Director: Pure Crete, 1989–2010; Pure Aviation, 1996–2010; Dir, Equity Creative Ltd, 1989–2001. Chair, Flood Risk Mgt Wales, 2005–10. Mem., Croydon BC, 1986–97 (Chm. of Housing, 1994–96; Leader of Council, 1996–97); Chm., London Boroughs Housing Cttee, 1994–96. Contested (Lab): Croydon S, 1987; Croydon Central, 1992. MP (Lab) Croydon Central, 1997–2005; contested (Lab) same seat, 2005. Team PPS, Dept of Constitutional Affairs, 2003–05. Member: Public Accounts Select Cttee, 1997–2003; Welsh Affairs Select Cttee, 2010–15; European Scrutiny Select Cttee, 2013–; Chairmen's Panel, 2015–. Sec., Parly Gp on Domestic Violence, 2003–05; Parly Ambassador, NSPCC, 2003–05. Chair: Lab. Finance and Industry Gp, 1998–2003 (Mem. Exec., 1994–; Vice Pres., 2003–); Deptl Cttee, Envmt, Transport and Regions, 1997–2003. Mem., Parly Assembly of the Council for Europe, 2010–15. Published parliamentary bills: Physical Punishment of Children (Prohibition) Bill, 2003; Regulation of Child Care Providers Bill, 2003; Regulation of Hormone Disrupting Chemicals Bill, 2004; School Meals and Nutrition Bill, 2005; Credit Card Regulation (Child Pornography) Bill, 2010; Multinational Motor Companies (duty of care to former employees) Bill, 2012; Regulation of Psychotherapists and Counsellors Bill, 2013; Sugar in Food and Drinks Bill, 2014; Bill criminalising Revenge Pornography, 2014 (incorporated into Criminal Justice and Courts Act, 2015); Electronic Cigarettes Bill, 2014; Internat. Trade Agreements (Security) Bill, 2014. *Recreations:* spending time with the family, singing. *Address:* House of Commons, SW1A 0AA.

**DAVIES, Glyn;** MP (C) Montgomeryshire, since 2010; *b* 16 Feb. 1944; *m* 1969, Bobbie; three *s* one *d. Educ:* Caereinion High Sch.; UCW, Aberystwyth. Mem. (C) Montgomeryshire DC, 1985–88 (Chm.). Chm., Develt Bd for Rural Wales, 1989–94. Mem. (C) Mid & W Wales, Nat. Assembly for Wales, 1999–2007. Contested (C) Montgomeryshire, 1997. *Recreations:* countryside, sport. *Address:* Cil Farm, Berriew, Welshpool, Montgomeryshire, Mid Wales SY21 8AZ. *T:* (01686) 640698.

**DAVIES, (Henry) Byron;** MP (C) Gower, since 2015; *b* Swansea, 4 Sept. 1952; *s* of William John Davies and Gladys Mary Davies; *m* 1978, Gill; one

*s. Educ:* Gowerton Boys' Grammar Sch., Swansea; Univ. of West London (LLB Hons). Officer, Metropolitan Police, 1971–2003; owner and dir of consultancy co. advising foreign govts on organised crime, 2003–11. Mem. (C) S Wales W, Nat. Assembly for Wales, 2011–May 2015. *Recreations:* general aviation, private pilot, cycling, Rugby. *Address:* House of Commons, SW1A 0AA. *Clubs:* Royal Air Force; Gowerton Conservative and Unionist.

**DAVIES, James Michael;** MP (C) Vale of Clwyd, since 2015; *b* St Asaph, 27 Feb. 1980; *s* of Michael Davies and Belinda Davies; *m* 2012, Nina Jones; one *s. Educ:* King's Sch., Chester; Christ's Coll., Cambridge (BA; MB BChir 2004; MA 2005). MRCGP 2008. Pre-registration House Officer, Glan Clwyd Hosp., 2004–05; Sen. House Officer, Countess of Chester Hosp., 2005–07; GP Registrar, City Walls Med. Centre, Chester, 2007–08; GP, Boughton Med. Gp, Chester, 2008–15; Partner, 2010–15. Mem. (C), Denbighshire CC, 2004–15. *Recreations:* travelling, walking, languages, local community regeneration, cinema, real ale and dining out, DIY. *Address:* House of Commons, SW1A 0AA. *T:* (020) 7219 4627. *E:* james.davies.mp@parliament.uk; (office) Hanover House, The Roe, St Asaph LL17 0LT. *T:* (01745) 583270. *Club:* Carlton.

**DAVIES, Mims;** MP (C) Eastleigh, since 2015; *b* Crawley, 2 June 1975; *m* Mark Davies; two *d. Educ:* Forest Grange Sch., Horsham; Royal Russell Sch., Croydon; Univ. of Swansea (BA Hons Politics with Internat. Relns). Radio presenter and events asst, The Wave, Swansea; radio presenter, Heartbeat FM, Knebworth; reporter and producer, BBC Southern Counties Radio; Communications Officer, Sussex Safer Roads Partnership. Member: Mid Sussex DC; Haywards Heath Town Council. *Recreations:* running, pop music, family time, sport. *Address:* House of Commons, SW1A 0AA. *T:* (020) 7219 6853. *E:* mims.davies.mp@parliament.uk. *W:* www.mimsdavies.org.uk. *Club:* Haywards Heath Harriers.

**DAVIES, Philip Andrew;** MP (C) Shipley, since 2005; *b* 5 Jan. 1972; *s* of Peter Davies and Marilyn (*née* Johnson, now Lifsey); *m* 1994, Debbie Hemsley (marr. diss. 2012); two *s. Educ:* Univ. of Huddersfield (BA Hons Histl and Pol Studies). Asda: various positions, 1993–2000; Customer Service Project Manager, 2000–04; Mktg Manager, 2004–05. Contested (C) Colne Valley, 2001. Member: Culture, Media and Sport Select Cttee, 2006–15; Backbench Business Cttee, 2010–12; Chairmen's Panel, 2010–; Justice Select Cttee, 2015–. Mem. Exec. Cttee, 1922 Cttee, 2006–12. *Recreation:* horse racing. *Address:* House of Commons, SW1A 0AA. *E:* philip.davies.mp@parliament.uk.

**DAVIS, Rt Hon. David (Michael);** PC 1997; MP (C) Haltemprice and Howden, 1997–June 2008 and since July 2008 (Boothferry, 1987–97); *b* 23 Dec. 1948; *s* of Ronald and Elizabeth Davis; *m* 1973, Doreen Margery Cook; one *s* two *d*. *Educ:* Warwick Univ. (BSc); London Business Sch. (MSc); Harvard (AMP). Joined Tate & Lyle, 1974: Strategic Planning Dir, 1984–87; Dir, 1987–89. PPS to Parly Under-Sec. of State, DTI, 1989–90; an Asst Govt Whip, 1990–93; Parly Sec., Office of Public Service and Science, Cabinet Office, 1993–94; Minister of State, FCO, 1994–97; Chm., Cons. Party, 2001–02; Shadow Sec. of State, ODPM, 2002–03; Shadow Home Sec., 2003–08. Chm., H of C Public Accounts Cttee, 1997–2001. Resigned seat June 2008 to contest by-election on civil liberties issue; re-elected July 2008. Non-exec. Dir, New City Agenda, 2014–. Mem., Financial Policy Cttee, CBI, 1977–79; Exec. Mem., Industrial Soc., 1985–87. Chm., Fedn of Cons. Students, 1973–74. *Recreations:* writing, flying, mountaineering. *Address:* House of Commons, SW1A 0AA.

**DAY, Martyn;** MP (SNP) Linlithgow and East Falkirk, since 2015; *b* Falkirk, 26 March 1971. Former bank worker. Mem. (SNP), W Lothian Council, 1999–2015. *Address:* House of Commons, SW1A 0AA.

**DEBBONAIRE, Thangam Rachel;** MP (Lab) Bristol West, since 2015; *b* 3 Aug. 1966; *née* Singh. *Educ:* Bradford Girls' Grammar Sch.; Chetham's Music Sch.; ARCM 1986; Univ. of Oxford; St John's City Coll. of Technol., Manchester; Bristol Univ. (MSc 1995). Professional cellist in string quartets, chamber music and soloist, 1977–2006; cellist, Royal Liverpool Philharmonic Orch., 1990–91; House-parent, girls boarding, Chetham's Sch. of Music, Manchester, 1989–91; Nat. Children's Officer, Women's Aid Fedn, 1991–98; Dir and lead ind. practitioner, Domestic Violence Responses, 1997–; Accreditation Officer, 2006–08, Res. and Fundraising Manager, 2008–15, Respect. *Publications:* (contrib.) Children Living with Domestic Violence, 1994; (jtly) Health Professionals Responding to Men for Safety, 2014; Responding to Domestic Violence in Diverse Communities, 2015. *Address:* House of Commons, SW1A 0AA. *W:* www.debbonaire.co.uk.

**DE PIERO, Gloria;** MP (Lab) Ashfield, since 2010; *b* Bradford, 21 Dec. 1972; *d* of Giorgio and Maddalena De Piero; *m* 2012, James Robinson. *Educ:* Yorkshire Martyrs Sch., Bradford; Bradford and Ilkley Coll.; Univ. of Westminster (BA Social Sci. 1996); Birkbeck Coll., Univ. of London (MSc Social and Political Theory 2001). Researcher, Jonathan Dimbleby prog., ITV, 1997–98; Producer/Reporter: On The Record, 1998–2002, Politics Show, 2002–03, BBC; Political Corresp., GMTV, 2003–10. Shadow Minister for Women and Equalities, 2013–15, for Young People and Voter Registration, 2015–. *Recreations:* karaoke, swimming. *Address:* House of Commons, SW1A 0AA. *T:* (020) 7219 7004, *Fax:* (020) 7219 0700. *E:* gloria.depiero.mp@parliament.uk.

**DINENAGE, Caroline;** MP (C) Gosport, since 2010; Parliamentary Under-Secretary of State, Department for Education and Ministry of Justice, since 2015; *b* Portsmouth, 28 Oct. 1971; *d* of Fred Dinenage, MBE and Beverley Dinenage; *m* 2014, (John) Mark Lancaster, *qv*; two *s* by a previous marriage. *Educ:* Univ. of Wales, Swansea (BA Hons English and Politics). Dir, Dinenage Ltd, 1996–. Mem. (C) Winchester CC, 1998–2003. Contested (C) Portsmouth S, 2005. PPS to Rt Hon. Nicola Morgan, 2014–15. Member: Sci. and Technol. Select Cttee, 2012–13; BIS Select Cttee, 2012–15; Vice Chairman: (RN), All-Party Parly Gp for Armed Forces, 2010–14; Associate Parly Gp for Manufg, 2012–; Chairman: All-Party Parly Gp on Local Growth, 2012–14; All-Party Parly Gp on Maths and Numeracy, 2014–. *Address:* House of Commons, SW1A 0AA. *T:* (020) 7219 7078. *E:* caroline.dinenage.mp@parliament.uk.

**DJANOGLY, Jonathan Simon;** MP (C) Huntingdon, since 2001; *b* 3 June 1965; *s* of Sir Harry Djanogly, CBE and Lady Djanogly; *m* 1991, Rebecca Silk; one *s* one *d*. *Educ:* University Coll. Sch.; Oxford Poly. (BA Hons); Guildford Law Sch. Admitted solicitor, 1990; Partner, S J Berwin LLP, 1998–2009. Chm., Pembroke VCT plc, 2012–; Consultant, King & Wood Mallesons LLP, 2012–. Mem. (C) Westminster LBC, 1994–2001. Contested (C) Oxford East, 1997. Shadow Minister, Constitutional, Legal and Home affairs, 2004–05; Shadow Solicitor Gen., and Shadow Trade and Industry Minister, 2005–10; Parly Under-Sec. of State, MoJ, 2010–12. Mem., Trade and Industry Select Cttee, 2001–05. *Recreations:* sports, arts. *Address:* House of Commons, SW1A 0AA. *T:* (020) 7219 2367.

**DOCHERTY, Martin John;** MP (SNP) West Dunbartonshire, since 2015; *b* 1971. *Educ:* Glasgow Coll. of Food Technol. (HND Business Admin 1997); Univ. of Essex (BA Politics); Glasgow Sch. of Art (MA 2004). W Dunbartonshire Community and Volunteering Services. Member (SNP): Clydebank DC, 1992; Glasgow CC, 2012–15. *Address:* House of Commons, SW1A 0AA.

**DODDS, Rt Hon. Nigel (Alexander),** OBE 1997; PC 2010; MP (DemU) Belfast North, since 2001; barrister; *b* 20 Aug. 1958; *s* of Joseph Alexander and Doreen Elizabeth Dodds; *m* 1985, Diana Jean Harris; two *s* one *d*. *Educ:* Portora Royal Sch., Enniskillen; St John's Coll., Cambridge (MA); Inst. of Professional Legal Studies, Belfast (Cert. of Professional Legal Studies). Called to the Bar, NI, 1981. Mem., Belfast City Council, 1985–2010 (Chairman: F and GP Cttee, 1985–87; Develt Cttee, 1997–99);

Lord Mayor of Belfast, 1988–89 and 1991–92; Alderman, Castle Area, 1989–97. Mem., NI Forum, 1996–98. Mem. (DemU) Belfast N, NI Assembly, 1998–2010; Minister: for Social Develt, NI, 1999–2000 and 2001–02; of Enterprise, Trade and Investment, NI, 2007–08; for Finance and Personnel, NI, 2008–09. Vice Pres., Assoc. of Local Authorities of NI, 1988–89. Mem., Senate, QUB, 1987–93. *Address:* House of Commons, SW1A 0AA.

**DOHERTY, Pat;** MP (SF) West Tyrone, since 2001; *b* Glasgow, 18 July 1945; *m* Mary; two *s* three *d*. Sinn Féin: Dir of Elections, 1984–85; Nat. Organiser, 1985–88; Vice-Pres., 1988–2009; Leader of delegn to Forum for Peace and Reconciliation, Dublin, 1994–96. Northern Ireland Assembly: Mem. (SF) W Tyrone, 1998–June 2012; Chm., Enterprise, Trade and Investment Cttee, 1999–2002. Contested (SF) West Tyrone, 1997. *Address:* (office) 1A Melvin Road, Strabane, Co. Tyrone BT82 9PP; c/o House of Commons, SW1A 0AA.

**DONALDSON, Rt Hon. Jeffrey (Mark);** PC 2007; MP Lagan Valley, since 1997 (UU, 1997–2003, DUP, since 2004); *b* 7 Dec. 1962; *s* of James Alexander Donaldson and Sarah Anne Donaldson; *m* 1987, Eleanor Mary Elizabeth Cousins; two *d*. *Educ:* Castlereagh Coll. (DipEE); Chartered Insurance Inst. (Financial Planning Cert.). Agent to Rt Hon. J. Enoch Powell, MP, 1983–85; Mem., NI Assembly, 1985–86; Partner in financial services/estate agency practice, 1986–97. Mem., NI Forum, 1996–98. Mem., Lagan Valley, NI Assembly, 2003–10 (UU, 2003–04, DUP, 2004–10). Jun. Minister, Office of the First Minister and Dep. First Minister, NI, 2008–09. Alderman, Lisburn CC, 2005–10. Hon. Sec., 1988–2000, Vice-Pres., 2000–03, UU Council. Chm., Causeway Inst. for Peace Building and Conflict Resolution, 2011–. *Recreations:* travelling, walking, reading, war graves and battlefield heritage. *Address:* House of Commons, SW1A 0AA. *T:* (020) 7219 3407; Old Town Hall, 29 Castle Street, Lisburn, Co. Antrim BT27 4DH. *T:* (028) 9266 8001.

**DONALDSON, Stuart Blair;** MP (SNP) West Aberdeenshire and Kincardine, since 2015; *s* of Bruce Donaldson and Maureen Donaldson. *Educ:* Banchory Acad.; Univ. of Glasgow (MA 2013). Formerly Parly Asst to Christian Allard, MSP. *Address:* House of Commons, SW1A 0AA.

**DONELAN, Michelle;** MP (C) Chippenham, since 2015; *b* Whitley, Cheshire, 8 April 1984; *d* of Michael and Kathryn Donelan. *Educ:* Univ. of York (BA Hons Hist. and Politics). Mktg asst on Marie Claire mag. and That's Life mag., Pacific Magazines, 2006–07; Mktg Exec., then Sen. Mktg Exec., Hist. Channel, AETN UK, 2007–10; Internat. Mktg Manager, World Wrestling Entertainment, 2010–14; mktg freelancer, Wilts, 2014–15. Contested (C) Wentworth and Dearne, 2010. *Recreations:* cycling, swimming, walking, cooking. *Address:* House of Commons, SW1A 0AA. *T:* 07794 040334. *E:* michelle.donelan.mp@parliament.uk.

**DORRIES, Nadine;** MP (C) Mid Bedfordshire, since 2005; *b* 21 May 1957; *d* of George and Sylvia Bargery; *m* 1984, Paul Dorries (marr. diss.); three *d*. *Educ:* Halewood Grange Comprehensive Sch., Liverpool; Warrington Dist Sch. of Nursing. Former nurse and businesswoman. Dir, BUPA. Advr to Oliver Letwin, MP. Contested (C) Hazel Grove, 2001. *Publications:* The Four Streets, 2014 (novel). *Address:* House of Commons, SW1A 0AA. *E:* dorriesn@parliament.uk. *Club:* Carlton.

**DOUBLE, Stephen Daniel;** MP (C) St Austell and Newquay, since 2015; *b* St Austell, 19 Dec. 1966; *m* 1986, Anne Bird; three *s*. *Educ:* Poltair Sch., St Austell. Barclays Bank, 1983–92; church pastor, 1992–2002. Director: Bay Direct Media Ltd, 2001–15; Phoenix Corporate Ltd, 2011–15. Mem. (C), Cornwall Council, 2009–15. *Address:* House of Commons, SW1A 0AA.

**DOUGHTY, Stephen John;** MP (Lab) Cardiff South and Penarth, since Nov. 2012; *b* Cardiff, 1980; *s* of Barry and Eileen Doughty. *Educ:* Llantwit Major Comprehensive Sch.; Lester B. Pearson United World Coll.; Corpus Christi Coll., Oxford (BA Hons 2001); St Andrews Univ. (MLitt 2003). Campaigns Coordinator, World Vision UK, 2004–06; Hd, Govt Relns, Oxfam GB, 2006–09; Special Advr, DFID, 2009–10; Hd, Oxfam Cymru/Wales, 2011–12. PPS to Shadow Chief Sec. to HM Treasury, 2013; an Opposition Whip, 2013–. *Recreations:* walking, music, travel, singing, outdoor pursuits. *Address:* House of Commons, SW1A 0AA. *T:* (020) 7219 5348. *E:* stephen.doughty.mp@parliament.uk.

**DOWD, James Patrick;** MP (Lab) Lewisham West and Penge, since 2010 (Lewisham West, 1992–2010); *b* Germany, 5 March 1951; *s* of late James Patrick Dowd and Elfriede Anna Dowd (*née* Janocha). *Educ:* Dalmain JM&I Sch., London; Sedgehill Comprehensive, London; London Nautical School. Apprentice telephone engineer, GPO, 1967–72; Station Manager, Heron petrol stations, 1972–73; Telecomms Engineer, Plessey Co., later GPT, 1973–92. Group Rep. and Br. Cttee, PO Engrg Union, 1967–72; Sen. Negotiator, ASTMS, then MSF. Lewisham Council: Councillor, 1974–94: Chief Whip; Chm. of Cttees; Dep. Leader; Dep. Mayor, 1987, 1991; Mayor, 1992. Former Mem., Lewisham and Southwark DHA. Contested (Lab): Beckenham, 1983; Lewisham W, 1987. An Opposition Whip, 1993–95; opposition frontbench spokesman on Northern Ireland, 1995–97; a Lord Comr of HM Treasury (Govt Whip), 1997–2001. Member: Select Cttee on Health, 2001–10; Select Cttee on Sci. and Technol., 2012–. Former school governor. *Recreations:* music, reading, theatre, Cornwall, being with friends. *Address:* House of Commons, SW1A 0AA. *T:* (020) 7219 4617. *Club:* Bromley Labour.

**DOWD, Peter;** MP (Lab) Bootle, since 2015; *b* Bootle, 20 June 1957. *Educ:* Liverpool Univ.; Lancaster Univ. CQSW. Health and social care worker, Merseyside. Member (Lab): Merseyside CC, 1981–86; Sefton BC, 1991– (Leader, Labour Gp, 2008–15; Leader of Council, 2011–15). *Address:* House of Commons, SW1A 0AA.

**DOWDEN, Oliver James,** CBE 2015; MP (C) Hertsmere, since 2015; *b* Park St, Herts; *m* Blythe; one *s* one *d. Educ:* Parmiters' Sch., Watford; Trinity Hall, Cambridge (BA). Teacher, Japan; lawyer, London; Account Dir, LLM; Dep. Campaigns Dir, Cons. Party; Man. Consultant, Hill and Knowlton Strategies, 2007; Dep. Dir, Political Ops, Cons. Party; Dep. COS and Advr to Prime Minister on policy and political issues, 2012–14. *Address:* House of Commons, SW1A 0AA.

**DOYLE-PRICE, Jackie;** MP (C) Thurrock, since 2010; an Assistant Government Whip, since 2015; *b* Sheffield, 5 Aug. 1969; *d* of Brian and Kathleen Doyle-Price. *Educ:* Notre Dame RC Sch., Sheffield; Univ. of Durham (BA Hons Econs/Politics). Asst Parly Officer, City of London, 1993–2000; Asst Private Sec. to Lord Mayor of City of London, 2000–05; Associate, FSA, 2005–10. Mem., Grays RAFA. *Recreations:* reading, theatre, music. *Address:* House of Commons, SW1A 0AA. *T:* (020) 7219 7171. *E:* jackie.doyleprice.mp@parliament.uk. *Club:* Grays Conservative.

**DRAX, Richard Grosvenor;** MP (C) South Dorset, since 2010; farmer; *b* 29 Jan. 1958; *s* of (Henry) Walter Plunkett-Ernle-Erle-Drax and Hon. Pamela Rose (*née* Weeks); *m* 1st, 1985, Zara Victoria Legge-Bourke (marr. diss. 1997); two *s* two *d*; 2nd, 1998, Eliza Sarah Dugdale; 3rd, 2009, Elsebet Bødtker. *Educ:* Harrow Sch.; Royal Agricl Coll., Cirencester (Dip. Rural Land Mgt 1990); Dip. Journalism 1995. Served Coldstream Guards, 1978–87. Journalist: Yorks Evening Press, 1991–96; Tyne Tees TV, Daily Express and Daily Telegraph, 1996–97; and reporter, BBC Radio Solent and BBC South Today, 1997–2006. *Address:* House of Commons, SW1A 0AA.

**DROMEY, Jack;** MP (Lab) Birmingham Erdington, since 2010; *b* 29 Sept. 1948; *m* 1982, Harriet Harman (*see* Rt Hon. H. Harman); two *s* one *d. Educ:* Cardinal Vaughan Grammar Sch. Sec., Brent Trades Council, 1976–78; Transport and General Workers' Union, later Unite: various posts from dist officer to nat. organiser, 1978–2003; Dep. Gen. Sec., 2003–10. Treas., Labour Party, 2004–10. Shadow Minister for Housing, 2010–13, for Home Affairs, 2013–15. Member, Select Committee: Business, Innovation and Skills, 2010; Regulatory Reform, 2010–15. *Address:* House of Commons, SW1A 0AA.

**DRUMMOND, Felicia Jane Beatrix;** MP (C) Portsmouth South, since 2015; *b* 16 June 1962; *d* of (George) Anthony Shepherd and Sarah Shepherd; *m* 1987, Hereward John Heneage Drummond; two *s* two *d. Educ:* Hull Univ. (BA SE Asian Studies 1983); Southampton Univ. (MA Global Politics and Internat. Relns 2007). Insce broker, 1983–87; Ofsted lay sch. inspector, 1994–99; Dir, Corporate Affairs, Cons. Middle East Council, 2010–11; Dep. Chm., Political, Portsmouth S Cons. Assoc., 2011–13. Member: Healthwatch; Community Health Council. Mem. (C) Winchester CC, 1996–99. Contested (C): Southampton Itchen, 2005; Portsmouth S, 2010. Trustee: Portsmouth CAB; Internat. Traditional Boatbuilding Coll., Portsmouth Historic Dockyard; ANA. Mem., Intelligence Corps, TA. *Address:* House of Commons, SW1A 0AA.

**DUDDRIDGE, James Philip;** MP (C) Rochford and Southend East, since 2005; *b* 26 Aug. 1971; *s* of Philip and Jennifer Duddridge; *m* 2004, Kathryn Brigid Thompson; two *s* one *d. Educ:* Univ. of Essex (BA Politics). With Barclays Bank, 1993–2002: Sales Dir, Ivory Coast, 1997–98; Sales Manager for unit trust business, UK, 1998–2001; Service Delivery Dir, Botswana, 2001–02; Account Dir, YouGov, 2001–05; Dir, Okavango Ltd, 2002–05. An Opposition Whip, 2008–10; a Lord Comr of HM Treasury (Govt Whip), 2010–12; Parly Under Sec. of State for Foreign and Commonwealth Affairs, 2014–15. Chm., Regulatory Reform Select Cttee, 2013–. *Recreations:* running, cycling, real ale. *Address:* House of Commons, SW1A 0AA. *T:* (020) 7219 4830, *Fax:* (020) 7219 3888. *E:* james@jamesduddridge.com. *Clubs:* Southend United Football, Southampton Football.

**DUGHER, Michael Vincent;** MP (Lab) Barnsley East, since 2010; *b* Doncaster, 26 April 1975; *s* of Robert Dugher and Isobel Dugher (*née* Archer); *m* 2004, Joanna Nunney; one *s* two *d. Educ:* St Mary's RC Sch., Edlington; McAuley RC Sch., Doncaster; Univ. of Nottingham (BA Hons Politics). Convenor, Notts and Derbys NUS, 1995–96; Nat. Chair, Labour Students, Lab. Party, 1997–98; Res. Officer, 1998–2000, Hd of Policy, 2000–01, AEEU; Special Adviser: to Minister for Transport, 2001–02; to Sec. of State for Defence, 2002–05; to Leader of H of C, 2005–06; UK Dir, Govt Relns, EDS, 2006–07; Special Advr to Govt Chief Whip, 2007–08; Chief Political Spokesman to Prime Minister, 2008–10. Shadow Minister for Defence Equipment, Support and Technol., 2010–11; PPS to Leader of the Opposition, 2011; Shadow Minister without Portfolio, Cabinet Office, 2011–13; Shadow Minister for Cabinet Office, 2013–14, for Transport, 2014–15, for Culture, Media and Sport, 2015–. Vice-Chair, Labour Party, 2012–13. *Publications:* (with J. Spellar) Fools Gold: dispelling the myth of the Tory economic legacy, 1999; (contrib.) Dictionary of Labour Biography, 2001. *Recreations:* football (watching), music (playing and listening), history. *Address:* House of Commons, SW1A 0AA; (office) West

Bank House, West Street, Hoyland, Barnsley S74 9EE. *T:* (01226) 743483. *E:* michael.dugher.mp @parliament.uk.

**DUNCAN, Rt Hon. Sir Alan (James Carter)**, KCMG 2014; PC 2010; MP (C) Rutland and Melton, since 1992; *b* 31 March 1957; 2nd *s* of late Wing Comdr J. G. Duncan, OBE and Anne Duncan (*née* Carter); civil partnership 2008, James Dunseath. *Educ:* Merchant Taylors' Sch.; St John's Coll., Oxford. Pres., Oxford Union, 1979. With Shell Internat. Petroleum, 1979–81; Kennedy Schol., Harvard Univ., 1981–82; oil trader, Marc Rich & Co., 1982–88; self-employed oil broker, 1988–92. PPS to Min. of State, DoH, 1993–94, to Chm. of Cons. Party, 1995–97; a Vice Chm. of Cons. Party, 1997–98; Parly Political Sec. to Leader of the Opposition, 1997; Opposition spokesman on health, 1998–99, on trade and industry, 1999–2001, on foreign affairs, 2001–03; Shadow Sec. of State for Constitutional Affairs, 2003–04, for Internat. Devslt, 2004–05, for Transport, 2005, for Trade and Industry, 2005–07, for Business, Enterprise and Regulatory Reform, 2007–09; Shadow Leader, H of C, 2009; Shadow Jun. Justice Minister for Prisons, 2009–10; Minister of State, DFID, 2010–14; Special Envoy to Yemen and to Oman, 2014–. Member: Select Cttee on Social Security, 1993–95; Intelligence and Security Cttee, 2015–. Contested (C) Barnsley W and Penistone, 1987. Vis. Parly Fellow, St Antony's Coll., Oxford, 2002–03. Freeman, City of London, 1980; Liveryman, Merchant Taylors' Co., 1987. *Publications:* An End to Illusions, 1993; (with D. Hobson) Saturn's Children: how the state devours liberty, prosperity and virtue, 1995. *Address:* House of Commons, SW1A 0AA. *Club:* Beefsteak.

**DUNCAN SMITH, Rt Hon. (George) Iain**; PC 2001; MP (C) Chingford and Woodford Green, since 1997 (Chingford, 1992–97); Secretary of State for Work and Pensions, since 2010; *b* 9 April 1954; *s* of late Group Captain W. G. G. Duncan Smith, DSO (Bar), DFC (2 Bars) and Pamela Mary Duncan Smith (*née* Summers); *m* 1982, Hon. Elizabeth Wynne Fremantle, *er d* of Baron Cottesloe; two *s* two *d. Educ:* HMS Conway (Cadet School); RMA Sandhurst; Dunchurch Coll. of Management. Scots Guards, 1975–81; ADC to Gen. Sir John Acland, 1979–81; GEC, 1981–88; Dir, Bellwinch (Property), 1988; Dir, Jane's Inf. Group, 1989–92. Vice-Chm., Fulham Cons. Assoc., 1991. Contested (C) Bradford West, 1987. Shadow Sec. of State for social security, 1997–99, for defence, 1999–2001; Leader, Cons. Party and Leader of the Opposition, 2001–03. Member, Select Committee: on Health, 1994–95; on Nolan, 1995; on Standards and Privileges, 1996–97. Sec., Cons. Backbench Cttee on Foreign and Commonwealth Affairs, 1992–97; Vice Chm., Cons. European Affairs Cttee, 1996–97; Mem., Cons. Party Adv. Council, 2003–. Chm. and Founder, Centre for Social Justice, 2004–10

(Patron, 2010–). Trustee: Lygon Alms-house, 1985–91; Whitefield Develt Trust. Freeman, City of London. *Publications:* The Devil's Tune (novel), 2003; Breakdown Britain, 2006; Breakthrough Britain, 2007; (jtly) Early Intervention: good parents, great kids, better citizens, 2009; various pamphlets on social security, European and defence issues; occasional journalism. *Recreations:* family, painting, fishing, cricket, tennis, shooting, opera, reading. *Address:* House of Commons, SW1A 0AA. *T:* (020) 7219 2667 and 3000.

**DUNLOP,** Baron *cr* 2015 (Life Peer), of Helensburgh in the County of Dunbarton; **Andrew James Dunlop;** Parliamentary Under-Secretary of State, Scotland Office, since 2015; *b* Helensburgh, 21 June 1959; *s* of Robert Jack Dunlop and Dorothy Shirley Dunlop; *m* 1991, Lucia Mary Elizabeth Campbell; three *d. Educ:* Trinity Coll., Glenalmond; Glasgow Acad.; Edinburgh Univ. (MA Hons Politics and Modern Hist.); King's Coll., London (Postgrad. Dip. European Competition Law). Midland Bank Internat., 1981–82; Hd of Policy and Res., Scottish Cons. Party, 1982–84; Cons. Res. Dept, 1984–86; Special Advr, Sec. of State for Defence, 1986–88; Prime Minister's Policy Unit, 1988–90; founder and Man. Dir, Politics Internat. Ltd, 1991–2008; Man. Dir, 2008–10, Exec. Chm., 2010–11, Interel Consulting UK; Mem. Mgt Bd, Interel Gp, Brussels, 2008–11; Special Advr to Prime Minister on Scotland and Devolution, 2012–15. Mem. Mgt Cttee, Sussex County, 2009–11, SE Region, 2011–12, Amateur Swimming Assoc. *Recreations:* swimming, tennis, sailing, gardening, ski-ing, following football. *Address:* House of Lords, SW1A 0PW. *Clubs:* Reform; Atlantis Horsham Swimming (Chm., 2008–12).

**DUNNE, Philip Martin;** MP (C) Ludlow, since 2005; Minister of State, Ministry of Defence, since 2015; *b* 14 Aug. 1958; *s* of Sir Thomas Raymond Dunne; *m* 1989, Domenica Margaret Anne Fraser; two *s* two *d. Educ:* Eton Coll.; Keble Coll., Oxford (BA 1980; MA 2006). S. G. Warburg & Co. Ltd, 1980–88; Dir, Corp. Develt, James Gulliver Associates, 1988–90; Partner, Phoenix Securities, 1991–97; a Man. Dir, Donaldson, Lufkin & Jenrette, 1997–2001; Dir, Business Develt, 2002–05, non-exec. Dir, 2006–09, Ruffer LLP. Co-founder, Dir, 1987–97, non-exec. Chm., 1997–2006, Ottakar's plc; non-exec. Chm., Baronsmead VCT 4 plc, 2001–10. Partner, Gatley Farms, 1987–. Mem. (C), S Shropshire DC, 2001–07. Asst Opposition Whip, 2008–10; Asst Govt Whip, 2010–12; Parly Under-Sec. of State, MoD, 2012–15. Member: Work and Pensions Select Cttee, 2005–06; Public Accounts Cttee, 2006–08; Treasury Select Cttee, 2007–08. Dep. Chm., Internat. Office, Cons. Party, 2008–10; Gov. (C) Westminster Foundn for Democracy, 2008–10. Dir, Juvenile Diabetes Res. Foundn, 1999–2005. *Address:* (office) 54 Broad Street, Ludlow, Shropshire SY8 1GP; House of Commons, SW1A 0AA.

**DURKAN, (John) Mark;** MP (SDLP) Foyle, since 2005; Leader, Social Democratic and Labour Party, 2001–10; *b* 26 June 1960; *s* of Brendan Durkan and Isobel Durkan (*née* Tinney); *m* 1993, Jackie Green; one *d. Educ:* St Columb's Coll., Derry; Queen's Univ., Belfast. Asst to John Hume, 1984–98. Mem. (SDLP) Derry CC, 1993–2000. Member: Forum for Peace and Reconciliation, Dublin, 1994–96; NI Forum (Talks Negotiator), 1996–98. Northern Ireland Assembly: Mem. (SDLP) Foyle, 1998–2010; Minister for Finance and Personnel, 1999–2001; Dep. First Minister, 2001–02; Chm., Cttee for Enterprise, Trade and Investment, 2007–09. Chairperson, SDLP, 1990–95. *Address:* (office) 23 Bishop Street, Derry BT48 6PR. *T:* (028) 7136 0700, *Fax:* (028) 7136 0808.

**EAGLE, Angela;** MP (Lab) Wallasey, since 1992; *b* 17 Feb. 1961; twin *d* of André and late Shirley Eagle; civil partnership 2008, Maria Exall. *Educ:* Formby High Sch.; St John's Coll., Oxford (BA PPE). Economic Directorate, CBI, 1984; Confederation of Health Service Employees: Researcher, 1984; Press Officer, 1986; Parly Officer, 1987–92. Parly Under-Sec. of State, DETR, 1997–98, DSS, 1998–2001, Home Office, 2001–02; Exchequer Sec. to HM Treasury, 2007–09; Minister of State (Minister for Pensions and Ageing Society), DWP, 2009–10; Shadow Chief Sec. to the Treasury, 2010–11; Shadow Leader, H of C, 2011–15; Shadow First Sec. of State and Shadow Sec. of State for Business, Innovation and Skills, 2015–. Mem., Nat. Women's Cttee, 1989–, Nat. Exec. Cttee, 2006–, Labour Party. Chair, Nat. Policy Forum, 2012–. Mem., BFI. *Recreations:* chess (Jun. Internat. Hons), cricket, cinema. *Address:* House of Commons, SW1A 0AA. *T:* (020) 7219 4074.
*See also M. Eagle.*

**EAGLE, Maria;** MP (Lab) Garston and Halewood, since 2010 (Liverpool, Garston, 1997–2010); *b* 17 Feb. 1961; twin *d* of André Eagle and late Shirley Eagle. *Educ:* Formby High Sch.; Pembroke Coll., Oxford (BA Hons); Coll. of Law, Lancaster Gate. Articles, Brian Thompson & Partners, Liverpool, 1990–92; Goldsmith Williams, Liverpool, 1992–95; Sen. Solicitor, Steven Irving & Co., Liverpool, 1994–97. Contested (Lab) Crosby, 1992. Parliamentary Under-Secretary of State: DWP, 2001–05; DfES, 2005–06; NI Office, 2006–07; MoJ, 2007–09; Govt Equalities Office, 2008–09; Minister of State, MoJ and Govt Equalities Office, 2009–10; Shadow Sec. of State for Transport, 2010–13, for Envmt, Food and Rural Affairs, 2013–15, for Defence, 2015–. *Address:* House of Commons, SW1A 0AA.
*See also A. Eagle.*

**EDWARDS, Jonathan;** MP (Plaid Cymru) Carmarthen East and Dinefwr, since 2010; *b* Capel Hendre, Carmarthenshire, 26 April 1976. *Educ:* Ysgol Gyfun Maes yr Yrfa; Univ. of Wales, Aberystwyth (BA Hist. and Politics; postgrad. degree in Internat. Hist.). COS to Rhodri Glyn Thomas, Mem., Nat. Assembly for Wales and Adam Price, MP; with Nat. Campaigns Directorate, Plaid Cymru, 2005–07; with Citizens Advice Cymru, 2007–. Plaid Cymru spokesman for: Business, Innovation and Skills, 2010–; Communities and Local Government, 2010–15; Culture, Olympics, Media and Sport, 2010–15; Transport, 2010–; Treasury, 2010–; Foreign Intervention, 2015–. Mem., Welsh Affairs Select Cttee, 2010–15. *Address:* House of Commons, SW1A 0AA.

**EFFORD, Clive Stanley;** MP (Lab) Eltham, since 1997; *b* 10 July 1958; *s* of Stanley Charles Efford and Mary Agnes Elizabeth Christina Caldwell; *m* 1981, Gillian Vallins; three *d. Educ:* Walworth Comprehensive Sch. Sen. Adventure Playground Leader; Asst to Warden, Pembroke Coll. Mission; former London taxi driver. Mem. (Lab) Greenwich LBC, 1986–98 (former Gp Sec.; Chief Whip; Chm., Social Services Cttee, Health and Envmt Cttee). Contested (Lab) Eltham, 1992. Shadow Minister for the Home Office, 2010–11, for Sports, Tourism and Gambling, 2011–15; PPS to successive Ministers for Housing, DCLG, 2008–10. Mem., Procedure Select Cttee, 1997–2000, Transport Select Cttee, 2002–09, H of C. Prelim. FA Coach's Badge. *Recreations:* sports, reading, cinema. *Address:* (office) 132 Westmount Road, Eltham, SE9 1UT. *T:* (020) 8850 5744. *Clubs:* Eltham Hill Working Man's, Woolwich Catholic.

**ELLIOTT, Julie;** MP (Lab) Sunderland Central, since 2010; *b* Whitburn, Sunderland, 1963; one *s* three *d. Educ:* Seaham Northlea Comprehensive Sch.; Newcastle Poly. (BA Govt and Public Policy). Regl Organiser, Labour Party, 1993–98; Agent, gen. election, Tynemouth, 1997; Regl Officer, Nat. Asthma Campaign, 1998–99; Regl Organiser, GMB, 1999–2010. Shadow Minister for Energy and Climate Change, 2013–15. Member: Eur. Scrutiny Select Cttee, 2010–15; Business, Innovation and Skills Select Cttee, 2011–13. *Address:* House of Commons, SW1A 0AA.

**ELLIOTT, Thomas;** MP (UU) Fermanagh and South Tyrone, since 2015; *b* 11 Dec. 1963; *s* of late John Elliott and of Noreen Elliott; *m* 1989, Anne; one *s* one *d. Educ:* Ballinamallard Primary Sch.; Duke of Westminster High Sch., Ballinamallard; Enniskillen Coll. of Agric. Self-employed farmer, 1981–. Mem. (pt-time), UDR/Royal Irish Regt, 1982–99. Mem. (UU), Fermanagh DC, 2001–10. Mem. (UU) Fermanagh and S Tyrone, NI Assembly, 2003–June 2015. Leader, Ulster Unionist Party, 2010–12. *Recreations:* community activity, sport, church. *Address:* 1 Regal Pass, Enniskillen, Co. Fermanagh BT74 7NT. *T:* (028) 6632 2028, *Fax:* (028) 6634 2846; House of Commons, SW1A 0AA. *E:* t.elliott6@btopenworld.com.

**ELLIS, Michael Tyrone;** MP (C) Northampton North, since 2010; *b* Northampton, 13 Oct. 1967; *s* of Jack Ellis and Margaret Ellis (*née* Surgenor). *Educ:* Wellingborough Sch.; Univ. of Buckingham (LLB); Inns of Court Sch. of Law (BVC). Called to the Bar, Middle Temple, 1993; in practice as barrister, 1993–2010. Mem. (C) Northants CC, 1997–2001. Member: Home Affairs Select Cttee, 2011–15; Jt Cttee on Statutory Instruments, 2010–; Chm., All-Party Parly Gp on the Queen's Diamond Jubilee, 2010–13. Pres., Commonwealth Jewish Council, 2012–14. *Recreations:* theatre, British Royal history. *Address:* House of Commons, SW1A 0AA. *T:* (020) 7219 7220, *Fax:* (020) 7219 6375. *E:* michael.ellis.mp@parliament.uk. *Club:* Carlton.

**ELLISON, Jane;** MP (C) Battersea, since 2010; Parliamentary Under-Secretary of State, Department of Health, since 2013; *b* Bradford, 15 Aug. 1964; *m* John Samiotis. *Educ:* St Hilda's Coll., Oxford (BA PPE). With John Lewis Partnership, London, 1986–2010: grad. trainee; Manager, Customer Direct Mktg; Sen. Manager, Edition, customer mag.; on secondment with music charity, Sing for Pleasure, 2004. Mem. (C) Barnet LBC, 1991–94, 2006–08. Contested (C): Barnsley E, Dec. 1996; Barnsley E and Mexborough, 1997; Tottenham, June 2000; Pendle, 2005. Member: Works and Pensions Select Cttee, 2012–13; Backbench Business Cttee, 2010–13. Trustee, Sing for Pleasure, 2008–. *Address:* House of Commons, SW1A 0AA.

**ELLMAN, Louise Joyce;** MP (Lab and Co-op) Liverpool Riverside, since 1997; *b* 14 Nov. 1945; *d* of late Harold and Annie Rosenberg; *m* 1967, Geoffrey David Ellman; one *s* one *d*. *Educ:* Manchester High Sch. for Girls; Hull Univ. (BA Hons); York Univ. (MPhil). Worked in further educn and on Open Univ., 1970–76. Member: Lancs CC, 1970–97 (Leader, Lab Gp, 1977–97; Leader, Council, 1981–97; Chm., 1981–85; Hon. Alderman, 1998–); W Lancs DC, 1974–87; Local Govt Adv. Cttee, Labour Party NEC, 1977–90; Regl Exec., NW Labour Party, 1985– (Chm., 1993–98). A Vice Pres., LGA, 1997, 2011–. Contested (Lab) Darwen, 1979. Member: Select Cttee on Envmt, Transport and Regl Affairs, 1997–2001; Select Cttee on Transport, 2002– (Chm., 2008–); Vice Pres., All Pty Parly Cttee against Anti-semitism, 2007–; Jt Sec., All Pty Gp against Trafficking, 2007–11; Treas., All Pty Parly Friends of the Bahá'ís Gp. Chm., PLP Regl Govt Gp, 1999. Chair: Jewish Labour Movement, 2004–; Labour-Regeneration Gp, 2005–10; Vice Chair: Labour Friends of Israel, 2004–; Liverpool Capital of Culture Gp, 2006–. Mem., Bd of Deputies of British Jews, 2007–. Vice-Chm., Lancashire Enterprises, 1982–97; Founder Mem., Co-operative Enterprises NW, 1979–; Founder Chm., NW Regl Assoc., 1992–93;

Mem., NW Partnership, 1993–97. Youngest mem., Lancs CC, 1970; youngest mem. and first woman to be Chm., 1981. *Address:* House of Commons, SW1A 0AA.

**ELLWOOD, Tobias;** MP (C) Bournemouth East, since 2005; Parliamentary Under-Secretary of State, Foreign and Commonwealth Office, since 2014; *b* 12 Aug. 1966; *s* of Peter Ellwood and Dr Caroline Ellwood; *m* 2005, Hannah Ryan. *Educ:* Vienna Internat. Sch.; Loughborough Univ. (BA Hons Design and Technol.); City Univ. Business Sch. (MBA); Kennedy Sch. of Govt, Harvard Univ. (Exec. Course on Nat. and Internat. Security). Served Army, RGJ, 1991–96. Researcher for Rt Hon. Tom King, 1996–97; Senior Business Develt Manager: London Stock Exchange, 1998–2002; Allen & Overy, 2002–04. Shadow Minister for culture, media and sport, 2007–10; PPS to Sec. of State for Defence, 2010–11, to Minister for Europe, 2011–13, to Sec. of State for Health, 2013–14. Mem., Parly Delegn to NATO, 2014–; Parly Advr to Prime Minister for NATO Summit, 2014. *Recreations:* private pilot, wind-surfing, travel, diving, landscape gardening, military history. *Address:* House of Commons, SW1A 0AA. *T:* (020) 7219 3000. *E:* tobias.ellwood.mp@parliament.uk.

**ELPHICKE, Charles;** MP (C) Dover, since 2010; a Lord Commissioner of HM Treasury (Government Whip), since 2015; *b* Huntingdon, 14 March 1971; *m* 1996, Natalie Ross (OBE 2015); one *s* one *d*. *Educ:* Felsted Sch.; Nottingham Univ. (LLB Hons). Called to the Bar, Middle Temple, 1994; admitted solicitor, 1998; Partner and Hd of Tax, Reed Smith, solicitors, 2001–05; Partner and Hd of Eur. Tax, Hunton & Williams, solicitors, 2006–10. Mem. (C) Lambeth LBC, 1994–98. Contested (C) St Albans, 2001. *Publications:* papers for Centre for Policy Studies. *Recreations:* sailing, making Britain a richer, more exciting place to be. *Address:* House of Commons, SW1A 0AA. *T:* (020) 7219 3000. *E:* charlie.elphicke.mp@parliament.uk. *Club:* Royal Cinque Ports Yacht.

**ENGEL, Natascha;** MP (Lab) North East Derbyshire, since 2005; Second Deputy Speaker of Ways and Means, and a Deputy Speaker, since 2015; *b* 9 April 1967; *d* of Achaz and Christina Engel; *m* 2001, David Salisbury Jones (marr. diss. 2012); three *s*. *Educ:* King's Coll., London (BA 1st Cl. Hons Mod. Langs); Westminster Press Dip. Journalism; Westminster Univ. (MA Tech. and Specialist Translation). Journalist, Dover Express, 1990; English and German teacher, Spain, 1990–92; teletext subtitler, 1992–97; GPMU Organiser, TUC Organising Acad., 1997–98; TU Liaison, Labour Party, 1998–2001; Prog. Dir, John Smith Inst., 2001–02; Co-ordinator, TU Political Fund Ballots, 2002–03. *Address:* House of Commons, SW1A 0AA. *T:* (020) 7219 3000. *E:* natascha.engel.mp@parliament.uk.

**ESTERSON, William;** MP (Lab) Sefton Central, since 2010; *b* 27 Oct. 1966; *s* of Derek and Joyce Esterson; *m* 1998, Caroline Herbert; one *s* one *d*. *Educ:* Rochester Mathematical Sch.; Leeds Univ. (BSc Maths and Phil. 1990). Accountancy trng; Dir, Leaps and Bounds (Trng) Ltd. Mem. (Lab) Medway Council, 1995–2010. Member: Envmt, Food and Rural Affairs Select Cttee, 2010–11; Educn Select Cttee, 2010–15; Communities and Local Govt Select Cttee, 2011–13; Treasury Select Cttee, 2015–. *Address:* House of Commons, SW1A 0AA.

**EUSTICE, (Charles) George;** MP (C) Camborne and Redruth, since 2010; Minister of State, Department for Environment, Food and Rural Affairs, since 2015; *b* Penzance, 1971; *s* of Paul Eustice and Adele Eustice. *Educ:* Truro Cathedral Sch.; Truro Sch.; Cornwall Coll.; Writtle Coll. Dir, Trevaskis Farm Ltd, 1996–99; Campaign Dir, No Campaign Against the Euro, 1999–2003; Hd of Press, Conservative Party, 2003–05; Press Sec. to Rt Hon. David Cameron, MP, 2005–07; Hd, External Relns, Conservative Party, 2008–09; Associate Dir, Portland PR, 2009–10. Parly Under-Sec. of State, DEFRA, 2013–15. *Recreation:* running. *Address:* House of Commons, SW1A 0AA. *T:* (020) 7219 7032. *E:* george.eustice.mp@parliament.uk.

**EVANS OF BOWES PARK,** Baroness *cr* 2014 (Life Peer), of Bowes Park in the London Borough of Haringey; **Natalie Jessica Evans;** a Baroness in Waiting (Government Whip), since 2015; *b* London, 29 Nov. 1975; *d* of Nicholas David Evans and Ann Elizabeth Evans; *m* 2010, James Oliver Wild. *Educ:* Henrietta Barnett Sch.; New Hall, Cambridge (BA Social and Political Sci. 1998). Hd of Policy, British Chambers of Commerce, 2006–08; Dep. Dir, Policy Exchange, 2008–11; Chief Operating Officer, 2011–12, Dir, 2012–15, New Schools Network. *Recreations:* cricket, football, theatre, travel, fine wine. *Address:* House of Lords, SW1A 0PW.

**EVANS, Christopher James;** MP (Lab Co-op) Islwyn, since 2010; *b* Llwynipia, Rhondda; *s* of Michael Alan Evans and Lynne Evans; *m* 2013, Julia Teresa Ockenden. *Educ:* Porth Co. Comp. Sch.; Pontypridd Coll.; Trinity Coll., Carmarthen (BA Hist.). Office Manager, Jack Brown Bookmakers Ltd, 1998–2001; Personal Account Manager, Lloyds TSB Bank plc, 2001–03; Marketing Exec., Univ. of Glamorgan, 2003–04; Area Sec., Union of Finance Staff, 2004–06; Parly Researcher, Don Touhig, MP, 2006–10. Contested (Lab) Cheltenham, 2005. *Recreations:* running, reading, watching most sports. *Address:* (office) 6 Woodfieldside Business Park, Penmaen Road, Pontllanfraith, Blackwood NP12 2DG. *T:* (01495) 231990.

**EVANS, Graham;** MP (C) Weaver Vale, since 2010; *b* Poynton, Cheshire, 10 Nov. 1963; *s* of Gordon Evans and Violet Evans; *m* 1995, Cheryl Browne; two *s* one *d*. *Educ:* Poynton High Sch.; Manchester Metropolitan Univ. (BA Hons Business Studies 2000); Postgrad. Dip. Mktg Mgt 2001. BAE Systems, 1982; sales mgt, Sun Chemical, 1988–99; sales mgt, Hewlett Packard, 1999–2004. Mem., Macclesfield BC, 2000–09. Contested (C) Worsley, 2005. MInstD. *Recreations:* cricket, football, Rugby, running, 5-a-side, British history (military, social and economic; specialist First World War historian). *Address:* House of Commons, SW1A 0AA. *T:* (020) 7219 7183. *E:* mail@grahamevansmp.com.

**EVANS, Nigel Martin;** MP (C) Ribble Valley, since 1992; *b* 10 Nov. 1957; *s* of late Albert Evans and Betty Evans. *Educ:* Swansea Univ. (BA Hons). Retail Newsagent, family business, 1979–90. West Glamorgan County Council: Councillor (C), 1985–91; Dep. Leader, 1989. Chm., Welsh Cons. Candidates Policy Gp, 1990; Pres., Cons. NW Parly Gp, 1991. Contested (C): Swansea West, 1987; Pontypridd, Feb. 1989; Ribble Valley, March 1991. PPS to Sec. of State for Employment, 1993–94, to Chancellor of Duchy of Lancaster, 1994–95; Opposition front bench spokesman on Welsh and constitutional affairs, 1997–2001; Shadow Welsh Sec., 2001–03; First Dep. Chm. of Ways and Means and a Dep. Speaker, H of C, 2010–13. Mem., Select Cttee on Transport, 1993, on Envmt, 1996–97, on Public Service, 1996–97, on Trade and Industry, 2003–05, on Culture, Media and Sport, 2005–09, on Internat. Develt, 2009–10; Sec., 1992–97, Chm., 2010–12, NW Gp of Cons. MPs; Secretary: Manufacturing Cttee; All-Party Tourism Cttee; Chairman: All-Party Music Gp, 1996–97 (Vice-Chm., 2002–10); All-Party Identity Fraud Gp, 2006–10; All-Party Egypt Gp, 2007–10; Co-Chm., All-Party Drugs Gp, 1997–2010; Pres., All-Party Beer Gp, 2010–; Patron, Parly Space Cttee, 2010–. Vice-Chm., Cons. Party (Wales), 1999–2001. Director: Made in the UK Ltd; Small Business Bureau. *Recreations:* tennis, swimming, theatre, tourism, new technology, defence, broadcasting. *Address:* Brooklyn Cottage, Main Street, Pendleton, Clitheroe, Lancs BB7 1PT. *T:* (01200) 443875; House of Commons, SW1A 0AA. *Clubs:* Carlton, Royal Automobile, Lansdowne, Groucho.

**EVENNETT, Rt Hon. David (Anthony);** PC 2015; MP (C) Bexleyheath and Crayford, since 2005; a Lord Commissioner of HM Treasury (Government Whip), since 2012; *b* 3 June 1949; *s* of late Norman Thomas Evennett and Irene Evennett; *m* 1975, Marilyn Anne Smith; two *s*. *Educ:* Buckhurst Hill County High School for Boys; London School of Economics and Political Science (BSc (Econ) Upper Second Hons, MSc (Econ)). School Master, Ilford County High School for Boys, 1972–74; Marine Insurance Broker, Lloyd's, 1974–81; Mem., Lloyd's, 1976–92; Dir, Lloyd's Underwriting Agency, 1982–91; Commercial Liaison Manager, Bexley Coll., 1997–2001; mgt lectr and consultant, 2001–05. Consultant, J & H Marsh and McLennan (UK), then Marsh (UK), Ltd,

1998–2000. Redbridge Borough Councillor, 1974–78. Contested (C) Hackney South and Shoreditch, 1979; MP (C) Erith and Crayford, 1983–97; contested (C) Bexleyheath and Crayford, 1997, 2001. PPS to Minister of State, Dept of Educn, 1992–93, to Sec. of State for Wales, 1993–95, to Minister of State, Home Office, 1995–96, to Sec. of State for Educn and Employment, 1996–97, to Sec. of State for Educn, 2010–12; an Opposition Whip, 2005–09; Shadow Minister for Univs and Skills (formerly Innovation, Univs and Skills), 2009–10. Member, Select Committee: on Educn, Science and the Arts, 1986–92; for Educn and Skills, 2005. *Recreations:* my family, reading, history, music, cinema. *Address:* House of Commons, SW1A 0AA. *Club:* Bexleyheath Conservative.

**FABRICANT, Michael Louis David;** MP (C) Lichfield, since 1997 (Mid-Staffordshire, 1992–97); *b* 12 June 1950; *s* of late Isaac Nathan Fabricant and of Helena (*née* Freed). *Educ:* Loughborough Univ. (BA Law and Econs); Univ. of Sussex (MSc Systems). CEng, FIET. Postgrad. doctoral res., mathematical econs, London Univ., Oxford Univ. and Univ. of S California, LA. Formerly: Broadcaster, current affairs, BBC Radio; Man. Dir, Commercial Radio Gp; Founder Dir, Internat. Broadcast Electronics and Investment Gp, 1979–91. PPS to Financial Sec., HM Treasury, 1996–97; Opposition front-bench spokesman on economic affairs, 2003–05; an Opposition Whip, 2005–10; a Lord Comr of HM Treasury (Govt Whip), 2010–12. Member, Select Committee: Nat. Heritage, 1993–96, 1997–2005; Culture, Media and Sport, 1997–99, 2001–05; Home Affairs, 1999–2001; Information, 2001–03 (Chm., 2001–03); Member: European Legislation Scrutiny Cttee B, 1993–97; Finance and Services Cttee, 2001–03; Liaison Cttee, 2001–03; Admin Cttee, 2015–; Dep. Chm., All Party Cable and Satellite Gp, 1997–99 (Treas., 1995–97); Vice Chairman: All Party Gp on Smoking and Health, 1997–2010; All Party Gp Anglo-German Gp, 1997–2010; All Party Gp on Film Industry, 1997–2010; Jt Chm., All Party Internet Gp, 1998–2003; Chairman: Royal Marines All Party Parly Gp, 2005–10 (Jt Chm., 1999–2005); Cons. Friends of America, 2008–; Dep. Chm., Cons. Parly Media Cttee, 1992–96. Vice Chm., Cons. Party, 2012–14. FCMI; FRSA. *Publications:* various newspaper articles and pamphlets. *Recreations:* fell-walking, reading, music (Mozart to rock), ski-ing, listening to the Archers. *Address:* House of Commons, SW1A 0AA. *Club:* Rottingdean (Sussex).

**FALLON, Rt Hon. Michael;** PC 2012; MP (C) Sevenoaks, since 1997; Secretary of State for Defence, since 2014; *b* 14 May 1952; *s* of late Martin Fallon, OBE, FRCSI and of Hazel Fallon; *m* 1986, Wendy Elisabeth, *e d* of late Peter Payne, Holme-on-Spalding Moor, Yorks; two *s*. *Educ:* St Andrews Univ. (MA Hons 1974). European Educnl Res. Trust, 1974–75; Opposition Whips Office, House of Lords, 1975–77; EEC Officer,

Cons. Res. Dept, 1977–79; Jt Man. Dir, European Consultants Ltd, 1979–81; Dir, Quality Care Homes plc, 1992–97; Chief Exec., Quality Care Develts Ltd, 1996–97; Man. Dir, Just Learning Ltd, 1996–2006; Director: Bannatyne Fitness Ltd, 1999–2000; Collins Stewart Tullett plc, 2004–06; Tullett Prebon plc, 2006–12; Attendo AB, 2008–12. Sec., Lord Home's Cttee on future of House of Lords, 1977–78; Assistant to Baroness Elles, 1979–83. MP (C) Darlington, 1983–92; contested (C) Darlington, 1992. PPS to Sec. of State for Energy, 1987–88; an Asst Govt Whip, 1988–90; a Lord Comr of HM Treasury, 1990; Parly Under-Sec. of State, DES, 1990–92; Opposition spokesman on trade and industry, 1997, on Treasury matters, 1997–98; Minister of State: BIS, 2012–14; DECC, 2013–14; Minister for Portsmouth, 2014. Mem., Treasury Select Cttee, 1999–2012; Chm., All Party Classics Gp, 2005–09. Mem., Exec., 1922 Cttee, 2005–07. Dep. Chm., Cons. and Unionist Party, 2010–12. Member: HEFCE, 1993–97; Adv. Council, Social Market Foundn, 1994–2001; Govt's Deregulation Task Force, 1994–97; Council, Centre for Policy Studies, 2009–. Dir, Internat. Care and Relief, 1997–2003; Pres., Royal London Soc. for the Blind, 2010–. Gov., Whitefield Schs, 1994–99. *Publications:* The Quango Explosion (jtly), 1978; Sovereign Members?, 1982; The Rise of the Euroquango, 1982; Brighter Schools, 1993; Social Mobility, 2007; contribs to journals. *Recreations:* books, ski-ing, visiting classical sites. *Address:* House of Commons, SW1A 0AA. *Club:* Academy.

**FARRELLY, (Christopher) Paul;** MP (Lab) Newcastle-under-Lyme, since 2001; *b* Newcastle-under-Lyme, 2 March 1962; *s* of late Thomas Farrelly and of Anne Farrelly (*née* King), *m* 1998, Victoria Perry; one *s* two *d*. *Educ:* St Edmund Hall, Oxford (BA Hons PPE). Manager, Corporate Finance Div., Barclays de Zoete Wedd, 1984–90; Corresp., Reuters Ltd, 1990–95; Dep. City and Business Ed., Independent on Sunday, 1995–97; City Ed., The Observer, 1997–2001. Mem., Culture, Media and Sport Select Cttee, 2005–. *Recreations:* Rugby, football, writing. *Address:* House of Commons, SW1A 0AA. *T:* (020) 7219 8262. *Clubs:* Holy Trinity Catholic, Halmer End Working Men's (Newcastle-under-Lyme); Trentham Rugby Union Football, Finchley Rugby Football, Commons and Lords Rugby Union Football.

**FARRON, Timothy James;** MP (Lib Dem) Westmorland and Lonsdale, since 2005; Leader, Liberal Democrats, since 2015; *b* 27 May 1970; *s* of Christopher Farron and Susan Farron (*née* Trenchard); *m* 2000, Rosemary Alison Cantley; two *s* two *d*. *Educ:* Univ. of Newcastle upon Tyne (BA Hons Politics 1991). Lancaster University: Adult Educn Officer, 1992–96; Special Needs Student Advr, 1996–98; Asst to Acad. Registrar, 1998–2002; Hd, Faculty Admin, St Martin's Coll., 2002–05. Member (Lib Dem): Lancs CC, 1993–2000; S Ribble BC, 1995–99; S Lakeland

DC, 2004–08. Pres., Liberal Democrats, 2011–14. Mem., Amnesty Internat., 1993–. Mem., Cumbria Wildlife Trust, 2003–. Mem. PCC, Milnthorpe St Thomas, 2004–. Chm., Milnthorpe Youth Gp, 2004–. *Recreations:* walking, football (both playing and watching, respectively as an average goalkeeper and a Blackburn Rovers fan), music. *Address:* House of Commons, SW1A 0AA; Acland House, Yard 2, Strickland Gate, Kendal LA9 4ND. *T:* (01539) 723403, *Fax:* (01539) 740800. *E:* tim@timfarron.co.uk. *Club:* Kendal and South Westmorland Liberal (Pres.).

**FAULKS,** Baron *cr* 2010 (Life Peer), of Donnington in the Royal County of Berkshire; **Edward Peter Lawless Faulks;** QC 1996; Minister of State, Ministry of Justice, since 2014; *b* 19 Aug. 1950; *s* of His Honour Peter Ronald Faulks, MC and Pamela Faulks (*née* Lawless); *m* 1990, Catherine Frances Turner, *d* of Lindsay Turner and Anthea Cadbury; two *s. Educ:* Wellington Coll.; Jesus Coll., Oxford (MA; Hon. Fellow 2014). FCIArb. Called to the Bar, Middle Temple, 1973, Bencher, 2002. Literary Agent, Curtis Brown, 1980–81; Asst Recorder, 1996–2000; Recorder, 2000–10. Chairman: Professional Negligence Bar Assoc., 2002–04; Res. Soc. of Conservative Lawyers, 2010–12. Special Advr to DCA on compensation culture, 2005–06. Mem., Commn on a Bill of Rights, 2012. *Publications:* (contributing ed.) Local Authority Liabilities, 1998, 5th edn 2012. *Recreations:* sports, the arts. *Address:* 33 Ladbroke Grove, W11 3AY; 1 Chancery Lane, WC2A 1LF. *T:* 0845 634 6666; House of Lords, SW1A 0PW. *Club:* Garrick.

**FELLOWS, Marion;** MP (SNP) Motherwell and Wishaw, since 2015; *b* 5 May 1949. *Educ:* Heriot-Watt Univ. (Accountancy and Finance). Lectr in Business Studies, W Lothian Coll. Mem. (SNP), N Lanarkshire Council, 2012–15. *Address:* House of Commons, SW1A 0AA.

**FERNANDES, Suella;** MP (C) Fareham, since 2015; *b* London, 3 April 1980; *d* of Chris Fernandes and Uma Fernandes. *Educ:* Heathfield Sch., Pinner; Queens' Coll., Cambridge (BA Hons Law 2002); Panthéon-Sorbonne Univ., Paris (LLM 2003); BVC 2005. Called to the Bar, Middle Temple, 2005; admitted to State Bar, NY, 2006; in practice as barrister specialising in planning, judicial review, immigration, No5 Chambers; Mem., Attorney Gen.'s C Panel of Treasury Counsel, 2010–15. Mem., Educn Select Cttee, 2015–. Parly Patron, Westminster Strategic Studies Gp, 2015–. Founder and Trustee, Africa Justice Foundn, 2010–14. Co-Founder and Gov., Michaela Community Sch., 2010–. *Address:* House of Commons, SW1A 0AA. *T:* (020) 7219 3000. *E:* suella.fernandes.mp@parliament.uk.

**FERRIER, Margaret;** MP (SNP) Rutherglen and Hamilton West, since 2015; *b* Glasgow; one *d.* Commercial Sales Supervisor, Terex Equipt Ltd, Motherwell, until 2015. *Address:* House of Commons, SW1A 0AA.

**FIELD, Rt Hon. Frank;** PC 1997; DL; MP (Lab) Birkenhead, since 1979; *b* 16 July 1942; *s* of late Walter and of Annie Field. *Educ:* St Clement Danes Grammar Sch.; Univ. of Hull (BSc (Econ)). Director: Child Poverty Action Gp, 1969–79; Low Pay Unit, 1974–80. Minister of State (Minister for Welfare Reform), DSS, 1997–98. Chairman: Select Cttee on Social Services, 1987–90; Select Cttee on Social Security, 1991–97; Jt Select Cttee on Draft Modern Slavery Bill, 2014; Select Cttee on Work and Pensions, 2015–; Co-Chm., All Party Parly Inquiry into hunger in UK, 2014. Chm., Pensions Reform Gp, 1999– (reports: Universal Protected Pension: modernising pensions for the millennium, 2001; Universal Protected Pension: the following report, 2002). Chairman: Ind. Review on Poverty and Life Chances, 2010 (report, Preventing Poor Children becoming Poor Adults, 2010); Modern Slavery Bill Evidence Rev., 2013 (report, Establishing Britain as a World Leader in the Fight against Modern Slavery, 2013). Vice Chm., Human Trafficking Foundn, 2011–. Co-Founder, Cool Earth, 2007. Chm., King James Bible Trust, 2007–. DL Merseyside, 2011. *Publications:* (ed jtly) Twentieth Century State Education, 1971; (ed jtly) Black Britons, 1971; (ed) Low Pay, 1973; Unequal Britain, 1974; (ed) Are Low Wages Inevitable?, 1976; (ed) Education and the Urban Crisis, 1976; (ed) The Conscript Army: a study of Britain's unemployed, 1976; (jtly) To Him Who Hath: a study of poverty and taxation, 1976; (with Ruth Lister) Wasted Labour, 1978 (Social Concern Book Award); (ed) The Wealth Report, 1979; Inequality in Britain: freedom, welfare and state, 1981; Poverty and Politics, 1982; The Wealth Report—2, 1983; (ed) Policies against Low Pay, 1984; The Minimum Wage: its potential and dangers, 1984; Freedom and Wealth in a Socialist Future, 1987; The Politics of Paradise, 1987; Losing Out: the emergence of Britain's underclass, 1989; An Agenda for Britain, 1993; (jtly) Europe Isn't Working, 1994; (jtly) Beyond Punishment: pathways from workfare, 1994; Making Welfare Work, 1995; How to Pay for the Future: building a stakeholders welfare, 1996; Stakeholder Welfare, 1997; Reforming Welfare, 1997; Reflections on Welfare Reform, 1998; The State of Dependency: welfare under Labour, 2000; Making Welfare Work: reconstructing welfare for the millennium, 2001; Neighbours from Hell: the politics of behaviour, 2003; The Ethic of Respect: a left wing cause, 2006; Attlee's Great Contemporaries, 2009; Saints and Heroes, 2010. *Address:* House of Commons, SW1A 0AA. *T:* (020) 7219 5193.

**FIELD, Rt Hon. Mark (Christopher);** PC 2015; MP (C) Cities of London and Westminster, since 2001; *b* 6 Oct. 1964; *s* of late Maj. Peter Field and Ulrike Field (*née* Peipe); *m* 1st, 1994, Michele Louise Acton (marr. diss. 2006); 2nd, 2007, Victoria Margaret Philadelphia Elphicke; one *s* one *d*. *Educ:* Reading Sch.; St Edmund Hall, Oxford (MA Hons Juris.); Coll. of Law, Chester. Trainee solicitor, Richards Butler, 1988–90; Solicitor, Freshfields, 1990–92; employment consultant, 1992–94; Man. Dir, Kellyfield Consulting (publishing/recruiting firm), 1994–2001. Adviser: Bd, Ellwood Atfield, 2011–; Cains, 2011–. Councillor (C), RBK&C, 1994–2002. An Opposition Whip, 2003–04; Shadow Minister for London, 2003–05; Shadow Financial Sec. to the Treasury, 2005; Shadow Minister for Culture, 2005–06. Member: Select Cttee on LCD, 2003, on Procedure, 2008–10; Intelligence and Security Cttee, 2010–15. Chm., All Party Parly Gp on Venture Capital and Private Equity, 2010–15 (Vice Chm., 2004–10); Vice-Chm., All Party Parly Gp on Bangladesh, 2009–, on Football, 2010–. Member Standing Committee for: Proceeds of Crime Act, 2002; Enterprise Act, 2002; Finance Act, 2002; Licensing Act, 2003; Housing Act, 2004; Railways Act, 2005; Finance Act (No. 2), 2005; Regn of Financial Services (Land Transactions) Act, 2006; Nat. Insurance Contributions Act, 2006; National Lottery Act, 2006; Crossrail Act, 2008; Finance Act, 2008; Nat. Insce Contribns Act, 2008; Dormant Bank and Building Socs Accounts Act, 2008; Business Rates Supplements Act, 2009; Finance Act, 2009. Mem., Adv. Cttee, London Sch. of Commerce, 2005–. Regular broadcaster on radio and TV and occasional newspaper columnist on H of C, economic and financial affairs, and London issues. *Publications:* Reforming the City (contrib.), 2009; Between the Crashes, 2013. *Recreations:* cricket, football, researching local history, reading political biographies and diaries, walking in London, listening to popular/rock music. *Address:* House of Commons, SW1A 0AA. *T:* (020) 7219 8155.

**FITZPATRICK, James, (Jim);** MP (Lab) Poplar and Limehouse, since 2010 (Poplar and Canning Town, 1997–2010); *b* 4 April 1952; *s* of James Fitzpatrick and Jean Fitzpatrick (*née* Stones). *Educ:* Holyrood Sch., Glasgow. Trainee, Tytrak Ltd, Glasgow, 1970–73; driver, Mintex Ltd, 1973–74; Firefighter, London Fire Brigade, 1974–97. PPS to Sec. of State for Health, 1999–2001; an Asst Govt Whip, 2001–02; a Lord Comr of HM Treasury (Govt Whip), 2002–03; Vice-Chamberlain of HM Household, 2003–05; Parliamentary Under-Secretary of State: ODPM, 2005–06; DTI, 2006–07; DfT, 2007–09; Minister of State, DEFRA, 2009–10; Shadow Minister for Envmt, Food and Rural Affairs, 2010, for Transport, 2010–13. Mem., NEC, Fire Bdes Union, 1988–97. Mem. Exec., Gtr London Lab. Party, 1988–2000 (Chm., 1991–2000). Fire Bde Long Service and Good Conduct Medal, 1994.

*Recreations:* cycling, reading, football (West Ham Utd), television and films. *Address:* House of Commons, SW1A 0AA. *T:* (020) 7219 5085.

**FLELLO, Robert Charles Douglas;** MP (Lab) Stoke-on-Trent South, since 2005; *b* 14 Jan. 1966; *s* of Douglas Flello and Valerie Swain; *m* 1990, Teresa (*née* Gifoli) (marr. diss.); one *d*, and one step *s*. *Educ:* University Coll. of N Wales, Bangor (BSc Hons). Consultant, Price Waterhouse, 1989–94; Manager, Arthur Andersen, 1994–99; Dir, Platts Flello Ltd, 1999–2003; CEO, Malachi Community Trust, 2003–04. Associate: Royal Inst. Taxation, 1990–; Soc. Financial Advrs, 1998–. *Recreations:* reading, running, ancient history, cooking, riding my motorbike. *Address:* House of Commons, SW1A 0AA; Ground Floor, Travers Court, City Road, Fenton, Stoke-on-Trent ST4 2PY. *T:* (01782) 844810, *Fax:* (01782) 593430.

**FLETCHER, Colleen Margaret;** MP (Lab) Coventry North East, since 2015; *b* Coventry, 23 Nov. 1954; *d* of William Charles Dalton and Dot Dalton; *m* Ian Richard Fletcher; two *s*. *Educ:* Lyng Hall Comprehensive Sch.; Henley Coll. GEC, Coventry; Customer Services Officer, Orbit Housing Gp. Mem. (Lab), Coventry CC, 1992–2000, 2002–04 and 2011–15. *Address:* House of Commons, SW1A 0AA.

**FLINT, Rt Hon. Caroline Louise;** PC 2008; MP (Lab) Don Valley, since 1997; *b* 20 Sept. 1961; *d* of late Wendy Flint (*née* Beasley); *m* 1st, 1987 (marr. diss. 1990); one *s* one *d*; 2nd, 2001, Phil Cole; one step *s*. *Educ:* Univ. of East Anglia (BA Hons American History and Lit.). Mgt Trainee, 1983–84; Policy Officer, 1984–86; GLC/ILEA; Head of Women's Unit, NUS, 1988–89; Principal Officer, Lambeth, 1989–93; Sen. Researcher and Political Officer, GMB, 1994–97. Parliamentary Private Secretary: to Minister of State, FCO, 1999–2000 and 2001–02, Minister for Energy, DTI, 2001; to Minister without Portfolio and Labour Party Chair, 2003; Parly Under-Sec. of State, Home Office, 2003–05; DoH, 2005–06; Minister of State, DoH, 2006–07; DWP, 2007–08; Minister for Yorks and the Humber, 2007–08; Minister for Housing, DCLG, 2008; Minister of State (Minister for Europe), FCO, 2008–09; Shadow Sec. of State for Communities and Local Govt, 2010–11, for Energy and Climate Change, 2011–15. *Recreations:* cinema, family and friends. *Address:* House of Commons, SW1A 0AA. *T:* (020) 7219 4407.

**FLYNN, Paul Phillip;** MP (Lab) Newport West, since 1987; *b* 9 Feb. 1935; *s* of late James Flynn and Kathleen Williams; *m* 1st, 1962, Anne Harvey (marr. diss. 1984); one *s* (one *d* decd); 2nd, 1985, Samantha Morgan, *d* of Douglas and Elsie Cumpstone; one step *s* one step *d*. *Educ:* St Illtyd's Coll., Cardiff. Steelworker, 1955–84; Researcher, 1984–87. Mem., Gwent CC, 1974–82. Contested (Lab) Denbigh, Oct. 1974. Frontbench spokesman on Wales, 1987, on social security, 1988–90. Mem., Gorsedd of Bards, 1991. Campaign for Freedom of Information Parly Award, 1991. *Publications:* Commons Knowledge: how to be a backbencher, 1997; Baglu 'Mlaen (autobiog.), 1998; Dragons led by Poodles, 1999; The Unusual Suspect, 2010; How to be an MP, 2012; Clockwinder Who Wouldn't Say No: the life of David Taylor MP, 2012. *Address:* House of Commons, SW1A 0AA. *Club:* Ringland Labour (Newport, Gwent).

**FOSTER, Kevin John;** MP (C) Torbay, since 2015; *b* Plymouth, 31 Dec. 1978; *s* of Michael Foster and late Linda Foster; partner, Hazel Noonan. *Educ:* Hele's Sch., Plympton; Univ. of Warwick (LLB Law 2000; LLM Internat. Econ. Law 2001); Inns of Court Sch. of Law (BVC 2002). Barman, Coventry Cons. Club, 2000–03; Asst to Philip Bradbourne, MEP, 2002–03; Paralegal, Howell and Co. Solicitors, 2003–04. Mem. (C), Coventry CC, 2002–14. Contested (C) Coventry S, 2010. *Recreations:* military history, cinema, music, church. *Address:* House of Commons, SW1A 0AA. *T:* 07985 446803. *E:* kevin.foster.mp@parliament.uk. *Clubs:* Preston Conservative (Paignton); Plympton Conservative (Plymouth).

**FOVARGUE, Yvonne Helen;** MP (Lab) Makerfield, since 2010; *b* Sale, 29 Nov. 1956; *d* of Kenneth Gibbon and Irene, (Renee), Gibbon (*née* Reed); one *d*; *m* 2009, Paul Kenny. *Educ:* Sale Girls Grammar Sch.; Leeds Univ. (BA Hons Eng.). Housing Officer, Manchester CC, 1979–86; Chief Exec., St Helens CAB, 1986–2010. Mem. (Lab) Warrington BC, 2004–10. Opposition Whip, 2011–13; Shadow Parly Under Sec. of State for Transport, 2013; Shadow Minister: for Defence, 2013–14, 2015; for Young People, 2014–15. Chm., All Party Parly Gp on Debt and Personal Finance, 2010–, on Legal Aid, 2010–. Mem., MENSA. *Recreations:* crime fiction, music of David Bowie. *Address:* (office) Wigan Investment Centre, Waterside Drive, Wigan WN3 5BA. *T:* (01942) 824029. *E:* yvonne.fovargue.mp@parliament.uk. *W:* www.twitter.com/Y_FovargueMP.

**FOX, Dr the Rt Hon. Liam;** PC 2010; MP (C) North Somerset, since 2010 (Woodspring, 1992–2010); *b* 22 Sept. 1961; *s* of William Fox and Catherine Young; *m* 2005, Dr Jesmé Baird. *Educ:* St Bride's High Sch., E Kilbride; Univ. of Glasgow (MB ChB 1983). MRCGP 1989. General Practitioner, Beaconsfield, 1987–91; Army MO (civilian), RAEC, 1981–91; Divl Surgeon, St John's Ambulance, 1987–91. Contested (C) Roxburgh and Berwickshire, 1987. PPS to Home Sec., 1993–94; an Asst Govt Whip, 1994–95; a Lord Comr of HM Treasury (Govt Whip), 1995–96; Parly Under-Sec. of State, FCO, 1996–97; Opposition spokesman on constitutional affairs, 1997–99, on health,

1999–2001; Shadow Health Sec., 2001–03; Co-Chm., Cons. Party, 2003–05; Shadow Foreign Sec., 2005; Shadow Defence Sec., 2005–10; Sec. of State for Defence, 2010–11. Mem., Select Cttee on Scottish Affairs, 1992; Secretary: Cons. back bench Health Cttee, 1992–93; Cons. West Country Members Group, 1992–93. *Publications:* Making Unionism Positive, 1988; (contrib.) Bearing the Standard, 1991; Rising Tides: facing the challenges of a new era, 2013; contrib. to House of Commons Magazine. *Recreations:* tennis, swimming, cinema, theatre. *Address:* House of Commons, SW1A 0AA. *T:* (020) 7219 4086.

**FOXCROFT, Victoria Jane;** MP (Lab) Lewisham, Deptford, since 2015. *Educ:* De Montfort Univ. (BA 2000). Research Officer, AEEU, 2002–05; Political Officer, Amicus the Union, 2005–09; Finance Sector Officer, Unite the Union, 2009–. Mem. (Lab) Lewisham LBC, 2010–14. *Address:* House of Commons, SW1A 0AA.

**FRANCOIS, Rt Hon. Mark (Gino);** PC 2010; MP (C) Rayleigh and Wickford, since 2010 (Rayleigh, 2001–10); Minister of State, Department for Communities and Local Government, since 2015; *b* London, 14 Aug. 1965; *m* 2000, Karen Thomas (marr. diss. 2006). *Educ:* Nicholas Comprehensive Sch., Basildon; Univ. of Bristol (BA 1986); King's Coll. London (MA 1987). Mgt trainee, Lloyds Bank, 1987; Consultant and Dir, Market Access Internat. Public Affairs Consultancy, 1988–95; Public Affairs Consultant, Francois Associates, 1996–2001. Mem. (C) Basildon DC, 1991–95. Opposition Jun. Whip, 2002; Shadow Econ. Sec., HM Treasury, 2004; Shadow Paymaster Gen., 2005–07; Opposition spokesman on Europe, 2007–09; Shadow Minister for Europe, 2009–10; Vice-Chamberlain of HM Household (Govt Whip), 2010–12; Minister of State, MoD, 2012–15. Mem., Envmtl Audit Cttee, H of C, 2001–05. Contested (C) Brent East, 1997. Served TA, 1983–89 (Lieut). Mem., RUSI. Fellow, Huguenot Soc. of GB and Ire., 2001–. Freeman, City of London, 2004; Liveryman, Co. of Wheelwrights, 2005–. Pres., Palace of Westminster Lions Club, 2006–12. *Recreations:* reading, travel, walking, history (including military history). *Address:* (office) 25 Bellingham Lane, Rayleigh, Essex SS6 7ED; c/o House of Commons, SW1A 0AA. *T:* (020) 7219 3000. *Clubs:* Carlton; Rayleigh Conservative (Pres., 2010–).

**FRAZER, Lucy Claire;** QC 2013; MP (C) South East Cambridgeshire, since 2015; *d* of Colin and Jocelyn Frazer; *m* 2002, David Leigh; one *s* one *d*. *Educ:* Leeds Girls' High Sch.; Newnham Coll., Cambridge (BA 1994). Called to the Bar, Middle Temple, 1996; in practice as barrister, 1998–2015. *Publications:* (contrib.) Rowlatt on Principal and Surety. *Address:* House of Commons, SW1A 0AA.

**FREEMAN, George William;** MP (C) Mid Norfolk, since 2010; Parliamentary Under-Secretary of State, Department for Business, Innovation and Skills and Department of Health, since 2014; b Cambridge, 12 July 1967; s of Arthur Freeman and Joanna Stockbridge (née Philipson); m 1996, Eleanor Holmes; one s one d. Educ: Radley Coll., Oxon; Girton Coll., Cambridge (BA Geog. 1989; MA). Parly Officer, NFU, 1990–92; Founder, Local Identity Agency, 1992–96; Dir, Early Stage Ventures, Merlin Biosciences, 1997–2001; CEO, Amedis Pharmaceuticals, 2001–03; Man. Dir, 4D Biomedical, 2003–10. PPS to Minister of State, DECC, 2010–12. Chm., All Party Parly Gp on Agricl Sci. and Technol., 2010; Govt Advr on Life Scis, 2011–13; Prime Ministerial Trade Envoy, 2013. Mem. Bd, Gtr Cambridge Partnership, 2005–09. Trustee, Cambridge Union Soc., 2005–08. Chm., The Norfolk Way, 2007–11. Contested (C) Stevenage, 2005. Recreations: sailing, wildfowling. Address: House of Commons, SW1A 0AA. T: (020) 7219 1940. E: george.freeman.mp@parliament.uk. Club: Norfolk (Norwich).

**FREER, Michael Whitney;** MP (C) Finchley and Golders Green, since 2010; b Manchester, 29 May 1960; s of Herbert and Marian Freer; civil partnership 2007, Angelo Crolla. Educ: Chadderton Grammar Sch., Manchester; St Aidan's Sch., Carlisle. Mem. (C) Barnet LBC, 1990–94 and 2001–10 (Leader, 2006–09). Exec. Mem., London Councils, 2008–09. Non-exec. Dir, London Develt Agency, 2008–10. Contested (C) Harrow West, 2005. Recreations: cycling, keep fit, learning French. Address: House of Commons, SW1A 0AA. T: (020) 7219 7071, Fax: (020) 7219 2211. E: mike.freer.mp@parliament.uk.

**FREUD,** Baron cr 2009 (Life Peer), of Eastry, in the County of Kent; **David Anthony Freud;** PC 2015; Minister of State (Minister for Welfare Reform), Department for Work and Pensions, since 2015; b London, 24 June 1950; s of Anton Walter Freud and Annette Vibeke Freud (née Krarup); m 1978, Priscilla Jane Dickinson; one s two d. Educ: Whitgift Sch.; Merton Coll., Oxford (BA PPE 1972; MA 1989). Journalist, Western Mail, 1972–75; Econs/Tax Reporter, and Lex Corresp., Financial Times, 1976–83; S. G. Warburg, later UBS Investment Bank, 1984–2003 (Vice Chm., Investment Banking, 2000–03); CEO, The Portland Trust, 2006–08. Author, ind. report for DWP, Reducing Dependency, Increasing Opportunity: options for the future of welfare to work, 2007; Advr, DWP, 2008. Shadow Minister for Welfare Reform, 2009–10; Parly Under-Sec. of State (Minister for Welfare Reform), DWP, 2010–15. Publications: Freud in the City, 2006. Recreations: swimming, cycling, ski-ing. Address: House of Lords, SW1A 0PW. T: (020) 7219 4907. E: freudd@parliament.uk. Club: Ski Club of GB.

**FULLER, Richard;** MP (C) Bedford, since 2010; b Bedford. Educ: University Coll., Oxford (BA); Harvard Business Sch. (MBA). Former Partner: technol. venture capital firm; mgt consultancy. Contested (C) Bedford, 2005. Nat. Chm., Young Conservatives, 1985–87. Address: House of Commons, SW1A 0AA.

**FYSH, Marcus John Hudson;** MP (C) Yeovil, since 2015; b Australia, 8 Nov. 1970; m; one d. Mercury Asset Mgt, 1993–2003; set up own business, 2003. Member (C): S Somerset DC; Somerset CC. Address: House of Commons, SW1A 0AA.

**GALE, Sir Roger (James),** Kt 2012; MP (C) North Thanet, since 1983; b Poole, Dorset, 20 Aug. 1943; s of Richard Byrne Gale and Phyllis Mary (née Rowell); m 1st, 1964, Wendy Dawn Bowman (marr. diss. 1967); 2nd, 1971, Susan Sampson (marr. diss.); one d; 3rd, 1980, Susan Gabrielle Marks; two s. Educ: Southbourne Prep. Sch.; Hardye's Sch., Dorchester; Guildhall Sch. of Music and Drama (LGSM). Freelance broadcaster, 1963–72; freelance reporter, BBC Radio, London, 1972–73; Producer, Current Affairs Gp, BBC Radio (progs included Newsbeat and Today), 1973–76; Producer/Dir, BBC Children's Television, 1976–79; Producer/Dir, Thames TV, and Editor, teenage unit, 1979–83. Joined Conservative Party, 1964; Mem., Cttee, Greater London Young Conservatives, 1964–65. PPS to Minister of State for Armed Forces, 1992–94. Member: Select Cttee on Televising of Proceedings of the House, 1988–91; Home Affairs Select Cttee, 1990–92; Broadcasting Select Cttee, 1997–2005; Procedure Select Cttee, 2010–15; All Party Parly Gp, Fund for Replacement of Animals in Med. Experiments, 1983–86; Chm., All Party Animal Welfare Gp, 1992–98; Mem., Chairman's Panel, 1997–. Vice Chm., Cons. Party, 2001–03. Founding Mem., Police and Parlt Scheme, 1996. Delegate, Council of Europe, 1987–89 and 2011–15. Contested Birmingham, Northfield, Oct. 1982 (Lab. majority, 289). Mem., Gen. Council, BBC, 1992–94. Founder, East Kent Development Assoc., 1984–86. Fellow: Industry and Parlt Trust, 1985; Parlt and Armed Forces Fellowship, 1992; Postgrad. Fellowship, Parlt Armed Forces Scheme, 2001–02. Pres., Cons. Animal Welfare Gp, 2003–. Special Constable, British Transport Police, 2003–06. Recreations: swimming, sailing. Address: House of Commons, Westminster, SW1A 0AA. E: galerj@parliament.uk. Clubs: Farmers, Lord's Taverners.

**GAPES, Michael John;** MP (Lab and Co-op) Ilford South, since 1992; b 4 Sept. 1952; s of late Frank William Gapes and of Emily Florence Gapes (née Jackson). Educ: Staples Road Infants' Sch., Loughton; Manford County Primary Sch., Chigwell; Buckhurst Hill County High Sch., Essex; Fitzwilliam Coll., Cambridge (MA Hons Econs 1975); Middlesex Polytechnic (Dip. Indust. Relations and Trade Union Studies 1976). VSO teacher, Swaziland, 1971–72; Sec., Cambridge Students' Union, 1973–74; Chm., Nat. Orgn of Labour Students, 1976–77. Admin. Officer, Middlesex Hosp., 1977; Nat. Student Organiser, Lab. Party, 1977–80; Res. Officer, Internat. Dept, Lab. Party, 1980–88; Sen. Internat. Officer, Lab. Party, 1988–92. Contested (Lab) Ilford North, 1983. PPS to Minister of State: NI Office, 1997–99; Home Office, 2001–02. Member: Foreign Affairs Select Cttee, 1992–97, 2010– (Chm., 2005–10); Defence Select Cttee, 1999–2001, 2003–05; Treas., 2010–13, Vice Chm., 2013–, British Gp, IPU; Chairman: UN All Party Parly Gp, 1997–2001; All Party Crossrail Gp, 2005–; Vice-Chm., All Party Parly Gp against Anti-Semitism, 1992–2005; Member: All Party Pakistan Gp, 1998; All Party Gp for the Tamils, 2009; Co-Chm., All Party EU Gp, 2010–12; Chm., PLP Children and Families' Cttee, 1994–95; Vice-Chm., PLP Defence Cttee, 1992–95 and 1996–97. Dep. Chm., Labour Friends of Israel, 1997–2005; Member: Labour Nat. Policy Forum, 1998–2005; Labour Friends of India, 1999–, of Palestine and the ME, 2009–, of the Czech Republic, 2012–; Labour ME Council, 2002–05. Mem., NATO Parly Assembly, 2002–05, 2010–. Chm., Westminster Foundn for Democracy, 2002–05. Member: Unite the Union; Co-operative Party. Member, Council: RIIA, 1996–99; VSO, 1997–2011. Vice Pres., Valentines Park Conservationists, 1998–2010; Member: Friends of Valentines Mansion, 2009–; Friends of Ilford Hosp. Chapel, 2000–. *Publications:* co-author of books on defence policy; Labour Party and Fabian Society pamphlets. *Recreations:* blues and jazz music, supporting West Ham United FC. *Address:* House of Commons, SW1A 0AA.

**GARDINER OF KIMBLE,** Baron *cr* 2010 (Life Peer), of Kimble in the County of Buckinghamshire; **John Eric Gardiner;** Captain of the Yeoman of the Guard (Deputy Chief Whip, House of Lords), since 2015; *b* London, 17 March 1956; *s* of Anthony Ernest Fiddes Gardiner and Heather Joan Gardiner (*née* Robarts); *m* 2004, Olivia Mirabel, sculptor, *e d* of Sir Richard Musgrave, 7th Bt. *Educ:* Uppingham Sch.; Royal Holloway Coll., Univ. of London (BA Mod. History and Politics). Farmer; Partner, C. M. Robarts and Son, 1992–. Countryside Alliance: Dir, Political Affairs, 1995–2004; Dep. Chief Exec., 2004–10; Bd Mem. and Exec. Dir, 2010–12. Chm., FACE (Fedn of Assocs for Hunting and Conservation) (UK), 1998–2012; Treas. Gen., FACE (Europe), 2000–12. Private Sec. to Chm., Cons. Party, 1989–95. A Lord in Waiting (Govt Whip), 2012–15; H of L Spokesperson for DCMS, 2012–; H of L Whip for Cabinet Office and DECC, 2012–. Mem., Select Cttee on HIV and Aids in UK, 2011. Cons. Party Whip, 2011–12; Cons. Dep. Chief Whip, 2013–. Chm., Vale of Aylesbury with Garth and S Berks Hunt, 1992–2006. Pres., Bucks Agricl Assoc.,

2007. *Recreations:* hunting, gardening. *Address:* House of Lords, SW1A 0PW. *E:* gardinerj@parliament.uk. *Club:* Pratt's.

**GARDINER, Barry Strachan;** MP (Lab) Brent North, since 1997; *b* 10 March 1957; *s* of late John Flannegan Gardiner and Sylvia Jean Strachan; *m* 1979, Caroline Anne Smith; three *s* one *d*. *Educ:* Haileybury; St Andrews Univ. (MA Hons). Corpus Christi Coll., Cambridge. ACII. Scottish Sec., SCM, 1979–81. John F. Kennedy Schol., Harvard Univ., 1983; General Average Adjuster, 1987–97. Parliamentary Under-Secretary of State: NI Office, 2004–05; DTI, 2005–06; DEFRA, 2006–07. Prime Minister's Special Envoy for Forests, 2007–08; Leader of Opposition's Special Envoy for Climate Change and the Envmt, 2010–15. *Publications:* articles in Philosophical Qly, Science, Lloyd's List, Insurance Internat. *Recreations:* music, bird watching, hill walking. *Address:* House of Commons, SW1A 0AA.

**GARNIER, Rt Hon. Sir Edward (Henry),** Kt 2012; PC 2015; QC 1995; MP (C) Harborough, since 1992; *b* 26 Oct. 1952; *s* of late Col William d'Arcy Garnier and Hon. Lavender Hyacinth (*née* de Grey); *m* 1982, Anna Caroline Mellows; two *s* one *d*. *Educ:* Wellington Coll.; Jesus Coll., Oxford (BA, MA). Called to the Bar, Middle Temple, 1976, Bencher, 2001; Asst Recorder, 1998–2000; a Recorder, 2000–. Vice-Pres., Hemsworth Assoc., 1987–. Contested: Wandsworth BC by-election, 1984; Tooting ILEA election, 1986; (C) Hemsworth, Gen. Election, 1987. PPS to Ministers of State, FCO, 1994–95; PPS to Attorney General and to Solicitor General, 1995–97, and to Chancellor of the Duchy of Lancaster, 1996–97; Opposition spokesman, Lord Chancellor's Dept, 1997–99; Shadow Attorney-Gen., 1999–2001; Shadow Minister: for Home Affairs, 2005–07; for Justice, 2007–09; Shadow Attorney-Gen., 2009–10; Solicitor Gen., 2010–12. Member: Home Affairs Select Cttee, 1992–95; Jt Cttee on Human Rights, 2014–; Sec., Cons. Foreign Affairs Cttee, 1992–94. Mem., Exec. Cttee, 1922 Cttee, 2001–05. Member: Howard League Commn on Sex in Prison, 2012–; Adv. Bd, Samaritans, 2013–. Patron, Ridley Eye Foundn, 2011–. UK Election Observer: Kenya, 1992; Bosnia, 1996. Vis. Parly Fellow, St Antony's Coll., Oxford, 1996–97. Mem. Bd, Great Britain–China Centre, 1998–2010; Trustee, China-Oxford Scholarship Fund, 2006–10, 2012–. Mem., Leics and Rutland Cttee, 1992–; Legal and Parly Cttee, 1994–2000, CLA. *Publications:* (contrib.) Halsbury's Laws of England, 4th edn, 1985; (contrib.) Bearing the Standard, 1991; (contrib.) Facing the Future, 1993; (contrib.) Lissack and Horlick on Bribery, 2nd edn 2014. *Recreations:* cricket, shooting, opera. *Address:* House of Commons, SW1A 0AA. *T:* (020) 7219 3000. *Clubs:* White's, Pratt's, Beefsteak; Vincent's (Oxford).

**GARNIER, Mark Robert Timothy;** MP (C) Wyre Forest, since 2010; *b* London, 26 Feb. 1963; *s* of Peter Garnier and Patricia Garnier (*née* Dowden); *m* 2001, Caroline Louise Joyce; two *s* one *d*. *Educ:* Charterhouse. Associate Director: W. I. Carr (Overseas Ltd), 1982–86; Swiss Bank Corp. Internat., 1986–88; Man. Dir, S China Securities (UK) Ltd, 1988–95; Exec. Dir, Daiwa (Europe Ltd), 1995–96; Associate Director: L. C. F. Edmond de Rothschild Securities, 1996–97; Bear Stearns, 1998; Dir, Meilen Asset Mgt, 1999–2005; Partner: CGR Capital LLP, 2006–08; Severn-Capital LLP, 2008–. Member: Treasury Select Cttee, 2010–; Finance Select Cttee, 2015–; Parly Commn on Banking Standards, 2012–13. FCSI (FSI 2007). Mem. Ct, Coachmakers' Co., 2003. *Recreations:* historic motor sport and aviation, target rifle shooting, photography, ski-ing. *Address:* House of Commons, SW1A 0AA. *T:* (020) 7219 7198. *E:* mark.garnier.mp@parliament.uk. *Clubs:* Carlton, Royal Automobile; North London Rifle.

**GAUKE, David Michael;** MP (C) South West Hertfordshire, since 2005; Financial Secretary, HM Treasury, since 2014; *b* 8 Oct. 1971; *s* of Jim Gauke and Susan Gauke (now Hall); *m* 2000, Rachel Katherine Rank; three *s*. *Educ:* Northgate High Sch., Ipswich; St Edmund Hall, Oxford; Chester Coll. of Law. Trainee solicitor and solicitor, Richards Butler, 1995–98; admitted, 1997; solicitor, Macfarlanes, 1999–2005. Exchequer Sec., HM Treasury, 2010–14. *Recreations:* cricket, football, walking, reading, family. *Address:* House of Commons, SW1A 0AA. *T:* (020) 7219 3000. *E:* david@davidgauke.com. *Clubs:* Rickmansworth Conservative; Tring Conservative.

**GETHINS, Stephen Patrick;** MP (SNP) Fife North East, since 2015; *b* Glasgow, 28 March 1976; *s* of James Gethins and Rhona Gethins; *m* 2013, Anya Hart Dyke; one *d*. *Educ:* Perth Acad.; Univ. of Dundee (LLB Hons); Univ. of Kent (MA Res.). EU Cttee of the Regions, 2005–07; Scotland Europa, 2007–09; Special Advr to First Minister, Scottish Govt, 2009–13; Chm., Adv. Bd, Scottish Global Forum, 2013–15. *Address:* House of Commons, SW1A 0AA. *T:* (020) 7219 5671. *E:* stephen.gethins.mp@parliament.uk. *Club:* Dundee United Football.

**GHANI, Nusrat;** MP (C) Wealden, since 2015; *d* of Abdul Ghani and Farzand Begum; *m* 2002, David Wheeldon; one *d*. *Educ:* Bordesley Green Girls' Sch.; Cadbury Sixth Form Coll.; Univ. of Central England; Univ. of Leeds (MA Internat. Relns). Health campaigner: Age UK; Breakthrough Breast Cancer; Strategic Communications and Public Affairs, BBC World Service and BBC World Service Trust. Mem., Home Affairs Select Cttee, 2015–; Chairman, All Party Parliamentary Group: on Ageing and Older People, 2015–; on Eye Health and Visual Impairment, 2015–; Member, All Party Parliamentary Group: on Domestic Violence,

2015–; on Women in Parlt, 2015–. Contested (C) Birmingham Ladywood, 2010. *Recreations:* cinema, music, reading, ski-ing, sailing, travel, walking on Ashdown Forest. *Address:* House of Commons, SW1A 0AA. *E:* nusrat.ghani.mp@parliament.uk.

**GIBB, Nicolas John;** MP (C) Bognor Regis and Littlehampton, since 1997; Minister of State, Department for Education, 2010–12 and since 2014; *b* 3 Sept. 1960; *s* of late John McLean Gibb and Eileen Mavern Gibb. *Educ:* Maidstone Grammar Sch.; Roundhay Sch., Leeds; Thornes House Sch., Wakefield; Univ. of Durham (BA Hons). ACA 1987. Chartered Accountant, KPMG, 1984–97. Opposition spokesman: on HM Treasury, 1998–99; on trade and industry, 1999–2001; on education, 2005–10. Member: Social Security Select Cttee, 1997–98; Public Accounts Cttee, 2001–03; Educn and Skills Select Cttee, 2003–05. Contested (C): Stoke-on-Trent Central, 1992; Rotherham, May 1994. *Address:* House of Commons, SW1A 0AA.

**GIBSON, Patricia;** MP (SNP) North Ayrshire and Arran, since 2015; *b* 12 May 1968; *née* Duffy; *m* 2007, Kenneth James Gibson. *Educ:* Univ. of Glasgow (MA 1991). Teacher of English, St Ninians High Sch., Giffnock, until 2015. Mem. (SNP), Glasgow CC, 2007–15. *Address:* House of Commons, SW1A 0AA.

**GILLAN, Rt Hon. Cheryl (Elise Kendall);** PC 2010; MP (C) Chesham and Amersham, since 1992; *b* 21 April 1952; *d* of Major Adam Mitchell Gillan and Mona Elsie Gillan (*née* Freeman); *m* 1985, John Coates Leeming. *Educ:* Cheltenham Ladies' Coll.; Coll. of Law. FCIM DipM. International Management Group, 1976–84; British Film Year, 1984–86; Ernst & Young, 1986–91; Dir, Kidsons Impey, 1991–93. PPS to Lord Privy Seal, 1994–95; Parly Under-Sec. of State, DFEE, 1995–97; Opposition frontbench spokesman: on trade and industry, 1997–98; on foreign and commonwealth affairs and overseas devel, 1998–2001; on home affairs, 2003–05; an Opposition Whip, 2001–03; Shadow Sec. of State for Wales, 2005–10; Sec. of State for Wales, 2010–12. Chm., Bow Group, 1987. Freeman, City of London, 1991; Liveryman, Marketors' Co., 1991. *Recreations:* golf, music, gardening, animals. *Address:* House of Commons, SW1A 0AA. *T:* (020) 7219 3000. *Club:* Royal Automobile.

**GLASS, Patricia;** MP (Lab) North West Durham, since 2010; *b* Esh Winning, Co. Durham; *m* Bob Glass; two *s*. Assistant Director of Education: Sunderland, 2004–06; Greenwich, 2006–08; Govt Advr on SEN for Yorks and Humber Reg., 2009–10. Mem., Educn Select Cttee, 2010–15. Mem., Lanchester Parish Council, 2007. *Address:* House of Commons, SW1A 0AA.

**GLEN, John Philip;** MP (C) Salisbury, since 2010; *b* Bath, 1 April 1974; *s* of Philip Glen and Thalia Glen (*née* Mitchenere); *m* 2008, Emma

Caroline O'Brien (*née* Stephens); one step s one step d. *Educ:* King Edward's Sch., Bath (Hd Boy); Mansfield Coll., Oxford (BA Mod. Hist. 1996; Pres. JCR 1995); Judge Inst., Univ. of Cambridge (MBA 2003). Accounts Asst, Fleet Support Gp, Chippenham, 1992–93; Parly Researcher to Gary Streeter, MP and Michael Bates, MP, 1996–97; Strategy Consultant, Accenture, 1997–2004, on secondment to Hd, Political Section, Conservative Res. Dept, 2000–01; Dep. Dir, 2004–05, Dir, 2005–06, Conservative Res. Dept; Sen. Advr to Global Hd of Strategy, Accenture, 2006–10. PPS to Sec. of State for Communities and Local Govt, 2012–15, to Sec. of State for Business, Innovation and Skills, 2015–. Member: Defence Select Cttee, 2010–12; Cttee on Arms Exports, 2010–12; Downing St Policy Bd, 2014–. JP Westminster, 2006–11. *Publications:* (contrib.) There is Such a Thing as Society, 2002. *Recreations:* family, church, eating out, travel, squash. *Address:* (office) Morrison Hall, 12 Brown Street, Salisbury, Wilts SP1 1HE; House of Commons, SW1A 0AA. *T:* (020) 7219 3000. *E:* john.glen.mp@parliament.uk.

**GLINDON, Mary;** MP (Lab) North Tyneside, since 2010; b 13 Jan. 1957; d of Margaret and Cecil Mulgrove; m 2000, Raymond Glindon; one d and one step s one step d. *Educ:* Sacred Heart Grammar Sch., Fenham; Newcastle upon Tyne Poly. (BSc Sociol. 1979). Clerical officer, CS, 1980–85; adminr, local govt, 1987–88; adminr/ community develt manager, Centre for Unemployment, 1988–2004; Adminr, NHS call centre, 2005; trainee dispenser, NHS, 2005–06; travel sales advr, call centre, 2006; sales asst in department store, 2006–08; Admin Officer, DWP and Child Maintenance and Enforcement Commn, 2008–10. Mem. (Lab) N Tyneside Council, 1995–2010 (Mayor, 1999–2000). Member: Envmt, Food and Rural Affairs Select Cttee, 2010–15; Transport Select Cttee, 2015–. *Address:* House of Commons, SW1A 0AA.

**GODSIFF, Roger Duncan;** MP (Lab) Birmingham Hall Green, since 2010 (Birmingham, Small Heath, 1992–97; Birmingham Sparkbrook and Small Heath, 1997–2010); b 28 June 1946; s of late George and of Gladys Godsiff; m 1977, Julia Brenda Morris; one s one d. *Educ:* Catford Comprehensive Sch. Bank clerk, 1965–70; political officer, APEX, 1970–90; senior research officer, GMB, 1990–92. Mem. (Lab) Lewisham BC, 1971–90 (Mayor, 1977). Contested (Lab) Birmingham, Yardley, 1983. Chm., British-Japanese Parly Gp, 1994–. Chm., Charlton Athletic Charitable Trust, 2004–. Gold and Silver Star, Order of Rising Sun (Japan), 2014. *Recreations:* sport - particularly football and cricket, listening to music, spending time with family. *Address:* House of Commons, SW1A 0AA. *Clubs:* Rowley Regis Labour; Charlton Athletic Supporters.

**GOLDSMITH, Frank Zacharias Robin, (Zac);** MP (C) Richmond Park, since 2010; b Westminster, 20 Jan. 1975; s of late Sir James Michael Goldsmith and of Lady Annabel Goldsmith (formerly Lady Annabel Vane Tempest Stewart); m 1st, 1999, Sheherazade Ventura-Bentley (marr. diss. 2012); one s two d; 2nd, 2013, Alice Miranda Rothschild; one d. *Educ:* Hawtreys; Eton Coll.; Internat. Honours Programme, Boston. Worked with Redefining Progress, San Francisco, 1994–95; joined Internat. Soc. for Ecology and Culture, 1995–97, based in Calif, Bristol and Ladakh, India (ran tourist educn prog. in Ladakh for part of time), later Assoc. Dir; Ed., 1997–2007, Dir, 2007–, The Ecologist mag. Co-founder, FARM, 2002. Dir, Ecosystems Ltd. Mem. Adv. Bd, JMG Foundn; Trustee: Royal Parks Foundn; Rainforest Foundn UK; Aspinall Foundn; Countryside Restoration Trust; Pres., Nat. Gardens Scheme, 2006–10. Speeches at numerous venues incl. Schumacher Meml Lects, Oxford Union, colls, schs and Think Tanks in UK. (Jtly) Beacon Prize for Young Philanthropist of the Year, 2003; Internat. Envmtl Leadership Award, Global Green USA, 2004. *Publications:* The Constant Economy: how to create a stable society, 2009; contrib. newspapers incl. The Times, Sunday Times, Daily Mail, Mail on Sunday, Independent, Guardian, Observer, Standard, Express, Daily Telegraph, Tribune and many regl newspapers; over 50 articles for The Ecologist; articles for other magazines incl. Country Life (contrib. and ed special edn, Dec. 2002), Big Issue, New Statesman, Spectator, Week, Global Agenda 2003, Geographical, Tatler and Vanity Fair. *Address:* House of Commons, SW1A 0AA. *Club:* Travellers.

**GOODMAN, Helen Catherine;** MP (Lab) Bishop Auckland, since 2005; b 2 Jan. 1958; d of Alan Goodman and Hanne Goodman; m 1988, Charles; two c. *Educ:* Lady Manners Sch., Bakewell; Somerville Coll., Oxford (BA 1979). HM Treasury, 1980–97, latterly Hd of Strategy Unit; Advr to Prime Minister of Czechoslovakia, 1990; Dir, Commn on Future of Multi Ethnic Britain, 1998; Hd of Strategy, Children's Soc., 1998–2002; Chief Exec., Nat. Assoc. of Toy and Leisure Libraries, 2002–05. Parly Sec., Office of the Leader of the H of C, 2007–08; Parly Under-Sec. of State, DWP, 2009–10. Shadow Minister: for Justice, 2010–11; for Culture, 2011–14; for Work and Pensions, 2014–15. Mem., Public Accounts Cttee, 2005–07. *Address:* House of Commons, SW1A 0AA. *T:* (020) 7219 4346. *E:* goodmanh@parliament.uk.

**GOODWILL, Robert;** MP (C) Scarborough and Whitby, since 2005; Parliamentary Under-Secretary of State, Department for Transport, since 2013; b 31 Dec. 1956; s of late Robert W. Goodwill and Joan Goodwill; m 1987, Maureen (*née* Short); two s one d. *Educ:* Bootham Sch., York; Univ. of Newcastle upon Tyne (BSc Hons Agriculture). Farmer, 1979–. Contested (C): Redcar, 1992; NW Leics, 1997; Cleveland and

Richmond, 1994, Yorks S, May 1998, EP elecns. MEP (C) Yorks and the Humber Reg., 1999–2004; Dep. Cons. Leader, EP, 2003–04. Opposition Whip, 2006–07; Shadow Transport Minister, 2007–10; an Asst Govt Whip, 2010–11; Govt Pairing Whip, 2011–13; a Lord Comr of HM Treasury (Govt Whip), 2012–13. *Recreations:* steam ploughing, travel, languages. *Address:* Southwood Farm, Terrington, York YO60 6QB. *T:* (01653) 648459; (constituency office) 21 Huntriss Row, Scarborough, N Yorks YO11 2ED. *E:* robert.goodwill.mp@parliament.uk.

**GOVE, Rt Hon. Michael (Andrew);** PC 2010; MP (C) Surrey Heath, since 2005; Lord Chancellor and Secretary of State for Justice, since 2015; *b* 26 Aug. 1967; *s* of Ernest and Christine Gove; *m* 2001, Sarah Vine; one *s* one *d*. *Educ:* Robert Gordon's Coll., Aberdeen; Lady Margaret Hall, Oxford (BA). Reporter, Aberdeen Press and Jl, 1989; researcher/reporter, Scottish TV, 1990–91; reporter, BBC News and Current Affairs, 1991–95; editor, 1995–2005, writer, 1995–2010, The Times. Sec. of State for Educn, 2010–14; Parly Sec. to HM Treasury (Govt Chief Whip), 2014–15. *Publications:* Michael Portillo, 1995; The Price of Peace: a study of the Northern Ireland peace process, 2000; Celsius 7/7, 2006. *Address:* House of Commons, SW1A 0AA. *T:* (020) 7219 3000.

**GRADY, Patrick John;** MP (SNP) Glasgow North, since 2015; *b* Inverness, 5 Feb. 1980. *Educ:* Inverness Royal Acad.; Univ. of Strathclyde. Work in London and in Malawi; campaigning and policy posts in charity and public sector. SNP Spokesperson on Internat. Develt, 2015–. Nat. Sec., SNP, 2012–. Contested (SNP) Glasgow N, 2010. *Address:* House of Commons, SW1A 0AA.

**GRAHAM, Richard;** MP (C) Gloucester, since 2010; *b* Reading, 4 April 1958; *s* of Robin and Judith Graham; *m* 1989, Anthea Knaggs; two *s* one *d*. *Educ:* Eton Coll.; Christ Church, Oxford (BA Hist. 1979); Investment Mgt Cert. 1998. Airline Manager, Cathay Pacific Airways and John Swire & Sons, 1980–86; HM Diplomatic Service, 1986–93: First Sec., Nairobi, Peking; Trade Comr, China, and Consul, Macau, 1989–92; Chief Rep. in China, Barings plc, 1993–95; Dir, ING Barings, 1995–97; Hd, Instnl Business, Baring Asset Mgt, 1997–2010. Director: Greater China Fund Inc., 1994–2004; Care 4 Children, 1999–2001; Chm., British Chamber of Commerce, Shanghai, 1995–97. Prime Minister's Trade Envoy to Indonesia, 2012–. Mem. (C) Cotswold DC, 2003–07. Contested (C) SW England, EP, 2004. PPS to Minister of State, FCO, 2010–14. Mem., Work and Pensions Select Cttee, 2010; Chm., All Party Parly China Gp, 2010–15; Founder Chm., All Party Parly Commonwealth Gp, 2012–13. *Recreations:* cricket, squash, watching Gloucester Rugby, walking. *Address:* House of Commons, SW1A 0AA. *T:* (020) 7219 7077. *E:*

richard.graham.mp@parliament.uk. *Clubs:* MCC, Lords and Commons Cricket, Gloucester City Winget Cricket.

**GRANT, Helen;** MP (C) Maidstone and the Weald, since 2010; *b* London, 28 Sept. 1961; *d* of Dr Julius Okuboye and Dr Gladys Spedding (*née* Butler); *m* 1991, Simon Julian Grant; two *s*. *Educ:* St Aidan's Sch., Carlisle; Trinity Sch., Carlisle; Univ. of Hull (LLB Hons); Guildford Coll. of Law (solicitors finals). Articled clerk, Cartmell Mawson and Maine, Carlisle; admitted solicitor, 1988; Clinical Negligence Solicitor, Hempsons, London, 1987–88; Equity Partner, Fayers & Co., S Wimbledon, 1988–94; Founder and Sen. Partner, Grants Solicitors LLP, 1996–. Non-exec. Dir, Croydon NHS PCT, 2005–07. Member: Family Div., Social Justice Policy Gp, 2006–08; Family Law Reform Commn, 2007–09, Centre for Social Justice; Equality and Diversity Cttee, Law Soc., 2008–09. Parliamentary Under-Secretary of State: (Women and Equalities), MoJ, 2012–13; (Women, Equalities, Sport and Tourism), DCMS, 2013–15. Mem., Justice Select Cttee, 2010–11; Vice Chm., Army Div., All Party Parly Gp for Armed Forces, 2010. Pres., Bd of Trustees, Maidstone Museums' Foundn, 2008–; Patron, Maidstone Br., Tomorrow's People, 2009–; Hon. Vice-Pres., Maidstone MENCAP Trust, 2010–. Hon. MInstRE 2010. *Publications:* contrib. to reports for Social Justice Policy Gp, Centre for Social Justice. *Recreations:* tennis, cinema, major sporting events, family life. *Address:* House of Commons, SW1A 0AA. *T:* (020) 7219 7107. *E:* helen.grant.mp@parliament.uk.

**GRANT, Peter;** MP (SNP) Glenrothes, since 2015.

**GRAY, James Whiteside;** MP (C) North Wiltshire, since 1997; *b* 7 Nov. 1954; *s* of Very Rev. John Rodger Gray, VRD, sometime Moderator, Gen. Assembly of C of S, and of Dr Sheila Gray (*née* Whiteside); *m* 1st, 1980, Sarah Ann Beale (marr. diss. 2007); two *s* one *d*; 2nd, 2009, Philippa Gay Mayo (*née* Keeble); one step *s* two step *d*. *Educ:* Hillhead Primary Sch., Glasgow; Glasgow High Sch.; Glasgow Univ. (MA Hons); Christ Church, Oxford. Grad. mgt trainee, P&O, 1977–78; Shipbroker, Anderson Hughes & Co., 1978–84; Mem., Baltic Exchange, 1978–91, 1997–; Dir, Baltic Futures Exchange, 1989–91; Man. Dir, GNI Freight Futures, 1985–92; Special Advr to Sec. of State, DoE, 1992–95; Dir, Westminster Strategy Ltd, 1995–97. Dep. Chm., Wandsworth Tooting Cons. Assoc., 1994–96. Contested (C) Ross, Cromarty and Skye, 1992. An Opposition Whip, 2000–01; Opposition front bench spokesman on defence, 2001–02, on countryside, 2002–05; Shadow Sec. of State for Scotland, 2005. Member, Select Committee: on Envmtl Affairs, 1997–2000; on DEFRA, 2007–10; on Procedure, 2010–15; on Defence, 2013–; on Admin, 2015–; Jt Chm., All-Party Minerals Gp, 1997–2001 and 2009–; Chairman: All-Party Multiple Sclerosis Gp, 2004–11; All-

Party Parly Gp for the Army, 2004–10; All-Party Parly Gp for Armed Forces, 2010–; Vice-Chairman: All-Party Parly Gp on Deafness, 2004–07; All-Party Parly Gp for Polar Regions, 2012–; Member: Speakers Panel of Chairmen, 2010–; Commons Finance and Services Cttee, 2010–13; Chm., Cons. Rural Action Gp, 2003–05; Cons. Defence and Foreign Affairs Policy Gp, 2006–07. Mem., UK Delegn, Council of Europe and WEU, 2007–08. Chm., Horse and Pony Taxation Cttee, 1999–2002. Trustee, Armed Forces Parly Trust (formerly Scheme), 2013– (Chm., 2013–) (Graduate, 1997–98, Post-grad. Scheme, 2001, Advanced Post-grad., 2010; rcds, 2003); Vis. Parly Fellow, St Antony's Coll., Oxford, 2005–06. Convenor, Poles Apart Conf., RUSI, 2013. Mem., Cons. Party Bd for SW, 2010–. Served HAC (TA), 1977–84 (Mem., Court of Assts, 2002–07); Vice-Pres., HAC Saddle Club. Vice-Chm., Charitable Properties Assoc., 2002–10; President: Chippenham Br., Multiple Sclerosis Soc., 2000–06 (Patron, Devizes Br., 2007–); Assoc. of British Riding Schs, 2001–; Consultant, British Horse Industry Confedn, 1999–2002. Patron, Mutual Support, 2006–. Freeman, City of London, 1982. *Publications:* Financial Risk Management in the Shipping Industry, 1985; Futures and Options for Shipping, 1987 (Lloyds of London Book Prize); Shipping Futures, 1990; Crown vs Parliament: who decides on going to war? (thesis), 2003; Poles Apart, 2013; (with M. Lomas) Who Takes Britain to War?, 2014. *Recreations:* countryside, riding horses, English local history, Polar regions. *Address:* House of Commons, SW1A 0AA. *T:* (020) 7219 6237. *Clubs:* Pratt's; Chippenham Constitutional (Pres., 1999–); Royal Wootton Bassett Conservative.

**GRAY, Neil Charles;** MP (SNP) Airdrie and Shotts, since 2015; *b* Orkney Isles, 16 March 1986; *m* Karlie; one *d. Educ:* Kirkwall Grammar Sch.; Stirling Univ. (BA 1st Cl. Hons Politics and Journalism 2008). Contract producer and reporter, BBC Radio Orkney, 2003–08; press and res. intern, SNP, Scottish Parlt, 2008; work in office of Alex Neil, MSP, 2008–15, Office Manager, 2011–15. *Address:* House of Commons, SW1A 0AA.

**GRAYLING, Rt Hon. Christopher (Stephen);** PC 2010; MP (C) Epsom and Ewell, since 2001; Leader of the House of Commons and Lord President of the Council, since 2015; *b* 1 April 1962; *s* of John Terence Grayling and Elizabeth Grayling; *m* 1987, Susan Dillistone; one *s* one *d. Educ:* Royal Grammar Sch., High Wycombe; Sidney Sussex Coll., Cambridge (MA Hist.). BBC News producer, 1985–88; producer and editor, Business Daily, Channel 4, 1988–91; Commissioning Editor, BBC Select, 1991–93; Dir, Charterhouse Prodns, 1993; Div. Dir, Workhouse Ltd, 1993–95; Dir, SSVC Gp, 1995–97; Change Consultant and Eur. Mktg Dir, Burson-Marsteller, 1997–2001. An Opposition Whip, 2002; Opposition front bench spokesman

on health, 2002–03, on higher and further educn, 2003–05; Shadow Leader, H of C, 2005; Shadow Secretary of State: for Transport, 2005–07; for Work and Pensions, 2007–09; Shadow Home Sec., 2009–10; Minister of State, DWP, 2010–12; Lord Chancellor and Sec. of State for Justice, 2012–15. *Publications:* The Bridgewater Heritage, 1984; A Land Fit for Heroes, 1985; The Story of Joseph Holt, 1985, 2nd edn 1999; (jtly) Just Another Star, 1988. *Recreations:* football, cricket. *Address:* House of Commons, SW1A 0AA. *T:* (020) 7219 8194.

**GREEN, Chris;** MP (C) Bolton West, since 2015; *b* 12 Aug. 1973. Engr, mass spectrometry industry. Contested (C) Manchester Withington, 2010. Mem., Sci. and Technol. Select Cttee, 2015–. *Address:* House of Commons, SW1A 0AA.

**GREEN, Rt Hon. Damian (Howard);** PC 2012; MP (C) Ashford, since 1997; *b* 17 Jan. 1956; *s* of Howard and late Audrey Green; *m* 1988, Alicia Collinson; two *d. Educ:* Reading Sch.; Balliol Coll., Oxford (MA 1st cl. Hons. PPE). Producer, BBC Financial Unit, 1980–82; Business Producer, Channel 4 News, 1982–84; Business News Ed., The Times, 1984–85; Business Ed., Channel 4 News, 1985–87; Presenter and City Ed., Business Daily prog., Channel 4, 1987–92; Prime Minister's Policy Unit, 1992–94; Public Affairs Advr, 1994–97. Opposition spokesman: on employment and higher educn; 1998–99; on the envmt, 1999–2001; Shadow Educn Sec., 2001–03; Shadow Transport Sec., 2003–04; Shadow Minister for Immigration, 2005–10; Minister of State: (Minister for Immigration), Home Office, 2010–12; (Minister for Policing, Criminal Justice and Victims), Home Office and MoJ, 2012–14. Chairman: European Mainstream Gp, 2014–; All-Party BBC Gp. Contested (C) Brent E, 1992. Trustee, Communities Develt Foundn, 1997–2001; Vice-Chm., John Smith Meml Trust, 2004–10. *Publications:* ITN Budget Factbook, annually 1984–86; A Better BBC, 1990; Communities in the Countryside, 1995; The Four Failures of the New Deal, 1998; Better Learning, 2002; More Than Markets, 2003; (with David Davis) Controlling Economic Migration, 2006. *Recreations:* cricket, football, opera, cinema. *Address:* House of Commons, SW1A 0AA. *T:* (020) 7219 3000.

**GREEN, Katherine Anne, (Kate),** OBE 2005; MP (Lab) Stretford and Urmston, since 2010; *b* 2 May 1960; *d* of Maurice Green and Jessie Craig Green (*née* Bruce); *m* 1985, Richard Duncan Mabb (marr. diss. 2006). *Educ:* Currie High Sch., Midlothian; Univ. of Edinburgh (LLB Hons 1982). Barclays Bank, 1982–97; Whitehall and Industry Gp Secondee to Home Office, 1997–99; Dir, NCOPF, 2000–04; Chief Exec., Child Poverty Action Gp, 2004–09. Member: Lord Chancellor's Adv. Cttee, City of London, 2001–09; Nat. Employment Panel, 2001–07; London Child Poverty Commn,

2006–09; Greater Manchester Poverty Commn, 2012–13. Shadow Minister: for Equalities, 2011–13; for Disabled People, 2013–15; for Women and Equalities, 2015–. Dir, Project Fresh Start, 2001–03. Trustee: Family and Parenting (formerly Nat. Family and Parenting) Inst., 2000–07 (Treas., 2006–07); Avenues Youth Project, 2000–05; Inst. for Fiscal Studies, 2004–09; Friends Provident Foundn, 2007–09; Webb Meml Trust, 2011–. JP City of London, 1993–2009. *Recreations:* theatre, swimming. *Address:* House of Commons, SW1A 0AA. *T:* (020) 7219 7162. *E:* kate.green.mp@parliament.uk.

**GREENING, Rt Hon. Justine;** PC 2011; MP (C) Putney, since 2005; Secretary of State for International Development, since 2012; *b* 30 April 1969. *Educ:* Oakwood Comprehensive Sch., Rotherham; Thomas Rotherham Coll.; Univ. of Southampton (BSc 1990); London Business Sch. (MBA 2000). ACA 1995. Audit Asst, Price Waterhouse, 1991–94; Audit Asst Manager, Revisuisse Price Waterhouse, 1995–96; Finance Manager, SmithKline Beecham, 1996–2001; Business Strategy Manager, GlaxoSmithKline, 2001–02; Sales and Mktg Finance Manager, Centrica, 2002–05. Econ. Sec., HM Treasury, 2010–11; Sec. of State for Transport, 2011–12. Mem. (C), Epping Town Council, 1999. Contested (C) Ealing, Acton and Shepherd's Bush, 2001. *Address:* (office) 3 Summerstown Road, SW17 0BQ; House of Commons, SW1A 0AA. *W:* www.justinegreening.co.uk.

**GREENWOOD, Lilian Rachel;** MP (Lab) Nottingham South, since 2010; *b* Bolton, Lancs, 26 March 1966; *d* of Harry Greenwood and Patricia Greenwood; three *d*; *m* 2008, Ravi Subramanian. *Educ:* Canon Slade Sch., Bolton; St Catharine's Coll., Cambridge (BA Hons 1987); South Bank Poly. (MSc). Research Officer: LACSAB, 1988–89; Civil and Public Services Assoc., 1989–92; Trainee Regl Officer, NUPE, 1992–93; UNISON: Regl Organiser, 1993–98; Regl Educn Officer, 1998–2002; Regl Manager, 2002–10. Shadow Sec. of State for Transport, 2015–. *Recreations:* running, walking, cycling, cinema. *Address:* (office) 12 Regent Street, Nottingham NG1 5BQ. *T:* (0115) 711 7000; House of Commons, SW1A 0AA. *E:* lilian.greenwood.mp@parliament.uk.

**GREENWOOD, Margaret;** MP (Lab) Wirral West, since 2015; *b* 14 March 1959. Teacher of English in secondary schs, further educn colleges and adult educn centres, Liverpool and Wirral; teacher of literacy to adult learners and adults with special needs; travel writer; website consultant. *Address:* House of Commons, SW1A 0AA.

**GRIEVE, Rt Hon. Dominic (Charles Roberts);** PC 2010; QC 2008; MP (C) Beaconsfield, since 1997; *b* Lambeth, London, 24 May 1956; *s* of William Percival Grieve, QC and Evelyn Grieve (*née* Mijouain); *m* 1990, Caroline

Hutton; two *s. Educ:* Westminster Sch.; Magdalen Coll., Oxford (MA Modern History); Poly. of Central London. Called to the Bar, Middle Temple, 1980, Bencher, 2004. Mem., Hammersmith and Fulham LBC, 1982–86. Contested (C) Norwood, 1987. Opposition front bench spokesman: for Scotland and on constitutional affairs, 1999–2001; on home affairs, 2001–03; on community cohesion, 2003–08; Shadow Attorney Gen., 2003–09; Shadow Home Sec., 2008–09; Shadow Sec. of State for Justice, 2009–10; Attorney Gen., 2010–14. Member: Jt Select Cttee on Statutory Instruments, 1997–2001; Select Cttee on Envmtl Audit, 1997–2001; Intelligence and Security Cttee, 2015–. Chm. Res. Cttee, 1992–95, Chm. Exec. Cttee, 2006–08, Finance and Gen. Purposes Cttee, 2006–, Soc. of Cons. Lawyers. Member: Council, Justice, 1997–; Franco-British Soc., 1997–2010 (Pres., 2011–); Luxembourg Soc., 1997–; Franco-British Council, 2010– (Vice Chm., 2011–). Hon. Recorder, Royal Bor. of Kingston-upon-Thames, 2012–. Lay visitor, police stations, 1990–96. Mem., London Dio. Synod, C of E, 1995–2001; a Dep. Church Warden. Gov., Ditchley Foundn, 2010–. *Recreations:* mountaineering, ski-ing, scuba diving, fell walking, travel, architecture. *Address:* House of Commons, SW1A 0AA. *T:* (020) 7219 6220; 1 Temple Garden Chambers, 1 Harcourt Buildings, Temple, EC4Y 9DA. *T:* (020) 7353 0407. *Club:* Garrick.

**GRIFFITH, Nia Rhiannon;** MP (Lab) Llanelli, since 2005; *b* 4 Dec. 1956; *d* of Prof. T. Gwynfor Griffith and Dr Rhiannon Griffith (*née* Howell); *m* (marr. diss.). *Educ:* Univ. of Oxford (BA 1st cl. Hons Mod. Foreign Langs 1979); UCNW, Bangor (PGCE 1980). Language teacher: Oldham, 1981–83; Queen Elizabeth Cambria Sch., Carmarthen, 1983–85; Hd of Langs Faculty, Gowerton Comp. Sch., Swansea, 1986–92; Advr and Schs Inspector, Estyn, 1992–97; Hd of Langs, Morriston Comp. Sch., Swansea, 1997–2005. Mem. (Lab), Carmarthen Town Council, 1987–99 (Sheriff, 1998; Dep. Mayor, 1998). Shadow Minister for Business, Innovation and Skills, 2010–11, for Wales, 2011–15; Shadow Sec. of State for Wales, 2015–. *Publications:* Ciao! Book 2: a textbook for teaching Italian, 1990; 100 Ideas for Teaching Languages, 2005. *Address:* (office) 6 Queen Victoria Road, Llanelli SA15 2TL; House of Commons, SW1A 0AA.

**GRIFFITHS, Andrew James;** MP (C) Burton, since 2010; *b* Wolverhampton, 19 Oct. 1970; *s* of Robert Griffiths and Harriet Griffiths (*née* Du'Rose); *m* 2013, Kate Kniveton. *Educ:* High Arcal Sch., Sedgley. Worked for family engrg business, 1996–2002; Advr to Cons. MEPs, 1999–2004; Chief of Staff: to Shadow Sec. of State for Envmt and Transport, 2004, for Family, 2004–05, for Culture, Media and Sport, 2005–07, for Community and Local Govt, 2007–09; to Chm., Cons. Party, 2009–10; Sec. to Bd, Cons. Party, 2009–10. Contested (C) Dudley N, 2001.

*Recreations:* supporting British brewing industry, football, cricket. *Address:* (office) Gothard House, 9 St Paul's Square, Burton on Trent, Staffs DE14 2EF. *T:* (01283) 568894. *E:* andrew.griffiths.mp@parliament.uk. *Clubs:* Carlton; Uttoxeter British Legion; Rolleston Working Men's.

**GUMMER, Benedict Michael;** MP (C) Ipswich, since 2010; Parliamentary Under-Secretary of State, Department of Health, since 2015; *b* London, 19 Feb. 1978; *s* of Baron Deben, PC. *Educ:* St Saviour's C of E Prim. Sch.; St John's College Sch., Cambridge; Tonbridge Sch.; Peterhouse, Cambridge (MA Hons). Company Dir, 2001–10; writer. *Publications:* The Scourging Angel: the black death in the British Isles, 2009. *Recreations:* music, reading, visiting Suffolk pubs with my friends. *Address:* House of Commons, SW1A 0AA. *E:* ben@bengummer.com.

**GWYNNE, Andrew John;** MP (Lab) Denton and Reddish, since 2005; *b* 4 June 1974; *s* of Richard John Gwynne and Margaret Elisabeth Gwynne (*née* Ridgway); *m* 2003, Allison Louise Dennis; two *s* one *d*. *Educ:* Univ. of Salford (BA Hons Politics and Contemp. Hist.); NE Wales Inst. of Higher Educn (HND Business and Finance). Asst to EDS Prog. Manager, ICL, Manchester, 1990–92; Mem., Year 2000 Team, Nat. Computing Centre, 1999–2000; European Co-ordinator, office of Arlene McCarthy, MEP, 2000–01; researcher, office of Andrew Bennett, MP, 2000–05. PPS to Minister of State, Home Office, 2005–07, to Home Sec., 2007–09, to Secretary of State, Children, Schs and Families, 2009–10; Shadow Minister: of Transport, 2010–11; for Health, 2011–15. Mem. (Lab) Tameside MBC, 1996–2008. *Recreations:* history, reading, computing, spending time with family. *Address:* House of Commons, SW1A 0AA. *T:* (020) 7219 4708. *E:* gwynnea@parliament.uk; (constituency office) Town Hall, Market Street, Denton M34 2AP. *T:* (0161) 320 1504, *Fax:* (0161) 320 1503.

**GYIMAH, Samuel Phillip;** MP (C) East Surrey, since 2010; Parliamentary Under-Secretary of State, Department for Education, since 2014; *b* Beaconsfield, Bucks, 10 Aug. 1976; *m* 2012, Dr Nicky Black. *Educ:* Achimota Secondary Sch., Ghana; Freman Coll., Herts; Somerville Coll., Oxford (BA PPE). Pres., Oxford Union, 1997. Investment Banker, Internat. Equities and Investment Banking Div., Goldman Sachs, 1999–2003; entrepreneur in trng, employment and Internet sectors, 2003–10. PPS to the Prime Minister, 2012–13; a Lord Comr of HM Treasury (Govt Whip), 2013–14; Parly Sec., Cabinet Office, 2014–15. Chm., Bow Gp, 2007. Gov., Haverstock Sch., 2004–07. *Publications:* (ed) From the Ashes…: the future of the Conservative Party, 2005; (jtly) Beyond the Banks, 2011. *Address:* House of Commons, SW1A 0AA. *T:* (020) 7219 3504. *E:* sam@samgyimah.com.

**HAIGH, Louise Margaret;** MP (Lab) Sheffield Heeley, since 2015; *b* Sheffield; 22 July 1987. *Educ:* Sheffield High Sch.; Nottingham Univ. Call centre worker; council youth services; Co-ordinator, All Party Parly Gp on Internat. Corporate Responsibility; Corporate Governance Policy Manager, Aviva plc. *Address:* House of Commons, SW1A 0AA.

**HALFON, Rt Hon. Robert;** PC 2015; MP (C) Harlow, since 2010; Minister of State (Minister without Portfolio), Cabinet Office, since 2015. *Educ:* Highgate Sch.; Exeter Univ. (BA Politics 1991; MA Russian and E Eur. Politics 1992). Formerly: res. and policy analyst to public affairs consultancies; freelance consultancy work; COS to Oliver Letwin, MP, 2001–05. Mem., Adv. Bd, Centre for Social Justice. Political Consultant to Cons. Friends of Israel, 2005–10. Member: Public Admin Select Cttee, 2010–14; Exec., 1922 Cttee, 2010–. Chair: Western Area Cons. Students, 1987–90; Exeter Univ. Cons. Assoc., 1989–90; Dep. Chair, Vauxhall Cons. Assoc., 1998–2000; Mem., Cons. Way Forward. Contested (C) Harlow, 2001, 2005. Mem. (C) Roydon PC, 2005–11. Trustee, Harlow Employability. Formerly: Gov., Passmores Sch.; Patron, Harlow Homeless Centre. *Publications:* contrib. articles to nat. newspapers. *Recreations:* reading, watches, Chelsea Football, countryside. *Address:* House of Commons, SW1A 0AA. *T:* (020) 7219 7223. *E:* Halfon4harlow@roberthalfon.com.

**HALL, Luke Anthony;** MP (C) Thornbury and Yate, since 2015; *b* S Glos, 8 July 1986. Shop worker, then Store Manager, Lidl, Yate; Area Manager, Farmfoods, until 2015. *Address:* House of Commons, SW1A 0AA.

**HAMILTON, Fabian;** MP (Lab) Leeds North East, since 1997; *b* 12 April 1955; *s* of late Mario Uziell-Hamilton and Her Honour Adrianne Uziell-Hamilton; *m* 1980, Rosemary Ratcliffe; one *s* two *d*. *Educ:* Brentwood Sch., Essex; Univ. of York (BA Hons). Graphic designer (own company), 1979–94; computer systems consultant, 1994–97. Leeds City Council: Mem. (Lab), 1987–97; Chm., Employment and Econ. Develt Cttee, 1994–96; Chm., Educn Cttee, 1996–98. Mem., Select Cttee on Foreign Affairs, 2001–10, on Political and Constitutional Reform, 2010–15. Contested (Lab) Leeds NE, 1992. Trustee, Heart Research UK (formerly Nat. Heart Res. Fund), 1999–2012. Gov., Northern Sch. of Contemporary Dance. *Recreations:* film, theatre, opera, photography, cycling. *Address:* House of Commons, SW1A 0AA. *T:* (020) 7219 3493.

**HAMMOND, Rt Hon. Philip;** PC 2010; MP (C) Runnymede and Weybridge, since 1997; Secretary of State for Foreign and Commonwealth Affairs, since 2014; *b* 4 Dec. 1955; *s* of Bernard Lawrence Hammond and Doris Rose Hammond; *m* 1991, Susan Carolyn, *d* of E. Williams-Walker; one *s* two *d*. *Educ:*

Shenfield Sch., Brentwood; University Coll., Oxford (Open Scholar, 1st cl. PPE, MA). Various posts, Speywood Labs Ltd, 1977–81; Dir, Speywood Medical Ltd, 1981–83; established and ran medical equipment distribution co., and dir, medical equipment manufg cos, 1983–94; Partner, CMA Consultants, 1993–95; Director: Castlemead Ltd, 1984–; Castlemead Homes Ltd, 1994–; Consort Resources Ltd, 2000–03. Consultant, Govt of Malawi, 1995–97. Contested (C) Newham NE, June 1994. Opposition spokesman on health and social services, 1998–2001, on trade and industry, 2001–02; on local and devolved govt, 2002–05; Shadow Chief Sec. to HM Treasury, 2005 and 2007–10; Shadow Sec. of State for Work and Pensions, 2005–07; Secretary of State: for Transport, 2010–11; for Defence, 2011–14. Mem., Select Cttee on Envmt, Transport and the Regions, 1997–98, on Trade and Industry, 2002. Sec., Cons. Parly Health Cttee, 1997–98. *Recreations:* reading, cinema, walking. *Address:* House of Commons, SW1A 0AA. *T:* (020) 7219 4055.

**HAMMOND, Stephen William;** MP (C) Wimbledon, since 2005; *b* 4 Feb. 1962; *s* of Bryan Norman Walter and Janice Eve Hammond; *m* 1991, Sally Patricia Brodie; one *d. Educ:* King Edward VI Sch., Southampton; Queen Mary Coll., London (BSc Econ Hons). Reed Stenhouse Investment Services, 1983–85; Canada Life, 1985–87; UBS Phillips & Drew, 1987–91; Dir, Kleinwort Benson Securities, 1991–98; Commerzbank, 1998–2003, Dir of Res., 1999–2001. Mem., Merton BC, 2002–06. Contested (C): Warwickshire North, 1997; Wimbledon, 2001. Shadow Minister for Transport, 2005–10; PPS to Sec. of State for Communities and Local Govt, 2010–12; Parly Under-Sec. of State, DfT, 2012–14. Chm., All Party Parly Gp for Wholesale Financial Markets, 2010–12. Chm. Cons. Friends of India, 2010–12. *Address:* House of Commons, SW1A 0AA. *T:* (020) 7219 1029. *E:* hammonds@parliament.uk. *Clubs:* Royal Wimbledon Golf, Wimbledon Hockey, Wimbledon Civic Forum (Pres.), Wimbledon Society.

**HANCOCK, Rt Hon. Matthew (John David);** PC 2014; MP (C) West Suffolk, since 2010; Minister for the Cabinet Office and Paymaster General, since 2015; *b* Chester, 2 Oct. 1978; *s* of Michael Hancock and Shirley Hills (now Carter); *m* 2006, Martha Hoyer Millar; two *s* one *d. Educ:* Farndon Co. Prim. Sch.; King's Sch., Chester; W Cheshire Coll.; Exeter Coll., Oxford (BA 1st Cl. PPE 1999); Christ's Coll., Cambridge (MPhil Econ 2003). Economist, Bank of England, 2000–05; COS to George Osborne, MP, 2005–10. Parly Under-Sec. of State for Skills, 2012–13, Minister of State (Minister for Skills and Enterprise), 2013–14, BIS and DfE; Minister of State (Minister for Business, Enterprise and Energy), BIS and DECC, 2014–15. Member: Public Accounts Cttee, 2010–12; Cttee on Standards and Privileges, 2010–12. *Publications:*

(with N. Zahawi) Masters of Nothing, 2011. *Recreations:* cricket, cooking, racing, walking with family. *Address:* House of Commons, SW1A 0AA. *T:* (020) 7219 7186. *E:* matthew. hancock.mp@parliament.uk.

**HANDS, Rt Hon. Gregory (William);** PC 2014; MP (C) Chelsea and Fulham, since 2010 (Hammersmith and Fulham, 2005–10); Chief Secretary to the Treasury, since 2015; *b* 14 Nov. 1965; *s* of Edward and Mavis Hands; *m* 2005, Irina Hundt; one *s* one *d. Educ:* Dr Challoner's Grammar Sch.; Robinson Coll., Cambridge (BA 1989). Banker, 1989–97. Mem. (C), Hammersmith and Fulham BC, 1998–2006. An Asst Govt Whip, 2011–13; Treas. of HM Household (Dep. Chief Whip), 2013–15. *Address:* House of Commons, SW1A 0AA.

**HANSON, Rt Hon. David (George);** PC 2007; MP (Lab) Delyn, since 1992; *b* 5 July 1957; *s* of late Brian George Hanson and of Glenda Doreen (*née* Jones); *m* 1986, Margaret Rose Mitchell; two *s* two *d. Educ:* Verdin Comprehensive, Winsford, Ches.; Hull Univ. (BA Hons, PGCE). Vice-Pres., Hull Univ. Students' Union, 1978–79. Management trainee, Co-op. Union/Plymouth Co-op. Soc., 1980–82; with Spastics Soc., 1982–89; Dir, RE-SOLV (Soc. for Prevention of Solvent Abuse), 1989–92. Councillor: Vale Royal BC, 1983–91 (Leader, Lab Gp and Council, 1989–91); Northwich Town Council, 1987–91. Contested (Lab): Eddisbury, 1983; Delyn, 1987; Cheshire W (European Parlt), 1984. PPS to Chief Sec. to HM Treasury, 1997–98; an Asst Govt Whip, 1998–99; Parly Under-Sec. of State, Wales Office, 1999–2001; PPS to the Prime Minister, 2001–05; Minister of State: NI Office, 2005–07; MoJ, 2007–09; Home Office, 2009–10; Shadow Treasury Minister, 2010–11; Shadow Minister for Police, 2011–13, for Immigration, 2013–15. *Recreations:* football, family, cinema. *Address:* House of Commons, SW1A 0AA. *T:* (020) 7219 5064; (constituency office) 64 Chester Street, Flint, Flintshire CH6 5DH. *T:* (01352) 763159.

**HARMAN, Rt Hon. Harriet;** PC 1997; QC 2001; MP (Lab) Camberwell and Peckham, since 1997 (Peckham, Oct. 1982–1997); *b* 30 July 1950; *d* of late John Bishop Harman, FRCS, FRCP, and of Anna Charlotte Harman; *m* 1982, Jack Dromey, *qv;* two *s* one *d. Educ:* St Paul's Girls' Sch.; York Univ. Brent Community Law Centre, 1974–78; Legal Officer, NCCL, 1978–82. Opposition Chief Sec. to the Treasury, 1992–94; opposition front bench spokesman: on employment, 1994–95; on health, 1995–96; on social security, 1996–97; Sec. of State for Social Security, 1997–98; Solicitor-Gen., 2001–05; Minister of State, DCA, subseq. MoJ, 2005–07; Lord Privy Seal and Leader of the House of Commons, and Minister for Women and for Equality, 2007–10; Dep. Leader and Chair of Labour Party, 2007–15; Shadow Sec. of State for Internat. Develt, 2010–11, for Culture, Media and Sport, 2011–15; Shadow Dep. Prime

Minister, 2011–15. Mem., NEC, Labour Party, 1993–98. *Publications:* Sex Discrimination in Schools, 1977; Justice Deserted: the subversion of the jury, 1979; The Century Gap, 1993. *Address:* House of Commons, SW1A 0AA.

**HARPER, Rt Hon. Mark;** PC 2015; MP (C) Forest of Dean, since 2005; Parliamentary Secretary to HM Treasury (Government Chief Whip), since 2015; *b* 26 Feb. 1970; *m* 1999, Margaret Whelan. *Educ:* Headlands Sch., Swindon; Swindon Coll.; Brasenose Coll., Oxford (BA 1991). Auditor, KPMG, 1991–95; Intel Corporation (UK) Ltd: Sen. Finance Analyst, 1995–97; Finance Manager, 1997–2000; Ops Manager, 2000–02; own accountancy practice, Forest of Dean, 2002–06. Contested (C) Forest of Dean, 2001. Shadow Minister: for Defence, 2005–07; for Disabled People, 2007–10; Parly Sec., Cabinet Office, 2010–12; Minister of State (Minister for Immigration), Home Office, 2012–14; Minister of State, DWP, 2014–15. *Address:* (office) 35 High Street, Cinderford, Glos GL14 2SL; House of Commons, SW1A 0AA.

**HARPHAM, (Robert) Harry;** MP (Lab) Sheffield, Brightside and Hillsborough, since 2015; *b* 21 Feb. 1954; *m* Gill Furniss. *Educ:* Northern Coll.; Univ. of Sheffield. NUM Mem. and rep., Clipstone Colliery, Nottingham. Mem. (Lab), Sheffield CC, 2000–15 (Dep. Leader, 2012; Cabinet Mem. for Homes and Neighbourhoods). *Address:* House of Commons, SW1A 0AA.

**HARRINGTON, Richard;** MP (C) Watford, since 2010; Parliamentary Under Secretary of State, Home Office, Department for Communities and Local Government and Department for International Development, since 2015; *b* Leeds, 4 Nov. 1957; *s* of John Harrington and Alma Harrington; *m* 1982, Jessie Benardette; two *s. Educ:* Leeds Grammar Sch.; Keble Coll., Oxford (MA Juris.). Graduate trainee, John Lewis Partnership, 1980–83; Co-Founder and Dir, Harvington Properties, 1983–; CEO, LSI Gp Hldgs plc, 1992–97. Non-exec. Dir, Eden Financial Ltd (formerly Eden Gp plc), 2005–. Vice Chm., Target Seats, Cons. Party, 2012–. *Recreations:* cinema, reading, taunting, citrology. *Address:* House of Commons, SW1A 0AA. *T:* (020) 7219 7180. *E:* richard.harrington.mp@parliament.uk. *Clubs:* Oriental; Oxhey Conservative; Town and Country (Watford).

**HARRIS, Carolyn;** MP (Lab) Swansea East, since 2015; *b* Swansea; *d* of Don and Pauline Marvelly; three *s. Educ:* Swansea Univ. Project Manager, Guiding Hands charity, 1998–2000; Wales Regl Dir, Community Logistics, 2000–03; Wales Regl Manager, children's cancer charity, 2003–05; Sen. Parly Asst and Constituency Manager, Office of Siân James, MP, 2005–15. *Address:* (office) 485 Llangyfelach Road, Brynhyfryd, Swansea SA5 8EA. *T:* (01792) 462059. *E:* carolyn.harris.mp@parliament.uk.

**HARRIS, Rebecca Elizabeth;** MP (C) Castle Point, since 2010; *b* Windsor, 22 Dec. 1967; *d* of Philip and Louise Harris; *m* Frank; one *s. Educ:* London Sch. of Econs and Pol Sci. (BSc). Mktg Dir, Phillimore & Co. Ltd (publishers), 1997–2007. Special Advr to Tim Yeo, MP, 2003–10. Mem. (C) Chichester DC, 1999–2003. Mem., Select Cttee for Business, Innovation and Skills, 2010–15, for Regulatory Reform, 2012–15. *Recreation:* gardening. *Address:* House of Commons, SW1A 0AA. *T:* (020) 7219 7602. *E:* rebecca.harris.mp@parliament.uk.

**HART, Simon Anthony;** MP (C) Carmarthen West and Pembrokeshire South, since 2010; *b* 15 Aug. 1963; *s* of Anthony Hart and Judith Hart (*née* Christie); *m* 1998, Abigail Kate Holland; one *s* one *d. Educ:* Radley Coll., Oxon; RAC Cirencester (Rural Estate Mgt). MRICS (ARICS 1985–99). Llewellyn Humphreys, Chartered Surveyors, 1988–98; Balfour, Burd & Benson, Chartered Surveyors, 1998–99; Regl Public Relns Officer, 1999, Dir of Campaign for Hunting, 1999–2003, Chief Exec., 2003–10, Countryside Alliance. Member: Pol and Constitutional Select Cttee, 2010–12; Welsh Affairs Select Cttee, 2012–15; Envmt, Food and Rural Affairs Select Cttee, 2015–. Master and Huntsman, S Pembrokeshire Hunt, 1988–99. Trustee, Sundorne Estate, 1995–. *Recreations:* all aspects of country sports, cricket. *Address:* House of Commons, SW1A 0AA. *Clubs:* Farmers; Cresselly Cricket.

**HASELHURST, Rt Hon. Sir Alan (Gordon Barraclough),** Kt 1995; PC 1999; MP (C) Saffron Walden, since July 1977; *b* 23 June 1937; *s* of late John Haselhurst and Alyse (*née* Barraclough); *m* 1977, Angela (*née* Bailey); two *s* one *d. Educ:* King Edward VI Sch., Birmingham; Cheltenham Coll.; Oriel Coll., Oxford. Pres., Oxford Univ. Conservative Assoc., 1958; Sec., Treas. and Librarian, Oxford Union Soc., 1959–60; Nat. Chm., Young Conservatives, 1966–68. MP (C) Middleton and Prestwich, 1970–Feb. 1974. PPS to Sec. of State for Educn, 1979–82. Chairman: of Ways and Means and a Dep. Speaker, H of C, 1997–2010; Admin Cttee, 2010–15; Member: Financial Services Cttee, 2010–; Audit Cttee, 2010–; Liaison Cttee, 2010–15; Ecclesiastical Cttee, 2010–15. Mem., H of C Select Cttee on European Legislation, 1982–97, on Catering, 1991–97, on Transport, 1992–97; Chm., All Party Parly Cricket Gp, 2010– (Hon. Sec. 1993–2010). Chm., Rights of Way Review Cttee, 1983–93. Commonwealth Parliamentary Association: Chm., UK Br., 2010–; Chm., Exec. Cttee, 2011–14. Chairman: Manchester Youth and Community Service, 1974–77; Commonwealth Youth Exchange Council, 1978–81; Chm. Trustees, Community Development (formerly Projects) Foundn, 1986–97. *Publications:* Occasionally Cricket, 1999; Eventually Cricket, 2001; Incidentally Cricket, 2003; Accidentally Cricket, 2009; Unusually Cricket, 2010; Fatally Cricket, 2013. *Recreations:*

gardening, theatre, music, watching cricket. *Address:* House of Commons, SW1A 0AA. *E:* alan.haselhurst.mp@parliament.uk. *Clubs:* MCC; Essex CC (Mem., Exec. Cttee, 1996–2008); Yorkshire CC; Middlesex CC.

**HAYES, Helen Elizabeth;** MP (Lab) Dulwich and West Norwood, since 2015; *b* 8 Aug. 1974. *Educ:* Balliol Coll., Oxford (BA Hons PPE); London Sch. of Econs and Pol Sci. (MSc Social Policy and Admin). MRTPI. Jt Man. Dir, Town Centres Ltd, subseq. Urban Practitioners, 1998–2012; Partner, Allies and Morrison, 2011–15. Mem. (Lab) Southwark LBC, 2010–15. *Address:* House of Commons, SW1A 0AA.

**HAYES, Rt Hon. John Henry;** PC 2013; MP (C) South Holland and The Deepings, since 1997; Senior Parliamentary Adviser to the Prime Minister, since 2013; Minister of State, Home Office, since 2015; *b* 23 June 1958; *s* of late Henry John Hayes and Lily Hayes; *m* 1997, Susan Jane Hopewell; two *s.* *Educ:* Colfe's Grammar Sch., London; Univ. of Nottingham (BA Hons, PGCE). Joined The Data Base Ltd, 1983, Dir, 1986–99. Mem., Nottinghamshire CC, 1985–98. Contested (C) Derbyshire NE, 1987, 1992. Shadow Schools Minister, 2000–01; Opposition Pairing Whip, 2001–02; Shadow Agriculture and Fisheries Minister, 2002–03; Shadow Housing and Planning Minister, 2003–05; Shadow Transport Minister, 2005; Shadow Minister: for Vocational Educn and Skills, 2005–07; for Lifelong Learning, Further and Higher Educn, 2007–10; Minister of State: for Further Educn Skills and Lifelong Learning, BIS and DFE, 2010–12; for Energy, DECC, 2012–13; (Minister without Portfolio), Cabinet Office, 2013–14; DfT, 2014–15. Member, Select Committee: Agriculture, 1997–99; Educn and Employment, 1998–99; Administration, 2001–02; Mem., Cttee of Selection, 2001–02. A Vice-Chm., Cons. Party, 1999–2000. Adjunct Associate Prof., Richmond, The American Internat. Univ. in London, 2002–10. *Recreations:* the arts (particularly English painting, poetry and prose), good food and wine, many sports (including darts and boxing), gardening, making jam, antiques, architecture, aesthetics. *Address:* House of Commons, SW1A 0AA. *T:* (020) 7219 1389. *Clubs:* Carlton; Spalding, Spalding Gentlemen's Soc. (Lincs).

**HAYMAN, Susan Mary;** MP (Lab) Workington, since 2015; *b* Upper Bucklebury, 28 July 1962; *d* of John Bentley and Rita Bentley; *m* 1997, Ross Hayman; one *s* one *d,* and one step *s* one step *d.* *Educ:* St Bartholomew's Comp. Sch., Newbury; Anglia Ruskin Univ. (BA Hons Eng. Lit.). Bookseller, Heffers Bookshop, 1984–86; proof-reader and copy editor, Goodfellow and Egan, 1986–88; self-employed proof-reader and copy editor, 1988–97; Asst to Tess Kingham, MP, 1997–2001, to Michael Foster, MP, 2001–05; Communications Consultant, Copper Consultancy, 2005–14; self-

employed communications consultant, 2014–15. Mem. (Lab) Cumbria CC, 2013–15. *Recreations:* music, theatre, gardening, walking the dog, fell walking. *Address:* House of Commons, SW1A 0AA. *T:* (020) 7219 4554. *E:* sue.hayman.mp@parliament.uk.

**HEALD, Sir Oliver,** Kt 2014; QC 2012; MP (C) North East Hertfordshire, since 1997 (North Hertfordshire, 1992–97); *b* 15 Dec. 1954; *s* of late John Anthony Heald and Joyce Heald; *m* 1979, Christine Whittle; one *s* two *d.* *Educ:* Reading Sch.; Pembroke Coll., Cambridge. Called to the Bar, Middle Temple, 1977, Bencher, 2013; practice in E Anglia and London, 1977–95 and 1997–2001. Contested (C) Southwark and Bermondsey, 1987. PPS to Minister of Agric., Fisheries and Food, 1994–95; Parly Under-Sec. of State, DSS, 1995–97; an Opposition Whip, 1997–2000; Opposition spokesman: on home affairs, 2000–01; on health, 2001–02; on work and pensions, 2002–03; Shadow Leader, H of C, 2003–05; Shadow Sec. of State for Constitutional Affairs, and Shadow Chancellor of Duchy of Lancaster, 2005–07; Solicitor General, 2012–14. Member: Employment Select Cttee, 1992–94; Admin Select Cttee, 1998–2000; Select Cttee on Modernisation of H of C, 2003–05; Select Cttee on Work and Pensions, 2007–12; Cttee on Standards in Public Life, 2008–12; Cttee of Selection, 2009–10; Cttee on Standards and Privileges, 2010–12; Ecclesiastical Cttee, 2010–12; Governance Select Cttee, 2014–15. Vice-Chm., Rules Cttee, Council of Europe, 2012. Chm. of Exec., Soc. of Conservative Lawyers, 2007–12. *Recreations:* sports, family. *Address:* House of Commons, SW1A 0AA.

**HEALEY, Rt Hon. John;** PC 2008; MP (Lab) Wentworth and Dearne, since 2010 (Wentworth, 1997–2010); *b* 13 Feb. 1960; *s* of Aidan Healey OBE and Jean Healey; *m* 1993, Jackie Bate; one *s.* *Educ:* Christ's Coll., Cambridge (schol., BA 1982). Charity campaigner, 1984–90; Campaigns Manager, Issue Communications, 1990–92; Head of Communications, MSF, 1992–94; Campaigns Dir, TUC, 1994–97. PPS to Chancellor of the Exchequer, 1999–2001; Parly Under-Sec. of State, DFES, 2001–02; Econ. Sec., 2002–05; Financial Sec., 2005–07, HM Treasury; Minister of State (Minister for Local Govt), 2007–09, (Minister for Housing), 2009–10, DCLG; Shadow Minister for Housing, 2010; Shadow Sec. of State for Health, 2010–11; Shadow Minister for Housing and Planning, 2015–. Contested (Lab) Ryedale, 1992. *Address:* House of Commons, SW1A 0AA. *E:* john.healey.mp@parliament.uk.

**HEAPPEY, James Stephen;** MP (C) Wells, since 2015; *b* Nuneaton, 30 Jan. 1981; *s* of Stephen and Anita Heappey; *m* 2009, Kate; one *s* one *d.* *Educ:* Queen Elizabeth's Hosp., Bristol; Univ. of Birmingham (BA Hons Pol Sci.); RMA, Sandhurst. Platoon Comdr, 1st Bn, Royal Glos, Berks and Wilts Regt, 2004–06; ADC to GOC, NI, 2006–07; The Rifles: Regtl Signals Officer,

4th Bn, 2007–09; Adjt, 2nd Bn, 2009–11; Exec. Officer, Army Gen. Staff, 2011–12. Parly Asst to Rt Hon. Dr Liam Fox, MP, 2012–13; consultant project manager, 2013–14. *Recreations:* cooking, cricket, golf, Rugby, tennis, family. *Address:* House of Commons, SW1A 0AA. *T:* (020) 7219 4289; 5 Cathedral View Offices, Wookey Hole Road, Wells, Som BA5 2BT. *T:* (01749) 343255. *E:* james.heappey.mp@parliament.uk.

**HEATON-HARRIS, Christopher;** MP (C) Daventry, since 2010; *b* 28 Nov. 1967; *s* of David Barry Heaton-Harris and Ann Geraldine Heaton-Harris; *m* 1990, Jayne Yvonne Carlow; two *d*. *Educ:* Tiffin Grammar Sch. for Boys, Kingston upon Thames. Dir, What 4 Ltd, 1995–2003. Contested (C) Leicester South, 1997, July 2004. MEP (C) East Midlands, 1999–2009. Pres., EU Sports Platform, 2009–10. *Recreation:* grade 5 soccer referee. *Address:* (office) 78 St George's Avenue, Northampton NN2 6JF; House of Commons, SW1A 0AA.

**HEATON-JONES, Peter;** MP (C) North Devon, since 2015; *b* Kingston upon Thames, 2 Aug. 1963; *s* of Richard Howard Heaton-Jones and Eileen Heaton-Jones (*née* Lewis). *Educ:* Esher Grammar Sch.; Southlands Coll. (BA Hons Sociol. and Geog. Univ. of London); London Coll. of Printing (CNAA Dip. Journalism). Sen. Broadcast Journalist, BBC, 1986–97; Hd, Mktg, ABC, Australia, 1998–2000; freelance broadcaster and media consultant, 2000–06; Press Sec., NSW Parlt, 2007–08; Agent, Cons. Party, 2008–10; Sen. Parly Asst, 2010–15. Mem. (C) Swindon BC, 2010–14. *Address:* House of Commons, SW1A 0AA. *E:* peter. heatonjones.mp@parliament.uk.

**HENDERSON, Gordon;** MP (C) Sittingbourne and Sheppey, since 2010; *b* Gillingham, Kent, 27 Jan. 1948; *s* of William John Butler Henderson and Pauline Henderson (*née* Pullen); *m* 1993, Louise Claire Crowder; one *s* two *d*. *Educ:* Fort Luton Secondary Sch. for Boys. Woolworths, 1964–79; restaurateur, 1979–83; Agent, Cons. Party, 1983–85; GEC Marconi, 1985–93; Unwins Wine Gp, 1993–2003; Beams UK Ltd, 2003–08; mgt consultant, 2008–10. Mem. (C) Kent CC, 1989–93. Contested (C): Luton S, 2001; Sittingbourne and Sheppey, 2005. *Recreations:* reading, writing. *Address:* House of Commons, SW1A 0AA. *T:* (020) 7219 7144; (office) Top Floor, Unit 10, Periwinkle Court, Church Street, Milton Regis, Sittingbourne, Kent ME10 2JZ. *E:* gordon.henderson.mp@ parliament.uk.

**HENDRICK, Mark Phillip,** CEng; MP (Lab and Co-op) Preston, since Nov. 2000; *b* 2 Nov. 1958; *s* of Brian Francis Hendrick and Jennifer (*née* Chapman); *m* 2008, Yannan Yu. *Educ:* Liverpool Poly. (BSc Hons Electrical and Electronic Engrg); Univ. of Manchester (MSc Computer Sci.; Cert Ed). CEng 1987. Trainee Technician, Signal and Telecommunications, BR, 1975–78; Student

Engr, 1979–81; RSRE Malvern, MoD, 1979; Special Systems Unit, STC plc, 1980; AEG Telefunken, Seligenstadt, Germany, 1981; Design Engr, Daresbury Lab., SERC, 1982–84 and 1985–88; Lectr, Stockport Coll., 1989–94. MEP (Lab and Co-op) Lancashire Central, 1994–99; contested (Lab) NW Reg., 1999. PPS to Sec. of State, DEFRA, 2003–06, FCO, 2006–07, to Minister of Justice, 2007–08. Member: Internat. Develt Select Cttee, 2008–10; Foreign Affairs Select Cttee, 2012–; Chm., All Party Parly China Gp, 2010–12. *Recreations:* football supporter (Manchester City and Preston North End), travel, chess, German and French. *Address:* c/o House of Commons, SW1A 0AA; (constituency office) PTMC, Marsh Lane, Preston PR1 8UQ. *T:* (01772) 883575. *Clubs:* Parkfield Labour; Lonsdale (Preston).

**HENDRY, Andrew Egan Henderson, (Drew);** MP (SNP) Inverness, Nairn, Badenoch and Strathspey, since 2015; *b* 31 May 1964; *m* Jackie; four c. Shop worker, latterly Dir, multinat. appliance manufr; Founder and Chm., Teclan Ltd, 1999–. Mem. (SNP), Highland Council, 2007–15 (Leader, SNP Gp, 2011–15; Leader of Council, 2012–15). Vice Pres., Conf. of Maritime Peripheral Regions, 2012–. *Address:* House of Commons, SW1A 0AA.

**HEPBURN, Stephen;** MP (Lab) Jarrow, since 1997; *b* 6 Dec. 1959; *s* of Peter and Margaret Hepburn. *Educ:* Springfield Comprehensive Sch., Jarrow; Newcastle Univ. Former Res. Asst to Donald Dixon, MP. Mem. (Lab) S Tyneside MBC, 1985–97 (Chair: Finance Cttee, 1989–90; Tyne & Wear Pensions, 1989–97; Dep. Leader, 1990–97). Member: Defence Select Cttee, 2000–01; NI Affairs Select Cttee, 2004–; Scottish Affairs Select Cttee, 2015–; Vice Chm., All Party Parly Shipbuilding and Ship Repair Gp; Secretary: All Party Football Gp; All Party Football Team. President: Bilton Hall Boxing Club; Jarrovians RFC; Jarrow FC. *Recreation:* sports. *Address:* House of Commons, SW1A 0AA. *T:* (constituency office) (0191) 420 0648. *Clubs:* Neon (Jarrow); Iona (Hebburn).

**HERBERT, Rt Hon. Nicholas Le Quesne, (Rt Hon. Nick);** PC 2010; MP (C) Arundel and South Downs, since 2005; *b* 7 April 1963; civil partnership 2008, Jason Eades. *Educ:* Haileybury; Magdalene Coll., Cambridge (BA Hons 1985). British Field Sports Soc., 1990–96, latterly Dir of Political Affairs; Chief Exec., Business for Sterling, 1998–2000; Dir, Reform, 2002–05. Contested (C) Berwick-upon-Tweed, 1997. Shadow Sec. of State for Justice, 2007–09, for Envmt, Food and Rural Affairs, 2009–10; Minister of State, MoJ and Home Office, 2010–12. *Address:* House of Commons, SW1A 0AA.

**HERMON, Sylvia, (Lady Hermon);** MP North Down, since 2001 (UU, 2001–10; Ind, since 2010); *b* 11 Aug. 1955; *d* of Robert and Mary

Paisley; *m* 1988, Sir John (Charles) Hermon, OBE, QPM (*d* 2008); two *s*. *Educ:* UCW, Aberystwyth (LLB 1st Cl. Hons); Coll. of Law, Chester. Lectr in Law, QUB, 1978–88; PR Consultant, 1993–96. *Publications:* A Guide to EEC Law in Northern Ireland, 1986. *Recreations:* swimming, ornithology. *Address:* House of Commons, SW1A 0AA.

**HILLIER, Meg;** MP (Lab and Co-op) Hackney South and Shoreditch, since 2005; *b* 14 Feb. 1969; *m* 1997; one *s* two *d*. *Educ:* St Hilda's Coll., Oxford (BA Hons PPE); City Univ. (Dip. Newspaper Journalism). Reporter, S Yorks Times, 1991; Petty Officer, P & O European Ferries, 1992; PR Officer, Newlon Housing Gp, 1993; reporter, 1994–95, features editor, 1995–98, Housing Today; freelance, 1998–2000. Mem. (Lab) Islington BC, 1994–2002 (Chair, Neighbourhood Services Cttee, 1995–97); Mayor, Islington, 1998–99. Mem. (Lab) NE, London Assembly, GLA, 2000–04. Mem. Bd, Transport for London, 2004–05. PPS to Sec. of State for Communities and Local Govt, 2006–07; Parly Under-Sec. of State, Home Office, 2007–10; Shadow Sec. of State for Energy and Climate Change, 2010–11. Mem., Public Accounts Select Cttee, 2011– (Chm., 2015–). Trustee, War Memls Trust, 2001–. *Recreations:* local history, cycling. *Address:* House of Commons, SW1A 0AA.

**HINDS, Damian Patrick George;** MP (C) East Hampshire, since 2010; Exchequer Secretary, HM Treasury, since 2015; *b* London, 27 Nov. 1969; *s* of Francis Hinds and Bridget Hinds; *m* 2007, Jacqui Morel; one *s* two *d*. *Educ:* St Ambrose Grammar Sch., Altrincham; Trinity Coll., Oxford (BA PPE 1992). Res. analyst, Mercer Mgt Consulting, 1992–95; Holiday Inn: Pricing Manager, 1995–96, Mktg Manager, 1996–99, Holiday Inn Europe; Vice Pres., e-Commerce, 2000–01, Vice Pres., Commercial, 2001–03, Holiday Inn and Intercontinental, EMEA; Strategy Dir, Greene King plc, 2005–07; freelance advr to hotel trade, 2003–05 and 2007–10. An Asst Govt Whip, 2014–15. *Recreation:* music. *Address:* House of Commons, SW1A 0AA. *T:* (020) 7219 7057. *E:* damian. hinds.mp@parliament.uk.

**HOARE, Simon James;** MP (C) North Dorset, since 2015; *b* Cardiff, 28 June 1969; *s* of Colin and Maria Hoare; *m* 2000, Kate, *y d* of William Lund, FRCS; three *d*. *Educ:* Bishop Hannon High Sch., Cardiff; Greyfriars, Oxford (BA Hons Modern Hist.). Business and public affairs consultant to land owners, farmers, public sector and property develt cos; family business in oil sector; Man. Dir, Community Connect Ltd, 2002–15. Member (C): W Oxfordshire DC, 2004–15 (Cabinet Mem., Resources, 2007–15); Oxfordshire CC, 2013–15. *Recreations:* gardening, collecting, horse racing, family. *Address:* House of Commons, SW1A 0AA. *T:* (020) 7219 5697. *E:* simon.

hoare.mp@parliament.uk. *Clubs:* Garrick, Royal Over-Seas League; Blandford Constitutional; Newport Boat (Pembrokeshire).

**HODGE, Rt Hon. Dame Margaret (Eve),** DBE 2015 (MBE 1978); PC 2003; MP (Lab) Barking, since June 1994; *b* 8 Sept. 1944; *d* of late Hans and Lisbeth Oppenheimer; *m* 1st, 1968, Andrew Watson (marr. diss. 1978); one *s* one *d*; 2nd, 1978, Henry Egar Garfield Hodge (later Hon. Sir Henry Hodge, OBE) (*d* 2009); two *d*. *Educ:* Bromley High Sch.; Oxford High Sch.; LSE (BSc Econ 1966). Teaching and internat. market research, 1966–73. London Borough of Islington: Councillor, 1973–94; Chair of Housing, 1975–79; Dep. Leader, 1981; Leader, 1982–92. Chair: Assoc. of London Authorities, 1984–92; London Res. Centre, 1985–92; Vice-Chair, AMA, 1991–92. Member: HO Adv. Cttee on Race Relations, 1988–92; Local Govt Commn, 1993–94; Board, Central and Inner London North TEC, 1990–92; Labour Party Local Govt Cttee, 1983–92. Parly Under-Sec. of State, DfEE, 1998–2001; Minister of State, DFES, 2001–05; Minister of State: (Minister for Employment and Welfare Reform (formerly for Work), DWP, 2005–06; DTI, 2006–07; DCMS, 2007–08 and 2009–10. Chair: Educn Select Cttee, H of C, 1997–98; Public Accounts Select Cttee, 2010–15; London Gp of Labour MPs, 1996–98; former mem., govt and local govt bodies. Sen. Consultant, Price Waterhouse, 1992–94. Director: London First, 1992; (non-exec.) UCH and Middlesex Hosp., 1992–94. Chair: Circle 33 Housing Trust, 1993–96; Fabian Soc., 1997–98. Gov., LSE, 1990–99; Mem. Council, Univ. of London, 1994–98. Hon. Fellow, Polytechnic of North London. Hon. DCL City, 1993; DUniv South Wales, 2014. Freeman, City of London, 2013. *Publications:* Quality, Equality and Democracy, 1991; Beyond the Town Hall, 1994; Elected Mayors and Democracy, 1997; contribs to numerous jls and newspapers. *Recreations:* family, opera, piano, travel, cooking. *Address:* c/o House of Commons, SW1A 0AA.

**HODGSON, Sharon;** MP (Lab) Washington and Sunderland West, since 2010 (Gateshead East and Washington West, 2005–10); *b* 1 April 1966; *d* of Joan Cohen (*née* Wilson); *m* 1990, Alan Hodgson; one *s* one *d*. *Educ:* Heathfield Sen. High Sch., Gateshead; Newcastle Coll. Payroll/account clerk, Tyneside Safety Glass, 1982–88; Northern Rock Bldg Soc., Gosforth, 1988–92; Payroll administrator, Burgess Microswitch, 1992–94; Administrator, Total Learning Challenge, 1998–99; Lab. Party Orgnr, 1999–2002; Labour Link Co-ordinator, UNISON, 2002–05. PPS to Minister of State, Home Office, 2006–07; to Minister of State, MoD, 2007–08; to Minister of State, DoH, 2008–09; an Asst Govt Whip, 2009–10; Opposition Whip, 2010; Shadow Minister: for Children and Families, 2010–13; for Women and Equalities, 2013–15. Mem., Children, Schs and Families Select Cttee, 2007–09. *Address:* (office) Units 1–1a, Vermont

House, Concord, Washington, Tyne and Wear NE37 2SQ; House of Commons, SW1A 0AA. *W:* www.sharonhodgson.org.

**HOEY, Catharine Letitia;** MP (Lab) Vauxhall, since June 1989; *b* 21 June 1946; *d* of Thomas Henry and Letitia Jane Hoey. *Educ:* Lylehill Primary Sch.; Belfast Royal Acad.; Ulster Coll. of Physical Educn (Dip. in PE); City of London Coll. (BSc Econs). Lectr, Southwark Coll., 1972–76; Sen. Lectr, Kingsway Coll., 1976–85; Educnl Advr, London Football Clubs, 1985–89. PPS to Minister of State (Minister for Welfare Reform), DSS, 1997–98; Parliamentary Under-Secretary of State: Home Office, 1998–99; DCMS (Minister for Sport), 1999–2001. Mayor of London's Comr for Sport, 2009–. Chairman: Countryside Alliance, 2005–14; London Sport, 2014–. Hon. Pres., Clay Pigeon Shooting Assoc.; Hon. Vice Pres., British Wheelchair Basketball. *Address:* House of Commons, SW1A 0AA. *T:* (020) 7219 3000. *Club:* Surrey CC (Hon. Vice Pres.).

**HOLLERN, Catherine Molloy;** MP (Lab) Blackburn, since 2015; *b* Dumbarton, 12 April 1955; two *d*; partner, John. Work study manager, Newman's Footwear; Contracts Manager, Blackburn Coll. Mem. (Lab), Blackburn with Darwen Council, until 2015 (Leader Lab Gp, 2004–15; Leader of Council, 2004–07 and 2010–15). *Address:* House of Commons, SW1A 0AA.

**HOLLINGBERY, George;** MP (C) Meon Valley, since 2010; a Lord Commissioner of HM Treasury (Government Whip), since 2015; *b* 12 Oct. 1963; *m* 1991, Janette Marie White; one *s* two *d*. *Educ:* Radley Coll.; Lady Margaret Hall, Oxford (BA Human Scis 1985); Wharton Sch., Univ. of Pennsylvania (MBA 1991). Stockbroker, Robert Fleming Securities, 1985–89; non-exec. Dir and shareholder, Lister Bestcare Ltd, 1991–95; Dir and Founder, Pet Depot Ltd, 1994–99; Chm. and Founder, Companion Care Vet. Gp, 1998–2001; property investment business, 2005–. Mem. (C) Winchester CC, 1999–2010. Contested (C) Winchester, 2005. PPS to Secretary of State for Home Dept, 2012–15. Mem., Communities and Local Govt Select Cttee, 2010–15. Mem. Exec., 1922 Cttee, 2012–. *Address:* House of Commons, SW1A 0AA.

**HOLLINRAKE, Kevin Paul;** MP (C) Thirsk and Malton, since 2015; *b* Easingwold, 28 Sept. 1963; *m* Nikky; four *c*. *Educ:* Easingwold Sch.; Sheffield Poly. Prudential Property Services: Branch Manager, Haxby, then Burnley, Lancs, 1985–87; Area Manager, 1987–91; Jt Founder and Man. Dir, Hunters Property Gp, 1992–; Co-owner, Vizzihome, 2008–13; Chm., Shoptility.com, 2013–. *Address:* House of Commons, SW1A 0AA.

**HOLLOBONE, Philip Thomas;** MP (C) Kettering, since 2005; *b* 7 Nov. 1964. *Educ:* Dulwich Coll.; Lady Margaret Hall, Oxford (MA 1987). Industry res. analyst, 1987–2003. Served TA, 1984–93. Member (C): Bromley BC, 1990–94; Kettering BC, 2003–. Contested (C): Lewisham E, 1997; Kettering, 2001. *Address:* House of Commons, SW1A 0AA.

**HOLLOWAY, Adam James Harold;** MP (C) Gravesham, since 2005; *b* 1965; *s* of Rev. Roger Holloway, OBE and Anne (*née* Alsop). *Educ:* Cranleigh Sch.; Magdalene Coll., Cambridge (BA Social and Pol Sci. 1987); RMA Sandhurst; Imperial Coll. of Sci. and Technol. (MBA). Travelled with the Afghan Resistance, 1982; classroom asst, Pace Coll., Soweto, S Africa, 1985. Grenadier Guards, 1987–92 (Captain); service in Gulf War, 1991. Presenter, 1992–94: World in Action (undercover, living homeless in London for 3 months, as homeless psychiatric patient for 2 months, as Muslim refugee in Serb territory, Bosnia, living homeless in NYC for 2 weeks); Disguises (reports from UK and Balkans); Sen. Reporter, ITN, 1994–97: Bosnia reporter, Sarajevo, 1994; News at Ten Special Reports; Reporter, Tonight with Trevor MacDonald (undercover as asylum seeker), 2001; Iraq War (Northern front) reports for ITN and Sky News, 2003. PPS to Minister of State, FCO, 2011–12. Member: Defence Select Cttee, 2006–10 and 2012–14; Public Admin Select Cttee, 2014–15; Foreign Affairs Select Cttee, 2015–. Dep. Chm., Cons. Middle East Council, 2010–. Chm., Council for Arab-British Understanding, 2009–14. Trustee: Christian Aid, 1997–2001; MapAction, 2004–10. *Publications:* In Blood Stepp'd in Too Far?: towards a realistic policy for Afghanistan, 2009. *Recreation:* being with my family and godchildren. *Address:* House of Commons, SW1A 0AA. *T:* (020) 7219 3000; c/o 440 Strand, WC2R 0QS. *E:* hollowaya@parliament.uk, ajhholloway@gmail.com. *Clubs:* Pratt's; Gravesend Conservative, Northfleet Conservative.

**HOPKINS, Kelvin Peter;** MP (Lab) Luton North, since 1997; *b* 22 Aug. 1941; *s* of late Prof. Harold Horace Hopkins, FRS and Joan Avery Frost; *m* 1965, Patricia Mabel Langley; one *s* one *d*. *Educ:* Nottingham Univ. (BA Hons Politics, Economics, Maths with Stats). Economic Dept, TUC, 1969–70 and 1973–77; Lectr, St Albans Coll. of Further Educn, 1971–73; Policy and Res. Officer, NALGO, then UNISON, 1977–94. Member: Public Administration Select Cttee, 2002–10 and 2011–; Transport Select Cttee, 2010–11; Eur. Scrutiny Cttee, 2007–; Chm., All Party Parly Gp on Alcohol Misuse, 1998–2001, for Social Sci. and Policy, 2010–; Co-Chm., All Party Parly Gp for Further Educn and Lifelong Learning, 2005–; Secretary: All Party Parly Gp for Jazz Appreciation, 1997–2001; All Party Parly Gp on Conflict Issues, 2007–10. Founder Mem., Old Testament Prophets, 1997–. Columnist, Socialist Campaign Gp News, 1998–2008. Gov., Luton Sixth Form Coll., 1993–. Hon. Fellow: Univ. of Luton, 1993; Univ. of Bedfordshire, 2010. *Publications:* NALGO papers. *Recreations:* music, wine, collecting antique glassware. *Address:* House of Commons, Westminster, SW1A 0AA. *T:* (020) 7219 6670; (home) (01582) 722913; 3 Union Street, Luton LU1 3AN. *T:* (01582) 488208.

**HOPKINS, Kristan Frederick;** MP (C) Keighley, since 2010; Vice Chamberlain of HM Household (Government Whip), since 2015; *b* 8 June 1963; one *d. Educ:* Leeds Univ. (BA). Served Army, Duke of Wellington's Regt. Lectr (pt-time) in media theory, communications and digital media. Chairman: Bradford Vision; Yorks and Humber Regl Housing Bd. Mem. (C) Bradford MDC, 1998–2010 (Leader, 2006–10). Parly Under-Sec. of State, DCLG, 2013–15. Contested (C): Leeds W, 2001; Halifax, 2005. *Address:* House of Commons, SW1A 0AA.

**HOSIE, Stewart;** MP (SNP) Dundee East, since 2005; *b* 3 Jan. 1963; *m* 1997, Shona Robison; one *d. Educ:* Carnoustie High Sch.; Dundee Coll. of Technol. Gp Inf. Systems Manager, MIH, 1988–93; systems analyst, 1993–96; Year 2000/EMU Project Manager, Stakis/Hilton, 1996–2000. Nat. Sec., 1999–2003, Dep. Leader, 2014–, SNP. Contested (SNP): Kirkcaldy, 1992, 1997; Kirkcaldy, Scottish Parlt, 1999. *Address:* (office) 8 Old Glamis Road, Dundee DD3 8HP; House of Commons, SW1A 0AA.

**HOWARTH, Rt Hon. George (Edward);** PC 2005; MP (Lab) Knowsley, since 2010 (Knowsley North, Nov. 1986–1997; Knowsley North and Sefton East, 1997–2010); *b* 29 June 1949; *m* 1977, Julie Rodgers; two *s* (one *d* decd). *Educ:* Liverpool Polytechnic. Formerly: engineer; teacher; Chief Exec., Wales TUC's Co-operative Centre, 1984–86. Former Mem., Huyton UDC; Mem., Knowsley BC, 1975–86 (Dep. Leader, 1982). Parliamentary Under-Secretary of State: Home Office, 1997–99; NI Office, 1999–2001. Mem., Intelligence and Security Cttee, 2015–. *Address:* House of Commons, SW1A 0AA.

**HOWARTH, Sir (James) Gerald (Douglas),** Kt 2012; MP (C) Aldershot, since 1997; *b* 12 Sept. 1947; *s* of late James Howarth and Mary Howarth, Hurley, Berks; *m* 1973, Elizabeth Jane, *d* of late Michael and Muriel Squibb, Crowborough, Sussex; two *s* one *d. Educ:* Haileybury and ISC Jun. Sch.; Bloxham Sch.; Southampton Univ. (BA Hons). Commnd RAFVR, 1968. Gen. Sec., Soc. for Individual Freedom, 1969–71; entered internat. banking, 1971; Bank of America Internat., 1971–77; European Arab Bank, 1977–81 (Manager, 1979–81); Syndication Manager, Standard Chartered Bank, 1981–83; Dir, Richard Unwin Internat., 1983–87; Jt Man. Dir, Taskforce Communications, 1993–96. Dir, Freedom Under Law, 1973–77; estabd Dicey Trust, 1976. Mem., Hounslow BC, 1982–83. MP (C) Cannock and Burntwood, 1983–92. Parliamentary Private Secretary: to Parly Under-Sec. of State for Energy, 1987–90; to Minister for Housing and Planning, 1990–91; to Rt Hon. Margaret Thatcher, MP, 1991–92; Shadow

Defence Minister, 2002–10; Parly Under-Sec. of State, MoD, 2010–12. Member: Select Cttee on Sound Broadcasting, 1987–92; Home Affairs Select Cttee, 1997–2001; Defence Select Cttee, 2001–03. Chairman: Lords and Commons Family and Child Protection Gp, 1999–2005; All Party RAF Gp, 2005; Vice-Chairman: Parly Aerospace Gp, 1997; All-Party Photography Gp, 2004–; Jt Sec., Cons. Parly Aviation Cttee, 1983–87; Vice-Chm., Cons. Parly Envmt, Transport and the Regions Cttee, 1997–99; Jt Vice-Chm., Cons. Parly Home Affairs Cttee, 2000–02. Mem. Exec., 1922 Cttee, 1999–2002; Chm., 92 Gp, 2001–07, 2013–. Chm., Conservative Way Forward, 2013–. Pres., British Air Display Assoc. (formerly Air Display Assoc. Europe), 2002–; Mem. Council, Air League. Trustee: Vulcan to the Sky Trust, 2006–; British Forces Foundn, 2008–. Jt Patron, Aerobility (formerly British Disabled Flying Assoc.), 2009–. CRAeS 2004. Liveryman, Hon. Co. of Air Pilots (formerly GAPAN), 2011. Britannia Airways Parly Pilot of the Year, 1988. Contributor to No Turning Back Gp pubns. *Recreations:* flying (private pilot's licence, 1965), photography, walking up hills, normal family pursuits. *Address:* House of Commons, SW1A 0AA. *T:* (020) 7219 5650.

**HOWE,** 7th Earl *cr* 1821; **Frederick Richard Penn Curzon;** PC 2013; Baron Howe, 1788; Baron Curzon, 1794; Viscount Curzon, 1802; farmer; Parliamentary Under-Secretary of State, Ministry of Defence, since 2015; Deputy Leader, House of Lords, since 2015; Chairman, London and Provincial Antique Dealers' Association, 1999–2010, Honorary President, since 2010; *b* 29 Jan. 1951; *s* of Chambré George William Penn Curzon (*d* 1976) (*g s* of 3rd Earl) and Enid Jane Victoria Curzon (*née* Fergusson) (*d* 1997); *S* cousin, 1984; *m* 1983, Elizabeth Helen Stuart, DL; one *s* three *d. Educ:* Rugby School; Christ Church, Oxford (MA Hons Lit. Hum.; Chancellor's Prize for Latin Verse, 1973). AIB. Entered Barclays Bank Ltd, 1973; Manager, 1982; Sen. Manager, 1984–87. Director: Adam & Co., 1987–90; Provident Life Assoc. Ltd, 1988–91. A Lord in Waiting (Govt Whip), 1991–92; front bench spokesman, H of L, on employment and transport, 1991, on environment and defence, 1992; Parly Sec., MAFF, 1992–95; Parly Under-Sec. of State, MoD, 1995–97; opposition front bench spokesman on health, H of L, 1997–2010; Parly Under-Sec. of State, DoH, 2010–15; elected Mem., H of L, 1999. Governor: King William IV Naval Foundation, 1984–; Trident Trust, 1985–2008; Milton's Cottage, 1985–2012 (Chm., 2006–11); Member: Council, RNLI, 1997–2014 (Pres., Chilterns Br., 1985–); Council of Mgt, Restoration of Appearance and Function Trust, 2000–10 (Chm., 2008–10); President: S Bucks Assoc. for the Disabled, 1984–; Nat. Soc. for Epilepsy, 1986–2010 (Vice-Pres., 1984–86); Penn Country Br., CPRE, 1986–92; Abbeyfield Beaconsfield Soc., 1991–2013. Patron: Demand, 2000–10; Chiltern Soc., 2001–.

Hon. FRCP 2008. *Recreations:* spending time with family, music. *Heir: s* Viscount Curzon. *Address:* c/o House of Lords, SW1A 0PW.

**HOWELL, John Michael,** OBE 2000; DPhil; MP (C) Henley, since June 2008; *b* London, 27 July 1955; *s* of Alexander J. Howell and Gladys S. Howell; *m* 1987, Alison Parker; one *s* two *d. Educ:* Battersea Grammar Sch.; Univ. of Edinburgh (MA 1978); St John's Coll., Oxford (DPhil 1981). Ernst & Young, 1987–96; Business Presenter, BBC World Service TV, 1996–97; Director: Fifth World Prodns Ltd, 1996–2003; Media Presentation Consultants Ltd, 2005–08. Mem. (C), Oxfordshire CC, 2004–09 (Cabinet Mem. for Change Mgt, 2005–08). PPS to Leader, H of C, 2010–14, to Minister of State, DCLG, 2010–12. Member: Justice Select Cttee, 2014–; Executive, 1922 Cttee, 2014–. *Publications:* Neolithic Northern France, 1983; Understanding Eastern Europe: the context of change, 1994. *Recreations:* music, theatre. *Address:* House of Commons, SW1A 0AA. *T:* (020) 7219 4828, 7219 6676, *Fax:* (020) 7219 2606. *E:* howellJm@parliament.uk; PO Box 84, Watlington, Oxon OX49 5XD. *T:* (01491) 613072. *Club:* Leander (Henley).

**HOWLETT, Ben;** MP (C) Bath, since 2015; *b* Colchester, 21 Aug. 1986; *s* of Clive Howlett and Beverley Howlett; partner, Josh Jones. *Educ:* Manningtree High Sch.; Colchester Sixth Form Coll.; Durham Univ. (BA Hons Hist. and Politics 2007); Univ. of Cambridge (MA Econ. Hist. 2008). Recruitment Consultant, Venn Gp, 2008–10; Managing Consultant, Finegreen Associates, 2010–15. *Recreations:* running (Bath half), Bath Rugby fan, charity work (healthcare and mental health), cooking, socialising, school governor. *Address:* House of Commons, SW1A 0AA. *T:* (020) 7219 8755. *E:* ben.howlett.mp@parliament.uk.

**HOYLE, Rt Hon. Lindsay (Harvey);** PC 2013; MP (Lab) Chorley, since 1997; Chairman of Ways and Means and a Deputy Speaker, House of Commons, since 2010; *b* 10 June 1957; *s* of Baron Hoyle; *m* 1st, Lynda Anne Fowler (marr. diss. 1982); 2nd, Catherine Swindley; two *d. Educ:* Adlington County Sch.; Lord's Coll., Bolton. Owner of building co.; Man. Dir, textile printing co. Mem. (Lab) Chorley BC, 1980–98 (Dep. Leader, 1995–97; Chair, Economic Develt and Tourist Cttee); Mayor, 1997–98. Member: Trade and Industry Select Cttee, 1998–2010; H of C Catering Cttee, 1997–2005; European Scrutiny Cttee, 2005–10; Finance Select Cttee, 2010–; All Pty Rugby League Gp, 1997– (Vice Chm., 1997–); All Pty Cricket Gp, 1997– (Treas., 1998–); All Pty Parly Gp on Financial Educn for Young People; Unite Parly Gp; Vice Chm., All Pty Tourism Gp, 1999–; Chm., All Pty BVI Gp, 2007–10; Pres., All Pty Gp on Gibraltar, 2001–. Member: Royal Lancs Agricl Show Soc.; Unite the Union. Hon. Colonel: C (64) Med. Sqdn (Vols); 5 Gen. Support Med. Regt. *Recreations:*

Rugby League (former Chm., Chorley Lynx), cricket, football. *Address:* House of Commons, SW1A 0AA. *T:* (020) 7219 3000. *Clubs:* Adlington Cricket, Chorley Cricket.

**HUDDLESTON, Nigel Paul;** MP (C) Worcestershire Mid, since 2015; *b* Lincs, 13 Oct. 1970; *m* 1999, Melissa Peters; one *s* one *d. Educ:* Robert Pattinson Comprehensive Sch., N Hykeham; Christ Church, Oxford (BA Hons PPE 1992); Anderson Sch. of Mgt, Univ. of Calif, Los Angeles (MBA 1998). Sen. Manager, Arthur Andersen Business Consulting, 1993–2002; Dir, Strategy Practice, Deloitte Consulting, 2002–10; Industry Hd of Travel, Google, 2011–15. Mem. (C) St Albans DC, 2011–15. Contested (C) Luton S, 2010. *Address:* House of Commons, SW1A 0AA.

**HUNT, Rt Hon. Jeremy;** PC 2010; MP (C) South West Surrey, since 2005; Secretary of State for Health, since 2012; *b* 1 Nov. 1966; *s* of Adm. Sir Nicholas John Streynsham Hunt, GCB, LVO; *m* 2009, Lucia Guo; one *s* one *d. Educ:* Charterhouse; Magdalen Coll., Oxford (BA 1st Cl. Hons PPE 1988). Co-Founder and Man. Dir, Hotcourses, 1991–2005; Co-Founder, Hotcourses Foundn, 2004. Shadow Sec. of State for Culture, Media and Sport, 2007–10; Sec. of State for Culture, Olympics, Media and Sport, 2010–12. *Recreation:* Latin music and dancing. *Address:* 23 Red Lion Lane, Farnham, Surrey GU9 7QN. *T:* (01252) 712536, *Fax:* (01428) 607498. *E:* huntj@parliament.uk.

**HUNT, Hon. Tristram Julian William,** PhD; FRHistS; MP (Lab) Stoke-on-Trent Central, since 2010; Senior Lecturer in Modern British History, Queen Mary University of London, since 2010 (Lecturer, 2003–10); *b* 31 May 1974; *s* of Baron Hunt of Chesterton, CB, FRS; *m* 2004, Juliet Thornback; one *s* two *d. Educ:* University Coll. Sch.; Trinity Coll., Cambridge (BA 1995; PhD 2000); Univ. of Chicago (Exchange Fellow). FRHistS 2005. Sen. researcher, Labour Party election campaign, 1997; Special Advr to Parly Under-Sec. of State, DTI, 1998–2001; Res. Fellow, IPPR, 2001; Associate Fellow, Centre for Hist. and Econs, King's Coll., Cambridge, 2001–02. Vis. Prof., Arizona State Univ., 2004–05. Author and presenter, television: Civil War (series), 2002; Isaac Newton: Great Briton, 2002; British Middle Class, 2005; The Protestant Revolution (series), 2007. Trustee: Heritage Lottery Fund, 2005–10; Nat. Heritage Meml Fund, 2005–10; History of Parliament Trust, 2011–. Shadow Sec. of State for Educn, 2013–15. *Publications:* The English Civil War, 2002, 3rd edn 2006; Building Jerusalem: the rise and fall of the Victorian city, 2004, 2nd edn 2005; Friedrich Engels: the frock-coated communist, 2009 (Elizabeth Longford Histl Biog. Prize, 2010); Ten Cities that made an Empire, 2014; contribs to History Today, Jl Social Hist. *Recreations:* Victorian urban architecture, fresh-water swimming, ceramics, book-browsing. *Address:*

c/o Georgina Capel Associates Ltd, 29 Wardour Street, W1D 6PS. *T:* (020) 7734 2414, *Fax:* (020) 7734 8101; House of Commons, SW1A 0AA. *E:* tristram.hunt.mp@parliament.uk.

**HUQ, Dr Rupa Asha;** MP (Lab) Ealing Central and Acton, since 2015; *b* Ealing, 2 April 1972; *d* of late Muhammad Huq and of Roshan Huq. *Educ:* Montpelier Primary Sch.; Notting Hill and Ealing High Sch.; Newnham Coll., Cambridge (BA Hons Social and Pol Scis with Law 1993); Univ. of E London (PhD Cultural Studies 1999). Asst to Carole Tongue, MEP, Strasbourg, 1996; Lectr, Manchester Univ., 1998–2004 (Leverhulme Trust Fellow); Sen. Lectr in Sociol. and Criminol., Kingston Univ., 2004–15. Dep. Mayoress of Ealing, 2010–11. Contested (Lab): North West, EP, 2004; Chesham and Amersham, 2005. *Publications:* Beyond Subculture, 2006; On the Edge: the contested cultures of English suburbia, 2013; Making Sense of Suburbia Through Popular Culture, 2013; contrib. articles to Guardian, Tribune, THES. *Address:* House of Commons, SW1A 0AA.

**HURD, Nicholas Richard;** MP (C) Ruislip, Northwood and Pinner, since 2010 (Ruislip Northwood, 2005–10); *b* 13 May 1962; *s* of Baron Hurd of Westwell, CH, CBE, PC and Tatiana Elizabeth Michelle Hurd; *m* 1st, 1988, Kim Richards (marr. diss.); two *s* two *d*; 2nd, 2010, Lady Clare Kerr, *er d* of Marquess of Lothian, PC, QC (Scot.); one *s* one *d*. *Educ:* Eton Coll.; Exeter Coll., Oxford (BA Classics 1985). Investment Manager, Morgan Grenfell, 1985–90; Corporate Finance Exec., Crown Communications, 1990–92; Managing Director: Passport Magazine Directories, 1992–94; Robert Fleming Do Brasil, 1994–2000; Business Develt Dir, Band-X Ltd, 2000–04; COS to Tim Yeo, MP, 2004–05. Shadow Minister for Charities, Social Enterprise and Volunteering, 2008–10; Parly Sec., Cabinet Office, 2010–14. Trustee, Greenhouse Sports Charity, 2004–. *Recreations:* sport, music. *Address:* House of Commons, SW1A 0AA. *T:* and *Fax:* (020) 7219 1053. *E:* nick.hurd.mp@parliament.uk.

**HUSSAIN, Imran;** MP (Lab) Bradford East, since 2015; *b* 7 June 1978. *Educ:* Univ. of Huddersfield (LLB). Called to the Bar, Lincoln's Inn. Mem. (Lab), City of Bradford MDC, 2002– (Dep. Leader, 2010–15). *Address:* House of Commons, SW1A 0AA. *T:* (020) 7219 8636. *E:* imran.hussain.mp@parliament.uk.

**IRRANCA-DAVIES, (Ifor) Huw;** MP (Lab) Ogmore, since Feb. 2002; *b* 22 Jan. 1963; *s* of Gethin Davies and Anne Teresa Davies; *m* 1991, Joanna Teresa Irranca; three *s*. *Educ:* Crewe and Alsager Coll. (BA Hons Combined Studies); Swansea Inst. of Higher Educn (MSc Eur. Leisure Resource Mgt (Univ. of Wales Award)). Recreation Asst, then Duty Manager, Lliw Valley BC, 1986–89; Manager, CLM Ltd and Serco Ltd, 1989–92; Facilities Manager, Swansea Coll.,

1994–96; Sen. Lectr, Swansea Inst. of Higher Educn, 1996–2002. An Asst Govt Whip, 2006–07; Parly Under-Sec. of State, Wales Office, 2007–08, DEFRA, 2008–10; Shadow Minister for Energy, 2010–11, for Food and Farming, 2011–15. Chm., Envmtl Audit Select Cttee, 2015–. All-Party Parliamentary Groups: Chm., Recognition of Munitions Workers; Co-Chm., Patient and Public Involvement in Health and Social Care; Vice Chairman: Energy Intensive Industries; British Council; University. *Recreations:* family activities, hill-walking, cycling, reading biographies and historical fiction, Rugby. *Address:* House of Commons, SW1A 0AA. *T:* (020) 7219 2952.

**JACKSON, Stewart James;** MP (C) Peterborough, since 2005; *b* 31 Jan. 1965; *s* of Raymond Thomas Jackson and Sylvia Alice Theresa Jackson; *m* 1999, Sarah O'Grady; one *d*. *Educ:* Royal Holloway Coll., Univ. of London (BA Hons (Econs and Public Admin) 1988); Thames Valley Univ. (MA Human Resource Mgt). MCIPD 2001. Pres., Univ. of London, 1988–89. Retail Banker, Lloyds TSB, 1993–98; Business Services Manager, AZTEC (Trng and Enterprise Council for SW London), 1998–2000; Business Advr, Human Resources, Business Link for London, 2000–05. Mem. (C) Ealing BC, 1990–98. Contested (C) Brent S, 1997, Peterborough, 2001. *Recreations:* family, cinema, travel, biographies, local history. *Address:* House of Commons, SW1A 0AA. *T:* (020) 7219 8286. *E:* jacksonsj@parliament.uk. *Club:* Peterborough Conservative.

**JAMES, Margot;** MP (C) Stourbridge, since 2010; an Assistant Government Whip, since 2015; *b* Coventry, 1958; *d* of Maurice James; partner, Jay. *Educ:* Millfield Sch., Som; London Sch. of Econs and Pol Sci. (BSc Econs and Govt). Work in sales and mktg for Maurice James Industries; consulting firm; Co-founder, Shire Health, 1986–98; Hd, Eur. Healthcare, 1998, Regl Pres., Pharmaceutical Div., 2005, Ogilvy & Mather. Non-exec. Dir, Parkside NHS Trust, 1998–2003. Mem. (C) Kensington and Chelsea LBC, 2006–08. Contested (C) Holborn and St Pancras, 2005. Mem., Business, Innovation and Skills Select Cttee, 2010–12; PPS to Minister for Trade and Investment, BIS and FCO, 2012, to Leader of H of C, 2014–15. *Address:* House of Commons, SW1A 0AA.

**JARVIS, Daniel Owen Woolgar,** MBE 2011; MP (Lab) Barnsley Central, since March 2011; *b* Nottingham, 30 Nov. 1972; *m* 2001, Caroline (*d* 2010); one *s* one *d*; *m* 2013, Rachel Jarvis; one *d*. *Educ:* Aberystwyth Univ.; RMA Sandhurst. Served Parachute Regt; deployed to Kosovo, Sierra Leone, NI, Iraq and Afghanistan; ADC to Gen. Sir Mike Jackson; Adjutant, 3 Para; Staff Planner, Perm. Jt HQ Northwood and Army HQ, Salisbury; Co. Comdr, Special Forces Support Gp. Shadow Culture Minister, 2011–13,

Shadow Justice Minister, 2013. Mem., Business, Innovation and Skills Select Cttee, 2011–12. *Address:* House of Commons, SW1A 0AA.

**JAVID, Rt Hon. Sajid;** PC 2014; MP (C) Bromsgrove, since 2010; Secretary of State for Business, Innovation and Skills and President, Board of Trade, since 2015; *b* Rochdale, 5 Dec. 1969; *m* 1997, Laura; one *s* three *d*. *Educ:* Univ. of Exeter (BA Hons Econs and Politics 1991). Analyst and Associate, 1991–94, Vice Pres., 1994–2000, Chase Manhattan Bank, N. A.; Dir, 2000–04, Man. Dir, 2004–09, Deutsche Bank AG; Mem. Bd, Deutsche Bank Internat. Ltd, 2007–09. Economic Sec., 2012–13, Financial Sec., 2013–14, HM Treasury; Minister for Equalities, 2014; Sec. of State for Culture, Media and Sport, 2014–15. *Address:* House of Commons, SW1A 0AA. *T:* (020) 7219 7027. *E:* sajid.javid.mp@parliament.uk.

**JAYAWARDENA, Ranil Malcolm;** MP (C) North East Hampshire, since 2015; *b* London, 3 Sept. 1986; *s* of Nalin Mahinda Jayawardena and Indira Maureen Jayawardena; *m* 2011, Alison Lyn Roberts; one *d*. *Educ:* Robert May's Sch., Odiham; Alton Coll., Alton; London Sch. of Econs and Political Sci. (BSc Hons). Various roles, from commercial banking to gp exec. functions, Lloyds Banking Gp, 2008–15. Mem., Basingstoke and Deane BC, 2008–15 (Dep. Leader, 2012–15). Mem., Home Affairs Select Cttee, 2015–. *Recreations:* cricket, golf, tennis, shooting, walking, local history, film, theatre. *Address:* House of Commons, SW1A 0AA. *T:* (020) 7219 3637. *E:* ranil.jayawardena.mp@parliament.uk.

**JENKIN, Hon. Bernard Christison;** MP (C) Harwich and North Essex, since 2010 (Colchester North, 1992–97; North Essex, 1997–2010); *b* 9 April 1959; *s* of Lord Jenkin of Roding, PC; *m* 1988, Anne Caroline Strutt (Baroness Jenkin of Kennington); two *s*. *Educ:* Highgate Sch.; William Ellis Sch.; Corpus Christi Coll., Cambridge (BA Hons Eng. Lit., MA). Ford Motor Co., 1983–86; 3i, 1986–88; Hill Samuel Bank, 1988–89; Legal & General Ventures, 1989–92. Contested (C) Glasgow Central, 1987. PPS to Sec. of State for Scotland, 1995–97; Opposition spokesman on constitutional affairs, 1997–98, on transport, 1998–99; Opposition front bench spokesman on transport, and for London, 1999–2001; Shadow Defence Sec., 2001–03; Shadow Sec. of State for the Regions, 2003–04; Shadow Minister for Energy, 2005; Dep. Chm., Conservative Party (Candidates), 2005–06. Chm., Select Cttee on Public Admin, 2010–; Member: Select Cttee on Social Security, 1992–97; Select Cttee on Defence, 2006–10; Sec., Cons. Backbench Small Business Cttee, 1992–97; Jt Sec., Cons. Backbench Foreign Affairs Cttee, 1994–95; Mem. Exec., 1922 Cttee, 2010–. Vice Pres., Combat Stress, 2009–. Mem., St Paul's Cathedral Council, 2005–. Pres., Cambridge Union Soc., 1982. *Publications:* (jtly) Defence Acquisition for the Twenty-First Century, 2015. *Recreations:* family,

music (esp. opera), fishing, shooting, sailing, skiing, DIY, arguing the Conservative cause. *Address:* House of Commons, SW1A 0AA. *T:* (020) 7219 3000. *Clubs:* Pratt's; Colchester Conservative.

**JENKYNS, Andrea Marie;** MP (C) Morley and Outwood, since 2015; *b* Beverley, 16 June 1974; *d* of late Clifford Jenkyns. *Educ:* Marton Primary Sch., Holderness; Open Univ. (Dip. Econs); Univ. of Lincoln (BA Internat. Relns and Politics 2014). Soprano singer and songwriter; music tutor in secondary schs, Lincs CC; musical theatre dir, two children's performing arts academies. Mem. (C), Lincs CC, 2009–13. Trustee, MRSA Action UK. *Address:* House of Commons, SW1A 0AA.

**JENRICK, Robert;** MP (C) Newark, since June 2014; *b* Wolverhampton, 1982; *m* 2009, Michal Berkner; three *d*. *Educ:* Wolverhampton Grammar Sch.; St John's Coll., Cambridge (BA 1st Cl. Hist. 2003); Univ. of Pennsylvania (Thouron Fellow 2004); Coll. of Law (Grad. Dip. Law 2005); BPP Law Sch. (Legal Practice Course 2006). Trainee solicitor, Skadden Arps, Slate, Meagher & Flom LLP, 2006–08; admitted as solicitor, 2008; Solicitor, Sullivan & Cromwell LLP, 2008–10; Sen. Exec. and Internat. Man. Dir, Decorative Arts Div., Christie's, 2010–14. PPS to Parly Under-Sec. for Energy and Climate Change, 2014–15, to Employment Minister, 2015. Mem., Health Select Cttee, 2014–15. Contested (C) Newcastle-under-Lyme, 2010. *Address:* House of Commons, SW1A 0AA; Belvedere, 29a London Road, Newark-on-Trent NG24 1TN.

**JOHNSON, Rt Hon. Alan (Arthur);** PC 2003; MP (Lab) Kingston-upon-Hull West and Hessle, since 1997; *b* 17 May 1950; *s* of late Lillian May and Stephen Arthur Johnson; *m* 1st, 1968, Judith Elizabeth Cox (marr. diss.); one *s* one *d* (and one *d* decd); 2nd, 1991, Laura Jane Patient; one *s*. *Educ:* Sloane Grammar School, Chelsea. Postman, 1968; UCW Branch Official, 1976; UCW Exec. Council, 1981; UCW National Officer, 1987–93; Gen. Sec., UCW, 1993–95; Jt Gen. Sec., CWU, 1995–97. PPS to Financial Sec. to the Treasury, 1997–99, to Paymaster General, 1999; Parly Under-Sec. of State, 1999–2001, Minister of State, 2001–03, DTI; Minister of State, DFES, 2003–04; Secretary of State: for Work and Pensions, 2004–05; for Trade and Industry, 2005–06; for Educn and Skills, 2006–07; for Health, 2007–09; for Home Dept, 2009–10; Shadow Sec. of State for Home Dept, 2010; Shadow Chancellor of the Exchequer, 2010–11. Mem., Trade and Industry Select Cttee, 1997. Mem. Gen. Council, TUC, 1994–95; Exec. Mem., Postal, Telegraph and Telephone Internat., 1994–97; Mem., Labour Party NEC, 1995–97; Dir, Unity Trust Bank plc. Duke of Edinburgh Commonwealth Study Conf., 1992. Gov., Ruskin Coll., 1992–97. *Publications:* This Boy: a memoir of a childhood, 2013 (Orwell Prize, 2014; Ondaatje Prize, 2014); Please, Mister

Postman: a memoir, 2014. *Recreations:* music, tennis, reading, football, cookery, radio. *Address:* House of Commons, SW1A 0AA.

**JOHNSON, (Alexander) Boris (de Pfeffel);** Mayor of London (C), 2008–May 2016; MP (C) Uxbridge and South Ruislip, since 2015; *b* 19 June 1964; *s* of Stanley Patrick Johnson and Charlotte Maria Johnson (*née* Fawcett); *m* 1st, 1987, Allegra Mostyn-Owen (marr. diss. 1993); 2nd, 1993, Marina Wheeler; two *s* two *d*. *Educ:* Eton (King's Schol.); Balliol Coll., Oxford (Brackenbury Schol.; Pres., Oxford Union). LEK Partnership, one week, 1987; The Times, 1987–88; Daily Telegraph, 1988–99: EC Correspondent, 1989–94; Asst Ed. and Chief Pol Columnist, 1994–99; Ed., The Spectator, 1999–2005. MP (C) Henley, 2001–June 2008. Opposition frontbench spokesman on higher educn, 2005–07. Jt Vice-Chm., Cons. Party, 2003–04. Commentator of the Year, 1997, Columnist of the Year, 2005, What the Papers Say Awards, 1997; Editors' Editor of the Year, 2003; Columnist of the Year, British Press Awards, 2004; Politician of the Year, Spectator Parliamentarian of the Year Awards, 2008, 2012; Politician of the Year, Political Studies Assoc., 2008; Politician of the Year, GQ Men of the Year Awards, 2008, 2012. *Publications:* Friends, Voters, Countrymen, 2001; Lend Me Your Ears: the essential Boris Johnson, 2003; Seventy Two Virgins (novel), 2004; The Dream of Rome, 2006; Life in the Fast Lane: the Johnson guide to cars, 2007; The Perils of the Pushy Parents, 2007; Johnson's Life of London, 2011; The Churchill Factor: how one man made history, 2014. *Recreations:* painting, cricket. *Address:* (until May 2016) Greater London Authority, City Hall, Queen's Walk, SE1 2AA; House of Commons, SW1A 0AA. *Club:* Beefsteak.

*See also J. E. Johnson.*

**JOHNSON, Diana Ruth;** MP (Lab) Kingston upon Hull North, since 2005; *b* 25 July 1966; *d* of late Eric Johnson and Ruth Johnson. *Educ:* Northwich Co. Grammar Sch. for Girls, later Leftwich High Sch.; Sir John Deane's Sixth Form Coll., Cheshire; Queen Mary Coll., Univ. of London (LLB 1988). Volunteer/locum lawyer, Tower Hamlets Law Centre, 1991–94; lawyer: N Lewisham Law Centre, 1995–99; Paddington Law Centre, 1999–2002. Member (Lab): Tower Hamlets LBC, 1994–2002; London Assembly, GLA, March 2003–2004. Mem., Metropolitan Police Authy, 2003–04. Non-executive Director: Newham Healthcare Trust, 1998–2001; Tower Hamlets PCT, 2001–05. Vis. Legal Mem., Mental Health Act Commn, 1995–98. Contested (Lab) Brentwood and Ongar, 2001. PPS to Minister of State, DWP, 2005–06, to Chief Sec. to HM Treasury, 2006–07; an Asst Govt Whip, 2007–10; Parly Under-Sec. of State, DCSF, 2009–10; Shadow Minister for Health, 2010, for Home Office, 2010–15. *Recreations:* cinema, books, theatre, fan of Hull City Football Club, walking. *Address:* (office) Sycamore Suite, Community Enterprise Centre, Cottingham Road, Hull HU5 2DH. *E:* johnsond@parliament.uk. *W:* www.dianajohnson.co.uk, www.twitter.com/DianaJohnsonMP; House of Commons, SW1A 0AA.

**JOHNSON, Gareth Alan;** MP (C) Dartford, since 2010; *b* Bromley, 12 Oct. 1969; *s* of Alan and Ruth Johnson; *m* 1997, Wendy Morris; one *s* one *d*. *Educ:* Dartford Grammar Sch.; Coll. of Law. Admitted solicitor, 1997; Solicitor, Thomas Boyd Whyte, Solicitors, 1997–2003. Contested (C) Dartford, 2005. *Recreation:* cricket. *Address:* House of Commons, SW1A 0AA. *E:* gareth.johnson.mp@parliament.uk.

**JOHNSON, Joseph Edmund;** MP (C) Orpington, since 2010; Minister of State (Minister for Universities and Science), Department for Business, Innovation and Skills, since 2015; *b* London, Dec. 1971; *s* of Stanley Patrick Johnson and Charlotte Maria Fawcett; *m* 2005, Amelia Gentleman; one *s* one *d*. *Educ:* Eton Coll.; Balliol Coll., Oxford (MA 1st cl. Mod. Hist.); Inst. d'Etudes Européennes, Brussels (Licence Spéciale); INSEAD, Fontainebleau (MBA 2000). Corporate financier, Investment Banking Div., Deutsche Bank, 1996–97; Financial Times: Lex columnist, 1997–99; Paris corresp., 2001–05; S Asia Bureau Chief, 2005–08; Associate Ed. and Ed., Lex column, 2008–10. PPS to Mark Prisk, Minister of State for Business and Enterprise, 2010–12; an Asst Govt Whip, 2012–14; Hd of No 10 Policy Unit, and Chair, Policy Adv. Bd, 2013–15; Parly Sec., 2013–14, Minister of State, 2014–15, Cabinet Office. *Publications:* (with Martine Orange) The Man Who Tried to Buy the World, 2003; (ed jtly) Reconnecting Britain and India: ideas for an enhanced partnership, 2011. *Recreations:* trekking, writing, tennis. *Address:* House of Commons, SW1A 0AA. *E:* jo.johnson.mp@parliament.uk.

*See also A. B. de P. Johnson.*

**JONES, Andrew Hanson;** MP (C) Harrogate and Knaresborough, since 2010; Parliamentary Under-Secretary of State, Department for Transport, since 2015; *b* Leeds, 28 Nov. 1963; *s* of Richard and Jean Jones. *Educ:* Bradford Grammar Sch.; Leeds Univ. (BA English 1985). Marketing Manager: Kingfisher plc, 1985–88, 1996–98; Going Places, 1989–96; Account Dir, M&C Saatchi, 1998–2000; The Mktg Store, Leeds, 2000–05; Mktg consultant, 2005–10, incl. Bettys and Taylors of Harrogate, 2006–08. Mem. (C) Harrogate BC, 2003–11 (Cabinet Mem., Finance and Resources, 2006–10). Contested (C) Harrogate and Knaresborough, 2001. Mem., Regulatory Reform Select Cttee, 2010–15. Apprenticeship Ambassador, 2012–15. Chm., Bow Gp, 1999–2000. *Recreations:* cricket, walking. *Address:* 57 East Parade, Harrogate, N Yorks HG1 5LQ. *T:* (01423) 529614. *E:* andrew.jones.mp@parliament.uk. *Clubs:* Carlton, MCC; Yorkshire CC.

**JONES, Rt Hon. David (Ian);** PC 2012; MP (C) Clwyd West, since 2005; *b* 22 March 1952; *s* of Bryn and Elspeth Savage Jones; *m* 1982, Sara Eluned Tudor; two *s. Educ:* Ruabon Grammar Sch.; University Coll. London (LLB); Coll. of Law. Admitted Solicitor, 1976; Sen. Partner, David Jones & Co., Llandudno, 1985–2009. Mem. (C) N Wales, Nat. Assembly for Wales, 2002–03. Parly Under-Sec. of State, Wales Office, 2010–12; Sec. of State for Wales, 2012–14. Contested (C): Conwy, 1997; City of Chester, 2001. *Recreation:* travel. *Address:* House of Commons, SW1A 0AA. *T:* (020) 7219 8070. *E:* david.jones.mp@parliament.uk.

**JONES, Gerald;** MP (Lab) Merthyr Tydfil and Rhymney, since 2015; *b* Caerphilly, 21 Aug. 1970; *s* of Colin and Patricia Jones; partner, Tyrone Powell. *Educ:* Bedwelly Comprehensive Sch.; Ystrad Mynach Coll. Grants Liaison Officer, Cardiff CC, 1999–2000; Community Develt Officer, Gwent Assoc. of Voluntary Orgns, 2001–05 and 2009–12. Mem. (Lab) Caerphilly CBC, 1995–2015 (Dep. Leader, 2004–08 and 2012–15). *Recreations:* cinema, reading, music. *Address:* House of Commons, SW1A 0AA. *T:* (020) 7219 5874. *E:* gerald.jones.mp@parliament.uk.

**JONES, Graham Peter;** MP (Lab) Hyndburn, since 2010; *b* 2 March 1966; partner, Kimberley Whitehead; one *s* one *d. Educ:* BA (Hons) Applied Social Studies. Graphic Designer, 1992–2010. Member (Lab): Hyndburn BC, 2002–10; Lancs CC, 2009–10. *Address:* House of Commons, SW1A 0AA.

**JONES, Helen Mary;** MP (Lab) Warrington North, since 1997; *b* 24 Dec. 1954; *d* of late Robert Edward Jones and of Mary Scanlan; *m* 1988, Michael Vobe; one *s. Educ:* Ursuline Convent, Chester; UCL; Chester Coll.; Univ. of Liverpool; Manchester Metropolitan Univ. BA, PGCE, MEd, CPE, LSF. Teacher of English; Develt Officer, Mind; Justice and Peace Officer, Liverpool; Solicitor. Contested (Lab): Shropshire N, 1983; Lancashire Central, EP elecn, 1984; Ellesmere Port and Neston, 1987. An Asst Govt Whip, 2008–09; Vice-Chamberlain of HM Household, 2009–10. Chm., Petitions Select Cttee, 2015–. *Address:* House of Commons, SW1A 0AA; 67 Bewsey Street, Warrington, Cheshire WA2 7JQ.

**JONES, Kevan David;** MP (Lab) North Durham, since 2001; *b* 25 April 1964. *Educ:* Univ. of Southern Maine, USA; Newcastle upon Tyne Poly. (BA). Political Officer, 1989–2001, Regl Organiser, 1992–99, Sen. Organiser, 1999–2001, GMB. Newcastle upon Tyne City Council: Mem. (Lab), 1990–2001; Chair of Public Health, 1993–97; Chief Whip, 1994–2000; Chair and Cabinet Mem. for Develt and Transport, 1997–2001. Parly Under-Sec. of State and Minister for Veterans, MoD, 2008–10; Shadow Minister for Armed Forces, 2010–15. Mem.,

Select Cttee on Defence, 2001–09. Chair, 1998–2000, Vice-Chair, 2000–01, Northern Regl Lab. Party. Mem., Commonwealth War Graves Commn, 2010–. *Address:* c/o House of Commons, SW1A 0AA; (office) Fulforth Centre, Front Street, Sacriston, Co. Durham DH7 6JT. *T:* (0191) 371 8834. *Club:* Sacriston Workmen's.

**JONES, Marcus Charles;** MP (C) Nuneaton, since 2010; Parliamentary Under-Secretary of State, Department for Communities and Local Government, since 2015; *b* 5 April 1974; *s* of Brian and Jean Jones; *m* 2004, Suzanne Clarke; one *s* one *d. Educ:* St Thomas More Sch., Nuneaton; King Edward VI Coll., Nuneaton. Conveyancing Manager, Tustain Jones & Co., Solicitors, 1999–2010. Mem. (C) Nuneaton and Bedworth BC, 2005–10 (Leader, 2008–09). *Address:* House of Commons, SW1A 0AA.

**JONES, Susan Elan;** MP (Lab) Clwyd South, since 2010; *b* Wrexham, 1 June 1968; *d* of Richard James and Margaret Eirlys Jones. *Educ:* Grango Comprehensive Sch., Rhosllannerchrugog; Ruabon Comprehensive Sch.; Univ. of Bristol (BA 1989); Univ. of Wales, Cardiff (MA 1992). English teacher: Tomakomai English Sch., Japan, 1990–91; Atsuma Bd of Educn, Japan, 1992–94; Corporate Develt Fundraiser, Muscular Dystrophy Campaign, 1995–96; fundraiser, USPG, 1997–2002; Dir, CARIS Haringey, 2002–05; Fundraising Exec., Housing Justice, 2005–10. Mem. (Lab) Southwark LBC, 2006–09 (Dep. Opposition Leader, 2007–09). *Publications:* (contrib.) The Red Book of the Voluntary Sector, 2014. *Recreation:* classical music. *Address:* House of Commons, SW1A 0AA. *E:* susan.jones.mp@parliament.uk.

**KANE, Michael Joseph Patrick;** MP (Lab) Wythenshawe and Sale East, since Feb. 2014; *b* Wythenshawe, 9 Jan. 1969; *s* of Joseph Kane and Kathleen Kane (*née* McGirl); *m* 1996, Sandra Bracegirdle. *Educ:* St Paul's RC High Sch.; Manchester Metropolitan Univ. (BA Social Scis 1997; PGCE 1999). Teacher, Springfield Primary Sch., 2000–08; Parliamentary Assistant: to Rt Hon. James Purnell, MP, 2008–10; to Jonathan Reynolds, MP, 2010–11; Sen. Exec. Asst, Tameside Council, 2011–14. Mem. (Lab) Manchester CC, 1991–2008. Nat. Chair, 2010–13, Actg Chief Exec., 2014, Movement for Change. *Recreations:* playing flute and bagpipes, Manchester City FC. *Address:* House of Commons, SW1A 0AA. *T:* (constituency office) (0161) 499 7900. *E:* mike.kane.mp@parliament.uk. *Club:* Stretford Wheelers.

**KAUFMAN, Rt Hon. Sir Gerald (Bernard),** Kt 2004; PC 1978; MP (Lab) Manchester, Gorton, since 1983 (Manchester, Ardwick, 1970–83); Father of the House, since 2015; *b* 21 June 1930; *s* of Louis and Jane Kaufman. *Educ:* Leeds Grammar Sch.; The Queen's Coll., Oxford. Asst Gen.-Sec., Fabian Soc., 1954–55; Political Staff, Daily Mirror, 1955–64; Political

Correspondent, New Statesman, 1964–65; Parly Press Liaison Officer, Labour Party, 1965–70. Parly Under-Sec. of State, DoE, 1974–75, Dept of Industry, 1975; Minister of State, Dept of Industry, 1975–79; Shadow Envmt Sec., 1980–83; Shadow Home Sec., 1983–87; Shadow Foreign Sec., 1987–92. Chm., Select Cttee on Nat. Heritage, 1992–97, on Culture, Media and Sport, 1997–2005. Chairman: All-Party Dance Gp, 2006–; All-Party Opera Gp, 2010–; Mem., Parly Cttee of PLP, 1980–92. Mem., Labour Party NEC, 1991–92. Mem., Royal Commn on H of L reform, 1999. Chm., Booker Prize Judges, 1999. HPk (Pakistan), 1999. *Publications:* (jtly) How to Live Under Labour, 1964; (ed) The Left, 1966; To Build the Promised Land, 1973; How to be a Minister, 1980, 2nd edn 1997; (ed) Renewal: Labour's Britain in the 1980s, 1983; My Life in the Silver Screen, 1985; Inside the Promised Land, 1986; Meet Me in St Louis, 1994. *Recreations:* travel, going to the pictures. *Address:* 87 Charlbert Court, Eamont Street, NW8 7DA. *T:* (office) (020) 7219 3000.

**KAWCZYNSKI, Daniel;** MP (C) Shrewsbury and Atcham, since 2005; *b* 24 Jan. 1972; *s* of Leonard and Halina Kawczynski; *m* 2000, Kate Lumb (marr. diss. 2011); one *d. Educ:* Univ. of Stirling (BA Hons Business Studies with French 1994). Internat. export consultant in telecommunications industry, Middle E, 1994–2004. Contested (C) Ealing Southall, 2001. PPS to Minister of State for Agriculture and Food, 2010–12, to Sec. of State for Wales, 2012–14. Member: Envmt, Food and Rural Affairs Select Cttee, 2005–07; Justice Select Cttee, 2007–09; Internat. Develt Select Cttee, 2008–10; Foreign Affairs Select Cttee, 2015–; Chairman: All Party Gp for Dairy Farmers, 2006; All Party Parly Gp for Saudi Arabia, 2007–15; All Party Parly Gp for Libya, 2008–; British Middle E and N Africa Council, 2012–. *Publications:* Seeking Gaddafi, 2010. *Address:* House of Commons, SW1A 0AA. *E:* kawczynskid@parliament.uk.

**KEELEY, Barbara Mary;** MP (Lab) Worsley and Eccles South, since 2010 (Worsley, 2005–10); *b* 26 March 1952; *d* of late Edward and Joan Keeley; *m* Colin Huggett. *Educ:* Univ. of Salford (BA 1st Cl. Hons Pols and Contemp. Hist.). Field Systems Engr and Systems Engrg Manager, IBM UK, until 1989; community regeneration advr, 1989–94; Area Manager, BITC, 1994–95; local govt and voluntary sector, 1995–2001; Consultant, researching policy issues, Princess Royal Trust for Carers, 2001–05. PPS to Parly Sec., Cabinet Office, then Minister of State, DWP, 2006–07, to Minister for Women and Equality, 2007–08; an Asst Govt Whip, 2008–09; Parly Sec., Leader of H of C, 2009–10; Shadow Minister: for Care Services, 2010; for Communities and Local Govt, 2010–11; for Treasury, 2015–. Mem., Health Select Cttee, 2011–15. Chair, PLP Women's Cttee, 2007–08. Mem., Trafford MBC, 1995–2004 (Cabinet Mem., 1999–2004). Dir, Pathfinder Children's Trust, 2002–04. *Recreations:*

running, watching cricket, listening to live music. *Address:* c/o House of Commons, SW1A 0AA. *T:* (020) 7219 8025. *W:* www.barbarakeeley.co.uk.

**KEEN OF ELIE,** Baron *cr* 2015 (Life Peer), of Elie in Fife; **Richard Sanderson Keen;** QC (Scot.) 1993; Advocate General for Scotland, since 2015; *b* 29 March 1954; *s* of Derek Michael Keen and Jean Sanderson Keen; *m* 1978, Jane Carolyn Anderson; one *s* one *d. Educ:* King's Sch., Rochester; Dollar Acad.; Edinburgh Univ. (LLB Hons 1976; Beckman Schol.). Admitted Faculty of Advocates, 1980 (Treas., 2006–07; Dean, 2007–14); Standing Jun. Counsel in Scotland to DTI, 1986–93. Called to the Bar, Middle Temple, 2009, Bencher, 2011; Mem., Blackstone Chambers, London, 2011–. Chairman: Appeals Cttee, ICAS, 1996–2001; Police Appeals Tribunal, 2004–10. Chm., Scottish Cons. and Unionist Party, 2014–. *Recreations:* golf, ski-ing, shooting, opera. *Address:* The Castle, Elie, Fife KY9 1DN; 27 Ann Street, Edinburgh EH4 1PL. *Clubs:* New (Edinburgh); Golf House (Elie); Hon. Co. of Edinburgh Golfers (Muirfield).

**KENDALL, Elizabeth Louise;** MP (Lab) Leicester West, since 2010; *b* 1971. *Educ:* Watford Grammar Sch. for Girls; Queens' Coll., Cambridge (BA 1st Cl. Hons Hist. 1993). Special Advr to Harriet Harman, MP, 1997–98; Res. Fellow, King's Fund; Associate Dir, Health, Social Care and Children's Early Years, IPPR; Dir, Maternity Alliance; Special Advr to Patricia Hewitt, MP, 2004–07; Dir, Ambulance Service Network, 2008–10. Shadow Minister for Care and Older People, 2011–15. Mem., Educn Select Cttee, 2010. *Address:* House of Commons, SW1A 0AA.

**KENNEDY, Seema Louise Ghiassi;** MP (C) South Ribble, since 2015; *b* Blackburn, 1974; *m* 2003, Paul Kennedy; three *s. Educ:* Westholme Sch., Blackburn; Pembroke Coll., Cambridge (BA Oriental Studies 1997); Université Sorbonne Nouvelle (Licence 1996). Solicitor, Slaughter and May, 2000–03; Associate Solicitor, Bevan Brittan, 2003–06; Dir, Tustin Develts, 2006–. *Recreations:* walking, opera, family. *Address:* House of Commons, SW1A 0AA. *T:* (020) 7219 4412. *E:* seema.kennedy.mp@parliament.uk.

**KEREVAN, George;** MP (SNP) East Lothian, since 2015; *b* Glasgow, 28 Sept. 1949; *m* Angela. *Educ:* Univ. of Glasgow. Lectr in Econs, Napier Univ., Edinburgh; Associate Ed., Scotsman, 2000–09; Producer, What If Prodns (Television) Ltd, 2000–06; producer of documentary films for Discovery, Hist. Channel and PBS. Former Chm., Edinburgh Tourist Bd; Member, Board: Edinburgh Internat. Fest.; Edinburgh Internat. Film Fest; Founder, Edinburgh Sci. Fest.; Co-organiser, Prestwick World Fest. of Flight. Mem. (Lab) Edinburgh CC, 1984–96. Contested (SNP) Edinburgh E, 2010. *Address:* House of Commons, SW1A 0AA.

**KERR, Calum Robert;** MP (SNP) Berwickshire, Roxburgh and Selkirk, since 2015; *b* Galashiels, 5 April 1972; *m* Ros; three *c. Educ:* Peebles High Sch.; St Andrews Univ. (MA Hons Modern Hist. 1994). Account Manager, Philips Business Communications, 1995–98; Channel Account Manager, 1998–2003, High Touch Account Manager, 2004–09, Nortel Networks; Avaya: Named Account Manager, 2009–12; Practice Consultant - Sales Acceleration, 2012–13; Practice Leader - Sales Mgt Excellence, 2014–15. *Address:* House of Commons, SW1A 0AA.

**KHAN, Rt Hon. Sadiq (Aman);** PC 2009; MP (Lab) Tooting, since 2005; *b* 8 Oct. 1970; *s* of late Amanullah Ahmad Khan and of Sehrun Nisa Khan; *m* 1994, Saadiya Ahmad; two *d. Educ:* Ernest Bevin Secondary Comprehensive Sch.; Univ. of N London (LLB Hons 1992); Coll. of Law, Guildford. Christian Fisher Solicitors: trainee solicitor, 1993–95; Solicitor, 1995–98; Partner, 1998–2000; Equity Partner: Christian Fisher Khan Solicitors, 2000–02; and Co-founder, Christian Khan Solicitors, 2002–04. Vis. Lectr, Univ. of N London and London Metropolitan Univ., 1998–2004. Mem. (Lab), Wandsworth BC, 1994–2006; Dep. Leader of Labour Gp, 1996–2001; Hon. Alderman, 2006. PPS to Lord Privy Seal and Leader of H of C, 2007; Govt Whip, 2007–08; Parly Under-Sec. of State, DCLG, 2008–09; Minister of State, DfT, 2009–10; Shadow Sec. of State for Transport, 2010; Shadow Lord Chancellor and Sec. of State for Justice, 2010–15; Shadow Minister for London, 2013–15. Chm., All-Party Parly Gp for Citizens Advice, 2006–08. Chair, Liberty, 2001–04; Founding Mem., Human Rights Lawyers Assoc., 2003. Exec. Mem., Fabian Soc., 2006– (Vice Chair, 2007; Chair, 2008–10); Vice Chair, Legal Action Gp, 1999–2004; Patron, Progress, 2005. *Publications:* Challenging Racism, 2003; Police Misconduct: Legal Remedies, 2005; Fairness not Favours, 2008; Punishment and Reform: how our justice system can help cut crime, 2011. *Recreations:* playing and watching sport, cinema, family, friends, local community. *Address:* House of Commons, SW1A 0AA. *T:* (020) 7219 6967, *Fax:* (020) 7219 6477. *E:* sadiqkhanmp@parliament.uk.

**KINAHAN, Daniel de Burgh;** DL; MP (UU) South Antrim, since 2015; *b* Belfast, 14 April 1958; *s* of Sir Robert George Caldwell Kinahan and of Coralie Kinahan (*née* de Burgh); *m* 1991, Anna Marguerite Bence-Trower; one *s* three *d. Educ:* Stowe Sch., Bucks; Royal Military Acad., Sandhurst; Edinburgh Univ. (BCom). Served Blues and Royals, 1977–84. Asst PR Manager, Short Bros, 1985–88; Rep. for Ireland and NI, Christie's, 1988–2003; estabd Danny Kinahan Fine Art and Castle Upton Gall., 2003–. Mem. (UU) S Antrim BC, 2005–09. Mem. (UU) S Antrim, NI Assembly, 2009–June 2015. Sqdn Leader, N Irish Horse (TA), 1988–89 (Hon. Col, 2013–). High Sheriff, Antrim, 1996. *Recreations:* tennis, football, walking, all sport, history, travel,

reading. *Address:* Castle Upton, Templepatrick, Co. Antrim BT39 0AH. *T:* (028) 9443 3480. *E:* danny@castleuptongallery.com. *Club:* Reform (Belfast).

**KINNOCK, Stephen Nathan;** MP (Lab) Aberavon, since 2015; *b* Tredegar, 1 Jan. 1970; *s* of Baron Kinnock, PC and Baroness Kinnock of Holyhead; *m* 1996, Helle Thorning-Schmidt; two *d. Educ:* Drayton Manor Comp. Sch.; Queens' Coll., Cambridge (BA Mod. Langs French and Spanish 1992); Coll. of Europe, Bruges. Policy Researcher for Gary Titley, MEP, 1993–94; Consultant, Lancashire Enterprises, 1994–96; British Council: Business Develt Manager, Dep. Dir, then Dir, Brussels, 1996–2003; Director: Contract Mgt Change Prog., 2003–05; St Petersburg, 2005–08; Sierra Leone, 2008; Dir, Hd of Europe and Central Asia, WEF, 2009–12; Man. Dir, Global Leadership and Technol. Exchange, Xyntéo AS, 2012–15. *Recreations:* football, gym. *Address:* (office) Unit 7, Water Street Business Centre, Water Street, Port Talbot SA12 6LF. *T:* (01639) 897660. *E:* stephen.kinnock.mp@parliament.uk.

**KIRBY, Simon Gerard;** MP (C) Brighton Kemptown, since 2010; an Assistant Government Whip, since 2015; *b* Hastings, 22 Dec. 1964; *m* 1992, Elizabeth Radford; four *s* two *d. Educ:* Hastings Grammar Sch.; Open Univ. (BSc Hons). Man. Dir, C-Side Ltd, 1989–2001. Member (C): E Sussex CC, 1992–93, 2005–09; Brighton BC, 1995–97; Brighton and Hove CC, 1996–99; Mid Sussex DC, 1999–2001. *Address:* House of Commons, SW1A 0AA. *T:* (020) 7219 7024. *E:* simon.kirby.mp@parliament.uk.

**KNIGHT, Rt Hon. Sir Gregory,** Kt 2013; PC 1995; MP (C) East Yorkshire, since 2001; writer, consultant solicitor; *b* 4 April 1949; *s* of late George Knight and Isabella Knight (*née* Bell). *Educ:* Alderman Newton's Grammar School, Leicester; College of Law, Guildford. Self employed solicitor, 1973–83. Member: Leicester City Council, 1976–79; Leicestershire County Council, 1977–83 (Chm., Public Protection Cttee). MP (C) Derby North, 1983–97; contested (C) same seat, 1997. PPS to the Minister of State: Home Office, 1987; Foreign Office, 1988–89; an Asst Govt Whip, 1989–90; a Lord Comr of HM Treasury, 1990–93; Dep. Govt Chief Whip and Treas. of HM Household, 1993–96; Minister of State, DTI, 1996–97; Shadow Dep. Leader, H of C, 2001–03; Opposition front bench spokesman: on transport and envmt, 2003–05; on transport, 2005–06; Vice-Chamberlain of HM Household (Govt Whip), 2012–13. Chm., H of C Procedure Select Cttee, 2005–12. Vice Chm., Cons. Candidates' Assoc., 1998–2001. Dir, Leicester Theatre Trust, 1979–85 (Chm., Finance Cttee, 1982–83). *Publications:* (jtly) Westminster Words, 1988; Honourable Insults: a century of political insult, 1990; Parliamentary Sauce: more political insults, 1992; Right Honourable Insults, 1998; Naughty Graffiti, 2005; Dishonourable Insults,

2011; pamphlets and articles for law, motoring and entertainment publications. *Recreation:* driving classic cars and making music. *Address:* House of Commons, SW1A 0AA. *Club:* Bridlington Conservative.

**KNIGHT, Julian Carlton;** MP (C) Solihull, since 2015; *b* Chester, 5 Jan. 1972; *s* of Carlton and Valerie Knight; *m* 2014, Philippa Harrison. *Educ:* Chester Catholic High Sch.; Hull Univ. (BA Hons). Field sales exec., News Internat., 1995–98; staff writer, Reader's Digest, 1998–2002; personal finance and consumer affairs reporter, BBC News, 2002–07; Money and Property Ed., Independent, 2007–15. *Publications:* Wills, Probate and Inheritance Tax for Dummies, 2004, 2nd edn 2008; Retiring Wealthy, 2005; Cricket for Dummies, 2006, 2nd edn 2013; (with M. Pattison) British Politics for Dummies, 2010, 2nd edn 2015; Eurocrisis for Dummies, 2012. *Recreations:* tennis, cricket, golf, football, cycling, the arts. *Address:* House of Commons, SW1A 0AA. *T:* (020) 7219 3577. *E:* julian.knight.mp@parliament.uk.

**KWARTENG, Dr Kwasi Alfred Addo;** MP (C) Spelthorne, since 2010; *b* London, 26 May 1975; *s* of Alfred and Charlotte Kwarteng. *Educ:* Eton Coll. (King's Schol.; Newcastle Schol.); Trinity Coll., Cambridge (BA 1996; MA; PhD 2000); Harvard Univ. (Kennedy Schol.). Financial Analyst: JP Morgan, then WestLB, 2000–04; Odey Asset Mgt, 2004–06; journalist and author, 2006–10. Member: Transport Cttee, 2010–13; Work and Pensions Cttee, 2013–15. Chm., Bow Gp, 2005–06. Trustee, History of Parliament Trust, 2011–. Contested (C): Brent E, 2005; London Assembly, GLA, 2008. *Publications:* Gridlock Nation (with J. Dupont), 2011; Ghosts of Empire, 2011; War and Gold, 2014; Thatcher's Trial, 2015. *Recreations:* music, history. *Address:* House of Commons, SW1A 0AA.

**KYLE, Dr Peter;** MP (Lab) Hove, since 2015; *b* Rustington, 9 Sept. 1970; *s* of Leslie Kyle and Joanna Murrell (*née* Davies). *Educ:* Felpham Community Coll.; Sussex Univ. (BA Hons Geog., Envmtl Studies and Internat. Develt 1999; DPhil Community Econ. Develt 2003). Dir, Children on the Edge, 1992–96; Co-Founder, Fat Sand Films, 2003–06; Dep. CEO, ACEVO, 2007–13; Chief Exec., Working for Youth, 2013–15. Non-exec. Dir, CAF Bank, 2011–. *Address:* House of Commons, SW1A 0AA; (office) 99 Church Road, Hove BN3 2BA. *E:* peter.kyle.mp@parliament.uk.

**LAING, Eleanor Fulton;** MP (C) Epping Forest, since 1997; First Deputy Chairman of Ways and Means, and a Deputy Speaker, House of Commons, since 2013; *b* 1 Feb. 1958; *d* of late Matthew and Betty Pritchard; *m* 1983, Alan Laing (marr. diss. 2003); one *s. Educ:* St Columba's Sch., Kilmacolm; Edinburgh Univ. (Pres., Union, 1980–81; BA, LLB 1982). Solicitor, Edinburgh and London, 1983–89; Special Advr to Rt Hon.

John MacGregor, MP, 1989–94. Contested (C) Paisley N, 1987. An Opposition Whip, 1999–2000; frontbench opposition spokesman on constitutional affairs, 2000–01, on educn, 2001–03, on women and equality, 2004–07; Shadow Sec. of State for Scotland, 2005; Shadow Minister for Justice, 2007–10. *Recreations:* theatre, music, golf, Agatha Christie Society. *Address:* House of Commons, SW1A 0AA.

**LAMB, Rt Hon. Norman (Peter);** PC 2014; MP (Lib Dem) North Norfolk, since 2001; *b* 16 Sept. 1957; *s* of late Hubert Horace Lamb and of Beatrice Moira Lamb; *m* 1984, Mary Elizabeth Green; two *s. Educ:* Wymondham Coll., Norfolk; Leicester Univ. (LLB). Sen. Asst Solicitor, Norwich CC, 1984–86; Solicitor, 1986–87, Partner, 1987–2001, Steele & Co. Lib Dem spokesman for health, 2007–10; an Asst Govt Whip, and Chief Parly and Political Advr to the Dep. Prime Minister, 2010–12; Parly Under-Sec. of State (Minister for Employment Relns, Consumer and Postal Affairs), BIS, 2012; Minister of State, DoH, 2012–15. *Publications:* Remedies in the Employment Tribunal, 1998. *Recreations:* football, walking. *Address:* House of Commons, SW1A 0AA. *T:* (020) 7219 0542; (office) Unit 4, The Garden Centre, Nursery Drive, Norwich Road, North Walsham, Norfolk NR28 0DR.

**LAMMY, Rt Hon. David (Lindon);** PC 2008; MP (Lab) Tottenham, since June 2000; *b* 19 July 1972; *s* of David and Rosalind Lammy; *m* 2005, Nicola Green; two *s. Educ:* King's Sch., Peterborough; SOAS, London Univ. (LLB Hons 1993); Harvard Law Sch. (LLM 1997). Called to the Bar, Lincoln's Inn; Attorney, Howard Rice, Calif, 1997–98; with D. J. Freeman, 1998–2000. Mem. (Lab), London Assembly, GLA, May–June 2000. PPS to Sec. of State for Educn and Skills, 2001–02; Parliamentary Under-Secretary of State: DoH, 2002–03; DCA, 2003–05; DCMS, 2005–07; DIUS, 2007–08; Minister of State, DIUS, then BIS, 2008–10. Member: Procedure Cttee, 2001; Public Admin Cttee, 2001; Chair, All Party Parly Gp on Fatherhood, 2013–, on Crossrail2, 2013–, on Race and Equality, on Wellbeing Economics, on London-Stansted-Cambridge Corridor. Member: Gen. Synod, C of E, 1999–2002; Archbishops' Council, 1999–2002. Trustee, ActionAid, 2001–06. *Publications:* Out of the Ashes: Britain after the riots, 2011. *Recreations:* film, theatre, live music, Spurs FC. *Address:* c/o House of Commons, SW1A 0AA. *T:* (020) 7219 0767.

**LANCASTER, (John) Mark,** TD 2002; DSc; MP (C) Milton Keynes North, since 2010 (Milton Keynes North East, 2005–10); Parliamentary Under-Secretary of State, Ministry of Defence, since 2015; *b* 12 May 1970; *s* of Rev. Ronald Lancaster, MBE; *m* (marr. diss.); one *d; m* 2014, Caroline Dinenage, *qv;* two step *s. Educ:* Kimbolton Sch., Cambs; Buckingham Univ. (BSc 1992; DSc 2007); Exeter Univ. (MBA 1993). Served Army, RE, 1988–90; Officer, TA, RE,

1990–. Dir, Kimbolton Fireworks Ltd, 1993–2005. PPS to Sec. of State for Internat. Develt, 2010–12; a Lord Comr of HM Treasury (Govt Whip), 2012–15. Mem. (C) Huntingdon DC, 1995–99. Consultant, Palmer Capital Partners, 2010–12. *Publications:* (contrib.) Fireworks Principles and Practice, 3rd edn 1998. *Recreations:* collector and restorer of classic British motorcycles, avid football supporter. *Address:* House of Commons, SW1A 0AA. *E:* lancasterm@parliament.uk.

**LATHAM, Pauline,** OBE 1992; MP (C) Mid Derbyshire, since 2010; *b* Lincs, 4 Feb. 1948; *m* 1968, Derek Latham; two *s* one *d. Educ:* Bramcote Hills Tech. Grammar Sch. Proprietor, Humble Pie, 1976–87; Dir, Michael St Develt, 1982–. Member (C): Derbys CC, 1987–93; Derby CC, 1992–96 and 1998–2010 (Mayor, 2007–08). Contested (C): Broxtowe, 2001; E Midlands, EP, 1999, 2004. Mem., Internat. Develt Select Cttee, 2010–. *Address:* House of Commons, SW1A 0AA.

**LAVERY, Ian;** MP (Lab) Wansbeck, since 2010; *b* Newcastle upon Tyne, 6 Jan. 1963; *s* of John Robert Lavery and Patricia Lavery; *m* 1986, Hilary Lavery; two *s. Educ:* New Coll., Durham (HNC Mining Engrg). Miner, National Coal Board: Lynemouth Colliery, 1980; Ellington Colliery, 1981–92; National Union of Mineworkers: Mem., Nat. Exec. Cttee, 1992–2010; Gen. Sec., Northumberland Area, 1992–2002; Pres., 2002. Mem. (Lab) Wansbeck DC, 1995–2002. Member, Select Committee: on NI Affairs, 2010–11; on Regulatory Reform, 2010–15; on Energy and Climate Change, 2010–. *Address:* House of Commons, SW1A 0AA.

**LAW, Christopher Murray Alexander;** MP (SNP) Dundee West, since 2015; *b* Edinburgh, 21 Oct. 1969; *s* of John and Jean Law. *Educ:* Madras Coll., St Andrews; Dundee Coll. of Further Educn (C&G Catering); Univ. of St Andrews (MA 1st Cl. Hons Social Anthropol.; postgrad. dip. in IT). Raleigh Internat., Namibia; organiser, motorbike expeditions in Himalayas; proprietor, Freewheeling Tours; businessman in financial sector. Mem., Scottish Affairs Cttee, 2015–; Vice Chm., All Party Parly Gp on Canada, 2015–, on Wine and Spirits, 2015–, on Whisky, 2015–. *Recreations:* reading, travel, motorcycles. *Address:* (office) 2 Marshall Street, Lochee, Dundee DD2 3BR. *T:* (01382) 848906. *E:* chris.law.mp@ parliament.uk.

**LEADSOM, Andrea Jacqueline;** MP (C) South Northamptonshire, since 2010; Minister of State, Department of Energy and Climate Change, since 2015; *b* Aylesbury, 13 May 1963; *d* of Richard Salmon and Judy Crompton (*née* Kitchin); *m* 1993, Ben Leadsom; two *s* one *d. Educ:* Tonbridge Girls' Grammar Sch.; Warwick Univ. (BA Hons). Fixed Interest and Treasury, BZW, 1987–91; Financial Instns Dir, Barclays Bank, 1993–97; Man. Dir, DPFM Ltd, 1997–99; Sen.

Investment Officer, Invesco Perpetual, 1999–2009. Mem. (C) S Oxfordshire DC, 2003–07. Econ. Sec., HM Treasury, 2014–15. Contested (C) Knowsley S, 2005. *Address:* House of Commons, SW1A 0AA. *T:* (020) 7219 7149. *E:* andrea.leadsom.mp@parliament.uk.

**LEE, Phillip James;** MP (C) Bracknell, since 2010; *b* Taplow, Bucks, 28 Sept. 1970; *s* of Antony and Marilyn Lee. *Educ:* Sir William Borlase Sch., Marlow, Bucks; King's Coll. London (BSc Hons Human Biol. 1993); Keble Coll., Oxford (MSc Human Biol. 1994); St Mary's Hosp. Med. Sch., London (MB BS 1999). House Officer: Wexham Park Hosp., Slough, 1999–2000; St Mary's Hosp., London, 2000; Sen. House Officer, Stoke Mandeville Hosp., Aylesbury, 2000–02; GP, Thames Valley, 2002–. Mem., Energy and Climate Change Select Cttee, 2010–15; Vice Chm., Parly Space Cttee, 2010–; Vice Chm., Cons. Middle East Council, 2010–. *Recreations:* cricket, water ski-ing, football, ski-ing. *Address:* House of Commons, SW1A 0AA. *T:* (020) 7219 1270. *E:* phillip@phillip-lee.com.

**LEFROY, Jeremy John Elton;** MP (C) Stafford, since 2010; *b* London, 30 May 1959; *s* of Rev. Christopher John Elton Lefroy and Sarah Ursula Lefroy (*née* Blacking); *m* 1985, Dr Janet Elizabeth MacKay; one *s* one *d. Educ:* Highgate Sch.; King's Coll., Cambridge (BA 1980; MA 1984). ACA 1985. Gen. Manager, 1989–91, Man. Dir, 1991–2000, African Coffee Co. Ltd, Moshi, Tanzania; Dir, African Speciality Products Ltd, Keele, 2000–. Dir, Tanzania Coffee Bd, 1997–99. Mem. (C) Newcastle-under-Lyme BC, 2003–07. *Recreations:* music (playing, singing, listening), walking, cricket, tennis, badminton. *Address:* House of Commons, SW1A 0AA. *T:* (020) 7219 7154. *E:* jeremy.lefroy.mp@parliament.uk.

**LEIGH, Sir Edward (Julian Egerton),** Kt 2013; MP (C) Gainsborough, since 1997 (Gainsborough and Horncastle, 1983–97); *b* 20 July 1950; *s* of Sir Neville Egerton Leigh, KCVO; *m* 1984, Mary Goodman; three *s* three *d. Educ:* St Philip's Sch., Kensington; Oratory Sch., Berks; French Lycée, London; UC, Durham Univ. (BA Hons). Called to the Bar, Inner Temple, 1977. Mem., Cons. Res. Dept, seconded to office of Leader of Opposition, GLC, 1973–75; Prin. Correspondence Sec. to Rt Hon. Margaret Thatcher, MP, 1975–76. Member (C): Richmond Borough Council, 1974–78; GLC, 1977–81. Contested (C) Teesside, Middlesbrough, Oct. 1974. PPS to Minister of State, Home Office, 1990; Parly Under-Sec. of State, DTI, 1990–93. Chairman: Public Accounts Cttee, H of C, 2001–10; Public Accounts Commn, H of C, 2011–; Backbench Cttee on Foreign Affairs, Defence, Internat. Develt, 2011–; All-Party Parly Gp on France, 2010– (Mem., 1983–); All-Party Parly Gp on Italy, 2015–; Secretary: Conservative backbench Cttees on agric., defence and employment, 1983–90; All-Party Parly Gp on Insurance, 2010– (Mem.,

1993–); Vice Chm., Conservative Back bench Cttees on foreign affairs and social security, 1997–2001; Financial Advr to HM Treasury, 2010–11. Delegate, Parly Assembly, Council of Europe, 2011–. Chm., Nat. Council for Civil Defence, 1980–82; Dir, Coalition for Peace Through Security, 1982–83. Kt of Honour and Devotion, SMO Malta, 1994. *Publications:* Right Thinking, 1979; Responsible Individualism, 1994; Monastery of the Mind, 2012. *Recreations:* walking, reading. *Address:* House of Commons, SW1A 0AA.

**LESLIE, Charlotte Ann;** MP (C) Bristol North West, since 2010; *b* Liverpool, Aug. 1978; *d* of Ian and Jane Leslie. *Educ:* Badminton Sch.; Millfield Sch.; Balliol Coll., Oxford (BA Lit. Hum.). Special Advr to Shadow Sec. of State for Educn and Skills, 2006; Educn Associate, Young Foundn, 2008. Member: Educn Select Cttee, 2010–13; Health Select Cttee, 2013–15. Back Bencher of the Year, Spectator, 2013. *Address:* House of Commons, SW1A 0AA. *T:* (020) 7219 7026, *Fax:* (020) 7219 0921. *E:* charlotte. leslie.mp@parliament.uk.

**LESLIE, Christopher Michael;** MP (Lab) Nottingham East, since 2010; *b* 28 June 1972; *s* of Michael N. Leslie and Dania K. Leslie; *m* Nicola Murphy; one *d*. *Educ:* Bingley Grammar Sch.; Univ. of Leeds (BA Hons Pol. and Parly Studies 1994; MA Indust. and Labour Studies 1996). Research Assistant: Rep. Bernie Sanders, US Congress, 1992; Gordon Brown, MP, 1993; Adminr, Bradford Labour Party, 1995–97; Researcher, Barry Seal, MEP, 1997. Dir, New Local Govt Network, 2005–10. MP (Lab) Shipley, 1997–2005; contested (Lab) same seat, 2005. PPS to Minister of State, Cabinet Office, 1998–2001; Parly Sec., Cabinet Office, 2001–02; Parly Under-Sec., ODPM, 2002–03; Parly Under-Sec. of State, DCA, 2003–05; Shadow Financial Sec. to HM Treasury, 2010–13; Shadow Chief Sec. to HM Treasury, 2013–15; Shadow Chancellor of the Exchequer, 2015. Mem. (Lab), Bradford MDC, 1994–98. *Recreations:* music, tennis, travel. *Address:* House of Commons, SW1A 0AA.

**LETWIN, Rt Hon. Oliver;** PC 2002; PhD; MP (C) West Dorset, since 1997; Minister for Government Policy, Cabinet Office, since 2010; Chancellor of the Duchy of Lancaster, since 2014; *b* 19 May 1956; *s* of late Prof. William Letwin; *m* 1984, Isabel Grace Davidson; one *s* one *d* (twins). *Educ:* Eton Coll.; Trinity Coll., Cambridge (BA, MA, PhD 1982). Vis. Fellow, Princeton Univ., 1981; Research Fellow, Darwin Coll., Cambridge, 1982–83; Special Advr, DES, 1982–83; Mem., Prime Minister's Policy Unit, 1983–86; with N. M. Rothschild & Sons Ltd, 1986–2003 (Dir, 1991–2003; non-exec. Dir, 2005–09). Opposition front-bench spokesman on constitutional affairs, 1998–99, on Treasury affairs, 1999–2000; Shadow Chief Sec. to HM Treasury, 2000–01; Shadow Home Sec.,

2001–03; Shadow Chancellor, 2003–05; Shadow Sec. of State for Envmt, Food and Rural Affairs, 2005; Chairman: Conservative Policy Review, 2005–10; Conservative Res. Dept, 2005–10; Conservative Policy Forum, 2010–. FRSA 1991. *Publications:* Ethics, Emotion and the Unity of the Self, 1984; Aims of Schooling, 1985; Privatising the World, 1987; Drift to Union, 1990; The Purpose of Politics, 1999; numerous articles in learned and popular jls. *Recreations:* ski-ing, tennis, walking. *Address:* House of Commons, SW1A 0AA. *T:* (020) 7219 3000.

**LEWELL-BUCK, Emma Louise;** MP (Lab) South Shields, since May 2013; *b* South Shields, 8 Nov. 1978; *d* of David and Linda Lewell; *m* 2010, Simon John Paul Buck. *Educ:* Northumbria Univ. (BA Hons Politics and Media Studies 2002); Durham Univ. (MSW 2008). Sales asst, Fenwick Ltd, 1998–2002; sessional playworker, N Tyneside Council, 2001–02; customer services, Traidcraft plc, 2002–05; Child Protection Social Worker: Sunderland CC, 2007–10; Newcastle CC, 2010–13. Mem. (Lab) S Tyneside Council, 2004–13 (Lead Mem., Adult Social Care and Support Services, 2009–13). PPS to Shadow Sec. of State for NI, 2013–15. *Recreations:* walking, spending time with friends and family, travelling, foreign languages, reading. *Address:* House of Commons, SW1A 0AA. *T:* (020) 7219 4468, *Fax:* (020) 7219 0264; (office) Ede House, 143 Westoe Road, South Shields, Tyne and Wear NE33 3PD. *T:* (0191) 427 1240, *Fax:* (0191) 427 6418. *E:* emma.lewell-buck.mp@parliament.uk.

**LEWIS, Brandon;** MP (C) Great Yarmouth, since 2010; Minister of State, Department for Communities and Local Government, since 2014; *b* 20 June 1971; *m* 1999, Justine Yolande Rappolt; one *s* one *d*. *Educ:* Forest Sch.; Univ. of Buckingham (BSc Hons Econs; LLB); King's Coll. London (LLM Commercial Law). Called to the Bar, Inner Temple. Dir, Woodlands Schs Ltd, 2001–12. Mem. (C) Brentwood BC, 1998–2009 (Leader, 2004–09). Parly Under-Sec. of State, DCLG, 2012–14. Mem. Council, Univ. of Buckingham, 2014–. *Recreations:* running, cycling, cinema, triathlon. *Address:* House of Commons, SW1A 0AA. *T:* (020) 7219 7231, *Fax:* (020) 7219 6558. *E:* brandon.lewis.mp@parliament.uk. *Club:* Carlton.

**LEWIS, Clive Anthony;** MP (Lab) Norwich South, since 2015; *b* London, 11 Sept. 1971. *Educ:* Univ. of Bradford (Econs). Pres., Univ. of Bradford Students' Union; Vice Pres., NUS. News reporter, BBC TV, incl. Chief Political Reporter, Eastern Reg.; technician, BBC. Served TA (Infantry Officer) (in Afghanistan, 2009). Mem., Public Accounts Select Cttee, 2015–. *Address:* House of Commons, SW1A 0AA.

**LEWIS, Ivan;** MP (Lab) Bury South, since 1997; *b* 4 March 1967; *s* of Joel and Gloria Lewis; *m* 1990, Juliette (marr. diss.), *d* of Leslie and Joyce Fox; two *s*. *Educ:* William Hulme's

Grammar Sch.; Stand Coll.; Bury Coll. of FE. Co-ordinator, Contact Community Care Gp, 1986–89; Jewish Social Services: Community Worker, 1989–91; Community Care Manager, 1991–92; Chief Exec., 1992–97. Mem., Bury MBC, 1990–98. PPS to Sec. of State for Trade and Industry, 1999–2001; Parly Under-Sec. of State, DfES, 2001–05; Econ. Sec., HM Treasury, 2005–06; Parliamentary Under-Secretary of State: for Care Services, DoH, 2006–08; DFID, 2008–09; Minister of State, FCO, 2009–10; Shadow Sec. of State for Culture, Media and Sport, 2010–11, for Internat. Develt, 2011–13, for NI, 2013–15. Member: H of C Deregulation Select Cttee, 1997–99; Health Select Cttee, 1999; Sec., All Party Parly Gp on Parenting, 1998–2001; Dep. Chm., Labour Friends of Israel, 1997–2001; Vice Chm., Inter-Parly Council Against Anti-Semitism, 1998–2001. Trustee, Holocaust Educnl Trust. *Recreation:* supporter of Manchester City FC. *Address:* House of Commons, SW1A 0AA; 381 Bury New Road, Prestwich, Manchester M25 1AW. *T:* (0161) 773 5500. *E:* ivanlewis@burysouth.fsnet.co.uk. *W:* www.ivanlewis.org.uk.

**LEWIS, Rt Hon. Dr Julian Murray;** PC 2015; MP (C) New Forest East, since 1997; *b* 26 Sept. 1951; *s* of late Samuel Lewis, tailor and designer, and Hilda Lewis. *Educ:* Dynevor Grammar Sch., Swansea; Balliol Coll., Oxford (MA 1977); St Antony's Coll., Oxford (DPhil 1981). Sec., Oxford Union, 1972. Seaman, RNR, 1979–82. Res. in defence studies, 1975–77, 1978–81; Sec., Campaign for Representative Democracy, 1977–78; Res. Dir and Dir, Coalition for Peace Through Security, 1981–85; Dir, Policy Res. Associates, 1985–; Dep. Dir, Cons. Res. Dept, 1990–96. Contested (C) Swansea W, 1983. Opposition Whip, 2001–02; Shadow Defence Minister, 2002–04, 2005–10; Shadow Minister for the Cabinet Office, 2004–05. Member: Select Cttee on Welsh Affairs, 1998–2001; Select Cttee on Defence, 2000–01 and 2015– (Chm., 2015–); Exec., 1922 Cttee, 2001; Intelligence and Security Cttee, 2010–15; Sec., Cons. Parly Defence Cttee, 1997–2001; Vice-Chairman: Cons. Parly Foreign Affairs Cttee, 2000–01; Cons. Parly European Affairs Cttee, 2000–01. Parly Chm., First Defence, 2004–09. Mem., Armed Forces Parly Scheme (RAF), 1998, 2000, (RN), 2004, (RCDS), 2006, (Jt Services), 2008. Vis. Sen. Res. Fellow, Centre for Defence Studies, Dept of War Studies, KCL, 2010–. Trustee, 1998–2001, Vice-Pres., 2001–07, Pres., 2007–09, British Military Powerboat Trust. Trench Gascoigne Essay Prize, RUSI, 2005 and 2007; Dissertation Prize, RCDS, 2006. *Publications:* Changing Direction: British military planning for post-war strategic defence 1942–47, 1988, 2nd edn 2003; Who's Left?: an index of Labour MPs and left-wing causes 1985–1992, 1992; Labour's CND Cover-up, 1992; Racing Ace: the fights and flights of 'Kink' Kinkead,

DSO, DSC★, DFC★, 2011; political pamphlets. *Recreations:* history, fiction, films, music, photography. *Address:* House of Commons, SW1A 0AA. *T:* (020) 7219 4179. *Clubs:* Athenæum; Totton Conservative.

**LIDDELL-GRAINGER, Ian Richard Peregrine;** MP (C) Bridgwater and West Somerset, since 2010 (Bridgwater, 2001–10); *b* 23 Feb. 1959; *s* of late David Ian Liddell-Grainger of Ayton and of Anne Mary Sibylla Liddell-Grainger *(née* Smith); *m* Jill Nesbit; one *s* two *d*. *Educ:* Wellesley House Sch., Kent; Millfield Sch., Somerset; S of Scotland Agricl Coll., Edinburgh (NCA). Farmer, Berwicks, 1980–85; Man. Dir, property mgt and develt co., 1985–. Mem., Tynedale DC, 1989–95. Contested (C) Torridge and Devon West, 1997. Major, Queen's Div., TA (formerly with 6th (Vol.) Bn), RRF. *Address:* (office) 16 Northgate, Bridgwater, Somerset TA6 3EU; c/o House of Commons, SW1A 0AA.

**LIDINGTON, Rt Hon. David (Roy),** PhD; PC 2010; MP (C) Aylesbury, since 1992; Minister of State, Foreign and Commonwealth Office, since 2010; *b* 30 June 1956; *s* of Roy N. and Rosa Lidington; *m* 1989, Helen Mary Farquhar Parry; four *s* (incl. twins). *Educ:* Haberdashers' Aske's Sch., Elstree; Sidney Sussex Coll., Cambridge (MA, PhD). British Petroleum plc, 1983–86; RTZ plc, 1986–87; Special Adviser to: Home Sec., 1987–89; Foreign Sec., 1989–90; Consultant, PPU Ltd, 1991–92. PPS to Leader of the Opposition, 1997–99; Opposition front-bench spokesman on: home affairs, 1999–2001; HM Treasury affairs, 2001–02; environment, food and rural affairs, 2002–03; NI, 2003–07; foreign affairs, 2007–10. *Publications:* articles on Tudor history. *Recreations:* history, choral singing. *Address:* House of Commons, SW1A 0AA. *T:* (020) 7219 3000; 100 Walton Street, Aylesbury, Bucks HP21 7QP. *T:* (01296) 482102.

**LILLEY, Rt Hon. Peter Bruce;** PC 1990; MP (C) Hitchin and Harpenden, since 1997 (St Albans, 1983–97); *b* 23 Aug. 1943; *s* of Arnold Francis Lilley and Lilian *(née* Elliott); *m* 1979, Gail Ansell. *Educ:* Dulwich Coll.; Clare Coll., Cambridge. MA; FInstPet 1978. Economic consultant in underdeveloped countries, 1966–72; investment advisor on energy industries, 1972–84. Chm., London Oil Analysts Gp, 1979–80; Partner, 1980–86, Dir, 1986–87, W. Greenwell & Co., later Greenwell Montagu. Consultant Dir, Cons. Res. Dept, 1979–83. Chm., Bow Group, 1972–75. Contested (C) Tottenham, Oct. 1974. PPS to Ministers for Local Govt, Jan.–Oct. 1984, to Chancellor of the Exchequer, 1984–87; Economic Sec. to HM Treasury, 1987–89, Financial Sec., 1989–90; Secretary of State: for Trade and Industry, 1990–92; for Social Security, 1992–97; front bench Opposition spokesman on HM Treasury, 1997–98. Co-Chair, All Party Parly Gp, Trade Out of Poverty, 2010–; Chair, Jt Cttee of Financial Services Bill, 2011–12; Member:

Energy and Climate Change Select Cttee, 2012–15; Envmtl Audit Cttee, 2015–. Dep. Leader, Cons. Party, 1998–99. *Publications:* (with S. Brittan) Delusion of Incomes Policy, 1977; (contrib.) Skidelsky: End of the Keynesian Era, 1980; various pamphlets. *Address:* House of Commons, SW1A 0AA. *T:* (020) 7219 3000. *Clubs:* Carlton, Beefsteak.

**LONG BAILEY, Rebecca;** MP (Lab) Salford and Eccles, since 2015; *b* 22 Sept. 1979; *m*; one *c. Educ:* Catholic High Sch., Chester; Manchester Metropolitan Univ. (BA Politics and Sociol.). Landlord and Tenant Solicitor, Halliwells, 2003–07; Solicitor (Healthcare), Hill Dickinson LLP, 2007–. *Address:* House of Commons, SW1A 0AA.

**LOPRESTI, Jack;** MP (C) Filton and Bradley Stoke, since 2010; *b* Bristol, 23 Aug. 1969; *s* of Domenico and Grace Lopresti; *m* 1992, Lucinda Catherine Lovell Cope; two *s* one *d. Educ:* Brislington Comprehensive Sch. Worked for family catering and ice cream business, 1985–97; consultant and manager, financial services and residential property, 1997–2007. Mem. (C) Bristol CC, 1999–2007. Contested: (C) Bristol E, 2001; SW, Eur. Parlt, 2004. Territorial Army, 2006–12: gunner, 266 Battery, RA (Glos Vol. Artillery); served with 29 Commando RA in Afghanistan. Mem., RUSI. Member: Gen. George Patton Histl Soc.; Internat. Churchill Centre. *Recreations:* running, hill-walking, military and political history. *Address:* House of Commons, SW1A 0AA. *T:* (020) 7219 7070. *E:* jack.lopresti.mp@parliament.uk. *Club:* Military and Naval.

**LORD, Jonathan George Caladine;** MP (C) Woking, since 2010; *b* Oldham, 17 Sept. 1962; *s* of His Honour John Herent Lord and of (June) Ann Lord (*née* Caladine); *m* 2000, Caroline Commander; one *s* one *d. Educ:* Shrewsbury Sch.; Kent Sch., Connecticut (Schol.); Merton Coll., Oxford (BA Hist. 1985). Dir, Saatchi & Saatchi, 1998–2000; campaign manager, Anne Milton, MP, gen. election, 2005. Member (C): Westminster CC, 1994–2002 (Dep. Leader, 1998–2000); Surrey CC, 2009–11. Contested (C) Oldham W and Royton, 1997. Chm., Guildford Cons. Assoc., 2006–10; Dep. Chm., Surrey Area Conservatives, 2007–09. *Recreations:* cricket, theatre, walking in the Surrey Hills. *Address:* House of Commons, SW1A 0AA. *T:* (020) 7219 6913. *E:* jonathan.lord.mp@parliament.uk.

**LOUGHTON, Timothy Paul;** MP (C) East Worthing and Shoreham, since 1997; *b* 30 May 1962; *s* of Rev. Michael Loughton and Pamela Dorothy Loughton (*née* Brandon); *m* 1992, Elizabeth Juliet MacLauchlan; one *s* two *d. Educ:* Priory Sch., Lewes; Univ. of Warwick (BA 1st cl. Hons); Clare Coll., Cambridge. Joined Montagu Loebl Stanley, then Fleming Private Asset Mgt, 1984, Dir 1992–2000. Formerly: Member: Wandsworth CHC; Substance Misuse Cttee,

Wandsworth HA; Battersea Sector Policing Gp; Vice-Chm., Wandsworth Alcohol Gp. Joined Conservative Party, 1977; various posts in local assocs in Lewes, Warwick Univ., Cambridge Univ. and Battersea, 1978–91; Dep. Chm., Battersea Cons. Assoc., 1994–96. Contested (C) Sheffield Brightside, 1992. Opposition spokesman: for envmt, transport and the regions, 2000–01; for health, 2001–07; for children, 2003–10; Parly Under-Sec. of State for Children and Families, DFE, 2010–12. Member: Finance Bill Standing Cttee, 1997–98; Envmtl Audit Select Cttee, 1997–2001; Jt House Cttee on Financial Services and Markets Bill, 1999; Home Affairs Select Cttee, 2014–15; Treasurer: Parly Maritime Gp, 1997–2008; Parly Animal Welfare Gp, 2001–07; Parly Archaeology Gp, 2002–10; Vice Chairman: All Party Autism Gp; All Party Cardiac Risk in the Young Gp, 2005–09; Parly Gp for Children, 2005–10, 2014–; All Party Parly Child Protection Gp, 2013–; Chairman: All Party Gp for Wholesale Financial Mkts, 2005–10; Cons. Disability Gp, 1998–2006; All Party Parliamentary Group: on British Mus.; on 1001 Critical Days; on Wine and Spirits; Jt Chm., Parly Mental Health Gp, 2005–10; Mem., Exec. Cttee, Inter Parly Union (UK), 2006–10 and 2013–. Captain, Commons and Lords Hockey Team, 2003–. Member: Sussex Archaeol Soc.; BM Soc. *Recreations:* archaeology, classics, wine, ski-ing, tennis, hockey. *Address:* House of Commons, SW1A 0AA.

**LUCAS, Dr Caroline;** MP (Green) Brighton Pavilion, since 2010; *b* 9 Dec. 1960; *d* of Peter and Valerie Lucas; *m* 1991, Richard Le Quesne Savage; two *s. Educ:* Exeter Univ. (BA English Lit. 1983; PhD 1989). Oxfam: Press Officer, 1989–91; Communications Officer for Asia, 1991–93; Policy Adviser on trade and envmt, 1993–97; on secondment to Trade Team, DFID, 1997–98; Team Leader, Trade and Investment Policy Team, 1998–99. Mem., Oxford CC, 1993–97. European Parliament: Mem. (Green) SE Region, England, 1999–2010; Mem., Cttee on Internat. Trade, 1999–2010, on Transport and Tourism, 1999–2004, on Envmt, Public Health and Food Safety, 2004–10; Mem., Palestine Delegn, 1999–2010. Green Party: Mem., 1986–; Nat. Press Officer, 1987–89; Co-Chair, 1989–90; Leader, 2008–12. *Publications:* (as Caroline Le Quesne) Writing for Women, 1989; Reforming World Trade: the social and environmental priorities, 1996; (as Caroline Lucas): (with Mike Woodin) Green Alternatives to Globalisation, 2004; Honourable Friends?: Parliament and the fight for change, 2015. *Recreations:* gardening, walking, piano playing. *Address:* House of Commons, SW1A 0AA.

**LUCAS, Ian Colin;** MP (Lab) Wrexham, since 2001; *b* 18 Sept. 1960; *s* of Colin and Alice Lucas; *m* 1986, Norah Anne (*née* Sudd); one *s* one *d. Educ:* New Coll., Oxford (BA Jurisprudence). Articled Clerk, then Solicitor, Russell-Cooke, Potter and Chapman Solicitors, Putney and

Kingston, 1983–85; Solicitor: Percy, Hughes and Roberts, Chester, 1985–86; Lees, Moore and Price, Birkenhead, 1986–87; Kirwan Nicholas Jones, then Roberts Moore Nicholas Jones, Birkenhead and Wrexham, 1987–92; D. R. Crawford, Oswestry, 1992–97; Sole Principal, Crawford Lucas, Oswestry, 1997–2000; Partner, Stevens Lucas, Oswestry and Chirk, 2001. Contested (Lab) N Shropshire, 1997. An Asst Govt Whip, 2008–09; Parly Under-Sec. of State, BIS, 2009–10; Shadow Minister: BIS, 2010–11; FCO, 2011–14; Defence, 2014–15. Non-exec. Dir, Robert Jones and Agnes Hunt Hosp., Gobowen, Shropshire, 1997–2001. *Recreations:* history, sport, art. *Address:* (office) Vernon House, 41 Rhosddu Road, Wrexham LL11 2NS. *T:* (01978) 355743.

**LUMLEY, Karen Elizabeth;** MP (C) Redditch, since 2010; *b* 28 March 1964; *d* of Derek and Sylvia Allott; *m* 1984, Richard Gareth Lumley; one *s* one *d*. *Educ:* Rugby High Sch. for Girls; E Warwicks Coll., Rugby. Trainee accountant, Ford Motor Co., 1982–84; Co. Sec., RKL Geological Services Ltd, 1985–. Member (C): Wrexham BC (Gp Leader, 1991–96); Clwyd CC, 1993–96; Redditch BC, 2001–03. Contested (C) Delyn, 1997; Redditch, 2001, 2005. *Recreations:* knitting, cooking, reading. *Address:* House of Commons, SW1A 0AA. *T:* (020) 7219 7133. *E:* karen.lumley.mp@parliament.uk.

**LYNCH, Holly Jamie;** MP (Lab) Halifax, since 2015; *b* Northowram, 8 Oct. 1986; *m* 2014, Chris Walker. *Educ:* Brighouse High Sch.; Lancaster Univ. With Matrix Technol. Solutions; Communications Officer for Linda McAvan, MEP. Co-Chair, All Party Parly Gp on Population, Develt and Reproductive Health, 2015–; Mem., Envmtl Audit Cttee, 2015–. *Address:* House of Commons, SW1A 0AA.

**McCABE, Stephen James;** MP (Lab) Birmingham Selly Oak, since 2010 (Birmingham, Hall Green, 1997–2010); *b* 4 Aug. 1955; *s* of late James and Margaret McCabe; *m* 1991; one *s* one *d*. *Educ:* Univ. of Bradford (MA); Moray House Coll., Edinburgh (Dip. and CQSW). Social worker, Generic Team, 1977–79, Intermediate Treatment Worker, 1979–83, Wolverhampton; Manager, The Priory, Newbury, 1983–85; Lectr in Social Services, NE Worcs Coll., 1986–89; social policy researcher, BASW, and part-time child care worker, Solihull, 1989–91; Educn Advr, CCETSW, 1991–97. An Asst Govt Whip, 2006–07; a Lord Comr, HM Treasury (Govt Whip), 2007–10. *Recreations:* cooking, hill-walking, reading, football. *Address:* House of Commons, SW1A 0AA. *T:* (020) 7219 3509.

**McCAIG, Callum;** MP (SNP) Aberdeen South, since 2015; *b* 6 Jan. 1985. *Educ:* Cults Acad.; Edinburgh Univ. (MA Politics). Parly Asst to Maureen Watt, MSP, 2006. Mem. (SNP)

Aberdeen CC, 2007–15 (Leader of Council, 2011–12; Leader, SNP Gp, 2011–15). *Address:* House of Commons, SW1A 0AA.

**McCARTHY, Kerry;** MP (Lab) Bristol East, since 2005; *b* 26 March 1965; *d* of late Oliver Thomas Haughney and of Sheila Ann Rix (*née* Smith); name changed to McCarthy, 1992. *Educ:* Univ. of Liverpool (BA Hons Russian, Politics and Linguistics); City of London Poly. Legal Asst, S Beds Magistrates' Court, 1986–88; Litigation Asst, Neves (Solicitors), 1988–89; trainee, Wilde Sapte, 1992–94; admitted solicitor, 1994; Lawyer, Abbey National Treasury Services plc, 1994–96; Sen. Counsel, Merrill Lynch Europe plc, 1996–99; Lawyer, Labour Party, 2001; Regl Dir, Britain in Europe, 2002–04; Hd, Public Policy, Waterfront Partnership, 2004–05. Dir, London Luton Airport Ltd, 1999–2003. PPS to Minister of State, Dept of Health, 2007, to Sec. of State for Internat. Develt, 2007–09; an Asst Govt Whip, 2009–10; Shadow Minister for Work and Pensions, 2010; Shadow Econ. Sec. to HM Treasury, 2010–11; Shadow Foreign Office Minister, 2011–15; Shadow Sec. of State for Envmt, Food and Rural Affairs, 2015–. Mem., Treasury Select Cttee, 2005–07. Mem. (Lab) Luton BC, 1995–96 and 1999–2003. *Recreations:* travel, scuba-diving, music. *Address:* House of Commons, SW1A 0AA. *T:* (020) 7219 4510. *E:* mccarthyk@parliament.uk; (constituency) 326a Church Road, Bristol BS5 8AJ. *T:* (0117) 939 9901, *Fax:* (0117) 939 9902. *Club:* St George Labour (Bristol).

**McCARTNEY, Jason Alexander;** MP (C) Colne Valley, since 2010; *b* Harrogate, 29 Jan. 1968; *s* of Wing Comdr Robert McCartney and Jean McCartney; two *d*. *Educ:* Lancaster Royal Grammar Sch.; RAF Coll., Cranwell; Leeds Trinity University Coll. (Postgrad. Dip. Broadcast Journalism). Officer, RAF, 1988–97; journalist, Radio Cleveland and Leeds, BBC, 1997–98; journalist and presenter, ITV Yorkshire, 1998–2007; Sen. Lectr, Leeds Metropolitan Univ., 2008–10. Member: Transport Select Cttee, 2013–15; Culture, Media and Sport Cttee, 2015–; 1922 Exec. Cttee, 2013–. *Recreations:* Huddersfield Town AFC, Huddersfield Giants RLFC, Yorkshire CCC, tennis, eating Hinchcliffe's Pies. *Address:* Upperbridge House, 24 Huddersfield Road, Holmfirth HD9 2JS. *T:* (01484) 688364, 688378; House of Commons, SW1A 0AA. *E:* jason.mccartney.mp@parliament.uk. *Club:* Royal Air Force.

**McCARTNEY, Karl Ian;** JP; MP (C) Lincoln, since 2010; *b* St Catherine's, Birkenhead, 25 Oct. 1968; *s* of John McCartney and Brenda McCartney (*née* Weir); *m* 1999, Cordelia Pyne; two *s*. *Educ:* Woodfall Lane Prim. and Jun. Schs; Birkenhead Sch. for Boys; Neston High Sch.; Willink Sch.; St David's University Coll., Wales (BA Hons Geog. 1991; Pres., Student Union, 1991–92); Kingston Business Sch., Kingston Univ. (MBA 1998). Logistics Analyst, Hasbro,

1992–93; Agent and Researcher, Conservative Central Office, 1993–96; Corporate Affairs, Corp. of London, 1996–2001. Dir, MLSystems, mgt consultancy, 1999–. Campaign Dir, 2007–10, Dep. Chm., 2010–12, Sir Keith Park Meml Campaign. Member: Transport Select Cttee, 2012–; 1922 Exec. Cttee, 2012–. Contested (C) Lincoln, 2005. JP Dartford, later Maidstone, then Lincoln, 1999–. *Recreations:* myriad of sports—football, Rugby, cricket, croquet, snowboarding, shooting; classic cars, green laning, trains, gardens, architecture, history, dance music, relaxing with family and friends, cooking. *Address:* Lincoln Conservative Association, 1A Farrier Road, Lincoln LN6 3RU; House of Commons, SW1A 0AA. *T:* (020) 7219 7221. *E:* karl.mccartney.mp@parliament.uk.

**McDONAGH, Siobhain Ann;** MP (Lab) Mitcham and Morden, since 1997; *b* 20 Feb. 1960; *d* of Cumin McDonagh and Breda McDonagh (*née* Doogue). *Educ:* Holy Cross Convent; Essex Univ. (BA Hons 1981). Clerical Officer, DHSS, 1981–82; Wandsworth Council: Admin. Asst, 1982–83; Receptionist, Homeless Persons Unit, 1983–86; Housing Advr, Housing Aid Centre, 1986–88; Develt Co-ordinator, Battersea Churches Housing Trust, 1988–97. An Asst Govt Whip, 2007–08. Mem., South Mitcham Community Centre, 1988. *Recreations:* shopping, music, women's magazines. *Address:* 1 Crown Road, Morden SM4 5DD. *T:* (020) 8542 4835.

**McDONALD, Andrew Joseph;** MP (Lab) Middlesbrough, since Nov. 2012; *b* Middlesbrough, 8 March 1958; *m* 1987, Sally. *Educ:* Leeds Poly. (BA Hons). Admitted Solicitor, 1990. Wilson-McDonald Solicitors, 1990–94; McDonald Solicitors, 1994–99; Thompson's Solicitors, 1999–2012. PPS to Shadow Attorney Gen., 2013, to Shadow Minister for Business, Innovation and Skills, 2013–15. Mem. (Lab) Middlesbrough Council, 1995–99. Governor: Abingdon Primary Sch., Middlesbrough, 1995–2010; Middlesbrough Coll., 2012–. *Address:* House of Commons, SW1A 0AA; (office) Unit 4 Broadcasting House, Newport Road, Middlesbrough TS1 5JA.

**McDONALD, Stewart Malcolm;** MP (SNP) Glasgow South, since 2015; *b* Glasgow, 24 Aug. 1986. *Educ:* Govan High Sch. Tour guide, Canary Is; work on campaigns and res. for MSPs. Mem., Transport Select Cttee, 2015–. *Address:* House of Commons, SW1A 0AA.

**McDONALD, Stuart Campbell;** MP (SNP) Cumbernauld, Kilsyth and Kirkintilloch East, since 2015; *b* Glasgow, 2 May 1978. *Educ:* Kilsyth Acad.; Univ. of Edinburgh (LLB Hons; DipLP 2001). Legal trainee, Simpson and Marwick, Solicitors, 2001–03; Solicitor, NHS Central Legal Office, 2003–05; Human Rights Solicitor, Immigration Adv. Service, 2005–09; Researcher, then Sen. Researcher, Scottish Parlt, 2009–13;

Sen. Researcher and Hd of Information, Yes Scotland HQ, 2013–14; work for anti-racism charity, 2014–15. SNP spokesperson on immigration, asylum and border control, 2015–. Mem., Home Affairs Select Cttee, 2015–. *Address:* House of Commons, SW1A 0AA.

**McDONNELL, Dr Alasdair;** MP (SDLP) Belfast South, since 2005; Leader, Social Democratic and Labour Party, since 2011; general medical practitioner, since 1979; *b* Cushendall, Co. Antrim, 1 Sept. 1949; *s* of Charles McDonnell and Margaret (*née* McIlhatton); *m* 1998, Olivia Nugent; two *s* two *d*. *Educ:* St MacNissi's Coll.; Garron Tower; University Coll., Dublin Med. Sch. (MB, BCh, BAO 1974). Jun. hosp. med. posts, 1975–79. Mem. (SDLP) Belfast CC, 1977–2001; Dep. Mayor, Belfast, 1995–96. Mem. (SDLP) Belfast S, Northern Ireland Assembly, 1998–June 2015. Contested (SDLP) Belfast South, 1979, 1982, 1983, 1987, 1992, 1997, 2001. Dep. Leader, SDLP, 2004–10. *Address:* House of Commons, SW1A 0AA; 22 Derryvolgie Avenue, Belfast BT9 6FN.

**McDONNELL, John Martin;** MP (Lab) Hayes and Harlington, since 1997; *b* 8 Sept. 1951; *s* of Robert and Elsie McDonnell; *m* 1st, 1971, Marilyn Jean Cooper (marr. diss. 1987); two *d*; 2nd, 1995, Cynthia Marie Pinto; one *s*. *Educ:* Great Yarmouth Grammar Sch.; Burnley Technical Coll.; Brunel Univ. (BSc); Birkbeck Coll., Univ. of London (MSc Politics and Sociology). Prodn worker, 1968–72; Research Assistant: NUM, 1976–78; TUC, 1978–82; full-time GLC Councillor, Hillingdon, Hayes and Harlington, 1982–86; Dep. Leader, GLC, 1984–85; Chm., GLC F and GP Cttee, 1982–85; Prin. Policy Advr, Camden Bor. Council, 1985–87; Secretary: Assoc. of London Authorities, 1987–95; Assoc. of London Govt, 1995–97. Editor, Labour Herald, 1985–88. Member: Gtr London Lab. Party Regl Exec. Cttee, 1982–87; for Gtr London, Lab. Party Nat. Policy Forum, 1993–; Chairman: Lab. Party Irish Soc.; Labour Repn Cttee. Advr, Guildford Four Relatives Campaign, 1984–; Chair, Britain and Ireland Human Rights Centre, 1992–; Founding Mem., Friends of Ireland, 1998–. Contested (Lab): Hampstead and Highgate, 1983; Hayes and Harlington, 1992. Shadow Chancellor of Exchequer, 2015–. Secretary: All Pty Britain-Kenya Gp of MPs, 1997–; All Pty Kurdish Gp, 1997–; All Pty Irish in Britain Parly Gp, 1999–; All Pty Gp on Endometriosis; Chair, All Party Punjabi Community in Britain Gp of MPs, 1999–; Secretary: Fire Brigades Union Parly Gp; Justice Unions Parly Gp; NUJ Parly Gp; PCS Trade Union Gp; Chair: Socialist Campaign Gp of MPs, 1998–; PCS Parly Gp; Labour Repn Cttee; Left Economists Adv. Panel; Co-ordinator, RMT Parly Gp. Housefather (pt-time) of family unit, children's home, 1972–87. Chairman: Hayes and Harlington Community Develt Forum, 1997–; Barra Hall Regeneration Cttee; Friends of Lake Farm; Friends of Minet Country Park;

Mem., Hayes Horticultural Show Assoc.; Hon. Vice Pres., Hayes FC; Patron, Hayes CC. *Publications:* articles and pamphlets incl. contribs to Labour Herald, Briefing, Tribune, Campaign News. *Recreations:* gardening, reading, cycling, music, theatre, cinema, Wayfarer dinghy sailing, supporting Liverpool, Hayes and Yeading Football Clubs, football refereeing; generally fermenting the overthrow of capitalism. *Address:* House of Commons, SW1A 0AA; Beverley, Cedar Avenue, Hayes, Middx UB3 2NE. *Clubs:* London Irish, Blues West 14; Hillingdon Irish Society; St Claret's, Working Men's (Hayes); Hayes and Harlington Community Centre.

**McFADDEN, Rt Hon. Patrick;** PC 2008; MP (Lab) Wolverhampton South East, since 2005; *b* 26 March 1965; *s* of James and Annie McFadden; *m* Marianna; one *s* one *d. Educ:* Holyrood Sec. Sch., Glasgow; Univ. of Edinburgh (MA Hons Pols 1988). Res. Asst to Rt Hon. Donald Dewar, MP, 1988–93; Advr to Rt Hon. John Smith, MP, 1993–94; Policy Advr to Rt Hon. Tony Blair, MP, 1994–2001; Political Sec. to the Prime Minister, 2002–05. Parly Sec. (Minister for Social Exclusion), Cabinet Office, 2006–07; Minister of State, BERR, later BIS, 2007–10; Shadow Sec. of State for Business, 2010; Shadow Minister of State for Europe, 2014–15. *Recreations:* sport, reading. *Address:* House of Commons, SW1A 0AA. *T:* (020) 7219 4036, *Fax:* (020) 7219 5665.

**McGARRY, Natalie;** MP (SNP) Glasgow East, since 2015; *b* Fife, 7 Sept. 1981; partner, David Meikle. *Educ:* Univ. of Aberdeen (law degree). Policy advr in voluntary sector. Columnist: Scotsman, Herald. SNP spokesperson on disabilities, 2015–. *Address:* House of Commons, SW1A 0AA.

**McGINN, Conor Patrick;** MP (Lab) St Helens North, since 2015; *b* Co. Armagh, 31 July 1984; *m*; one *s.* Worked in charity sector and managed health projects; Pol Advr to Labour defence team. Mem., Defence Select Cttee, 2015–. *Address:* House of Commons, SW1A 0AA. *Club:* Windle Labour.

**McGOVERN, Alison;** MP (Lab) Wirral South, since 2010; *b* 30 Dec. 1980; *d* of Mike and Ann McGovern; *m* 2008, Ashwin Kumar; one *d. Educ:* Wirral Grammar Sch. for Girls; University Coll. London (BA Philosophy). Researcher, H of C, 2002–06; Public Affairs Manager: Network Rail, 2006–08; Art Fund, 2008–09; Creativity, Culture and Educn, 2009. Mem. (Lab) Southwark LBC, 2006–10. PPS to Rt Hon. Gordon Brown, MP, 2010. *Address:* House of Commons, SW1A 0AA.

**McINNES, Elizabeth Anne;** MP (Lab) Heywood and Middleton, since Oct. 2014; *b* Oldham, Lancs, 30 March 1959; *d* of George Frederick McInnes and Margaret Elizabeth McInnes; partner, Stephen John Duxbury; one *s. Educ:* Hathershaw Comp. Sch., Oldham; St Anne's Coll., Oxford (BA Hons Biochem. 1981);

Surrey Univ. (MSc Clin. Biochem. 1983). Trainee Clin. Scientist, Greenwich District Hosp., 1981–83; Basic Grade Biochemist, Royal Hallamshire Hosp., Sheffield, 1983–87; Sen. Clin. Scientist, Pennine Acute Hosps NHS Trust, 1987–2014. Chair, Nat. Health Sector Cttee, Unite, 2013–14. Mem., Rossendale BC, 2010–14. *Recreations:* hill-walking, camping, art, music. *Address:* House of Commons, SW1A 0AA. *T:* (020) 7219 0684. *E:* mcinnesl@parliament.uk.

**MACKESON-SANDBACH, Antoinette, (Mrs M. R. Sherratt);** MP (C) Eddisbury, since 2015; *b* London, 15 Feb. 1969; *d* of Ian and Annie Mackeson-Sandbach; one *d* (one *s* decd); *m* 2012, Matthew Robin Sherratt. *Educ:* West Heath; Haileybury Coll.; Nottingham Univ. (BA Hons Law; LLM Internat. Law). Called to the Bar, Lincoln's Inn, 1993; in practice as barrister, 9 Bedford Row, 1995–2006; farmer, 2006–11. Mem. (C) Wales N, Nat. Assembly for Wales, 2011–15; Shadow Minister: for Rural Affairs, 2011–14; for Envmt and Energy, 2014–15. *Address:* House of Commons, SW1A 0AA. *T:* (020) 7219 3000. *E:* antoinette.sandbach.mp@parliament.uk.

**MACKINLAY, Craig;** JP; MP (C) South Thanet, since 2015; *b* Chatham, 7 Oct. 1966; *s* of Colin Francis Mackinlay and Margaret Elizabeth Mackinlay; *m* 2011, Katalin Madi. *Educ:* Rainham Mark Grammar Sch., Rainham; Univ. of Birmingham (BSc Hons Zool. and Comparative Physiol.). FCA 1992; CTA 1993. Self-employed Partner, Beak Kemmenoe, Chatham. Mem. (C), Medway Council, 2007–15. JP N Kent. *Recreations:* sailing, shooting, travel. *Address:* House of Commons, SW1A 0AA. *T:* (020) 7219 4442. *E:* craig@craigmackinlay.com. *Clubs:* Carlton; Castle (Rochester).

**McKINNELL, Catherine;** MP (Lab) Newcastle upon Tyne North, since 2010; *b* Newcastle upon Tyne, 8 June 1976; *d* of John Grady and Agnes Grady (*née* Miller); *m* 2006, James Rhys McKinnell; one *s* one *d. Educ:* Sacred Heart Comprehensive Sch., Fenham, Newcastle upon Tyne; Univ. of Edinburgh (MA Hons Politics and Hist.); Univ. of Northumbria (Postgrad. DipLaw, CPE and Legal Practise Course). Admitted Solicitor 2004; Dickinson Dees LLP, 2002–09. Shadow Solicitor Gen., 2010–11; Shadow Minister for Children, 2011–15; Shadow Attorney Gen., 2015–. Member: Northumbria Assoc.; Unite the Union. Mem., Tyneside Cinema. *Recreations:* swimming, gardening, travel. *Address:* House of Commons, SW1A 0AA. *T:* (020) 7219 7115. *Club:* Tyneside Irish Centre.

**MACKINTOSH, David James;** MP (C) Northampton South, since 2015; *b* Northampton, 2 April 1979; *s* of James Mackintosh and Dolores Mackintosh. *Educ:* Roade Sch., Northants; Univ. of Durham. Member (C): Northamptonshire CC, 2009–; Northampton

BC, 2011–15 (Leader, 2011–15). *Address:* House of Commons, SW1A 0AA. *T:* (020) 7219 5756. *E:* david.mackintosh.mp@parliament.uk.

**McLAUGHLIN, (Elizabeth) Anne;** MP (SNP) Glasgow North East, since 2015; *b* Greenock, 8 March 1966; *d* of John Robert McLaughlin and Elizabeth Fulton McLaughlin (*née* Purdie). *Educ:* Port Glasgow High Sch.; Royal Scottish Acad. of Music and Drama and Univ. of Glasgow (BA Dramatic Studies 1987). Anniversary Co-ordinator, Sense Scotland, 1994–96; Scottish Fundraising Manager, ICRF, 1996–2000; Staff Fundraiser, ScottishPower, 2000–01; Man. Dir, Business for Scotland, 2001–06; Internal Communications Exec., SNP HQ, 2002–06; Political Advr to Aileen Campbell, MSP, 2007–08; Communications Manager, Community Business Technol. Developers, Galle, Sri Lanka, 2008; Campaign Co-ordinator, SNP, Glasgow E by-election, 2008; Political Advr to Robert Doris, MSP, 2008–09. MSP (SNP) Glasgow, Feb. 2009–2011; contested (SNP): Glasgow Provan, Scottish Parlt, 2011; Inverclyde, June 2011. *Publications:* (ed) Tall Tales, Short Stories, 1995. *Recreations:* blogging (http:indygalgoestoholyrood.blogspot.com), travel, languages, creative writing, photography. *Address:* House of Commons, SW1A 0AA.

**McLOUGHLIN, Rt Hon. Patrick (Allen);** PC 2005; MP (C) Derbyshire Dales, since 2010 (West Derbyshire, May 1986–2010); Secretary of State for Transport, since 2012; *b* 30 Nov. 1957; *s* of Patrick and Gladys Victoria McLoughlin; *m* 1984, Lynne Newman; one *s* one *d*. *Educ:* Cardinal Griffin Roman Catholic Sch., Cannock. Mineworker, Littleton Colliery, 1979–85; Marketing Official, NCB, 1985–86. PPS to Sec. of State for Trade and Industry, 1988–89; Parly Under-Sec. of State, Dept of Transport, 1989–92, Dept of Employment, 1992–93, DTI, 1993–94; an Asst Govt Whip, 1995–96; a Lord Comr of HM Treasury (Govt Whip), 1996–97; Opposition Pairing Whip, 1997–98; Dep. Opposition Chief Whip, 1998–2005; Opposition Chief Whip, 2005–10; Parly Sec. to HM Treasury (Govt Chief Whip), 2010–12. *Address:* House of Commons, SW1A 0AA.

**McNALLY, John;** MP (SNP) Falkirk, since 2015; *b* Denny, 1 Feb. 1951; *s* of John and Rose McNally; *m* 1980, Sandra Chalmers; one *s* one *d*. *Educ:* St Patrick's Primary Sch., Denny; St Modan's High Sch., Stirling. Hairdresser, 1965–; salon owner, 1970–. Mem. (SNP), Falkirk Council, 2005–15. *Recreations:* cycling, golf. *Address:* House of Commons, SW1A 0AA. *T:* (020) 7219 6525.

**MacNEIL, Angus Brendan;** MP (SNP) Na h-Eileanan An Iar, since 2005; *b* 21 July 1970; *m* 1998, Jane Douglas. *Educ:* Castlebay Secondary Sch., Isle of Barra; Nicolson Inst., Stornoway; Strathclyde Univ. (BEng 1992); Jordanhill Coll. (PGCE 1996). Civil Engr, Lilley Construction

Ltd, 1992–93; reporter, BBC Radio, Inverness, 1993–95; teacher, Salen Primary Sch., Mull, 1996–98; Gaelic Develt Officer, Lochaber, 1998–99; Lectr in Educn (part-time), Inverness Coll., 1999–2000; teacher, various schs incl. Lochaber and Fort William, 2000–03; teacher and crofter, Isle of Barra, 2003–05. Contested (SNP) Inverness E, Nairn and Lochaber, 2001. *Address:* (office) 31 Bayhead Street, Stornoway, Isle of Lewis, Outer Hebrides HS1 2DU; House of Commons, SW1A 0AA.

**McPARTLAND, Stephen;** MP (C) Stevenage, since 2010; *b* 9 Aug. 1976; *m* Emma. *Educ:* Liverpool Coll.; Liverpool Univ. (BA Hist. 1997); Liverpool John Moores Univ. (MSc Technol. Mgt 1998). Agent, NE Herts Cons. Assoc., 2001–08; Membership Dir, British Amer. Business, 2008–10. *Address:* House of Commons, SW1A 0AA.

**MACTAGGART, Rt Hon. Fiona;** PC 2015; MP (Lab) Slough, since 1997; *b* 12 Sept. 1953; *d* of Sir Ian Auld Mactaggart, 3rd Bt and Rosemary, *d* of Sir Herbert Williams, 1st Bt, MP. *Educ:* Cheltenham Ladies' Coll.; King's Coll., London (BA Hons); Inst. of Educn, London (MA). Gen. Sec., London Students' Organisation, 1977–78; Vice-Pres., 1978–80, Nat. Sec., 1980–81, NUS; Gen. Sec., Jt Council for Welfare of Immigrants, 1982–86. Mem. (Lab) Wandsworth BC, 1986–90 (Leader of the Opposition, 1988–90). Teacher, Lyndhurst Sch., Camberwell, 1988–92; Lectr, Inst. of Educn, 1992–97. PPS to Sec. of State for Culture, Media and Sport, 1997–2001; Parly Under-Sec. of State, Home Office, 2003–06. Member: Public Admin Cttee, 1997–98; Educn and Skills, then Children, Schs and Families Cttee, 2006–10; Jt Cttee on Human Rights, 2009–10; Health Cttee, 2010; Public Accounts Cttee, 2011–14; Intelligence and Security Cttee, 2014–. Chm., PLP Women's Cttee, 2001–03, 2008–10, 2011–. Chm., Liberty (NCCL), 1994–96. *Address:* House of Commons, SW1A 0AA.

**MADDERS, Justin;** MP (Lab) Ellesmere Port and Neston, since 2015; *b* Manchester, 22 Nov. 1972; *m* Nicole Meardon; three *s*. *Educ:* Univ. of Sheffield. Solicitor, 1998–2015. Member (Lab): Ellesmere Port and Neston BC, 1998–2009 (Leader, 2007–09); Cheshire W and Chester Council, 2009–15 (Leader of Opposition, 2011–14). *Address:* House of Commons, SW1A 0AA. *T:* (020) 7219 6584. *E:* justin.madders.mp@parliament.uk.

**MAHMOOD, Khalid;** MP (Lab) Birmingham Perry Barr, since 2001; *b* 13 July 1961. Formerly: engr, advr, Danish Internat. Trade Union. Mem., Birmingham CC, 1990–93. *Address:* c/o House of Commons, SW1A 0AA.

**MAHMOOD, Shabana;** MP (Lab) Birmingham Ladywood, since 2010; *b* Small Heath, Birmingham, 17 Sept. 1980; *d* of Mahmood Ahmed. *Educ:* Lincoln Coll., Oxford (LLB). Called to the Bar, Gray's Inn, 2004; employed as barrister, Berrymans Lace Mawer, 2004–07. Mem., Work and Pensions Select Cttee, 2010; Shadow Home Office Minister, 2010–11; Shadow Minister: for Higher Educn, BIS, 2011–13; for Univs and Sci., BIS, 2013; for the Treasury, 2013–15; Shadow Chief Sec. to the Treasury, 2015. *Address:* House of Commons, SW1A 0AA.

**MAIN, Anne;** MP (C) St Albans, since 2005; *b* 17 May 1957; *d* of late George and of Rita Wiseman; *m* 1st, 1978, Stephen Tonks (*d* 1991); one *s* two *d*; 2nd, 1995, Andrew Jonathan Main; one *s*. *Educ:* Bishop of Llandaff Secondary Sch., Cardiff; Univ. Coll. of Wales, Swansea (BA 1978); Univ. of Sheffield (PGCE 1978). Teacher of English and Drama, Feltham Comp. Sch., 1979–80; supply posts, Bristol, 1991–94. Member (C): Beaconsfield Parish Council, 1999–2002; S Bucks DC, 2001–05. *Address:* (office) 104 High Street, London Colney, St Albans, Herts AL2 1QL; House of Commons, SW1A 0AA.

**MAK, Alan;** MP (C) Havant, since 2015; *b* York, 19 Nov. 1983. *Educ:* St Peter's Sch., York; Peterhouse, Cambridge (BA Hons Law 2005); Oxford Inst. of Legal Practice (DipLP 2006). Parly researcher, Hon. Ed Vaizey, MP, 2006–07; Trainee Solicitor, 2007–09, Solicitor, 2009–14, Clifford Chance LLP; Founder, two small businesses, 2014. Chm., All Party Parly Gp for Entrepreneurship, 2015–. Trustee, Magic Breakfast, 2009–15 (Pres., 2011–15); Founder and Chm., Young Professionals' Br., RBL, 2011–15. FRSA 2008. *Recreations:* watching and playing sport, films, travel. *Address:* House of Commons, SW1A 0AA. *T:* (020) 7219 3000. *E:* alan.mak.mp@parliament.uk.

**MALHOTRA, Seema;** MP (Lab and Co-op) Feltham and Heston, since Dec. 2011; *b* Hammersmith, London, 7 Aug. 1972; *d* of late Sushil Kumar Malhotra and of Usha Malhotra; *m* 2005, Sushil Saluja. *Educ:* Green Sch., Isleworth; Univ. of Warwick (BA Hons Politics and Philosophy 1994); Univ. of Massachusetts (Schol.); Aston Univ. (MSc Business IT 1995). Mgt Consultant, Accenture, 1995–2003; Sen. Manager, PricewaterhouseCoopers, 2003–07; Advisor: to Minister for W Midlands, 2007–09; to Chair, Council of Regl Ministers, 2008–09; to video games industry on child safety agenda, 2008; Prog. Leader, cross-govt prog. to increase diversity in public appts, 2009–10; Pol Advr to Actg Leader of Opposition, 2010; Strategic Prog. Advr, UK Interactive Entertainment Assoc., 2011. Shadow Minister for Home Office, 2015; Shadow Chief Sec. to Treasury, 2015–. Mem., Justice Select Cttee, 2012–13. Chair, Young Fabians, 1999–2000; Fabian Society: Exec. Mem., 2000–; Chair, 2005–06; Founder and Dir, Fabian Women's Network, 2005–. Fellow, British American Project, 2007. FRSA. *Publications:* (contrib.) Dictionary of Labour Biography, 2001; (contrib.) From the Workhouse to Welfare, 2009.

*Recreations:* running, cinema, music, gardening, playing the guitar. *Address:* House of Commons, SW1A 0AA. *T:* (020) 7219 8957. *E:* seema. malhotra.mp@parliament.uk.

**MALTHOUSE, Christopher Laurie, (Kit);** MP (C) Hampshire North West, since 2015; Member (C) West Central, London Assembly, Greater London Authority, since 2008; *b* Liverpool, 27 Oct. 1966; *s* of John Christopher Malthouse and Susan Malthouse; *m* 2007, Juliana Farha; one *s* one *d*; one *s* by a previous marriage. *Educ:* Liverpool Coll.; Newcastle Univ. (BA Jt Hons Pols and Econs). Mem., ICAEW, 1997. Touche Ross & Co., 1992–97; Finance Officer, Cannock Gp, 1997–2001; Chm., County Hldgs, 2001–; Chief Exec., 2005–08; Finance Dir, 2008–, Alpha Strategic plc. Contested (C) Liverpool Wavertree, 1997. Mem., Westminster CC, 1998–2006 (Dep. Leader, 2001–05). Dep. Mayor of London, Policing, 2008–12, Business and Enterprise, 2012–15. Chairman: Hydrogen London, 2008–15; London & Partners, 2014–15; Vice Chair, London Enterprise Panel, 2012–15. *Publications:* (contrib.) A Blue Tomorrow, 2001. *Recreations:* baking bread and policies, writing poetry and prose, watching others dance and play, childcare. *Address:* Greater London Authority, City Hall, The Queen's Walk, SE1 2AA. *T:* (020) 7983 4099. *E:* kit.malthouse@london.gov.uk; House of Commons, SW1A 0AA.

**MANN, John;** MP (Lab) Bassetlaw, since 2001; *b* 10 Jan. 1960; *s* of James Mann and Brenda (*née* Cleavin); *m* 1986, Joanna White; one *s* two *d*. *Educ:* Manchester Univ. (BA Econ). MIPD. Hd of Res. and Educn, AEU, 1988–90; Nat. Trng Officer, TUC, 1990–95; Liaison Officer, Nat. Trade Union and Lab Party, 1995–2000. Dir, Abraxas Communications Ltd, 1998–2001. Mem. (Lab), Lambeth BC, 1986–90. Mem., Treasury Select Cttee, 2003–05, 2009–. Mem., Editl Adv. Panel, People Management, 2005–. *Publications:* (with Phil Woolas) Labour and Youth: the missing generation, 1985; The Real Deal: drug policy that works, 2006. *Recreations:* football, cricket, hill walking. *Address:* House of Commons, SW1A 0AA. *Clubs:* Manton Miners'; Worksop Town.

**MANN, Scott Leslie;** MP (C) North Cornwall, since 2015; *b* 24 June 1977; *s* of Eugene Mann and Peggy Mann; one *d*. *Educ:* Wadebridge Boys' Sch.; Wadebridge Comp. Sch.; St Austell Coll. (BTEC Business Diploma). Gardener, 1994–97; butcher, 1995–98; postman, 1995–2015; retail worker, 1997–2000. Mem., Cornwall Council, 2009–. Mem., Wadebridge Angling Assoc. *Recreations:* fishing, road cycling, running. *Address:* (office) 10 Market House Arcade, Bodmin Fore Street, Bodmin, Cornwall PL31 2JA. *T:* (01208) 74337. *E:* scott@scottmann.org.uk. *Clubs:* United and Cecil; Wadebridge Cricket (Hon. Vice Pres., 2013–).

**MARRIS, Robert;** MP (Lab) Wolverhampton South West, 2001–10 and since 2015; *b* 8 April 1955; *s* of Dr Charles Marris and Margaret Chetwode Marris, JP; partner, Julia Pursehouse. *Educ:* St Edward's Sch., Oxford; Univ. of British Columbia (BA Sociology and Hist. (double 1st) 1976; MA Hist. 1979). Trucker, 1977–79; trolley bus driver, 1979–82; law student, Birmingham Poly., 1982–84; articled clerk, 1985–87; solicitor, 1987. Regl Officer, Stafford, NUT, 2011–13. Contested (Lab) Wolverhampton SW, 2010. *Recreations:* Wolves, Canadiana, bicycling. *Address:* House of Commons, SW1A 0AA.

**MARSDEN, Gordon;** MP (Lab) Blackpool South, since 1997; *b* 28 Nov. 1953; *s* of late George Henry Marsden and Joyce Marsden. *Educ:* Stockport Grammar Sch.; New Coll., Oxford (BA 1st cl. Hons History; MA); Warburg Inst., London Univ. (postgrad. res.); Harvard Univ. (Kennedy Schol. in Internat. Relations). Tutor and Associate Lectr, Arts Faculty, Open Univ., 1977–97; PR Consultant, 1980–85; Chief Public Affairs Advr, English Heritage, 1984–85; Editor, History Today, 1985–97; Consultant Ed., New Socialist, 1989–90. Chm., Fabian Soc., 2000–01. Contested (Lab) Blackpool S, 1992. PPS, Lord Chancellor's Dept, 2001–03, to Sec. of State for Culture, Media and Sport, 2003–05; Shadow Minister for Skills and FE, 2010–13, for Transport, 2013–15. Mem., Select Cttee on Educn and Employment, 1998–2001, 2005–07, on Innovation, Univs and Skills, 2007–10. Vice-Pres., All Party Arts and Heritage Gp, 2000–; Chair: All Party Skills Gp, 2006–10; All Party Estonia Gp, 2008–; All Party Veterans Gp, 2010–; Co-Chair, All Party Osteoporosis Gp, 2011–; Vice-Pres., PLP Educn and Employment Cttee, 1998–2001; Mem., Ecclesiastical Cttee, 1998–2015. Pres., British Destinations (formerly British Resorts, later British Resorts and Destinations) Assoc., 1998–. Mem. Bd, Inst. of Historical Res., 1995–2001. Trustee, History Today, 2005–14. Vis. Parly Fellow, St Antony's Coll., Oxford, 2003; Centenary Fellow, Historical Assoc., 2006–07. *Publications:* (ed) Victorian Values: personalities and perspectives in Nineteenth Century society, 1990, 2nd edn 1998; (contrib.) The English Question, 2000; (contrib.) The History of Censorship, 2002; contrib. History Today, Independent, Times, Tribune, THES. *Recreations:* world music, travel, medieval culture. *Address:* House of Commons, SW1A 0AA. *T:* (020) 7219 1262.

**MASKELL, Rachael Helen;** MP (Lab) York Central, since 2015; *b* 5 July 1972. *Educ:* Univ. of E Anglia (BSc Physiotherapy 1994). Physiotherapist in hosps incl. Barnet Gen. Hosp.; Hd of Health, Unite, until 2015. Mem., Health Select Cttee, 2015–. *Address:* House of Commons, SW1A 0AA.

**MASKEY, Paul;** MP (SF) Belfast West, since June 2011; *b* Belfast, 10 June 1967; *s* of Alexander and Teresa Maskey; *m* Patricia; two *c. Educ:* Edmund Rice Coll. Co-ordinator, Fáilte Feirste Thiar; has worked as florist and glass cutter. Mem. (SF) Belfast CC, 2001–09 (Leader, SF Gp, until 2009). Mem. (SF) Belfast W, NI Assembly, 2007–July 2012. *Recreations:* football, walking. *Address:* Sinn Féin, 51–55 Falls Road, Belfast BT12 4PD. *T:* (028) 9034 7350, *Fax:* (028) 9034 7360. *E:* westbelfastmp@sinnfein.ie.

**MATHESON, Christian;** MP (Lab) City of Chester, since 2015; *b* Cheshire, 2 Jan. 1968; *m* Katherine; two *d. Educ:* London Sch. of Econs and Pol Sci. Formerly Manager in electricity industry; roles with Unite Union. Mem., Culture, Media and Sport Select Cttee, 2015–. *Address:* House of Commons, SW1A 0AA.

**MATHIAS, Tania Wyn;** MP (C) Twickenham, since 2015; *d* of Roger Wynn Mathias and Vivienne Desiree Mathias. *Educ:* St Paul's Girls' Sch.; St Catherine's Coll. and Christ Church, Oxford (MB BCh 1988). Refugee Affairs Officer and Health Officer, UNRWA, 1991–93. NHS medical doctor. Mem. (C) Richmond upon Thames LBC, 2010–15. *Recreations:* bird watching, documentary film making. *Address:* House of Commons, SW1A 0AA. *E:* drtania. mathias.mp@parliament.uk.

**MAUDE OF HORSHAM, Baron** *cr* 2015 (Life Peer), of Shipley in the County of West Sussex; **Francis Anthony Aylmer Maude;** PC 1992; Minister of State (Minister for Trade and Investment), Department for Business, Innovation and Skills and Foreign and Commonwealth Office, since 2015; *b* 4 July 1953; *s* of Baron Maude of Stratford-upon-Avon, TD, PC; *m* 1984, Christina Jane, *yr d* of late Peter Hadfield, Shrewsbury; two *s* three *d. Educ:* Abingdon Sch.; Corpus Christi Coll., Cambridge (MA (Hons) History; Avory Studentship; Halse Prize). Called to Bar, Inner Temple, 1977 (scholar; Forster Boulton Prize), Bencher, 2011. Councillor, Westminster CC, 1978–84. MP (C) Warwicks N, 1983–92; contested (C) Warwicks N, 1992; MP (C) Horsham, 1997–2015. PPS to Minister of State for Employment, 1984–85; an Asst Government Whip, 1985–87; Parly Under Sec. of State, DTI, 1987–89; Minister of State, FCO, 1989–90; Financial Sec. to HM Treasury, 1990–92; Shadow Chancellor, 1998–2000; Shadow Foreign Sec., 2000–01; Chm., Conservative Party, 2005–07; Shadow Minister for the Cabinet Office and Shadow Chancellor of the Duchy of Lancaster, 2007–10; Minister for the Cabinet Office and Paymaster Gen., 2010–15. Chm., Govt's Deregulation Task Force, 1994–97. Director: Salomon Brothers, 1992–93; Asda Gp, 1992–99; Man. Dir, 1993–97, Adv. Dir, 1997–98, Morgan Stanley & Co.; Dep. Chm., Benfield Gp, 2003–08; Chairman: Incepta Gp, 2004–06; Mission Marketing Gp, 2006–09. *Recreations:* ski-ing, cricket, reading, music. *Address:* House of Lords, SW1A 0PW.

**MAY, Rt Hon. Theresa Mary;** PC 2003; MP (C) Maidenhead, since 1997; Secretary of State for the Home Department, since 2010; *b* 1 Oct. 1956; *d* of Rev. Hubert Brasier and Zaidee Brasier (*née* Barnes); *m* 1980, Philip John May. *Educ:* St Hugh's Coll., Oxford (MA). Bank of England, 1977–83; Inter-Bank Res. Orgn, 1983–85; Assoc. for Payment Clearing Services, 1985–97 (Hd of European Affairs Unit, 1989–96). Mem. (C), Merton LBC, 1986–94. Contested (C): Durham NW, 1992; Barking, June 1994. Opposition frontbench spokesman on educn and employment, 1998–99; Shadow Secretary of State: for Educn and Employment, 1999–2001; for Transport, Local Govt and the Regions, 2001–02; for Transport, 2002; for Envmt and Transport, 2003–04; for the Family, 2004–05, also for Culture, Media and Sport, 2005; Chm., Cons. Party, 2002–03; Shadow Leader, H of C, 2005–09; Shadow Minister for Women, 2007–10; Shadow Sec. of State for Work and Pensions, 2009–10; Minister for Women and for Equalities, 2010–12. *Recreations:* walking, cooking. *Address:* House of Commons, SW1A 0AA. *Clubs:* Maidenhead Conservative; Leander.

**MAYNARD, Paul Christopher;** MP (C) Blackpool North and Cleveleys, since 2010; *b* Crewe, 16 Dec. 1975; *s* of Brian and Rosemary Maynard. *Educ:* University Coll., Oxford (BA Hons Modern Hist.). Special Advr to Dr Liam Fox, MP, 1999–2007. Contested (C) Twickenham, 2005. *Address:* House of Commons, SW1A 0AA.

**MEACHER, Rt Hon. Michael (Hugh);** PC 1997; MP (Lab) Oldham West and Royton, since 1997 (Oldham West, 1970–97); *b* 4 Nov. 1939; *s* of late George Hubert and Doris May Meacher; *m* 1st, 1962, Molly Christine (*née* Reid) (Baroness Meacher) (marr. diss. 1987); two *s* two *d*; 2nd, 1988, Mrs Lucianne Sawyer. *Educ:* Berkhamsted Sch., Herts; New College, Oxford (Greats, Class 1 1962); LSE (DSA 1963). Sec. to Danilo Dolci Trust, 1964; Research Fellow in Social Gerontology, Univ. of Essex, 1965–66; Lecturer in Social Administration: Univ. of York, 1967–69; London Sch. of Economics, 1970. Parly Under-Secretary of State: DoI, 1974–75; DHSS, 1975–76; Dept of Trade, 1976–79; Mem., Shadow Cabinet, 1983–97; chief opposition spokesman on health and social security, 1983–87, on employment, 1987–89, on social security, 1989–92, on development and co-operation, 1992–93, on Citizen's Charter, 1993–94, on transport, 1994–95, on employment, 1995–96, on envmtl protection, 1996–97; Minister of State (Minister for the Envmt), DETR, 1997–2001, DEFRA, 2001–03. Mem., Treasury Select Cttee, 1980–83 (a Chm. of its sub-cttee). Chm., Labour Co-ordinating Cttee, 1978–83; Member: Campaign for Press Freedom; Labour Party NEC, 1983–88. Vis. Prof., Univ. of Surrey, Dept of Sociology, 1980–87. *Publications:* Taken for a Ride: Special Residential Homes for the Elderly Mentally Infirm, a study of separatism in social policy, 1972; Fabian pamphlets incl. The Care of the Old, 1969; Wealth: Labour's Achilles Heel, in Labour and Equality, ed P. Townsend and N. Bosanquet, 1972; Socialism with a Human Face, 1981; Diffusing Power: the key to Socialist revival, 1992; Destination of the Species: the riddle of human existence, 2010; The State We Need: keys to the renaissance of Britain, 2013; numerous articles. *Recreations:* music, sport, reading. *Address:* House of Commons, SW1A 0AA; 34 Kingscliffe Gardens, SW19 6NR.

**MEALE, Sir (Joseph) Alan,** Kt 2011; MP (Lab) Mansfield, since 1987; *b* 31 July 1949; *s* of late Albert Henry and Elizabeth Meale; *m* 1983, Diana Gilhespy; one *s* one *d*. *Educ:* St Joseph's RC School; Ruskin College, Oxford; Sheffield Hallam Univ. (MA 1997). Seaman, British Merchant Navy, 1964–68; engineering worker, 1968–75; Nat. Employment Develt Officer, NACRO, 1977–80; Asst to Gen. Sec., ASLEF, 1980–83; Parly and Political Advisor to Michael Meacher, MP, 1983–87. An Opposition Whip, 1992–94; PPS to Dep. Leader of Lab. Party, 1994–97, to Dep. Prime Minister, 1997–98; Parly Under-Sec. of State, DETR, 1998–99. Mem., Select Cttee on Home Affairs, 1989–92; Chair, Cross Rail Select Cttee, 2005–08; Treas., Parly All Party Football Gp, 1989; Chairman: British Cyprus Cttee, 1992–; British Section, CPA Cyprus Gp, 2007–; Member: Parly Court of Referees, 1997–; Speaker's Panel, H of C, 2010–. Council of Europe: Mem., 2000–; First Vice-Pres., 2002–; President: Envmt, Agric., Local and Regl Democracy Cttee, 2008–; Eur. Prize Cttee, 2011–; Chief Whip, Council of Europe and Western EU British Delegn, 2007–; Mem., Socialist Bureau, 2011–; Leader, Labour Gp, 2012–; Mem., Eur. Interim Security and Defence Cttee, Western EU, 2012–. Fellow and Postgrad. Fellow, Industry and Parly Trust, 1989; Fellow, Armed Forces Parly Scheme (ranked Major). UK Parly Rep., Retired Mems Assoc., 2011–; Pres., Retired Miners Assoc., 2013–. Vice-Pres., Executive, Portland Coll. Trust, 1988–2011. Member: Exec., SSAFA, 1989–97; War Pensions Bd, 1989–97. Comr, Commonwealth War Graves Commn, 2002–10. Pres., Mansfield Town AFC, 2004–09. *Recreations:* reading, owner and breeder of thoroughbred horses, writing. *Address:* 85 West Gate, Mansfield, Notts NG18 1RT. *T:* (01623) 660531; House of Commons, SW1A 0AA. *Club:* Woodhouse Working Men's.

**MEARNS, Ian;** MP (Lab) Gateshead, since 2010; *b* Newcastle upon Tyne, April 1957; partner, Anne. *Educ:* St Mary's RC Primary Sch., Forest Hall; St Mary's RC Tech. Sch., Newcastle upon Tyne. With Northern Gas, 1974–85. Chair: Educn Comm, UNESCO, 1993–2000; Scrutiny Policy Rev. Gp, NE Assembly. Council Rep., LGA (Vice-Pres., 2010–11; Vice-Chair: Envmt Bd; Culture Tourism and Sport Bd; Mem., Educn Exec.). Mem. (Lab) Gateshead Council,

1983–2010 (Dep. Leader, 2002–10). Mem., Educn Select Cttee, 2010–. *Address:* House of Commons, SW1A 0AA.

**MENZIES, Mark;** MP (C) Fylde, since 2010; *b* Irvine, 18 May 1971; *s* of Andrew Menzies and Mary Isobel Menzies. *Educ:* Keil Sch., Dumbarton; Univ. of Glasgow (MA Hons Econ. and Social Hist.). With Marks & Spencer plc, 1994–95; Mktg Manager, Asda Stores Ltd, 1995–2007; Hd, Local Mktg, Wm Morrison Supermarkets plc, 2008–10. Contested (C): Glasgow Govan, 2001; Selby, 2005. PPS to Minister for Energy, 2010–12, to Minister for Housing, 2012–13, to Minister for Internat. Devel, 2013–14. *Recreations:* ski-ing, walking, cinema. *Address:* House of Commons, SW1A 0AA. *T:* (020) 7219 7073, *Fax:* (020) 7219 2235. *E:* mark.menzies.mp@parliament.uk.

**MERCER, Johnny;** MP (C) Plymouth Moor View, since 2015; *b* Dartford, Kent, 17 Aug. 1981; *s* of Andrew Mercer and Margaret Mercer; *m* Felicity Cornelius; two *d. Educ:* Eastbourne Coll.; Royal Mil. Acad. Sandhurst. Intern, City of London, 2000–02; Officer, Army, 2002–14. *Address:* House of Commons, SW1A 0AA. *E:* johnny.mercer.mp@parliament.uk.

**MERRIMAN, Huw William;** MP (C) Bexhill and Battle, since 2015; *b* Brackley, Northants, 13 July 1973; *s* of Richard and Ann Merriman; *m* 2001, Victoria Powdrill; three *d. Educ:* Buckingham Co. Secondary Sch.; Aylesbury Coll. of Further Educn; Durham Univ. (BA Hons Law); Inns of Court Sch. of Law. Called to the Bar, Inner Temple, 1996; in practice as barrister, 1997; Man. Dir, Lehman Bros in Admin, 2008–15. Mem. (C), Wealden DC, 2007–15. Contested (C) NE Derbys, 2010. *Recreations:* cooking, gardening, beekeeping. *Address:* House of Commons, SW1A 0AA. *T:* (020) 7219 8712. *E:* huw.merriman.mp@parliament.uk. *Clubs:* Farmers; Bexhill Conservative.

**METCALFE, Stephen James;** MP (C) South Basildon and East Thurrock, since 2010; *b* Walthamstow, 9 Jan. 1966; *s* of David John and Valerie Metcalfe; *m* 1988, Angela Claire Giblett; one *s* one *d. Educ:* Loughton Sch.; Buckhurst Hill Co. High Sch. Order Clerk, Burrup Matthieson, 1985–86; Metloc Printers Ltd: Sales Exec., 1986–87; Studio Manager, 1987–92; Dir, 1992–2011. Mem. (C) Epping Forest DC, 2003–07. Contested (C) Ilford S, 2005. PPS to Sec. of State for Justice, 2014–. Mem., Sci. and Technol. Select Cttee, 2010–15; Dep. Chm., Parly Scientific Cttee, 2014–. *Publications:* wine appreciation, theatre, Rugby, football. *Address:* House of Commons, SW1A 0AA. *T:* (020) 7219 7009. *E:* stephen.metcalfe.mp@parliament.uk.

**MILIBAND, Rt Hon. Edward;** PC 2007; MP (Lab) Doncaster North, since 2005; *b* 24 Dec. 1969; *s* of late Ralph Miliband and of Marion Miliband (*née* Kozak); *m* 2011, Justine Thornton; two *s. Educ:* Corpus Christi Coll., Oxford (BA);

London Sch. of Economics (MSc (Econ)). TV journalist; speechwriter and researcher for Harriet Harman, MP, 1993, for Rt Hon. Gordon Brown, MP, 1994–97; Special Advr to Chancellor of the Exchequer, 1997–2002; Lectr in Govt, Harvard Univ., 2002–04; Chm., Council of Econ. Advrs, HM Treasury, 2004–05. Parly Sec., Cabinet Office, 2006–07; Chancellor of the Duchy of Lancaster and Minister for the Cabinet Office, 2007–08; Sec. of State for Energy and Climate Change, 2008–10; Shadow Sec. of State for Energy and Climate Change, 2010; Leader of the Labour Party and Leader of the Opposition, 2010–15. *Address:* House of Commons, SW1A 0AA.

**MILLER, Rt Hon. Maria (Frances Lewis);** PC 2012; MP (C) Basingstoke, since 2005; *b* 26 March 1964; *d* of John and June Lewis; *m* 1990, Iain George Miller; two *s* one *d. Educ:* London Sch. of Econs (BSc Hons Econs 1985). Advertising Exec., Grey Advertising, 1985–90; Advertising and Mktg Manager, Texaco, 1990–95; Director: Grey Advertising, 1995–2000; Rowland Co., then PR21, 2000–02. Shadow Minister: for Education, 2005–06; for Family Welfare incl. CSA, 2006–07; for Family, 2007–10; Parly Under-Sec. of State, DWP, 2010–12; Sec. of State for Culture, Media and Sport and Minister for Women and for Equalities, 2012–14. Chm., Women and Equalities Select Cttee, 2015–. Pres., Wolverhampton NE Cons. Assoc., 2001–; Chm., Wimbledon Cons. Assoc., 2002–03. *Recreation:* three children. *Address:* House of Commons, SW1A 0AA. *T:* (020) 7219 3000. *E:* maria.miller.mp@parliament.uk.

**MILLING, Amanda Anne;** MP (C) Cannock Chase, since 2015; *b* Burton upon Trent, 12 March 1975; *d* of Humphrey and Patricia Milling. *Educ:* Moreton Hall Sch.; University Coll. London (BSc Hons Econs). Researcher, SW1 Res., 1997–99; Quaestor Research and Marketing Strategists: Sen. Res. Exec., 1999–2000; Res. Manager, 2000–03; Associate Dir, 2003–06; Res. Dir, 2006–10; Dir, Optimisa Res., 2010–14. *Recreation:* running. *Address:* House of Commons, SW1A 0AA. *T:* (020) 7219 8356. *E:* amanda.milling.mp@parliament.uk.

**MILLS, Nigel John;** MP (C) Amber Valley, since 2010; *b* Jacksdale, 1974; *s* of John and Rosemary Mills; *m* 2013, Alice Elizabeth Ward. *Educ:* Univ. of Newcastle upon Tyne (BA Classics). ACA 2000. Tax Adviser: PricewaterhouseCoopers, 1998–2010; Deloitte, 2010. Mem. (C) Amber Valley BC, 2004–11; Heanor and Loscoe Town Council, 2007–11. Member, Select Committee: on Admin, 2010–; on NI Affairs, 2011–; on Work and Pensions, 2012–15; Public Accounts, 2015–. *Address:* House of Commons, SW1A 0AA.

**MILTON, Rt Hon. Anne (Frances);** PC 2015; MP (C) Guildford, since 2005; Treasurer of HM Household (Deputy Chief Whip), since 2015; *b* 3 Nov. 1955; *d* of late Patrick Turner and Nesta

Turner; *m* Dr Graham Henderson; three *s* one *d*. *Educ:* Haywards Heath Grammar Sch.; St Bartholomew's Hospital Sch. of Nursing (RGN 1977). Staff Nurse, 1977–78, Research Nurse, 1978–81, St Bartholomew's Hosp.; District Nursing Sister: City and Hackney HA, 1981–83; St Thomas' Hosp., London, 1983–85; Med. Advr on Housing for E London and City HA, 1985–2000; self-employed med. advr to social housing providers, 2000–05. Parly Under-Sec. of State, DoH, 2010–12; a Lord Comr of HM Treasury (Govt Whip), 2012–14; Vice-Chamberlain of HM Household (Govt Whip), 2014–15. *Publications:* contrib. Lancet. *Recreations:* gardening, reading, music. *Address:* House of Commons, SW1A 0AA. *T:* (020) 7219 8392. *E:* anne.milton.mp@parliament.uk.

**MITCHELL, Rt Hon. Andrew (John Bower);** PC 2010; MP (C) Sutton Coldfield, since 2001; *b* 23 March 1956; *s* of Sir David Bower Mitchell and Pamela Elaine (*née* Haward); *m* 1985, Sharon Denise (*née* Bennett); two *d*. *Educ:* Rugby; Jesus Coll., Cambridge (MA History). 1st RTR (Short Service (Limited) Commission), 1975; served with UNFICYP. Pres., Cambridge Union, 1978; Chm., Cambridge Univ. Conservatives, 1977; rep. GB in E–SU American debating tour, 1978. Internat. and Corp. business, Lazard Brothers & Co., 1979–87, Consultant, 1987–92; Dir, Lazard Gp Cos, 1997–2009. Senior Strategy Adviser: Boots Co., 1997–2001; Accenture (formerly Andersen Consulting), 1997–2009; Investec, 2013–. Director: Miller Insce Gp, 1997–2001; Commer Gp, 1998–2002; Financial Dynamics Holdings, 1998–2002. Advr to Bd, Hakluyt, 1998–2001. Contested (C) Sunderland South, 1983. MP (C) Gedling, 1987–97; contested (C) same seat, 1997. A Vice-Chm., Cons. Party, with special responsibility for candidates, 1992–93; an Asst Govt Whip, 1992–94; a Lord Comr of HM Treasury (Govt Whip), 1994–95; Parly Under Sec. of State, DSS, 1995–97; Opposition front bench spokesman: economic affairs, 2003–04; police and home affairs, 2004–05; Shadow Sec. of State for internat. devlt, 2005–10; Sec. of State for Internat. Devlt, 2010–12; Parly Sec. to HM Treasury (Govt Chief Whip), 2012. Sec., One Nation Gp of Conservative MPs, 1989–92, 2005–. Chm., Coningsby Club, 1983; President: Islington North Conservatives, 1996–2006 (Chm., 1983–85); Gedling Cons. Assoc., 2004–. Vice-Chm., 1998–2010, Trustee, 2010–, Alexandra Rose Charity. Member Council: SOS Sahel, 1991–2010; GAP, 2000–05. *Recreations:* ski-ing, music, travel, wine. *Address:* 30 Gibson Square, N1 0RD. *T:* (020) 7226 5519; 8 Tudor Road, Sutton Coldfield B73 6BA. *T:* (0121) 355 5519. *Clubs:* Cambridge Union Society (Cambridge); Carlton and District Constitutional (Gedling); Sutton Coldfield Conservative.

**MOLLOY, Francie;** MP (SF) Mid Ulster, since March 2013; *b* Derrymagowan, Co. Tyrone, 16 Dec. 1950; *m*; two *s* two *d*. *Educ:* St Patrick's Intermediate Sch., Dungannon; Newry Further Educn Coll. Apprentice fitter/welder, Felden Govt Trng Centre, Belfast; fitter/welder, Planet/Powerscreen, Ulster; full-time political activist, 1980; Dir of Elections for Bobby Sands, 1981. Mem. (SF) Dungannon and S Tyrone BC, 1985–89 and 1993 (Mayor, 2001–02 and 2005–06; Dep. Mayor, 2003–04). Mem. (SF) NI Assembly, 1998–2013. Chm., Finance and Personnel Cttee, 1999–2003, Dep. Speaker, 2006–07 and 2007–11, Principal Dep. Speaker, 2011–13, NI Assembly. Contested (SF) NI, EP, 1994. *Address:* c/o Sinn Féin, 55 Falls Road, Belfast BT12 4PD.

**MONAGHAN, Carol, (Mrs Feargal Dalton);** MP (SNP) Glasgow North West, since 2015; *b* Glasgow, 2 Aug. 1972; *m* Feargal Dalton; one *s* two *d*. *Educ:* Univ. of Strathclyde (BSc Hons Laser Physics and Optoelectronics 1993); PGCE Physics and Maths. Teacher, Glasgow schs; Hd of Physics and Hd of Sci., Hyndland Secondary Sch., until 2015. Lectr, Univ. of Glasgow; consultant, Scottish Qualifications Authy. Mem., Sci. and Technol. Select Cttee, 2015–. *Address:* House of Commons, SW1A 0AA.

**MONAGHAN, Dr Paul William;** MP (SNP) Caithness, Sutherland and Easter Ross, since 2015; *b* Montrose, 1965; *s* of William Monaghan and Margaret Monaghan (*née* Innes); partner, Stephanie Anderson; one *d*. *Educ:* Inverness Royal Acad.; Univ. of Stirling (BA Hons 1st Psychol. and Sociol.; PhD Social Policy 2004). MBPsS 1999. Hd, Planning and Develt, Northern Constabulary, 2003–08; Dir and Gen. Manager, Highland Homeless Trust, 2008–15. FInstLM 2007. *Recreations:* travel, cycling. *Address:* House of Commons, SW1A 0AA. *T:* (020) 7219 8485. *E:* paul.monaghan.mp@parliament.uk.

**MOON, Madeleine;** MP (Lab) Bridgend, since 2005; *b* 27 March 1950; *d* of Albert Edward and Hilda Ironside; *m* Stephen John Moon (*d* 2015); one *s*. *Educ:* Madeley Coll. (Cert Ed 1971); Keele Univ. (BEd 1972); University Coll., Cardiff (CQSW, DipSW 1980). Social Services Directorate: Mid Glamorgan CC, 1980–96; City and Co. of Swansea, 1996–2002; Care Standards Inspectorate for Wales, 2002–05. Member (Lab): Porthcawl Town Council, 1990–2000 (Mayor, 1992–93, 1995–96); Ogwr BC, 1991–96; Bridgend CBC, 1995–2005. PPS to Minister of State, DCSF, 2007–08, to Minister of State, DECC, 2008–10. Member: Envmt, Food and Rural Affairs Select Cttee, 2005–07; Defence Select Cttee, 2009–. *Recreations:* travel, theatre, films, reading, walking, looking for things I have put in a safe place! *Address:* House of Commons, SW1A 0AA. *E:* moonm@parliament.uk.

**MORDAUNT, Penelope Mary;** MP (C) Portsmouth North, since 2010; Minister of State, Ministry of Defence, since 2015; *b* Torquay, 4 March 1973; *d* of John Edward Patrick Mordaunt and late Jennifer Mordaunt and step *d* of Sylvia Mordaunt. *Educ:* Oaklands RC Comprehensive

Sch., Waterlooville; Reading Univ. (BA Hons Philosophy 1995). Aid worker, 1991–92; spokesman, Freight Transport Assoc., 1997–99; Hd, Foreign Press, George Bush's presidential campaign, 2000; Hd of Broadcasting, Cons. Party, 1999–2001; Director: RBKC, 2001–03; Media Intelligence Partners, 2004–06; Diabetes UK, 2006–09. Dep. Dir, Big Lottery Fund, 2003–05. Parly Under-Sec. of State, DCLG, 2014–15. *Recreations:* astronomy, painting, hospital volunteer, RNR, dance and music. *Address:* House of Commons, SW1A 0AA. *T:* (020) 7219 7129, *Fax:* (020) 7219 3592. *E:* penny. mordaunt.mp@parliament.uk.

**MORDEN, Jessica;** MP (Lab) Newport East, since 2005; *b* 29 May 1968; *d* of Mick and Margaret Morden. *Educ:* Croesyceiliog Comp. Sch., Cwmbran; Univ. of Birmingham (BA Hons Hist. 1989). Researcher: to Huw Edwards, MP, 1991–92; to Llew Smith, MP, 1992–93; Organiser, SE Wales, Welsh Lab. Party, 1993–98; Elections Officer, Labour Party, 1998–99; Gen. Sec., Welsh Labour Party, 1999–2005. *Recreations:* gym, film. *Address:* House of Commons, SW1A 0AA. *T:* (020) 7219 6213, (constituency) (01633) 841725. *E:* jessica.morden.mp@parliament.uk. *Club:* Ringland Labour (Newport).

**MORGAN, Rt Hon. Nicola (Ann);** PC 2014; MP (C) Loughborough, since 2010; Secretary of State for Education, and Minister for Women and Equality, since 2014; *b* Kingston upon Thames, 10 Oct. 1972; *d* of Peter M. Griffith and Jennifer C. Griffith; *m* 2000, Jonathan Morgan; one *s. Educ:* Surbiton High Sch.; St Hugh's Coll., Oxford (MA Law); Guildford Law Sch. Admitted as solicitor, 1996; in practice as solicitor, specialising in corporate law: Theodore Goddard, 1994–97; Allen & Overy, 1998–2002; Travers Smith, 2002–10. An Asst Govt Whip, 2012–13; Economic Sec., 2013–14, Financial Sec., 2014, HM Treasury. *Recreations:* running, ski-ing, spending time with family. *Address:* House of Commons, SW1A 0AA. *T:* (020) 7219 7224, (constituency) (01509) 262723. *E:* nicky. morgan.mp@parliament.uk.

**MORRIS, Anne Marie;** MP (C) Newton Abbot, since 2010; *b* London, 1957; *d* of late John Backes and of Margaret Agg; partner, Roger Kendrick. *Educ:* Hertford Coll., Oxford (BA PPP/Juris.); Open Univ. (MBA 1997); Harvard Univ. (Leadership Prog. 2004). Admitted solicitor, 1982; trainee solicitor, Withers, London, 1981–83; Corporate Finance Lawyer, Norton Rose, London, 1983–85; Corporate, Commercial, Banking Lawyer, Crossman Block, London, 1985; Asset Finance Lawyer, Sinclair Roche & Temperley, Singapore, 1986–88; Corporate Finance Lawyer, 1988–90, Hd, Educn and Trng, 1990–93, Allen & Overy; Dir, Professional and Business Devlt, Baker & McKenzie, 1993–95; Dir, Mktg and Business Devlt, Simmons & Simmons, 1995–97; Mktg Dir, Tax and Legal Services, EMEA,

PricewaterhouseCoopers, 1997–99; Global Marketing Director: Ernst & Young, 1999–2002; Linklaters, 2002–05; Man. Dir, Manteion Ltd, 2005–. Mem., W Sussex CC, 2005–07 (Chm., Health Overview and Scrutiny Cttee). PPS, BIS, 2015–. Founder and Chair, All Party Parly Gp for Micro Businesses, 2011–15; Chair, All Party Parly Gp for Small Businesses, 2015. Sec., Bolney Br., Arundel and S Downs Cons. Assoc., 2003. Member: Cttee, Nat. Legal Educn and Trng Gp, 1990–94 (Chm., 1990–94); Lord Chancellor's Adv. Gp on Legal Educn, 1992–93; Cttee, Nat. Professional Services Mktg Gp, 1994–97; wkg party to develop personal mgt standards, Law Soc., 1994–95; Bd, Eur. Mentoring and Coaching Council, 2008–09; Work and Pensions Select Cttee, 2012–15; Specialist Assessor, Law, HEFC, 1992–93. Mem. Bd of Studies, Oxford Inst. of Legal Practice, 1990–2004; non-exec. Mem. Bd, Southampton Univ., 2005–06. Associate Gov., Rydon Sch., 2010–; former Gov., Newton Abbot Coll. FRSA 2000; FCIM 2002; MInstD 2001. *Address:* Templer House, Sandford Orleigh, Newton Abbot, Devon TQ12 2SQ. *T:* (01626) 368277. *E:* annemarie@annemariemorris.co.uk.

**MORRIS, David;** MP (C) Morecambe and Lunesdale, since 2010; *b* Leigh, Lancs, 3 Jan. 1966; *s* of Captain Alan Lewis Morris and Vera White; *m* (marr. diss.); two *s. Educ:* St Andrew's Sch., Nassau. Company director, 1990–2010. Contested (C): Blackpool S, 2001; Carmarthen W and S Pembrokeshire, 2005. Mem., Select Cttee on Sci. and Technol., 2010–14, on Political and Constitutional Reform, 2014–15. Chairman, All-Party Groups: Bahamas, 2014–; Bovine TB, 2014–; Coastal and Marine, 2014–. UK Govt Self Employment Ambassador, 2014–. Chm., Cons. Friends of Nuclear Energy, 2010–. Lt Comdr, RN, Parly Armed Forces Scheme, 2010. Master Mariner, 2014. *Recreations:* music, classic cars. *Address:* House of Commons, SW1A 0AA. *T:* (020) 7219 7234.

**MORRIS, Grahame;** MP (Lab) Easington, since 2010; *b* 13 March 1961; *s* of late Richard and Constance Morris; *m* 1986, Michelle Hughes; two *s. Educ:* Peterlee Howletch Secondary Sch.; Newcastle Coll. (BTEC ONC); Newcastle Poly. (BTEC HNC Med. Lab. Scis). Med. lab. SO, Sunderland Royal Infirmary, 1980–87; researcher and constituency caseworker to John Cummings, MP, 1987–2010. Non-exec. Dir, City Hosps Sunderland NHS Trust, 1997–2005. Mem. (Lab) Easington DC, 1987–2003. Mem., Health Select Cttee, 2010–15. *Address:* House of Commons, SW1A 0AA.

**MORRIS, James;** MP (C) Halesowen and Rowley Regis, since 2010; *b* Nottingham, 4 Feb. 1967; *m* 1995, Anna Mellitt; one *s* one *d. Educ:* Univ. of Birmingham (BA Eng. Lit.); Univ. of Oxford (postgrad.); Cranfield Sch. of Mgt (MBA). IT/software entrepreneur, 1996–2006; Managing Director: Torington Interactive, 1996–2001; Vice-Versa Ltd, 2001–06; Chief Exec., Localis,

2008–10. *Publications:* (ed jtly) Big Ideas: building on Conservative fundamentals, 2008; (ed jtly) Million Vote Mandate, 2008; (ed jtly) Can Localism Deliver?, 2009. *Recreations:* spending time with family, cricket, theatre, music. *Address:* House of Commons, SW1A 0AA. *T:* (020) 7219 7080. *E:* james.morris.mp@parliament.uk.

**MORTON, Wendy;** MP (C) Aldridge-Brownhills, since 2015; *b* Northallerton, 1967; *d* of Thomas and Edna Hunter; *m* 1990, David Morton. *Educ:* Wensleydale Sch., N Yorks; Open Univ. (MBA). Exec. Officer, FCO, 1987–89; sales and marketing: HMCO Europe; Centrostyle; Dir, DM Electronics Ltd, 1991–. *Recreations:* walking, running, cooking, Rotary. *Address:* House of Commons, SW1A 0AA. *T:* (020) 7219 8784. *E:* wendy.morton.mp@parliament.uk.

**MOWAT, David John;** MP (C) Warrington South, since 2010; *b* Rugby, 1957; *s* of John and Pat Mowat; *m* 1983, Veronica Mann; one *s* three *d. Educ:* Lawrence Sheriff Grammar Sch., Rugby; Imperial Coll., London (BSc Civil Engrg). ACA 1981. Chartered Accountant, 1981–2002, Partner, 1989–2002, Arthur Andersen, London; Global Man. Partner for Energy, Accenture, 2002–05. Mem. (C) Macclesfield BC, 2007–08. PPS to Financial Sec. to HM Treasury, 2012–. *Recreations:* chess, golf, Rugby Union and League, theatre. *Address:* (office) 1 Stafford Road, Warrington, Cheshire WA4 6RP. *T:* (01925) 231267; House of Commons, SW1A 0AA. *E:* david.mowat.mp@parliament.uk. *Clubs:* Carlton; Warrington.

**MULHOLLAND, Gregory Thomas;** MP (Lib Dem) Leeds North West, since 2005; *b* 31 Aug. 1970; *m* 2004, Raegan Melita Hatton; three *d. Educ:* St Ambrose Coll., Altrincham; Univ. of York (BA 1991; MA 1995). Account handler, several marketing and sales promotion agencies, 1997–2002. Mem. (Lib Dem), Leeds CC, 2003–05 (Lead Mem., Corp. Services and Metro (W Yorks PTA)). *Address:* (office) Wainwright House, 12 Holt Park Centre, Holt Road, Leeds LS16 7SR; House of Commons, SW1A 0AA.

**MULLIN, (William Arthur) Roger;** MP (SNP) Kirkcaldy and Cowdenbeath, since 2015. *Educ:* Univ. of Edinburgh (MA Hons Sociol. 1977); Stow Coll., Glasgow (HNC Electrical and Electronic Engrg). Tutor in Social Scis, Univ. of Edinburgh, 1977–79; Lectr in Industrial Sociol., W Lothian Coll., 1979–80; Sen. Lectr and Depute Hd, Centre for Industrial Studies, Glenrothes Coll., 1980–85; Hd of Dept, Stevenson Coll. of FE, 1985–86; Sen. Partner, Roger Mullin Associates, 1986–99; Man. Dir, Inter-ed Ltd, 1993–2012; freelance writer, researcher, 2014–15. Consultant to orgns incl. UNESCO, UNFAO, UNIDO, UNDP, ILO, IBRD and Asian Develt Bank. Associate Lectr and Ext. PhD Supervisor, Open Univ., 1978–2002; MBA Ext. Lectr and thesis supervisor, Stirling Univ., 2001–15. Director: Red Lead Arts Ltd, Belfast, 2004–05; Momentous Change Ltd, 2012–14. Hon. Prof., Stirling Univ. Mgt Sch., 2010–15. Internat. Progs Advr, Australian Acad., 1996–97; Columnist, TES Scotland. Advr to Lifelong Learning Inquiry, Enterprise and Lifelong Learning Cttee, Scottish Parlt, 2001–02. Member: Industrial Adv. Panel, Inst. of Biomed. and Life Scis, Univ. of Glasgow, 1997–2003; Internat. Adv. Gp, ICOD Canada. Chm., Bd of Trustees, Stirling Univ. Student Union, 2010–11. Hon. Pres., Univ. of Paisley, 1995–98. MIPD 1988. *Publications:* (contrib.) Multi-Party Britain, 1979; (contrib.) The Referendum Experience, Scotland 1979, 1981; Career Goals and Educational Attainment: what is the link?, 2004; (contrib.) Public and Third Sector Leadership, 2014; contrib. Bull. Scottish Politics. *Address:* (office) East Shop, Law's Close, 343 High Street, Kirkcaldy, Fife KY1 1JN. *T:* (01592) 747359, (020) 7219 6069. *E:* roger.mullin.mp@parliament.uk.

**MUNDELL, Rt Hon. David (Gordon);** PC 2010; MP (C) Dumfriesshire, Clydesdale and Tweeddale, since 2005; Secretary of State, Scotland Office, since 2015; *b* 27 May 1962; *s* of Dorah Mundell; *m* 1987, Lynda Jane Carmichael (marr. diss. 2012); two *s* one *d. Educ:* Lockerbie Acad.; Edinburgh Univ. (LLB Hons 1984); Univ. of Strathclyde Business Sch. (MBA 1991). Trainee Solicitor, Tindal Oatts, Glasgow, 1985–87; Solicitor, Maxwell Waddell, Glasgow, 1987–89; Sen. Corporate Lawyer, Biggart Baillie & Gifford, Glasgow, 1989–91; Group Legal Advr Scotland, BT, 1991–98; Head of Nat. Affairs, BT Scotland, 1998–99. MSP (C) S of Scotland, 1999–2005. Shadow Sec. of State for Scotland, 2005–10; Parly Under-Sec. of State, Scotland Office, 2010–15. Member: Law Soc. of Scotland, 1986–; Law Soc., 1992–. *Recreations:* family and friends, travel. *Address:* House of Commons, SW1A 0AA.

**MURRAY, Ian;** MP (Lab) Edinburgh South, since 2010; *b* Edinburgh, 10 Aug. 1976; *s* of James Brownlie Murray and Lena Murray; partner, Hannah Catherine Woolfson. *Educ:* Wester Hailes Educn Centre; Univ. of Edinburgh (MA Hons Social Policy and Law). Investment Administrator: WM Co., 1998; AEGON UK, 1998–99; Dir, Ops, Worldart.com, 2000–02; Dir, 100mph Events Ltd, 2002–; Partner, Alibi Bars LLP, 2005–11. Mem. (Lab) Edinburgh CC, 2003–10. PPS to Shadow Sec. of State for Culture, Media and Sport, 2010–11; Shadow Minister for Employee Relns, Postal and Consumer Affairs, 2011–13, for Trade and Investment (incl. Employment Relns and Postal Affairs), 2013–15; Shadow Sec. of State for Scotland, 2015–. Member: Business, Innovation and Skills Select Cttee, 2010–11; Envmtl Audit Select Cttee, 2010–12. *Address:* (office) 31 Minto Street, Edinburgh EH9 2BT. *T:* (0131) 662 4520, *Fax:* (0131) 662 1990. *E:* ian.murray.mp@parliament.uk.

**MURRAY, Sheryll;** MP (C) South East Cornwall, since 2010; *b* Millbrook, Cornwall, 4 Feb. 1956; *d* of Edgar and Elaine Hickman; *m* 1986, Neil Murray (*d* 2011); one *s* one *d. Educ:* Torpoint Sch. Insce underwriter, 1972–88; GP receptionist, 1990–2010. Mem. (C) Cornwall CC, 2001–05. *Address:* Windsor Place, Liskeard, Cornwall PL14 4BH. *T:* (01579) 344428. *E:* sheryll@sheryllmurray.com.

**MURRISON, Dr Andrew William;** MP (C) South West Wiltshire, since 2010 (Westbury, 2001–10); *b* 24 April 1961; *s* of William Gordon Murrison, RD and Marion Murrison (*née* Horn); *m* 1994, Jennifer Jane Munden; five *d. Educ:* Harwich High Sch.; The Harwich Sch.; BRNC Dartmouth; Bristol Univ. (MB ChB 1984; MD 1996); Hughes Hall, Cambridge (DPH 1996). MFOM 1994. Med. Officer, RN, 1981–2000, 2003 (Surg. Comdr); Med. Officer, RNR; Consultant Occupational Physician, 1996–2001. Opposition front bench spokesman on health, 2003–05, on defence, 2005–10; PPS to Sec. of State for Health, 2010–12; Parly Under-Sec. of State, MoD, 2012–14, NI Office, 2014–15. Chm., All Party Parly Gp on Morocco, 2010–12. Prime Minister's Special Rep., Centenary Commemoration of First World War, 2011–. *Publications: Tommy This an' Tommy That,* 2011; contribs to various biomed. pubns. *Recreations:* sailing, ski-ing. *Address:* House of Commons, SW1A 0AA.

**NANDY, Lisa Eva;** MP (Lab) Wigan, since 2010; *b* Manchester, 9 Aug. 1979; *d* of Dipak Nandy. *Educ:* Parrs Wood Comp. Sch., Manchester; Univ. of Newcastle upon Tyne (BA Hons Pols 2001); Birkbeck, Univ. of London (MSc Pols and Govt 2005). Researcher to Neil Gerrard, MP, 2001–03; Policy Researcher, Centrepoint, 2003–05; Policy Advr, Children's Soc., 2005–10. Mem. (Lab) Hammersmith and Fulham LBC, 2006–10. Shadow Minister for Children and Families, 2012–15; Shadow Sec. of State for Energy and Climate Change, 2015–. *Recreations:* theatre, Rugby League. *Address:* House of Commons, SW1A 0AA. *T:* (020) 7219 7188. *E:* lisa.nandy.mp@parliament.uk.

**NASH,** Baron *cr* 2013 (Life Peer), of Ewelme in the County of Oxfordshire; **John Alfred Stoddard Nash;** Parliamentary Under-Secretary of State, Department for Education, since 2013; *b* Bahrain, 22 March 1949; *s* of Lewis John and Josephine Nash; *m* 1983, Caroline Jennifer Paul; one *s* one *d. Educ:* Milton Abbey Sch.; Corpus Christi Coll., Oxford (MA Law). Called to the Bar, Inner Temple, 1972. Chm., 1988–2002, non-exec. Partner, 2002–12, Sovereign Capital. Non-exec. Dir, DfE, 2010–13. Chm., British Venture Capital Assoc., 1988–89. Chairman: Future (charity), 2005–; Pimlico Acad., 2008–. *Recreation:* golf. *Address:* Department for Education, Sanctuary Buildings, Great Smith Street, SW1P 3BT. *Clubs:* Athenaeum, Turf.

**NEILL, Robert James Macgillivray;** MP (C) Bromley and Chislehurst, since June 2006; *b* 24 June 1952; *s* of John Macgillivray Neill and Elsie May Neill (*née* Chaston); *m* 2009, Daphne White. *Educ:* London Sch. of Econs (LLB Hons 1973). Called to the Bar, Middle Temple, 1975; barrister in private practice, 1975–2006. Member (C): Havering BC, 1974–90 (Chm., Envmt and Social Services Cttees); Romford, GLC, 1985–86; Greater London Authority: Mem. (C) Bexley and Bromley, London Assembly, 2000–08; Leader, Cons. Gp, 2000–02, 2004–06; Chair, Planning and Spatial Develt Cttee, 2002–04. Shadow Minister for Local Govt, 2007–10; Parly Under-Sec. of State, DCLG, 2010–12. Mem., Select Cttee on Justice and Constitutional Affairs, 2006–10; Chm., Select Cttee on Justice, 2015–. Mem., UK Delegn to Parly Assembly of Council of Europe, 2012–. Vice Chm., Cons. Party, 2012–. Dep. Chm., Commn on London Governance, 2004–06. Leader, London Fire and Civil Defence Authy, 1985–87. Mem., Metropolitan Police Authy, 2004–08. Regl Chm., Gtr London Cons. Party, 1996–99 (Dep. Chm., 1993–96). Contested (C) Dagenham, 1983 and 1987. Mem., UK Delegn, Cttee of Regions of EU, 2002–08. Non-exec. Dir, NE London HA, 2002–06. *Recreations:* opera, travel, sailing. *Address:* House of Commons, SW1A 0AA. *Club:* Carlton.

**NEVILLE-ROLFE,** Baroness *cr* 2013 (Life Peer), of Chilmark in the County of Wiltshire; **Lucy Jeanne Neville-Rolfe,** DBE 2012; CMG 2005; FCIS; Parliamentary Under-Secretary of State, Department for Business, Innovation and Skills, since 2014, and Department for Culture, Media and Sport, since 2015; *b* 2 Jan. 1953; *d* of late Edmund and Margaret Neville-Rolfe; *m* Sir Richard John Packer, KCB; four *s. Educ:* Somerville Coll., Oxford (BA PPE; MA; Hon. Fellow, 2003). FCIS 2010. Joined MAFF, 1973; Pvte Sec. to Minister of Agric., Fisheries and Food, 1977–79; EC Sheepmeat and Milk, 1979–86; Land Use, 1986–88; Food Safety Act, 1988–90; Head of Personnel, 1990–92; Mem., Prime Minister's Policy Unit, 1992–94; Under Sec., 1994; Dir, Deregulation Unit, DTI, then Better Regulation Unit, Cabinet Office, 1995–97; Tesco plc: Gp Dir of Corporate Affairs, 1997–2006, and Company Sec., 2003–06; Exec. Dir, Corporate and Legal Affairs, 2006–13. Non-executive Director: John Laing Construction, 1991–92; Bd of Mgt, FCO, 2000–05; Carbon Trust, 2008–13; ITV plc, 2010–14; Chm., Dobbies Garden Centres plc, 2007–11. Member: Dep. Prime Minister's Local Govt Funding Cttee, 2003–04; ESRC Panel on Cultures of Consumption, 2003–07; Corporate Leaders Gp on Climate Change, 2005–; Foresight Obesity Project, 2005–07; China Britain Business Council, 2005–13; UK India Business Council, 2008–13; Efficiency Bd, Cabinet Office, 2010–; Strategic Adv. Gp, UKTI, 2011–. Member: Bd of Mgt, British Retail Consortium, 1998–2012

(Dep. Chair, 2003–12); Econs and Eur. Cttees, CBI, 1998–; UNICE Task Force on Enlargement, 1999–2004. Pres., EuroCommerce, 2012–15 (Vice Pres., 1998–2008). Gov., London Business Sch., 2011–. *Recreations:* cricket, racing, gardening, art, architecture, theatre.

**NEWLANDS, Gavin Andrew Stuart;** MP (SNP) Paisley and Renfrewshire North, since 2015; *b* Paisley, 2 Feb. 1980; *s* of Gordon Newlands and Isabel Newlands; *m* 2008, Lynn Single; two *d. Educ:* Trinity High Sch., Renfrew. Business Analyst, McDonald's Restaurants Ltd, 2005–07; Asst Manager, then Business Analyst, later Business Manager, AG Restaurants Ltd, 2007–15. *Recreations:* spending time with family, Rugby, football (watching), golf. *Address:* (office) 6 Porterfield Road, Renfrew PA4 8HG. *T:* (0141) 378 0600. *E:* gavin.newlands.mp@parliament.uk. *Club:* Paisley Rugby.

**NEWTON, Sarah;** MP (C) Truro and Falmouth, since 2010; an Assistant Government Whip, since 2015; *m* Alan Newton; one *s* two *d. Educ:* Falmouth Sch.; King's Coll. London (BA Hist.); Grad. Sch. of Internat. Studies, USA. Formerly: Mktg Officer for IBIS, then Citibank; Director: American Express; Age Concern England; Internat. Longevity Centre. Former Mem. (C) Merton LBC. Member: Admin Select Cttee, 2010–12; Welfare Reform Bill Cttee, 2011; Sci. and Technol. Select Cttee, 2012–15; Care Bill Cttee, 2014; Ecclesiastical Cttee, 2014–15. Dep. Chm., Cons. Party, 2012–. FRSA. *Address:* House of Commons, SW1A 0AA.

**NICOLSON, John;** MP (SNP) Dunbartonshire East, since 2015; *b* Glasgow, 1961; *s* of John Donald Nicolson and Marion Stant; partner, Juliano Zini. *Educ:* Univ. of Glasgow (MA Hons); Harvard Univ. (Harkness Fellow; Kennedy Schol.). Speech writer, US Senate, 1985–87; freelance journalist and broadcaster, 1987–2015: reporter for Newsnight, Assignment, Public Eye, Panorama, On the Record; presenter: News 24; BBC Breakfast; ITV News; contrib. The Times, Sunday Times, Observer, Sunday Telegraph, Guardian. SNP spokesperson on Culture, Media and Sport, 2015–. *Recreations:* travel, reading, music, cooking, art, exploring derelict buildings. *Address:* House of Commons, SW1A 0AA. *T:* (020) 7219 6857. *E:* john.nicolson.mp@parliament.uk.

**NOKES, Caroline;** MP (C) Romsey and Southampton North, since 2010; *b* Lyndhurst, 26 June 1972; *d* of Roy James Perry; one *d. Educ:* La Sagesse Convent, Romsey; Peter Symonds Coll.; Univ. of Sussex (BA Hons). Researcher for Roy Perry, MEP, 1994–2004; Chief Exec., Nat. Pony Soc., 2008–09. Mem. (C) Test Valley BC, 1999–2011 (Exec. Mem. for Leisure, 2001–10). *Recreations:* riding, cookery. *Address:* House of Commons, SW1A 0AA. *T:* (020) 7219 1468. *E:* caroline.nokes.mp@parliament.uk.

**NORMAN, (Alexander) Jesse;** MP (C) Hereford and South Herefordshire, since 2010; *b* London, 23 June 1962; *s* of Sir Torquil (Patrick Alexander) Norman, CBE; *m* 1992, Kate, *d* of Baron Bingham of Cornhill (Life Peer), KG, PC; two *s* one *d. Educ:* Eton Coll.; Merton Coll., Oxford (Open Exhibnr; BA Classics); University Coll. London (MPhil; PhD Philosophy 2003). Project Dir, Sabre Foundn, 1989–91; Manager, then Asst Dir, 1991–97, Dir, 1997, BZW; Teaching Fellow and Lectr, UCL, 1998–2003; Lectr, Birkbeck Coll., London, 2003; Exec. Dir, Policy Exchange, 2005–06. Hon. Res. Fellow, UCL, 2005–10. Director: Classical Opera Co., 2004–; Roundhouse, 2007–. Trustee: Kindle Centre, 2007–10; Hay Fest., 2008–. Chm., Select Cttee on Culture, Media and Sport, 2015–. Patron: Herefordshire Riding for Disabled, 2009–; No 1 Ledbury Rd, 2010–; Music Pool, 2010–; Herefords Mind, 2011–. Pres., Hereford Hosp. Radio, 2011–; Vice President: Ross Horticl Soc., 2011–; Herefords and Glos Canal Trust, 2011–. *Publications:* The Achievement of Michael Oakeshott, 1992; Breaking the Habits of a Lifetime: Poland's first steps to the market, 1992; After Euclid: visual reasoning and the epistemology of diagrams, 2006; Compassionate Conservatism, 2006; Compassionate Economics, 2008; Churchill's Legacy, 2009; The Big Society, 2010; Edmund Burke: philosopher, politician, prophet, 2013; pamphlets, essays, journalism and academic articles. *Recreations:* music, especially jazz and opera, hill-walking, sports, cinema. *Address:* House of Commons, SW1A 0AA; Suite 3, Penn House, Broad Street, Hereford HR4 9AP. *E:* jesse.norman.mp@parliament.uk. *Club:* Westfields Football.

**NUTTALL, David John;** MP (C) Bury North, ·since 2010; *b* Sheffield, 25 March 1962; *s* of Roy Nuttall and Kathleen Nuttall; *m* 2004, Susan Smith (*née* Finn). *Educ:* Aston Comp. Sch., Rotherham; Univ. of London (LLB ext.). Admitted solicitor, 1990, NP, 1998; Taylor Son & Co., later Taylors, solicitors: trainee legal exec., 1980–88; Legal Exec. and Articled Clerk, 1988–90; Partner, 1990–98; Sen. Partner, 1998–2006; NP, Nuttall's Notaries, 2006–10. Contested (C): Sheffield Hillsborough, 1997; Morecambe and Lunesdale, 2001; Bury N, 2005; Yorkshire and the Humber, EP, 1999. *Recreations:* walking, watching cricket and football, bird watching. *Address:* House of Commons, SW1A 0AA. *T:* (020) 7219 7030. *E:* david.nuttall.mp@parliament.uk. *Club:* Salisbury Conservative (Bury).

**OFFORD, Dr Matthew James,** FRGS; MP (C) Hendon, since 2010; *b* Alton, Hants, 3 Sept. 1969; *s* of Christopher and Hilda Offord; *m* 2010, Claire Michelle Rowles. *Educ:* Amery Hill Sch., Alton; Nottingham Trent Univ. (BA Hons); Lancaster Univ. (MA); King's Coll. London (PhD 2011). FRGS 2005. Political analyst, BBC, 2001–10. Mem. (C) Barnet BC, 2002–10 (Dep. Leader, 2006–09). Chm., Hendon Cons. Assoc.,

2004–07. Contested (C) Barnsley E and Mexborough, 2001. *Recreations:* scuba diving, sailing, swimming, reading, travel, wine. *Address:* House of Commons, SW1A 0AA. *T:* (020) 7219 7083. *E:* matthew.offord.mp@parliament.uk.

**O'HARA, Brendan;** MP (SNP) Argyll and Bute, since 2015; *b* Glasgow, 27 April 1963; *m* Catherine; two *d*. *Educ:* St Andrew's Secondary Sch., Carntyne; Univ. of Strathclyde (BA Econ. Hist. and Modern Hist. 1992). Work with Glasgow DC; television producer, STV, Sky Sports, BBC; TV programmes include: Comedy Connections; Movie Connections; The Football Years; Scotland's Greatest Album; Road to Referendum. Contested (SNP): Glasgow Springburn, 1987; Glasgow Central, 1992. *Address:* House of Commons, SW1A 0AA.

**O'NEILL OF GATLEY,** Baron *cr* 2015 (Life Peer), of Gatley in the County of Greater Manchester; **Terence James, (Jim) O'Neill;** Commercial Secretary, HM Treasury, since 2015; Visiting Research Fellow, Breugel, since 2013; *b* Manchester, 17 March 1957; *s* of late Terence and Kathleen O'Neill; *m* 1983, Caroline; two *c*. *Educ:* Burnage High Sch., Manchester; Univ. of Sheffield (BA Econs 1978; MA 1979); Univ. of Surrey (PhD 1983). Economist: Bank of America, 1982–83; Internal Treasury Mgt, Marine Midland Bank, 1983–88; Swiss Bank Corp., 1988–95 (Hd of Global Res., 1991–95); Goldman Sachs: Economist and Partner, 1995–2013; Co-Hd, Global Econs Res. and Chief Currency Economist, 1995–2001; Hd, Global Econs Res., 2001–08; Chief Economist, 2001–10; Hd of Global Econs, Commodities and Strategy Res., 2008–10; Chm., Goldman Sachs Asset Mgt, 2010–13. Creator of acronym, BRICs (Brazil, Russia, India and China as the growth opportunities of the future), 2001. Chm., City Growth Commn, 2013–14. Non-exec. Dir, DFE, 2013–. Hon. DLitt Sheffield, 2014. *Publications:* The Growth Map: economic opportunity in the BRICs and beyond, 2011; The BRIC Road to Growth, 2013. *Recreations:* sport, tennis, running, football, travel.

**ONN, Melanie;** MP (Lab) Great Grimsby, since 2015; *b* Great Grimsby, 19 June 1979; *d* of Jacqueline Jagger; *m* 2014, Christopher Jenkinson; one *s*. *Educ:* Healing Comprehensive Sch., Grimsby; Franklin Coll., Grimsby; Middlesex Univ. (BA Hons Politics, Philosophy and Internat. Studies 2000). Labour Party: Facilities Adminr, 2000–03; Communications Officer to Gen. Sec., 2003–06; Compliance Officer, 2006–10; Hd of Compliance, 2010; Regl Organiser, Yorks and Humber, Unison, 2010–15. *Address:* House of Commons, SW1A 0AA. *T:* (020) 7219 6282; (office) 112 Cleethorpe Road, Grimsby, NE Lincs DN31 3HW. *T:* (01472) 359584. *E:* melanie.onn.mp@parliament.uk.

**ONWURAH, Chinyelu Susan, (Chi);** MP (Lab) Newcastle upon Tyne Central, since 2010; *b* Wallsend, 12 April 1965. *Educ:* Kenton Sch.; Imperial Coll., London (BEng Electrical Engrg 1987); Manchester Business Sch. (MBA 2002). CEng 2003. With Nortel, 1987–95; Cable & Wireless, 1995–99; Director: product strategy, Global Telesystems UK, 1999–2000; mkt develt, Teligent, 2000–01; Partner, Hammatan Ventures, 2001–04; Hd, telecoms technol., Ofcom, 2004–10. Shadow Minister: for innovation and sci., BIS, 2010–13; Cabinet Office, 2013–15. *Address:* House of Commons, SW1A 0AA.

**OPPERMAN, Guy Thomas;** MP (C) Hexham, since 2010; an Assistant Government Whip, since 2015; *b* Marlborough, Wilts, 18 May 1965; *s* of Michael Opperman and Julia Opperman. *Educ:* Univ. of Lille (Dip. 1st Cl. 1984); Univ. of Buckingham (LLB 1986). Farmer, Africa, 1987; called to the Bar, Middle Temple, 1989; in practice as a barrister, 1989–2010. Dir, TD Chrome Ltd, family engrg business, until 2009. Mem. (C) Wilts CC, 1995–99. Contested (C): N Swindon, 1997; Caernarfon, 2005. *Publications:* over 100 articles. *Recreations:* amateur steeplechase jockey, writing. *Address:* House of Commons, SW1A 0AA; (constituency office) 1 Meal Market, Hexham NE46 1NF. *Club:* Albert Edward (Hexham).

**OSAMOR, Kate Ofunne;** MP (Lab and Co-op) Edmonton, since 2015; *b* N London, 15 Aug. 1968. *Educ:* Creighton Comprehensive Sch.; Univ. of E London (BA Hons Third World Studies 2006). Big issue; NHS Exec. Asst, Camidoc GP Out of Hours, 2002–10; Black and Ethnic Minorities Labour, 2012–13; NHS Practice Manager: Sterndale Surgery, 2012–13; Park Lodge Med. Centre, 2013–15. Member: Petitions Select Cttee, 2015–; Educn Select Cttee, 2015–. Mem., Nat. Exec., Labour Party, 2014–. *Address:* House of Commons, SW1A 0AA.

**OSBORNE, Rt Hon. George (Gideon Oliver);** PC 2010; MP (C) Tatton, since 2001; Chancellor of the Exchequer, since 2010; First Secretary of State, since 2015; *b* 23 May 1971; *s* and *heir* of Sir Peter George Osborne, Bt; *m* 1998, Hon. Frances Victoria, *d* of Baron Howell of Guildford, PC; one *s* one *d*. *Educ:* St Paul's Sch., London; Davidson Coll., N Carolina (Dean Rusk Schol.); Magdalen Coll., Oxford (MA Hons Mod. Hist.). Freelance journalist, 1993; Hd, Pol Sect., Cons. Res. Dept, 1994–95; Special Advr, MAFF, 1995–97; Pol Office, 10 Downing St, 1997; Pol Sec. to Leader of Opposition, 1997–2001; Sec. to Shadow Cabinet, 1997–2001. An Opposition Whip, 2003; Opposition frontbench spokesman on Treasury, 2003–04; Shadow Chief Sec. to HM Treasury, 2004–05; Shadow Chancellor of the Exchequer, 2005–10. Member: Public Accounts Cttee, 2001–03, Public Accounts Commn, 2002–03, H of C; Select Cttee on Transport,

2003. Trustee, Arts and Business, 2006–10. Vice-Pres., E Cheshire Hospice, 2001–. *Address:* House of Commons, SW1A 0AA. *T:* (020) 7219 8214.

**OSWALD, Kirsten Frances;** MP (SNP) East Renfrewshire, since 2015; *b* Dundee, 21 Dec. 1972; *d* of Ed and Helen Oswald; *m* Davinder Bedi; two *s*. *Educ:* Carnoustie High Sch.; Univ. of Glasgow (MA Hons Hist. 2005). HR, Motherwell Coll., 1998–2002; Hd of HR, South Lanarks Coll., 2002–15. SNP spokesperson on armed forces and veterans, 2015–. *Address:* House of Commons, SW1A 0AA.

**OWEN, Albert;** MP (Lab) Ynys Môn, since 2001; *b* 10 Aug. 1959; *s* of late William Owen and Doreen Owen (*née* Woods); *m* 1983, Angela Margaret Magee; two *d*. *Educ:* Holyhead Comprehensive Sch.; Coleg Harlech; Univ. of York (BA Hons Politics 1997). Merchant seafarer, 1975–92; full-time educn, 1992–97; Manager, Centre for the Unwaged (advice, trng and information centre), 1997–2001. *Recreations:* travel by train, cooking, gardening, walking, running, cycling. *Address:* House of Commons, SW1A 0AA; (constituency office) Ty Cledwyn, 18a Thomas Street, Holyhead, Anglesey LL65 1RR. *T:* (01407) 765750.

**PAISLEY, Hon. Ian Richard Kyle;** MP (DemU) North Antrim, since 2010; *b* 12 Dec. 1966; *s* of Baron Bannside, PC and of Baroness Paisley of St George's; *m* 1990, Fiona Margaret Elizabeth Currie; two *s* two *d*. *Educ:* Shaftesbury House Coll.; Methodist Coll.; Queen's Univ., Belfast (BA Hons Modern History; MSSc Irish Politics 1995). Res. Asst for Dr Ian Paisley, MP, H of C, 1989–2010. Member: NI Forum for Political Dialogue, 1996–98; NI Police Bd, 2001–10. Justice spokesman, DUP, 1992–2002. Mem. (DemU) Antrim N, NI Assembly, 1998–2010. Jun. Minister, Office of First Minister and Dep. First Minister, NI, 2007–08. Fellow, Sch. of Leadership, Maryland State Univ., 1997. Royal Humane Soc. Testimonial, 1999. *Publications:* Reasonable Doubt: the case for the UDR Four, 1991; Echoes: Protestant identity in Northern Ireland, 1994; Peace Deal?, 1998; Ian Paisley: a life in photographs, 2004; articles in jls. *Recreations:* my children, Chinese food, cinema, Rugby, motorcycling. *Address:* House of Commons, SW1A 0AA; 9–11 Church Street, Ballymena, Co. Antrim BT43 6DD.

**PARISH, Neil Quentin Gordon;** MP (C) Tiverton and Honiton, since 2010; *b* 26 May 1956; *s* of Reginald Thomas Parish and Kathleen Susan Mary Parish; *m* 1981, Susan Gail; one *s* one *d*. *Educ:* Brymore Sch., Somerset. Left sch. at 16 to run farm of 100 acres; farm increased to 300 acres, dairy and arable, 1990. Member (C): Sedgemoor DC, 1983–95 (Dep. Leader, 1989–95); Somerset CC, 1989–93; Parish Council, 1985–. European Parliament: Mem. (C) SW Region, England, 1999–2009; spokesman on agriculture and on fisheries; Chairman: Agric. and

Rural Develt Cttee, 1999–2009; Animal Welfare Intergroup, 2007–09; Member: Envmt Cttee, 2001–09; Fisheries Cttee, 2002–09; Chm., Select Cttee on Envmt, Food and Rural Affairs, 2015–. Mem., EU Australian and NZ delegn. Contested (C) Torfaen, 1997. *Recreations:* swimming, walking. *Address:* House of Commons, SW1A 0AA.

**PATEL, Rt Hon. Priti;** PC 2015; MP (C) Witham, since 2010; Minister of State (Minister for Employment), Department for Work and Pensions, since 2015; *b* London, 29 March 1972; *d* of Sushil K. Patel and Anjana Patel; *m* 2004, Alex Sawyer; one *s*. *Educ:* Westfield Girls' Sch., Watford; Keele Univ. (BA Econs); Univ. of Essex (Dip. British Govt). Dep. Press Sec. to Rt Hon. William Hague, 1997–2000; Associate Dir, Shandwick, 2000–03; Corporate Relns Manager, Diageo plc, 2003–07; Dir, Corporate Communications, Weber Shandwick, 2007–10. Exchequer Sec., HM Treasury, 2014–15. *Recreations:* cricket, horseracing, rock music, travel. *Address:* House of Commons, SW1A 0AA. *T:* (020) 7219 3000. *E:* priti.patel.mp@parliament.uk.

**PATERSON, Rt Hon. Owen (William);** PC 2010; MP (C) North Shropshire, since 1997; *b* 24 June 1956; *s* of late Alfred Paterson and Cynthia Paterson (*née* Owen); *m* 1980, Hon. Rose Emily Ridley; two *s* one *d*. *Educ:* Radley Coll.; Corpus Christi Coll., Cambridge (MA Hist.). British Leather Co.: Sales Dir, 1980; Man. Dir, 1993–97. Pres., European Tanners' Confedn, 1996–97. Contested (C) Wrexham, 1992. Opposition Whip, 2000–01; PPS to Leader of Opposition, 2001–03; Shadow Minster for DEFRA, 2003–05; Shadow Minister of State for Transport, 2005–07; Shadow Sec. of State for NI, 2007–10; Secretary of State: for NI, 2010–12; for Envmt, Food and Rural Affairs, 2012–14. *Recreations:* travel, history, trees, riding, hunting, racing, poultry. *Address:* House of Commons, SW1A 0AA.

**PATERSON, Steven;** MP (SNP) Stirling, since 2015; *b* Stirling, 25 April 1975. *Educ:* Cambusbarron Prim. Sch.; Stirling High Sch.; Univ. of Stirling (BA Hons Hist. and Politics). Visitor Attraction Asst, Argyll, The Isles, Loch Lomond, Stirling and the Trossachs, Scottish Tourist Bd, then VisitScotland, 1997–2006; Media and Communications Manager for Bruce Crawford, MSP, 2006–15. Mem. (SNP), Stirling Council, 2007–15. *Address:* (office) Springfield House, Laurelhill Business Park, Stirling FK7 9JQ. *T:* (01786) 406375. *E:* steven.paterson.mp@parliament.uk.

**PAWSEY, Mark;** MP (C) Rugby, since 2010; *b* Meriden, 16 Jan. 1957; *s* of James Francis Pawsey; *m* 1984, Tracy Harris; two *s* two *d*. *Educ:* Reading Univ. (BSc Estate Mgt 1978). Trainee Surveyor, Strutt & Parker, 1978–79; Account Manager, Autobar Vending Supplied Ltd, 1979–82; Founder and Man. Dir, Central Catering

Supplies, 1982–2008. Mem., Communities and Local Govt Select Cttee, 2010–15. Contested (C) Nuneaton, 2005. *Recreations:* Rugby football, planting woodland, cooking. *Address:* House of Commons, SW1A 0AA. *E:* mark.pawsey.mp@parliament.uk.

**PEARCE, Teresa;** MP (Lab) Erith and Thamesmead, since 2010; *b* Southport, 1 Feb. 1955; *d* of Arthur and Josephine Farrington; two *d. Educ:* St Thomas More RC Sch., Eltham. Inland Revenue, 1975–79; Knox Cropper, 1989–99; Sen. Manager, Pricewaterhouse Coopers, 1999–2009. Mem. (Lab) Bexley LBC, 1998–2002. Mem., Erith Slopes Socialist Book Club. *Recreations:* cinema, reading, travel. *Address:* House of Commons, SW1A 0AA. *T:* (020) 7210 6936. *E:* teresa.pearce.mp@parliament.uk. *W:* www.teresapearce.org.uk.

**PENNING, Rt Hon. Michael (Allan);** PC 2014; MP (C) Hemel Hempstead, since 2005; Minister of State, Home Office and Ministry of Justice, since 2014; *b* 28 Sept. 1957; *s* of Brian and Freda Penning; *m* 1988, Angela Louden; two *d. Educ:* Appleton Comp. Sch., Benfleet; King Edmund Comp. Sch., Rochford. Served Grenadier Guards, 1974–79; RAMC, 1979–81; Essex Fire and Rescue Service, 1981–88; freelance media consultant, 1999–2000; Dep. Hd, News and Media, Conservative Party, 2000–04. Parly Under-Sec. of State, DfT, 2010–12; Minister of State: NI Office, 2012–13; DWP, 2013–14. Contested (C) Thurrock, 2001. GSM 1976. *Recreations:* keen angler, passionate Rugby Union supporter. *Address:* House of Commons, SW1A 0AA. *T:* (020) 7219 3000. *E:* penningm@parliament.uk.

**PENNYCOOK, Matthew Thomas;** MP (Lab) Greenwich and Woolwich, since 2015; *b* 29 Oct. 1982; partner, Joanna. *Educ:* London Sch. of Econs and Pol Sci. (BA 1st Cl. Hons Internat. Relns and Hist.); Balliol Coll., Oxford (Schol.; MPhil Internat. Relns (Dist.)). Volunteer, Child Poverty Action Gp; sen. roles in charity and voluntary sectors, incl. Fair Pay Network; Sen. Res. and Policy Analyst, Resolution Foundn. Mem., Energy and Climate Change Select Cttee, 2015–. Mem. (Lab) Greenwich LBC, 2010–15. *Address:* House of Commons, SW1A 0AA.

**PENROSE, John David;** MP (C) Weston-super-Mare, since 2005; a Lord Commissioner of HM Treasury (Government Whip), since 2014; Parliamentary Secretary, Cabinet Office, since 2015; *b* 22 June 1964; *s* of late David Goronwe Penrose and of Anna Jill Penrose (who *m* 1995, Tom Lawrie); *m* 1995, Hon. Diana Mary Harding (Baroness Harding of Winscombe); two *d. Educ:* Ipswich Sch.; Downing Coll., Cambridge (BA Hons 1986); Columbia Univ., NY (MBA 1991). J. P. Morgan, 1986–90; McKinsey & Co., 1992–94; Commercial Dir, Academic Books Div., Thomson Publishing, 1995–96; Man. Dir, Longman sch. textbooks for UK and Africa,

Pearson plc, 1996–2000; Chm., Logotron, 2001–08. Contested (C): Ealing Southall, 1997; Weston-super-Mare, 2001. PPS to Chm., Cons. Policy Rev., 2006–08; Shadow Minister for Business, 2009–10; Parly Under-Sec. of State, DCMS, 2010–12; an Asst Govt Whip, 2013–14. Mem., Amnesty Internat. Mem., Blagdon and Dist Beekeeping Club. *Recreations:* fishing, beekeeping, listening to other people's opinions. *Address:* House of Commons, SW1A 0AA. *Clubs:* Weston-super-Mare Conservative; Weston-super-Mare Constitutional.

**PERCY, Andrew;** MP (C) Brigg and Goole, since 2010; *b* Hull, 1977. *Educ:* York Univ. (BA Hons); Leeds Univ. (PGCE). History teacher in schs in E Yorks and N Lincs; MP's researcher; pt-time primary sch. teacher. Mem. (C) Hull CC, 2000–10. Contested (C) Normanton, 2005. Member, Select Committee: on Procedure, 2010–11; on Regulatory Reform, 2010–15; on Standing Orders, 2011–; on Health, 2012–; on NI Affairs, 2012–15; Panel of Chairs, 2015–. *Address:* House of Commons, SW1A 0AA.

**PERKINS, (Matthew) Toby;** MP (Lab) Chesterfield, since 2010; *b* 12 Aug. 1970; *s* of Victor F. Perkins and late Teresa Perkins; *m* 1996, Susan Beverley Francis; one *s* one *d. Educ:* Trinity Sch., Leamington Spa; Silverdale Sch., Sheffield. Telephone sales, CCS Media, 1991–95; Prime Time Recruitment: Recruitment Consultant, 1995–97; Branch Manager, 1997–99; Area Manager, 2000–02; estabd Club Rugby, 2005–10; Dir, Birdholme Children's Centre Nursery, 2007–10. Mem. (Lab) Chesterfield BC, 2003–11. Shadow Educn Minister, 2010–11; Shadow Business Minister, 2011–. Member: Communities and Local Govt Select Cttee, 2010; Jt Cttee on Statutory Instruments, 2010–15. Former player, Chesterfield, Sheffield Tigers and Derbys Rugby Union; qualified Rugby coach, 2006. *Address:* House of Commons, SW1A 0AA.

**PERRY, Claire Louise;** MP (C) Devizes, since 2010; Parliamentary Under-Secretary of State, Department for Transport, since 2014; *b* Bromsgrove, 3 April 1964; *d* of David Richens and Joanna Richens; *m* 1996, Clayton Perry (marr. diss. 2014); one *s* two *d. Educ:* Brasenose Coll., Oxford (BA Hons Geog. 1985); Harvard Business Sch. (MBA 1990). Vice Pres., Bank of America, 1985–88; Engagement Manager, McKinsey & Co., 1990–94; Dir and Hd of Equities E-commerce, Credit Suisse, 1994–2000. PPS to Sec. of State for Defence, 2011–12; an Asst Govt Whip, 2013–14. Adviser to Prime Minister on preventing the commercialisation and sexualisation of childhood, 2012–. *Recreations:* gardening, cycling, reading. *Address:* House of Commons, SW1A 0AA. *T:* (020) 7219 7050. *E:* claire.perry.mp@parliament.uk.

**PHILLIPS, Jessica Rose;** MP (Lab) Birmingham Yardley, since 2015; *b* Yardley, 9 Oct. 1981; *m* Tom Phillips; two *s. Educ:* Univ. of Leeds (BA Jt

Hons Econ. and Social Hist. and Social Policy 2003); Univ. of Birmingham (Postgrad. Dip. Public Sector Mgt 2013). Project and Event Manager, Health Links, 2008–10; Business Develt Manager, Sandwell Women's Aid, 2010–15. Mem. (Lab), Birmingham CC, 2012–. Mem., Women and Equalities Select Cttee, 2015–. Victims' Champion, Birmingham, 2011. *Address:* House of Commons, SW1A 0AA.

**PHILLIPS, Stephen James;** QC 2009; MP (C) Sleaford and North Hykeham, since 2010; a Recorder, since 2009; *b* London, 9 March 1970; *s* of late Stewart Charles Phillips and of Janice Frances Phillips (*née* Woodall, now Pavey); *m* 1998, Fiona Jane Parkin (marr. diss. 2013); one *s* two *d*. *Educ:* Canford Sch.; Oriel Coll., Oxford (BA Juris 1991; BCL 1992). Late 14/20 King's Hussars and Welsh Guards. Called to the Bar, Lincoln's Inn, 1993; in practice specialising in commercial litigation. Chm. of Govs, Frank Barnes Sch. for Deaf Children, 2006–10. Member: European Scrutiny Cttee, 2010–15; Public Accounts Cttee, 2014–. *Recreation:* getting muddy with my kids. *Address:* 7 King's Bench Walk, Temple, EC4Y 7DS. *T:* (020) 7910 8300, *Fax:* (020) 7910 8400. *E:* clerks@7kbw.com; House of Commons, SW1A 0AA. *Club:* Cavalry and Guards.

**PHILLIPSON, Bridget Maeve;** MP (Lab) Houghton and Sunderland South, since 2010; *b* Gateshead, 19 Dec. 1983; *d* of Clare Phillipson; *m* 2009, Lawrence Dimery; one *d*. *Educ:* St Robert of Newminster Catholic Sch., Washington; Hertford Coll., Oxford (BA Hons Modern Hist. 2005). Sunderland CC, 2005–07; Manager, Wearside Women in Need refuge, 2007–10. Mem., Lab Party Nat. Policy Forum, 2002–04. Chm., Oxford Univ. Labour Club, 2003. *Recreations:* reading, music, dog-walking. *Address:* House of Commons, SW1A 0AA. *T:* (020) 7219 7087. *E:* bridget.phillipson.mp@parliament.uk.

**PHILP, Chris;** MP (C) Croydon South, since 2015; *b* Bromley, 6 July 1976; *s* of Brian Philp and Edna Philp; *m* 2009, Elizabeth Purves; one *s* one *d* (twins). *Educ:* St Olave's Grammar Sch., Orpington; University Coll., Oxford (MPhys 1st Cl.). Analyst, McKinsey & Co., 1998–2000; Co-Founder and Dir, Blueheath, 2000–04; Co-Founder and Chief Executive Officer: Pluto Capital, 2004–15; Pluto Finance. Contested (C) Hampstead and Kilburn, 2010. *Publications:* (ed) Conservative Revival, 2006. *Recreations:* football, ski-ing, riding. *Address:* House of Commons, SW1A 0AA. *T:* (020) 7219 3000. *E:* chris.philp.mp@parliament.uk.

**PICKLES, Rt Hon. Sir Eric (Jack),** Kt 2015; PC 2010; MP (C) Brentwood and Ongar, since 1992; *b* 20 April 1952; *m* 1976, Irene. *Educ:* Greenhead Grammar Sch.; Leeds Polytechnic. Joined Conservative Party, 1968; Young Conservatives: Area Chm., 1976–78; Nat. Vice-Chm., 1978–80; Nat. Chm., 1980–81;

Conservative Party: Member: Nat. Union Exec. Cttee, 1975–91; One Nation Forum, 1987–91; Nat. Local Govt Adv. Cttee, 1985– (Chm., 1992–93); Lectr, Cons. Agents Examination Courses, 1988–; Local Govt Editor, Newsline, 1990–92; a Vice-Chm., 1993–97; Dep. Chm., 2005–07. Bradford Council: Councillor, 1979–91; Chm., Social Services, 1982–84; Chm., Educn, 1984–86; Leader, Cons. Gp, 1987–91; Leader of Council, 1988–90. Dep. Leader, Cons. Gp, AMA, 1989–91. PPS to Minister for Industry, 1993; Opposition frontbench spokesman on social security, 1998–2001; Shadow Transport Minister, 2001–02; Shadow Sec. of State for Local Govt and the Regions, 2002–07, for Communities and Local Govt, 2007–09; Sec. of State for Communities and Local Govt, 2010–15. Chm., All Party Film Gp, 1997–2004; Vice-Chm., Cons. Envmt, Transport and Regions Cttee, 1997–98. Chm., Conservative Party, 2009–10. UK Envoy on post-Holocaust Issues, 2015–. Mem., Council of Europe, 1997–. Mem., Yorks Area RHA, 1982–90. *Recreations:* film buff, opera, serious walking. *Address:* House of Commons, SW1A 0AA.

**PINCHER, Christopher John;** MP (C) Tamworth, since 2010; *b* Walsall, 24 Sept. 1969; *s* of John and Sandra Pincher. *Educ:* Ounsdale Sch., Wombourne, Staffs; London Sch. of Econs and Pol Sci. (BSc (Econ) Govt and Hist. 1991). Exec., outsourcing practice, Accenture, 1993–2010. PPS to Foreign Sec., 2015–; Mem., Energy and Climate Change Select Cttee, 2010–15. *Recreations:* horse racing, motor sports, history. *Address:* House of Commons, SW1A 0AA. *T:* (020) 7219 7169. *E:* christopher. pincher.mp@parliament.uk. *Club:* Travellers.

**POULTER, Dr Daniel Leonard James;** MP (C) Central Suffolk and North Ipswich, since 2010; *b* Beckenham, 30 Oct. 1978. *Educ:* Univ. of Bristol (LLB Hons); Univ. of London (MB BS); King's Coll., London (AKC). Medical doctor specialising in obstetrics and gynaecol. Mem. (C) Hastings BC, 2006–07; Dep. Leader, Reigate and Banstead BC, 2008–10. Parly Under-Sec. of State, DoH, 2012–15. Member: Health Select Cttee, 2011–12; House of Lords Reform Cttee, 2011–12. *Publications:* articles in field of women's health. *Recreations:* Rugby, cricket, golf. *Address:* House of Commons, SW1A 0AA. *E:* daniel. poulter.mp@parliament.uk.

**POUND, Stephen Pelham;** MP (Lab) Ealing North, since 1997; *b* 3 July 1948; *s* of late Pelham Pound and Dominica James; *m* 1976, Marilyn Anne Griffiths; one *s* two *d*. *Educ:* London Sch. of Economics (BSc Econ., Dip. Indust. Relations). Seaman, 1967–69; Bus Conductor, 1969–70; Hosp. Porter, 1970–79; student, 1980–84; Housing Officer, Camden Council, 1984–88; Homeless Persons Officer, Hammersmith and Fulham Council, 1988–90; Housing Officer, Paddington Churches HA, 1990–97. Councillor,

London Borough of Ealing, 1982–98; Mayor of Ealing, 1995–96. Opposition Whip, 2010; Shadow Minister of State for NI, 2011–15. *Recreations:* Fulham FC, cricket, walking, collecting comics. *Address:* House of Commons, SW1A 0AA. *T:* (020) 7219 6238; 115 Milton Road, Hanwell, W7 1LG. *Clubs:* St Joseph's Catholic Social; Fulham Football Club Supporters'.

**POW, Rebecca Faye;** MP (C) Taunton Deane, since 2015; *b* Somerset, 10 Oct. 1960; *m* Charles Clark; three *c. Educ:* Wye Coll., Univ. of London (BSc Hons Rural Envmt Studies 1982). Presenter, producer and dir, HTV, ITV West and Channel 4, 1989–2005, incl. Envmt Corresp., HTV; producer and presenter, Farming Today, BBC Radio 4; work for NFU; Dir, Pow Prodns, PR co., 1988–. Member: Envmtl Audit Cttee, 2015–; Envmt Food and Rural Affairs Select Cttee, 2015–. Trustee, Somerset Wildlife Trust. *Address:* House of Commons, SW1A 0AA.

**POWELL, Lucy Maria;** MP (Lab) Manchester Central, since Nov. 2012; *b* Manchester, 10 Oct. 1974; *d* of John Lloyd Powell and Mary Powell; *m* 2009, James Williamson; one *s* one *d* and one step *s. Educ:* Parrs Wood High Sch.; Somerville Coll., Oxford; King's Coll. London (BSc Chem.). Parly asst to Glenda Jackson, MP, 1997–98, to Beverley Hughes, MP, 1998–99; PR rôle, later Hd, Regl Campaigning, then Campaign Dir, Britain in Europe, 1999–2005; Gov. relns, 2006–07; Leader, Manchester Innovation Fund project, 2007–10, NESTA; Manager, Labour Party leadership campaign for Rt Hon. Edward Miliband, 2010; Actg COS, then Dep. COS to Leader of Opposition, 2010–12; Shadow Minister for Childcare and Children, 2013–14, for Cabinet Office, 2014–15; Shadow Sec. of State for Educn, 2015–. Mem., Transport Select Cttee, 2012–13. *Address:* House of Commons, SW1A 0AA.

**PRENTIS, Hon. Victoria Mary Boswell;** MP (C) Banbury, since 2015; *b* Banbury, 24 March 1971; *d* of Baron Boswell of Aynho; *m* 1996, Sebastian Hugh Runton Prentis; two *d* (one *s* decd). *Educ:* Royal Holloway and Bedford New Coll., London (BA Hons English Lit.); Downing Coll., Cambridge (MA Law). Called to the Bar, Middle Temple, 1995; with Govt Legal Service, latterly Sen. CS, 1997–2014. *Recreations:* the countryside, detective fiction, cider making, fundraising. *Address:* House of Commons, SW1A 0AA. *T:* (020) 7219 8756. *E:* victoria. prentis.mp@parliament.uk. *Clubs:* Carlton, Farmers.

**PRIOR OF BRAMPTON,** Baron *cr* 2015 (Life Peer), of Swannington in the County of Norfolk; **David Gifford Leathes Prior;** Parliamentary Under-Secretary of State, Department of Health, since 2015; chairman and director of various private companies; *b* 3 Dec. 1954; *s* of Baron Prior, PC; *m* 1987, Caroline Henrietta Holmes; twin *s* and *d. Educ:* Charterhouse; Pembroke

Coll., Cambridge (Exhibnr; MA Law 1976). Called to the Bar, Gray's Inn, 1977; Commercial Dir, British Steel, 1980–87. MP (C) N Norfolk, 1997–2001; contested (C) same seat, 2001. Vice Chm., 1998–99, Dep. Chm. and Chief Exec., 1999–2001, Conservative Party. Chm., Norfolk and Norwich University Hospital Trust, 2002–06 and 2007–13; Chm., Care Quality Commn, 2013–15. *Recreations:* gardening, farming, most sports. *Address:* Swannington Manor, Swannington, Norwich NR9 5NR. *T:* (01603) 861560. *Club:* Royal Automobile.

**PRISK, (Michael) Mark;** MP (C) Hertford and Stortford, since 2001; Prime Minister's Investment Envoy to the Nordic and Baltic Nations, since 2014; *b* 12 June 1962; *s* of Michael Raymond Prisk and June Irene Prisk; *m* 1989, Lesley Jane Titcomb. *Educ:* Truro Sch., Cornwall; Univ. of Reading (BSc Hons Land Mgt). Knight Frank & Rutley, 1983–85; Chartered Surveyor, 1985–; Dir, Derrick, Wade & Waters, 1989–91; Principal: Mark Prisk Connection, 1991–97; mp2, 1997–2001. Shadow Financial Sec., 2002–03; Shadow Paymaster Gen., 2003–04; Opposition Whip, 2004–05; Shadow Minister, Small Business and Enterprise, 2005–08, Business, 2008–10; Minister of State, BIS, 2010–12; Minister of State (Minister for Housing), DCLG, 2012–13. Contested (C): Newham NW, 1992; Wansdyke, 1997. Nat. Vice Chm., FCS, 1981–82; Trustee: Industry and Parliament Trust, 2007–; Parliament Choir, 2014–. Dir, Edward Stanfords Ltd, 2014–. Chm., Youth for Peace through NATO, 1983–85. Chm. Governors, Stratford GM Sch., 1992–93. *Recreations:* piano, choral music, Rugby and cricket supporter. *Address:* House of Commons, SW1A 0AA. *T:* (020) 7219 3000.

**PRITCHARD, Mark Andrew;** MP (C) The Wrekin, since 2005; *b* 22 Nov. 1966; *s* of late Francis Pritchard and of Romona Pritchard; *m* 1997, Sondra Janae Spaeth (marr. diss. 2013). *Educ:* London Guildhall Univ. (MA Mktg Mgt); CIM Postgrad. Dip. Mktg; Elim Coll. (Cert. Theol. and Pastoral Studies); Univ. of Buckingham (MA Internat. Diplomacy, 2013). Parly researcher, 1994–95; founder and owner: Pritchard Communications Ltd, 1999–2007; Next Steps Mkt Res. Ltd, 2002–06. Member: Harrow BC, 1993–94; Woking BC, 2000–03. Contested (C) Warley, 2001. Member: Envmtl Audit Select Cttee, 2005–07; DWP Select Cttee, 2006–08; Welsh Affairs Select Cttee, 2007–10; Transport Select Cttee, 2008–10; Jt Nat. Security Strategy Cttee, 2010–; DFID Select Cttee, 2012–; Speaker's Panel, 2013–; Vice Chairman: All Party Parly Gp on Social Care, 2005; ASEAN Parly Gp, 2010–; Parly Gp for Abolition of Death Penalty, 2012–; Secretary: Cons. Parly Defence Cttee, 2006; Cons. Parly Foreign Affairs Gp, 2006; 1922 Cttee, 2010–12; Vice Chm., Cons. Parly Foreign Affairs and Defence Cttee; Mem., Cons. Homeland Security Team, 2006–; Founding Mem. and Comr, Cons. Human Rights Commn,

2006–; Mem. Bd, Parliamentarians for Global Action, 2007–. Member: Parly Delegn to NATO, 2010–14; British Irish Parly Assembly, 2013–. Dep. Chm., Internat. Office, Cons. Party, 2010–12. Member: Council, Bow Gp, 1993–94; Bd, Cons. Councillors Assoc., 2002–05. *Recreations:* writing comedy, trainee bird watcher, jazz, ski-ing, animal welfare. *Address:* c/o House of Commons, SW1A 0AA. *T:* (020) 7219 3000. *E:* pritchardm@parliament.uk.

**PUGH, Dr John David;** MP (Lib Dem) Southport, since 2001; *b* 28 June 1948; *s* of James and Patricia Pugh; *m* 1971, Annette; one *s* three *d*. *Educ:* Maidstone Grammar Sch.; Durham Univ.; PhD Manchester; MPhil Nottingham; MA Liverpool. Head: Social Studies, Salesian High Sch., Bootle, 1972–83; Philosophy and Religious Studies, Merchant Taylors' Sch., Crosby, 1983–2001. Mem. (Lib Dem) Sefton MBC, 1987–2002 (Leader, Lib Dem Gp, 1992–2001; Leader of Council, 2000–01). *Publications:* The Christian Understanding of God, 1990. *Recreation:* cycling. *Address:* House of Commons, SW1A 0AA; 27 The Walk, Birkdale, Southport, Lancs PR8 4BG. *T:* (01704) 569025. *Club:* National Liberal.

**PURSGLOVE, Thomas Christopher John;** MP (C) Corby, since 2015; *b* 5 Nov. 1988. *Educ:* Sir Christopher Hatton Sch., Wellingborough; Queen Mary Coll., Univ. of London (BA Politics). Pt-time work for Rt Hon. Douglas Hogg, MP, 2008–10; Parly Asst to Christopher Heaton-Harris, MP, 2010–15; Dir, Together Against Wind, 2014–. Mem. (C), Wellingborough BC, 2007–15. *Recreations:* cricket, swimming, golf. *Address:* House of Commons, SW1A 0AA.

**QUIN, Jeremy Mark;** MP (C) Horsham, since 2015; *b* Aylesbury, 24 Sept. 1968; *s* of Rev. David Quin and late Elizabeth Quin; *m* 2003, Joanna Healey. *Educ:* St Albans Sch.; Hertford Coll., Oxford (BA Hons Mod. Hist. 1990). Natwest Wood Mackenzie & Co. Ltd, 1990–99; BT Alex Brown, 1999–2000; a Man. Dir, Deutsche Bank, 2000–15. Mem., Work and Pensions Select Cttee, 2015–. Contested (C) Meirionnydd Nant Conwy, 1997. *Address:* House of Commons, SW1A 0AA. *E:* jeremy.quin.mp@parliament.uk.

**QUINCE, Will;** MP (C) Colchester, since 2015; *b* Ascot; *s* of Nigel Anthony Quince and Jane Frances Quince; *m* 2009, Elinor Ann; one *d* (one *s* decd). *Educ:* Windsor Boys' Sch.; Univ. of Wales, Aberystwyth (LLB Hons Law); Univ. of West of England (DipLP 2012). Mkt Develt Exec., Concur Technologies Ltd, 2005–06; Customer Develt Manager, Britvic Soft Drinks plc, 2006–10; trainee solicitor, Asher Prior Bates, 2010–13; Solicitor, Thompson Smith and Puxon, 2013–15. Member (C): E Herts DC, 2007–08; Colchester BC, 2011–. *Address:* 66 Prettygate Road, Colchester, Essex CO3 4ED. *T:* 07944 098398. *E:* will.quince.mp@parliament.uk.

**QURESHI, Yasmin;** MP (Lab) Bolton South East, since 2010; *b* Pakistan, 5 July 1963; *d* of Mohammad Qureshi and Sakina Beg; *m* 2008, Nadeem Ashraf Butt. *Educ:* Westfield Sch.; South Bank Poly. (BA Law 1984); Council of Legal Educn; University Coll. London (LLM 1987). Called to the Bar, Lincoln's Inn, 1985; in practice as barrister, 1987–; Crown Prosecutor, CPS, 1987–2000; Hd, Criminal Legal Section, UN Mission, Kosovo, 2000–01; Dir, Dept of Judicial Admin, Kosovo, 2001–02; Policy Adviser, CPS, 2002–04; Human Rights Advr to Mayor of London, 2004–08; barrister: 2 King's Bench Walk Chambers, 2004–08; Kenworthy's Chambers, Manchester, 2008–10. Contested (Lab) Brent E, 2005. Mem., Justice Select Cttee, 2010–15. *Address:* House of Commons, SW1A 0AA.

**RAAB, Dominic Rennie;** MP (C) Esher and Walton, since 2010; Parliamentary Under-Secretary of State, Ministry of Justice, since 2015; *b* Bucks, 25 Feb. 1974; *m* 2005, Erika Rey. *Educ:* Dr Challoner's Grammar Sch., Amersham; Lady Margaret Hall, Oxford (BA Law); Jesus Coll., Cambridge (LLM). Internat. lawyer; Linklaters, incl. secondments to Liberty and in Brussels advising on EU and WTO law, 1998–2000; entered FCO, 2000; advr on legal issues, 2000–03; First Sec. (Legal), The Hague, 2003–06; COS to Shadow Home Sec., 2006–08, to Shadow Justice Sec., 2008–10. Member: Jt Cttee on Human Rights, 2010–13; Educn Select Cttee, 2013–15. *Publications:* The Assault on Liberty: what went wrong with rights, 2009. *Recreations:* sport (karate black belt 3rd dan, boxing), theatre, travel. *Address:* House of Commons, SW1A 0AA.

**RAYNER, Angela;** MP (Lab) Ashton-under-Lyne, since 2015; *b* Stockport, 28 March 1980; *d* of Martyn and Lynne Bowen; one *s*; *m* 2010, Mark Rayner; two *s*. *Educ:* Bridgehall Primary Sch.; Avondale High Sch.; Stockport Coll. (British Sign Lang., Care, Counselling). Home help, private sector and local govt, 1998–2005. Trade union lay activist, 2002–15. Samaritan, 1997–2000. *Address:* House of Commons, SW1A 0AA. *T:* (020) 7219 8782. *E:* angela.rayner.mp@ parliament.uk.

**REDWOOD, Rt Hon. John (Alan);** PC 1993; DPhil; MP (C) Wokingham, since 1987; *b* 15 June 1951; *s* of William Charles Redwood and Amy Emma Redwood (*née* Champion); *m* 1974, Gail Felicity Chippington (marr. diss. 2004); one *s* one *d*. *Educ:* Kent Coll., Canterbury; Magdalen and St Antony's Colls, Oxford; MA, DPhil Oxon. MCSI. Fellow, All Souls Coll., Oxford, 1972–87, 2003–05, 2007–. Investment Adviser, Robert Fleming & Co., 1973–77; Investment Manager and Dir, N. M. Rothschild & Sons, 1977–87; Norcros plc: Dir, 1985–89; Jt Dep. Chm., 1986–87; non-exec. Chm., 1987–89. Non-executive Chairman: Hare Hatch Hldgs Ltd (formerly Mabey Securities), 1999–2008; Concentric plc, 2003–08; Pan Asset Capital Mgt, 2007–09; non-exec. Dir, BNB, 2001–07.

Investment Advr, CS (formerly Evercore) Pan Asset, 2007–. Adviser, Treasury and Civil Service Select Cttee, 1981; Head of PM's Policy Unit, 1983–85. Councillor, Oxfordshire CC, 1973–77. Parly Under Sec. of State, DTI, 1989–90; Minister of State: DTI, 1990–92; DoE, 1992–93; Sec. of State for Wales, 1993–95; Opposition front bench spokesman on trade and industry, 1997–99, on the envmt, 1999–2000; Shadow Sec. of State for De-regulation, 2004–05. Head, Cons. Parly Campaigns Unit, 2000–01; Chairman: Cons. Party Policy Review on Econ. Competitiveness, 2005–10; Cons. Economic Affairs Cttee, 2010–. Vis. Prof., Middx Business Sch., 2000–. Governor of various schools, 1974–83. Qualified Ind. Financial Advr, CISI, 2012. *Publications:* Reason, Ridicule and Religion, 1976; Public Enterprise in Crisis, 1980; (with John Hatch) Value for Money Audits, 1981; (with John Hatch) Controlling Public Industries, 1982; Going for Broke, 1984; Equity for Everyman, 1986; Popular Capitalism, 1988; The Global Marketplace, 1994; The Single Currency, 1995; Action Not Words, 1996; Our Currency, Our Country, 1997; The Death of Britain?, 1999; Stars and Strife, 2001; Just Say No, 2001; Singing the Blues, 2004; Superpower Struggles, 2005; I Want to Make a Difference, 2006; After the Credit Crunch, 2009; The Future of the Euro, 2012; pamphlets on Cons. matters. *Recreations:* water sports, village cricket, daily blog (www.johnredwood.com). *W:* www.johnredwoodsdiary.com. *Address:* House of Commons, SW1A 0AA. *T:* (office) (020) 7219 4205, (home) (020) 7976 6603.

**REED, Jamieson Ronald, (Jamie);** MP (Lab) Copeland, since 2005; *b* 4 Aug. 1973; *s* of Ronald and Gloria Reed; *m*; three *s* one *d. Educ:* Whitehaven Sch.; Manchester Univ. (BA English 1994); Univ. of Leicester (MA Mass Communications 2000). Researcher: EP, 1995–97; and Advr, Labour Gp, Cumbria CC, 1997–2000; Manager, TU and Community Sellafield Campaign, 2000–01; Public Affairs, BNFL, 2001–05. *Recreations:* spending time with my family, American literature, modern history, music, football, fell walking, Rugby League. *Address:* House of Commons, SW1A 0AA. *T:* (office) (01946) 816723. *E:* andersenj@parliament.uk.

**REED, Steven Mark Ward,** OBE 2013; MP (Lab) Croydon North, since Nov. 2012; *b* St Albans, 12 Nov. 1963; *s* of Royston and Thelma Reed. *Educ:* Sheffield Univ. (BA English). Thomson, 1990–97; Law Soc., 1997–2001; Home Office, 1997–98; Pannell Kerr Forster, Accountants, 1998–99; Thomson, 2001–02; Wolters Kluwer, 2002–08. Mem. (Lab) Lambeth LBC, 1998–12 (Leader, 2006–12). Member: Exec. Bd, for Housing, 2009–10, for Children and Young People's Services, 2010–12, London Councils; Bd, London Enterprise Partnership, 2010–12; Chm., London Young People's Educn and Skills Bd, 2010–12; Co-Chair, Nine Elms

Strategy Bd, 2010–12; Dep. Chm., LGA, 2010–12; Chm., Central London Forward; Chair, Cooperative Councils Innovation Network, 2010–12 (Patron, 2012–). *Address:* House of Commons, SW1A 0AA; (office) 908 London Road, Thornton Heath CR7 7PE.

**REES, Christina Elizabeth;** MP (Lab) Neath, since 2015; *b* 21 Feb. 1954; *m* 1981, Rt Hon. Ronald Davies (marr. diss. 2000); one *d. Educ:* Cynffig Comprehensive Sch.; Ystrad Mynach Coll.; Univ. of Wales Coll. of Cardiff (LLB Hons 1995). Auditor, S Glamorgan CC, 1979–84; Constituency Sec., H of C, 1984–96; called to the Bar, 1996; in practice as barrister, Cardiff, 1997–98; Develt Officer and Nat. Coach, Wales Squash and Racketball, 2003–15; Squash Professional, Vale Hotel, 2004–14. Mem. (Lab): Mid-Glamorgan CC, 1988–95; Porthcawl Town Council, 2012–15; Bridgend CBC, 2012–15. Member: Welsh Affairs Select Cttee, 2015–; Justice Select Cttee, 2015–. Contested (Lab): Arfon, Nat. Assembly for Wales, 2011; Wales, EP, 2014. JP 1990. Female Coach of Year, Sport Wales, 2008. *Address:* House of Commons, SW1A 0AA.

**REES-MOGG, Jacob William;** MP (C) North East Somerset, since 2010; *b* 24 May 1969; *s* of Baron Rees-Mogg and of Gillian Shakespeare Rees-Mogg (*née* Morris); *m* 2007, Helena de Chair; three *s* one *d. Educ:* Eton Coll.; Trinity Coll., Oxford (BA Hist. 1991). Investment Analyst, J. Rothschild Investment Mgt, 1991–93; Dir, Lloyd George Mgt, Hong Kong, 1992–96, London, 1996–2007; Sen. Partner and Founder, Somerset Capital Mgt, 2007–. Contested (C): Central Fife, 1997; The Wrekin, 2001. Member, Select Committee: on Procedure, 2010–15; on Eur. Scrutiny, 2010–; Treasury, 2015–. *Address:* House of Commons, SW1A 0AA; Gournay Court, West Harptree, Somerset BS40 6EB. *T:* (01761) 221027.

**REEVES, Rachel Jane;** MP (Lab) Leeds West, since 2010; *b* 13 Feb. 1979; *d* of Graham Reeves and Sally Reeves. *Educ:* New Coll., Oxford (BA Hons PPE); London Sch. of Econs and Pol Sci. (MSc Econs). Economist: Bank of England, 2000–02, 2003–09; British Embassy, Washington, 2002–03; Business Planner, Halifax Bank of Scotland, 2006–09. Shadow Chief Sec. to the Treasury, 2011–13; Shadow Sec. of State for Work and Pensions, 2013–15. Contested (Lab) Bromley and Chislehurst, 2005, June 2006. *Publications:* Why Vote Labour?, 2010; contrib. Jl of Pol Econ. *Recreations:* swimming, walking, tennis, theatre. *Address:* House of Commons, SW1A 0AA; (office) Unit 8A, Bramley Shopping Centre, Bramley, Leeds LS13 2ET. *T:* (0113) 255 2311. *E:* rreevesmp@gmail.com.

**REYNOLDS, Emma;** MP (Lab) Wolverhampton North East, since 2010; *b* Wolverhampton, 2 Nov. 1977. *Educ:* Wadham Coll., Oxford (BA PPE). Policy Researcher,

Small Business Europe, Brussels, 2001–03; Pol Advr to Pres., Party of Eur. Socialists, 2004–06; Special Advr to Minister of State for Europe, FCO, 2006–07, to Parly Sec. to HM Treasury (Govt Chief Whip), 2007–08; Sen. Consultant, Cogitamus Ltd, 2009–10. Shadow Minister for Housing, 2013–15; Shadow Sec. of State for Communities and Local Govt, 2015. *Recreations:* running, swimming, cinema. *Address:* (office) 492A Stafford Street, Wolverhampton WV10 6AN. *E:* emma.reynolds.mp@parliament.uk.

**REYNOLDS, Jonathan Neil;** MP (Lab Co-op) Stalybridge and Hyde, since 2010; *b* 28 Aug. 1980; *s* of Keith and Judith Reynolds; *m* 2008, Claire Johnston; one *s* one *d. Educ:* Houghton Kepier Comprehensive Sch.; Sunderland City Coll.; Manchester Univ. (BA Politics and Modern Hist.); BPP Law Sch., Manchester. Political asst to James Purnell, MP; trainee solicitor, Addleshaw Goddard LLP, Manchester until 2010. Mem. (Lab Co-op) Tameside MBC, 2007–11. Mem., Select Cttee on Sci. and Technol., 2010–12; Sec., All Party Parly Gp on the Armed Forces, 2010–. *Address:* House of Commons, SW1A 0AA.

**RIMMER, Marie Elizabeth,** CBE 2005; MP (Lab) St Helens South and Whiston, since 2015; *b* St Helens, 27 April 1947. With Pilkington Glass, 1962–99, incl. Stats and Accounts Dept, buyer of engrg equipt for glass prodn lines, and Health and Safety Advr, Float Glass Manufg. Mem. (Lab), St Helens MBC, 1978– (Leader, 1985–93, 1999–2013). Trustee, St Helens Hope Centre. *Address:* House of Commons, SW1A 0AA.

**RITCHIE, Margaret;** MP (SDLP) South Down, since 2010; *b* 25 March 1958; *d* of late John Ritchie and Rose Ritchie (*née* Drumm). *Educ:* Queen's Univ., Belfast (BA). Mem. (SDLP) Down DC, 1985–2009. Mem., NI Forum, 1996. Parly Asst to Edward McGrady, MP, 1987–2003. Mem. (SDLP) S Down, NI Assembly, 2003–12; Minister for Social Develt, NI, 2007–10. Mem., Envmt, Food and Rural Affairs Select Cttee, 2012–. Leader, SDLP, 2010–11. *Address:* (office) 32 Saul Street, Downpatrick, Co. Down BT30 6NQ.

**ROBERTSON, Rt Hon. Angus;** PC 2015; MP (SNP) Moray, since 2001; *b* 28 Sept. 1969. *Educ:* Broughton High Sch., Edinburgh; Univ. of Aberdeen (MA 1991). News Editor, Austrian Broadcasting Corp., 1991; reporter, BBC, Austria, etc, 1991–99; communications consultant and journalist, 1999–. SNP spokesman on foreign affairs, 2001–15, on defence, 2003; SNP Leader, H of C, 2007–. SNP Campaign Director: Scottish Parlt elections 2007 and 2011, Scottish independence referendum, 2014. Mem., Intelligence and Security Cttee, 2015–. Contested (SNP) Midlothian, Scottish Parlt, 1999. *Address:* (constituency office) 9 Wards Road, Elgin, Moray IV30 1NL; c/o House of Commons, SW1A 0AA.

**ROBERTSON, Laurence Anthony;** MP (C) Tewkesbury, since 1997; *b* 29 March 1958; *s* of James Robertson and Jean (*née* Larkin); *m* 1989, Susan (*née* Lees) (marr. diss. 2014); two step *d; m* 2015, Anne Marie (*née* Adams). *Educ:* St James C of E Sch., Farnworth; Farnworth Grammar Sch.; Bolton Inst. Higher Educn. Work study engr, 1976–82; industrial consultant, 1982–92; charity fundraising, 1992–97 (raised about £2 million for various charities). Contested (C): Makerfield, 1987; Ashfield, 1992. An Opposition Whip, 2001–03; Opposition front bench spokesman on economic affairs, 2003–05; Shadow Minister for NI, 2005–10. Chm., NI Affairs Select Cttee, 2010–; Member: Envmt Audit Select Cttee, 1997–99; Social Security Select Cttee, 1999–2001; European Scrutiny Select Cttee, 1999–2002; Educn and Skills Select Cttee, 2001; Jt Cttee on Consolidation of Bills, 1997–2001; Chm., All Party Gp on Ethiopia and Djibouti, 2009–; Jt Chm., All Party Gp on Racing and Bloodstock, 2010–; Co-Chm., British Irish Parly Assembly, 2011–. Secretary: Cons. Back Bench Constitutional Cttee, 1997–2001; 92 Gp, 2001–02. *Recreations:* sport (ran 6 marathons), particularly horseracing and golf, reading, writing, history. *Address:* House of Commons, SW1A 0AA. *T:* (020) 7219 4196; 22 High Street, Tewkesbury GL20 6DL. *T:* (01684) 291640.

**ROBINSON, Gavin James;** MP (DemU) Belfast East, since 2015; *b* Belfast, 22 Nov. 1984; *s* of John Calvert Robinson and Claire Allison Robinson (*née* Nesbitt); *m* 2011, Lindsay Witherow. *Educ:* Grosvenor Grammar Sch.; Univ. of Ulster (LLB Hons Law); Queen's Univ., Belfast (MA Irish Politics; CPLS). Called to the Bar, NI, 2008; Special Advr to First Minister of NI, 2011–12, 2013–15. Mem. (DemU), Belfast CC, 2010–15 (Alderman, 2012–15; Gp Leader, DUP); Lord Mayor of Belfast, 2012–13. *Recreations:* Rugby, reading, cooking, travel. *Address:* House of Commons, SW1A 0AA. *E:* g.j.robinson@ hotmail.co.uk. *Club:* Ulster Reform.

**ROBINSON, Geoffrey;** MP (Lab) Coventry North West, since March 1976; *b* 25 May 1938; *s* of Robert Norman Robinson and Dorothy Jane Robinson (*née* Skelly); *m* 1967, Marie Elena Giorgio; one *s* one *d. Educ:* Emanuel School; Cambridge and Yale Univs. Labour Party Research Assistant, 1965–68; Senior Executive, Industrial Reorganisation Corporation, 1968–70; Financial Controller, British Leyland, 1971–72; Managing Director, Leyland Innocenti, Milan, 1972–73; Chief Exec., Jaguar Cars, Coventry, 1973–75; Chief Exec. (unpaid), Meriden Motor Cycle Workers' Co-op., 1978–80 (Dir, 1980–82). Chm., TransTec PLC, 1986–97. Dir, W Midlands Enterprise Bd, 1980–84. Opposition spokesman on science, 1982–83, on regional affairs and industry, 1983–86; HM Paymaster General, 1997–98. *Publications:* The Unconventional Minister: my life inside New

Labour, 2000. *Recreations:* reading, architecture, gardens, football. *Address:* House of Commons, SW1A 0AA. *T:* (020) 7219 3000.

**ROBINSON, Mary Josephine;** MP (C) Cheadle, since 2015; *b* 23 Aug. 1955; *m* Stephen Robinson; four *c.* Co-founder, Robinson Rose, Accountants, until 2008; proprietor, Mary Felicity Design, 2008. Mem. (C), S Ribble BC, 2007–13. Mem., Communities and Local Govt Select Cttee, 2015–. *Address:* House of Commons, SW1A 0AA.

**ROSINDELL, Andrew;** MP (C) Romford, since 2001; *b* Romford, 17 March 1966; *s* of Frederick William Rosindell and Eileen Rosina Rosindell (*née* Clark). *Educ:* Rise Park Jun. and Infant Sch.; Marshalls Park Secondary Sch. Researcher and freelance journalist, and Res. Asst to Vivian Bendall, MP, 1986–97; Dir, 1997–99, Internat. Dir, 1999–2005, Eur. Foundn. Mem., London Accident Prevention Council, 1990–95. Mem. (C) Havering BC, 1990–2002 (Vice-Chm., Housing Cttee, 1996–97; Hon. Alderman, 2007–); Chm., N Romford Community Area Forum, 1998–2002. Contested (C): Glasgow Provan, 1992; Thurrock, 1997. An Opposition Whip, 2005–07; Shadow Home Affairs Minister and spokesman on Animal Welfare, 2007–10; Member: Deregulation and Regulatory Reform Select Cttee, 2001–05; Constitutional Affairs Select Cttee, 2004–05; Foreign Affairs Select Cttee, 2010–; Jt Cttee on Statutory Instruments, 2002–04; NI Grand Cttee, 2006–07; All Party Parliamentary Groups: Secretary: Falkland Is, 2001–; S Pacific Is, 2009–; Belize, 2010–; Jt Chm., British-Swiss, 2010–; Vice-Chairman: Iceland, 2005–; Bermuda, 2005–; Channel Is, 2006–; Madagascar, 2007–; British Indian Ocean Territory (Chagos Is), 2008–; Gibraltar, 2010– (Sec., 2001–02); Queen's Diamond Jubilee, 2010–; Vice Chm. and Sec., Cayman Is, 2010–; Chairman: Montserrat, 2005–; British-Manx (formerly Anglo-Manx), 2005–; Greyhound, 2006–; St George's Day, 2007–; Flags and Heraldry, 2008–; Australia/NZ, 2010– (Sec., 2001–10); Zoos and Aquariums, 2010– (Sec., 2007–10); Canada, 2010– (Sec., 2008–10); British Overseas Territory, 2010–; Turks and Caicos Is, 2010–; Mauritius, 2010–; Pitcairn Is, 2010–; Liechtenstein, 2010– (Sec., 2005–10); Central America, 2011– (Sec., 2010–11); Founding Chm., Polar Regs (Arctic and Antarctic), 2011–14; Co-Chairman: Mongolia, 2010–; St Lucia, 2012–; Treasurer: Danish, 2005– (Jt Treas., 2001–05); Botswana, 2010–; Mem., Panel of Chairs, 2010–. Member: Commonwealth Parly Assoc., 2001– (Mem. Exec. Cttee, 2010–); Inter-Parly Union, 2001– (Mem. Exec. Cttee, 2010–); British-American Parly Gp, 2001–; Adv. Bd, Commonwealth Exchange, 2013–. Fellow, Industry and Parlt Trust India Fellowship, 2009; Mem., British-Irish Parly Assembly, 2010–. Armed Forces Parly Scheme (RM), 2002–03; (RAF), 2005–07, (Army), 2009–13. Chairman: Royal Soc. of St George, Houses of Parlt Br., 2009–; Palace of Westminster Philatelic Soc., 2010–. Sec., Cons. 92 Gp, 2003–06; Mem., No Turning Back Gp. Parly Advr, Guild of Travel and Tourism, 2008–. Joined Cons. Party and Young Conservatives, 1981; Chairman: Romford YC, 1983–84 (Pres., 2006–); Gtr London YC, 1987–88; Nat. YC, 1993–94; Eur. YC, 1993–97; Vice-Pres., Conservative Future, 2013–; Conservative Party: Mem., Nat. Union Exec. Cttee, 1986–88 and 1992–94; Vice-Chm., 2004–05; Pres., Gibraltar Br., 2004–; Chm., Romford Cons. Assoc., 1998–2001. Chm., Cons. Friends of Gibraltar, 2002–, of Australia and NZ, 2010–; Pres., Cons. Friends of Taiwan, 2011–; Member: Cons. Middle East Council, 2005–; Cons. Friends of Israel, 2001–, India, 2005–, America, 2008–; Pres., Cons. Commonwealth Assoc., 2013. Chairman: Internat. Young Democrat Union, 1998–2002; UK-Norfolk Island Friendship Gp, 2009–; Zimbabwe-Rhodesia Relief Fund, 2010–. Pres., Caribbean Young Democrat Union, 2001–; Co-Pres., British-Middle E and N Africa Council, 2012–; Vice-Pres., Constitutional Monarchy Assoc. Member: Council, Freedom Assoc., 2005–; Flag Inst., 2008–; Bd of Govs, Westminster Foundn for Democracy, 2010–; Council, Canada UK Colloquium, 2010–; Hon. Bd Mem., Iman Foundn, 2011–. Pres., Romford Sqdn ATC, 2002–; Hon. Member: HMS Antrim Assoc., 2008–; Romford Lions Club, 2008– (Vice-Pres., 2010–); Burma Star (SW Essex Br.), 2010–; Romford Cons. and Constitutional Club, 2001–; Falkland Is Assoc., 2001–; Vice President: Romford and Dist Scout Assoc., 1995–; Romford RBL Band and Corps of Drums, 2010–; Romford Rotary Club, 2010–; Flag Inst., 2014–. Member: Salvation Army, Romford Citadel, 1973–82; St Edward the Confessor Ch, Romford Market, 1988–; St Alban Protomartyr Ch, Romford, 2001–. Member: RAFA; RBL; Essex Wildlife Trust, 2007–; British Overseas Territories Conservation Forum, 2003–; Trustee, Friends of British Overseas Territories, 2014–. Governor: Bower Park Sch., Romford, 1989–90; Dame Tipping C of E Sch., Havering-atte-Bower, 1990–2002. Vice-Pres., Romford FC; Hon. Mem., Havering-atte-Bower CC. Trustee, Retired Greyhound Trust, 2010–. Patron: Justice for Dogs; Remus Meml Horse Sanctuary, 2005–; Assoc. of British Counties, 2007–; Lennox Children's Cancer Fund, 2009–; Romford Cons. Business and Enterprise Club, 2012–; British Monarchist Soc., 2013–. Hon. Member: Staffs Bull Terrier Club; E Anglian Staffs Bull Terrier Club; Romford Lions, 2007. Freeman, City of London, 2003. *Publications:* (jtly) Defending Our Great Heritage, 1993. *Recreations:* Staffordshire bull terriers, travel, philately, history. *Address:* House of Commons, SW1A 0AA. *T:* (020) 7219 8475; (constituency office) 85 Western Road, Romford, Essex RM1 3LS. *T:* (01708) 766700, (home) (01708) 761186. *E:*

andrew@rosindell.com, andrew.rosindell.mp@ parliament.uk. *Clubs:* Romford Conservative and Constitutional; Romford Golf (Hon.).

**ROTHERAM, Steven Philip;** MP (Lab) Liverpool Walton, since 2010; *b* 4 Nov. 1961; *s* of Harry and Dorothy Rotheram; *m* 1989, Sandra; one *s* two *d. Educ:* Ruffwood Comprehensive Sch.; Kirkby Further Educn Coll.; Liverpool John Moores Univ. (MA Urban Renaissance). Work in construction sector, 1978–89; instructor, 1989–2001; Director: SIP Property Develt LLP, 2006–; SPR Consultants. Dir, Liverpool Inst. for Performing Arts, 2004–10. Mem. (Lab) Liverpool CC, 2002–11 (Lord Mayor, 2008). *Address:* House of Commons, SW1A 0AA.

**RUDD, Rt Hon. Amber;** PC 2015; MP (C) Hastings and Rye, since 2010; Secretary of State, Department of Energy and Climate Change, since 2015; *b* London, 16 Aug. 1963; *m* 1991, Adrian Anthony Gill (marr. diss.); one *s* one *d. Educ:* Queen's Coll., London; Edinburgh Univ. (MA Hons Hist. 1986). With J P Morgan, London and NY, 1986–87; Director: Lawnstone Ltd, 1988–97; MacArthur & Co., 1997–99; CEO, Investors Noticeboard Ltd, 1999–2001; Consultant, I-Search Ltd, 2001–03; Man. Dir and Sen. Consultant, Lawnstone Ltd, 2003–10. Columnist, Corporate Financier, 2003–10. Contested (C) Liverpool Garston, 2005. PPS to Chancellor of Exchequer, 2012–13; an Asst Govt Whip, 2013 14; Parly Under-Sec. of State, DECC, 2014–15. Mem., Envmt, Food and Rural Affairs Select Cttee, 2010–12. *Address:* House of Commons, SW1A 0AA.

**RUTLEY, David Henry;** MP (C) Macclesfield, since 2010; *b* Gravesend, Kent, 7 March 1961; *s* of John Rutley and Birthe Rutley; *m* 1994, Rachel Faber; two *s* two *d. Educ:* Lewes Priory Sch.; London Sch. of Econs and Pol Sci. (BSc Econ 1985); Harvard Business Sch. (MBA 1989). Business Develt Dir, PepsiCo Internat., 1991–94; Special Advr to Cabinet Office, MAFF, HM Treasury, 1994–96; Dir, Business Effectiveness, Safeway Stores, 1996–2000; Dir, Financial Services and Dir, E-commerce, Asda Stores, 2000–05; Sales and Mktg Dir, Halifax Gen. Insce, 2005–07; Business Consultant, 2008–09, Mktg Dir, 2009–10, Barclays Bank. Contested (C) St Albans, 1997. Parliamentary Private Secretary: to Minister for Immigration, 2010–12; to Minister for Policing and Criminal Justice, 2012–14; to Minister for Europe, 2014–15; to Sec. of State for Work and Pensions, 2015–. Mem., Treasury Select Cttee, 2010; Sec., All Party Parly Gp on National Parks, 2012– (Vice-Chm., 2010–12); Co-Chm., All Party Parly Gp on Mountaineering, 2010–. *Recreations:* family, walking in the Peak District, mountaineering, church. *Address:* House of Commons, SW1A 0AA. *T:* (020) 7219 7106. *E:* david.rutley.mp@ parliament.uk.

**RYAN, Rt Hon. Joan (Marie);** PC 2007; MP (Lab) Enfield North, 1997–2010 and since 2015; consultant in communications and strategy; Advisor, Global Tamil Forum, since 2012 (Chief Executive Officer, 2010–12); *b* 8 Sept. 1955; *d* of late Michael Joseph Ryan and Dolores Marie Ryan (*née* Joyce); *m* 1998, Martin Hegarty; one *s* one *d*, and one step *s* one step *d. Educ:* City of Liverpool Coll. of Higher Educn (BA Hons 1979); South Bank Poly. (MSc 1983); Avery Hill Coll. (PGCE 1984). Sociology, Soc. Sci., Religious Studies and Eur. Politics Teacher, and Hd of Year, Hurlingham and Chelsea Secondary Sch., Fulham, 1984–89; Head of Pastoral Educn, Hawksmoor Sixth Form Coll., Fulham, 1989–94; Head of Humanities, William Morris Acad., Hammersmith, 1994–97. Mem. (Lab) Barnet LBC, 1990–98. Contested (Lab) Enfield N, 2010. An Asst Govt Whip, 2002–03; a Lord Comr of HM Treasury (Govt Whip), 2003–06; Parly Under-Sec. of State, Home Office, 2006–07; Special Rep. to Cyprus, 2007–10. Dir, Labour No 2 AV, 2010–12. Chair, Riders for Health, 2010–. Oral history interviewer, Imperial War Mus., 1984–86. *Recreations:* visiting historic buildings, cinema, learning to sail. *Address:* House of Commons, SW1A 0AA.

**SALMOND, Rt Hon. Alexander Elliot Anderson;** PC 2007; MP (SNP) Gordon, since 2015; Member (SNP) Aberdeenshire East, Scottish Parliament, since 2011 (Gordon, 2007–11); *b* 31 Dec. 1954; *s* of Robert F. F. Salmond and late Mary S. Milne; *m* 1981, Moira F. McGlashan. *Educ:* Linlithgow Acad.; St Andrews Univ. (MA Hons). Govt Econ. Service, 1980; Asst Agricl and Fisheries Economist, DAFS, 1978–80; Energy Economist, Royal Bank of Scotland plc, 1980–87. Scottish National Party: Mem. Nat. Exec., 1981–; Vice-Chair (Publicity), 1985–87; Sen. Vice-Convener (Dep. Leader) (formerly Sen. Vice-Chair), 1987–90; Leader, 1990–2000 and 2004–14. MP (SNP) Banff and Buchan, 1987–2010. SNP parly spokesperson on energy, treasury and fishing, 1987–88, on economy, energy, environment and poll tax, 1988–97, on constitution and fishing, 1997–2005; on foreign affairs, 2015–. Mem. (SNP) Banff & Buchan, Scottish Parlt, 1999–2001; Ldr of the Opposition, 1999–2000; First Minister, 2007–14. Vis. Prof of Economics, Univ. of Strathclyde, 2003–. *Publications:* The Dream Shall Never Die: 100 days that changed Scotland forever (autobiog.), 2015; articles and conference papers on oil and gas economics; contribs to Scottish Government Yearbook, Fraser of Allander Economic Commentary, Petroleum Review, Opec Bulletin, etc. *Address:* Scottish Parliament, Edinburgh EH99 1SP; 84 North Street, Inverurie, Aberdeenshire AB51 4QX; House of Commons, SW1A 0AA.

**SAVILLE ROBERTS, Elizabeth;** MP (Plaid Cymru) Dwyfor Meirionnydd, since 2015; *b* London, 16 Dec. 1964; *d* of Nicholas and Nancy Saville; *m* 1994, Dewi Wyn Roberts; twin *d*.

*Educ:* Univ. of Wales, Aberystwyth (BA Hons Celtic Studies 1987); Bi-lingual Postgrad. Cert. for Personal Assts 1988; NCTJ 1991; Coleg Meirion-Dwyfor, Dolgellau (PGCE 1996). Sec., French and Russian Depts, QMC, 1988–89; staff reporter, Retail Newsagent, 1989–90; news reporter, Herald Newspapers, 1990–92; Lectr, 1993–2001, Hd, Canolfan Sgiliaithth, 2001–12, Coleg Meirion-Dwyfor; Dir of Bilingualism, Grŵp Llandrillo, Menai, 2012–14. Mem. (Plaid Cymru) Gwynedd CC, 2004–15. *Recreations:* horse riding, hill walking, art, history, poetry. *Address:* Angorfa, Heol Meurig, Dolgellau, Gwynedd LL40 1LN. *T:* (01341) 422661. *E:* liz.savilleroberts.mp@parliament.uk.

**SCULLY, Paul Stuart;** MP (C) Sutton and Cheam, since 2015; *b* Rugby, 29 April 1968; *s* of Basil and Joan Scully; *m* 1990, Emma; one *s* one *d*. *Educ:* Bedford Sch.; Univ. of Reading. Political Assistant: office of Andrew Pelling, MP, 2005–07; office of Shailesh Vara, MP, 2007–09; office of Alok Sharma, MP, 2010–12; Partner, Nudge Factory Ltd, 2011–. Mem. (C) Sutton LBC, 2006–10 (Leader of Opposition, 2006–10). *Address:* (office) Donnington House, 2a Sutton Court Road, Sutton, Surrey SM1 4SY. *T:* (020) 8642 3791. *E:* info@scully.org.

**SELOUS, Andrew Edmund Armstrong;** MP (C) South West Bedfordshire, since 2001; Parliamentary Under-Secretary of State, Ministry of Justice, and an Assistant Government Whip, since 2014; *b* 27 April 1962; *s* of late Gerald M. B. Selous, OBE, VRD, and Miranda Selous (*née* Casey); *m* 1993, Harriet Marston; three *d*. *Educ:* London Sch. of Econs (BSc Econ). ACII 1993. Great Lakes Re (UK) PLC, 1991–2001. Served TA, HAC and RRF, 1981–94. *Recreation:* family life. *Address:* House of Commons, SW1A 0AA. *Clubs:* Leighton Buzzard Conservative, Dunstable Conservative.

**SHAH, Naseem Akhter;** MP (Lab) Bradford West, since 2015; *b* 13 Nov. 1973; *d* of Zoora Shah; two *s* one *d*. Carer for children with disabilities; advocate for women with disabilities and their carers; work for Samaritans; work with NHS in commng services; Chm., Sharing Voices Bradford, mental health charity, 2012. *Address:* House of Commons, SW1A 0AA.

**SHANNON, (Richard) James;** MP (DemU) Strangford, since 2010; *b* Omagh, 25 March 1955; *s* of Richard James Shannon and Mona Rebecca Rhoda Shannon; *m* 1987, Sandra George; three *s*. *Educ:* Ballywalter Primary Sch.; Coleraine Academical Instn. Served UDR, 1974–75 and 1976–77; 102 Light Air Defence Regt, RA, 1978–89. Ards Borough Council: Mem. (DemU), 1985–2010; Mayor, 1991–92; Alderman, 1997–2010. Mem., NI Forum, 1996–98; Mem. (DemU) Strangford, NI Assembly, 1998–2010. GSM (NI) 1974. *Recreations:* field sports, football, Ulster-Scots

language and culture. *Address:* (office) 34a Frances Street, Newtownards, Co. Down BT23 7DN. *T:* (028) 9182 7990.

**SHAPPS, Rt Hon. Grant;** PC 2010; MP (C) Welwyn Hatfield, since 2005; Minister of State: Department for International Development, since 2015; Foreign and Commonwealth Office, since 2015; *b* 14 Sept. 1968; *s* of Tony and Beryl Shapps; *m* 1997, Belinda Goldstone; two *s* one *d* (of whom one *s* one *d* are twins); *Educ:* Watford Grammar Sch.; Cassio Coll., Watford (business and finance); Manchester Polytech. (HND Business and Finance). Founded Printhouse Corp. (design, web and print co.), 1990, Chm., 2000–. Contested (C) Welwyn Hatfield, 2001. Shadow Housing Minister, 2007–10; Minister of State, DCLG, 2010–12; Minister of State (Minister without Portfolio), Cabinet Office, 2012–15. Mem., Public Admin Select Cttee, 2005–07. Vice Chm. (Campaigning), 2005–07, Chm., 2012–15, Cons. Party. *Recreation:* private pilot with IMC and night qualifications. *Address:* House of Commons, SW1A 0AA. *T:* (020) 7219 8497, *Fax:* (020) 7219 0659. *E:* grant@shapps.com.

**SHARMA, Alok;** MP (C) Reading West, since 2010; *b* 7 Sept. 1967; *m*; two *d*. *Educ:* Blue Coat Sch., Reading; Salford Univ. (BSc Applied Physics with Electronics 1988). CA. Accountancy and corporate finance advr. *Address:* House of Commons, SW1A 0AA.

**SHARMA, Virendra;** MP (Lab) Ealing and Southall, since July 2007; *b* 5 April 1947; *s* of Dr Lekh Raj Sharma and R. P. Sharma; *m* 1968, Nirmala; one *s* one *d*. *Educ:* London Sch. of Econs (MA 1979). Started working life as bus conductor; subseq. in voluntary sector; Day Services Manager for people with learning disabilities, Hillingdon, 1996–2007. Mem. (Lab) Ealing BC, 1982–2010. Member: Jt Cttee on Human Rights, 2007–15; Health Select Cttee, 2010–15; Internat. Develt Cttee, 2015–. Chm., Indo-British All Party Parly Gp. Nat. Ethnic Minorities Officer, Lab Party, 1986–92. *Recreations:* reading, walking. *Address:* House of Commons, SW1A 0AA. *T:* (020) 7219 6080. *E:* sharmav@parliament.uk.

**SHEERMAN, Barry John;** MP (Lab) Huddersfield, since 1983 (Huddersfield East, 1979–83); *b* 17 Aug. 1940; *s* of late Albert William Sheerman and Florence Sheerman (*née* Pike); *m* 1965 Pamela Elizabeth (*née* Brenchley); one *s* three *d*. *Educ:* Hampton Grammar Sch.; LSE (BSc (Econs) Hons; MSc Hons). Lectr, Univ. Coll. of Swansea, 1966–79. Visiting Professor: of Social Enterprise, Huddersfield Univ.; Inst. of Educn, London Univ. Chairman: Policy Connect, 1995–; Urban Mines. An opposition front bench spokesman on: employment, dealing with training, small business and tourism, 1983–88; home affairs, dealing with police, prisons, crime prevention, drugs, civil defence and fire service, 1988–92; disabled people's rights, 1992–94. Mem., Public Accounts Cttee, 1981–83; Co-

Chm., Educn and Employment Select Cttee, 1999–2001 (Chm., Sub-Cttee on Educn, 1999–2001); Chm., Select Cttee on Educn and Skills, 2001–10; Chairman: Parly Adv. Council on Transport Safety, 1981–; Labour Campaign for Criminal Justice, 1989–92; Labour Party Commn on Sch.-to-Work; Co-Chm., Parly Manufg Industry Gp, 1993–; Vice-Chm., Parly Univ. Gp, 1994–2012. Chm., Parly Gps for Sustainable Waste Mgt, 1995–, and for Manufg, Design and Innovation, 1999–; Chm., Cross-Party Adv. Gp on Preparation for EMU, 1998–, on European Economic Reform, 2005–. Mem., Sec. of State for Trade and Industry's Manufg Task Force, 1999–2002. Chairman: World Bank Business Partnerships for Develt Cttee, 2001–03; Global Road Safety Partnership, 2001–. Chm., John Clive Trust. FRSA; FRGS 1989; FCGI 2005. Hon. Dr: Kingston, 2007; Bradford, 2007. *Publications:* (jtly) Harold Laski: a life on the Left, 1993; pamphlets on education and training, tourism, and justice. *Address:* House of Commons, SW1A 0AA. *W:* www.twitter.com/bsheermanmp.

**SHELBROOKE, Alec Edward;** MP (C) Elmet and Rothwell, since 2010; *b* 10 Jan. 1976; *s* of Derek and Patricia Shelbrooke; *m* 2011, Susan Spencer. *Educ:* St George's C of E Comp. Sch., Gravesend; Brunel Univ. (BEng Hons 1998). Project mgt, Univ. of Leeds, 1999–2010. Mem. (C), Leeds CC, 2004–10. Contested (C) Wakefield, 2005. *Address:* House of Commons, SW1A 0AA.

**SHEPPARD, Thomas;** MP (SNP) Edinburgh East, since 2015; *b* Coleraine, NI, 6 March 1959; partner, Catherine Louise Burton; two step *d*. *Educ:* Aberdeen Univ. (MA Sociol. and Politics 1982). Vice Pres., NUS, 1982–84; work in PR and campaigns: Capa Ltd, 1984–86; Camden LBC, 1986–88; Islington LBC, 1988–93; Edinburgh DC, 1993–94; Asst Gen. Sec., Labour Party in Scotland, 1994–97; Dir, Stand Comedy Club, 1998–2015. Mem. (Lab) Hackney LBC, 1986–94 (Dep. Leader, 1990–94). *Address:* House of Commons, SW1A 0AA. *E:* tommy. sheppard.mp@parliament.uk.

**SHERRIFF, Paula Michelle;** MP (Lab) Dewsbury, since 2015; *b* Alexandria, Scotland. Victim support rôle, Police Service, 1993–2003; community healthcare, NHS, 2003–13; private healthcare sector, 2013–15. Chair, Pontefract Business Forum. Mem. (Lab) Wakefield Council, 2012–15. *Address:* House of Commons, SW1A 0AA. *E:* paula.sherriff.mp@parliament.uk.

**SHIELDS,** Baroness *cr* 2014 (Life Peer), of Maida Vale in the City of Westminster; **Joanna Shields,** OBE 2014; Parliamentary Under-Secretary of State, Department for Culture, Media and Sport, since 2015; *b* 12 July 1962; holds dual US/UK nationality; *m* Andrew Stevenson; one *s*. *Educ:* Pennsylvania State Univ.; George Washington Univ. (MBA). Man. Dir, Europe, RealNetworks International, 2001–03; Man. Dir, EMEA, Google Inc., 2005–07; CEO, Bebo Inc., 2007–08; Vice Pres., Aol, 2007–09; Vice Pres. and Man. Dir, EMEA, Facebook, 2010–12; Chief Exec., 2012–14, Chm., 2014–15, Tech City UK. Non-exec. Dir, London Stock Exchange Gp 2014–. UK Business Ambassador for Digital Industries, 2012–. Trustee, American Sch. in London, 2013–.

**SHUKER, Gavin;** MP (Lab and Co-op) Luton South, since 2010; *b* 10 Oct. 1981; *m* 2007, Lucie Moore; one *d*. *Educ:* Icknield High Sch.; Luton Sixth Form Coll.; Girton Coll., Cambridge (BA Soc. and Pol Sci. 2003). Associate Pastor, Cambridge, 2003–06, Church Leader, Luton 2006–, City Life Church; charity worker, Fusion UK, 2003–08; Endis Ltd, 2008–10. Shadow Minister for Water and Waste, 2011–13, for Internat. Develt, 2013–15. *Address:* House of Commons, SW1A 0AA.

**SIDDIQ, Tulip, (Mrs C. W. St J. Percy);** MP (Lab) Hampstead and Kilburn, since 2015; *b* London, 16 Sept. 1982; *d* of Dr Shafiq Siddiq and Sheikh Rehana; *m* 2013, Christian William St John Percy. *Educ:* University Coll. London (BA); King's Coll. London (MA); Birkbeck, Univ. of London (MSc). Work for Amnesty Internat.; researcher: Philip Gould Associates; GLA; Brunswick Gp LLP. Mem. (Lab) Camden LBC, 2010–14 (Cabinet Mem. for Culture and Communities, 2010–14). *Address:* House of Commons, SW1A 0AA. *T:* (020) 7219 3000.

**SIMPSON, David;** MP (DemU) Upper Bann, since 2005; *b* 16 Feb. 1959; *m* Elaine Elizabeth; one adopted *s* two adopted *d*. *Educ:* Killicomaine High Sch.; Coll. of Business Studies, Belfast. Businessman. Mem. (DemU), Craigavon BC, 2001–10; Mayor of Craigavon, 2004–05. Mem. (DemU) Upper Bann, NI Assembly, 2003–10. *Address:* (office) 13 Thomas Street, Portadown, Craigavon, Co. Armagh BT62 3NP; House of Commons, SW1A 0AA.

**SIMPSON, Rt Hon. Keith (Robert);** PC 2015; MP (C) Broadland, since 2010 (Mid Norfolk, 1997–2010); *b* 29 March 1949; *s* of Harry Simpson and Jean Simpson (*née* Day); *m* 1984, Pepita Hollingsworth; one *s*. *Educ:* Thorpe Grammar Sch.; Univ. of Hull (BA Hons 1970). Postgrad. res., KCL, 1970–72; Sen. Lectr in War Studies, RMA Sandhurst, 1973–86; Hd of Oversea and Defence Section, Cons. Res. Dept, 1986–88; Special Advr to Sec. of State for Defence, 1988–90; Dir, Cranfield Security Studies Inst., Cranfield Univ., 1991–97. Opposition front bench spokesman on defence, 1998–99 and 2002–05, on agriculture, 2001–02, on foreign affairs, 2005–10; on Opposition Whip, 1999–2001; PPS to Foreign Sec., 2010–. Member: DEFRA Select Cttee, 2001–02; Parly Intelligence and Security Cttee, 2015–. Sec., Cons. backbench Defence Cttee, 1997–98; Mem., H of C Catering Cttee, 1997–98; Chm.,

Cons. History Gp, 2003–. Member: Lord Chancellor's Adv. Council on Nat. Records and Archives, 2006–08; Prime Minister's First World War Centenary Adv. Gp, 2013–. Member: RUSI, 1970–; IISS, 1975–; British Commn for Mil. History, 1980–; Comr, Commonwealth War Graves Commn, 2008–. Trustee, Hist. of Parlt Trust, 2005–10. *Publications:* The Old Contemptibles, 1981; (ed) A Nation in Arms, 1985; History of the German Army, 1985; (ed) The War the Infantry Knew 1914–1919, 1987; Waffen SS, 1990. *Recreations:* collecting books, cinema, visiting restaurants, walking battlefields, observing ambitious people. *Address:* House of Commons, SW1A 0AA. *T:* (020) 7219 4053.

**SKIDMORE, Christopher James,** FRHistS; MP (C) Kingswood, since 2010; author, since 2004; *b* Bristol, 17 May 1981; *s* of Robert and Elaine Skidmore. *Educ:* Bristol Grammar Sch.; Christ Church, Oxford (BA Hons Double First; MSt). FRHistS 2010. Advr, Cons. Party, 2006–09; Tutor, 2009–10, Hon. Res. Fellow, 2012–, Bristol Univ. Member: Health Select Cttee, 2010–13; Educn Select Cttee, 2012–14; Policy Bd, No 10 Downing St, 2013–. FRSA. *Publications:* Edward VI: the lost king, 2007; Death and the Virgin, 2010; After the Coalition, 2011; Britannia Unchained, 2012; Bosworth: the birth of the Tudors, 2013. *Address:* House of Commons, SW1A 0AA. *T:* (020) 7219 7094. *E:* chris.skidmore.mp@parliament.uk.

**SKINNER, Dennis Edward;** MP (Lab) Bolsover, since 1970; *b* 11 Feb. 1932; good working-class mining stock; *m* 1960; one *s* two *d. Educ:* Tupton Hall Grammar Sch.; Ruskin Coll., Oxford. Miner, Parkhouse Colliery and Glapwell Colliery, 1949–70. Mem., Nat. Exec. Cttee of Labour Party, 1978–92, 1994–98, 1999–; Vice-Chm., Labour Party, 1987–88, Chm., 1988–89; Pres., Derbyshire Miners (NUM), 1966–70; Pres., NE Derbys Constituency Labour Party, 1968–71; Derbyshire CC, 1964–70; Clay Cross UDC, 1960–70. *Publications:* Sailing Close to the Wind: reminiscences, 2014. *Recreations:* tennis, cycling, walking. *Address:* House of Commons, SW1A 0AA. *T:* (01773) 581027. *Clubs:* Miners' Welfares in Derbyshire; Bestwood Working Men's.

**SLAUGHTER, Andrew Francis;** MP (Lab) Hammersmith, since 2010 (Ealing, Acton and Shepherd's Bush, 2005–10); *b* 29 Sept. 1960; *s* of late Alfred Frederick Slaughter and Marie Frances Slaughter. *Educ:* Univ. of Exeter; Coll. of Law; Inns of Court Sch. of Law. Called to the Bar, Middle Temple, 1993; barrister, Bridewell Chambers, 1993–2006, Lamb Chambers, 2006–. Mem., Hammersmith and Fulham LBC, 1986–2006 (Dep. Leader, 1991–96; Leader, 1996–2005). *Address:* House of Commons, SW1A 0AA. *T:* (020) 7219 4990.

**SMEETH, Ruth Lauren;** MP (Lab) Stoke-on-Trent North, since 2015; *b* Edinburgh, 29 June 1979; *d* of Lucille Kelly; *m* 2004, Michael Smeeth.

*Educ:* Downend Comprehensive Sch.; Alton Sixth Form Coll.; Birmingham Univ. (BSocSc Hons; Postgrad. Dip. PR). Sen. researcher, Amicus/AEEU, 2000–04; Hd of Govt Relns, Sodexo, 2004–05; Dir, Public Affairs, Bicom, 2005–07; Public Affairs Manager, Nestlé UK, 2007; Campaign Co-ordinator, CST, 2008–10; Dep. Dir, Hope Not Hate, 2010–15. *Recreations:* cinema, reading, travel. *Address:* House of Commons, SW1A 0AA. *T:* (020) 7219 4844. *E:* ruth.smeeth.mp@parliament.uk. *Club:* Naval and Military.

**SMITH, Rt Hon. Andrew (David);** PC 1997; MP (Lab) Oxford East, since 1987; *b* 1 Feb. 1951; *m*; one step *s. Educ:* Reading Grammar Sch.; St John's Coll., Oxford. Joined Labour Party, 1973. Mem., Oxford City Council, 1976–87 (Chairman: Recreation Cttee, 1980–83; Planning Cttee, 1984–87). Opposition spokesman on higher and continuing educn, 1988–92, on Treasury and Economic Affairs, 1992–94, on transport, 1996–97; Shadow Chief Sec. to HM Treasury, 1994–96; Minister of State, DFEE, 1997–99; Chief Sec. to HM Treasury, 1999–2002; Sec. of State for Work and Pensions, 2002–04. Contested (Lab) Oxford E, 1983. Chm., Bd, Oxford Brookes Univ. (formerly Oxford Poly.), 1987–93. *Address:* Unit A, Bishops Mews, Transport Way, Oxford OX4 6HD; House of Commons, SW1A 0AA.

**SMITH, Angela Christine;** MP (Lab) Penistone and Stocksbridge, since 2010 (Sheffield Hillsborough, 2005–10); *b* 16 Aug. 1961; *d* of Thomas Edward Smith and Patricia Ann Smith; *m* 2005, Steven Wilson; one step *s* one step *d. Educ:* Univ. of Nottingham (BA 1st cl. Hons (English studies) 1990); Newnham Coll., Cambridge. Lectr, Dearne Valley Coll., Wath on Dearne, 1994–2003. Mem., Sheffield CC, 1996–2005 (Chm., Finance, 1998–99; Cabinet Mem. for Educn and Trng, 2002–05). Opposition Whip, 2010–11; Shadow Dep. Leader of the House, 2011–14; Shadow Minister, DEFRA, 2014–15. *Recreations:* hill-walking, bird watching, cooking. *Address:* Area Regeneration Centre, Town Hall, Manchester Road, Stocksbridge S36 2DT. *T:* (0114) 283 1855, *Fax:* (0114) 283 1850; House of Commons, SW1A 0AA. *T:* (020) 7219 6713. *E:* smithac@parliament.uk.

**SMITH, Catherine;** MP (Lab) Lancaster and Fleetwood, since 2015; *b* Barrow-in-Furness, 16 July 1985; *d* of Alan and Joyce Smith. *Educ:* Lancaster Univ. (BA Hons Gender and Sociol. 2006). Campaigns and Policy Officer, British Assoc. of Social Workers, 2011–15. Contested (Lab) Wyre and Preston N, 2010. *Address:* House of Commons, SW1A 0AA. *T:* (020) 7219 6001. *E:* cat.smith.mp@parliament.uk.

**SMITH, Chloe;** MP (C) Norwich North, since July 2009; *b* May 1982; *d* of David and Claire Smith; *m* 2013, Sandy McFadzean. *Educ:* Univ. of York (BA Hons 1st Class Eng. Lit.). Mgt

Consultant, Deloitte, until 2009. An Asst Govt Whip, 2010–11; Economic Sec., HM Treasury, 2011–12; Parly Under-Sec. of State, Cabinet Office, 2012–13. *Address:* House of Commons, SW1A 0AA.

**SMITH, Henry Edward Millar;** MP (C) Crawley, since 2010; *b* Epsom, 14 May 1969; *s* of John Edwin Smith and Josephine Anne Smith (*née* Millar); *m* 1994, Jennifer Lois Ricks; one *s* one *d* (and one *s* decd). *Educ:* University Coll. London (BA Hons Philosophy 1991). Mem. (C) W Sussex CC, 1997–2010 (Leader, 2003–10). Contested (C) Crawley, 2001, 2005. *Publications:* (jtly) Direct Democracy, 2005. *Recreations:* family, ski-ing, vexillology. *Address:* House of Commons, SW1A 0AA. *T:* (020) 7219 7043. *E:* henry.smith.mp@parliament.uk.

**SMITH, Jeffrey;** MP (Lab) Manchester Withington, since 2015; *b* Withington, 26 Jan. 1963; *s* of Allan Smith and Deidre Smith. *Educ:* Old Moat Primary Sch.; Univ. of Manchester (BA(Econ) Hons 1984). Event manager, 1985–2010; DJ, 1992–2011. Mem. (Lab) Manchester CC, 1997–2015 (Executive Member: for Educn and Children's Services; for Finance; for Housing and Regeneration). Mem., Envmtl Audit Select Cttee, 2015–. Mem. Bd, Southway. Governor: Old Moat Primary Sch.; Parrs Wood High Sch. *Address:* House of Commons, SW1A 0AA.

**SMITH, Julian;** MP (C) Skipton and Ripon, since 2010; an Assistant Government Whip, since 2015; *b* Stirling, 30 Aug. 1971; *m* 2003, Amanda. *Educ:* Balfron Sch.; Millfield Sch.; Univ. of Birmingham (BA Hons English and Hist.). Founder and Man. Dir, Arq Internat., recruitment co., 1999–2010, non-exec. Dir, 2010–12. *Address:* House of Commons, SW1A 0AA.

**SMITH, Nicholas Desmond John;** MP (Lab) Blaenau Gwent, since 2010; *b* Cardiff, 14 Jan. 1960; *s* of William Thomas Smith and Alma Anne Smith; *m* (marr. diss.); two *d. Educ:* Coventry Univ. (BA Hist., Pols and Internat. Relns 1981); Birkbeck Coll., London (MSc Econ. and Social Change 1991). Constituency Organiser to Frank Dobson, MP, 1989–91; Organiser, Wales Labour Party, 1991–93; Hd, Membership Develt, Labour Party, 1993–98; consultant on internat. campaigning, 1998–2000; Campaign Manager, Public Policy, NSPCC, 2000–04; Sec. Gen., Eur. Parly Labour Party, 2005–06; Dir, Policy and Partnerships, Royal Coll. of Speech and Lang. Therapists, 2006–10. PPS to Shadow Work and Pensions Sec., 2010–11, to Shadow Foreign Sec., 2011–15. Mem., Public Accounts Cttee, 2010–. Member: Aneurin Bevan Soc.; Fabian Soc. FRGS. *Recreations:* hiking, singing, reading, chess. *Address:* House of Commons, SW1A 0AA. *T:* (020) 7219 7018. *E:* nick.smith.mp@parliament.uk.

**SMITH, Owen;** MP (Lab) Pontypridd, since 2010; *b* Morecambe, Lancs, 2 May 1970; *s* of Prof. David Burton Smith; *m* 1995, Liz; two *s* one *d. Educ:* Sussex Univ. (BA Hist. and French). Producer, BBC Radio and TV, 1992–2002; Govt Special Advr to Wales Office, 2002, to NI Office, 2003–05; Hd, Govt Affairs, Pfizer Ltd, 2005–07; Dir, Corporate Affairs and Health Econs, Amgen Ltd, 2008–09. Shadow Minister, Wales Office, 2010–11; Mem., Shadow Health Team, 2010–11; Shadow Exchequer Sec. 2011–12; Shadow Sec. of State for Wales, 2012–15, for Work and Pensions, 2015–. Contested (Lab) Blaenau Gwent, June 2006. *Recreations:* family, fishing, reading, Rugby. *Address:* House of Commons, SW1A 0AA. *T:* (020) 7219 7128, (constituency office) (01443) 401122. *E:* owen.smith.mp@parliament.uk. *Club:* Pontypridd Rugby Football.

**SMITH, Royston Matthew,** GM 2012; MP (C) Southampton, Itchen, since 2015; *b* Harefield, Southampton, 13 May 1964; *s* of Frank Wilmot Smith and Marie Cecilia Smith (*née* Page). RAF Kinloss (Nimrod), 1980–83; RAF St Mawgan (Nimrod), 1983–86; RAF Lyneham (Hercules C130), 1986–88; RAF Laarbruch, Germany (Tornado GR4), 1988–90; maintenance engr, BA, Heathrow, 1990–2006. Mem. (C), Southampton CC, 2000– (Leader of Council, 2010–12). Mem., Hants Fire and Rescue Authy, 2000–15 (Chm., 2009–15). Gov., Southampton Solent Univ. Contested (C) Southampton, Itchen, 2010. *Address:* House of Commons, SW1A 0AA.

**SMYTH, Karin;** MP (Lab) Bristol South, since 2015; *b* London, 8 Sept. 1964; *m;* three *s. Educ:* Bishopshalt Sch.; Uxbridge Tech. Coll.; Univ. of E Anglia (BA Econ. and Social Studies 1988); Univ. of Bath (MBA 1995). Joined NHS as Manager, 1988; Pol Asst to Valerie Davey, MP, 1997–2001; non-exec. Dir, Bristol N PCT, 2002–06; Ind. Project and Interim Manager, 2008–10; Locality Manager, South Bristol Consortium, 2010–. Mem., Public Accounts Select Cttee, 2015–. Trustee, Bristol Deaf Centre, 2007–08. Governor: St Werburgh's Park Nursery Sch. and Children's Centre; St Thomas More Secondary Sch., 1996–2000. *Address:* House of Commons, SW1A 0AA.

**SOAMES, Rt Hon. Sir (Arthur) Nicholas (Winston),** Kt 2014; PC 2011; MP (C) Mid Sussex, since 1997 (Crawley, 1983–97); *b* 12 Feb. 1948; *s* of Baron Soames, GCMG, GCVO, CH, CBE, PC and Lady Soames, LG, DBE; *m* 1st, 1981, Catherine Weatherall (marr. diss. 1990); one *s;* 2nd, 1993, Serena, *d* of Sir John L. E. Smith, CH, CBE; one *s* one *d. Educ:* Eton. Served 11th Hussars (PAO), 1967–70 (2nd Lieut); Equerry to the Prince of Wales, 1970–72; Asst Dir, Sedgwick Group, 1976–82. PPS to Minister of State for Employment, 1984–85, to Sec. of State, DoE, 1987–89, to Sec. of State, DTI, 1989–90; Parly Sec., MAFF, 1992–94; Minister of State for the Armed Forces, MoD, 1994–97;

Shadow Defence Sec., 2003–05. Pres., Conservative Middle East Council, 2010–. Mem., Commonwealth War Graves Commn, 2003–08. *Recreation:* country pursuits. *Address:* House of Commons, SW1A 0AA. *T:* (020) 7219 3000. *Clubs:* White's, Turf, Pratt's, Beefsteak.

**SOLLOWAY, Amanda Jane;** MP (C) Derby North, since 2015; *b* 6 June 1961. *Educ:* Bramcote Hills Grammar Sch. Tennis player; Hd of Trng and Develt, Baird Clothing, 1998–2009; mgt consultant, 2009–. Mem., Business, Innovation and Skills Select Cttee, 2015–. Chair, Cons. Friends of Internat. Develt. Mem., Ockbrook and Borrowash Parish Council, 2011. FCIPD. *Publications:* (with A. Cartwright) Emotional Intelligence: activities for developing you and your business, 2009. *Address:* House of Commons, SW1A 0AA.

**SOUBRY, Rt Hon. Anna (Mary);** PC 2015; MP (C) Broxtowe, since 2010; Minister of State (Minister for Business and Enterprise), Department for Business, Innovation and Skills, since 2015; *b* Lincoln, 7 Dec. 1956; *d* of David and Frances Soubry; two *d*; partner, Neil Davidson, CBE. *Educ:* Hartland Comprehensive Sch., Worksop; Univ. of Birmingham (LLB). Presenter and reporter, Central Television, 1984–92; called to the Bar, Inner Temple, 1995; in practice as barrister, 1995–2010. Parly Under-Sec. of State, DoH, 2012–13; Parly Under-Sec. of State, 2013–14, Minister of State, 2014–15, MoD. Contested (C) Gedling, 2005. *Recreations:* gardening, cooking, ski-ing, watching football, cricket and Rugby. *Address:* House of Commons, SW1A 0AA. *T:* (020) 7219 7211. *E:* anna.soubry.mp@parliament.uk.

**SPELLAR, Rt Hon. John (Francis);** PC 2001; MP (Lab) Warley, since 1997 (Warley West, 1992–97); *b* 5 Aug. 1947; *s* of William David and Phyllis Kathleen Spellar; *m* 1981, Anne Rosalind Wilmot (*d* 2003); one *d*. *Educ:* Bromley Parish Primary Sch.; Dulwich Coll.; St Edmund Hall, Oxford (BA PPE). Electrical, Electronic, Telecommunication and Plumbing Union: Res. Officer, 1969–76; Nat. Officer, 1976–92. Contested (Lab) Bromley, 1970. MP (Lab) Birmingham Northfield, 1982–83; contested (Lab) same seat, 1983, 1987. Parly Under-Sec. of State, 1997–99, Minister of State, 1999–2001, MoD; Minister of State (Minister for Transport), DTLR, then DFT, 2001–03; Minister of State, NI Office, 2003–05; Comptroller of HM Household, 2008–10; Opposition Dep. Chief Whip, 2010; Opposition Dep. Spokesman on Foreign Affairs, 2010–15. *Recreation:* gardening. *Address:* House of Commons, SW1A 0AA. *T:* (020) 7219 0674. *Clubs:* Bromley Labour; Brandhall Labour.

**SPELMAN, Rt Hon. Caroline (Alice);** PC 2010; MP (C) Meriden, since 1997; Second Church Estates Commissioner, since 2015; *b* 4 May 1958; *d* of Marshall Cormack and Helen Margaret Greenfield; *m* 1987, Mark Gerald Spelman; two *s* one *d*. *Educ:* Herts and Essex Grammar Sch. for Girls; Queen Mary Coll., London (BA 1st cl. Hons European Studies). Sugar Beet Advr, NFU, 1981–84; Dep. Dir, European Confedn of Sugar Beet Growers, Paris, 1984–89; Dir, Spelman, Cormack and Associates (food and biotechnology consultancy), 1989–2009. Contested (C) Bassetlaw, 1992. Shadow Secretary of State: for internat. develt, 2001–03; for envmt, 2003–04; for local and devolved govt affairs, 2004–05; DCLG, 2006–07; Shadow Minister: for women, 2001–04; ODPM, 2005–06; Chm., Cons. Party, 2007–09; Shadow Sec. of State for Communities and Local Govt, 2009–10; Sec. of State for Envmt, Food and Rural Affairs, 2010–12. Member: Envmtl Audit Cttee, 2013–15; Jt Cttee on Modern Slavery Bill, 2014. Chm., Parliament Choir, 2013–15. Vice-Pres., Tearfund, 2013–. *Publications:* The Non-Food Uses of Agricultural Raw Materials, 1994. *Recreations:* tennis, hockey, singing. *Address:* House of Commons, SW1A 0AA. *T:* (020) 7219 4189.

**SPENCER, Mark Steven;** MP (C) Sherwood, since 2010; *b* 20 Jan. 1970; *s* of Cyril and Dorothy Spencer; *m* Claire; one *s* one *d*. *Educ:* Colonel Frank Seely Sch., Calverton; Shuttleworth Agricl Coll. (Nat. Cert. Agric.). Farmer, Spring Lane Farm, Nottingham; Proprietor, Floralands Garden Village, Lambley. Member (C): Gedling BC, 2003–; Notts CC, 2005–. *Address:* House of Commons, SW1A 0AA.

**STARMER, Sir Keir,** KCB 2014; QC 2002; MP (Lab) Holborn and St Pancras, since 2015; *b* 2 Sept. 1962; *s* of Rod and late Jo Starmer; *m* 2007, Victoria Alexander; one *s* one *d*. *Educ:* Reigate Grammar Sch.; Leeds Univ. (LLB 1st Cl. Hons 1985); St Edmund Hall, Oxford (BCL 1986; Hon. Fellow, 2012). Called to the Bar: Middle Temple, 1987, Bencher, 2009; St Lucia, 1997; St Vincent, 1997; Belize, 2002. Dir of Public Prosecutions, 2008–13. Fellow, Human Rights Centre, Essex Univ., 1998–. Human Rights Advr to NI Policing Bd, 2003–08. Mem., Foreign Sec.'s Adv. Panel on the Death Penalty, 2002–08. Mem., Governance Adv. Bd, British Council, 2002–07. Mem. Council, Justice, 1999–2008. DUniv Essex, 2011; Hon. DLaws Leeds, 2012. Human Rights Lawyer of the Year Award, Justice/Liberty, 2001. *Publications:* (ed) Justice in Error, 1995; Three Pillars of Liberty: political rights and freedom in the UK, 1996; Signing up for Human Rights: the UK and international standards, 1998; (ed) Miscarriages of Justice, 1999; European Human Rights Law, 1999; Blackstone's Human Rights Digest, 2001; Criminal Justice, Police Powers and Human Rights, 2001; (contrib.) Human Rights Principles, 2001; (contrib.) Mithani's Directors' Disqualification, 2001; (contrib.) Human Rights and Civil Practice, 2001; contribs to Public Law. *Recreations:* football, classical music. *Address:* House of Commons, SW1A 0AA.

**STEPHENS, Christopher;** MP (SNP) Glasgow South West, since 2015; *b* Glasgow, 20 March 1973; *m. Educ:* Trinity High Sch., Renfrew. With Glasgow CC. Lead negotiator, UNISON, Glasgow. Mem., Nat. Exec. Cttee, SNP. Contested (SNP) Glasgow Pollock, Scottish Parlt, 2007, 2011. *Address:* House of Commons, SW1A 0AA.

**STEPHENSON, Andrew;** MP (C) Pendle, since 2010; *b* 17 Feb. 1981; *s* of Malcolm and Ann Stephenson. *Educ:* Poynton Co. High Sch.; Royal Holloway, Univ. of London (BSc Business Mgt 2002). Partner, Stephenson and Threader, 2002–10. Mem. (C), Macclesfield BC, 2003–07. Vice Chm., (Youth) Conservative Party, 2010–13. *Address:* House of Commons, SW1A 0AA.

**STEVENS, Jo;** MP (Lab) Cardiff Central, since 2015; *b* Swansea, 6 Sept. 1966. *Educ:* Ysgol Uwchradd Argoed; Elfed High Sch.; Univ. of Manchester (LLB Hons 1988); Manchester Poly. (CPE 1989). Admitted Solicitor, 1991; Solicitor and Dir, Thompsons Solicitors, 1989–2015. *Recreations:* football, cricket, Rugby, darts. *Address:* House of Commons, SW1A 0AA. *E:* jo.stevens.mp@parliament.uk. *Clubs:* Cardiff City Football, Glamorgan County Cricket.

**STEVENSON, (Andrew) John;** MP (C) Carlisle, since 2010; *b* Aberdeen, 4 July 1963; *s* of Andrew Lochart Stevenson and Jane Wilson Stevenson. *Educ:* Aberdeen Grammar Sch.; Dundee Univ. (MA Hons Hist. and Pols); Chester Law Coll. Admitted solicitor, 1990; Partner, Bendles Solicitors, Carlisle, 1994–. Mem. (C) Carlisle CC, 1999–2010. *Recreation:* sport. *Address:* Wood Villa, Great Corby, Carlisle CA4 8LL. *E:* john.stevenson.mp@parliament.uk.

**STEWART, Iain Aitken;** MP (C) Milton Keynes South, since 2010; *b* 18 Sept. 1972; *s* of James Stewart and Leila Stewart. *Educ:* Hutchesons' Grammar Sch., Glasgow; Univ. of Exeter (BA Pols 1993); Chartered Mgt Inst. (Dip. Mgt 2006). Trainee chartered accountant, Coopers & Lybrand, 1993–94; Hd, Research, Scottish Cons Party, 1994–98; Dep. Dir, 1998–2001, Dir, 2001–06, Parly Resources Unit, H of C; Associate, Odgers Berndtson (formerly Odgers, Ray & Berndtson), 2006–10. Contested (C) Glasgow Rutherglen, Scottish Parlt, 1999; contested (C) Milton Keynes SW, 2001, 2005. PPS to Sec. of State for Transport, 2013–15, to Sec. of State for Scotland, 2015–. Mem., Transport Select Cttee, 2010–13. Mem. (C), Shenley Brook End and Tattenhoe Parish Council, 2005–11. *Address:* House of Commons, SW1A 0AA.

**STEWART, Col Robert Alexander, (Bob),** DSO 1993; MP (C) Beckenham, since 2010; *b* 7 July 1949; *s* of late. A. A. Stewart, MC and Marguerita Joan Stewart; *m* 1st (marr. diss. 1993); one *s* one *d*; 2nd, 1994, Claire Podbielski; one *s* three *d*. *Educ:* Chigwell Sch.; RMA Sandhurst;

Univ. of Wales, Aberystwyth (BSc 1st Cl. Hons Internat. Politics). Commnd, Cheshire Regt, 1969; Instructor, RMA, 1979–80; Army Staff Coll., Camberley, 1981; Company Comdr, N Ireland, 1982–83; Staff Officer, MoD, 1984–85; 2 i/c 1st Bn Cheshire Regt, 1986–87; JSSC 1988; MA to Chm., NATO Mil. Cttee, HQ NATO, Brussels, 1989–91; CO, 1st Bn Cheshire Regt, 1991–93; Chief of Policy, SHAPE, 1994–95; resigned Regular Army, 1996; JSDC, 1997–98. Sen. Consultant, Public Affairs, Hill & Knowlton (UK) Ltd, 1996–98; Sen. Vice Pres., WorldSpace UK, 1998–2001; Dir, Action Leadership, 2001–10. Mem., Defence Select Cttee, 2010–; Chm., All-Party Parly Gp for Army, 2010–. Non-exec. Chm., Premier Gold Resources, 2012–15. Chm., Ind. Defence Media Assoc., 2003–10. Patron: Elifar Foundn, 2007–; Bede Griffiths Charitable Trust (UK), 2014–. Companion, RAF Regt Officers' Dinner Club. *Publications:* Broken Lives, 1993; Thoughts on Leadership, 2004; Leadership under Pressure, 2009. *Recreations:* writing, history. *Address:* House of Commons, SW1A 0AA. *T:* 07771 863894. *Clubs:* Army and Navy, Royal Air Force.

**STEWART, Roderick James Nugent, (Rory),** OBE 2004; MP (C) Penrith and The Border, since 2010; Parliamentary Under-Secretary of State, Department for Environment, Food and Rural Affairs, since 2015; *b* 3 Jan. 1973; *s* of Brian Thomas Webster Stewart, CMG; *m* 2012, Shoshana Clark; one *s*. *Educ:* Eton; Balliol Coll., Oxford (MA). Served Black Watch (RHR), 1991–92. Entered FCO, 1995; Second Secretary, Jakarta, 1997–99; Montenegro, 1999–2000; crossed Iran, Afghanistan, Pakistan, India and Nepal on foot, 2000–02; Dep. Governorate Co-ordinator, Al Amarah, Coalition Provisional Authy, 2003–04; Sen. Advr, Nasiriyah, 2004; Fellow, Carr Center, Harvard Univ., 2004–05; Chief Exec., Turquoise Mt Foundn, Afghanistan, 2005–08; Ryan Family Prof. of Human Rights and Dir, Carr Center for Human Rights Policy, Harvard Univ., 2008–10. Member: Foreign Affairs Select Cttee, 2010–15; Defence Select Cttee, 2014–15 (Chm., 2014–15). Gov., Internat. Res. Develt Council, 2008–10. Presenter, The Legacy of Lawrence of Arabia, 2010, Afghanistan: the Great Game, 2012, BBC TV. FRSL 2008. DUniv Stirling, 2009; Hon. Dr American Univ. Paris, 2011. Livingston Medal, RSGS, 2010. *Publications:* The Places in Between, 2004 (Ondaatje Prize, RSL, 2005); Occupational Hazards, 2006; (jtly) Can Intervention Work?, 2011; The Marches, 2014. *Recreations:* walking, history, trees. *Address:* House of Commons, SW1A 0AA. *Clubs:* Athenæum, Travellers, Beefsteak.

**STOWELL OF BEESTON,** Baroness *cr* 2011 (Life Peer), of Beeston in the County of Nottinghamshire; **Tina Wendy Stowell,** MBE 1996; PC 2014; Leader of the House of Lords and Lord Privy Seal, since 2014; *b* Nottingham, 2 July 1967; *d* of David and

Margaret Stowell. *Educ:* Chilwell Comprehensive; Broxtowe Coll. of Further Educn. PA to Dir, RAF Regt, MoD, 1986–88; PA to Counsellor (Defence Supply), Defence Section, British Embassy, Washington, 1988–91; PA to Chief Press Sec., Press Office, Prime Minister's Office, 1991–96; various posts, private sector cos, 1996–98; Dep. Chief of Staff to Leader of Cons. Party and Leader of the Opposition, 1998–2001; BBC: Dep. Sec., 2001–03; Hd of Communications to Chm. and Governing Body, 2003–08; Hd of Corporate Affairs, 2008–10; independent strategic communications consultant, 2010–11; Dir, Tina Stowell Associates, 2010–11. A Baroness in Waiting (Govt Whip), 2011–13; Parly Under-Sec. of State, DCLG, 2013–14. *Address:* House of Lords, SW1A 0PW. *T:* (020) 7219 5353. *E:* stowellt@parliament.uk. *W:* www.tinastowell.co.uk, www.twitter.com/tinastowell.

**STREETER, Gary Nicholas;** MP (C) South West Devon, since 1997 (Plymouth Sutton, 1992–97); *b* 2 Oct. 1955; *s* of Kenneth Victor Streeter and Shirley Nellie (*née* Keable); *m* 1978, Janet Stevens; one *s* one *d*. *Educ:* Tiverton Grammar Sch.; King's Coll., London (LLB 1st cl. Hons). Articled at Coward Chance, London, 1978–80; admitted solicitor, 1980; joined Foot & Bowden, solicitors, Plymouth, 1980, Partner, 1984–99. Plymouth City Council: Mem., 1986–92; Chm., Housing Cttee, 1989–91. PPS to Solicitor-General, 1993–95, and to Attorney-General, 1994–95; an Asst Govt Whip, 1995–96; Parly Sec., Lord Chancellor's Dept, 1996–97; Opposition front bench spokesman on European affairs, 1997–98; Shadow Sec. of State for Internat. Develt, 1998–2001; Shadow Minister of State for Foreign Affairs, 2003–04. Member: Panel of Chairs (formerly Chairmen's Panel), 2008–15; Speaker's Cttee overseeing Electoral Commn, 2008–; Ecclesiastical Cttee, 2010–15; Chairman: Christians in Parliament, 2010–; Westminster Foundn for Democracy, 2010–. A Vice Chm., Cons. Party, 2001–02; Chm., Cons. Party Internat. Office, 2005–08. *Publications:* (ed) There is Such a Thing as Society, 2002. *Recreation:* lover of cricket and Rugby. *Address:* House of Commons, SW1A 0AA. *T:* (020) 7219 4070.

**STREETING, Wesley Paul William;** MP (Lab) Ilford North, since 2015; *b* London, 21 Jan. 1983. *Educ:* Westminster City Sch.; Selwyn Coll., Cambridge (BA Hist.). Pres., Cambridge Univ. Students' Union, 2004–05; Vice Pres. (Educn), 2006–10, Pres., 2008–10, NUS; Chief Exec., Helena Kennedy Foundn, 2010–12; Hd of Educn, Stonewall, 2012–13; Associate, Magic Breakfast, 2015. Mem. (Lab) Redbridge LBC, 2010– (Dep. Leader, 2014–15). *Recreations:* theatre, cinema, walking, travelling. *Address:* House of Commons, SW1A 0AA. *T:* (020) 7219 6132. *E:* wes.streeting.mp@parliament.uk.

**STRIDE, Melvyn John;** MP (C) Central Devon, since 2010; a Lord Commissioner of HM Treasury (Government Whip), since 2015; *b* 30 Sept. 1961; *m* 2005, Michelle King Hughes; three *d*. *Educ:* Portsmouth Grammar Sch.; St Edmund Hall, Oxford (BA PPE 1984). President: Oxford Univ. Cons. Assoc., 1981; Oxford Union, 1984. Founder and Owner, Venture Mktg Gp, 1987–. An Asst Govt Whip, 2014–15. *Address:* House of Commons, SW1A 0AA.

**STRINGER, Graham Eric;** MP (Lab) Blackley and Broughton, since 2010 (Manchester Blackley, 1997–2010); *b* 17 Feb. 1950; *s* of late Albert Stringer and Brenda Stringer; *m* 1999, Kathryn Carr; one *s*, and one step *s* one step *d*. *Educ:* Moston Brook High Sch.; Sheffield Univ. (BSc Hons Chemistry). Analytical chemist. Mem. (Lab), Manchester City Council, 1979–98 (Leader, 1984–96; Chm., Policy and Resources Cttee); Chm., Manchester Airport, 1996–97. Parly Sec., Cabinet Office, 1999–2001; a Lord Comr of HM Treasury (Govt Whip), 2001–02. *Address:* House of Commons, SW1A 0AA.

**STUART, Rt Hon. Gisela (Gschaider);** PC 2015; MP (Lab) Birmingham Edgbaston, since 1997; *b* 26 Nov. 1955; *d* of late Martin and of Liane Gschaider; *m* 1st, 1980, Robert Scott Stuart (marr. diss. 2000); two *s*; 2nd, 2010, Derek John Scott (*d* 2012). *Educ:* Staatliche Realschule, Vilsbiburg; Manchester Poly.; London Univ. (LLB 1991). Dep. Dir, London Book Fair, 1982; Law Lectr, Worcester Coll. of Technol., 1992–97; res. in pension law, Birmingham Univ., 1995–97. PPS to Minister of State, Home Office, 1998–99; Parly Under-Sec. of State, DoH, 1999–2001. Member: Social Security Select Cttee, 1997–98; Foreign Affairs Select Cttee, 2001–10; Defence Select Cttee, 2010–15; Intelligence and Security Cttee, 2015–; Chair, All Party Parly Gp on Kazakhstan, 2015–. Mem. Presidium, Convention on Future of Europe. Associate Ed., 2001–05, Ed., 2006–, The House mag. Member: Ext. Bd, Birmingham Business Sch., 2007–; London Univ. Ext. Prog., 2008–. Trustee: Henry Jackson Soc., 2006–; Reading Force, 2014–; Armed Forces Parly Scheme, 2014–. Hon. Dr Aston, 2008; DUniv Birmingham City, 2015. Bundesverdienstkreuz (Germany), 2008. *Publications:* The Making of Europe's Constitution, 2003. *Address:* House of Commons, SW1A 0AA. *T:* (020) 7219 3000. *E:* stuartg@parliament.uk.

**STUART, Graham Charles;** MP (C) Beverley and Holderness, since 2005; *b* 12 March 1962; *s* of late Dr Peter Stuart and of Joan Stuart; *m* 1989, Anne Crawshaw; two *d*. *Educ:* Glenalmond Coll.; Selwyn Coll., Cambridge. Dir, CSL Publishing Ltd, 1987–. Mem. (C) Cambridge CC, 1998–2004 (Leader, Cons. Gp, 2000–04): Chairman: Educn Select Cttee, 2010–15; All Party Parly Gp on Rural Services. Vice-Pres., Globe Internat., 2007–. Chm., Cambridge Univ. Cons. Assoc., 1985. *Recreations:* cricket, cycling, motorcycling. *Address:* House of Commons, SW1A 0AA. *T:* (020) 7219 4340. *E:* graham@ grahamstuart.com.

**STURDY, Julian Charles;** MP (C) York Outer, since 2010; *b* Yorks, 1971; *s* of Robert William Sturdy; *m* Victoria; one *s* one *d. Educ:* Harper Adams Univ. Farming and property business. Mem., Harrogate BC, 2002–07. Contested (C) Scunthorpe, 2005. *Address:* House of Commons, SW1A 0AA.

**SUNAK, Rishi;** MP (C) Richmond, Yorks, since 2015; *b* 12 May 1980; *m* 2009, Akshatha, *d* of N. R. Narayana Murthy; two *d. Educ:* Winchester Coll.; Oxford (BA 1st Cl. Hons PPE 2001); Stanford Univ. (Fulbright Schol.; MBA 2006). Analyst, then Exec. Dir, Merchant Banking, Goldman Sachs, 2001–04; Partner, TCI, London, 2006; Co-Founder, investment firm; Hd, Black and Minority Ethnic Res. Unit, Policy Exchange. Dir, Catamaran Ventures. Mem., Envmt, Food and Rural Affairs Select Cttee, 2015–. *Address:* House of Commons, SW1A 0AA.

**SWAYNE, Rt Hon. Desmond (Angus),** TD 2000; PC 2011; MP (C) New Forest West, since 1997; Minister of State, Department for International Development, since 2014; *b* 20 Aug. 1956; *s* of George Joseph Swayne and Elizabeth McAlister Swayne (*née* Gibson); *m* 1987, Moira Cecily Teek; one *s* two *d. Educ:* Bedford Sch.; Univ. of St Andrews (MTh). Schoolmaster: Charterhouse, 1980–81; Wrekin Coll., 1982–87; Systems Manager, Royal Bank of Scotland, 1988–96. Opposition front bench spokesman on health, Jan.–Sept. 2001, on defence, 2001–02, on NI, 2003–04; Opposition Whip, 2002–03; PPS to Leader of the Opposition, 2004–10, to Prime Minister, 2010–12; a Lord Comr of HM Treasury (Govt Whip), 2012–13; Vice Chamberlain of HM Household (Dep. Chief Whip), 2013–14. TA Officer, 1987–. Prison visitor, 1989–. *Address:* House of Commons, SW1A 0AA. *Clubs:* Cavalry and Guards; Serpentine Swimming.

**SWIRE, Rt Hon. Hugo (George William);** PC 2011; MP (C) East Devon, since 2001; Minister of State, Foreign and Commonwealth Office, since 2012; *b* 30 Nov. 1959; *s* of late Humphrey Roger Swire and of Philippa Sophia Montgomerie (she *m* 2004, 7th Marquess Townshend); *m* 1996, Alexandra, (Sasha), Petruška Mina, *d* of late Sir John William Frederic Nott, KCB; two *d. Educ:* Eton; Univ. of St Andrews; RMA Sandhurst. Lieut, 1 Bn Grenadier Guards, 1980–83; Head, Develt Office, Nat. Gall. 1988–92; Sotheby's, 1992–2001: Dep. Dir, 1996–97; Dir, 1997–2001. Contested (Scottish C and Unionist) Greenock and Inverclyde, 1997. Shadow Minister for the Arts, 2004–05, for Culture, 2005; Shadow Sec. of State for Culture, Media and Sport, 2005–07; Minister of State, NI Office, 2010–12. FRSA 1993. *Address:* House of Commons, SW1A 0AA. *Clubs:* White's, Pratt's, Beefsteak; Exmouth Conservative (Pres., 2005–).

**SYMS, Robert Andrew Raymond;** MP (C) Poole, since 1997; *b* 15 Aug. 1956; *s* of Raymond Syms and Mary Syms (*née* Brain); *m* 2000, Fiona Mellersh (separated 2007), *d* of Air Vice-Marshal F. R. L. Mellersh, CB, DFC and bar; one *s* one *d. Educ:* Colston's Sch., Bristol. Dir, C. Syms & Sons Ltd, family building and plant hire gp, 1975–. Mem., Wessex RHA, 1988–90. Member (C): N Wilts DC, 1983–87 (Vice Chm., 1984–87); Leader, Cons. Gp, 1984–87); Wilts CC, 1985–97. Contested (C) Walsall N, 1992. PPS to Chm., Conservative Party, 1999; opposition front bench spokesman on the envmt, 1999–2001; an Opposition Whip, 2003; opposition spokesman, DCLG (formerly ODPM), 2003–07; an Asst Govt Whip, 2012–13. Chairman: Regulatory Reform Select Cttee, 2010–12; HS2 (formerly High Speed Rail) Select Cttee, 2014–; Member: Health Select Cttee, 1997–2000 and 2007–10; Procedure Select Cttee, 1998–99; Transport Select Cttee, 2001–03; Liaison Cttee, 2010–12; Vice-Chm., Cons. back bench Constitutional Cttee, 1997–2001. A Vice-Chm., Cons. Party, 2001–03. N Wiltshire Conservative Association: Treas., 1982–83; Dep. Chm., 1983–84; Chm., 1984–96; Vice Pres., 1986–88. FCIOB 1999. *Recreations:* reading, travel, cycling. *Address:* House of Commons, SW1A 0AA; c/o Poole Conservative Association, 38 Sandbanks Road, Poole BH14 8BX. *T:* (01202) 739922.

**TAMI, Mark Richard;** MP (Lab) Alyn and Deeside, since 2001; *b* 3 Oct. 1962; *s* of Michael John Tami and Patricia Tami; *m* 1992, Sally Daniels; two *s. Educ:* Enfield Grammar Sch.; UCW, Swansea (BA Hons). Head of Res. and Communications, 1992–99, Head of Policy, 1999–2001, AEEU. An Asst Govt Whip, 2007–10; an Opposition Whip, 2010–11; Opposition Asst Chief Whip, 2011–15. Chm., Welsh PLP, 2006–. *Publications:* Votes for All: compulsory voting in elections, 2000. *Recreations:* football, cricket, antiques. *Address:* House of Commons, SW1A 0AA.

**TAYLOR OF HOLBEACH,** Baron *cr* 2006 (Life Peer), of South Holland in the County of Lincolnshire; **John Derek Taylor,** CBE 1992; PC 2014; Captain of the Honourable Corps of Gentlemen at Arms (Government Chief Whip in House of Lords), since 2014; Deputy Chairman, Conservative Party, and Chairman, National Conservative Convention, 2000–03; *b* 12 Nov. 1943; *s* of late Percy Otto Taylor and Ethel Taylor (*née* Brocklehurst); *m* 1968, Julia Aileen Cunnington, *d* of late Leslie and Evelyn Cunnington, Bedford; two *s. Educ:* Holbeach Primary Sch.; St Felix Sch., Felixstowe; Bedford Sch. Dir, family horticultural and farming businesses, 1968–2010. Dir, 1990–2009, Chm., 2000–09, Springfields Horticl Soc. Ltd, and associated cos. Chairman: EC Working Party on European Bulb Industry, 1982; NFU Bulb Sub-cttee, 1982–87. Governor: Glasshouse Crops Res. Inst., 1984–88; Inst. of Horticl Res., 1987–90; Mem., Horticl Develt Council, 1986–91.

Member, Minister of Agriculture's Regional Panel: Eastern Reg., 1990–92; E Midlands Reg., 1992–96. Chm., Holbeach and E Elloe Hosp. Charitable Trust, 1989–2006, now Patron; Trustee, Brogdale Horticl Trust, 1998–2005. Mem., Lincoln Diocesan Bd of Finance, 1995–2001 (Mem., Assets Cttee, 1995–2001, 2003–12). East Midlands Conservative Council: Mem., Exec. Cttee, 1966–98; Hon. Treas., 1984–89; Chm., 1989–94; Mem., Cons. Bd of Finance, 1985–89; Mem., Cons. Bd of Mgt, 1996–98; National Union of Conservative Associations: Member: Exec. Cttee, 1966–68 and 1984–98; Gen. Purposes Cttee, 1988–98; Standing Rev. Cttee, 1988–98; Agents Employment Adv. Cttee, 1988–94; Agents Exam Bd, 1994–98; Vice Pres., 1994–97; Pres. and Cons. Conf. Chm., 1997–98; Chairman: Candidates Cttee, Cons. Party, 1997–98, 2002–05; Cons. Party Constitutional Review, 1998–2000; Cons. Agents' Superannuation Fund, 2006–10; Conservatives Abroad, 2001–08. House of Lords: Opposition Whip, 2006–10; Opposition Spokesman: on Envmt, and on Wales, 2006–07; on Work and Pensions, 2006–10; Shadow Minister, Environment, Food and Rural Affairs, 2007–10; govt spokesman for Cabinet Office, for work and pensions and for energy and climate change, 2010–11; a Lord in Waiting (Govt Whip), 2010–11; Parliamentary Under-Secretary of State: DEFRA, 2011–12; Home Office, 2012–14. Chm., Taylor Rev., Sci., Agriculture and Horticulture, 2010–. Founder Chm., local Young Cons. Br., 1964; Mem., Holland with Boston Cons. Assoc., 1964–95 (formerly Treas., Vice Chm., Chm. and Pres.); Pres., S Holland and The Deepings Cons. Assoc., 1995–2001, now Patron. Contested (C): Chesterfield, Feb. and Oct. 1974; Nottingham, EP elections, 1979. President: Lincs Agricl Soc., 2012; E of England Agricl Soc., 2014. FRSA 1994; ARAgS 2012; MIHort, 2013; FCIHort, 2014. Liveryman: Farmers' Co., 2009–; Gardeners' Co., 2010–. Peer of the Year, House Magazine Awards, 2011; Farm Business Personality of the Year, Business Mag., 2012. *Publications:* (ed) Taylor's Bulb Book, 1994. *Recreations:* English landscape and vernacular buildings, France, literature, arts, music. *Address:* House of Lords, SW1A 0PW. *Club:* Farmers.

**THEWLISS, Alison Emily;** MP (SNP) Glasgow Central, since 2015; *b* 13 Sept. 1982; *m*; two *c. Educ:* Univ. of Aberdeen. Mem. (SNP), Glasgow CC, 2007–15. SNP spokesperson on cities, 2015–. Mem., Communities and Local Govt Select Cttee, 2015–. Mem., Scottish CND. *Address:* House of Commons, SW1A 0AA.

**THOMAS, Derek Gordon;** MP (C) St Ives, since 2015; *b* 20 July 1972; *m*; two *s.* Apprentice Cornish mason; community worker, Chapel St Methodist Ch, Penzance and Mustard Seed, Helston; proprietor, construction business. Founder, Surviveale, outdoor adventure project, 1997–. Former Mem. (C), Penwith DC. Mem., Sci. and Technol. Select Cttee, 2015–. *Address:* House of Commons, SW1A 0AA.

**THOMAS, Gareth Richard;** MP (Lab) Harrow West, since 1997; *b* 15 July 1967; *s* of Howard and Susan Thomas. *Educ:* UCW, Aberystwyth (BScEcons Hons Politics 1988); Univ. of Greenwich (PGCE 1991); KCL (MA Imperial and Commonwealth Hist. 1997). Teacher, 1992–97. Mem. (Lab) Harrow BC, 1990–97. PPS to Minister Without Portfolio and Party Chairman, 2001–02, to Sec. of State for Educn and Skills, 2002–03; Parly Under-Sec. of State, 2003–08, Minister of State, 2008–10, DFID; Parly Under-Sec. of State, 2007–08, Minister of State, 2008–09, BERR. Chm., Parly Renewable and Sustainable Energy Gp, 1998–2003. Chm., Co-op Party, 2000–. *Recreations:* arts (member of the Tate, theatre, etc.), road running, supporting Arsenal, Swansea City FC and Harrow Borough FC, watching London Welsh RFC. *Address:* House of Commons, SW1A 0AA.

**THOMAS-SYMONDS, Nicklaus,** FRHistS; MP (Lab) Torfaen, since 2015; *b* Panteg, Torfaen, 26 May 1980; *s* of Jeffrey and Pamela Symonds; *m* 2006, Rebecca Thomas; two *d. Educ:* St Alban's RC High Sch., Pontypool; St Edmund Hall, Oxford (MA PPE); Univ. of Glamorgan (DipLaw); Cardiff Univ. (BVC). FRHistS 2012. Tutor and Lectr in Politics, St Edmund Hall, Oxford, 2002–15; called to the Bar, Lincoln's Inn, 2004; in practice as barrister, 2004–15. Secretary: Blaenavan Lab. Party, 2004–15; Torfaen CLP, 2009–15. *Publications:* Attlee: a life in politics, 2010; Nye: the political life of Aneurin Bevan, 2014; contrib. articles to British Hist., Llafur: Jl of Welsh People's Hist. Soc., Parly Affairs. *Recreations:* reading, watching football and Rugby. *Address:* House of Commons, SW1A 0AA. *T:* (020) 7219 4294. *E:* nick.thomassymonds.mp@ parliament.uk. *Club:* Elgan Working Men's (Blaenavon).

**THOMPSON, Owen;** MP (SNP) Midlothian, since 2015; *b* Glasgow; *s* of late Robert Thompson and of Margaret Thompson. *Educ:* Napier Univ. (BA Hons Accounting and Finance). Work for financial service cos. Mem. (SNP) Midlothian Council, 2005–15 (Dep. Leader, 2012–13; Leader, 2013–15). *Recreations:* football, computer games. *Address:* House of Commons, SW1A 0AA. *E:* owen.thompson.mp @parliament.uk.

**THOMSON, Michelle Rhonda;** MP for Edinburgh West, since 2015 (SNP, May–Oct. 2015, Ind, since Oct. 2015); *b* 11 March 1965; *m*; two *c. Educ:* Royal Scottish Acad. of Music and Drama; Abertay Univ. (MSc IT). Professional musician, 1985; Prog. Manager and Project Manager, Standard Life, 1991–2006; Prog. Manager and Portfolio Manager, Royal Bank of Scotland Gp, 2006–08; Dir, Your Property Shop, 2009–15. Founder Mem. and Exec. Bd Mem.,

Business for Scotland, 2012–14. Mem., Business, Innovation and Skills Select Cttee, 2015–. *Address:* House of Commons, SW1A 0AA.

**THORNBERRY, Emily;** MP (Lab) Islington South and Finsbury, since 2005; *b* 27 July 1960; *d* of late Sallie Thornberry; *m* 1991, Hon. Sir Christopher George Nugee; two *s* one *d. Educ:* Univ. of Kent (BA 1982). Called to the Bar, Gray's Inn, 1983; in practice, specialising in criminal law, 1985–. Shadow Energy and Climate Change Minister, 2010; Shadow Health and Social Care Minister, 2010–11; Shadow Attorney Gen., 2011–14. *Address:* (office) 65 Barnsbury Street, N1 1EK; House of Commons, SW1A 0AA. *E:* thornberrye@parliament.uk. *W:* www.emilythornberry.com.

**THROUP, Margaret Ann;** MP (C) Erewash, since 2015; *b* W Yorks, 27 Jan. 1957. *Educ:* Univ. of Manchester (BSc Hons Biol.). Biomed. scientist, Calderdale HA; sales exec., product manager, mktg manager, business develt; Dir, In-Vitro Diagnostic Div., pharmaceutical co.; business consultant. Member: Health Select Cttee, 2015–; Scottish Affairs Select Cttee, 2015–. *Address:* House of Commons, SW1A 0AA.

**TIMMS, Rt Hon. Stephen (Creswell);** PC 2006; MP (Lab) East Ham, since 1997 (Newham North East, June 1994–1997); *b* 29 July 1955; *s* of late Ronald James Timms and of Margaret Joyce Timms (*née* Johnson); *m* 1986, Hui-Leng Lim. *Educ:* Farnborough Grammar Sch.; Emmanuel Coll., Cambridge (MA, MPhil). Consultant, Logica, 1978–86; Ovum: Principal Consultant, 1986–94; Manager, Telecommunications Reports, 1994. Sec., Newham NE Labour Party, 1981–84. Newham Borough Council: Councillor (Lab), 1984–97; Chm., Planning Cttee, 1987–90; Leader, 1990–94. PPS to Minister of State, DFEE, 1997–98, to Sec. of State for NI, 1998; Parly Under-Sec. of State, DSS, 1998–99; Minister of State (Minister for Pensions), DSS, 1999; Financial Sec., HM Treasury, 1999–2001, 2004–05 and 2008–10; Minister of State: (Minister for School Standards), DFES, 2001–02; (Minister for e-commerce and Competitiveness, then for Energy, e-Commerce and Postal Services), DTI, 2002–04; (Minister for Pensions), DWP, 2005–06; Chief Sec. to HM Treasury, 2006–07; Minister of State: BERR, 2007–08; DWP, 2008; Parly Under-Sec. of State, BIS, 2009–10; Shadow Minister for Employment, 2010–15. Mem., H of C Treasury Select Cttee, 1996–97; Mem. Council, 1996–98, Hon. Treas., 1997–98, Parly IT Cttee. Mem., Plaistow Christian Fellowship; Chm., Christians on the Left (formerly Christian Socialist Movement), 2012– (Vice-Chm., 1996–99); Vice-Chm., Labour Party Faith Gps, 2007–. Trustee, Traidcraft Foundn, 2011–. Mem., Ramblers' Assoc. Hon. Pres., Telecommunications Users' Assoc., 1995–99. Hon. DEd E London, 2002. *Publications:* Broadband Communications: the commercial impact, 1986; ISDN: customer premises equipment, 1988; Broadband Communications: market strategies, 1992. *Address:* House of Commons, SW1A 0AA. *T:* (020) 7219 4000.

**TIMPSON, (Anthony) Edward;** MP (C) Crewe and Nantwich, since May 2008; Minister of State, Department for Education, since 2015; *b* Knutsford, Cheshire, 26 Dec. 1973; *s* of John Timpson, CBE and Alex Timpson, MBE; *m* 2002, Julia Helen Still; one *s* two *d. Educ:* Pownall Hall Sch.; Alderley Edge Co. Prim. Sch.; Stockport Grammar Jun. Sch.; Terra Nova Sch.; Uppingham Sch.; Durham Univ. (BA Hons Politics); Coll. of Law, London (LLB). Called to the Bar, Inner Temple, 1998; non-practising family law specialist. PPS to Home Secretary, 2010–12; Parly Under-Sec. of State, DfE, 2012–15. *Recreations:* football (watching and playing), cricket, marathon running, travel, playing with my children. *Address:* House of Commons, SW1A 0AA.

**TOLHURST, Kelly Jane;** MP (C) Rochester and Strood, since 2015; *b* Borstal, Rochester, 23 Aug. 1978; *d* of Morris and Christine Tolhurst. *Educ:* Chapter High Sch. Dir, Skipper UK Ltd, Rochester, 2002–. Mem. (C) Medway Council, 2011–. Member: Eur. Scrutiny Select Cttee, 2015–; Business, Innovation and Skills Select Cttee, 2015–. *Address:* House of Commons, SW1A 0AA. *T:* (020) 7219 5387. *E:* kelly.tolhurst.mp@parliament.uk.

**TOMLINSON, Justin Paul;** MP (C) North Swindon, since 2010; Parliamentary Under-Secretary of State, Department for Work and Pensions, since 2015; *b* 1976; *m* 2012, Joanne Wheeler. *Educ:* Harry Cheshire High Sch., Kidderminster; Oxford Brookes Univ. (BA Business and Mktg 1999). Sales and Mktg Manager, First Leisure, 1999–2000; Mktg Exec., Point to Point, 2000; Dir, TB Mktg Solutions Ltd, 2000–10. Mem. (C), Swindon BC, 2000–10. Mem., Public Accounts Cttee, 2012–14. Contested (C) N Swindon, 2005. *Address:* House of Commons, SW1A 0AA.

**TOMLINSON, Michael James;** MP (C) Mid Dorset and North Poole, since 2015; *b* Wokingham, 1 Oct. 1977; *s* of Howard and Heather Tomlinson; *m* 2000, Frances Mynors; one *s* two *d. Educ:* Univ. of London (BA Hons Classics). Called to the Bar, Middle Temple, 2002 (Queen Mother's Schol.). *Recreations:* all sports, reading, going to the beach with my family. *Address:* House of Commons, SW1A 0AA. *Clubs:* Hamworth Cricket, Poole Hockey.

**TRACEY, Craig Paul;** MP (C) North Warwickshire, since 2015; *b* Durham, 21 Aug. 1974; *s* of Edward and Joyce Tracey; *m* 2014, Karen. *Educ:* Framwellgate Moor Comprehensive Sch. Owner, Dunelm Insce Brokers, 1996–2015. Dir, Dunelm Business Consultants, 2014–. Member: Southern Staffs Employment and Skills Bd, 2014–. Founder Trustee, Lichfield

Garrick Th., 2012–. *Recreations:* local football, ski-ing. *Address:* House of Commons, SW1A 0AA. *T:* (020) 7219 5646. *E:* craig.tracey.mp@parliament.uk.

**TREDINNICK, David Arthur Stephen;** MP (C) Bosworth, since 1987; *b* 19 Jan. 1950; *m* 1983, Rebecca Jane Shott (marr diss. 2008); one *s* one *d*. *Educ:* Ludgrove Sch., Wokingham; Eton; Mons Officer Cadet Sch.; Graduate Business Sch., Cape Town Univ. (MBA); St John's Coll., Oxford (MLitt 1987). Trainee, E. B. Savoury Milln & Co., Stockbrokers, 1972; Account Exec., Quadrant International, 1974; Salesman, Kalle Infotec UK, 1976; Sales Manager, Word Processing, 1977–78; Consultant, Baird Communications, NY, 1978–79; Marketing Manager, Q1 Europe Ltd, 1979–81; Res. asst to Kenneth Warren, MP, and Angela Rumbold, CBE, MP, 1981–87; Dir, Malden Mitcham Properties (family business), 1985–. Contested (C) Cardiff S and Penarth, 1983. PPS to Minister of State, Welsh Office, 1991–94. Chm., Select Cttee on Statutory Instruments, 1997–2005; Member: Select Cttee on Health, 2010–15; Select Cttee on Sci. and Technol., 2013–15; Chairman: Jt Cttee on Statutory Instruments, 1997–2005; All-Party Parly Gp for Integrated Healthcare (formerly for Alternative and Complementary Medicine, then for Complementary and Integrated Medicine), 2006– (Treas., 1991–2002; Jt Chm., 2002–06); Treas., Parly Gp for World Sport, 1991–95; Secretary: Cons. backbench Defence Cttee, 1990–91; Cons. backbench Foreign Affairs Cttee, 1990–91. Chm., British Atlantic Gp of Young Politicians, 1989–91; Co-Chm., Future of Europe Trust, 1991–94; Chairman: Anglo East European Trade Co., 1990–97; Ukraine Business Agency, 1992–97. *Address:* House of Commons, SW1A 0AA. *T:* (020) 7219 4514.

**TREVELYAN, Anne-Marie Belinda;** MP (C) Berwick-upon-Tweed, since 2015; *b* London, 6 April 1969; *d* of (Donald) Leonard Beaton and Katherine Beaton; *m* 1998, John Henry Thornton Trevelyan; one *s* one *d*. *Educ:* St Paul's Girls' Sch., London; Oxford Poly. (BSc Hons Maths 1990). CA 1993. Contested (C) Berwick-upon-Tweed, 2010. *Recreations:* walking, cooking, tennis, tapestry, Berwick Rangers Football Supporters Club. *Address:* House of Commons, SW1A 0AA. *T:* (020) 7219 4437. *E:* annemarie.trevelyan.mp @parliament.uk.

**TRICKETT, Jon Hedley;** MP (Lab) Hemsworth, since Feb. 1996; *b* 2 July 1950; *s* of Lawrence and Rose Trickett; *m* 1969 (marr. diss.); one *s* one *d*; *m* 1994, Sarah Balfour; one *d*. *Educ:* Hull Univ. (BA Politics); Leeds Univ. (MA Pol Sociol). Builder/plumber, to 1985. Joined Labour Party, 1971; Leeds City Council: Councillor, Beeston Ward, 1985–96; Chair: Finance Cttee, 1986–89; Housing Cttee, 1988–89; Leader, 1989–96. Chm., Leeds City Development Co., 1989–96; Member of Board: Leeds Development Corp., 1992–96; Leeds Health Care, 1992–96;

Director: Leeds/Bradford Airport, 1988–96; Leeds Playhouse, 1988–96; Leeds Theatre Co., 1988–96. PPS to Minister Without Portfolio, 1997–98, to Sec. of State for Trade and Industry, 1998, to the Prime Minister, 2008–10; Shadow Minister of State, Cabinet Office, 2010–11; Shadow Minister for the Cabinet Office, 2011–13; Shadow Minister without Portfolio and Dep. Chair, Labour Party, 2013–15; Shadow Sec. of State for Communities and Local Govt, and Shadow Minister for Constitutional Convention, 2015–. Mem., Public Accounts Select Cttee, 2001–06. Mem., GMBATU. *Recreations:* cycling, sail-boarding. *Address:* Ground Floor, Moorthorpe Railway Station, Barnsley Road, South Kirkby, Pontefract, W Yorks WF9 3AT. *T:* (01977) 655695; House of Commons, SW1A 0AA. *Club:* Cyclists' Touring.

**TRUSS, Rt Hon. Elizabeth (Mary);** PC 2014; MP (C) South West Norfolk, since 2010; Secretary of State for Environment, Food and Rural Affairs, since 2014; *b* Oxford, 26 July 1975; *d* of John Kenneth Truss and Priscilla Mary Truss; *m* 2000, Hugh O'Leary; two *d*. *Educ:* Roundhay Sch., Leeds; Merton Coll., Oxford (MA PPE). Commercial Analyst, Shell International, 1996–2000; Commercial Manager and Regulatory Econs Dir, Cable & Wireless, 2000–05; Divl Man. Dir, Communication Gp, 2005–07; Dep. Dir, Reform, 2007–09. Parly Under-Sec. of State, DFE, 2012–14. Contested (C): Hemsworth, 2001; Calder Valley, 2005. *Recreations:* food, design, cinema. *Address:* House of Commons, SW1A 0AA. *T:* (020) 7219 7151. *E:* elizabeth.truss.mp@parliament.uk.

**TUGENDHAT, Thomas Georg John,** MBE 2010; MP (C) Tonbridge and Malling, since 2015; *b* 27 June 1973; *s* of Hon. Sir Michael George Tugendhat; *m* Anissia; one *s*. *Educ:* Bristol Univ. (BA Theol. 1995); Gonville and Caius Coll., Cambridge (MPhil Islamic Studies 1996). Volunteer, CSV, 1991–92; freelance journalist, Beirut, 1997–99; Founder and Manager, Fortune Promoseven, PR co., Lebanon, 1997–99; Mgt Consultant, First Consulting Ltd, 2000–01; Energy Analyst, Bloomberg LP, 2001–03; Dir, Lashkar & Co., 2013–. Officer, Territorial Army, 2003–: with RM, Iraq War as Intelligence Officer, 2003; Advr to Nat. Security Advr, Office of Nat. Security Council, Afghanistan, 2005–06; Advr to Gov., Helmand Province, 2006–07; with Army Strategy Br., 2009–10; MA to CDS, 2010–13. Mem., Admin and Constitutional Affairs Cttee, 2015–. *Address:* House of Commons, SW1A 0AA.

**TURLEY, Anna Catherine;** MP (Lab Co-op) Redcar, since 2015; *b* Dartford, 9 Oct. 1978. *Educ:* Ashford Sch., Kent; Greyfriars Hall, Oxford (BA Hons Hist.). Civil Servant, Home Office, 2001–05; Special Adviser: to Sec. of State for Work and Pensions, 2005; to Chancellor of Duchy of Lancaster, 2006–07; Dep. Dir, New

Local Govt Network, 2007–10. *Address:* House of Commons, SW1A 0AA. *T:* (020) 7219 5441. *E:* anna.turley.mp@parliament.uk.

**TURNER, Andrew John;** MP (C) Isle of Wight, since 2001; *b* Coventry, 24 Oct. 1953; *s* of late Eustace Albert Turner and Joyce Mary Turner (*née* Lowe); partner, Carole Dennett. *Educ:* Rugby Sch.; Keble Coll., Oxford (BA 1976, MA 1981); Birmingham Univ. (PGCE 1977); Henley Mgt Centre. Teacher of Econs and Geog., Rushden Boys' Comp. Sch., 1977, Lord Williams's Sch., Thame, 1978–84; Res. Officer, Cons. Central Office, 1984–86; Special Advr to Sec. of State for Social Services, 1986–88; Dir, Grant-maintained Schools Foundn, 1988–97; Dep. Dir, Educn Unit, IEA, 1998–2000; Head of Policy and Resources, Educn Dept, Southwark BC, 2000–01. Educn Consultant, 1997–2001, Dir, 2000–02, Empire Packet Co. A Vice-Chm., Conservative Party, 2003–05; Opposition front bench spokesman on charities, 2005–06. FRSA. *Recreations:* walking, the countryside, old movies, avoiding gardening. *Address:* House of Commons, SW1A 0AA; (home) Seal House, Sea Street, Newport, Isle of Wight PO30 5BW; (constituency office) Riverside Centre, The Quay, Newport, Isle of Wight PO30 2QR. *T:* (01983) 530808.

**TURNER, Karl;** MP (Lab) Kingston upon Hull East, since 2010; *b* East Hull, 15 April 1971; *s* of Ken Turner and Pat Turner. *Educ:* Bransholme High Sch.; Hull Coll.; Hull Univ. YTS, Hull CC; self-employed antiques dealer; called to the Bar, Middle Temple, 2005; in practice as a barrister, Max Gold Partnership, Hull, 2005–09; Wilberforce Chambers, Hull, 2009–. *Address:* House of Commons, SW1A 0AA.

**TWIGG, (John) Derek;** MP (Lab) Halton, since 1997; *b* 9 July 1959; *s* of Kenneth and Irene Twigg; *m* 1988, Mary Cassidy; one *s* one *d*. *Educ:* Bankfield High Sch., Widnes; Halton Coll. of Further Educn. Civil service posts, Department of Employment, and DFE, then DFEE, 1975–96; political consultant, 1996–97. Member (Lab): Cheshire CC, 1981–85; Halton DC, 1983–97. PPS to Minister of State, DTI, 1999–2001, to Sec. of State, DTLR, 2001–02; an Asst Govt Whip, 2002–03; a Lord Comr of HM Treasury (Govt Whip), 2003–04; Parliamentary Under-Secretary of State: DFES, 2004–05; DfT, 2005–06; MoD, 2006–08; Shadow Health Minister, 2010–11. Mem., Public Accounts Cttee, 1998–99. *Recreations:* hill walking, reading military history. *Address:* House of Commons, SW1A 0AA. *T:* (020) 7219 3000.

**TWIGG, Stephen;** MP (Lab and Co-op) Liverpool West Derby, since 2010; *b* 25 Dec. 1966; *s* of Ian David Twigg and late Jean Barbara Twigg. *Educ:* Southgate Comprehensive Sch.; Balliol Coll., Oxford (BA Hons). Pres., NUS, 1990–92; Parliamentary Officer: British Sect., Amnesty Internat., 1992–93; NCVO, 1993–94;

researcher, office of Margaret Hodge, MP, 1994–96. Mem. (Lab), Islington LBC, 1992–97. Gen. Sec., Fabian Soc., 1996–97 (Mem. Exec., 1997–). MP (Lab) Enfield, Southgate, 1997–2005; contested (Lab) same seat, 2005. Parly Sec., Privy Council Office, 2001–02; Parly Under-Sec. of State, DfEE, 2002–04, Minister of State, DfES, 2004–05; Shadow Sec. of State for Educn, 2011–13. Member: Select Cttee on Modernisation of H of C, 1998–2000; Select Cttee on Educn and Employment, 2000–01; Chm., Select Cttee on Internat. Develt, 2015–. Dir, Foreign Policy Centre, 2005–10 (Bd Mem., 1998–2005). Chairman: Labour Campaign for Electoral Reform, 1998–2001; Lab. Friends of Israel, 1998–2001. Dir, Crime Concern, 1997–2000. Dir, Special Projects, AEGIS Charitable Trust, 2005–10; Chm., Young People Now Foundn, 2006–08. Trustee, WEA, 2006–08 (Patron, 2008–); Chair of Trustees, Merseyside Domestic Violence Services, 2008–. Patron: Merseyside Motor Neurone Disease Assoc., 2011–; Amputees and Carers Support In Liverpool, 2011–. Mem., USDAW. Gov., Jubilee Primary Sch., 2006–07. *Address:* House of Commons, SW1A 0AA.

**TYRIE, Rt Hon. Andrew (Guy);** PC 2015; MP (C) Chichester, since 1997; *b* 15 Jan. 1957; *s* of late Derek and of Patricia Tyrie. *Educ:* Felsted Sch.; Trinity Coll., Oxford (MA); Coll. of Europe, Bruges; Wolfson Coll., Cambridge (MPhil). BP, 1981–83; Cons. Res. Dept, 1983–84; Special Adviser: to Sec. of State for the Envmt, 1985; to Minister for Arts, 1985–86; to Chancellor of the Exchequer, 1986–90; Fellow, Nuffield Coll., Oxford, 1990–91; Woodrow Wilson Scholar, Washington, 1991; Sen. Economist, EBRD, 1992–97. Contested (C) Houghton and Washington, 1992. Shadow Financial Sec., 2003–04; Shadow Paymaster Gen., 2004–05. Chairman: Treasury Select Cttee, 2010– (Mem., 2001–03, 2009–10); Parly Commn on Banking Standards, 2012–13; Member: Select Cttee on Public Admin, 1997–2001; Justice Cttee (formerly Constitutional Affairs Select Cttee), 2005–10; Public Accounts Commn, 1997–; Exec. Cttee, 1922 Cttee, 2005–06. *Publications:* The Prospects for Public Spending, 1996; Sense on EMU, 1998; Reforming the Lords, 1998; (jtly) Leviathan at Large, 2000; Mr Blair's Poodle, 2000; (jtly) Statism by Stealth, 2002; Mr Blair's Poodle Goes to War, 2004; (jtly) Account Rendered, 2011; many pamphlets on econ. and parly issues. *Recreation:* golf. *Address:* House of Commons, SW1A 0AA. *Clubs:* Garrick, MCC, Royal Automobile.

**UMUNNA, Chuka;** MP (Lab) Streatham, since 2010; *b* 17 Oct. 1978. *Educ:* St Dunstan's Coll., Catford; Univ. of Manchester (LLB English and French Law); Univ. of Burgundy; Nottingham Law Sch. Admitted Solicitor, 2004; with Herbert Smith, London, 2002–06, Rochman Landau, 2006–10. Shadow Sec. of State for Business, Innovation and Skills, 2011–15. Mem., Treasury

Select Cttee, 2010–11; Vice Chairman, All Party Parliamentary Group: on Nigeria, 2010–15; on Thameslink, 2010–15. Member: GMB; Unite; Fabian Soc.; Compass. *Publications:* (ed) Owning the Future: how Britain can make it in a fast-changing world, 2014. *Address:* House of Commons, SW1A 0AA.

**VAIZEY, Hon. Edward Henry Butler, (Ed);** MP (C) Wantage, since 2005; Minister of State, Department for Culture, Media and Sport and Department for Business, Innovation and Skills, since 2014; *b* 5 June 1968; *s* of Baron Vaizey and of Lady Vaizey, CBE; *m* 2005, Alexandra Mary Jane Holland; one *s* one *d. Educ:* St Paul's Sch., London; Merton Coll., Oxford (BA 1989, MA 2004); City Univ. (Dip. Law 1992). Desk Officer, Conservative Res. Dept, 1989–91; called to the Bar, Middle Temple, 1993, practised as barrister, 1993–96; Director: Public Policy Unit, 1996–97; Politics Internat., 1997–98; Consolidated Communications, 1998–2003; Chief Speech Writer to Leader of the Opposition, 2004. Opposition frontbench spokesman on the arts, 2006–10; Parliamentary Under-Secretary of State: BIS, 2010–11; DCMS, 2010–14. Contested (C) Bristol East, 1997. Exec. Dir, Edexcel Ltd, 2007–10. Vice-Chm., National Churches Trust, 2008–10; Trustee, Heritage of London Trust, 2009–10. Mem. Bd, Bush Th., 2009–10. Pres., Didcot Town FC, 2005–. Fellow, Radio Acad., 2015. Hon. FRIBA 2010. *Publications:* (ed with M. Gove and N. Boles) A Blue Tomorrow, 2001; (ed with M. McManus) The Blue Book on Transport, 2002; (ed) The Blue Book on Health, 2002. *Address:* House of Commons, SW1A 0AA. *T:* (020) 7219 3000. *E:* vaizeye@parliament.uk. *Club:* Soho House.

**VARA, Shailesh Lakhman;** MP (C) North West Cambridgeshire, since 2005; Parliamentary Under-Secretary of State: Ministry of Justice, since 2013; Department for Work and Pensions, since 2015; *b* 4 Sept. 1960; *s* of Lakhman Arjan Vara and Savita Vara (*née* Gadher); *m* 2002, Beverley Deanne Fear; two *s. Educ:* Aylesbury Grammar Sch.; Brunel Univ. (LLB; Hon. Fellow, 2010). Admitted Solicitor, 1990; articled, Richards Butler, 1988–90; Crossman Block, 1991–92; Payne Hicks Beach, 1992–93; CMS Cameron McKenna, 1994–2001. Shadow Dep. Leader of the H of C, 2006–10; an Asst Govt Whip, 2010–12. Mem., Select Cttee on Envmt, Food and Rural Affairs, 2005–06, on Admin, 2010–11, on Finance and Services, 2011–13. Chm., Cons. Parly Friends of India, 2008–10; Vice-Chm., Cons. China Parly Gp, 2009–10. A Vice-Chm., Cons. Party, 2001–05. Contested (C): Birmingham Ladywood, 1997; Northampton S, 2001. Treas., 2001–04, Vice Chm., 2006–09, Exec. Cttee, Soc. of Cons. Lawyers. Mem., Campaign Exec. Gp, Great Fen Project, 2005–10. Gov., Westminster Kingsway Coll., 2002–05. Vice-Pres., Huntingdonshire

CCC, 2007–. *Recreations:* travel, cricket, tae kwon do. *Address:* House of Commons, SW1A 0AA. *T:* (020) 7219 3000. *E:* varas@parliament.uk.

**VAZ, Rt Hon. (Nigel) Keith (Anthony Standish);** PC 2006; MP (Lab) Leicester East, since 1987; *b* Aden, 26 Nov. 1956; *s* of late Anthony Xavier Vaz and Merlyn Verona Vaz; *m* 1993, Maria Fernandes; one *s* one *d. Educ:* St Joseph's Convent, Aden; Latymer Upper Sch., Hammersmith; Gonville and Caius Coll., Cambridge (BA 1979); Coll. of Law, Lancaster Gate. Solicitor, Richmond-upon-Thames BC, 1982; Senior Solicitor, Islington BC, 1982–85; Solicitor, Highfields and Belgrave Law Centre, Leicester, 1985–87. Contested (Lab): Richmond and Barnes (gen. election), 1983; Surrey W (European Parlt election), 1984. Opposition front bench spokesman on inner cities and urban areas, 1992–97; PPS to Attorney Gen. and Solicitor Gen., 1997–99; Parly Sec., Lord Chancellor's Dept, 1999; Minister of State (Minister for Europe), FCO, 1999–2001. Member: Home Affairs Select Cttee, 1987–92 (Chm., 2007–); Constitutional Affairs Select Cttee, 2002–07. Chairman: All Party Hosiery and Knitwear Gp, 1987–92; Unison Gp of MPs, 1996–99; Indo-British Parly Gp, 1997–99 (Vice Pres., 1999–); Yemen Parly Gp, 1997–99, 2001–; Vice Chairman: Tribune Gp of MPs, 1992 (Treas., 1994); PLP Internat. Develt Gp, 1997–99; All Party Parly Gp to Holy See, 2006; Treas., All Party Parly Race and Community Gp, 2006. Labour Party: Mem., Regl Exec., 1994–96; Chm., Ethnic Minority Taskforce, 2006–; Vice Chm., Women's Race and Equality Cttee; Mem., NEC, 2007–; Trustee, Pension Regulator, 2008. Pres., India Develt Gp (UK) Ltd, 1992–. Chm., City 2020, Urban Policy Commn, 1993–99; Mem., Nat. Adv. Cttee, Crime Concern, 1989–93; Vice Chm., British Council, 1998–99. Mem., Clothing and Footwear Inst., 1988–94. Vice Pres., Assoc. of Dist Councils, 1993–97. Patron: Gingerbread, 1990–; Labour Party Race Action Gp, 2000–. Founder Patron: Naz Project London, 1999–; Next Steps Foundn, 2003; Silver Star Appeal, 2006. Jt Patron, UN Year of Tolerance, 1995; EU Ambassador, Year of Intercultural Dialogue, 2008. President: Leicester and S Leics RSPCA, 1988–99; Leicester Kidney Patients Assoc., 2000. Former Columnist: Tribune; Catholic Herald; New Life (Gujarat Samachar). *Address:* 144 Uppingham Road, Leicester LE5 0QF. *T:* (0116) 212 2028. *Clubs:* Safari (Leicester); Scraptoft Valley Working Men's.

*See also V. C. M. Vaz.*

**VAZ, Valerie Carol Marian;** MP (Lab) Walsall South, since 2010; *b* Aden, 7 Dec. 1954; *d* of late Anthony Xavier Vaz and Merlyn Verona Vaz (*née* Pereira); *m* 1992, Paul John Townsend; one *d. Educ:* Twickenham Co. Grammar Sch.; Bedford Coll., Univ. of London (BSc); Coll. of Law (CPE and Law Soc. final exam.). Articled clerk, Herbert Smith, 1982–84; admitted solicitor, 1984; local govt solicitor, London Bors of Brent and Hammersmith and Fulham, 1985–92; Townsend Vaz Solicitors, 1992–2001; Dep. Dist Judge, 1996–2000; Treasury Solicitor's Dept, 2001–10; MoJ, 2008–09 (on secondment). Mem. (Lab) Ealing LBC, 1986–90 (Dep. Leader, 1988–89). Member: Health Select Cttee, 2010–15; Regulatory Reform Cttee, 2010–15; Panel of Chairs, 2015–; All Party Parly Gp on Burma; Vice-Chair, Parly Labour Party. Mem., Lay Adv. Panel, Coll. of Optometrists, 2007. Presenter, Network East, BBC TV, 1987. Mem., Law Soc. *Recreations:* music, playing piano and guitar, gardening, member of National Trust and Kew Gardens. *Address:* House of Commons, SW1A 0AA. *T:* (020) 7219 7176, *Fax:* (020) 7219 5045. *E:* valerie.vaz.mp@parliament.uk.

See also Rt Hon. N. K. A. S. Vaz.

**VERMA,** Baroness *cr* 2006 (Life Peer), of Leicester in the County of Leicestershire; **Sandip Verma;** Parliamentary Under-Secretary of State, Department for International Development, since 2015; *b* 30 June 1959; *d* of S. S. and R. Rana; *m* 1977, Ashok Kumar Verma; one *s* one *d. Educ:* locally. Senior Partner, Domiciliary Care Services, 2000. Contested (C): Hull E, 2001; Wolverhampton SW, 2005. House of Lords: Opposition spokesperson on health, educn and skills, 2006–07, on innovation, univs and skills, 2007–10, on children, schs and families, 2007–08, 2009–10; an Opposition Whip, 2006–10; a Baroness in Waiting (Govt Whip), 2010–12; govt spokesman for Cabinet Office, 2010–12, internat. develt, 2010–11, women and equalities, 2010–12, business, innovation and skills, 2011–12; Parly Under-Sec. of State, DECC, 2012–15. Advr, Bright Distributors Ltd, 2006–. Exec. Mem., Ethnic Diversity Council, 2005–. Chm. (Political), Leics South Cons Assoc., 2006–08; Pres., City of Leics Cons. Assoc., 2008–09, 2010–11. Champion, Roko Breast Cancer, 2006–; Patron: Tory Reform Group, 2006–; Cons. British Asian Link, 2006–; Pakistan-India Friendship Soc., 2006–; Bucks Punjabi Internat. Soc., 2006–. *Recreations:* socialising, reading, walking, going to different parts of the world, arranging events, watching cricket. *Address:* House of Lords, SW1A 0PW. *T:* (office) (020) 7219 5216, (home) (0116) 270 1686, *Fax:* (0116) 270 1603. *E:* Vermas@parliament.uk.

**VICKERS, Martin John;** MP (C) Cleethorpes, since 2010; *b* Cleethorpes, 13 Sept. 1950; *m* 1981, Ann Gill; one *d. Educ:* Havelock Sch.; Grimsby Coll.; Univ. of Lincoln (BA Hons Politics 2004). In printing industry, 1967–78; in retail trade, 1978–94; Constituency Agent to Edward Leigh, MP, 1994–2010. Member (C): Great Grimsby BC, 1980–94; NE Lincs Council, 1999–2011 (Cabinet Mem., 2003–09). Contested (C) Cleethorpes, 2005. *Address:* House of Commons, SW1A 0AA.

**VILLIERS, Rt Hon. Theresa (Anne);** PC 2010; MP (C) Chipping Barnet, since 2005; Secretary of State for Northern Ireland, since 2012; *b* 5 March 1968; *d* of late George Villiers and of Virginia Villiers; *m* 1999, Sean David Henry Wilken, QC. *Educ:* Univ. of Bristol (LLB Hons 1990); Jesus Coll., Oxford (BCL Hons 1991). Called to the Bar, Inner Temple, 1992; Barrister specialising in chancery, insolvency and entertainment law, 1994–95; Lectr in Law, King's Coll., London, 1995–99. MEP (C) London Region, 1999–2005. Treas. and economic spokesman, 1999–2004, Dep. Leader, 2001–02, Cons. delegn to EP; EP Rapporteur for Investment Services Directive, 2002–05. Shadow Chief Sec. to HM Treasury, 2005–07; Shadow Sec. of State for Transport, 2007–10; Minister of State, DfT, 2010–12. *Publications:* (with Sean Wilken) Waiver, Variation and Estoppel, 1998; Tax Harmonisation: the impending threat, 2001; various articles in legal jls, incl. Lloyd's Maritime and Commercial Law Qly. *Address:* House of Commons, SW1A 0AA. *Club:* Middlesex CC.

**WALKER, Charles Ashley Rupert,** OBE 2015; MP (C) Broxbourne, since 2005; *b* 11 Sept. 1967; *s* of late Timothy Walker and of Carola Walker (*née* Ashton) (she *m* 1976, Rt Hon. Sir Christopher John Chataway, PC); *m* 1995, Fiona Jane Newman; two *s* one *d. Educ:* American Sch. of London; Univ. of Oregon (BSc Pol Sci. 1990). Communications Dir, CSG plc, 1997–2001; Director: Blue Arrow Ltd, 1999–2001; LSM Processing Ltd, 2002–04. Mem., Wandsworth LBC, 2002–. Contested (C) Ealing North, 2001. *Recreations:* fishing, cricket. *Address:* House of Commons, SW1A 0AA. *T:* (020) 7219 3000. *E:* walkerc@parliament.uk. *Clubs:* Waltham Cross Conservative; Hoddesdon Conservative.

**WALKER, Robin Caspar;** MP (C) Worcester, since 2010; *b* Worcs, 12 April 1978; *s* of Baron Walker of Worcester, PC, MBE and of Tessa (*née* Pout); *m* 2011, Charlotte Keenan. *Educ:* St Paul's Sch.; Balliol Coll., Oxford (Schol.; BA Ancient and Modern Hist. 2000). Chief Exec., Property Map Ltd, 2000–01; Res. Exec., i-Search Ltd, 2001–03; Finsbury Group: Exec., 2003–04; Sen. Exec., 2004–06; Associate Partner, 2006–09; Partner, 2009–10. Member: Welsh Affairs Select Cttee, 2011–12; BIS Select Cttee, 2012–15; PPS to Minister of State, NI, 2013–14, to Sec. of State, DEFRA, 2014–15. *Address:* House of Commons, SW1A 0AA.

**WALLACE, (Robert) Ben (Lobban);** MP (C) Wyre and Preston North, since 2010 (Lancaster and Wyre, 2005–10); Parliamentary Under-Secretary of State, NI Office, since 2015; *b* 15 May 1970; *m* 2001, Liza Cooke; two *s* one *d. Educ:* Millfield Sch., Somerset; RMA Sandhurst. Ski Instructor, Austrian Nat. Ski Sch., 1987–89; advertising, RGSH Boston, USA; commissioned, Scots Guards, 1991; Platoon Comdr, 1991–93 (despatches, 1992); Ops Officer, 1993, Intelligence, 1994–97; Co. Comdr, 1997; served

Windsor, London, N Ireland, Central America, BAOR, Egypt, Cyprus; retired 1998. EU Dir, QinetiQ, 2003–05. MSP (C) NE Scotland, 1999–2003; Mem., EU Cttee, health spokesman, Scottish Parlt. Shadow Minister of State for Scotland, 2006–10; PPS to Lord Chancellor and Sec. of State for Justice, 2010–12, to Minister without Portfolio, 2012–14; an Asst Govt Whip, 2014–15. Mem., Scottish Select Cttee, 2005–10, NI Grand Cttee, H of C, 2005–10; Chm., All Party Parly Gp on Iran, 2006–14. Mem., Queen's Body Guard for Scotland (Royal Co. of Archers), 2006–. Recreations: ski-ing, sailing, Rugby, horse racing. Address: House of Commons, SW1A 0AA; c/o Village Centre, Great Eccleston Village Centre, 59 High Street, Great Eccleston PR3 0YB. Club: Third Guards.

**WARBURTON, David John;** MP (C) Somerton and Frome, since 2015; b Burnham, Bucks, 28 Oct. 1965; s of John and Erica Warburton; m 2002, Harriet Katharine Baker-Bates; one s one d. Educ: Reading Sch.; Waingels Coll.; Royal Coll. of Music (Dip. RCM); King's Coll. London (MMus). Professional composer, 1992–95; Teacher of Music, Hurlingham and Chelsea Sch., and RCM Jun. Dept, 1995–99; Man. Dir, Music Solution Ltd, 1999–2002; Chief Exec., 2002–05; Chm., 2005–08, Pitch Entertainment Gp; Man. Partner, Oflang Partners LLP, 2008–15; Chm., MyHigh Ltd, 2012–15. Chm., Wells Cathedral Sch. Parents' Assoc., 2010–14; Mem., Capital Exec. Cttee, Shakespeare's Globe Th., 2008–10. Trustee, Ups and Downs Southwest, 2013–. Patron, Royal Bath and West Soc., 2013–. Member: MENSA, 1994–; ESU, 2008–. FRSA. Recreations: playing the piano and thinking out loud, both of which to the annoyance of friends and family. Address: House of Commons, SW1A 0AA.

**WARMAN, Matthew;** MP (C) Boston and Skegness, since 2015; b Enfield, London, 1 Sept. 1981; m Dr Rachel Weaver. Educ: Haberdashers' Aske's Boys' Sch.; Univ. of Durham (BA Hons English Lit. 2004). The Telegraph: writer, 1999–2009; Consumer Technol. Ed., 2008–13; Technol. Ed. (Hd of Technol.), 2013–15. Recreation: eating and consequential exercise. Address: House of Commons, SW1A 0AA. T: (020) 7219 8643. E: matt.warman.mp@parliament.uk.

**WATKINSON, Dame Angela (Eileen),** DBE 2013; MP (C) Hornchurch and Upminster, since 2010 (Upminster, 2001–10); b 18 Nov. 1941; m 1961, Roy Michael Watkinson (marr. diss.); one s two d. Educ: Wanstead County High Sch.; Anglia Poly. (HNC 1989). Bank of NSW, 1958–64; Special Sch. Sec., Essex CC, 1976–88; Cttee Clerk, Barking and Dagenham BC, 1988–89; Cttee Manager, Basildon DC, 1989–94. Member (C): Havering BC, 1994–98; Essex CC, 1997–2001. An Opposition Whip, 2002–04 and 2006–10; Shadow Minister: for Health and Educn in London, 2004–05; for Local Govt and

Communities, 2005; a Lord Comr of HM Treasury (Govt Whip), 2010–12. Mem., Work and Pensions Select Cttee, 2013–15. Member: Parly Assembly, Council of Europe, 2012–; Cttee on Standards in Public Life, 2013–. Freeman, City of London, 2004. Address: (office) 23 Butts Green Road, Hornchurch, Essex RM11 2JS; c/o House of Commons, SW1A 0AA.

**WATSON, Thomas;** MP (Lab) West Bromwich East, since 2001; b 8 Jan. 1967; s of Tony and Linda Watson; m 2000, Siobhan Corby. Educ: Hull Univ. Fundraiser, Save the Children, 1988–89; Chair, Nat. Orgn of Labour Students, 1992–93; Dep. Gen. Election Co-ordinator, Labour Party, 1993–97; Nat. Political Organiser, AEEU, 1997–2001. An Asst Govt Whip, 2004–05 and 2007–08; a Lord Comr of HM Treasury (Govt Whip), 2005–06; Parly Under-Sec. of State, MoD, 2006; a Parly Sec., Cabinet Office, 2008–09. Dep. Chm., Labour Party and Campaign Co-ordinator, 2011–13; Dep. Leader, Labour Party, 2015–. Recreation: gardening. Address: House of Commons, SW1A 0AA. Club: Friar Park and West Bromwich Labour.

**WEIR, Michael;** MP (SNP) Angus, since 2001; b 24 March 1957; s of James and Elizabeth Weir; m 1985, Anne Jack; two d. Educ: Arbroath High Sch.; Aberdeen Univ. (LLB). Solicitor: Charles Wood and Son, Kirkcaldy, 1981–83; Myers and Wills, Montrose, 1983–84; J. & D. G. Shiell, Brechin, 1984–2001. Dean, Faculty of Procurators and Solicitors in Angus, 2001. Mem. (SNP), Angus DC, 1984–88. Contested (SNP) Aberdeen S, 1987. Pres., Aberdeen Univ. Student Nationalist Assoc., 1979; Mem., Nat. Exec., Young Scottish Nationalists, 1982. Address: House of Commons, SW1A 0AA; (office) 16 Brothock Bridge, Arbroath, Angus DD11 1NG. T: (01241) 874522.

**WEST, Catherine Elizabeth;** MP (Lab) Hornsey and Wood Green, since 2015; b Mansfield, Vic, Australia; m 1996, Dr Colin Sutherland; one s one d. Educ: Univ. of Sydney (BA, BSW); Sch. of Oriental and African Studies, Univ. of London (MA Chinese Politics). Social worker, Australia; caseworker for David Lammy, MP, 2000. Mem., Islington LBC, 2000–14 (Leader of Opposition, 2004–10; Leader of Council, 2010–13). Chm., Transport and Envmt Cttee, London Councils, 2010–14. Recreations: swimming, cricket. Address: House of Commons, SW1A 0AA. T: (020) 7219 6141. E: catherine.west.mp@parliament.uk.

**WHARTON, James Stephen;** MP (C) Stockton South, since 2010; Parliamentary Under-Secretary of State, Department for Communities and Local Government, since 2015; b Stockton-on-Tees, 16 Feb. 1984; s of Stephen Wharton and Karen Wharton. Educ: Yarm Sch., Yarm; St Peter's Sch., York; Durham Univ. (LLB Hons); Coll. of Law, York. Admitted solicitor, 2008; Solicitor, BHP Law, Darlington and Stockton.

*Recreations:* walking, usually whilst delivering leaflets. *Address:* House of Commons, SW1A 0AA.

**WHATELY, Helen Olivia Bicknell;** MP (C) Faversham and Mid Kent, since 2015; *b* Surrey, 23 June 1976; *m* Marcus Whately; one *s* two *d. Educ:* Lady Margaret Hall, Oxford (BA PPE 1998). Consultant, PricewaterhouseCoopers, 1998–2001; Manager, Strategic Alliances Gp, AOL Europe, 2003–05; Sen. Manager, AOL UK, 2005–06; Advr to Shadow Sec. of State for Culture, Media and Sport, 2006–07; Engagement Manager, and Associate, McKinsey & Co., 2007–15. Mem., Health Select Cttee, 2015–; Co-Chair, All Pty Parly Gp on Healthcare, 2015–; Vice-Chair, All Pty Parly Gp on Mental Health, 2015–. Contested (C) Kingston and Surbiton, 2010. *Address:* House of Commons, SW1A 0AA.

**WHEELER, Heather;** MP (C) South Derbyshire, since 2010; *b* Norwich, 14 May 1959; *d* of Charles Peter Clough Wilkinson and Freda Mary Wilkinson; *m* 1986, Robert James Wheeler; one *d. Educ:* Grey Coat Hosp., Westminster. ACII 1985. Placing Manager, RICS Insce Services Ltd, 1977–87. Member (C): Wandsworth BC, 1982–86; S Derbys DC, 1995–2011 (Leader, 2007–10). Contested (C) Coventry S, 2001, 2005. Member, Select Committee: on Standards and Privileges, 2010–13; on Communities and Local Govt, 2011–15. Chm., All Party Parly Local Govt Gp, 2010–. Mem. Exec., 1922 Cttee, 2011–. *Recreations:* watching sport, DIY, listening to The Archers. *Address:* House of Commons, SW1A 0AA.

**WHITE, Christopher;** MP (C) Warwick and Leamington, since 2010; *b* 28 April 1967. *Educ:* Univ. of Manchester (BE); Univ. of Bath (MBA). Work at Longbridge with MG Rover; freelance PR consultant. Mem. (C) Warwick DC, 2007–10. Contested (C): Birmingham Hall Green, 2001; Warwick and Leamington, 2005. PPS to Minister of State for Policing Crime and Criminal Justice, 2015–, for Security, 2015–. Member: Internat. Develt Select Cttee, 2010–15; Business, Innovation and Skills Select Cttee, 2015–. Co-Chair, All Party Parly Gp on Manufg, 2010–; Chair, All Party Parliamentary Group on: Video Games, 2014–; Nat. Citizen Service, 2014–; Vice Chair, All Party Parly Gp on Poverty, 2010–15. Introd. Private Mem.'s Bill, resulting in Public Services (Social Value) Act, 2012. Mem. Bd and Vice Chm., Policy Connect. Trustee: Warwicks Assoc. of Youth Clubs; Webb Meml Trust, 2011–; Motionhouse Dance Charity, 2011–. *Address:* House of Commons, SW1A 0AA.

**WHITEFORD, Eilidh,** PhD; MP (SNP) Banff and Buchan, since 2010; *b* Aberdeen, 24 April 1969; *d* of Douglas Dodson Whiteford and Kathleen Whiteford (*née* MacLeod); *m* 2010, Stephen Smith. *Educ:* Banff Acad.; Univ. of Glasgow (MA Hons 1991; PhD 1998); Univ. of

Guelph (MA 1994). Lectr in Scottish Literature and Academic Develt Officer, Univ. of Glasgow, 1999; Co-ordinator, Scottish Carers' Alliance, 2001–03; Campaigns Manager, Scotland, Oxfam, 2003–09. *Recreation:* music. *Address:* House of Commons, SW1A 0AA. *T:* (020) 7219 7005. *E:* eilidh.whiteford.mp@parliament.uk.

**WHITEHEAD, Dr Alan Patrick Vincent;** MP (Lab) Southampton Test, since 1997; *b* 15 Sept. 1950; *m*; one *s* one *d. Educ:* Southampton Univ. (BA 1973; PhD 1976). Dep. Dir., 1976–79, Dir, 1979–83, Outset; Dir, British Inst. of Industrial Therapy, 1983–92; Prof. of Public Policy, Southampton Inst., 1992–97. Mem. (Lab), Southampton CC, 1980–92 (Leader, 1984–92). Parly Under-Sec. of State, DTLR, 2001–02. Member: Select Cttee on Envmt, Transport and Regions, 1997–99, on constitutional affairs, 2003–10, on Energy and Climate Change, 2008–; Envmtl Audit Select Cttee, 2010–15; Standards and Privileges Cttee, 2005–13; Chairman: All Party Ports Gp, 1998–2001; Parly Renewable and Sustainable Energy Gp, 2003–; Parly Sustainable Resource (formerly Waste) Gp, 2003–; British-Polish Parly Gp, 2008–. *Address:* House of Commons, SW1A 0AA. *T:* (020) 7219 3000.

**WHITFORD, Dr Philippa;** MP (SNP) Central Ayrshire, since 2015; *b* Belfast, 24 Dec. 1958; *d* of Philip Whitford and Elizabeth Whitford; *m* 1987, Hans Josef Pieper; one *s. Educ:* Douglas Acad., Milngavie; Univ. of Glasgow (MB ChB 1982; MD 1991). FRCSGlas 1986. Surgical training: Royal Victoria Hosp., Belfast, 1983–84; Belfast City Hosp., 1984; Glasgow Royal Infirmary, 1984–85; Registrar: Monklands Dist Gen. Hosp., Airdrie, 1985–86; Royal Hosp. for Sick Children, Glasgow, 1986–87; Canniesburn Hosp., Glasgow, 1987; Glasgow Royal Infirmary, 1987; Res. Fellow, Depts of Surgery and Biochem., Univ. of Glasgow, 1987–89; Registrar (Gen. Surgery), Inverclyde Royal Hosp., 1989–91; Volunteer Consultant Surgeon in Gen. Surgery and Urology, Ali Ahli Hosp., Gaza, 1991–92; Volunteer Health Care Planning and Gen. Surgery, Al Hamshary Hosp., Sidon, Lebanon Balsam Hosp., 1993; Sen. Registrar (Gen. Surgery and Breast Surgery), Aberdeen Royal Infirmary, 1994–96; Consultant Breast Cancer Surgeon, Crosshouse Hosp., Kilmarnock, 1996–2014. Lead clinician in breast cancer, Ayrshire and Arran Health Bd, 1996–2010. Mem., Health Select Cttee, 2015–. *Publications:* articles on breast cancer and surgery in British Jl of Surgery, British Jl of Cancer, Eur. Jl of Cancer. *Recreations:* singing, playing cello, painting. *Address:* (office) 14 Eglinton Street, Irvine KA12 8AS. *T:* (01294) 311160. *E:* philippa.whitford.mp @parliament.uk.

**WHITTAKER, Craig;** MP (C) Calder Valley, since 2010; *b* Radcliffe, Lancs, 30 Aug. 1962; *s* of Frank Whittaker and Marjorie Whittaker; *m* 2011, Elaine Wilkinson; one *s* two *d* by a previous marriage. *Educ:* Belmont State High Sch., NSW.

Restaurant Manager: Pizza Hut (Australia) Pty Ltd, 1980–84; Pizza Hut (UK) Ltd, 1984–85; Licensee: Liberty Taverns Ltd, 1985–86; J. W. Lees (Brewers) Ltd, 1986–88; Dir, Food Retail (Australia), Kezdem Pty Ltd, 1988–92; Retail Branch Manager, Wilkinson Home and Garden Stores, 1992–98; Retail Gen. Manager, PC World, DSG Internat. plc, 1998–2009. Mem. (C) Calderdale MBC, 2003–04, 2007–11 (Lead Mem., Children and Young People, 2007–10). Mem., Educn Select Cttee, 2010–15; Jt Chm., All Party Parly Gp on Street Children, 2011–; Chm., All Party Parly Gp on Looked After Children and Care Leavers, 2012–, on Adoption and Fostering, 2012–. Chm., Together for Looked-after Children charity, 2011–. *Recreations:* scuba diving, travel. *Address:* House of Commons, SW1A 0AA. *T:* (020) 7219 7031, *Fax:* (020) 7219 1054. *E:* craig.whittaker.mp@parliament.uk.

**WHITTINGDALE, Rt Hon. John (Flasby Lawrance),** OBE 1990; PC 2015; MP (C) Maldon, since 2010 (Colchester South and Maldon, 1992–97; Maldon and East Chelmsford, 1997–2010); Secretary of State for Culture, Media and Sport, since 2015; *b* 16 Oct. 1959; *s* of late John Whittingdale and of Margaret Esmé Scott Napier; *m* 1990, Ancilla Campbell Murfitt (marr. diss. 2008); one *s* one *d. Educ:* Sandroyd Sch.; Winchester Coll.; University Coll. London (BScEcon). Head of Political Section, Conservative Research Dept, 1982–84; Special Adviser to Sec. of State for Trade and Industry, 1984–87; Manager, N. M. Rothschild & Sons, 1987; Political Sec. to the Prime Minister, 1988–90; Private Sec. to Rt Hon. Margaret Thatcher, 1990–92. PPS to Minister of State for Educn, 1994–95, for Educn and Employment, 1995–96; an Opposition Whip, 1997–98; Opposition Treasury spokesman, 1998–99; PPS to Leader of the Opposition, 1999–2001; Shadow Sec. of State for Trade and Industry, 2001–02, for Culture, Media and Sport, 2002–03 and 2004–05, for Agriculture, Fisheries and Food, 2003–04. Member, Select Committee: on Health, 1993–97; on Trade and Industry, 2001; Chairman: Select Cttee on Culture, Media and Sport, 2005–15; Jt Cttee on Privacy and Injunctions, 2011–12. Sec., Conservative Parly Home Affairs Cttee, 1992–94; Mem. Exec., Cons. 1922 Cttee, 2005–15 (Vice Chm., 2006–15). Parly Mem., Cons. Party Bd, 2006–09. FRSA 2008. *Recreations:* cinema, music. *Address:* c/o House of Commons, SW1A 0AA. *Club:* Essex.

**WIGGIN, William David;** MP (C) North Herefordshire, since 2010 (Leominster, 2001–10); *b* 4 June 1966; *s* of Sir Alfred William, (Jerry), Wiggin, TD and of Rosemary Janet (*née* Orr, now Dale Harris); *m* 1999, Camilla Chilvers; two *s* one *d. Educ:* Eton; UCNW, Bangor (BA Hons Pure Econs). Trader: Rayner Coffee Internat., 1988–90; Mitsubishi Corp., 1990–91; Union Bank of Switzerland, 1991–94; Associate Dir, Dresdner Kleinwort Benson, 1994–98; Manager, Commerzbank, 1998–2001. Opposition

spokesman on envmt, 2003, on agric. and fisheries, 2005–09; Shadow Sec. of State for Wales, 2003–05; Opposition Whip, 2009–10; an Asst Govt Whip, 2010–12. *Recreations:* motor bikes, Hereford cattle, country sports. *Address:* House of Commons, SW1A 0AA. *Clubs:* Hurlingham, Annabel's.

**WILLIAMS OF TRAFFORD,** Baroness *cr* 2013 (Life Peer), of Hale in the County of Greater Manchester; **Susan Frances Maria Williams;** Parliamentary Under-Secretary of State, Department for Communities and Local Government, since 2015; *b* Cork, Ireland, 16 May 1967; *d* of John Henry McElroy and Mary McElroy; *m* 2005, Alexander Williams; one *s* two *d. Educ:* La Sagesse High Sch., Jesmond, Newcastle upon Tyne; Huddersfield Poly. (BSc Hons Applied Nutrition). Nutritionist, Multiple Sclerosis charity, 1992–2002. Mem. (C) Trafford MBC, 1998–2011 (Leader, 2004–09). NW Chm., Heritage Lottery Fund, 2011–12; CEO, Atlantic Gateway, 2012–14; Dir, NW Rail Campaign, 2011–14. A Baroness in Waiting (Govt Whip), 2014–15. Contested (C) Bolton West, 2010. *Recreations:* hill walking in Scotland, backgammon, pub quizzes. *Address:* House of Lords, SW1A 0PW.

**WILLIAMS, (Alun) Craig;** MP (C) Cardiff North, since 2015; *b* Welshpool, 7 June 1985; *s* of David Williams and Andrea Williams; *m* 2013, Clare Bath; one *s* one *d.* Mem. (C), Cardiff CC, 2008–15 (Chm., Economy Cttee, 2012–15). Dir, Cardiff Bus, 2011–15. *Recreations:* Rugby, real ale, walking, Welsh springer spaniels, school governor (primary). *Address:* House of Commons, SW1A 0AA. *T:* (020) 7219 8245. *E:* craig.williams.mp@parliament.uk. *Clubs:* Carlton; Cardiff and County.

**WILLIAMS, Hywel;** MP (Plaid Cymru) Arfon, since 2010 (Caernarfon, 2001–10); *b* 14 May 1953; *s* of late Robert Williams and of Jennie Page Williams; *m* 1st, 1977, Sian Davies (marr. diss. 1998); three *d*; 2nd, 2010, Dr Myfanwy Davies. *Educ:* Ysgol Glan y Mor, Pwllheli, Gwynedd; UC Cardiff (BSc Hons Psychol. 1974); UCNW, Bangor (CQSW 1980). Approved Social Worker (Mental Health), 1984. Social Worker: Child Care and Long Term Team, Social Services Dept, Mid Glam CC, 1974–76; Mental Health Team, Social Services Dept, Gwynedd CC, 1976–78 and 1980–84; Welsh Office funded project worker, 1985–91, Hd of Centre, 1991–93, N and W Wales Practice Centre, UCNW, Bangor; freelance lectr, consultant and author in social work and social policy, 1994–2001. CCETSW Cymru: Mem. Welsh Cttee and Chm., Welsh Lang. Sub-cttee, 1989–92; Mem., Welsh Lang. Pubns Adv. Panel, 1992–93. *Publications:* (contrib.) Social Work in Action in the 1980s, 1985; (compiled and ed) A Social Work Vocabulary, 1988; (gen. ed.) Child Care Terms, 1993; (contrib. and gen ed.) Social Work and the Welsh Language, 1994; (compiled and ed) An

Index of Trainers and Training, 1994; (contrib. and ed jtly) Gofal: a training and resource pack for community care in Wales, 1998; Speaking the Invisible, 2002. *Recreations:* walking, cinema, reading. *Address:* House of Commons, SW1A 0AA. *T:* (020) 7219 5021; 8 Stryd Y Castell, Caernarfon, Gwynedd LL15 1SE. *T:* (01286) 672076.

**WILLIAMS, Mark Fraser;** MP (Lib Dem) Ceredigion, since 2005; *b* 24 March 1966; *s* of Ronald and Pauline Williams; *m* 1997, Helen Refna Wyatt; one *s* three *d* (of whom one *s* one *d* are twins). *Educ:* University Coll. of Wales, Aberystwyth (BSc Econ 1987); Rolle Faculty of Educn, Univ. of Plymouth (PGCE 1993). Res. Asst to Lib, then Lib Dem, Peers and Constituency Asst to Geraint Howells, MP, 1987–92; Primary School Teacher: Madron Daniel Sch., Penzance, 1993–96; Forches Cross Sch., Barnstaple, 1997–2000; Dep. Hd, Llangors Church in Wales Sch., nr Brecon, 2000–05. Lib Dem spokesman on schools, 2005–06, on Wales, 2005–; Dep. Leader, Welsh Lib Dems, 2015–. Mem., Welsh Affairs Select Cttee, 2005–. Co-Chm., Lib Dem Backbench Cttee for political and constitutional reform, 2010–12, for Welsh Affairs, 2012–. Contested (Lib Dem): Monmouth, 1997; Ceredigion, Feb. 2000, 2001. Pres., Ceredigion Lib Dems, 1999–2000. *Recreations:* gardening, reading, biographies, walking. *Address:* 32 North Parade, Aberystwyth, Ceredigion SY23 2NF. *T:* (01970) 627721. *E:* williamsmf@parliament.uk.

**WILLIAMSON, Rt Hon. Gavin (Alexander);** PC 2015; MP (C) South Staffordshire, since 2010; *b* Scarborough, 25 June 1976; *s* of Ray and Beverley Williamson; *m* 2001, Joanne Elizabeth Eland; two *d*. *Educ:* Raincliffe Secondary Sch.; Scarborough Sixth Form Coll.; Univ. of Bradford (BSc Hons Social Scis). Glynwed Gp, 1998–2004; Gen. Manager, Aynsley China, 2004–08; Divl Man. Dir and Gp Dir, NPS Gp, 2008–10. Mem. (C) N Yorks CC, 2001–05. Contested (C) Blackpool N and Fleetwood, 2005. PPS to Minister of State for NI, 2011–12, to Sec. of State for Transport, 2012–13, to Prime Minister, 2013–. Mem., NI Affairs Select Cttee, 2010–11; Chm., All Party Parly Gp on Motor Neurone Disease, 2010–14; Co-Chm., Associate Parly Design and Innovation Gp, 2010–14. Mem., Exec. Cttee, UK Br., CPA, 2010–12. *Address:* House of Commons, SW1A 0AA.

**WILSON, Corri;** MP (SNP) Ayr, Carrick and Cumnock, since 2015; *b* Ayr, 1963; *d* of John and Mary Wilson; one *s* one *d*. *Educ:* West of Scotland Univ. New Deal Advr, DSS subseq. DWP, 1982–2003; project worker, Barnardo's, 2005–09; Police Custody Welfare Officer, Strathclyde Jt Police Bd, 2007–08; Dir, Caledonii Resources Ltd, 2012–. Mem. (SNP) S Ayrshire Council, 2012–. *Address:* House of Commons, SW1A 0AA. *E:* corri.wilson.mp@parliament.uk.

**WILSON, Philip;** MP (Lab) Sedgefield, since July 2007; *b* 31 May 1959; *s* of Bernard Wilson and Ivy Wilson (*née* Woods); *m* (marr. diss. 1999); two *s*. *Educ:* Trimdon Secondary Modern Sch.; Sedgefield Comprehensive Sch. Civil Servant, Dept for Nat. Savings, 1978–87; res. asst to Rt Hon. Tony Blair, MP, 1987–94; Labour Party organiser, 1994–97; Political Asst to Gen. Sec., Labour Party, 1997–99; Consultant, Brunswick Gp, 1999–2002; Dir, Fellows' Associates, 2002–07. *Recreations:* jazz, reading, writing. *Address:* House of Commons, SW1A 0AA. *T:* (020) 7219 4966. *E:* phil.wilson.mp@parliament.uk.

**WILSON, Robert O.;** MP (C) Reading East, since 2005; Parliamentary Secretary, Cabinet Office, since 2014; *b* 4 Jan. 1965; *m* one *s* three *d*. *Educ:* Wallingford Sch.; Univ. of Reading (BA Hist.). Entrepreneur, health and communications. Mem. (C), Reading BC, 1992–96, 2004–06. Shadow Minister for Higher Educn, 2007–09; an Opposition Whip, 2009–10; PPS to Sec. of State for Culture, Olympics, Media and Sport, 2010–12, for Health, 2012–13, to Chancellor of the Exchequer, 2013–14. Contested (C): Bolton NE, 1997; Carmarthen W and S Pembs, 2001. *Publications:* 5 Days to Power: the journey to coalition Britain, 2010; The Eye of the Storm, 2014. *Address:* (office) 12a South View Park, Marsack Street, Reading RG4 5AF; House of Commons, SW1A 0AA.

**WILSON, Samuel, (Sammy);** MP (DemU) East Antrim, since 2005; *b* 4 April 1953; *s* of Alexander and Mary Wilson. *Educ:* Methodist Coll., Belfast; The Queen's Univ., Belfast (BScEcon; PGCE). Teacher of Economics, 1975–83; Researcher in N Ireland Assembly, 1983–86. Councillor, Belfast CC, 1981–; Lord Mayor of Belfast, 1986–87 and 2000–01. Press Officer for Democratic Unionist Party, 1982–96. Contested (DemU) Antrim E, 2001. Mem. (DemU) Belfast E, 1998–2003, E Antrim, 2003–Aug. 2015, NI Assembly; Minister of the Envmt, 2008–09, of Finance and Personnel, 2009–13, NI. *Publications:* The Carson Trail, 1982; The Unionist Case—The Forum Report Answered, 1984; Data Response Questions in Economics, 1995. *Recreations:* reading, motor cycling, windsurfing, gardening. *Address:* East Antrim DUP, 116 Main Street, Larne BT40 1RG. *T:* (028) 2826 7722. *E:* barronj@parliament.uk.

**WINNICK, David Julian;** MP (Lab) Walsall North, since 1979; *b* Brighton, 26 June 1933; *s* of late Eugene and Rose Winnick; one *s*; *m* 1968, Bengi Rona (marr. diss.), *d* of Tarik and Zeynep Rona. *Educ:* secondary school; London Sch. of Economics (Dip. in Social Admin). Army National Service, 1951–53. Branch Secretary, Clerical and Administrative Workers' Union, 1956–62 (later APEX GMB; Mem. Exec. Council, 1978–88, Vice-Pres., 1983–88); Advertisement Manager, Tribune, 1963–66; employed by UKIAS, 1970–79 (Chm., 1984–90).

Member: Willesden Borough Council, 1959–64; London Borough of Brent Council, 1964–66 (Chair, Children Cttee, 1965–66). Contested (Lab) Harwich, 1964; MP (Lab) Croydon South, 1966–70; contested (Lab): Croydon Central, Oct. 1974; Walsall N, Nov. 1976. Member: Select Cttee on the Environment, 1979–83; Home Affairs Cttee, 1983–87, 1997–; Select Cttee on Procedure, 1989–97; Co-Chm., British-Irish Inter-Parly Body, 1997–2005 (Vice-Chm., 1993–97). Recreations: walking, cinema, theatre, reading. Address: House of Commons, SW1A 0AA.

**WINTERTON, Rt Hon. Rosalie, (Rt Hon. Rosie);** PC 2006; MP (Lab) Doncaster Central, since 1997; b 10 Aug. 1958; d of Gordon and Valerie Winterton. Educ: Doncaster Grammar Sch.; Hull Univ. (BA Hons Hist.). Asst to John Prescott, MP, 1980–86; Parliamentary Officer: London Borough of Southwark, 1986–88; RCN, 1988–90; Man. Dir, Connect Public Affairs, 1990–94; Hd, private office of John Prescott, MP, 1994–97. Parly Sec., LCD, 2001–03; Minister of State: DoH, 2003–07; DfT, 2007–08; DWP, 2008–09; BIS and DCLG, 2009–10; Minister for Yorkshire and the Humber, 2008–10; Shadow Leader, H of C, 2010; Shadow Chief Whip, 2010–. Recreations: sailing, reading. Address: House of Commons, SW1A 0AA.

**WISHART, Peter;** MP (SNP) Perth and North Perthshire, since 2005 (North Tayside, 2001–05); b 9 March 1962; s of Alex and Nan Wishart; m 1990, Carrie Lindsay (separated 2003); one s. Educ: Moray House Coll. of Educn. Community worker, 1984–85; musician with rock band, Runrig, 1985–2001. Chief Whip, SNP Gp, 2001–07, 2013–; Mem., Scottish Affairs Select Cttee, 2008–10 and 2015– (Chm., 2015–). SNP spokesperson: for Culture, Media and Sport, 2001–15; Internat. Develt, 2001–10; for Constitution and Home Affairs, 2007–15; Shadow Leader of the House, 2015–. Recreations: music, hillwalking. Address: (office) 35 Perth Street, Blairgowrie PH10 6DL; (office) 63 Glasgow Road, Perth PH2 0PE.

**WOLLASTON, Sarah;** MP (C) Totnes, since 2010; b 1962; m Adrian; one s two d. Educ: Tal Handaq Service Children's Sch., Malta; Watford Grammar Sch. for Girls; Guy's Hosp. Med. Sch. (BSc Pathol. 1983; MB BS 1986). DRCOG 1991; MRCGP 1992. Forensic med. examr, Devon and Cornwall Police, 1996–2001; GP, Chagford Health Centre, Devon, 1999–2010; Trainer, Peninsula Med. Sch., Plymouth, 2001–10; teacher, Exeter Postgrad. Centre until 2010. Mem., Health Select Cttee, 2010– (Chm., 2014–). Address: House of Commons, SW1A 0AA.

**WOOD, Michael Jon;** MP (C) Dudley South, since 2015; b 17 March 1976; s of Brian Wood and Jacqueline Susan Wood (née Priest); m 2008, Laura Chadderton; one s one d. Educ: Old

Swinford Hosp. Sch.; Univ. of Wales, Aberystwyth (BScEcon Hons Econs and Law 1997); Cardiff Univ. (Postgrad. DipLaw 1999). Asst to Earl of Stockton, MEP, 1999–2002; Policy Advr, Eur. Parlt, 2002–06; Sen. Researcher, JDS Associates, 2006–08; Constituency Organiser, Cons. Party, 2009–10; Caseworker to Andrew Griffiths, MP, 2010–11; Parly Asst, H of C, 2011–14. Mem. (C) Dudley MBC, 2014–. Address: House of Commons, SW1A 0AA.

**WOODCOCK, John Zak;** MP (Lab Co-op) Barrow and Furness, since 2010; b Sheffield, 14 Oct. 1978; m 2004, Amanda Telford; two d. Educ: Edinburgh Univ. (MA 2002). Journalist, Scotsman; Special Adviser: to Rt Hon. John Hutton, MP, 2005; to Cabinet Sec., 2005; to Sec. of State for Work and Pensions, 2005–07; to Sec. of State for Business, Enterprise and Regulatory Reform, 2007–08; to the Prime Minister, 2009. Shadow Transport Minister, 2010–12; Shadow Education Minister, 2015. Mem., Defence Select Cttee, 2010. Address: House of Commons, SW1A 0AA.

**WRAGG, William Peter;** MP (C) Hazel Grove, since 2015; b Stockport, 11 Dec. 1987; s of Peter Wragg and Julie Wragg. Educ: Poynton High Sch. and Sixth Form; Univ. of Manchester (BA Hist.); Liverpool John Moores Univ. (PGCE). Former primary sch. teacher. Mem. (C) Stockport Council, 2011–15. Address: House of Commons, SW1A 0AA.

**WRIGHT, Iain David;** MP (Lab) Hartlepool, since 2004; b 9 May 1972; m Tiffiny; three s one d. Educ: Manor Comprehensive Sch., Hartlepool; University Coll. London (BA, MA). ACA 2003. Deloitte & Touche, 1997–2003; chartered accountant, One NorthEast, 2003–04. Mem. (Lab), Hartlepool BC, 2002–05. Parly Under-Sec. of State, DCLG, 2007–09, DCSF, 2009–10. Chm., Select Cttee on Business, Innovations and Skills, 2015–. Address: (office) 23 South Road, Hartlepool TS26 9HD; House of Commons, SW1A 0AA.

**WRIGHT, Rt Hon. Jeremy (Paul);** PC 2014; QC 2014; MP (C) Kenilworth and Southam, since 2010 (Rugby and Kenilworth, 2005–10); Attorney General, since 2014; b 24 Oct. 1972; s of John and Audrey Wright; m 1998, Yvonne Salter; one s one d. Educ: Taunton Sch.; Trinity Sch., NYC; Univ. of Exeter (LLB Hons). Called to the Bar, Inner Temple, 1996; in practice on Midlands and Oxford Circuit, specialising in criminal law, 1996–2005. An Opposition Whip, 2007–10; a Lord Comr of HM Treasury (Govt Whip), 2010–12; Parly Under-Sec. of State, MoJ, 2012–14. Mem., Select Cttee on Constitutional Affairs, 2005–07. Trustee, Community Develt Fund, 2007–09. Recreations: golf, music, cinema. Address: House of Commons, SW1A 0AA. T: (020) 7219 8299. E: jeremy.wright.mp@parliament.uk.

**YOUNGER OF LECKIE,** 5th Viscount *cr* 1923, of Alloa, Clackmannanshire; **James Edward George Younger;** Bt 1911; a Lord in Waiting (Government Whip), since 2015; *b* 11 Nov. 1955; *e s* of 4th Viscount Younger of Leckie, KT, KCVO, TD, PC, DL and of Diana Rhona (*née* Tuck); *S* father, 2003; *m* 1988, Jennie Veronica (*née* Wootton); one *s* two *d. Educ:* Cargilfield Sch., Edinburgh; Winchester Coll.; St Andrews Univ. (MA Hons Medieval Hist. 1979); Henley Mgt Coll. (MBA 1993). MCIM 1994. Personnel Mgr, Coats Patons, 1979–84; Recruitment Consultant, Angela Mortimer Ltd, 1984–86; Exec. Search Consultant, Stephens Consultancies, 1986–92; Director: MacInnes Younger, 1992–94; HR, UBS Wealth Mgt, 1994–2004; Culliford Edmunds Associates, 2004–07; Consultant, Eban Internat., 2007–10. Chm., Bucks Cons. Constituency Assoc., 2006–10. Member: Assoc. of Cons. Peers, 2006–; Area Bd, Oxon and Bucks Conservatives, 2008–13; Chm., Milton Keynes Conservatives, 2011–13. Elected Mem., H of L, 2010. Cons. Party Whip, 2011–12; a Lord in Waiting (Govt Whip), 2012–13; Parly Under-Sec. of State, BIS, 2013–14. Vice Pres., War Widows' Assoc., 2012–. Mem., Royal Co. of Archers (Queen's Body Guard for Scotland). Pres., Highland Soc. of London, 2012–; Hon. Pres., Kate Kennedy Club Life Members Assoc., St Andrews Univ. *Recreations:* sailing, tennis, shooting, Highland dancing, ski-ing, country pursuits, cricket. *Heir: s* Hon. Alexander William George Younger, *b* 13 Nov. 1993. *Address:* The Old Vicarage, Dorton, Aylesbury, Bucks HP18 9NH. *T:* (01844) 238396. *E:* jeg.younger@virgin.net. *Club:* White Hunters Cricket (Hampshire).

**ZAHAWI, Nadhim;** MP (C) Stratford-on-Avon, since 2010; *b* Baghdad, 2 June 1967; *s* of Harith and Najda Zahawi; *m* 2004, Lana Saib; two *s* one *d. Educ:* University Coll. London (BSc Chem. Eng.). Marketing Director: Global Inc. Ltd, 1990–95; Allen (Hinckley) Ltd, 1995–98; Eur. Mktg Dir, Smith & Brooks Ltd, 1998–2000; CEO and Co-founder, YouGov plc, 2000–10. Non-exec. Dir, SThree plc, 2008–; Chief Strategy Officer, Gulf Keystone, 2015–. Mem., Foreign Affairs Select Cttee, 2014–. Mem. (C), Wandsworth BC, 1994–2006. Patron, Peace One Day, 2008–. *Publications:* (with M. Hancock) Masters of Nothing: the crash and how it will happen again unless we understand human nature, 2011. *Recreations:* show jumping, cinema, spending time with family and friends. *Address:* House of Commons, SW1A 0AA. *Clubs:* Annabel's, Soho House.

**ZEICHNER, Daniel Stephen;** MP (Lab) Cambridge, since 2015; *b* Beckenham, 9 Nov. 1956; *s* of Eric Zeichner and Mary Zeichner (*née* Mead); *Educ:* King's Coll., Cambridge (BA 1979). Milk roundsman, Co-op, 1976; trainee computer programmer, Cambs CC, 1979–81; computer programmer, Perkins Engines, Peterborough, 1981; Database Adminr, Pye Electronics, Cambridge, 1982; computer programmer, Whitbread, Reading and London, 1983; estabd and ran Red and Green Nurseries, Norfolk, retail and wholesale herbaceous plant specialists, 1983–91; computer programmer and systems designer, Norwich Union, 1984–91; Political Assistant: to John Garrett, MP, 1992–97; to Clive Needle, MEP, 1995–99; Labour Link Policy and Campaigns Officer, UNISON, 2002–15. Mem. (Lab), S Norfolk DC, 1995–2003. *Recreations:* enjoying music, especially at Cambridge's Kettles Yard, Cambridge United season ticket holder. *Address:* House of Commons, SW1A 0AA. *T:* (01223) 423252. *E:* daniel.zeichner.mp@parliament.uk.

# UK GENERAL ELECTION 2015 STATISTICS

STATE OF THE PARTIES AFTER THE 2015 GENERAL ELECTION

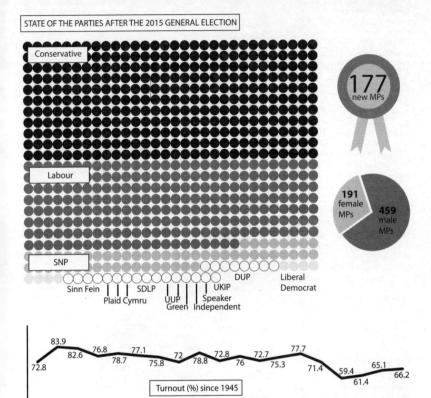

177 new MPs

191 female MPs    459 male MPs

Conservative
Labour
SNP
Sinn Fein    SDLP    DUP    Liberal Democrat
Plaid Cymru    UUP    Speaker    UKIP
Green    Independent

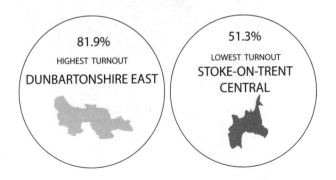

Turnout (%) since 1945

83.9
82.6
76.8
78.7
77.1
75.8
72
78.8
72.8
76
72.7
75.3
77.7
71.4
59.4
61.4
65.1
66.2
72.8

1945 1950 1951 1955 1959 1964 1966 1970 1974 1974 1979 1983 1987 1992 1997 2001 2005 2010 2015
(Feb.)(Oct.)

81.9%
HIGHEST TURNOUT
DUNBARTONSHIRE EAST

51.3%
LOWEST TURNOUT
STOKE-ON-TRENT CENTRAL

# UK GENERAL ELECTION 2010

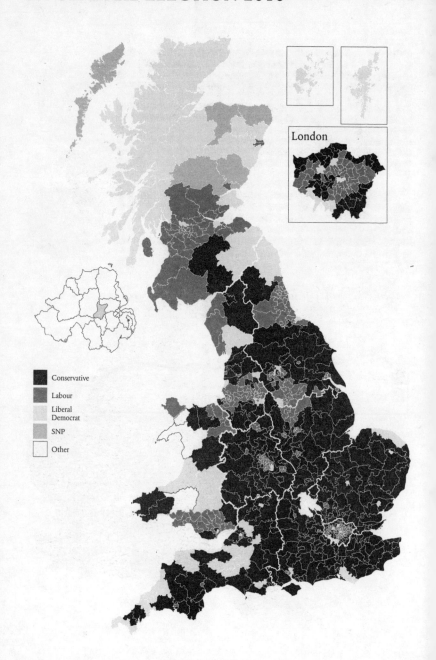

Conservative
Labour
Liberal
Democrat
SNP
Other

London